VOLUME

1

The

AMERICAN
HERITAGE
Pictorial History of the
PRESIDENTS
of the United States

Front endsheet: Crowds flock to the White House for Jackson's inaugural reception; Library of Congress

Back endsheet: A print depicting the first eleven American Presidents; Polk Home, Columbia, Tennessee

VOLUME

1

GEORGE WASHINGTON *through* RUTHERFORD B. HAYES

The

AMERICAN HERITAGE

Pictorial History of the

PRESIDENTS

of the United States

by the Editors of
AMERICAN HERITAGE
The Magazine of History

Editor in Charge
KENNETH W. LEISH

Foreword by
BRUCE CATTON

Published by
AMERICAN HERITAGE PUBLISHING CO., INC.

Book Trade Distribution by
SIMON AND SCHUSTER

AMERICAN HERITAGE
BOOK DIVISION

MANAGING DIRECTOR   Richard M. Ketchum

GENERAL EDITOR   Alvin M. Josephy, Jr.

Staff for this Book

EDITOR   Kenneth W. Leish

ASSOCIATE EDITORS   **David Jacobs**
Michael Harwood

PICTURE EDITOR   **Wesley Day**

ASSISTANT EDITORS   **Nancy Kelly**
John Phillips
Susan D. Eikov

COPY EDITORS   **Joan Wilkinson**
Brenda Bennerup
Ellen C. Ehrlich
Helen C. Dunn

PICTURE RESEARCHER   Carla Davidson

EDITORIAL ASSISTANT   Hilary E. Abramson

ART DIRECTOR   Chester Prosinski
Assistant: Margaret Chou

AMERICAN HERITAGE PUBLISHING CO., INC.

PRESIDENT   James Parton

CHAIRMAN, EDITORIAL COMMITTEE   Joseph J. Thorndike

EDITOR, AMERICAN HERITAGE MAGAZINE   Oliver Jensen

SENIOR ART DIRECTOR   Irwin Glusker

PUBLISHER, AMERICAN HERITAGE MAGAZINE   Darby Perry

PRESIDENTIAL BIOGRAPHIES
by

Wilson Sullivan
David Jacobs
Michael Harwood

Saul Braun
Joseph L. Gardner
Donald Young

Charles L. Mee, Jr.
Vincent Buranelli
Martin Luray

Sculptor Gutzon Borglum carved giant likenesses of four American Presidents—George Washington, Thomas Jefferson, Theodore Roosevelt, and Abraham Lincoln—in the granite face of Mt. Rushmore in South Dakota.

CONTENTS
OF VOLUME ONE

ADDITIONAL BIOGRAPHIES

FOREWORD

BY BRUCE CATTON

The highest and most significant office in the United States is of course the Presidency. It was created by the Founding Fathers, and since·their day it has been developed, strengthened, and marvelously expanded until it is much greater than it was originally designed to be. It is the principal instrument through which the people of the United States try to control their destiny in a complicated and uncertain world. Perhaps the best way to examine the office is to examine the lives and personalities of the men who have held it, because the Presidency today is in many ways the sum of large and small contributions made by the different Presidents.

At this writing there have been thirty-five of these men, and they make a mixed grill. Sometimes it seems that they have nothing much in common except the fact that for one reason or another the voters elevated them to high office. Some of them were surpassingly strong men and some of them were woefully weak; some of them ideally fitted the times they served, a few were obviously miscast, and still others were simply average men doing the best they could in a most demanding job. Each man was in his own day the man to whom the country looked for leadership, and by and large the leadership has usually been forthcoming. If the story of the Presidents proves nothing else, it testifies to the enormous stability of the office itself and of the nation that devised it.

The country does not always elect its most famous and talented men to the Presidency. The list of prominent Americans who were highly qualified for the job but never got it is long. It can be balanced by a list of Presidents who would hardly be remembered today, except by the historians of political life, if they had not entered the White House. (Who would recall Millard Fillmore, John Tyler, Franklin Pierce, Chester Alan Arthur, or Benjamin Harrison?) There are, on the list, some very good men who were overwhelmed by the immense problems that the Presidency brought them: James Buchanan, Andrew Johnson, and Ulysses S. Grant, for instance, were dedicated men who simply

faced more than they knew how to handle. Often enough, a man who seems poorly qualified for the office grows mightily once he gets in it—Andrew Jackson, for example, and Abraham Lincoln, to name only two. A time of crisis does not always bring forth a President who can cope with crisis—a strong President or two in the decade just before the Civil War might have saved the country an infinity of suffering, and the same is true of the early 1920's—but surprisingly often we get a big man just when we need one.

Indeed, the most interesting thing about the long roll call of men who have lived in the White House is that the average is so surprisingly high. One of our favorite jokes has to do with the offhand way in which we choose our Vice Presidents. Logically, these men ought to be dismal failures when tragedy puts them into the top job. Actually, they are not. Some were ineffective Presidents to be sure, but some were genuinely first-rate.

One thing that stands out is that the office of the Presidency has always been growing—partly because the times themselves have demanded it, but also because certain exceptional men have stretched the powers of the office in order to do things that needed to be done for the nation. Jefferson, Jackson, Lincoln, the two Roosevelts, Truman: each of them made the office bigger by boldly exerting its implied but unstated powers. Bear in mind, too, that none of the men who seized and exercised the undefined authority that becomes visible to the man in the White House was guilty of anything like Caesarism. Every man who ever lived in the White House understood that he was acting for something much bigger than himself. When he reached out for additional authority, he was getting it for the Presidency and not for himself.

Here they are, then—the men who have been Presidents of the United States. They make a pretty good group, all in all, and they have not failed us. Only a nation with sound instincts for the survival of freedom, democracy, and the national well-being could have chosen a group that stands the backward glance as well as this one does.

GEORGE WASHINGTON

Geophysics Washington, said an Anti-
federalist newspaper, has "the ostentation of an eastern bashaw." The first
President, a contemporary senator insisted, "has become in the hands of
Hamilton, the dishclout of every dirty speculation, as his name goes to wipe
away blame and silence all murmuring." On the eve of Washington's retirement, Benjamin Franklin's grandson, Benjamin Bache, crowed: "Every heart
. . . ought to beat high in exultation, that the name of Washington ceases from
this day to give a currency to political iniquity and to legalize corruption."

Other opponents accused him of stealing from the Treasury, of toadying to
the British, of being inept as a general. An embittered Tom Paine, imprisoned
by the French for revolutionary agitation, condemned Washington's neutrality in his case: "As to you, sir, treacherous in private friendship . . . and a
hypocrite in public life, the world will be puzzled to decide . . . whether you
have abandoned good principles, or whether you ever had any."

To most of his contemporaries, however, George Washington—commander
of the tattered colonial army, chairman of the Constitutional Convention,
first President of the United States—was indisputably first in war, first in
peace, and first in the hearts of his countrymen. Despite their political differences, Thomas Jefferson spoke for the nation in urging Washington to seek a
second term: "The confidence of the whole Union is centered in you . . ." he
told his chief. "North and South will hang together if they have you to hang
on." After Washington's death, Jefferson wrote: "Never did nature and fortune combine more perfectly to make a man great, and to place him in . . . an
everlasting remembrance."

But America would not be satisfied with the realities—glorious though they
were—of Washington's life. It wanted a flawless hero. Washington "was des-

Washington at sixty-three, by Gilbert Stuart

11

tined to a stature in death," writes historian Daniel Boorstin, "which he had never attained in life. . . . A deification which in European history might have required centuries was accomplished here in decades."

Thus, despite the political slander and bile that marred Washington's two administrations, the first President soon came to be regarded as a demigod. Mason Locke Weems, an Episcopal clergyman and itinerant bookseller, reaped enormous profits from his largely apocryphal biography of Washington, first published in 1800. Weems attributed all virtues to the first President, from extraordinary honesty, bravery, and wisdom to exceptional physical dexterity; in the fifth edition of the biography, printed in 1806, the legend of Washington and the cherry tree first appeared in type. Despite Weems's crass assurance to his publisher that the latter had "a great deal of money lying in the bones of old George," the myths he spawned engaged and still engage Americans.

Because of this literature of hero worship, because of Washington's own reticence, and because of his family's penchant for burning, editing, or giving away his private papers and letters, the personality of George Washington has remained obscure, distant, never quite credible. Perhaps historian W. E. Woodward was partially correct when he wrote that people think they do not understand Washington because they can find in him nothing that is not within themselves. "It was just in that quality that his greatness lay. He was the American common denominator, the average man deified and raised to the nth power."

In any case, American history has made the arduous passage from Washington mythology to balanced fact. We no longer imagine, with a facetious Nathaniel Hawthorne, that Washington "was born with his clothes on, and his hair powdered, and made a stately bow on his first appearance in the world." Nor given contemporary scholarship can we fully agree that he remains, any longer, "the man almost nobody knows."

The first President of the United States was born in royal Virginia's Westmoreland

This mug, probably made in Germany in 1776, is believed by some scholars to present the earliest depiction of Washington cutting down the cherry tree.

County, in a brick farmhouse, at 10 A.M. on February 11, 1732 (or February 22, according to the modern calendar adopted in 1752). His father was Augustine Washington, "a blond giant," according to biographer James T. Flexner, "fabulously strong but miraculously gentle . . . a nervous businessman." Augustine's second wife, Mary Ball Washington, was the mother of George and his three brothers—Samuel, John Augustine, and Charles—and two sisters. George also had two half brothers, Lawrence and Augustine, Jr., and a half sister, Jane.

The Washington mythology—nurtured by Weems and others—idealized Mary Washington as the perfect American mother. In reality, however, she was querulous and illiterate, and resented George's success because she felt that he neglected her. She refused to participate in any ceremony honoring him, deprecated his achievements, and despite the commander in chief's ample provisions for her financial needs, actually asked the Virginia legislature, at the height of the Revolutionary War, to come to her aid—to Washington's anger and embarrassment.

Attended from birth by slaves, George first moved with his parents some forty miles up the Potomac to a 2,500-acre tract named Epsewasson (later Mount Vernon) and in 1738 to a smaller plot, Ferry Farm, on the Rappahannock. When George was eleven, his father died, and thereafter Mary Washington's eldest child escaped her watchful eye whenever he could, fleeing to visit relatives and friends.

"Some men," Washington observed, "will gain as much experience in the course of three or four years as some will in ten or a dozen." And if experience is the best teacher, President Washington was well taught indeed. His education—acquired from members of his family, and perhaps also from a private tutor and from schoolteachers in Fredericksburg and Westmoreland County —was rudimentary, limited to accounting, utilitarian arithmetic, geometry, geography as a basis of surveying, and practical studies of the calendar and the zodiac. He was thoroughly practical—"a man of hands," wrote Woodward, "not without brains, but with hand and brain moving together. . . . He used thought only as a mode of action."

Nevertheless, the young Washington did occasionally find time for Alexander Pope, the Bible, *Tom Jones*, and *The Spectator*. And a list of maxims for correct social behavior caught his copybook fancy: the *Rules of Civility*, probably prepared by sixteenth-century Jesuits for the cultivation of French aristocrats. The maxims suggested that acceptable social conduct does not include cleaning one's teeth with the tablecloth, that "every action done in company ought to be with some sign of respect to those that are present," and that the correct man will remember to "bedew no man's face with Spittle, by approaching too near."

It was this copybook ethic that Washington carried with him in his careful ascent in Virginia society. His patron and tutor in this rise was his half brother Lawrence. It was Lawrence's marriage to Anne Fairfax, of the

Lawrence Washington became mentor to his favorite half brother, George, when their father died.

wealthy Virginia Fairfaxes, and the couple's frequent sojourns at Belvoir, the huge estate of Anne's father, that opened the gates of wealth and status to young George. As Lawrence's protégé, he often visited Belvoir, where George Fairfax (Anne's brother) and his wife, Sally, had taken up residence.

At sixteen, Washington accompanied George Fairfax on a month-long surveying tour of Lord Thomas Fairfax's vast lands beyond the Blue Ridge in the Shenandoah Valley. For his efforts Washington was paid $7.20 per day, a tidy fee for the time. The lodgings made available to them on this trip were not all that Washington could have wished. Of one place, he noted: "I . . . strip[p]ed myself very orderly and went in to ye Bed as they called it when to my Surprize I found it to be nothing but a Little Straw— Matted together without Sheets or anything else but only one thread Bear blanket with double its Weight of Vermin, such as Lice Fleas & c . . . I put on my Cloth[e]s and Lay as my Companions."

Wherever he went, Washington already commanded attention by his mere physical presence. Six-foot-two, lanky, and large-

boned (he wore a size 13 shoe), he had gray-blue eyes and brown hair. "In conversation he looks you full in the face," Captain George Mercer observed in 1760, "is deliberate, deferential, and engaging. . . . His movements and gestures are graceful, his walk majestic, and he is a splendid horseman." Meticulous in counting his possessions, he once actually calculated the number of seeds in a pound (troy weight) of red clover: 71,000. And he knew every foot of land he owned (1,459 acres purchased with surveying wages before he was nineteen). A few years later, during the French and Indian War, he would say of himself: "I have a constitution hardy enough to encounter and undergo the most severe trials, and, I flatter myself the resolution to face what any man durst."

In 1751 George accompanied Lawrence Washington to Barbados, where his half brother, ill with tuberculosis, hoped to regain his health. There, George contracted the smallpox that pock-marked his face permanently, but fortunately left him immune to the disease that later ravaged his Continental Army. In the following year, Lawrence Washington died, and George began his military career.

Commissioned a major in the militia, Washington was appointed adjutant of the southern district of Virginia. In the fall of 1753 he was given a historic assignment by Governor Robert Dinwiddie: to carry to the French at Fort Le Boeuf, three hundred miles away in the Ohio Valley, a royal ultimatum to cease fortifications and settlements there "within His Majesty's Dominions." Washington left on his mission on November 15. He stopped on the way to survey the site of a projected fort and, at Logstown on the north bank of the Ohio, urged the Indians, unsuccessfully, to accept the British as benign big brothers. Proceeding to Le Boeuf, he found the French adamant and cocky in their rejection of Britain's claims.

Having recorded a careful description of the fort in his notebook, Washington headed for home, on a trek through the frozen wilderness that can only be called heroic. The horses, hampered by deep snow, were unable to proceed, and Washington and his guide, Christopher Gist, had to continue on foot, through Indian-infested forests, to Williamsburg, more than five hundred miles away. Near Murthering Town, close to the Forks of the Ohio, an Indian, perhaps a French hireling, fired point-blank at Washington at fifteen paces but missed.

Washington had hoped that the Allegheny River would be frozen solid when he and Gist reached it, but it was not; masses of ice were crashing down the river. With one hatchet between them, the two men built a raft at a spot now within Pittsburgh's city limits, and then launched it into the icy cascade. "Before we were halfway over," Washington wrote later, "we were jammed in the ice, in such a manner that we expected every

THE
JOURNAL
OF
Major *George Washington,*
SENT BY THE
Hon. *ROBERT DINWIDDIE,* Esq;
His Majesty's Lieutenant-Governor, and
Commander in Chief of *VIRGINIA,*
TO THE
COMMANDANT
OF THE
FRENCH FORCES
ON
OHIO.
To WHICH ARE ADDED, THE
GOVERNOR's LETTER,
AND A TRANSLATION OF THE
FRENCH OFFICER's ANSWER.

WILLIAMSBURG:
Printed by WILLIAM HUNTER. 1754

After his trek back to Virginia from Fort Le Boeuf in the winter of 1753–54, Washington wrote a chronicle of his mission that brought him some renown.

14

Washington's brass telescope, still at Mount Vernon

moment our raft to sink and ourselves to perish. I put out my setting pole to try to stop the raft that the ice might pass by, when the rapidity of the stream threw it [the raft] with such violence against the pole that it jerked me out into ten feet of water but I fortunately saved myself by catching hold of one of the raft logs." Drenched and shivering, the men continued their march, reaching Will's Creek, some fifty miles from Winchester, on January 7, 1754.

The defiant reply of the French confirmed Governor Dinwiddie's conviction that British holdings in the Ohio Valley must be defended. For Washington there was the pleasure of seeing his report officially printed, plus £50 voted him by a grateful Virginia assembly. He said of the money: "I was employed to go on a journey in the winter (when I believe few or none would have undertaken it), and what did I get by it? My expenses borne."

Commissioned a lieutenant colonel by Dinwiddie in 1754, Washington was ordered back to the Ohio Valley to secure the site of the Ohio Company's fort, which was being built at the junction of the Allegheny and Monongahela rivers. En route he learned that the site had fallen to the French (they named it Fort Duquesne), and that enemy troops were advancing toward him in strength. At Great Meadows, Pennsylvania,

Washington's men surrounded and attacked a party of French soldiers without warning. Ten Frenchmen, including their chief officer, Joseph Coulon, the Sieur de Jumonville, were killed and twenty-one were captured.

Washington then entrenched at an abandoned fort he named "Necessity." It was "badly sited," notes historian Esmond Wright, "in an open, swampy hollow over which a nearby hill gave a commanding view." This was the first of several less-than-brilliant maneuvers that would earn for Washington the criticism of some military strategists. On July 3, a superior force, led by Jumonville's brother, compelled Washington to surrender and, taking advantage of the Virginian's ignorance of French, obtained his signature on a written admission that he had "assassinated" Jumonville.

Washington's hasty action in attacking the French party is sometimes credited with precipitating the Seven Years' War. But for Washington it would be indispensable experience in frontier military tactics, and a source of notoriety in the chancelleries of Europe. Disillusioned with what he considered Dinwiddie's mismanagement of Virginia's military establishment, and bitter because of a ruling that colonials could not rise above the rank of captain in the British army, Washington resigned his commission at the end of 1754.

After the Fort Necessity fiasco, Washington wrote: "I have heard the bullets whistle; and, believe me, there is something charming in the sound." But the bullets lost their charm in 1755. In May, Washington was appointed aide-de-camp to General Edward Braddock in a 1,300-man expedition against Fort Duquesne. At the Monongahela they met a French and Indian force. Braddock's men, trained in traditional European methods of battle, were surrounded and decimated by enemies adept at frontier warfare. Braddock himself was slain, and sixty-three of his eighty-six officers were killed or wounded. The regulars panicked and fled; according to Washington, the Virginia colonials alone "behaved like men and died like soldiers." Washington himself had two horses killed under him, and four bullets pierced his coat before he organized a retreat.

Returning to Virginia, Washington was named a colonel and commander in chief of the militia. He was thus called upon, at twenty-three, to defend the colony's 300-mile frontier from what was considered an imminent French and Indian attack. But inadequate troops and provisions, limited authority, and a royal governor who would not give him permission to seize Fort Duquesne, the key position in the West, made his task impossible. When even his right to command was challenged by an officer of the Maryland militia who held a royal commission, Washington rode all the way from Williamsburg to Boston to ask Governor William Shirley, the acting commander in chief of British forces in North America, to confirm his rank. In Boston, the proud young colonel was told to his great satisfaction that his rank was valid, though only when no British regulars were present.

For more than two years, Washington doggedly defended Virginia's long frontier with badly equipped, unpaid militiamen. Then, in 1758, a British force under General John Forbes was assigned to march on Fort Duquesne. Washington was selected to serve as Forbes's acting brigadier, and when the French abandoned and burned the fort, the main objective of his strategy for Virginia's defense was achieved. He resigned his commission and retired to sixteen years of publicly uneventful but privately joyous life.

Washington's marriage to the widow Martha Dandridge Custis on January 6, 1759, vastly increased his fortune. Plump and appealing, and reputedly the richest widow in the colony, Martha Washington added 17,-000 acres to George's 5,000, and 300 slaves to his 49. She also provided him with a town house in the capital at Williamsburg and with Daniel Custis' two children, the overindulged and indolent John Parke Custis and the epileptic Martha Parke Custis, who died at seventeen.

Martha Washington was good-natured, healthy, and prosaic. With the assistance of thirteen servants and seven workmen, she kept a fine household at Mount Vernon, which Washington leased from Lawrence's heirs until he inherited it in 1761. George called Martha "Patsy," and Martha, twenty-seven at the time of the marriage, called George, twenty-six, "Old Man." That their marriage was based primarily on love is unlikely. Indisputably, Washington had earlier fallen in love with George Fairfax's wife, Sally, the coquettish belle of the Williamsburg cotillions. On July 20, 1758, he had assured Martha, as a "faithful and affectionate friend," that her life was "now inseparable from [his]," recalling "that happy hour when we made our pledges to each other." Less than two months later, he directly avowed by letter his love for Mrs. Fairfax. "The world has no business to know the object of my love, declared in this manner to you," wrote the affianced soldier, "when I want to conceal it." There is no evidence that the love was consummated or that Martha knew of it. But his letters to Sally remain. Not all the glories of the Revolutionary command, nor even the splendors of the Presidency, Washington assured Sally near the end of his life, had "been able to eradicate from my mind those happy moments, the happiest of my life, which I have enjoyed in your company."

Nevertheless, he settled down with Martha at Mount Vernon and became a dutiful vestryman and church warden, punctual tobacco planter, land broker, speculator, and surveyor. Now one of the richest men in Virginia, Washington—in historian Shelby Little's words—"took up his duties as a Burgess, was publicly thanked for his great services to his country, and drafted a law to prevent hogs running at large in Winchester." From 1768 to 1774 he also served as a Fairfax County justice.

Everyone at Mount Vernon knew his place. "Mrs. Forbes," Washington said of his housekeeper, "will have a warm, decent and comfortable room to herself, to lodge in, and will eat of the Victuals of our Table, but not sit at it, at any time, *with us*, be her appearance what it may: for if this was *once admitted*, no line satisfactory to either party,

Mrs. Sally Fairfax, a Virginia neighbor, was the object of Washington's discreet but lifelong love.

perhaps, could be drawn thereafter." Welcome at the table or not, Mrs. Forbes had her hands full. Washington entertained lavishly in the tradition of the Virginia gentry, despite his complaint that his house was, at times, "a well resorted tavern."

He carefully supervised every detail of plantation production and management: accounts receivable and payable, mortgage payments due, the state of the crops and fertilizing experiments, the performance of brood mares. When he had time, he read books such as *A New System of Agriculture or a Speedy Way to Grow Rich.*

Washington's attitude toward his Negro slaves at first reflected that of the reigning plantation owners of his time. Slaves were property, efficient or not. His viewpoint changed, however. In the early 1770's he committed himself to the gradual abolition of the slave trade through legislation. Although he owned more slaves than he needed, he refused to sell them without their permission. Drawing a parallel between the tyranny of slavery and the tyranny of Britain toward the colonies, he nevertheless opposed freeing slaves who were content with their masters. Such action, he argued, would lead to "discontent on one side and resentment on the other."

Though an Anglican vestryman, Washington was not religious in a formal sense. On one occasion, however, he assured Sally Fairfax that "there is a Destiny which has the control of our actions not to be resisted by the strongest efforts of Human Nature." He willingly granted to all the right to travel "that road to heaven which to them shall seem the most direct, plainest, easiest, and least liable to exceptions."

By 1774, Washington had begun to participate actively in America's burgeoning economic and political revolution. He had opposed the Stamp Act and thoroughly approved Massachusetts' refusal to submit to British commercial restrictions. Angered by Britain's retaliatory closing of the port of Boston, he was present with Jefferson at the Raleigh Tavern in Williamsburg on May 27, 1774, after the Crown had dissolved the rebellious House of Burgesses. At this meeting, the Virginia legislators issued a vote of sympathy with their New England brothers, appointed delegates to a Virginia convention that would select representatives to a continental congress, and passed a resolution stating that an attack on one of the colonies would be considered an attack on all of them. Later that year, Washington was chosen to attend the First Continental Congress in Philadelphia, at which he sat silently but impressively, his sword at his side.

After being elected to command five Virginia militia companies, Washington was appointed a delegate to the Second Continental Congress of May, 1775; there he served on a committee charged with drafting regulations for a colonial army and a strategy for the defense of New York City. In that Second Congress, John Adams of Massachusetts nominated George Washington as commander in chief of a proposed Continental Army. He was elected unanimously. In assuming the post, Washington was humbly

Washington, painted in 1776 by C. W. Peale

magnanimous: "Though I am truly sensible of the high honor done me in this appointment, yet I feel great distress from a consciousness that my abilities and military experience may not be equal to the extensive and important trust." But he would accede to Congress' will, do his plain duty, and "exert every power I possess in the service for support of the glorious cause." Refusing a salary, he asked only that Congress bear his expenses.

In his General Orders, issued the next day, Washington appealed for a unified effort to end regionalism and colonial jealousies. Throughout the war, from the siege of Boston to Yorktown, he would be frustrated by the very sectionalism he abjured; by recalcitrant governors more concerned with their colonies' defenses than with those of the emerging nation; by chronic desertions, inadequate arms, desperately bad food and provisions, unreliable intelligence, and mercantile profiteering; and by limited terms of conscription that prolonged the war and increased the cost of training troops.

Washington took command of his troops in Cambridge, Massachusetts, on July 3, 1775. Lack of ammunition and cannon, however, delayed his first major move until March, 1776, when he fortified Dorchester

Heights, placing Boston and the British fleet in the port under threat of bombardment. The British evacuated the city on March 17, and Washington, having received an honorary doctorate from Harvard, led his troops to New York City, where, he correctly believed, the enemy would strike next.

In New York, Washington had 20,000 ill-trained troops. With them, he was expected to beat back a combined British assault force—then gathering at Staten Island—of some 32,000 crack redcoats under General William Howe and more than 30 war vessels and 400 transports under Sir William's brother, Admiral Richard Howe.

On July 4, 1776, a jubilant Congress proclaimed in the Declaration of Independence that the colonies were free of the Crown under "the Laws of Nature and of Nature's God." But in August, the brothers Howe moved in to seize control of New York Harbor and both the East and Hudson rivers. Facing encirclement, Washington dispatched 5,000 men to Brooklyn Heights, maintaining the rest of his forces in Manhattan.

William Howe defeated the colonials in the Battle of Long Island, inflicting 1,500 casualties. The Howes failed, however, to follow through by sailing up the East River and cutting Washington's forces in two. On August 29, Washington withdrew the rest of his Long Island troops to Manhattan.

Plagued by desertions, Washington's forces dwindled, while British ranks swelled. In September, Howe struck again in a massive landing at Kip's Bay, and facing no opposition from the terrified and retreating colonials (who earned Washington's cane-swinging rage), forced Washington north to Harlem Heights. When Congress rejected his proposal to burn New York, Washington stationed 7,500 men to guard the Hudson at both Fort Washington on the New York shore and Fort Lee on the New Jersey side. He then eluded Howe's advance up the East River by retreating to White Plains in October. Attacked there, he retreated again.

In November, Washington proceeded to Fort Lee only to see it captured by General Charles Cornwallis' troops, who scaled the

Palisades. (The British had taken Fort Washington two days earlier.) With 5,000 men, Washington retreated through New Jersey and crossed the Delaware into Pennsylvania. The British, now in firm control of New York City and most of New Jersey, sent a portion of their force to pursue him, garrisoning finally at Trenton and Bordentown. "I am wearied almost to death," Washington said. "I think the game is pretty near up."

But now, as at so many times when conditions seemed hopeless, Washington moved with daring and grandeur. On Christmas night, 1776, he and his men rowed silently across the ice-laden Delaware River to attack the sleeping encampment of British mercenaries at Trenton. The attack, in which some nine hundred Hessians were taken prisoner, constituted a major turning point in the war, the first of Washington's justly celebrated surprise maneuvers.

After the British captured Fort Washington, New York, in 1776, they moved to take Fort Lee, on the New Jersey side of the Hudson. Some 4,000 soldiers (below) crossed the river, climbed the Palisades, and just missed trapping the garrison, which fled.

Undeterred, a confident Lord Cornwallis moved toward Washington's new headquarters at Trenton's Assunpink Creek. Again Washington played the fox, leaving his Trenton campfires burning throughout the night of January 2, 1777, and moving to Princeton, where he surprised and routed a British garrison, cutting Cornwallis' line of supply. As the British pulled back to New York, Washington set up winter quarters in Morristown. He could well be proud, for in two spectacular moves he had regained most of New Jersey against vastly superior odds.

For their part, the British now resolved on a major new strategy: a thrust from Lake Champlain in the north to secure New England and New York, and to keep Washington busy on two fronts. But at Saratoga, 6,000 British troops under General John Burgoyne were defeated by some 17,000 Continentals led by General Horatio Gates. It was another turning point in the war, one that would rank with Yorktown.

The troops under Washington, however, faced a new period of despair. Howe, instead of coming to the aid of Burgoyne on Gates's southern flank, had chosen to take Philadelphia. Washington, with 10,500 troops,

marched south to meet Howe's 15,000 red-coats at Brandywine Creek on September 11, 1777. The Americans suffered 1,000 casualties in a clear defeat, but made an orderly retreat across the Schuylkill River. Howe entered Philadelphia on September 26. On October 4, in a daring if unsuccessful assault, Washington attacked Howe's main encampment at Germantown, Pennsylvania, and after losing 1,000 more men, retired for the winter to Valley Forge, twenty miles outside Philadelphia.

It was a black season for General Washington. Valley Forge was, he said, "a dreary kind of place, and uncomfortably provided." It was a vast understatement. His men faced bitter cold and frost without shoes or blankets, were forced to drink soup "full of burnt leaves and dirt," and wore lice-ridden clothes, while the British fattened and wined on Pennsylvania Dutch largesse. Before the winter was over, 3,000 of Washington's 9,000 men had deserted. As if bitter hardship in the field was not a great enough burden, Washington was also attacked in Congress. Epitomizing the prevailing hyper-critical mood was Jonathan Sargent's diatribe: "Thousands of Lives & Millions of property are yearly sacrificed to the Insufficiency of our Commander-in-Chief. . . ." But the British failure to attack Valley Forge allowed Washington's war-torn force to recover and to train.

In May, 1778, General Howe was replaced by Sir Henry Clinton, who left Philadelphia in June to march back through New Jersey to New York. Washington, in pursuit, met the British on June 28 at Monmouth, New Jersey, and held the field after angrily quashing a precipitate retreat of American forces under General Charles Lee. He then saw the British use one of his treasured tactics—withdrawal by night (to New York). Monmouth was the last major battle in the North. In February, 1778, the colonists received important news: France, impressed by the American victory at Saratoga, had entered the war in alliance with the colonies.

As Clinton initiated a series of hit-and-run raids in the North, the main British cam-paign under Cornwallis shifted to the South: Savannah was captured; an amphibious assault launched on Charleston took that city; and South Carolina was overrun as one of the worst American defeats took place at Camden on August 16, 1780. After a series of hard-fought battles in the South in the first half of 1781, Cornwallis marched to Virginia, where he brought his full force into Yorktown on August 1.

In the North, Washington's 9,000 Continentals were joined in 1781 by 7,800 French troops under the Comte de Rochambeau. A combined operation with the Comte de Grasse, the French naval commander in the West Indies, was planned for August. The objective: to trap Cornwallis by land and sea. Washington planned the march to Virginia skillfully, and when the French and American armies arrived there, Cornwallis found himself outnumbered two to one. French naval victories and the Franco-American siege convinced Cornwallis that his position was hopeless; he surrendered on October 17, 1781. It was the last major military engagement of the war.

What of Washington as military strategist and commander? It is clear that he made tactical blunders and that many of his contemporaries thought him too indecisive and too imperious for a republican commander. It is also true that he owed much to France, notably at Yorktown. But, the fact remains that Washington won the war.

Esmond Wright has written that "the explanation is not that Washington won [the war] but that Britain lost it, and to the terrain rather than to the enemy." But Washington won on many positive counts. He had unassailable and unflinching courage when it was needed most; the worst conditions brought out his best, in daring and in leadership. He believed in the "glorious cause" of America and, in the darkest moments, could envision its future greatness. And it is incontestable from contemporary descriptions that he possessed charisma, the magnetic aura of leadership that sways men.

On a purely military level he won because he knew his enemies and avoided meeting them on their terms. Faced with the disciplined ranks of Britain's troops, he concluded early: "We should on all occasions avoid a general action, nor put anything to the risk unless compelled by a necessity into which we ought never to be drawn." Accordingly, he became a master of tactical retreat, maneuver at night, and surprise attack.

Three extramilitary events reveal Washington's character and thinking during the Revolutionary period: the notorious Conway Cabal; Washington's firm rejection of a crown in an American monarchy; and his writing of the "Circular Letter to the Governors of All the States."

After his defeat of Burgoyne at Saratoga, General Gates enjoyed a seasonal glamour and applause. He became the focus of opposition to Washington's leadership. In 1777, the year of Gates's victory, Major General Thomas Conway, an Irish-born French officer serving with the colonial troops, wrote to Gates suggesting that the latter might well replace the "weak" Washington. The letter reached Washington, who simply informed Conway that he was aware of the latter's machinations. Further plotting prompted an avowal of congressional support for Washington, and Conway's schemes were aborted. Throughout the intrigue, Washington retained full self-control. Let generals who will, fight for status, he said. As for himself, he had only "one great end in view," the success of the Revolution.

After Yorktown, the unpaid Continental Army seethed over the public's ingratitude and neglect; civil affairs in 1782 bordered on anarchy. Washington was urged by a distinguished Philadelphia colonel, Lewis Nicola, to accept an American crown and thus mend the nation's sundered political fabric with a strong and popular monarchy. The General's reply to Nicola was prompt and vigorous: "Such ideas . . . I must view with abhorrence and reprehend with severity."

Washington's famed "Circular Letter to the Governors of All the States," written from Newburgh, New York, on June 8, 1783, is one of his very few formal statements of political philosophy. Noting the nation's great potential, Washington informed each of the states that if the nation's democratic experiment failed, only Americans could be blamed. "This is the time of their political probation," he wrote, ". . . this is the moment to establish or ruin their national Character for ever." He warned that a weak and eccentric union would enable European states to divide and conquer the country. To secure a more durable union, he advocated four "Pillars on which the glorious Fabrick of our Independency and National Character must be supported." These were "1st. An indissoluble Union of the States under an Federal Head. 2dly. A sacred regard to Public Justice. 3dly. The adoption of a proper Peace Establishment, and 4thly. The prevalence of that pacific and friendly Disposition, among the People of the United States, which will induce them to forget their local prejudices and policies, to make those mutual concessions which are requisite to the general prosperity, and in some instances, to sacrifice their individual advantages to the interest of the Community."

Washington himself set April 19, 1783, the anniversary of the Battle of Lexington, as the date of formal cessation of hostilities with England. He entered New York in triumph in November, welcomed by fireworks and waving flags. After toasting his retiring

Washington's mess chest, at right, was used by his orderlies to prepare his meals in the field.

officers' health at Fraunces' Tavern, he proceeded to Philadelphia, where he settled his expense account with Congress (declaring himself the loser) and resigned his commission at Annapolis in December.

Washington returned to Mount Vernon, his great mission accomplished. "At length," he said at fifty-one, "I am become a private citizen on the banks of the Potomac." He described himself as "a wearied traveller" who had "escaped the quicksands and mires which lay in his way." But he would know no retirement. The Articles of Confederation were proving wholly inadequate to the purposes of liberated colonies seeking union. Like other wealthy landowners and merchants, Washington was alarmed by a government unable to enforce its will, and shocked by such anarchic defiance of government as Shays' (anti-tax, anti-hard-money) Rebellion in Massachusetts. "Combustibles in every state," Washington said, needed only a spark to ignite the land.

In May, 1787, the Constitutional Convention met at Philadelphia. Among the delegates was George Washington of Virginia, who was welcomed to the city by enthusiastic crowds; on May 25 he was unanimously chosen president of the Convention.

If he had expressed hopes for a strong central government as a private citizen, in his new position Washington maintained an immaculate neutrality. Above fray and faction, he presided over the Convention with a grave and paternal silence, "a commanding witness to duty," as Clinton Rossiter has written, a hero "whose presence would raise hopes and quiet fears everywhere."

Washington's sole speech at the Convention urged the adoption of a ratio of 1 to 30,000, rather than 1 to 40,000, in House representation as more adequate "security for the rights and interests of the people." He also cast his vote for a strong Presidency.

Franklin said that often during the Constitutional Convention he had looked at the sun painted on Washington's chair (right) and had wondered if it implied dawn or dusk for the states. The signing of the Constitution convinced him it was a rising sun.

Then, having lent his enormous prestige to the new instrument of government, he returned to Mount Vernon to await the Constitution's ratification, believing it would "probably produce no small influence on the happiness of society through a long succession of ages to come."

With the Constitution ratified (New Hampshire's vote accomplished this on June 21, 1788), the United States had a strong federal government with authority to tax, to make its acts binding on the states, and to conduct foreign relations. Now once again the call went out to Mount Vernon. On February 4, 1789, the electoral college unanimously named George Washington the nation's first President. His Vice President was John Adams, the Northern half of the first balanced ticket. On April 16, Washington left his plantation for the nation's capital, then New York City. Despite his assurance that he had no "wish beyond that of living and dying an honest man on my own farm," he was now called, at the age of fifty-seven,

GEORGE WASHINGTON
PRESIDENT.
1792.

This medal commemorates an Indian treaty of 1792.

to lead a great experiment in democracy. He assumed the Presidency with no less foreboding than pride: "My movements to the chair of government," he said, "will be accompanied by feelings not unlike those of a culprit, who is going to the place of his execution." He had the comfort of knowing, however, that a hopeful, united nation stood by his side. Indeed, Pierce Butler, a Convention delegate, had written that the powers of the Presidency were "greater than I was disposed to make them. Nor . . . do I believe they would have been so great had not many of the members cast their eyes towards General Washington as President. . . ."

The President-elect was besieged by public applause, parades, and celebrations in a triumphal march from Mount Vernon to the capital. In New York, on April 30, 1789, Washington rode to Federal Hall, at the corner of Wall and Nassau streets, for the nation's first presidential inauguration. A jubilant, awed, and expectant crowd massed in the streets, looking up to the canopied portico, awaiting their champion and leader.

Then he appeared, majestic and tall, dressed in brown broadcloth and white silk stockings, his dress sword at his side. Robert Livingston, Chancellor of New York, lifted the Bible to administer the oath, which the Commander in Chief repeated, according to a newspaper account, with "devout fervency." Now President of the United States,

Washington bowed to kiss the Bible. Then Chancellor Livingston said: "It is done," and shouted, "Long live George Washington, President of the United States!"

To both houses of Congress, assembled in the Senate chamber, Washington delivered the first Inaugural Address, his "aspect grave, almost to sadness," said one observer. Acceding once again to the nation's summons from the "asylum" of Mount Vernon, the President deprecated his "inferior endowments from nature." Invoking God's aid, declining a salary, and asking—again—only for his expenses, Washington expressed the hope that ". . . no local prejudices or attachments, no separate views nor party animosities, will misdirect the comprehensive and equal eye" that ought to govern the nation above sectional interests. Liberty and "the republican model of government," he said, are *finally* staked on the experiment intrusted to the hands of the American people."

Washington wished to be a President above politics, above sectionalism, and, indeed, above all controversy. During his first administration he made nonpolitical tours of the thirteen states, North and South, in a symbolic gesture of American unity. He avoided all direct personal advocacy or involvement in congressional legislation and limited his messages to Congress to broad and optimistic homilies. But his hope of remaining completely above the fray was dashed by both Federalist and Republican opposition. Exasperated with Washington's sometimes glacial aloofness, John Adams called him "an old mutton head," and even Jefferson said on one occasion, "Curse on his virtues, they have undone his country."

But in the beginning there were only accolades, as George and Martha put in order the presidential office and household. Meanwhile, Congress debated what to call the new Chief Executive. The Senate, harried by its monarchist faction, debated the merits of "His Elective Majesty," "His Elective Highness," "His Highness, the President of the United States and Protector of the Rights of the Same," even "His Mighti-

President Washington had three executive mansions. In New York he lived first on Cherry Street (left), then on lower Broadway (center); in Philadelphia his home was on High Street (right). The White House, begun in 1792, was occupied in 1800.

ness." A more rational House of Representatives settled the matter. The Chief Executive would be styled, with elegant simplicity, "President of the United States."

Washington was acutely conscious of his immense power in setting precedents: "It is devoutly wished on my part," he said, "that these precedents may be fixed on true principles." If he made the wrong appointments as Chief Executive, he feared he "might perhaps raise a flame of opposition that could not easily, if ever, be extinguished. . . ." He believed that government officials should be appointed with rigorous care, on the basis of aptitude, residence, and "former merits and sufferings in the service." They should also be, he insisted, "just and candid men who are disposed to measure matters on a Continental Scale." In a bid for national unity, he appointed both Federalists and Antifederalists, with evident regard for geographic balance.

As his Secretary of State, Washington appointed Thomas Jefferson of Virginia, an ardent republican, Francophile, and democratic theorist. New York's Alexander Hamilton, Washington's Revolutionary aide-de-camp and confidant, and a major author of

The Federalist, became Secretary of the Treasury. Henry Knox of Massachusetts, his artillerist in the Revolution, was named Secretary of War, and Edmund Randolph, another of Washington's aides-de-camp and a prime mover in Virginia's ratification of the Constitution, was appointed Attorney General.

Washington believed that "the Constitution of the United States, and the laws made under it, must mark the line of [his] official conduct. . . ." He would, he wrote, neither stretch presidential powers "nor relax from them in any instance whatever, unless imperious circumstances shd. render the measure indispensable." Nevertheless, Washington had no qualms about asserting firm presidential authority in areas where the Constitution was silent or gray. The Constitution said nothing about a Cabinet of appointed officers, but Washington named a Cabinet—and a strong one. Nor did the Constitution say anything about the President's right to proclaim neutrality (clearly a negative corollary to Congress' power to declare war), but Washington nonetheless did so during the Franco-British war. Personally, or through subordinates, he was a strong President, asserting executive priority as the occasion demanded and as the law, positively or tacitly, allowed.

Of Washington's methods as Chief Executive, Jefferson later said: "His mind . . . was slow in operation . . . but sure in conclu-

sion. . . . Hearing all suggestions, he selected whatever was best . . . [but was] slow in readjustment." Neither hatred nor friendship, Jefferson added, could bias his decisions.

Deferential to Congress, Washington believed that a bill should be vetoed only if it were clearly unconstitutional. He had a rigid sense of the nation's tripartite system of checks and balances, but he had equal regard for his own presidential prerogatives. When an angry House of Representatives, controlled by Jefferson's Democratic-Republican party, demanded in 1796 that the President submit for its investigation all executive instructions and papers relating to Jay's controversial treaty with England, Washington reminded the House that its assent to this, or any treaty, was not legally required.

In a nation with no experience in strong elected executives, he worked slowly toward a presidential balance of dignity and candor. He believed that the President must in his "public character . . . maintain the dignity of Office, without subjecting himself to the imputation of superciliousness."

When, on a visit to Massachusetts, Washington was invited to call on Governor John Hancock, he maintained his national priority with cool courtesy: "The President of the United States," he wrote to Hancock, "presents his best respects to the Governor, and has the honor to inform him that he shall be at home, 'till 2 o'clock." Washington's re-

sponse to Hancock was supremely right. The President grasped—and grasped early—a central fact of American democracy: the President is not only elected by all the people, he embodies all the people. He is their ultimate representative.

This same conviction, reinforced by Washington's own patrician experience as a Virginia landowner, dictated a substantial degree of ritual pomp. Washington had no hesitation in forcing respect for the Presidency among European observers by moving through the capital in a yellow chariot adorned with gilded cupids and his coat of arms. The Executive Mansion, staffed by fourteen white servants and seven slaves, was managed with comparable splendor. Through doors opened by powdered and liveried lackeys, dignitaries and visitors moved twice weekly to the President's afternoon receptions and to "Lady" Washington's glacially formal levees.

Not all Americans were delighted by this display of executive elegance. The Antifederalists regarded the splendor as a harbinger of a new monarchy and aristocracy that had no place in buckskinned America. For their part, the Washingtons paid little heed to the clamor. They were learning that in assuming public stature they had relinquished all privacy. Besides, the new President had more on his mind than petty objections to his style of living. "There is a rank due to the United States among nations," he said, "which will be withheld, if not absolutely lost, by the reputation of weakness." It was on building the nation's strength that Washington concentrated. To sustain the new government, to secure the faith and allegiance of the nation's owning and controlling classes and of its farmers, laborers, and artisans, Washington knew he must first establish a strong financial system that would guarantee American money and credit and protect manufacture and trade.

The organization of America's basic financial structure was assigned to Alexander Hamilton, whose importance in the administration was second only to Washington's. Hamilton moved with swift efficiency to build his new system. In a deal with Jefferson and Madison, leaders of the Democratic-Republicans, he agreed to support the location of the new national capital on the Potomac, closer to the South, in exchange for the Virginians' approval of the federal government's assumption of state debts as a means of strengthening the central government. Hamilton also proposed that new bonds be issued, covering the federal debt at full value, and that a portion of the government's revenue be set aside regularly for payment of interest and principal.

In 1791, Hamilton suggested that the government form a corporation, the Bank of the United States, to issue bank notes backed by gold and silver as the official United States currency, and to serve as both the main depository of government funds and as the financial agent of the Treasury. It was to be a corporation supervised by the government but run by directors representing private stockholders. When agrarians and states' righters cried out against financial and political tyranny, and questioned Congress' constitutional right to charter a bank, Hamilton replied that this right was inherent in its power to tax, to regulate trade, and to defend the nation. In 1791, Washington signed the bill chartering the Bank. Also under Hamilton's aegis, a decimally based currency was adopted, an excise tax was imposed on whisky, and a protective tariff was adopted to favor domestic goods.

The Jeffersonians were incensed, Jefferson himself close to resignation over what he regarded as a flagrant collusion of financial and political oligarchies. Futilely Washington urged an end to both Hamilton's and Jefferson's "wounding suspicions and irritable charges," which had now reached a state of public vituperation. In 1792, however, both men agreed that only Washington's decision to accept a second term could even temporarily bridge the widening schism; Washington was unanimously re-elected.

The temper of the new federal government was tested by three events during Washington's second administration: the celebrated Whisky Rebellion; the machinations of the licentious Girondist French minister, Edmond Genêt; and the fierce public storm over John Jay's treaty with England.

In July, 1794, Washington was challenged by defiant whisky distillers in western Pennsylvania who abhorred the Federalist excise tax on their product. (It was difficult and expensive to transport corn to market, but when distilled into whisky, it became an easily movable cash crop—and their chief source of income.) They terrorized excise agents, forced troops guarding the chief excise inspector to surrender, and threatened to march on Pittsburgh. Alarmed that the revolt might spread, Washington called for some 15,000 state militiamen to check the insurgents and thus prove that the United States was "able [and] willing to support our government and laws." He and Hamilton both rode out to review the militia. There was little opposition to this demonstration of executive strength.

Throughout Washington's tenure as President, revolutionary France and its conflict with England remained as divisive an issue as Hamilton's fiscal programs. Washington's own policy was a formal and circumspect neutrality. But the tension was heightened in 1793 by the arrival in the United States of a new French minister, Citizen Edmond Genêt, who was messianically committed to recruiting American money and volunteers for France against Britain and gaining an advantageous commercial treaty for his

This Federalist cartoon has Washington and his troops marching out to meet an invasion by French republican "cannibals," while Jefferson, giving orders to his friends in a French accent, tries to impede the advance.

country. Playing on American antipathy toward Britain, the flamboyant Genêt harangued the populace and hired and armed United States privateers to prey on British ships and return them as prizes to American ports. "Ten thousand people in the streets of Philadelphia," said John Adams, "day after day threatened to drag Washington out of his house, and effect a revolution in the Government, or compel it to declare war in favor of the French revolution. . . ."

Washington and Hamilton, unmoved by the anti-British sentiment, were enraged by Genêt's activities. And when he threatened to appeal to the people for support (over Washington's head), even Jefferson, the Francophile, was upset. Washington demanded the minister's recall, but Genêt, fearful of returning to France (now under Jacobin control), appealed for and was granted asylum in the United States.

Despite Washington's firm declaration of neutrality, the British continued to impress American seamen and search United States ships on the pretext of hunting for deserters. They also continued to occupy military posts they had promised to abandon, and to incite the Indians to harass the Western frontier. The Maine-Canada boundary was also in dispute, as was the exclusion of American ships from West Indian trade.

To settle these issues, Washington sent Chief Justice John Jay to London in April, 1794. The contents of Jay's Treaty were not made public until March, 1795. Britain agreed to abandon the frontier military posts by 1796, to open her East and West Indian ports, to refer the Maine boundary dispute to a commission, and to negotiate ship-seizure claims, but she made no concession on trading rights, impressment, or the incitement of Indians. Moreover, the United States was denied the right to export many vital products to the West Indies.

The public and press exploded in wrath. Hamilton was stoned in the streets. The attacks on the treaty were aimed directly at Washington, phrased, said the President, in "such exaggerated and indecent terms as could scarcely be applied to a Nero, a notorious defaulter, or even to a common pickpocket." But Washington's prestige enabled him to withstand the assault. He signed the treaty in August, 1795. In another—more popular—treaty, with Spain, Washington secured the right of navigation on the Mississippi and the right to export from New Orleans duty-free for a period of three years.

In 1796, angered by Republican attacks and disillusioned by the calumny and abuses of the public, Washington reshuffled his Cabinet. After Jefferson and Hamilton resigned, the arch-Tory Timothy Pickering became Secretary of State, Oliver Wolcott headed the Treasury, and James McHenry was Secretary of War. Washington himself had become uncharacteristically partisan. "I shall not," he declared, ". . . bring a man into any office of consequence knowingly whose political tenets are adverse to the measures which the general government are pursuing; for this, in my opinion, would be a sort of political suicide."

The Antifederalist press attacked him for this policy. The President, said one newspaper, was "the scourge and misfortune of our country." Nor was Washington ever able to ignore such assaults. At a Cabinet meeting early in his administration, Jefferson recalled, Washington was visibly enraged by an attack in the press. "By god," Jefferson reports him as saying, "he had rather be on his own farm than to be made *emperor of the world.*"

In September, 1796, he was ready to deliver his Farewell Address, a speech—polished by Hamilton—that would have incalculable effect on United States foreign policy for generations. Warning against the debilitating effects of sectionalism and excessive party spirit, the retiring President abjured "the insidious wiles of foreign influence." He inveighed against permanent alliances and permanent animosities, urging only "temporary alliances for extraordinary emergencies."

For himself, Washington added: "I anticipate with pleasing expectation that retreat, in which I promise myself to realize, without alloy, the sweet enjoyment of partaking, in the midst of my fellow-citizens, the benign influence of good Laws under a free Government—the ever favourite object of my heart. . . ."

Now sixty-five, the old soldier was able to go home at last. But he had put his stamp on the American Presidency forever. He had sought information "from all quarters" and judged the conflicting data "more independently than any man" John Adams "ever knew." He had, as Jefferson said, "decided the course to be pursued . . . kept the government steadily in it, unaffected by the agitation."

"It was no easy task," wrote Clinton Rossiter, "to be the first occupant of a mistrusted office under a dubious Constitution." It is unmistakably true that Washington made the government of America work as only he, at his point in time, could. He built the peace on which it was based; he presided over the formulation of its legal structure; he nurtured and governed its birth. As Rossiter said, "He fulfilled the hopes of the friends of the Constitution and spiked the fears of its critics."

In retirement Washington was content "to make, and sell, a little flour. . . . To repair houses going fast to ruin. . . . To amuse myself in agriculture and rural pursuits. . . . Now and then to meet friends I esteem. . . ." But his retirement was not entirely bucolic. President Adams, alarmed by declining relations with France, named him commander of a provisional army on alert. Washington defended prosecutions under the hated and unconstitutional Alien and Sedition Acts as necessary to prevent "a disunion of the states." And he scored the Republicans for condemning every Federalist act.

But the life of the planter and landowner prevailed, as Washington began his "diurnal course with the sun." At night, he said, he felt "tired and disinclined" to write or read. Besides, he concluded, he might soon be "looking into Domesday Book."

On Saturday, December 14, 1799, the Commander in Chief, suffering from a tracheal infection (possibly tuberculosis), prepared to pay "the debt which we all must pay." "I am not afraid to go," he said. Just before he died he put the fingers of his left hand on his right wrist and counted his pulse, his lips moving.

He was buried in a vault at the foot of Mount Vernon's hill, "embalmed," said one newspaper, "by the tears of *America.*"

—WILSON SULLIVAN

G. Washington [signature]

A PICTURE PORTFOLIO

*This cotton handkerchief, probably made in
1777, depicts Washington as a wartime hero.*

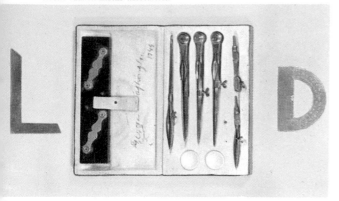

After learning the surveyor's craft with his father's tools, Washington acquired the set of drafting instruments above — probably in 1749, the date inside the case. That year he received an appointment as surveyor of Culpeper County.

On the map below, Washington sketched the land he traversed on his journey up the Ohio Valley to Fort Le Boeuf, near Lake Erie, in 1753–54. In May, 1754, he led the English troops that struck the first blow in the Seven Years' War, at a spot just northwest of the mountain spur the map shows running northward from the Allegheny Range.

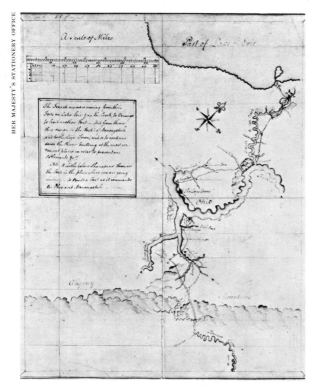

ADVENTURES OF
A YOUNG VIRGINIAN

What route could the young Virginian, left without a father at eleven, take to future wealth and fame? Military service was one way. His mother said No to a proposal that George join the British navy when he was fourteen. But six years later, after he had become a surveyor and the owner of almost 1,500 acres of land, and after his beloved half brother Lawrence had died of tuberculosis, George joined the Virginia militia as a major. It was the first step on a long—and dangerous—road. Several times it seemed unlikely that he would live long enough to achieve a great future. Although he was exceptionally strong and vigorous, he suffered from malaria, smallpox, pleurisy, dysentery, and perhaps even typhoid, all before he was thirty. As a soldier, he underwent constant exposure to foul weather. On his way back from an expedition to Fort Le Boeuf in 1753, he almost drowned when he fell off his raft in the icy Allegheny River, and he was shot at (and missed) by an Indian standing less than fifty feet away. In the terrible massacre of General Braddock's troops in 1755, only a third of the officers emerged unhurt, but Washington was one of them, although four bullets had punctured his coat and two horses had been shot under him. Virginia's Governor Robert Dinwiddie, who made Washington commander in chief of the colony's militia in 1755, thought him a "braw laddie." And so he was. But he was also a lucky one.

Charles Willson Peale painted the portrait of Washington at left in 1772. It is the earliest known picture of the future President, who is wearing his Virginia militia colonel's uniform. The gilt crescent-shaped gorget around his neck identifies him as an officer.

General Braddock falls from his horse, mortally hurt, while a French and Indian war party decimates his close-ranked troops, in the Edwin Willard Deming painting below of the July, 1755, Battle of the Wilderness. The figure to the right of Braddock may be Washington, his aide-de-camp. The debacle temporarily ended the English attempt to take French Fort Duquesne.

The unusual identification of the figures in this charming water color, done about 1780, suggests that the anonymous artist was a Pennsylvania German.

"SAFE HARBOR"

I am now, I believe, fixed at this seat with an agreeable consort for life," Washington wrote from Mount Vernon in 1759, "and hope to find more happiness in retirement than I ever experienced amidst a wide and bustling world. . . ." Out of the Army and married to the wealthy, capable Martha Custis, Washington passed fifteen pleasant years as a more or less private man. He was chosen a member of the House of Burgesses, was made a justice of Fairfax County, and was always busy as master of Mount Vernon. But life was not without its trials and tragedies. As stepfather to his wife's two children, he agonized through the delicate Patsy Custis' five-year struggle with epilepsy and her death in 1773. The behavior of Jack Custis drove Washington to express a sarcastic wish that schooling would make Jack "fit for more useful purposes than a horse racer." A schoolmaster subsequently voiced the opinion that Jack was the most "indolent" and "surprisingly voluptuous" young man he had ever seen. But Washington was unable to bring himself to apply badly needed discipline, and Martha was a very indulgent mother. Jack lounged his way through an abbreviated education and married early. These were Washington's happiest years. Then, in 1775, his peace, and America's, were broken. "I am embarked," he wrote a few days before going to Boston as commander in chief of the Revolutionary forces, "on a wide ocean, boundless in its prospect, and in which, perhaps, no safe harbor is to be found."

Charles Willson Peale painted the miniature (above) of Martha Washington, on ivory, around 1776. The General wore it in a gold locket around his neck for the rest of the war.

Below are Martha's children, John Parke (Jack) and Martha Parke (Patsy) Custis, as painted by John Wollaston.

COMMANDER IN CHIEF

Washington's troops forced the British to leave Boston in March, 1776, but for months afterward there was little to cheer the rebels: an expedition against Canada failed, New York fell, and Washington was chased across New Jersey in a calamitous retreat. His army finally came to rest in December on the Pennsylvania side of the Delaware River—ostensibly to defend Philadelphia, but actually, it seemed, to await the inevitable crushing blow by the British, or worse, to endure dissolution through despair, desertion, and the departure of militiamen as enlistment terms ended. Manifestly, Washington needed to kindle enthusiasm; thus, he told Congress he would go on the offensive "as soon as there shall be the least probability of doing it." He took the initiative with an advance across the Delaware on Christmas night. The battle at Trenton the following morning, in which the American soldiers killed or captured almost 1,000 Hessians, gave the rebel cause a crucial new lease on life.

Congress ordered the above medal struck to commemorate the British evacuation of Boston on March 17, 1776. It depicts Washington and members of his staff on Dorchester Heights, where the Americans, in a surprise move, had set up artillery, making untenable the British position in the city below.

As darkness fell on Christmas night, the army began its tortuous crossing of the Delaware, as shown in the painting at right by Edward Hicks. Despite high winds, freezing temperature, and thudding ice floes, the maneuver was completed before dawn.

The above painting of the Battle of Princeton is the work of Washington's stepgrandson (and Robert E. Lee's father-in-law), George Washington Parke Custis. General Hugh Mercer, kneeling at right, led the troops that made the first contact with the British and was mortally wounded by a bayonet. Washington, at left, rallied the American soldiers, overran the British position, and then chased the fleeing enemy, crying, "It is a fine fox chase, my boys."

The 9,000 soldiers who encamped at Valley Forge (right) lacked blankets, clothing, shoes, and, as the desperate proclamation seen at far right indicates, sufficient food.

TRIUMPHS
AND TRAVAILS

Washington avoided a pitched battle with a British force sent to retake Trenton; he led his army around the enemy flank in a night march and on January 3, 1777, attacked the British post at Princeton. The operation cleared most of western New Jersey of the British, but it was the last major American victory in the area for eighteen months. General Howe took Philadelphia that September, and in December, Washington's troops set up winter quarters at Valley Forge. That incredibly bitter season was profitable in one way: Baron von Steuben, a German officer, drilled the ragged rebel soldiers. The discipline paid off in June, 1778: at the Battle of Monmouth, after General Charles Lee ordered an American retreat, Washington was able to rally Lee's men from the verge of a rout and managed to hold the field against a large body of British veterans. His motley army had finally come of age.

By His Excellency

GEORGE WASHINGTON, Esquire, GENERAL and COMMANDER in CHIEF of the Forces of the United States of America.

BY Virtue of the Power and Direction to Me especially given, I hereby enjoin and require all Persons residing within seventy Miles of my Head Quarters to thresh one Half of their Grain by the 1st Day of February, and the other Half by the 1st Day of March next ensuing, on Pain, in Case of Failure, of having all that shall remain in Sheaves after the Period above mentioned, seized by the Commissaries and Quarter-Masters of the Army, and paid for as Straw.

GIVEN under my Hand, at Head Quarters, near the Valley Forge, in Philadelphia County, this 20th Day of December, 1777.

G. WASHINGTON.

By His Excellency's Command,
ROBERT H. HARRISON, Sec'y.

37

Emanuel Leutze's painting shows Washington, in a fury, taking charge of the retreating troops at Monmouth.

At left, General Lee, relieved of command and stung by a dressing down from Washington, sags in his saddle.

HEROES OF THE REVOLUTION

INDEPENDENCE NATIONAL HISTORICAL COLLECTION

DANIEL MORGAN

Morgan changed the course of the Revolutionary War in the South in 1781 when he won the Battle of Cowpens. A large, rough-and-tumble man, he had run away from his home near the Delaware River at eighteen and had settled in the Shenandoah Valley, where he became a teamster, farmer, and backwoods fighter. He was wounded during the French and Indian War: a ball hit him in the neck and tore out through his face, resulting in a permanent scar. As the American rebellion began, Congress called for "expert riflemen"; Morgan, then thirty-nine, raised a company of Virginia sharpshooters and in three weeks marched the six hundred miles to Boston. His company joined the drive to Quebec, where Morgan was captured. After an exchange of prisoners in 1776, Morgan was given command of a rifle regiment and made a colonel. He and his buckskinned troops distinguished themselves with Gates, in the North, and with Washington, near Philadelphia. Because Congress would not promote him, Morgan tried to resign in 1779, but came back to help Gates in the wake of the Camden defeat, at last becoming a brigadier general. After Cowpens, illness forced him to retire. He served his country again, notably during the Whisky Rebellion in 1794 and as a one-term congressman late in the century. Morgan died in 1802.

INDEPENDENCE NATIONAL HISTORICAL COLLECTION

JOHN PAUL JONES

Born a gardener's son at Kirkbean, Scotland, in 1747, Jones went to sea at thirteen and won his first command (of a trading vessel) at twenty-one. In 1775 he was commissioned an officer in the infant American Navy and became a raider, taking prizes and threatening coastal towns on both sides of the Atlantic. Tories called him a pirate, and "the nurses of Scotland hushed their crying charges [or so Disraeli wrote] by the whisper of his name. . . ." Hot-tempered and arrogant, to his associates Jones was a difficult man. Yet his faults were outweighed by the tactical skill, single-mindedness, and bravery he displayed, as in the famous battle off Flamborough Head on September 23, 1779. In command of a motley fleet, he engaged a British convoy bound for the Baltic, and with his flagship, the ancient East Indiaman *Bonhomme Richard*, captured the bigger, better-armed *Serapis* after a long and terrible encounter that so shattered the old *Richard* it sank some thirty-six hours later. Refused flag rank due to the opposition of other officers, and bereft, in 1783, of an American Navy to serve, Jones went to Europe. In 1788, he became a rear admiral in the navy of the Russian Empress, Catherine the Great. Intrigue against him forced his retirement, however, and in 1790 he went to France, where he died two years later.

NATHANAEL GREENE

"He came to us," Henry Knox declared, "the . . . most untutored being I ever met with, but, in less than twelve months, he was equal to any General officer in the army, and very superior to most of them." A congenital limp kept Nathanael Greene from becoming a Rhode Island militia officer in 1774, but he joined as a private, and in the spring of 1775 was made commander of the troops raised to aid Massachusetts at the siege of Boston. By August, 1776, when he was thirty-three, he was a major general in the Continental Army. He fought at Trenton and Germantown, and at Valley Forge he reluctantly accepted appointment as quartermaster general. He left that job after two years because of a row with Congress. Taking charge of the war in the South in 1780, he waged a brilliant campaign of attrition against a superior force. As Greene described it, "We fight, get beat, rise and fight again." The British, cut down piecemeal while seeking the decisive battle Greene refused to give them, were compelled, by the autumn of 1781, to quit all their forts in the interior and hole up, under siege, in Charleston. Showered with honors, but physically and financially exhausted by the war, Greene was only forty-three years old when he died in 1786 on an estate that had been presented to him by a grateful state of Georgia.

GEORGE ROGERS CLARK

Child of the Virginia frontier, surveyor, and explorer, Clark was twenty-four when in 1777 he was made responsible for protecting Kentucky from British-supported Indian raids. He chose an outrageously bold course: invasion of the distant Illinois country and seizure of Detroit to stop the flow of arms. By stealth, bravery, and bluff, his band of guerrillas took the towns of Kaskaskia, Cahokia, Prairie du Rocher, and Vincennes. He won offers of peace from many Indian nations, and after Vincennes was captured by the British, he retook it. Clark never reached Detroit; control of the Old Northwest remained in armed dispute for two years after Yorktown. But at the end Clark held most of that savage theater, a fact reflected in the terms of the Treaty of Paris. He then became a commissioner of land grants and of Indian affairs. Unpaid for his military service (although Virginia gave him a sword and some land), he involved himself in unsuccessful colonizing projects in the West. He accepted a general's commission from France and would have led an attack on Spanish Louisiana, but Washington issued a proclamation against the venture. Indigent, discredited, finally a dependent cripple, Clark died near Louisville in 1818. He was the older brother of William Clark, co-leader of the famous Lewis and Clark expedition.

VICTORY AT YORKTOWN

ABOVE AND BELOW: MUSÉE DE VERSAILLES, COURTESY OF COLONIAL WILLIAMSBURG

After ravaging Virginia during the spring of 1781, Lord Cornwallis brought his troops to Yorktown to await reinforcements. Besieged there by Franco-American forces under Washington and Rochambeau, and prevented by the French navy from escaping by sea, Cornwallis realized that his situation was hopeless. The painting above, by eyewitness Louis Van Blarenberghe, shows the French marching into the siege positions; below, the surrendering redcoats parade between the French (rear) and the Americans on October 18, 1781.

MOUNT VERNON

After the war, Washington settled into what he hoped would be permanent repose as planter and host at Mount Vernon. His estate, once known as Epsewasson, had been in the family since the seventeenth century and had been renamed Mount Vernon, after British Admiral Edward Vernon, by Washington's half brother Lawrence. After leasing the property in 1754 from his widowed sister-in-law (he inherited it when she died in 1761), the General added a second story and wings to the main house, imported furniture for it, and planted trees around it. Gradually he added to the original 2,126 acres; this growth continued until the plantation encompassed more than 8,000 acres, including five farms. Between 1783 and 1787, the banquet hall and the cupola atop the hipped roof were finished, outbuildings were added or improved, and the bowling green in front of the mansion was graded. Washington found directing these improvements and looking after the farming exceedingly satisfying, but the nation needed him, and he was called away: first to attend the Constitutional Convention in 1787, then to assume the Presidency two years later.

An unknown artist painted this view of the Mount Vernon mansion circa 1790. In the foreground the Washington family strolls on the bowling green. Nelly Custis, Martha's granddaughter, is at the left. Washington, with cane, and Martha walk arm in arm. The pair at the right is thought to be young George Custis and his tutor.

The high secretary below was a late addition to Washington's study. He bought it in Philadelphia as he prepared for retirement from the Presidency. The desk was willed to Dr. James Craik, a friend since 1754 and one of the attending physicians at Washington's deathbed. It was reacquired for Mount Vernon from the doctor's descendants in 1905.

The Palladian window above is considered to be one of the most striking details in the handsome New Room—the banquet hall completed in 1787. The curtains are of dimity, with green satin festoons.

An excellent sample of early Virginia architecture, the West Parlor (below) was probably finished just before Washington moved into the house with his new bride. The Washington portrait is by C. W. Peale.

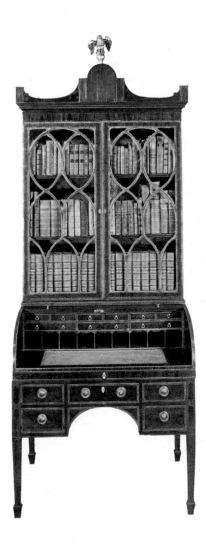

45

THE FIRST PRESIDENT

Before he left Mount Vernon in the spring of 1789, the President-elect confessed to Henry Knox deep misgivings about his new role. He felt, he said, like a felon on the way to be hanged; he foresaw "an ocean of difficulties." His journey north was a triumph. On April 23, a week before the inaugural, he was rowed across New York Bay from Elizabethtown to the temporary federal capital at New York. Cannon boomed and thousands of citizens on the shore cheered emotionally. The city was full to overflowing; one visitor exclaimed, "We shall remain here if we have to sleep in tents as many will have to do." On April 30, the first President was sworn in on the balcony of Federal Hall. Then he retired inside to deliver his Inaugural Address. Despite the city's joy and the dignity of the occasion, Washington's extreme discomfort was evident to Senator Maclay of Pennsylvania, who noted how the President fidgeted and fumbled with his papers. And Massachusetts Congressman Fisher Ames wrote of Washington's "modesty, actually shaking; his voice deep, a little tremulous, and so low as to call for close attention. . . ." The General was right; his greatest trial had begun.

In New York Bay, Washington's triumphal barge (left), bearing federal, state, and city dignitaries, and "rowed by thirteen pilots of this harbor, dressed in white uniform," neared the landing at the foot of Wall Street, while gaily decorated ships and the cannon on the Battery fired thirteen-gun salutes. The New York Daily Advertiser *referred to the event as "animated and moving beyond description."*

Amos Doolittle made the engraving below of Washington's inauguration at Federal Hall from a drawing by eyewitness Peter Lacour. After administering the oath, Chancellor Robert R. Livingston cried out, "Long live George Washington, President of the United States!" and the spectators, clogging the roadways and the rooftops and windows of the buildings along Wall and Broad streets, echoed his words.

FEDERALIST COLOSSUS

He was a revolutionary who considered the frame of the government he revolted against "the best in the world"; he was admired as a political philosopher—the brilliant advocate of strong central rule—and hated as the highhanded, egocentric party boss, even by many who shared his political beliefs.

This was Alexander Hamilton—next to the President, the dominant figure of Washington's administration. Born of a common-law marriage in the Caribbean in 1755 or 1757, Hamilton came to New York in 1772 for an education. At King's College (later Columbia), he became a leader of the unrest that led to the Revolution. While serving as an officer under Washington, he began to develop his theories of democratic rule and to campaign for a convention to enlarge the powers of the federal government. To survive, Hamilton thought, the nation would have to be what it was not under the Articles of Confederation—firmly united, with the separatist tendencies of the states kept in check, able to defend itself against attack, and dependable in economic matters. Hamilton favored government support of American commerce and the encouragement of an educated, well-to-do ruling class, whose interests would be closely tied to interests of the nation.

Many of his aristocratic ideas, drawn from the British model, clashed with strong republican feelings in the states. His plan for government did not attract support at the Constitutional Convention in 1787, and at the end of that long conclave he admitted (according to Madison) that "No man's ideas were more remote [from the final draft of the Constitution] than his own were known to be." Even so, he had been a member of the Committee of Style that produced the finished document; he pleaded for its unanimous approval by the delegates, and then went home to begin writing, with the help of Madison and Jay, arguments in favor of ratification—*The Federalist* papers. He believed that the new Constitution, imperfect though it might be, offered a viable alternative to the "anarchy and convulsion" he saw rapidly engulfing the Confederation.

Appointed Secretary of the Treasury by Washington in 1789, he continued to strengthen the federal powers. At his insistence the United States assumed full responsibility for its Revolutionary debts, and for the war debts of the states. This served to unite the wealthy creditor class behind the central government and stabilize the economy. With an excise on whisky, he confirmed the government's right to tax. Perhaps most important, his arguments in favor of the creation of a national bank—the doctrine of implied powers—gave the Constitution the flexibility it would need to cope with the changing demands of passing decades.

Hamilton was, as Thomas Jefferson once said, "a colossus" to the Federalist party. He was more, however: he was a colossus in the history of democratic government.

This portrait of Hamilton is by John Trumbull.

WASHINGTON'S APPOINTEES

JOHN JAY

First Chief Justice of the Supreme Court, the cultured and diligent Jay—born in New York City in 1745—was a noted lawyer and a member of both Continental Congresses. He served as minister to Spain from 1780 to 1782, and then participated in the peace talks in Paris. His insistence that the American commissioners be regarded as representatives of the United States, not of the "Colonies," delayed the negotiations and may have cost the United States possession of Canada, which the British might have been willing to cede in exchange for an early end to the war. Jay also shared responsibility with John Adams for suing for peace without consultation with France. The final treaty was signed in September, 1783, and Jay returned home early the next year to serve as secretary of foreign affairs. An advocate of a strong central government, he wrote five *Federalist* papers. He was named Chief Justice by Washington, but went to England in 1794 to cope with the threat of a new war. His success was limited, for the treaty bearing his name did not include British recognition of American neutrality rights. He returned to New York to find himself elected governor, and held that office for six years, retiring to private life at the age of fifty-five. Twenty-eight years later, Jay died in Bedford, New York.

JAMES WILSON

A university-educated Scot, James Wilson arrived in the colonies in 1765, at the age of twenty-three. He was soon appointed Latin tutor at the College of Philadelphia, and began studying law. By 1774, he had a large practice in southern Pennsylvania. Elected to Congress in 1775, 1782, and 1785, he signed the Declaration of Independence and spoke as a strong nationalist. In his political philosophy there was also a strain of democratic theory, but he made enemies among the rights-of-man idealists when he opposed the democratic Pennsylvania constitution of 1776. His philosophy and debating skills influenced the federal Constitution in 1787; among his contributions to the Convention was his daring advocacy of direct election of the nation's Chief Executive. He asked Washington for the job of Chief Justice in the new government, but was made an associate justice instead. On the bench and in law lectures, he promulgated his Federalist ideas further, trying to establish himself as an American Blackstone. He did not quite achieve that eminence, partly because he had become deeply involved in land speculation and was caught short by a recession in the 1790's; hounded by creditors, he began to fall apart emotionally. Wilson contracted malaria in 1798 and died that same year in an inn at Edenton, North Carolina.

HENRY KNOX

There was, wrote Washington, "no one whom I have loved more sincerely" than General Knox. Seventh of his Scotch-Irish parents' ten sons, Knox was born in Boston in 1750, quit school early to support his widowed mother, and celebrated coming of age by opening The London Book-Store in Boston in 1771. A soldier while still in his teens, he rose rapidly in rank during the Revolution, becoming Washington's artillery commander in 1775 and brigadier general the following year. He hauled cannon over the mountains from Fort Ticonderoga to Dorchester Heights, forcing the British to evacuate Boston. He fought in the battles around New York and in the surprise attack on Trenton, and gave Washington dependable support in numerous other engagements, including Yorktown. A major general by 1781, Knox commanded the Army post at West Point, where soon the military academy he had suggested would be founded. He was named Secretary of War in 1785, and retained the position under Washington, unsuccessfully urging the construction of a strong military establishment. Huge, energetic, self-confident, he "retired" in 1794 and began a many-sided business and political career, mostly in Maine. A chicken bone, stuck in his intestinal tract, ended General Knox's life in 1806.

EDMUND RANDOLPH

Scion of a leading Virginia family, Randolph studied at William and Mary and in his father's law office before commencing a remarkably rapid rise to national prominence. An aide-de-camp to Washington during the Revolution, he became attorney general of his state at twenty-three. He was elected to the Continental Congress three years later, in 1779, and to the governorship of Virginia in 1786. As a delegate to the Constitutional Convention, he presented the Virginia Plan —the foundation of the finished Constitution. But he opposed a one-man executive branch, criticized the breadth of power given the central government by the Constitution, and refused to sign that document in Philadelphia. In the crucial Virginia Ratification Convention, however, he supported adoption of the document as the practical course. Washington made him Attorney General and, after Jefferson resigned, Secretary of State. Randolph served capably in that difficult post until the summer of 1795; then rumors (the accuracy of which is still in doubt) of corrupt dealings with a French diplomat resulted in Randolph's resignation. He returned to his private law practice and, in 1807, led the successful defense of former Vice President Aaron Burr at his trial for treason. Edmund Randolph was sixty years old when he died in 1813.

AN EXCISEMAN. Carrying off two Kegs of Whiskey, is pursued by two farmers, intending to tar and feather him, he runs for 'Squire Vultures to divide with him; but is met on the way by his evil genius who claps an hook in his nose, leads him off to a Gallows, where he is immediately hanged.

The unpopular exciseman, confiscating tax evaders' whisky, comes to a bad end in this antifederal cartoon.

THE WHISKY REBELLION

Washington considered the development of a firm national government, based on the new Constitution, his prime responsibility as President. The most crucial test of federal strength—and one of the most important events of his administration—came in 1794. In western Pennsylvania, an organized rebellion broke out over the federal excise tax on whisky. Responding to the crisis, President Washington affirmed the taxation powers of Congress and the legitimacy of executive and judicial responsibility for enforcing the laws. "If the laws are to be so trampled upon with impunity," he warned, "and a minority . . . is to dictate to the majority, there is an end put, at one stroke, to republican government." To assure that the uprising would be controlled before it became a general Antifederalist conflagration, Washington called for the enlistment of an army, and he and Secretary of the Treasury Alexander Hamilton rode with the 12,000-man force as it marched off toward insurrectionist territory. This display of executive determination brought to an end the Whisky Rebellion without one shot having to be fired.

Pittsburgh Allegheny County

I DO ~~solemnly~~ promise, ~~henceforth~~ to submit to the Laws of the United States; that I will not directly nor indirectly oppose the execution of the Acts for raising a Revenue on Distilled Spirits and Stills, and that I will support as far as the Laws require the civil authority in affording the protection due to all officers and other Citizens.

September 11, 1794.

The few "Whisky Boys" who were caught in the federal army's sweep through western Pennsylvania were allowed to sign the oath at right, and to go free. Two were imprisoned, but they were later pardoned by Washington.

In the painting below by eyewitness Frederick Kemmelmeyer, Washington actively assumes his presidential role as Commander in Chief of the armed forces, reviewing some of the troops raised against the whisky rebels.

In this family portrait by Edward Savage, two of Martha's grandchildren, George Washington Parke Custis and Eleanor Parke Custis, join the Washingtons around a table spread with a map of the Potomac River. Martha points to the site of the federal capital, under construction when Washington died.

Attended by his wife, three physicians, and members of his household, Washington died quietly the night of December 14, 1799. "With perfect resignation and a full possession of his reason," wrote his secretary, Tobias Lear, "he closed his well spent life."

NEW-YORK HISTORICAL SOCIETY, OLDS COLLECTION

"THE WEARIED TRAVELLER"

To the wearied traveller, who sees a resting-place, and is bending his body to lean thereon, I now compare myself," Washington wrote, with poetic poignancy, on his next-to-last day as President. "The remainder of my life . . . will be occupied in rural amusement." He predicted he would not stir more than twenty miles from Mount Vernon the rest of his days. But complete withdrawal was neither his style, nor his lot; John Adams' troubles, the war crisis of 1798, and the building of the nearby federal city all engaged his energies from time to time. Even so, he devoted long hours to the running of his plantation, played host to numerous guests, enjoyed the company of the chatty, cheery Martha, and indulged himself by letting his correspondence slide a bit. Though he had jokingly "entered into an engagement" with friends "not to quitt the theatre of this world" before the turn of the new century (so Martha wrote), Washington signed his will in July, 1799, and died in December of that year, defaulting on his "contract" by just eighteen days.

C. W. Peale painted him during the Revolutionary War.

Joseph Wright portrayed General Washington in 1784.

Adams thought this Savage portrait was the best.

This painting by A. V. Wertmuller was done in 1794.

A MAN
OF MANY FACES

The first President was one of the most frequently painted, drawn, and sculpted men of his time. "*In for a penny, in for a pound,* is an old adage," he remarked amusedly in 1785. "I am so hackneyed to the touches of the painter's pencil, that I am *now* altogether at their beck; and sit, 'like Patience on a monument,' whilst they are delineating the lines of my face. It is a proof, among many others, of what habit and custom can accomplish. At first I was as impatient at the request, and as restive under the operation, as a colt is of the saddle. The next time I submitted very reluctantly, but with less flouncing. Now, no dray-horse moves more readily to his thill than I to the painter's chair." Some of the portraits reveal, in the set of his jaw, Washington's chronic problems with false teeth; most fail to show the President's true complexion—sallow, scarred, and pock-marked. But from most of the numerous attempts to portray him—even though they are so various it is sometimes hard to believe they are all paintings of the same man—there emanates a sense of dignity, of seriousness bordering on sadness, and of the artists' consciousness of their subject as a hero.

The above sketch, by Benjamin Latrobe, is reputed to have been drawn at the Mount Vernon dinner table.

Jean Antoine Houdon, the French sculptor, came to the United States in 1785 and made the life mask below for a bust of Washington. Experts point out that pressure of the plaster sometimes reshapes the face, making such a mask an inexact impression.

MONUMENT TO A HERO

Almost 556 feet tall, the Washington Monument towers over the spacious Capital city, its white marble facing tinted by the changing light of day, glowing under floodlights at night, and echoed in the long reflecting pool. The idea of a national memorial to Washington was conceived in 1833, and the design was more or less settled on in 1836, but the cornerstone was not laid until Independence Day, 1848, and by 1858 only 156 feet of obelisk had been erected. No work at all was done on it for the next twenty years—a period of turmoil for the nation. Construction began again in 1878, and six years later, on a blustery December day, the monument was finally finished.

In the 1875 cartoon above, the spirit of Washington chides Columbia for failing to finish his monument.

The exotic design at left was entered in the Washington National Monument Society's contest.

The winner of that competition, opposite, was the work of Robert Mills. The Monument Society then eliminated the neoclassic temple base, with its heroic sculpture of Washington in a war chariot. Even so, the monument cost $1,187,710 to build.

NATIONAL ARCHIVES

FACTS IN SUMMARY: GEORGE WASHINGTON

CHRONOLOGY

UNITED STATES		WASHINGTON
	1732	*Born February 11 (February 22, n.s.)*
	1748	*Joins surveying expedition to Shenandoah*
	1749	*Appointed county surveyor*
	1751	*Visits Barbados*
	1752	*Lawrence Washington dies*
		Receives commission in Virginia militia
	1753	*Delivers ultimatum to French at Fort Le Boeuf*
French and Indian War begins	1754	*Attacks French party near Fort Duquesne*
		Capitulates at Fort Necessity
	1755	*Serves as aide to General Braddock*
		Appointed commander in chief of militia
French abandon Ohio Valley	1758	*Elected to House of Burgesses*
		Resigns commission
	1759	*Marries Martha Custis*
	1761	*Inherits Mount Vernon*

UNITED STATES		WASHINGTON
Treaty of Paris	1763	
Stamp Act	1765	
Townshend Acts	1767	
Massachusetts Circular Letter	1768	*Becomes a justice of Fairfax County*
House of Burgesses dissolved	1769	
Boston Massacre	1770	*Secures Ohio Valley lands for veterans of French and Indian War*
Boston Tea Party	1773	
Intolerable Acts	1774	*Delegate to First Continental Congress*
First Continental Congress		
Lexington and Concord	1775	*Delegate to Second Continental Congress*
Bunker Hill		
Second Continental Congress		*Elected commander in chief of Army*
British evacuate Boston	1776	*Siege of Boston*
Declaration of Independence		*Loses N.Y. in battles of Long Island and White Plains*
		Retreats through N.J.
		Takes Trenton
Burgoyne surrenders at Saratoga	1777	*Takes Princeton*
		Defeated at Brandywine and Germantown
Articles of Confederation adopted		*Winters at Valley Forge*
		Conway Cabal exposed
Franco-American alliance	1778	*Wins Battle of Monmouth*
Spain enters war	1779	
British take Charleston	1780	
Articles of Confederation ratified	1781	*Receives surrender of Cornwallis at Yorktown*
Treaty of Paris	1783	*Bids farewell to officers*
		Resigns commission
Constitutional Convention	1787	*Elected president of Constitutional Convention*
Constitution ratified	1788	
French Revolution	1789	*Elected President*
Bill of Rights		
Capital moved to Philadelphia	1790	*Signs assumption bill*
Emergence of rival parties		
District of Columbia established	1791	*Signs National Bank charter*
		Approves excise tax
	1792	*Re-elected President*
Jefferson resigns as Secretary of State	1793	*Issues Neutrality Proclamation*
		Demands recall of Genêt
Jay's Treaty signed in London	1794	*Suppresses Whisky Rebellion*

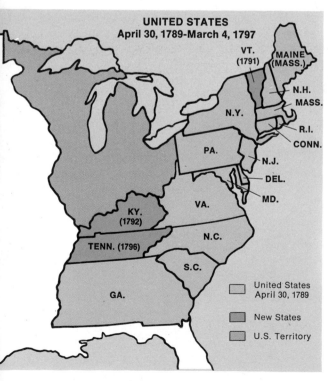

UNITED STATES
April 30, 1789–March 4, 1797

VT. (1791)
MAINE (MASS.)
N.H.
MASS.
N.Y.
R.I.
CONN.
PA.
N.J.
DEL.
MD.
VA.
KY. (1792)
TENN. (1796)
N.C.
S.C.
GA.

United States April 30, 1789
New States
U.S. Territory

Hamilton resigns from Cabinet	1795	*Reorganizes Cabinet*
Pinckney's Treaty signed in Madrid		
John Adams elected President	1796	*Publishes Farewell Address*
	1797	*Retires to Mount Vernon*
Undeclared naval war with France	1798	*Appointed commander of provisional army*
	1799	*Dies December 14*

BIOGRAPHICAL FACTS

BIRTH: Pope's Creek (Wakefield), Westmoreland County, Va., Feb. 11, 1732 (Feb. 22, new style)

ANCESTRY: English

FATHER: Augustine Washington; b. Westmoreland County, Va., 1694; d. King George County, Va., April 12, 1743

FATHER'S OCCUPATION: Planter

MOTHER: Mary Ball Washington; b. Lancaster County, Va., 1708; d. near Fredericksburg, Va., Aug. 25, 1789

BROTHERS: Samuel (1734–1781); John Augustine (1736–1787); Charles (1738–1799)

SISTERS: Elizabeth (1733–1797); Mildred (1739–1740)

HALF BROTHERS: Lawrence (1718–1752); Augustine (1720–1735)

HALF SISTER: Jane (1722–1735)

WIFE: Martha Dandridge Custis; b. New Kent County, Va., June 21, 1731; d. Mount Vernon, Va., May 22, 1802

MARRIAGE: Kent County, Va., Jan. 6, 1759

CHILDREN: None (adopted two children from his wife's first marriage)

HOME: Mount Vernon, Va.

EDUCATION: Private tutoring by family

RELIGIOUS AFFILIATION: Episcopalian

OCCUPATIONS BEFORE PRESIDENCY: Surveyor; soldier; planter

MILITARY SERVICE: Virginia militia (1752–1758); commander in chief of Continental Army (1775–1783)

PRE-PRESIDENTIAL OFFICES: Member of Virginia House of Burgesses; Justice of Fairfax County; Delegate to First and Second Continental Congresses; President of Constitutional Convention

POLITICAL PARTY: Favored Federalists

AGE AT INAUGURATION: 57

OCCUPATION AFTER PRESIDENCY: Planter

DEATH: Mount Vernon, Va., Dec. 14, 1799

PLACE OF BURIAL: Mount Vernon, Va.

ELECTION OF 1789

(In 1789 and 1792, each elector voted for two men.)

CANDIDATES	ELECTORAL VOTE
George Washington	69
John Adams	34
John Jay	9
Nine others	26

FIRST ADMINISTRATION

INAUGURATION: April 30, 1789; Federal Hall, New York City

VICE PRESIDENT: John Adams

SECRETARY OF STATE: Thomas Jefferson

SECRETARY OF THE TREASURY: Alexander Hamilton

SECRETARY OF WAR: Henry Knox

ATTORNEY GENERAL: Edmund Randolph

POSTMASTER GENERAL: Samuel Osgood; Timothy Pickering (from Aug. 19, 1791)

SUPREME COURT APPOINTMENTS: John Jay, Chief Justice (1789); John Rutledge (1789); William Cushing (1789); Robert H. Harrison (1789); James Wilson (1789); John Blair (1789); James Iredell (1790); Thomas Johnson (1791)

FIRST CONGRESS (March 4, 1789–March 4, 1791):
Senate: 17 Federalists; 9 Antifederalists
House: 38 Federalists; 26 Antifederalists

SECOND CONGRESS (March 4, 1791–March 4, 1793):
Senate: 16 Federalists; 13 Democratic-Republicans
House: 37 Federalists; 33 Democratic-Republicans

STATES ADMITTED: Vermont (1791); Kentucky (1792)

ELECTION OF 1792

CANDIDATES	ELECTORAL VOTE
George Washington	132
John Adams	77
George Clinton	50
Two others	5

SECOND ADMINISTRATION

INAUGURATION: March 4, 1793; Federal Hall, Philadelphia

VICE PRESIDENT: John Adams

SECRETARY OF STATE: Thomas Jefferson; Edmund Randolph (from Jan. 2, 1794); Timothy Pickering (from Aug. 20, 1795)

SECRETARY OF THE TREASURY: Alexander Hamilton; Oliver Wolcott, Jr. (from Feb. 2, 1795)

SECRETARY OF WAR: Henry Knox; Timothy Pickering (from Jan. 2, 1795); James McHenry (from Feb. 6, 1796)

ATTORNEY GENERAL: Edmund Randolph; William Bradford (from Jan. 29, 1794); Charles Lee (from Dec. 10, 1795)

POSTMASTER GENERAL: Timothy Pickering; Joseph Habersham (from Feb. 25, 1795)

SUPREME COURT APPOINTMENTS: William Paterson (1793); John Rutledge, Chief Justice (1795); Samuel Chase (1796); Oliver Ellsworth, Chief Justice (1796)

THIRD CONGRESS (March 4, 1793–March 4, 1795):
Senate: 17 Federalists; 13 Democratic-Republicans
House: 57 Democratic-Republicans; 48 Federalists

FOURTH CONGRESS (March 4, 1795–March 4, 1797):
Senate: 19 Federalists; 13 Democratic-Republicans
House: 54 Federalists; 52 Democratic-Republicans

STATE ADMITTED: Tennessee (1796)

JOHN ADAMS

J ohn Adams was not born into the First Family of America; he founded it. Although his Puritan ancestors were active in local affairs, the Adamses of Massachusetts remained typical colonial farmers until John and Susanna Boylston Adams of Braintree parish had their first son. In this Adams, born on October 19, 1735, there developed a brilliance of intellect and a uniqueness of character that he passed to his sons and they to theirs. But if character separated John Adams from his forefathers and distinguished his descendants, it also forbade rapport between the Adamses and the American people, to whose service they were totally devoted.

That John Adams became President at all is one more tribute to the Founding Fathers of the United States: it is doubtful that he could progress very far in modern politics. Early in his career, when he began to devote himself to the cause of American independence, he maintained a legalistic posture high above the issues in which his fellow patriots were emotionally involved. He was haughty, condescending, self-righteous, cantankerous, throughout his life; he was so aloof that even the people with whom he joined forces were not always sure he was on their side. Yet they were delighted when he was, for he was incorruptible and extraordinarily intelligent, and he had the courage to stand by his convictions at any cost. Another facet of the prismatic Adams character was introspectiveness. He could be unusually objective about himself: the self-portraiture in his diary might have been written by a disinterested party. He called himself "puffy, vain, conceited." He wrote that vanity was his "cardinal folly," and often his contemporaries paid tribute to his perceptiveness by agreeing with him.

While his offspring appear to have been born with the Adams character, John Adams had to develop it. In his youth he much preferred farm chores

John Adams in 1798, painted by William Winstanley

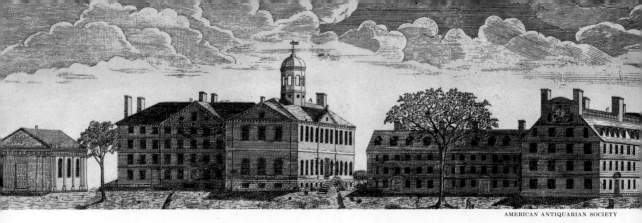

to schoolwork, and he studied agriculture (which remained his hobby for life) more than Latin. But his parents had provided a model for him: his uncle Joseph Adams, a Harvard graduate who had been a schoolmaster and then a clergyman of some stature. Thus in 1751, at the age of sixteen, Adams entered Harvard. There, two years later, he began his diary. To our knowledge, no earlier Adams had worked out his ideas in writing, but John felt a need to do so. As historian James Truslow Adams (no relation) put it, "that insatiable desire to write, write, write" entered the Adams genes and became a hereditary compulsion.

After graduating from Harvard, Adams was employed as master of the grammar school in Worcester, Massachusetts. From the start, teaching was at best barely tolerable for him. Adams was at that time softspoken and introverted, almost shy. The boys—there were fifty of them in his class, ranging in age from five to fifteen—at first behaved with some restraint, testing him, making certain that a wolf was not hidden beneath the sheepskin. Before long the pupils had the measure of their master and took the upper hand. They were to Adams "little runtlings, just capable of lisping A, B,C, and troubling the master"; the classroom became for him a "school of affliction." Yet the apparent alternative, the ministry, seemed no less depressing. Adams was bathed in gloom until the summer of 1756, when he began finding nightly retreat in the law offices of James Putnam. Two years later he left teaching, passed the bar examination, and began practicing law at Braintree.

In order to observe the methods of more experienced lawyers, Adams attended trials

Paul Revere made this engraving of Harvard in 1767, twelve years after Adams' graduation from college.

throughout the surrounding counties. One of the attorneys he greatly admired was fiery James Otis of Boston, advocate general of the vice admiralty. When, early in 1761, Otis resigned his court-appointed office to argue the colonial case against the Writs of Assistance before the chief justice of Massachusetts, Adams attended the hearing.

The Writs of Assistance were legal permits giving inspectors the right to enter and search any ship, warehouse, or private home where smuggled goods were thought to be hidden. Although colonial courts had long been empowered to issue writs, it had not often been necessary or prudent to do so. After the Seven Years' War, however, Parliament found itself in debt while colonial prosperity had never been healthier, especially in Massachusetts, and the courts were ordered to issue writs. It was difficult enough to suddenly enforce a long-ignored law, but to complicate matters further for England, King George II died. Traditionally, all writs automatically expired six months after the death of a monarch, and according to Otis the English decision not to withdraw the writs was in opposition to British law. Moreover, Otis added emotionally, enforcement of the writs was a violation of an Englishman's established right to freedom from intrusion in his own home.

Sixty years later John Adams would write that in the council chamber where Otis spoke "the child Independence was born." Adams' diary of the time makes only passing mention of the speech, but retrospective drama was characteristic of Adams' writing.

64

Beneath the cold, intellectual façade, under the detachment and pomposity, was a John Adams who was more romantic than he ever would have admitted. He could be quite sentimental, and he felt with incredible depth. He fell in and out of love as often as a schoolgirl. He cherished the ladies and pampered them and left them untouched—by him anyway—on their pedestals. An early sweetheart, Hannah Quincy, tempered her affection for him because she thought no ordinary woman could ever return the immeasurable quantity of love that John Adams had in him to give. On his part Adams longed for a wife and family, but he was cautious, and he proposed marriage only once—to Abigail Smith. They were married in 1764.

Hannah Quincy had been right: Abigail Smith Adams was no ordinary woman. She read more than a lady was supposed to; she was smarter than a woman ought to have been; and she spoke out when convention called for feminine silence. She was the perfect wife for Adams, for she managed to keep the cold, impersonal statesman out of the home and the devoted, at times even tender, family man in. She humored his hypochondria and made light of his constant premonitions of early death. Adams did not emerge as a public figure until after his marriage. True, the national issues were growing in intensity, but he still had elements of the timid schoolmaster in him. Now they disappeared, replaced by a directness—sometimes even a flair—that suited the role he was about to play.

For one thing, he began to spend more time with his cousin Samuel. Sam Adams, bankrupt businessman, radical, patriot, scholar, teacher, rabble-rouser—depending on who was describing him—was in 1764 the Boston tax collector who opposed the taxes he was supposed to collect. Thirteen years older than John, Sam had the vision to look beyond the superficiality of individual issues to the larger issues that were dividing Crown

and colonies. Although John Adams would remain considerably more cautious than his cousin, he too began to view each issue as part of the whole.

The Stamp Act of 1765 provides a case in point. The surface issue was censorship: because the act would require the colonials to purchase stamps for every printed document, from wills to playing cards, from insurance policies to newspapers, the Crown would have the opportunity to refuse to sell stamps for material it regarded as unfavorable. But the real issue, just as it had been with the Writs of Assistance, was taxation without representation, and that—so the saying was beginning to go—was tyranny. When word came that the act had been passed, angered colonials swung into action. The militant Sons of Liberty stormed and wrecked the home of Massachusetts-born Lieutenant Governor Thomas Hutchinson, and Sam Adams organized a blockade of the custom house to prevent the stamps from being distributed. John Adams wrote a series of brilliant articles for the Boston *Gazette*, condemning the act purely on legal grounds, turning for premises to British law, claiming that it was "inconsistent with the spirit of the common law and of the essential fundamental principles of the British constitution that we should be subject to any tax imposed by the British Parliament; because we are not represented in that assembly in any sense. . . ." When a Massachusetts General Court was called for October,

The bland entries in John Adams' diary, right, bespeak the tedium of his teaching days in Worcester.

he wrote a list of recommendations for the Braintree delegate. To his surprise, forty towns in Massachusetts adopted as their own his Braintree Instructions, which made John Adams a figure of importance.

Of the actions of the Sons of Liberty he was extremely critical. To oppose an unjust law in court, to petition, to call a congress—these were legal rights; but to react with vigilante vandalism was not. Such was John Adams' position until the courts were suddenly closed. The government's reasoning was clear enough: all legal documents had to be stamped; the colonials would not permit distribution of the stamps; therefore the business of the law could no longer proceed. Shaken from his perch, Adams saw the weakness in his commitment to legality. How does one employ legal channels when the channels are closed? Even after the Stamp Act was repealed and the courts reopened, Adams was troubled: the Crown had closed the courts once, and could do so again.

Although he remained a moderate, favoring legal petition as the first weapon of protest, Adams no longer equated forceful resistance with treason. He grew closer to Sam Adams and James Otis, and when he refused the governor's appointment to the lucrative post of advocate general of the admiralty, he was acknowledged by the people of Boston as a patriot, albeit a stuffy one.

But Adams placed his political career on the block before it even got going. On March 5, 1770, a squad of soldiers under the command of Captain Thomas Preston paraded past a crowd of Bostonians. During the customary exchange of insults, the crowd became a mob; stones were thrown, shots were fired, five civilians were killed and several injured. When no other lawyer would agree to defend the soldiers involved in the Boston Massacre, the objective John Adams announced that he would be the defense attorney. Before the trial began, Adams was persuaded to become a candidate for the provincial legislature. Having no confidence in the judgment of the people, he was sure that the defender of British soldiers could not possibly win; but he entered the race anyway and, much to his surprise, won by the considerable ratio of 4 to 1.

Though the people who elected him admired his courage in standing forward for the defendants, they were not prepared for Adams' success in court. Preston was acquitted, two of the soldiers were convicted of minor infractions and given light sentences, and the rest were exonerated. Adams was ostracized: the Sons of Liberty called

The print below depicts the "Indians" at the height of the Boston Tea Party. Although he did not participate, John Adams called the event "magnificent."

him a deserter, the patriot press turned against him, and, perhaps most painful of all, Sam Adams wrote a series of articles signed VINDEX, which implied collusion between defense and royalist court. To make matters worse, the royalists began wooing John Adams, assuming that he had come over to their side. The sensitivity he was usually capable of controlling asserted itself: he packed up and went back to Braintree. "Farewell politics," he wrote in his diary.

He kept to his farewell for two and a half years. Then, late in 1772, Parliament introduced reforms to provincial courts. Some letters by Thomas Hutchinson, which proved that the courts had been rigged previously and that the new "reforms" were calculated to make the courts entirely subordinate to the Crown, were intercepted by Benjamin Franklin and sent to Sam Adams, who published them. On January 4, 1773, the first of a series of eight long articles decrying the situation appeared in the *Gazette* over the signature of John Adams. In May the legislature nominated him to sit in the upper chamber of the House of Representatives; and when the governor vetoed his name, Adams was returned to patriot graces.

In the autumn of 1773, the much-scarred umbilical cord between Crown and colonies was stretched to the breaking point. Three years earlier, Parliament had repealed most of the duties on colonial imports imposed by the Townshend Acts but had left the tax on tea. The colonists had evaded the tax by smuggling tea from the Netherlands, while tea leaves were rotting in London warehouses. But now the East India Company, heavily indebted to the government, was nearly bankrupt, and Parliament awarded it exclusive right to the sale of tea in the American colonies. This was the last straw for the colonials; they would not have their economy ruined by monopolies. On the evening of December 16, 1773, the merchant ship *Dartmouth*, first of three tea-bearing vessels to dock in Boston Harbor, was the site of a masquerade fete attended by a group of Indian-guised Bostonians, who summarily tossed the cargo overboard. The

The locket above was a gift to Abigail from John Adams as he left for France in 1778. The fatalistic inscription reads, "I yield whatever is is right."

party spread to the other ships when they arrived. This time John Adams approved.

The ministers of George III responded to the Boston Tea Party by passing the "Intolerable Acts," which closed Boston Harbor and appointed a military governor for Massachusetts. Although the sternest provisions were aimed at New England, the implications of the acts were clear throughout the colonies, and in Philadelphia on September 5, 1774, the First Continental Congress convened in protest. John Adams, delegate from Massachusetts, labored for passage of the Suffolk Resolves (named for Boston's county), which advocated outright resistance to the Intolerable Acts. The Resolves were accepted, and Adams returned home one of the most influential men in the province.

At the Second Continental Congress, in 1775, John Adams was the most vigorous delegate. He urged that regionalism be sacrificed for the good of all the colonies, that each state contribute to a single continental army, that George Washington be commander of that army. He served on the committee that drew up the Declaration of Independence and was its foremost defender when it was attacked by moderates. He favored a union of states into a single government and actively backed the Articles of Confederation, which created a United States of America and remained in force until the Constitution was ratified in 1788. Adams debated almost every issue and was a member

The paintings above of Abigail Adams Smith, left, and her parents, John and Abigail Adams, were done in London in the 1780's. Ralph Earl painted Mrs. Adams; Mather Brown, the others.

of more than ninety different committees.

Past forty and rotund, Adams was not cut out for soldiering, so while the Revolution was being fought, he became a diplomat. In 1778 and again two years later he was sent to France, but he got along with neither Benjamin Franklin, the American minister, nor the Comte de Vergennes, the French foreign minister. In The Hague, however, Adams successfully negotiated a large loan in 1782. Then he returned to France, where with Franklin and Jay on September 3, 1783, he signed the Treaty of Paris, wherein Great Britain acknowledged the existence of a separate and independent United States of America. Two years later he became the first American minister to the Court of St. James's. In London, John Adams was a proud, aggressive, uncompromising defender of American interests. But his approach to the British probably made little difference, for almost every American attempt to establish friendship and commercial relations with England was received coldly. In 1788, after three frustrating years in London, Adams asked to be recalled.

When he arrived home a new government was being formed under the recently ratified Constitution. Adams believed—and he was by no means alone in his belief—that the Vice Presidency belonged to him almost as automatically as the Presidency did to George Washington; but while the General was elected unanimously, Adams won with a plurality of only 34 out of 69 electoral votes. The widely distributed balloting was engineered by Alexander Hamilton, who thereby planted the seeds of a feud from which neither man would profit.

Adams' attempts to interpret and define the responsibilities of the Vice Presidency as presented in the Constitution were complicated by his concern with petty details. He pondered whether he should be his own man or the President's, whether he should be an independent statesman in the Senate, over which he presided, or an impartial monitor. He asked the Senate for advice: should he address the chamber standing or sitting? "Gentlemen," he said, "I am possessed of two separate powers—the one in *esse*, the other in *passe* [Vice President of the United States but President of the Senate] . . . when the President comes into the Senate, what shall I be?" Who cares? thought Senator William Maclay, a huge, rugged Pennsylvania lawyer, advocate of democratic simplicity and keeper of the journal that gives us our most thorough glimpse into the early years of the Senate. Adams was fond of official titles, without which, he thought, "governments cannot be raised nor supported." Writing that Adams "may go and dream about titles, for he will get none," Maclay and his side prevailed. But behind his back, some senators did acquiesce in the

Vice President's affection for titles by awarding him one of his own: His Rotundity.

With the matter of titles settled against him, Adams, according to Maclay, continued to infuriate the Senate with his condescension. Before debate on any issue could begin, the Vice President insisted on addressing to the chamber a lecture on the constitutional responsibilities of the Senate. During debate, he was arbitrary and prejudiced in his decisions regarding who could and who could not participate. Before a vote could be taken, he would, like a schoolmaster talking to children, summarize the issue, or his own interpretation of it, and unhesitatingly instruct the senators how to vote.

By philosophy Adams was a Federalist. He did not trust the masses, and he acknowledged a "natural division [between] the gentlemen and the simple men." But by temperament he was simply not a party man. However opinionated he might have been, he was not faithful to ideological dogma. Hamilton seems to have gathered as much, and throughout Washington's first administration, he looked for signs of the Vice President's unreliability. As Senate president, Adams had broken twenty tie votes—all in accordance with the position of Washington, who more often than not sided with the Hamiltonians. Therefore, Hamilton had no grounds on which to oppose Adams.

Adams stood for re-election because he wanted to be President. In his second term in the second office, he had less to do—there were fewer tie votes—and he came to hate the job. Once he had been a mover of events, a great debater, a figure in controversy; now he was a loyal, passive observer. To Abigail he wrote, "My country has in its wisdom contrived for me the most insignificant office that ever the invention of man contrived or his imagination conceived."

The election of 1796 was the first bipartisan election in the United States. The Constitution had made no provisions for parties, and candidates were selected by congressional caucus. Candidates for the Presidency and Vice Presidency were listed together on a ballot that did not differentiate between the offices. Each elector voted twice, and the highest and next-highest vote getters became President and Vice President. The Federalists nominated Adams and Thomas Pinckney; the Democratic-Republicans, Jefferson and Aaron Burr. Wanting to be the power behind the President and anticipating that he would never be able to control Adams, Hamilton quietly worked for the election of Pinckney to the Presidency. His own power, however, was less than he had estimated, and his plan backfired. Adams won, but by just three votes, and Jefferson became Vice President.

The circumstances under which Adams took office could hardly have been worse. In the first place, he succeeded the Father of His Country—a tough act to follow. To Adams it was unjust that he should have to wallow in the muck of party politics that George Washington had for the most part been able to remain above. But wallow he did: unlike Washington—the living legend, the gallant warrior—Adams, the chubby intellectual, could find no support in the idolizing masses. Forced to seek support from the party, he retained Washington's largely Hamiltonian Cabinet—a mistake. Finally, Adams was saddled with a Vice President who had not wanted the office and who belonged to—indeed led—the opposition.

By taking Jefferson into his confidence, Adams hoped that they could labor together effectively. But a gap had developed between them. Jefferson had read articles by Adams condemning some aspects of the French Revolution and had called Adams a monarchist. His son John Quincy Adams had written answers to the Jefferson-endorsed works of Thomas Paine; when reissued, the articles were attributed to the elder Adams, and the gap was broadened. At the outset of their administration, as the crisis with France intensified, their mutual desire to avoid war might have succeeded in closing the rift to some extent; but after Jefferson, on the grounds that the Vice President belonged to the legislative branch of the government and could not participate in executive discussions, refused to go to

France as a special envoy, they seldom saw each other. They were further estranged on the issue of the Naturalization, Alien, and Sedition Acts, and by the end of the administration, the President and Jefferson were not even on speaking terms.

Adams also tried to get on with Alexander Hamilton, but that did not work either. Hamilton simply could not rid himself of the notion that every presidential concession meant that Adams might be handled. A cycle developed: the President would give an inch, Hamilton would take a foot, and Adams the next time would give nothing at all. Adams' persistence and courage could take the form of either stubborn inflexibility or admirable determination—depending on whom he was dealing with—but on the surface he retained that old air of shyness that Hamilton could not see through. The Adams-Hamilton conflict marred the whole of the administration and wrecked the political future of Adams, Hamilton, and the Federalist party.

The crisis with France was the principal issue of Adams' administration. For his part, Adams was not sympathetic to the French revolutionists, but he had long been biased against Great Britain; so he immediately became a man in the middle. By nature, the Federalists favored aristocratic England; and the Democratic-Republicans, revolutionary France. France itself regarded the United States as favorable to Britain, especially since the completion of Jay's Treaty, and the Federalist-dominated Congress did little to contradict the French impression. In France, citizens with pro-American sympathies were imprisoned; the French assumed that every American vessel was bound toward a British port; and when Adams dispatched General Charles Pinckney to Paris to see what could be done about stopping French harassment of American ships, Talleyrand, the French foreign minister, refused to see him. The Hamiltonians were poised for battle, and the President urged an increase in the strength of the armed forces. Determined to negotiate before firing, however, Adams tried diplomacy again, dispatching Pinckney and two other ministers

to Paris. Talleyrand sent a trio of his own to see them under a cloak of carefully contrived secrecy. In confidential undertones, the French agents said that Talleyrand would listen favorably to any American proposal if the United States would issue a large loan to France and make Talleyrand's attentions worth his while. Informed of the attempted blackmail, Adams sent the diplomats' report to Congress, but for the names of the French agents, he substituted the initials X, Y, and Z. Congress released the report to the public, which became infected with what Jefferson called the XYZ fever, a national passion to avenge the French insult. Always anti-French, Hamilton fed the militant attitude, writing that any defender of France was "a fool, a madman, or a traitor."

He implied, of course, that John Adams was one or all of these. Although the President was in favor of preparedness—he signed military appropriations and urged George Washington to resume command of the armed services—he was not himself stricken with XYZ fever. Still determined to negotiate, he insisted on Talleyrand's assurance that representatives of the United States would be treated with courtesy in Paris. Thoroughly embarrassed by the furor that the XYZ Affair had caused, the French minister agreed, reasoning that further hostility toward the United States would simply provide England with another ally. Another American minister to the French Republic was dispatched (over the objections of Hamilton, who later pressured Adams into changing the delegation to a mission of three, two of whom were Hamiltonians); and with the Treaty of Morfontaine on September 30, 1800, the good relations between the United States and France were restored. The settlement had great personal value for Adams, who soon after its conclusion composed his own epitaph: "Here lies John Adams, who took upon himself the responsibility of the peace with France in the year 1800."

The Federalist party was badly shaken by the XYZ Affair. Hamilton had expected that congressional passage of military bills would inspire France to declare war, thereby

In the print above, L'Insurgente *surrenders to the* U.S.S. Constellation *in 1799. America captured eighty-four French vessels in the undeclared war.*

discrediting the pro-French Republicans. That, of course, had not worked. Moreover, the Republican press had called the whole affair a hoax, insinuating that the diplomats whose report had fostered the XYZ fever had made themselves unavailable to conciliation. Adams received blows from both sides —from the Federalists for not going to war with France and from the Republicans for stimulating panic by promoting congressional passage of the military bills.

In 1798, the majority Federalists tried to utilize the national enthusiasm for war to silence their critics; they sponsored and passed the Naturalization, Alien, and Sedition Acts. During the height of the French crisis, Frenchmen in America were widely assumed to favor their homeland, while many non-French Europeans were known to sympathize with the principles of the French Revolution. Forgetting—or choosing to ignore—the similarity between the French and the American struggles for independence, the Federalists first passed the Naturalization Act, raising the period of residency required for American citizenship to fourteen years. Then came the Alien Act, which gave the President power to expel all foreigners he considered dangerous, and the Alien Ene-

mies Act, which gave him the right to deport or imprison any native of a nation at war with the United States. Finally, the Sedition Act forbade "insurrection, riot, unlawful assembly" and prescribed fines and jail terms for "false, scandalous and malicious writing" about the President, Congress, or nation. A case can be made for the necessity of such legislation, but the Federalists employed the acts to silence opponents. Closing their ranks against what they considered an assault on freedom of speech and the press, the Jeffersonians declared that the Alien and Sedition Acts were violations of constitutionally guaranteed rights. State courts were urged to disregard the acts, and many did.

The Alien and Sedition Acts conformed with the political philosophy of John Adams, and he signed them, thus losing what little Republican admiration his stand on France had won him; but the instinctive, sensitive Adams in practice ignored them, thereby giving Hamilton fresh ammunition. In fact, Hamilton himself had grave doubts about the constitutionality of the Alien and Sedition Acts, but he could not resist the opportunity to abuse the President. When Adams failed to deport Joseph Priestly, an English radical whose outspoken advocacy of the French Revolution had scandalized the Federalists, and when he pardoned John Fries, who had been condemned to death for leading a violent Pennsylvania uprising against the war taxes voted in 1798, Hamilton wrote an open *Letter Concerning the Public Conduct and Character of John Adams*. Dealing mostly with the President's handling of the French crisis, the document was too obscure to be read by the simple people and too illogical to impress the nation's leaders. It did, however, have disastrous results for Adams.

His administration had been stormy, but Adams was cautiously optimistic about winning the second term he so desperately wanted. He had purged his Cabinet of two Hamiltonian spies, his generosity regarding the Alien and Sedition Acts defendants had by and large compensated for his earlier unpopular support of the acts, and the peace with France had deprived the Jeffersonians of a monumental issue. But when Hamilton's letter was published, Adams' optimism was dissipated, for if the document was an almost meaningless hodgepodge of unreadable rhetoric, it was also a crystal-clear statement that the Federalists were deeply divided. The letter irritated even Charles Pinckney, the Hamiltonian "vice presidential" candidate in 1800, who, to his credit, announced that he would not be a party to a plan to divert votes from Adams.

Meanwhile, the White House, though far from finished, was ready for occupancy. Abigail was ill, and Adams arrived from Philadelphia without her. On November 1, 1800, he became the first Chief Executive to sleep in the Mansion. Reflecting on the potential of the White House as a symbol in the affections of Americans, he composed a prayer that Franklin Delano Roosevelt later had carved on the mantel of the State Dining Room: "I pray Heaven to bestow the best of Blessings on this House and all that shall hereafter inhabit it. May none but honest and wise men ever rule under this roof." When Mrs. Adams finally arrived, she hung a clothesline and a Stuart portrait of George Washington; the outcome of the election would determine what else she would do.

Adams and Pinckney were opposed again by Jefferson and Burr, and Burr's powerful New York machine proved decisive. The President had no trouble at all placing the blame for his defeat: "Mr. Hamilton has carried his eggs to a fine market," he wrote. "The very two men of all the world that he was most jealous of are now placed over him." In a letter to a friend Adams confided that his defeat was a good thing, as he expected to die soon. His last official act was the appointment of John Marshall as Chief Justice of the Supreme Court.

Disappointed and bitter, Adams left Washington by stagecoach on the morning of Jefferson's inauguration, conspicuously absenting himself from it. Retiring to Quincy (formerly Braintree), Massachusetts, he became a farmer, insisting that he had not been so cheerful "since some sin to me unknown involved me in politics." He gathered together his diaries and started work on an autobiography.

Perhaps his affront to Jefferson bothered him, for on the first day of 1812, Adams wrote a genial letter to Monticello. "I wish you Sir many happy New Years and that you may enter the next and many succeeding Years with as animating Prospects for the Public as those at present before Us." He signed it "Friend," and Jefferson—by what was almost return mail in those days— wrote back on January 21: "A letter from you calls up recollections very dear to my mind. It carries me back to the times when, beset with difficulties and dangers, we were fellow laborers in the same cause, struggling for what is most valuable to man, his right of self-government." The two ex-Presidents thus began an extensive correspondence, exchanging ideas about current affairs from time to time, but devoting themselves mainly to nostalgic reminiscences or philosophical bantering. Jefferson shared Adams' misery when Abigail died of typhoid in 1818, and Adams' joy when John Quincy Adams was elected President of the United States.

John Adams died at ninety on, appropriately, the Fourth of July, 1826, the fiftieth anniversary of the Declaration of Independence. His last words were "Jefferson still survives." But Jefferson in fact did not. He had died at Monticello several hours earlier.

—DAVID JACOBS

John Adams

A PICTURE PORTFOLIO

John Adams' spectacles lie on the tulipwood desk bought when he was in Europe. The desk is now at the family home in Quincy, Massachusetts.

THE BOSTON MASSACRE

John Adams was thirty-five when he undertook as important a case as any ever "tried in any court or country of the world." With typical dramatic flair the young attorney thus described his upcoming defense of the officer and soldiers indicted for murder in the Boston Massacre of 1770. Adams for some time had foreseen the inevitable clash of military and citizenry: with the British troop build-ups that followed the colonists' protests against English tax measures, Adams had said that the danger "appeared in full view before me." He viewed his acceptance of the case as a kind of martyrdom, for the defendants' cause was universally unpopular. But shortly before the trial began he was chosen a Boston delegate to the General Court, the electorate apparently acknowledging his courage and integrity in the delicate legal situation. The jury acquitted six soldiers, and the remaining two received token punishment. Adams could rest assured that justice and the law had been served. But the radical press of John's cousin Sam Adams, disappointed at the loss of a guilty verdict and a propaganda plum, upbraided Adams in the months that followed. After one term in the General Court, Adams retired to Braintree, declaring himself "an infirm man" and feeling much put upon. Yet he could not long remain detached from public life, and by 1774 he was named a Massachusetts delegate to the Continental Congress in Philadelphia, where he would help to shape a new nation.

The fresco above of the Boston Massacre is located in the National Capitol. It depicts the height of the crisis: one of the mob has been shot, and the redcoats, taunted by the angry crowd, continue their retaliation.

The portrait at left by Benjamin Blyth shows John Adams in 1776. At thirty-one, he was a prominent attorney.

The stamp below was authorized under the hated Stamp Act of 1765, the first direct taxation of the colonies by the Crown. Stamps were required for all newspapers, pamphlets, and legal documents. Violent protests ensued, and the seeds of permanent dissension were sown.

75

The painting below, probably by John Trumbull, is the quintessence of Ben Franklin, diplomat. Parisian high society had never encountered anyone quite like him: he blended the elements of simple American frontiersman (complete with coonskin hat) with charming and sophisticated conversation and an unerring sense of timing. He captivated statesman and citizen alike, and he was undeniably a great favorite with the ladies of court society. John Adams said that he could *"never obtain the favor of [his] company in a morning before breakfast."*

"A FRIEND
TO HUMAN KIND"

He was seventy years old, and though he had "retired" almost three decades before, Benjamin Franklin found himself clomping down the ship's ramp onto French soil on behalf of his country. He had come to ask for help—for support and money—and all his talk about what France might gain from American independence would be just so much salesmanship; nevertheless, the French were delighted to see him. They displayed his portrait in shop windows, stamped his image on coins and jewelry, held banquets in his honor. When John Adams arrived two years later, in 1778, he was astonished. Franklin's reputation, he noted, was so universal that "there was scarcely a peasant or a citizen, a *valet de chambre*, coachman or footman, a lady's chambermaid or a scullion in a kitchen who was not familiar with it, and who did not consider him a friend to human kind."

Europe had known Ben Franklin for a long time. *Poor Richard's Almanack* had been translated, his scientific experiments widely duplicated, and even the great Mozart had composed an adagio for the armonica, a musical instrument of Franklin's invention. But France held a special admiration for the Philadelphian, for while Franklin suited their romantic portrait of the wise and simple American, he also belonged alongside Voltaire and Defoe and Montesquieu in the Age of Enlightenment, that international phenomenon which France thought purely French.

Franklin was wise but by no account simple, and he was perfectly willing to accept the role in which the French had cast him. Before long, John Adams grew impatient with Franklin; Adams had come to deal in diplomacy, not to participate in "continual dissipation," nor to dress like a Daniel Boone and recite little wisdoms. Openly critical, he deplored the Franklin-led commission, its waste and inefficiency, and he was recalled. What John Adams had neglected to consider was that Benjamin Franklin was accomplishing a great deal.

Adams could not even enjoy the luxury of being alone with his resentment during the voyage home; instead, he was accompanied by a French official gushing admiration for Franklin. At one point Adams erupted: "It is universally believed in France, England and all of Europe," he said, "that his electric wand has accomplished this Revolution. But nothing is more groundless. He has done very little."

Adams returned to Europe in 1780 and negotiated a Dutch loan large enough to reduce American dependency on France. This proved valuable during the Paris peace negotiations, for Franklin had in fact become overly acquiescent to French plans to participate in the talks. France would be better served by a continuing war between the United States and Great Britain than by American independence; thus Adams and the third American commissioner, John Jay, overruled Franklin's efforts to have the French present at the parleys. The treaty was concluded in 1783 with a minimum of French interference.

Franklin irritated Adams even after his death in 1790. While the aura around Franklin's name grew, John Adams insisted that he had been "the vainest man and the falsest character I have ever met with. . . ."

The Adams house, opposite, is shown as it appeared in 1787, when John bought it for some £600. Dr. Cotton Tufts, Abigail's uncle, negotiated the transaction while Adams was minister to the Court of St. James's. The house was constructed in 1731.

The china used by the Adams family in the White House in 1800 (left) is now displayed at Peacefield.

Adams' first addition to the house was an extension containing the Long Room (below). The furniture, purchased in France, was the first to be used in the White House. The portraits of Abigail, John Quincy, and John are copies of originals now hanging in the Executive Mansion in Washington.

PEACEFIELD

In 1787, John Adams was anxious to get home. He had been ambassador to England for two years and a diplomat in Europe for seven before that. His latest post had brought only disappointment; a lasting amity with Britain seemed as far away as ever, and in 1788 he resigned. Although he and Abigail were eager to return to Massachusetts, they must have been somewhat uneasy about the house they were to occupy, for they had bought it unseen while still in England. The modest home was in Braintree, and contained only a paneled parlor and dining room on the ground floor and two bedrooms and three smaller rooms above. The kitchen and servants' quarters were in a separate building. Abigail said at first sight that the building looked like "a wren's house."

The Adamses were not to remain long at Peacefield, as John named it, for with the election of 1789 and John's ascension to the Vice Presidency they soon would be living in New York. The seat of government shortly would shift to Philadelphia, and through the 1790's John Adams spent little time at Peacefield except for periodic visits. During his Presidency, Adams added to the house a gabled extension, including the Long Room on the ground floor and a capacious second-story study. Since farming was a lifelong delight to Adams, he also erected a complex of barns and stables.

John Adams retired happily to Quincy following his Presidency; he had twenty-six years to devote to family, farming, and correspondence. Subsequent Adams generations made their own contributions to the Old House, as it came to be called, notably a stone library, adjacent to the house, for John Quincy's books and letters, and the connection of the kitchen to the main building. The house was last used as a residence in 1927 and now is a national historic site.

FULL
OF
LOVE
FOR
THEE
AND
THINE

JOHN ADAMS

The love that filled the early-nineteenth-century jug at left was a bipartisan liquid, intended for the lips of both Federalist Thees and Republican Thines. To one side of the message is a portrait of John Adams, and to the other, a picture of James Madison.

In his magnanimous letter (below) to John Adams after the presidential election of 1796, Thomas Jefferson lashed out at mutual adversary Alexander Hamilton, who had tried to subvert Adams' victory. At the advice of Democratic-Republican party organizer James Madison, however, the letter was never sent.

Dear Sir   Monticello Dec. 28. 1796

The public & the public papers have been much occupied lately in placing us in a point of opposition to each other. I trust with confidence that less of it has been felt by ourselves personally. in the retired canton where I am, I learn little of what is passing: pamphlets I see never; papers but a few; and the fewer the happier. our latest intelligence from Philadelphia at present is of the 16th inst. but tho' at that date your election to the first magistracy seems not to have been known as a fact, yet with me it has never been doubted. I knew it impossible you should lose a vote North of the Delaware. & even if that of Pensylvania should be against you in the mass, yet that you would get enough South of that to place your succession out of danger. I have never one single moment expected a different issue; & tho' I know I shall not be believed, yet it is not the less true that I have never wished it. my neighbors, as my compurgators, could aver that fact, because they see my occupations & my attachment to them. indeed it is possible that you may be cheated of your succession by a trick worthy the subtlety of your arch-friend of New York, who has been able to make of your real friends tools to defeat their & your just wishes. most probably he will be disappointed as to you. & my inclinations place me out of his reach. I leave to

FRIENDLY RIVALS

You and I," wrote Vice President John Adams to Thomas Jefferson in 1796, "must look down from the battlements of heaven if we ever have the pleasure of seeing it." From Monticello, Jefferson answered that he agreed, adding that politics was "a subject I never loved and now hate." The two men were both nominees in the first contested presidential election of the young nation's life, and they saw no reason to alter their cordial twenty-year-long relationship. Meanwhile, a Democratic-Republican handbill in wide circulation asserted that "*Thomas Jefferson* . . . first framed the sacred political sentence that all men are *born* equal. *John Adams* says this is all farce and falsehood. . . . Which of these . . . will you have for your President?" The Federalist press, in turn, called Jefferson an enemy of the Constitution, an atheist, freethinker, and coward. Just as President Washington had feared, "the daemon of party spirit" penetrated American politics and possessed the election. But while their countrymen spat venom at one another, the two principal candidates, aloof from the indignity of campaigning, continued when they could their old correspondence. The election results were predictably regional: Jefferson's strength came from the South, Adams' from the North, and they shared the Middle Atlantic states. Adams won, but Jefferson, with just three electoral votes fewer, became Vice President.

THOMAS PINCKNEY

Because John Adams' relationship with the Federalist party was more an alliance than allegiance, Alexander Hamilton tried to arrange the election so that the vice presidential candidate, Thomas Pinckney, would be elected President. Hamilton, however, was not always a perceptive judge of men, and Pinckney later proved less faithful to the party than Adams: he was an advocate of states' rights; he not only opposed Hamilton's efforts to have war declared with France, but he was against Adams' military build-up during the crisis; and as a congressman from South Carolina, he voted against the Sedition Act. Born in Charleston in 1750, Pinckney was raised and educated in England, graduating from Oxford. He returned to South Carolina and became an officer in the militia in 1775. After the Revolution, he was appointed minister to Great Britain, where he served until 1795, when he was sent to Spain to negotiate a settlement of U.S.-Spanish borders in North America. Returning home a year later, he probably would have won the Vice Presidency but for Hamilton's meddling. When the New England electors heard that Hamilton was trying to secure more votes for Pinckney than for Adams, they cast their votes for Adams and Jefferson, and Pinckney received only fifty-nine votes. After two terms in Congress (1797–1801), he quit politics and devoted his life to agriculture until his death in 1828.

YEARS OF TURMOIL

After the Alien and Sedition Acts were passed in 1798, a Newark man was fined one hundred dollars for wishing out loud that a cannon wadding would lodge in the President's backside; a county official in New York was manacled and driven two hundred miles to jail for his anti-administration remarks; Congressman Matthew Lyon of Vermont was sentenced to four months for calling Adams pompous and selfish in a personal letter. But the Federalist "Reign of Terror" was short lived: so harsh was the wording of the acts that just being a Republican was almost tantamount to sedition, and there were too many Republicans to jail them all. Public outrage began working against the Federalists. Representative Lyon was easily re-elected while serving his jail term. Vice President Jefferson made capital of the widespread indignation, spread a rumor that the Federalists were about to crown Adams king, and convinced the Kentucky and Virginia legislatures to declare the acts unconstitutional and therefore inapplicable in those states. The uproar dimmed national interest in the undeclared naval war with France and overshadowed Adams' successful peace negotiations. Condemned by the Republicans for signing the Alien and Sedition Acts and disowned by most Federalists for making peace with France, Adams was through. A Federalist congressman said he hoped the President would break his neck; he was not charged with sedition. The elections came and Adams went, the Alien and Sedition Acts went, and so did Federalist possession of the Presidency forever.

In 1799 John Fries organized a regiment of seven hundred Pennsylvania Dutchmen to oppose collection of the taxes Congress had imposed in anticipation of a French war. Crying "Dämm de President, dämm de Congresz, dämm de Arischdokratz!" and bolstered by their wives, whose weapons were pots of boiling water, they forceably ejected the tax collectors. When President Adams sent troops to put down the insurrection, Fries was captured, tried, and sentenced to death. Although the contemporary print at left shows Adams turning his back on Mrs. Fries's pleas for mercy, the President went against the advice of his party and granted a full pardon.

Although Congress never declared war against France, it could not resist the temptation to commemorate a victorious battle. In 1800, the congressional medal shown above was awarded to Thomas Truxton, commander of the Constellation. It shows his frigate pursuing France's La Vengeance, which was subsequently captured.

In 1798, Federalist Roger Griswold insulted Republican Matthew Lyon in the House of Representatives, and Lyon spat in his face. Two weeks later, Griswold struck back with his cane; Lyon picked up the fireplace tongs, and Congress' first good brawl (left) was under way.

84   *John Adams' most ambitious, exhausting, and often frustrating efforts during his Presidency were devoted to making peace with France. When the Treaty of Morfontaine was signed in 1800, he regarded it as the single achievement for which he should most be remembered.*

Artists Francesco and J. B. Piranesi, uncle and nephew, may well have been witnesses to the signing of the treaty, for their studio was in Morfontaine. Their hand-colored print, above, illustrates the festivities of October 3, 1800, in honor of the conclusion of the crisis.

85

FEDERAL CITY

In 1790 Congress authorized the establishment of a permanent seat for the national government. The act provided for the transfer of operations from Philadelphia to Washington (which the President always called "Federal City") in 1800, but no one could foresee the frustrations and delays which would attend the ambitious project. The builders' efforts were continually thwarted by supply and labor shortages and by congressional frugality. The lawmakers and the Supreme Court were wedged into the lone completed wing of the Capitol; the congressmen were "utterly secluded from Society" in the sparsely populated city. At the other end of muddy Pennsylvania Avenue, Abigail Adams found the unfinished White House damp, chilly, and ill-lit. But as the century progressed, the Potomac tract blossomed, as Washington had once envisioned, into a model of "Grandeur, Simplicity and Convenience."

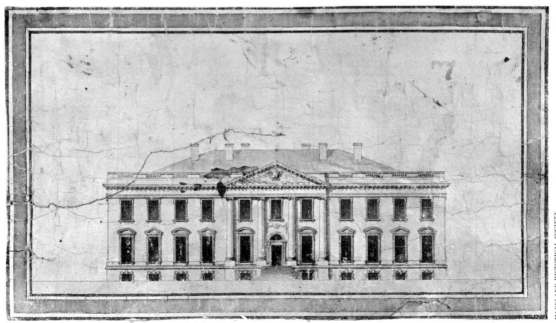

Irish-born James Hoban won $500 for his design for the Executive Mansion (above). His competitors included Thomas Jefferson and Capitol designer William Thornton, whose plans also reflected the mid-eighteenth-century Palladian style. Construction on Washington's oldest public building began in 1792, but it was not completed by the 1800 deadline.

This serene vista (left), from an 1801 engraving, depicts a Georgetown-Federal City area quite different from that described by John and Abigail Adams when, in November of 1800, they became the first First Family to occupy the President's permanent residence. Abigail found Georgetown the "very dirtiest hole I ever saw," and was candid in her reactions to the stump-strewn landscape and the swampy nature of field and road alike. She allowed, perhaps ambiguously, that the region was indeed "capable of every improvement."

As construction lagged, the Capitol could boast only a north wing, as seen in the 1800 water color below by William Birch.

FACTS IN SUMMARY: JOHN ADAMS

CHRONOLOGY

UNITED STATES		ADAMS
	1735	*Born October 19*
	1751	*Enters Harvard*
French and Indian War	1754	
	1758	*Admitted to the bar*
James Otis opposes Writs of Assistance	1761	
Sugar Act	1764	*Marries Abigail Smith*
Stamp Act	1765	*Denounces Stamp Act*
Townshend Acts	1767	
Boston Massacre	1770	*Elected to General Court*
		Defends Thomas Preston
Boston Tea Party	1773	
Intolerable Acts	1774	*Delegate to First Continental Congress*
First Continental Congress		
Lexington and Concord	1775	*Delegate to Second Continental Congress*
Bunker Hill		
Second Continental Congress		*Nominates Washington as commander in chief*
Declaration of Independence	1776	*Signs Declaration of Independence*
Burgoyne surrenders at Saratoga	1777	*Elected commissioner to France*
Articles of Confederation adopted		
Franco-American Alliance	1778	*Sails to France*
	1779	*Returns to Boston*
		Drafts Mass. constitution
		Sails to Europe
	1780	*Negotiates treaty with Netherlands*
Articles of Confederation ratified	1781	
British surrender at Yorktown		
	1782	*Secures loan and recognition from Dutch*

		1783	*Signs Treaty of Paris*
		1784	*Named minister to England*
Constitutional Convention		1787	.
Constitution ratified		1788	*Returns to U.S.*
Washington elected President		1789	*Elected Vice President*
Bill of Rights			
Emergence of rival parties		1791	
		1792	*Re-elected Vice President*
Neutrality Proclamation		1793	
Whisky Rebellion		1794	
Jay's Treaty			
Suspension of Franco-American relations		1796	*Elected President*
		1797	*Appoints commission to negotiate with French*
Undeclared naval war with France		1798	*XYZ Affair*
			Creates Navy Department
			Appoints Washington to command Army
			Signs Alien and Sedition Acts
Fries Uprising		1799	*Appoints second commission to France*
Death of Washington			
Treaty of Morfontaine		1800	*Moves to White House*
			Loses presidential election
Jefferson inaugurated President		1801	*Appoints John Marshall as Chief Justice*
			Ends presidential term
Madison elected President		1808	
War with England		1812	*Resumes correspondence with Jefferson*
		1818	*Death of Abigail Adams*
John Quincy Adams elected President		1825	
Jefferson dies July 4		1826	*Dies July 4*

BIOGRAPHICAL FACTS

BIRTH: Braintree (Quincy), Mass., Oct. 19, 1735

ANCESTRY: English

FATHER: John Adams; b. Braintree (Quincy), Mass., Jan. 28, 1691; d. Braintree (Quincy), Mass., May 25, 1761

FATHER'S OCCUPATIONS: Farmer; cordwainer

MOTHER: Susanna Boylston Adams; b. March 5, 1699; d. April 17, 1797

BROTHERS: Peter Boylston (1738–1823); Elihu (1741–1775)

WIFE: Abigail Smith; b. Weymouth, Mass., Nov. 11, 1744; d. Quincy, Mass., Oct. 28, 1818

MARRIAGE: Weymouth, Mass., Oct. 25, 1764

CHILDREN: Abigail Amelia (1765–1813); John Quincy (1767–1848); Susanna (1768–1770); Charles (1770–1800); Thomas Boylston (1772–1832)

HOME: Peacefield, Quincy, Mass.

EDUCATION: Attended private schools in Braintree; received B.A. (1755) and M.A. (1758) from Harvard

RELIGIOUS AFFILIATION: Unitarian

OCCUPATIONS BEFORE PRESIDENCY: Teacher; farmer; lawyer

PRE-PRESIDENTIAL OFFICES: Rep. to Mass. General Court; Delegate to First and Second Continental Congresses; Member of Provincial Congress of Mass.; Delegate to Mass. Constitutional Convention; Commissioner to France; Minister to Netherlands and England; Vice President

POLITICAL PARTY: Federalist

AGE AT INAUGURATION: 61

OCCUPATION AFTER PRESIDENCY: Writer

DEATH: Quincy, Mass., July 4, 1826

AGE AT DEATH: 90

PLACE OF BURIAL: First Unitarian Church, Quincy, Mass.

ELECTION OF 1796

(Each elector voted for two men.)

CANDIDATES	ELECTORAL VOTE
John Adams Federalist	71
Thomas Jefferson Democratic-Republican	68
Thomas Pinckney Federalist	59
Aaron Burr Democratic-Republican	30
Samuel Adams Democratic-Republican	15
Oliver Ellsworth Federalist	11
Seven others	22

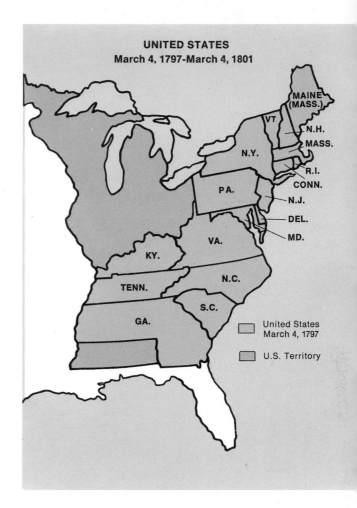

UNITED STATES
March 4, 1797–March 4, 1801

MAINE (MASS.) — VT — N.H. — MASS. — N.Y. — R.I. — CONN. — PA. — N.J. — DEL. — MD. — VA. — KY. — N.C. — TENN. — S.C. — GA.

United States March 4, 1797

U.S. Territory

THE ADAMS ADMINISTRATION

INAUGURATION: March 4, 1797; Federal Hall, Philadelphia

VICE PRESIDENT: Thomas Jefferson

SECRETARY OF STATE: Timothy Pickering; John Marshall (from June 6, 1800)

SECRETARY OF THE TREASURY: Oliver Wolcott, Jr.; Samuel Dexter (from Jan. 1, 1801)

SECRETARY OF WAR: James McHenry; Samuel Dexter (from June 12, 1800)

ATTORNEY GENERAL: Charles Lee

POSTMASTER GENERAL: Joseph Habersham

SECRETARY OF THE NAVY: Benjamin Stoddert

SUPREME COURT APPOINTMENTS: Bushrod Washington (1798); Alfred Moore (1799); John Marshall, Chief Justice (1801)

FIFTH CONGRESS (March 4, 1797–March 4, 1799):
Senate: 20 Federalists; 12 Democratic-Republicans
House: 58 Federalists; 48 Democratic-Republicans

SIXTH CONGRESS (March 4, 1799–March 4, 1801):
Senate: 19 Federalists; 13 Democratic-Republicans
House: 64 Federalists; 42 Democratic-Republicans

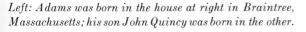

Left: Adams was born in the house at right in Braintree, Massachusetts; his son John Quincy was born in the other.

THOMAS JEFFERSON

Near the foot of the road that leads up to Monticello, a granite obelisk, visible through the gates of a graveyard, bears these words: "Here was buried Thomas Jefferson, author of the Declaration of American Independence, of the Statute of Virginia for Religious Freedom, and father of the University of Virginia."

This epitaph, composed by Jefferson himself, was modest for a man who had also served as minister to France, governor of Virginia, the first Secretary of State, the second Vice President, and—for two remarkable terms—the third President of the United States.

Perhaps Jefferson knew that history would read and write carefully between his lines. And it did. "The principles of Jefferson," Abraham Lincoln would say, "are the definitions and axioms of a free society." To other admirers he would become "a man of steel clothed in homespun" and "the Apostle of Americanism." To his detractors and enemies, however, he was less than anointed: "a howling atheist," an agent of Napoleon, a lecher, worshiping "some infamous prostitute, under the title of the Goddess of Reason." Alexander Hamilton derided Jefferson's "womanish attachment to France," and was convinced that his disinterest and republicanism actually concealed a thirst for power.

Admiration and attack notwithstanding, the range of Jefferson's interests and skills was almost incredible. Pre-eminently a statesman and politician, he was also an adept writer, lawyer, farmer, naturalist, architect, musician, linguist, classicist, philosopher, scientist, geographer, surveyor, botanist, ethnologist, and paleontologist. He was interested in everything, from the origin of the rainbow to the habitat of the wild turkey, from fossils and Newtonian physics to calculus, Anglo-Saxon grammar, and the condition of Negroes in

Thomas Jefferson, painted by Rembrandt Peale in 1805

Santo Domingo. Books, he said, were the "greatest of all amusements." He read Cicero in Latin, Plato in Greek, Montesquieu in French, Cervantes in Spanish. To fathom the poet Ossian, he studied Gaelic. He compiled Indian vocabularies. And even on a backbreaking, three-mile-an-hour, ten-day stagecoach trip from Williamsburg to Philadelphia in 1775, he made notes on fauna and flora and odd coins. As a naturalist, he recorded the growth of trees and flowers, the appearance of birds, the advance and recess of frost. As an inventive farmer, he introduced the moldboard plow to the American Philosophical Society, which he headed from 1796 to 1815. A connoisseur of art, he had one of the finest collections of sculpture and paintings in America.

For all his activities, however, Jefferson was essentially a home-centered, contemplative man. Wherever he was—in France or Philadelphia, among scholars or kings—he was always eager to return to Monticello. "But the enormities of the times in which I have lived," he said in 1809, "have forced me to take a part in resisting them, and to commit myself on the boisterous ocean of political passions."

Jefferson's departure from his "country" (as he always called Virginia) to make his entrance into politics was no less than epochal for the United States. "Jefferson's was to be the leading mind of the first age of our national life," historian Daniel Boorstin concludes, "and therefore in a powerful position for shaping the American intellectual character."

Thomas Jefferson was born, one of ten children, on April 13, 1743, midway through the reign of George II. His birthplace was "Shadwell" in Goochland (now Albemarle) County on Virginia's western frontier. His parents were Peter Jefferson, a prosperous tobacco plantation owner and surveyor, and Jane (Randolph) Jefferson, daughter of one of Virginia's first families, descended from English and Scottish nobility, "to which," Jefferson would wryly add in old age, "let everyone ascribe the . . . merit he chooses."

Thomas' early education was entrusted to the Reverend Mr. William Douglas, for whom Jefferson appears to have had little regard, but from whom he acquired the rudiments of Latin, Greek, and French. When Peter Jefferson died in 1757, Thomas left Douglas' tutelage and studied for two years in a log cabin classroom under the iconoclastic Reverend Mr. James Maury, whom Jefferson described as a "correct classical scholar," and under whose guidance he mastered several languages and was introduced to natural philosophy and geology.

On January 14, 1760, Jefferson wrote a decisive letter to his guardian, Colonel John Harvie, in which he asked for permission to attend William and Mary in Williamsburg. "By going to the College," he reasoned, "I shall get a more universal Acquaintance, which may hereafter be serviceable to me; & I suppose I can pursue my studies in the Greek & Latin as well there as here, & likewise learn something of the Mathematics." Jefferson left the frontier for Williamsburg in March, 1760, and enrolled at the college. The gay capital of colonial Virginia must have been an abrupt change for the provincial student, who nursed at least one hangover from an Apollo Tavern carouse. "I never could have thought," he recorded for posterity on that occasion, "the succeeding

The College of William and Mary is shown at left as it looked in colonial times. It was the second oldest college in the colonies, having opened in 1694, fifty-eight years after the establishment of Harvard. The structures are, from left to right, Brafferton Hall, which housed Indian students, the Wren, or main, building, and the home of the school's president.

sun would have seen me so wretched as I now am!"

Sensitive, shy, and soft spoken, Jefferson was "Long Tom," well over six feet tall, slender, broad-shouldered, his jaw set square, his hands large, his limbs disproportionately long. A gangling, freckled, hazel-eyed redhead, he was a sloucher and a lounger. But his brilliant mind brought him to the attention of the intellectuals of Williamsburg, including his mentor at the college, Dr. William Small, professor of mathematics, natural history, and moral philosophy.

Jefferson graduated from William and Mary in April, 1762, and became an apprentice in the Williamsburg office of George Wythe, one of Virginia's leading jurists. Wythe joined Small in introducing the promising scholar to Virginia's royal governor, Francis Fauquier, at whose table this improbable threesome would often be honored at dinner, where the discussion of politics, literature, music, and philosophy was easily the main course. Though unimpressed by the argot of law, Jefferson was admitted to the bar of the General Court in 1767. He did well as a lawyer, numbering among his clients such prominent Virginia families as the Randolphs, Pendletons, and Pages.

On January 1, 1772, Jefferson married a well-to-do widow, Martha (Wayles) Skelton, in the Anglican rite. He was twenty-eight, she twenty-three. Martha, or Patty, as Jefferson called her, was beautiful, graceful, and high-spirited. A year after the marriage, her father died, leaving her 40,000 acres of land and 135 slaves. But she also inherited a large debt, which accounted in part for Jefferson's subsequent financial troubles.

Moving into the still uncompleted Monticello (construction had begun in 1769), the newlyweds were at first restricted to Jefferson's one-room bachelor quarters. Martha Jefferson was to bear Thomas six children, of whom only Martha ("Patsy") and Maria ("Polly") lived to maturity. Throughout her marriage, Mrs. Jefferson was wracked by chronic miscarriages, contributing to her ill health and to her early death at thirty-three.

In December, 1768, Jefferson had been elected to the Virginia House of Burgesses; he retained his seat there until the royal dissolution of the House in 1775. One of his first acts as a legislator was to introduce, unsuccessfully, a bill to permit owners to free their slaves. Jefferson also held the posts of Albemarle County lieutenant (1770) and Albemarle County surveyor (1773). While not an outstanding public speaker, he excelled as a committeeman and was recognized early as an accomplished writer.

On March 12, 1773, Jefferson and other members of Virginia's radical, anti-British group drew up resolves creating the Virginia Committee of Correspondence to maintain secret contact with the North. The closing of the port of Boston in 1774 resulted in a resolution to side with the Northern rebels; Jefferson championed proclamation of a symbolic fast day to protest the British tyranny in Massachusetts. When the governor of Virginia, the Earl of Dunmore, dissolved the House of Burgesses, Jefferson and his fellow rebels met on May 27, 1774, at the Raleigh Tavern, declaring that "an attack on any one colony should be considered as an attack on the whole." They also agreed that Virginia's counties should elect delegates to a convention that would select representatives

At this portable writing desk Jefferson composed the first draft of the Declaration of Independence.

to the Continental Congress. Albemarle County chose Jefferson as its delegate to the Virginia convention, but dysentery prevented him from attending. He drafted, however, an eloquent protest against royal policy: *A Summary View of the Rights of British America.* It was rejected by the Virginians as too bold, but it made Jefferson a major spokesman for republican America.

Addressed directly to George III, *A Summary View* is a classic of political advocacy and polemic. Jefferson's case for colonial grievances against the Crown was based not merely on evident commercial and political injustice, but also on the natural rights of Englishmen themselves—inherent and irrevocable rights that the King would not have dared to contravene in his own country. "Kings," he reminded George, "are the servants, not the proprietors of the people." Denying all parliamentary authority over the American states, Jefferson informed the sovereign that the colonies' initial submission to him had been voluntary, clearly implying that what had been freely given could also, in tyranny, be withdrawn.

Demanding freedom of world trade in goods that Britain could not use, and an end to taxation of a people not represented in London, Jefferson ridiculed the idea that 160,000 electors in Britain should tyrannize America's four million people through a capricious Parliament, subject, in colonial matters, to the whims and delays of a callous King. Special trade privileges for Britain were acceptable, said Jefferson, still hoping for conciliation, but despotic rule was not.

A Summary View hit the colonies—and Europe—with tremendous force. Jefferson was promptly proscribed by Parliament in a bill of attainder, still another British violation of British law.

In the summer of 1775, he was elected to serve as alternate to Peyton Randolph, a Virginia delegate at the Second Continental Congress. By this time, the fighting at Lexington was history. "This accident," Jefferson said, "has cut off any hope of reconciliation." At the Congress, Jefferson made no speeches, but served on two committees.

Because both his wife and daughter were ill, Jefferson left for Monticello in December of 1775. He found Virginia enraged by Lord Dunmore's punitive burning of Norfolk in January, 1776. Saddened by the death of his mother and suffering from migraine headaches, Jefferson did not return to Philadelphia until May. Less than one month later, on June 7, Virginia's Richard Henry Lee rose to propose a resolution that would change forever the course of human history. Be it resolved, Lee declared, "That these United Colonies are and of right ought to be free and independent states, that they are absolved from all allegiance to the British crown, and that all political connection between them and the state of Great Britain is and ought to be, totally dissolved."

Congress, delaying its vote on the Lee resolution until July 1, appointed a committee of five to draft a formal Declaration of Independence: Thomas Jefferson of Virginia, John Adams of Massachusetts, Benjamin Franklin of Pennsylvania, Roger Sherman of Connecticut, and Robert R. Livingston of New York. The committee, deferring to the thirty-three-year-old Jefferson's established skill as a writer and advocate (he had just written the preamble to the Virginia constitution), delegated him to draft the Declaration. From June 11 to June 28 he worked on it, polishing, changing, rewriting. After amendments by Adams and Franklin were incorporated, the committee submitted the document to the Congress on June 28, 1776.

Jefferson's original draft contained more than 1,800 words. Congress expunged 460, including a stunning condemnation of slavery, as Long Tom sat mute and hurt, and the redoubtable Adams defended the document, word by word. Approved by Congress on July 2, the Declaration was issued to the nation and the world on July 4, 1776.

The Declaration did not merely express American thought; it changed it, inspired it, and committed it to the principle of freedom for all men. Expressing the eighteenth century's faith in human reason and contempt for unearned authority, the document rang with optimism, with the equation of desire and achievement. Jefferson wrote as if tyranny had never been truly binding, as if man had just been born and was building his first house of government. As in *A Summary View*, he carefully catalogued the King's "long train of abuses and usurpations": his legislative, commercial, and judicial despotism; his absentee bureaucracy; his naval depredations; his onerous mercantile taxes; his incitement of American Indians against the colonists; his most unprincely and unchristian conduct.

But the Declaration was—and remains—epochal, not merely as a formal document of rebellion by one specific nation against an-

other. Its greatness lies in its soaring affirmation of unassailable human liberty. Men were to be free, Jefferson wrote, not merely because they wanted to, or because tyranny was intrinsically unjust. Men were to be free because they were, in fact, free under "the laws of nature and of nature's God." Human rights were not magnanimously granted by monarchs and therefore retractable. Human rights were an indissoluble birthright given by God and therefore inalienable. And first among these were the rights of "life, liberty, and the pursuit of happiness." Government's only just function was to secure and advance these rights; when a government ceased to perform this function, it was the duty of men to rebel against it and form another.

Accordingly, America now declared itself thirteen "free and independent states . . . absolved from all allegiance to the British crown." Accordingly, too, America stated the creed of liberty by which it would judge events, and *be* judged for ages to come.

His major task completed, Jefferson remained in Congress for the first debates on the Articles of Confederation, and then left for Monticello in September of 1776. There was, after all, much Revolutionary work to be done at home in Virginia. On October 7, Jefferson entered the Old Dominion's newly designated House of Delegates, where he remained until 1779. In the House, Jefferson spearheaded prodigious legislative achievements. Of one hundred and twenty-six reform bills he sired, at least one hundred

Above is Jefferson's rough manuscript of words that subsequent generations would learn by heart at school.

95

passed. The law of primogeniture and entails was abolished. The criminal law was revised. Although his bill to establish a system of general education failed to pass, it remained a model for future laws.

In 1779, Jefferson introduced the Act for Establishing Religious Freedom, which was not, however, adopted until 1786. This classic bill guaranteed that "no man shall be compelled to frequent or support any religious worship, place, or ministry whatsoever," and that "all men shall be free to profess, and by argument to maintain, their opinions in matters of religion, and that the same shall in nowise diminish, enlarge, or affect their civil capacities." Jefferson reasoned that "our civil rights have no dependence on our religious opinions, more than our opinions in physics or geometry," and that official attempts to impose an established state religion breed only hypocrisy and corruption of the very faith they purport to espouse. Although not a churchgoer himself, Jefferson was, nonetheless, deeply religious. He described himself as "a real Christian," subscribing to the ethics of Jesus, if not the metaphysics of Christianity.

On June 1, 1779, Jefferson succeeded Patrick Henry as wartime governor. From the

Among Thomas Jefferson's many inventions for his household was the revolving music stand above.

start, his administration was beset by ills. Objectively, Jefferson was plagued by an inadequate militia and by border harassments by Indians. Fear of an impending British invasion, for which Virginians were unprepared, pervaded the state. Subjectively, Jefferson was less effective as an executive than as a seer, committeeman, and draftsman. He eschewed, even in war, the use of illegal or arbitrary executive means toward just ends. When Britain finally invaded Virginia in force, he resigned, urging his replacement by a military governor, and retired to Monticello. On June 4, 1781, the British pursued him to Monticello, and he fled to Poplar Forest, a cottage one hundred miles away.

An angered House of Delegates, after electing Thomas Nelson, Jr., military governor, ordered an inquiry into Jefferson's conduct as governor and his failure to organize an adequate militia. A more clement House, in December, 1781, absolved Jefferson of guilt.

On September 6, 1782, Jefferson's wife died. Although he had been determined never to return to politics, the loneliness of his mansion now caused him "to seek relief from personal woe in public activity." In June of 1783, he was elected a delegate to the Continental Congress, where his legislative proposals were formidable. He suggested the adoption of a national dollar, subdivided into tenths and hundredths—a measure approved during Washington's administration with the concurrence of Alexander Hamilton. His Report of Government for the Western Territory (core of the later Ordinance of 1787) advocated the exclusion of slavery in all Western territories after 1800. He also drew up a schema for the final peace treaty with Great Britain, and a report that would establish procedure in the drafting of commercial agreements.

In May, 1784, Jefferson was appointed to assist Franklin and Adams in Europe in the preparation of consular treaties. A year later, he was named Franklin's successor as minister to France, a post he held until October of 1789. Franklin's homespun wit and forthrightness had won the heart of Paris, but

Jefferson's beloved daughter "Patsy" is shown here as she looked around 1786, when she was in Paris.

Jefferson evaded comparisons, adroitly insisting that he had come not to replace Franklin, only to succeed him. As minister, Jefferson presented America's revolutionary case with erudition and dexterity, hailed France tactfully as a counterpoise to a common British antagonist, and negotiated a consular convention.

"On France itself," Nathan Schachner writes, "Jefferson was of two minds. He envied the French their architecture, sculpture, painting, and music; but nothing else. Fresh from the spaciousness of America, where institutions, no matter how far behind the ideal, at least were liberal and progressive, where the people walked with an independent air and poverty was practically unknown, the swarming alleys of Paris, the contrast between resplendent Court and the hopeless masses . . . filled him with a sense of horror." To see the world, Jefferson would say, is to love America all the more.

In a sense, Jefferson never really left home; his eye was ever on Virginia. While in France, he designed the buildings for the new state capital at Richmond, worked on plans for his beloved Monticello, and heard the glad news that his Act for Establishing Religious Freedom had passed the Virginia legislature in 1786. From Paris, too, reviewing the newly adopted Constitution by mail with his friend James Madison, he insisted on the prompt inclusion of a bill of rights.

Despite official United States neutrality in France's revolution, Jefferson was patently sympathetic with the more moderate revolutionists, who were at once the source of his diplomatic data and contacts and the object of his special concern. He proposed to the Marquis de Lafayette a new charter for France, and to Lafayette's aunt, Madame de Tessé, a procedural form for the French Assembly of Notables. In later years Jefferson would maintain that every cultivated and traveled man would prefer France as a principal alternative to his own country.

Still, Jefferson was glad to start for home in October, 1789, to return to family, farm, and books. As he approached Monticello, two days before Christmas, his servants spotted his phaeton and followed it up the steep hill to the mansion. "When the door of the carriage was opened," his daughter Martha recorded, "they received him in their arms and bore him to the house, crowding round and kissing his hands and feet, some blubbering and crying, others laughing. It seemed impossible to satisfy their anxiety to touch and kiss the very earth which bore him."

On his return from Europe, Jefferson's basic philosophy, modified at least marginally by the French revolutionary experience, was already clear. He had, above all, a confirmed and unsullied faith in America, viewing it in candent Biblical terms as a promised land. But America's abundance and promise, Jefferson argued in 1789, was no cause for pride. The United States, he said, must "show by example the sufficiency of human reason for the care of human affairs and that the will of the majority, the Natural Law of every society, is the only sure guardian of the rights of man."

Impressed by the ideology of the Enlightenment, Jefferson shared its faith in reason, science, and human perfectibility. "We believed," he would say in retrospect in 1823, "that man was a rational animal, endowed by nature with rights and with an innate sense of justice . . . that he could be restrained from wrong and protected in right, by moderate powers confided to persons of his own choice, and held to their duties by dependence on his own will." He believed also in the superiority of agrarian virtue, unsullied by industry and commerce. "Those who labor in the earth," Jefferson had said in his *Notes on Virginia*, "are the chosen people of God. . . ." Urging American reliance on the products of Europe, already hopelessly corrupted by factories, he turned with contempt on the urban community: "The mobs of great cities add just so much to the support of pure government, as sores do to the strength of the human body."

Bacon, Newton, and Locke were for Jefferson a "trinity of the three greatest men the world had ever produced." He admired Bacon for his theory of inductive reasoning from observed fact, for his theory of movement from clinically measurable data to hypothesis, experiment, and control. He valued Newton for his revolutionary description of a physical world governed by predictable laws of cause and effect, applicable no less to human conduct than to the elements. Locke became his fountainhead for his concept of natural human rights, founded not on the will of man but in the very substance of the natural order, rights discoverable to human reason. He admired, too, Locke's belief that man protected his natural rights to life, liberty, and property in voluntary mutual contract, organizing a protective government, desirable and sufferable only if its selected leaders lived up to its terms.

Appointed by Washington in December, 1789, as the first Secretary of State, Jefferson arrived in New York to assume his duties in March of the following year. It was a difficult tenure. Although he collaborated with Hamilton on the federal government's assumption of state debts, in exchange for Hamilton's concession that the new national capital be located on the banks of the Potomac, he was distressed to see Washington espouse Hamilton's plan for a central Bank of the United States—to Jefferson an insidious concentration of wealth. As an agrarian, he regarded banks as parasitic.

Unhappy over Hamilton's leading role in the administration, Jefferson asked to retire by the end of 1792. He was persuaded by the President to stay on at least another year to avoid overt Federalist-Republican dissension within the government. During this period, his coinage and monetary system was adopted with Hamilton's approval, and Jefferson had to deal with a major political problem—the French appointment of Citizen Edmond Genêt as minister to the United States. Jefferson said in 1793 that rather than see the French Revolution fail he "would . . . have seen half the earth desolated." But when Genêt, despite America's officially stated neutrality in the Franco-British conflict, "spoke of going over President Washington's head" in direct appeal to the American people for assistance against England, Jefferson was nonplused. He recommended Genêt's prompt expulsion.

Disappointed by France and still frustrated by Hamilton, Jefferson was now determined to resign and held Washington to his promise to let him go at the end of 1793. On January 16, 1794, Jefferson was back at Monticello. His retirement would be brief, however. In 1796, the Republicans, incensed by the reign of wealth and privilege and by Jay's Treaty, nominated Jefferson and Aaron Burr to oppose John Adams in his bid for the Presidency. Jefferson lost the election to Adams by three electoral votes, thus becoming Vice President for four more years of Federalist frustration.

Republican sentiment against the Federalists became frenetic with the passage of the Alien and Sedition Acts, which they viewed as an odious attempt to silence or intimidate all opposition. "Against us," Jefferson wrote, "are . . . all the officers of the government, all who want to be officers, all timid men who prefer the calm of despotism to the boisterous sea of liberty. . . ." Now

Jefferson abandoned all semblance of impartiality and plunged into overt leadership of the emerging Republican party. The Alien and Sedition Acts, he told Madison in June of 1800, were "so palpably in the teeth of the Constitution as to show they [the Federalists] mean to pay no respect to it."

To counter the federal government and reassert the states' rights to political freedom, Jefferson pushed through the Kentucky legislature (and Madison through Virginia's) a series of resolutions declaring the Alien and Sedition Acts unconstitutional. In Kentucky, Jefferson argued a primary brief of the Southern case. "Where powers are assumed which have not been delegated," he said, "a nullification of the act is the rightful remedy."

In 1800, Jefferson was nominated by the Republicans for the Presidency of the United States. His running mate was Aaron Burr; his opponents, John Adams, seeking re-election, and Charles Pinckney. Jefferson's basic concept of the federal role, as he approached the election, was presented in a lucid letter of 1799 to Elbridge Gerry. "I am for preserving to the States," he wrote, "the powers not yielded by them to the Union. . . . I am not for transferring all the powers of the States to the General Government, and all those of that government to the executive branch." He said he preferred "a government rigorously frugal and simple," its savings promptly applied to discharging the national debt, its attitude firmly fixed against bureaucracy based on spoils. Dismissing a standing army as a coercive menace to liberty, and urging a navy limited to coastal patrol, he advocated a strong militia as adequate to maintaining the social order, short of invasion. He urged free trade with all.

Despite five years of ministry in France, Jefferson advocated "little or no diplomatic establishment" and opposed foreign alliances. In another assault on the Alien and Sedition Acts, he declared himself "against all violations of the Constitution to silence by force and not by reason the complaints or criticisms, just or unjust, of our citizens

This 1800 cartoon attacked Jefferson for his letter to Philip Mazzei, an Italian friend, in which he violently accused the Federalists of despotism.

against the conduct of their agents." In light of Jefferson's conduct as President, these statements take on ironic significance: although he did cut the American diplomatic corps to the bone, he was to reverse or abridge all the rest of these principles.

But now he faced a vicious campaign, a toxic stew of license and spleen. The Federalists were badly split, Hamilton openly warring with Adams. Hamilton raged against Jefferson, determined to prevent that "atheist in religion, and a fanatic in politics, from getting possession of the helm of state." It was a newspaper and pamphlet war, too, waged pre-eminently by Philip Freneau's Jeffersonian *National Gazette* and John Fenno's Hamiltonian *U.S. Gazette*. Jefferson was attacked as a drunkard, the father of numerous mulattoes, and an atheist. "Our churches will be prostrated," cried the *New-England Palladium*. "There is scarcely a possibility," added the *Connecticut Courant*,

AARON BURR

Aaron Burr possessed the brilliance, wit, and charm of a born leader. But he was an egomaniac who forever sowed the seeds of his own failure. Rising rapidly in the New York State Republican party, he received thirty electoral votes in the presidential election of 1796. Named as Jefferson's running mate four years later, he campaigned vigorously in New York and was largely responsible for the Republican victory. But when the electoral count showed him tied with Jefferson, his ambition overrode his common sense, and he declined to remove himself from competition, thus earning Jefferson's lasting distrust. Having failed to win the President's support for a second term as Vice President, and having lost his state's gubernatorial election, an embittered Burr challenged Alexander Hamilton to a duel and killed him. He then became involved in a scheme apparently aimed at separating at least part of the West from the United States, and conquering Mexico. Blinded by dreams of glory, he raised an army, but it was pitifully small, and he was arrested before he could do any damage. Charged with treason, Burr was brought to trial before Chief Justice John Marshall in 1807. Jefferson demanded a verdict of guilty, but the anti-Jefferson Chief Justice conducted the trial in a manner that led to Burr's acquittal. Burr then left for Europe, where he continued his intrigues fruitlessly. He died in New York in 1836.

"that we shall escape a *Civil War*. . . . Murder, robbery, rape, adultery, and incest will be openly taught and practiced. . . ."

While there was a definite understanding that Jefferson was running for the Presidency and Burr for the Vice Presidency, the method of voting demanded that state electors cast votes for two men, without distinguishing between their choices for the first and second offices. When Jefferson and Burr received the same number of votes, the election was thus thrust into a seething Federalist-controlled House of Representatives. The tie was not broken until thirty-six ballots had been cast, and then only because Hamilton, hating Jefferson less than he hated Burr, swung the Federalist vote in Jefferson's favor.

President at fifty-seven, Jefferson was the first Chief Executive inaugurated in Washington; he was sworn in, ironically, by the arch-Federalist, Chief Justice John Marshall, who had been appointed by Adams in the closing weeks of his administration.

Jefferson, conscious that he and Burr had forged the nation's first viable opposition party, held out the olive branch to old enemies. In a noble Inaugural Address, Jefferson urged conciliation and an end to sectionalism, and tried to set at rest the fear that he planned a new revolution. "We are all republicans," he said, "we are all federalists." Hailing "a rising nation, spread over a wise and fruitful land . . . advancing rapidly to destinies beyond the reach of mortal eye," Jefferson asked an end to political bitterness. "Every difference of opinion," he said, "is not a difference of principle. We have called by different names brethren of the same principle." It was a candid appeal for practical consensus toward shared ends. Jefferson promised "a wise and frugal government, which shall restrain men from injuring one another, [but] which shall leave them otherwise free to regulate their own pursuits." Then Jefferson—the architect of the Kentucky Resolutions, which gave the Union one of its first major hints of nullification—turned to those who had threatened secession in the North. "If there be any among us who would wish to dissolve this Union or to change its republican form, let them stand undisturbed as monuments of the safety with which error of opinion may be tolerated where reason is left free to combat it."

His oath sworn, President Jefferson moved to strike the Federalists down. The Federalist excise tax and Judiciary Act were repealed, several of Adams' midnight judgeship appointments were declared null and void, and victims of the Alien and Sedition Acts were pardoned. By 1803, a political patronage balance had been restored.

Jefferson's first major foreign crisis began in 1801. European commercial powers—and the United States—had long paid Africa's Barbary Coast pirates annual fees to protect their vessels from raids. When the Pasha of Tripoli demanded that America increase its payments, the United States refused, and the Pasha declared war. Jefferson ordered the fleet to the Mediterranean. In 1804, Tripolitans took the American warship *Philadelphia*, which had run aground, and United States frigates bombarded Tripoli. His purpose, Jefferson said, was to bludgeon "the Barbarians of Tripoli to the desire of peace on proper terms by the sufferings of war."

The Philadelphia, *captured and manned by Tripolitans in the war with the Barbary pirates, was destroyed in a fire (below) set by American raiders.*

Later, William Eaton, the American consul at Tunis, marched with a small force from Libya to the Tripolitan town of Derna and seized it. A treaty favorable to the United States was signed in 1805.

Easily the most important event in Jefferson's first term was his purchase of the Louisiana Territory, which doubled the size of the United States. By the Treaty of San Ildefonso in 1800, Spain had ceded to France its rights to the port of New Orleans and, by extension, to the Mississippi and the vast province of Louisiana. Realizing that free navigation of the Mississippi and the use of New Orleans for storage were crucial to the commerce of the nation, and fearful of new French territorial designs in the West, Jefferson moved to purchase New Orleans in 1803. Given two million dollars by Congress to use for that purpose, he dispatched James Monroe to Paris to join Robert Livingston, who was already negotiating with Napoleon.

Livingston was delighted to learn that Napoleon was willing to offer more than just New Orleans. "They ask of me only one town in Louisiana," the dictator declared, "but I already consider the colony as entirely lost." By the time Monroe arrived, France had ceded to the United States the vast continental slice of land from the Mississippi to the Rockies for sixteen million dollars. Aware that his ministers had far exceeded their congressional instructions and

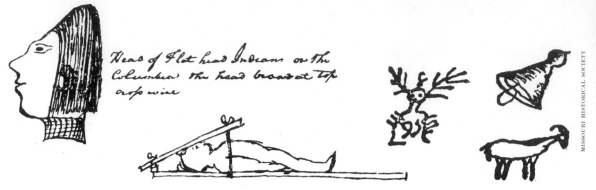

These sketches, taken from the journal of Lewis and Clark, show, from left to right, a flat-headed Chinook; the method used to shape the skulls of infants; a rock painting; an Indian hat; and a bighorn sheep.

constitutional authority, Jefferson decided nevertheless to confront a special session of Congress with the accomplished fact. The Senate and House authorized the purchase, and Jefferson signed the treaty with France on October 20, 1803.

Jefferson's first presidential term was also distinguished by his commissioning of the Lewis and Clark expedition to map the Missouri River and to increase American knowledge of the Western lands. The expedition, begun in May, 1804, concluded when Meriwether Lewis reported to the President on January 10, 1807.

Jefferson, meanwhile, had projected a presidential image wholly new to official Washington. While he served French food—to the chagrin of chauvinists—he also abolished the levee, a quasi-monarchical, ritualistic reception favored by both Presidents Washington and Adams, and maintained in the White House the informality of Monticello. Anthony Merry, Britain's minister, spoke in 1804 of Jefferson's "yarn stockings and slippers down at the heels," describing his general appearance as "very much like that of a tall, large-boned farmer. . . ."

Without question, the diffident patrician had become the hero of America's common man. Jefferson's achievement in gaining this stature was, Dumas Malone has written, "due in considerable part to his identification of himself with causes for which time was fighting. . . . His unchallenged leadership was due, not to self-assertiveness and imperiousness of will, but to the fact that circumstance had made him a symbolic figure, and that to an acute intelligence and

unceasing industry he joined a dauntless and contagious faith."

With a record highlighted by the Louisiana Purchase, the victory over the Barbary pirates, and the repeal of the hated Federalist excise tax, Jefferson sought and decisively won re-election as President in 1804. Burr, who killed Alexander Hamilton in a duel in July, had already been replaced as Jefferson's running mate by New York's governor, George Clinton. The Democratic-Republicans took the South, Pennsylvania, New York, and even conservative Massachusetts, for a total of 162 electoral votes against 14 for Federalists Charles Pinckney and Rufus King. Jefferson could not know then that his second term would end in as much public rancor as his first had ended in exultation.

In 1806 the United States was confronted with naval harassment by both London and Paris, who, blockading each other's ports, seized American ships and impressed American seamen. Jefferson responded with less belligerence than he had shown toward Tripoli: he overtly rejected war with either European power. Though angered in 1807 by Britain's attack on the United States frigate *Chesapeake* and the capture of its crew on the grounds that four of the sailors were British deserters, Jefferson still refused to tarnish his administration with war. His solution was an embargo, terminating all foreign commerce by the United States.

The embargo not only failed to reverse British and French naval policy, but called down the wrath of the nation on Jefferson's head. "A whole people," thundered Josiah Quincy, "is laboring under a most grievous oppression. All the business of the nation is deranged. . . . All its industry stagnant."

"The embargo," writes historian Leonard Levy, "begun as a means of coercing and starving England and France into respect for American rights, rapidly became an instrument of coercion against American citizens. To avoid foreign war, Jefferson made domestic war." The regular army, which Jefferson had opposed, was increased, and the United States Navy and militia were ordered to enforce the embargo. "Congress," the President insisted, "must legalize all *means* which may be necessary to obtain its *end*."

A federal judge in Charleston, himself appointed by Jefferson, attacked the Embargo Act as "an unsanctioned encroachment upon individual liberty." Senator Samuel White of Delaware charged that it put "the whole country under military law," and permitted unwarranted search, seizure, and arrest on the merest suspicion of intent to export. "To this day," Levy concludes, the embargo "remains the most repressive and unconstitutional legislation ever enacted by Congress in time of peace."

By February 21, 1809, Jefferson had asked Congress to lift the embargo against all but French and British shipping, and to lift it entirely by June 1, 1809. It was left to Madison, historian Stuart Gerry Brown notes, "to develop a better policy if he could, or else go to war."

Jefferson's second term was marred by still another major departure from civil liberties. Former Vice President Aaron Burr, who had tried unsuccessfully to lead a revolt of Western states (possibly intending to unite them with Mexico, with himself as emperor of a new kingdom), was tried for treason and acquitted by a federal court under Chief Justice John Marshall. Before the verdict was in, Jefferson made it clear that he thought Burr should be found guilty. It was a grave departure from ideology for the author of *A Summary View* and the Declaration of Independence, and for the man who had successfully urged the adoption of the Bill of Rights, guaranteeing fair trial by jury.

His less-than-splendid second term notwithstanding, many urged Jefferson to seek a third. He declined, however. For Jefferson, the Presidency had been "a splendid misery," bringing "nothing but unceasing drudgery and daily loss of friends."

In retirement at sixty-six, Jefferson became "Old Sachem," the Sage of Monticello. "I resume with delight," he said, "the character and pursuits for which nature designed me. I talk of ploughs and harrows," he wrote in 1810, "of seeding and harvesting, with my neighbors, and of politics, too, if they choose . . . and feel, at length, the blessing of being free to say and do what I please." Old correspondence was renewed. "I have given up newspapers in exchange for Tacitus and Thucydides," he wrote to John Adams in 1812 after their eleven-year silence.

Up at dawn, Jefferson wrote and read until breakfast. He rode six or eight miles on horseback each day, overseeing his lands and farms. He supervised his gristmill, nail factory, and furniture shop; built a dumb-waiter and weather vanes; and delighted in spoiling his beloved great-grandchildren. He kept a full house of family and friends; at times, there were as many as seventy overnight guests. Even in near-bankruptcy—in 1826 his friends throughout the nation raised nearly sixteen thousand dollars to bail him out of debt—he kept Monticello as a haven.

He found time to advise Presidents Madison and Monroe when they asked. But his primary interest in retirement was the founding of the University of Virginia. He

MONTICELLO

JEFFERSON LOTTERY.
Register No. 1979
MANAGERS.
John Brockenborough,
Philip Norb. Nicholas,
Richard Anderson.
Combination Nos. 3 15 31
This Ticket will entitle the holder thereof to such prize as may be drawn to its numbers in the JEFFERSON LOTTERY.
Richmond, April, 1826.
For the Managers,
Wm. Grattan, Printer.

A public lottery was initiated in 1826 to bail the ex-President out of debt, but the idea was abandoned when his friends raised some $16,000 themselves.

was involved in the selection of its professors, its library books, its curriculum. He designed its buildings and directly supervised its construction. And he presented at the founding of this first nonsectarian American university a classic definition of academic freedom: "This institution," he said, "will be based on the illimitable freedom of the human mind. For here we are not afraid to follow truth wherever it may lead, nor to tolerate any error so long as reason is left free to combat it."

In retirement, too, Jefferson refined and enlarged his philosophy of freedom. He refused to look back to past authority. "Some men," he wrote, "look at constitutions with sanctimonious reverence, and deem them like the ark of the covenant, too sacred to be touched. . . . Laws and institutions must go hand in hand with the progress of the human mind."

Jefferson retained a vibrant and undiminished faith in democracy. "The only orthodox object . . . of government," he wrote in 1812, "is to secure the greatest degree of happiness possible to the general mass. . . ." Where else, he reasoned, will we "find the origin of *just* powers, if not in the majority of the society?" But although he insisted that the will of the majority prevail, he was equally insistent that the rights of minorities be protected.

Jefferson also retained his faith in the exemplary mission of America. In the Revolution, he maintained, we were not "acting for ourselves alone, but for the whole human race. The event of our experiment is to show whether man can be trusted with self-government."

In his final years, Jefferson held to conservative concepts of federal and state power. Despite his own unorthodox acts as Chief Executive, he insisted that he was opposed to "a very energetic government" as "always oppressive." The states, he maintained, were "the wisest conservative power ever contrived by man."

Jefferson opposed a strong Supreme Court —especially under Federalist control—reviewing the constitutionality of acts passed by an elected Congress and signed by an elected President. "The great object of my fear," he wrote in 1821, "is the Federal Judiciary." He cited the Court's potential reign as an oligarchy, insisting that the Constitution had "erected no such single tribunal," independent of "the will of the nation."

Forced by events to modify soaring theory in searing practice, Jefferson left behind him a rich but paradoxical heritage. Conservatives have admired his opposition to "energetic government," his defense of states' rights, his opposition to the Supreme Court, his frugality with public funds, and his patrician good sense. Liberals have applauded his vigorous use of executive power, his defense of minorities, his commitment to ·civil liberties, and his defiance of precedent.

It would be facile even to suggest that Jefferson was, or remains, all things to all men. It would be more accurate to say that he has emerged as America's foremost prophet and spokesman of liberty.

For himself, Jefferson remained confident that history would corroborate that men had indeed been created equal and would continue to prefer the "boisterous sea of liberty" to "the calm of despotism." And when all is said, the Jeffersonian tradition, as Boorstin has written, does remain "our principal check on the demands of irresponsible power."

On July 4, 1826, the fiftieth anniversary of the Declaration of Independence, the third President of the United States died, a few hours before his old friend, John Adams. He had fought to stay alive for that day, awaking on the third of July in delirium to mutter instructions that the Virginia Committee of Safety must be warned of the British approach. Ten days before his death, Long Tom wrote one of his last and strongest dicta of liberty. Urging that America remain to the world "the signal of arousing men to burst [their] chains," he said: "The mass of mankind has not been born with saddles on their backs, nor a favored few, booted and spurred, ready to ride them legitimately, by the Grace of God."

—WILSON SULLIVAN

Th Jefferson

A PICTURE PORTFOLIO

This victory flag celebrated Jefferson's assumption of the Presidency after the election of 1800.

"HE SOON SEIZED
UPON MY HEART"

Youth is not rich in time; it may be poor," wrote the poet Edward Young; "Part with it as with money, sparing. . . ." These lines, copied out by Thomas Jefferson in his student days, could stand as the young man's credo, and as an explanation for his rapid rise in colonial politics. He wasted little time, studied diligently, and quickly made his mark. He was practicing law at twenty-three. One year later he became a member of the colonial legislature, and was soon part of the anti-British faction that led the House of Burgesses in its most rebellious acts. His address to George III, *A Summary View of the Rights of British America*, made him a world figure at thirty-one. Draftsman of the Declaration of Independence, and then governor of Virginia, he was chosen to succeed the legendary Franklin as minister to France in 1785. "He was," said John Adams of Jefferson, "so prompt, frank, explicit and decisive upon committees and in conversation . . . that he soon seized upon my heart."

A Swiss painter, Pierre Eugene Du Smitière, made the above portrait of Jefferson in 1775. That same year, the thirty-three-year-old Virginian attended the Continental Congress at Philadelphia and wrote the Declaration of Independence in a room in a bricklayer's house.

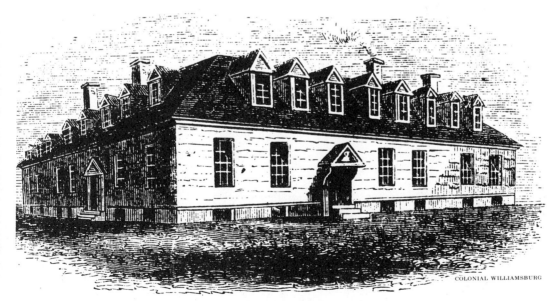

The Raleigh Tavern in Williamsburg, above, was a meeting place for the Virginia Revolutionaries. At left is the Governor's Palace, where Jefferson, then a student at William and Mary, often dined with Governor Francis Fauquier. When Jefferson became governor of Virginia during the Revolution, he lived at the Palace.

107

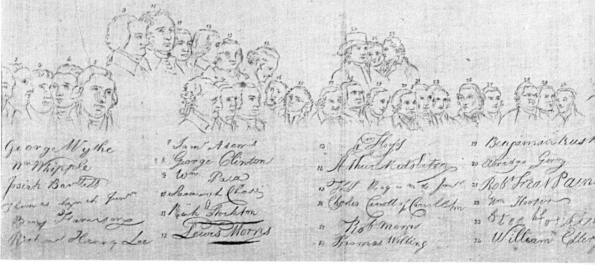

This print, on a cotton kerchief, depicts the adoption of the Declaration of Independence.

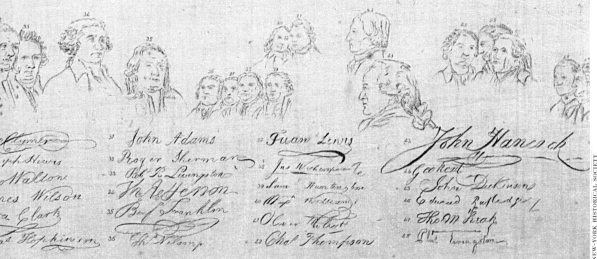

Shown standing in front of the table are Adams, Sherman, Livingston, Jefferson, and Franklin.

Jefferson, a widower, fell in love with the beautiful Maria Cosway, above, during his second summer in France. But she was already married, and their affair was platonic and brief.

"It was wise," Jefferson wrote of France in tumult, "to have 2 passports"—one from the King, one from the elected representatives. The passport below bears the signature of Louis XVI.

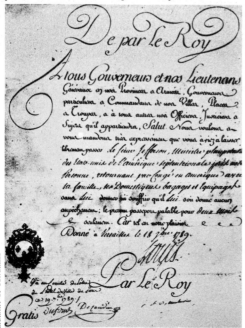

A "SAVAGE" ABROAD

Behold me at length on the vaunted scene of Europe!" wrote the new United States minister to France, Thomas Jefferson, to a friend in 1785. "You are, perhaps, curious to know how this new scene has struck a savage of the mountains of America. Not advantageously, I assure you. I find the general fate of humanity here most deplorable." He was shocked by the contrasts in French society. "The truth of Voltaire's observation offers itself perpetually, that every man here must be either the hammer or the anvil," he said. And the quality of the foremost hammers—the royalty—did not impress him. "There is not a crowned head in Europe," he wrote to George Washington in 1788, "whose talents or merits would entitle him to be elected a vestryman by . . . any parish in America." Jefferson remained officially aloof from the revolutionary movement in France, but he sympathized with it and participated as an adviser, particularly in the formation of France's new political institutions. Having toured the provinces, he counseled Lafayette: "Ferret people out of their hovels, as I have done, look into their kettles . . . loll on their beds. . . . You shall [then] be able to apply your knowledge to the softening of their beds, or the throwing a morsel of meat into their kettle of vegetables." Meanwhile, as a diplomat, Jefferson worked out a commercial treaty with Prussia and a consular agreement with France, traveled widely, observed and listened, and sent home a great variety of information on Europe. His stay abroad was both enjoyable and stimulating, and after his return to the United States, the Virginian looked upon France as his second home.

Louis XVI of France, left, was willing to re-form his government, and on July 11, 1789, Jefferson wrote that peaceful revolution seemed assured. But the King was easily swayed by advisers. Three days after Jefferson wrote his letter, the Bastille was attacked.

"They took all the arms, discharged the prisoners, and such of the garrison as were not killed in the first moment of fury . . . cut off [the heads of the governor and lieutenant governor] and sent them through the city in triumph." So wrote the American minister, describing the fall of the Bastille, below.

A MOMENTOUS PURCHASE

Almost from the start of Washington's administration, Jefferson had criticized the Federalists for stretching the Constitution beyond the intentions of the Founding Fathers. But the major achievement of his own first term as President, the Louisiana Purchase, set a loose-constructionist precedent of profound importance. Jefferson believed that France, which had been given title to Spanish lands beyond the Mississippi, was a threat to American commerce on the river, and he feared that the United States might have to fight a major war to assert its rights of navigation; he was also afraid that European wars might spread to North America if the French retained the Louisiana region. The President saw the future of the United States in continental terms; two years before the purchase was made he had begun to plan an expedition to explore the Northwest to the Pacific. When it seemed that Napoleon might be willing to sell Florida and some of the land on the lower Mississippi, Jefferson sent American diplomats to France to open negotiations, even though the Constitution did not mention a federal right to buy new territory. But when the United States was suddenly offered 828,000 square miles of land, extending westward to the Rockies, the President agonized over the constitutional question. He considered asking for an amendment to legalize the act, and finally supported the purchase, hoping, he said, "that the good sense of our country will correct the evil of loose construction when it shall produce its ill effects."

UNDER ☆ MY ☆ ☆WINGS

EVERY THING PROSPERS

New Orleans (above) was a prosperous city in 1803, the year it became American. The strategic location of this port, controlling all the ocean-bound trade of the Mississippi, was one reason for the Louisiana Purchase.

JEFFERSON'S APPOINTEES

ROBERT R. LIVINGSTON

Robert R. Livingston's role in the negotiation of the Louisiana Purchase in 1803 capped a notable public career. He had served on a wide range of committees during four terms in the Continental Congress, and he had helped draft the Declaration of Independence, although he did not sign it because the New York convention had not so authorized him. Livingston then organized the new nation's department of foreign affairs and, as its first foreign secretary, oversaw the signing of the Treaty of Paris. He was a key figure in the formation of New York's state government, helping to draw up its constitution. From 1777 to 1801 he was New York State chancellor, in which capacity he administered the presidential oath to George Washington in 1789. Livingston split with the Federalists because he felt that he had not received his just share of patronage and became Jefferson's minister to France in 1801. When Napoleon offered to sell all of Louisiana to the United States, Livingston, along with James Monroe, boldly exceeded his authority and accepted. He had backed Robert Fulton's development of the steamship *Clermont*, and when he retired in 1804 Livingston continued to exercise the monopoly on steam navigation he had obtained from the state of New York in 1798. He died in 1813 at the age of sixty-six.

ALBERT GALLATIN

Swiss-born Albert Gallatin came to America in 1780 when he was nineteen; by 1790 he was a member of the Pennsylvania legislature, evincing a Jeffersonian liberalism and an interest in public finance. Elected to the United States Senate in 1794, he demanded that the Secretary of the Treasury issue reports on past expenses, and was unseated by Federalists who maintained that he had not been a citizen long enough to serve in the Senate. A congressman from 1795 to 1801, Gallatin helped create a standing finance committee and continued to urge financial reforms. As Secretary of the Treasury under Jefferson and Madison, he favored light taxes and little spending; but although he reduced the national debt, the prewar embargoes and the War of 1812 ruined his attempts to bring about lasting fiscal stability. He served on the peace delegation to Ghent, negotiated commercial treaties with Britain, and became minister to France and then to England. Returning to America, he served from 1831 until 1839 as president of the National Bank. Gallatin was also the first president of the University of the City of New York, the founder of the American Ethnological Society, and the president of the New-York Historical Society. In the last years of his life, he conducted valuable studies of Indian tribes. He died in 1849.

MERIWETHER LEWIS

At twenty-nine, Meriwether Lewis was pre-eminently qualified for the task assigned him in 1803 by Thomas Jefferson: to lead an overland expedition to the Pacific. Lewis, raised in Virginia and Georgia, was an expert hunter and amateur naturalist. Six years in various military outposts had tested his leadership and familiarized him with Indian affairs. Lewis had become Jefferson's private secretary in 1801, and they frequently discussed Jefferson's long-held dream of Northwest exploration. In the spring of 1804, forty-eight men under Lewis and William Clark began their trek to the headwaters of the Missouri River and beyond. They wintered in North Dakota and by August of 1805 approached the Continental Divide. They descended the Clearwater and Columbia rivers, reaching the Pacific Ocean in November. On the return trip, Lewis took a different route than Clark and encountered hostile Indians. Later he was accidentally wounded by one of his own men; but the parties rejoined and arrived in St. Louis in September of 1806 to the surprise and joy of a country that had presumed them lost. Lewis had justified Jefferson's faith in him by making voluminous notes which were of great value to scientists, explorers, and students. He became governor of Louisiana, a post he held until his death in 1809.

BOTH: INDEPENDENCE NATIONAL HISTORICAL PARK

WILLIAM CLARK

William Clark was happily surprised when Meriwether Lewis asked him to help lead an expedition to the Northwest in 1803. The younger brother of George Rogers Clark, he had served in the Army from 1792 to 1796, and had participated in several fierce battles with the Indians, including the one at Fallen Timbers in Ohio in 1794, during which he had met Lewis for the first time. After retiring from the Army, Clark had traveled widely in the West, and Lewis knew that his thorough knowledge of Indian affairs and his experiences as a frontiersman made him an ideal choice for co-leader of the exploration party. Clark's bent for map making and his skill at drawing birds and animals also contributed heavily to the mission's success. After the expedition's return in 1806, Clark became superintendent of Indian affairs for the Louisiana (later Missouri) Territory; in 1813, he became governor of the region. During the War of 1812, Clark was instrumental in defending the West from British-incited Indian attacks. Postwar treaties were periodically broken by rebellious tribes, but Clark often took the side of the Indians against the federal government, and as a result won their esteem and kept uprisings to a minimum. Clark remained active in Western affairs until his death at the age of sixty-eight on September 1, 1838.

In the war with the Barbary States, the former American consul at Tunis, William Eaton, carried out an incredible unauthorized military mission against Tripoli. He marched a patchwork army five hundred miles across the desert (above) from Alexandria to Derna, which he captured, helping to bring about a peace treaty.

A TROUBLED TERM

Foreign affairs made Jefferson's second term a rocky one. The Napoleonic Wars resulted in restrictions on American shipping by the belligerents, impressment of American sailors, and the British attack on the frigate *Chesapeake*. Jefferson responded with the Nonimportation and Embargo acts, but these were not effective and were bitterly resented by many Americans. There were some successes, however: a treaty was signed with the Barbary pirates; Spain was induced to cease harassing the Southern and Western frontiers; and Congress made it illegal to import slaves. But by 1809 Jefferson was glad to be leaving office. "Never did a prisoner, released from his chains, feel such relief as I shall on shaking off the shackles of power," he wrote on March 2. "Nature intended me," the President added wistfully, "for the tranquil pursuits of science. . . ."

In 1805 Jefferson found himself in the midst of the war between England and France. The above cartoon, symbolic of the war's effect on American trade, depicts King George and Napoleon robbing the President.

On June 22, 1807, the American frigate Chesapeake sailed out of Hampton Roads, Virginia, bound for the Mediterranean, with four British sailors in her crew. She was intercepted by the British Leopard, and when she refused permission for a search, the Leopard fired a crippling broadside (left) and seized the four deserters. American anger at the incident led to the embargo.

117

JUDICIAL GIANT

John Marshall had "one original . . . almost supernatural faculty," said a contemporary, William Wirt: he could grasp an argument in a law court by "a single glance of his mind." This amazing capacity for concentration and insight was obvious to others even in Marshall's youth: he needed only about a month's formal study and a few years of practice to become one of Virginia's leading lawyers. And although he had never held a judicial post prior to his appointment to the Supreme Court, he became a superb Chief Justice.

Born near Germantown, Virginia, in 1755, Marshall served in the Revolution as an officer, was elected a state assemblyman, and was Virginia's most prominent Federalist by the time he was forty. Although he turned down several important national posts because he preferred to practice law, he did agree to accept an assignment to France in 1797, a mission that resulted in the XYZ Affair. He was elected to Congress in 1799, and in May, 1800, President John Adams convinced Marshall to become Secretary of State; the following year, Adams made him, concurrently, Chief Justice. It was Marshall, therefore, who swore in his distant cousin and political enemy, Thomas Jefferson, as the nation's third President.

Out of the Jefferson-Marshall antagonism came one of the Supreme Court's most momentous precedents: that the Court could declare an act of Congress unconstitutional. John Adams had spent his final night in the White House making last-gasp appointments designed to preserve Federalist power in the government. Among them were a number of justices of the peace for the District of Columbia. In the rush, some of the commissions were never delivered, and Jefferson decided to hold on to them. One of the men waiting for his commission was William Marbury; he asked the Supreme Court to demand that Secretary of State Madison deliver the commissions, being aware that the Court had been empowered to do so by the Judiciary Act of 1789. Marshall was sympathetic, but he knew that the Court was at a crossroads in terms of prestige, and that if it did issue the order, Jefferson and Madison would ignore it. He did not want to rule against Marbury, so he delivered his precedent-setting opinion, *Marbury v. Madison*, in which he scathingly criticized Madison and Jefferson for not giving Marbury his commission, but declared that the section of law that empowered the Court to issue the order was unconstitutional. Jefferson called Marshall's careful logic "twistifications," but Marshall had made the first assertion of what was to be the greatest power of the Supreme Court.

Marshall served as Chief Justice for more than thirty-four years. It was very much his Court; of 1,106 decisions handed down, he dissented on only 9. He established protections for private property; he expanded the powers of the federal government and restricted those of the states; most important, although he never again found it necessary to declare a law unconstitutional, he made the Court the nation's final arbiter on the acceptability of laws.

John Marshall, portrayed by Rembrandt Peale

When one pen on the polygraph above was moved, the other moved in the same way. Jefferson adapted the machine so that he could make copies of his letters as he wrote them.

Below is a page from one product of Jefferson's study of American Indian languages—a comparative vocabulary. In the left-hand column the languages are identified, followed by the different words for "fog," "rain," and "snow."

English	fog	rain	snow
French	brouillard	pluie	neige
Delaware	aäuän	suuklan	uüna
Unami		su-ka-laan	guun
Monsi		su-ka-laan	guun
Chippewa		ke-me-wan	ac-guun
Knisteneaux	pakishikow	kimiwoin	counah
Algonquin	awinni	ke-mi-woine	so gui po
Tawa		ke-mi-wan	ac-guun
Shawanee		ke-me-wani / kimmawane	guun-i-cooke
Nanticoke	houge,wen	urniaow / su-ko-ran	quo-no guun
Mohiccon		sokangan / so-he-gan	washana wa-scha-ni
Unquachog		suhetun	soachpo
Oneida	lishwandauh	yoconnoal	onaieghta
Cayuga			
Onondaga	ojinquara / tiawenohku	na-jelshtaronti	ogera
Miami	uoonuah	petilinive / petilamuah	monetwa / monatuah
Cherokee		oc caiscuh kamuhan	ainhache sun

"ALWAYS DOING"

John F. Kennedy once described a group of Nobel Prize winners, dining in the Executive Mansion, as "the most extraordinary collection of talent . . . that has ever been gathered together at the White House—with the possible exception of when Thomas Jefferson dined alone." Merely dipping at random into Jefferson's achievements in the arts and sciences reveals the variety of his talents. He developed a distinctively American style of architecture by combining Roman models with inexpensive American materials. His experiments with rice growing (for which he once smuggled seeds out of Italy) made the United States a major rice producer, and his ideas on education and architecture were embodied in the University of Virginia. The urge to learn and to educate others led him in many directions. From 1797 to 1815, he served as president of the American Philosophical Society, a scientific organization. He collected the bones of prehistoric animals, Indian vocabularies, paintings and sculpture, and great books (his library formed the basis of the new Library of Congress after the first had been burned by the British in 1814). And his writings cover a vast range of subjects, including morals, botany, legislative procedure, comparative literature, philosophy, and marriage. As Jefferson himself once wrote, "Determine never to be idle. . . . It is wonderful how much may be done if we are always doing."

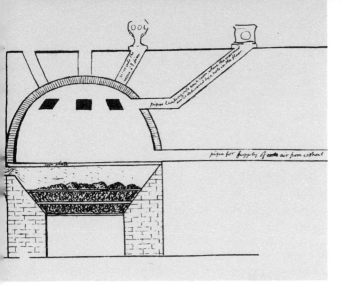

The central-heating plant, left, was another of Jefferson's inventions. The upward shafts are a chimney and heat pipes; the horizontal one carried air to the fire.

Jefferson's design for the rotunda at the University of Virginia, below, was derived from Palladio's drawing of the Roman Pantheon. However, the rotunda design was considerably less massive than that of its classical model, with taller pillars, a simpler portico, and a more graceful unity.

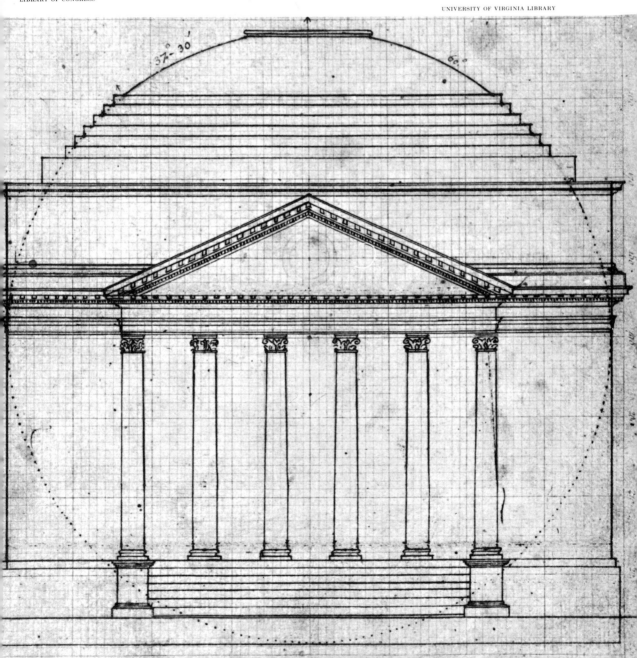

Monticello ("little mountain") was begun in 1769 and was livable, though uncompleted, when Jefferson left for France. His travels gave him new ideas for the mansion, and work on it was renewed while he was Secretary of State. Not until his Presidency was over did the thirty-two-room house (below) assume its final form.

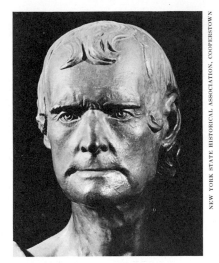

*John H. I. Browere made the life mask
of Jefferson, above, in October, 1825.*

MONTICELLO

Jefferson, declared the
Marquis de Chastellux after visiting Monticello in 1782, "is the first American who
has consulted the Fine Arts to know how he
should shelter himself from the weather."
Seven years later, Jefferson began a major
remodeling of his home, finally finishing it in
1808. In addition to the classical design, Jefferson was responsible for such ingenious devices as clocks that told the day as well as
the hour, folding ladders, a dumb-waiter
(hidden in a fireplace) on which wine could
be elevated from the cellar, swivel chairs,
and hanging beds. In 1809 he retired to
Monticello, where, until he died in 1826, he
played the genial and generous host, while
falling ever further into debt. Captain Edmund Bacon, his overseer, felt that the
Sage's "gangs" of guests took advantage of
him. They came year round, but were most
numerous in summer. Bacon remarked that
the twenty-six spare horse stalls at Monticello were frequently not sufficient for the
visitors' mounts. "I have often sent a wagon-
load of hay up to the stable," the overseer
said, "and the next morning there would not
be enough left to make a bird's nest."

FACTS IN SUMMARY: THOMAS JEFFERSON

CHRONOLOGY

UNITED STATES		JEFFERSON		UNITED STATES		JEFFERSON
					1785	*Named minister to France*
	1743	*Born April 13*				
	1762	*Graduates from College of William and Mary*		Constitutional Convention	1787	
Townshend Acts	1767	*Admitted to the bar*		Washington elected President	1789	*Appointed Secretary of State*
	1768	*Elected to Virginia House of Burgesses*		Bill of Rights		
Boston Massacre	1770	*Appointed Albemarle County lieutenant*			1791	*Leads opposition to Hamilton*
	1772	*Marries Martha Skelton*		Genêt Affair	1793	*Resigns Secretaryship*
Boston Tea Party	1773	*Appointed Albemarle County surveyor*		Adams wins Presidency	1796	*Elected Vice President*
First Continental Congress	1774	*Writes* A Summary View of the Rights of British America		Naval war with France	1798	*Drafts Kentucky Resolutions*
				Alien and Sedition Acts		
				Treaty of Morfontaine	1800	*Ties with Burr in presidential election*
Lexington and Concord	1775	*Elected alternate delegate to Second Continental Congress*		Tripoli declares war against U.S.	1801	*Elected President*
Second Continental Congress						*Dispatches Navy to Mediterranean*
Declaration of Independence	1776	*Drafts Declaration of Independence*			1802	*Repeals excise tax and Judiciary Act of 1801*
		Elected to Virginia House of Delegates		Ohio admitted as 17th state	1803	*Approves Louisiana Purchase*
Articles of Confederation adopted	1777			Louisiana Purchase		*Commissions Lewis and Clark expedition*
	1779	*Introduces Act for Establishing Religious Freedom*		Burr-Hamilton duel	1804	*Re-elected President*
		Elected governor of Virginia		Peace with Tripoli	1805	
British invade Virginia	1781	*Resigns as governor*		Chesapeake-Leopard Affair	1807	*Signs Embargo Act*
Siege of Yorktown				Madison inaugurated	1809	*Signs Nonintercourse Act*
Treaty of Paris	1783	*Drafts Virginia constitution*		Washington burned	1814	*Sells books to Congress*
		Elected to Continental Congress			1819	*Becomes rector of University of Virginia*
				John Adams dies July 4	1826	*Dies July 4*

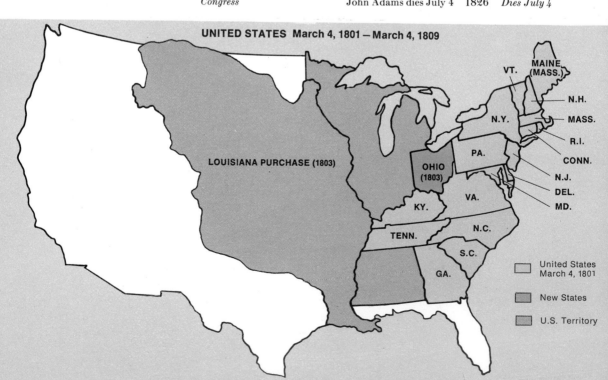

UNITED STATES March 4, 1801 — March 4, 1809

LOUISIANA PURCHASE (1803)

MAINE (MASS.)
VT.
N.H.
N.Y.
MASS.
R.I.
PA.
CONN.
OHIO (1803)
N.J.
DEL.
MD.
VA.
KY.
TENN.
N.C.
S.C.
GA.

☐ United States March 4, 1801
☐ New States
☐ U.S. Territory

BIOGRAPHICAL FACTS

BIRTH: "Shadwell," Goochland (now Albemarle) County, Virginia, April 13, 1743

ANCESTRY: Welsh

FATHER: Peter Jefferson; b. Chesterfield County, Va., Feb. 29, 1708; d. "Shadwell," Va., Aug. 17, 1757

FATHER'S OCCUPATIONS: Planter; surveyor

MOTHER: Jane Randolph Jefferson; b. London, England, Feb. 9, 1720; d. "Shadwell," Va., March 31, 1776

BROTHER: Randolph (1755–1815)

SISTERS: Jane (1740–1765); Mary (1741–1760); Martha (1746–1811); Lucy (1752–1784); Anna Scott (1755–?)

WIFE: Martha Wayles Skelton; b. Charles City County, Va., Oct. 19, 1748; d. "Monticello," Va., Sept. 6, 1782

MARRIAGE: Charles City County, Va., Jan. 1, 1772

CHILDREN: Martha (1772–1836); Maria (1778–1804); Lucy Elizabeth (1782–1785); (two daughters and a son died in infancy)

HOME: "Monticello," Charlottesville, Va.

EDUCATION: Private tutoring; attended country school in Albemarle County, Va.; received B.A. from College of William and Mary (1762)

RELIGIOUS AFFILIATION: No denomination

OCCUPATIONS BEFORE PRESIDENCY: Planter; lawyer; writer; philosopher; scientist; architect

PRE-PRESIDENTIAL OFFICES: Member of Virginia House of Burgesses; County Lieutenant; County Surveyor; Deputy Delegate to Second Continental Congress; Member of Virginia House of Delegates; Governor of Virginia; Commissioner to France; Minister to France; Secretary of State; Vice President

POLITICAL PARTY: Democratic-Republican

AGE AT INAUGURATION: 57

OCCUPATIONS AFTER PRESIDENCY: Planter; writer; educator

DEATH: "Monticello," Charlottesville, Va., July 4, 1826

PLACE OF BURIAL: "Monticello," Charlottesville, Va.

ELECTION OF 1800

(Each elector voted for two men. A tie between Jefferson and Burr resulted, and the House of Representatives elected Jefferson President.)

CANDIDATES	ELECTORAL VOTE
Thomas Jefferson Democratic-Republican	73
Aaron Burr Democratic-Republican	73
John Adams Federalist	65
Charles C. Pinckney Federalist	64
John Jay Federalist	1

FIRST ADMINISTRATION

INAUGURATION: March 4, 1801; Senate Chamber, Washington, D.C.

VICE PRESIDENT: Aaron Burr

SECRETARY OF STATE: James Madison

SECRETARY OF THE TREASURY: Samuel Dexter; Albert Gallatin (from May 14, 1801)

SECRETARY OF WAR: Henry Dearborn

ATTORNEY GENERAL: Levi Lincoln

POSTMASTER GENERAL: Joseph Habersham; Gideon Granger (from Nov. 28, 1801)

SECRETARY OF THE NAVY: Benjamin Stoddert; Robert Smith (from July 27, 1801)

SUPREME COURT APPOINTMENT: William Johnson (1804)

SEVENTH CONGRESS (March 4, 1801–March 4, 1803):
Senate: 18 Democratic-Republicans; 14 Federalists
House: 69 Democratic-Republicans; 36 Federalists

EIGHTH CONGRESS (March 4, 1803–March 4, 1805):
Senate: 25 Democratic-Republicans; 9 Federalists
House: 102 Democratic-Republicans; 39 Federalists

STATE ADMITTED: Ohio (1803)

END OF PRESIDENTIAL TERM: March 4, 1805

ELECTION OF 1804

(The Twelfth Amendment, ratified in September, 1804, provided for separate voting for President and Vice President, and precluded a repetition of the Jefferson-Burr tie of 1800.)

CANDIDATES	ELECTORAL VOTE
Thomas Jefferson Democratic-Republican	162
Charles C. Pinckney Federalist	14

SECOND ADMINISTRATION

INAUGURATION: March 4, 1805; Senate Chamber, Washington, D.C.

VICE PRESIDENT: George Clinton

SECRETARY OF STATE: James Madison

SECRETARY OF THE TREASURY: Albert Gallatin

SECRETARY OF WAR: Henry Dearborn

ATTORNEY GENERAL: John Breckinridge: Caesar A. Rodney (from Jan. 20, 1807)

POSTMASTER GENERAL: Gideon Granger

SECRETARY OF THE NAVY: Robert Smith

SUPREME COURT APPOINTMENTS: Brockholst Livingston (1806); Thomas Todd (1807)

NINTH CONGRESS (March 4, 1805–March 4, 1807):
Senate: 27 Democratic-Republicans; 7 Federalists
House: 116 Democratic-Republicans; 25 Federalists

TENTH CONGRESS (March 4, 1807–March 4, 1809):
Senate: 28 Democratic-Republicans; 6 Federalists
House: 118 Democratic-Republicans; 24 Federalists

END OF PRESIDENTIAL TERM: March 4, 1809

THE FOURTH PRESIDENT (1809–1817)

JAMES MADISON

As Father of the Constitution, congressman, chief organizer of the Democratic-Republican party, Secretary of State, and President, James Madison was, figuratively, a giant in the history of the United States. Physically, however, he was (in the words of Washington Irving) a "withered little apple-John." Brittle and sickly, at five feet six and barely one hundred pounds he was the smallest of the American Presidents. He had bright blue eyes under bushy eyebrows, a pale complexion, scraggly white hair, and lips permanently pinched as though pursed in unending contemplation. A naturally restrained delivery combined with a slight vocal disability made his speeches almost inaudible.

But what James Madison had to say was usually worth hearing. A bookish man, most at ease in his library, he was nonetheless a good conversationalist, knowledgeable of course, but witty, earthy, and satirical, too. He might have preferred a discussion of Greek philosophy with his friend Thomas Jefferson, but he was quite capable of making small talk with his wife's guests and charming them with his ingratiating smile.

Born in his maternal grandmother's home at Port Conway, Virginia, on March 16, 1751, he was, like Washington and Jefferson, a scion of the powerful planter aristocracy. The Madison plantation in the Virginia Piedmont stretched for thousands of acres and touched the wild Appalachian frontier at Montpelier, site of the wooden house where James was raised. His mother taught him to read and write, and his father, a justice of the peace, taught him by example the obligations to community service that the planter class assumed. He had plenty of playmates, almost all of whom were children of his father's slaves. At night he often lay awake in fear, listening to the Indian raiding parties emerging from the mountain forests close by, their spine-chill-

President Madison, by John Vanderlyn

ing war whoops echoing through the valley. Both the companionship of his boyhood days and the trauma of the nights made lasting impressions on James Madison: as an adult he would remain at once bitterly anti-Indian and emphatically antislavery.

At the age of eleven, Madison was sent to the school of Donald Robertson, a Scot who spoke English and other languages with so pronounced a burr that James joked about having to learn "Scottish French." After 1767, however, Madison was educated at home under the tutelage of young Reverend Thomas Martin, Princeton, class of 1764.

Virginia gentry customarily sent their sons either abroad to college or to William and Mary in Williamsburg; to send them to school in another colony was almost tantamount to treason. But in 1769, when he was eighteen, James Madison entered the College of New Jersey at Princeton. His father claimed that the climate of Williamsburg was the primary reason; but while it was true that James was frail and sickly, "climate" may have had a double meaning. William and Mary's administration was doing nothing to stop the violent persecution of Virginia Baptists, and its Episcopalian president was known to favor the establishment of a state church, which the Madisons opposed.

Unlike William and Mary, which catered almost exclusively to Virginians, Princeton attracted students from all the colonies. There Madison began to understand the absurdity of the idea—much too prevalent—that one owed all his patriotic allegiance to his native province. In the same way, Princeton's theological broad-mindedness and avowed tolerance of religious dissent confirmed Madison's conviction that no sect could claim a privileged place in any society.

Madison was a dedicated student, a natural scholar who retained and applied what he learned. At Princeton he studied Locke and Montesquieu and, like Jefferson, could, when the time came, immediately apply their philosophies to the reality of the American situation. John Locke held that every nation is a compact between government and governed: should one party violate the compact, the other is entitled to react in any way deemed necessary to secure his rights. Investigating the machinery of free government, Baron de Montesquieu (Charles Louis de Secondat) concluded that maintenance of freedom depended on a separation of executive, legislative, and judicial powers so that each could check and balance the others.

After receiving his B.A. in 1771, Madison considered becoming a minister, and he remained at Princeton for another year to study Hebrew and ethics. He changed his mind about the ministry, however, and returned home in doubt about his future. His studies and extracurricular interests had weakened his physical condition, and his deteriorated health left him tense, depressed, and uncertain for more than two years.

Then came the Revolution. American independence was to James Madison a great moral and philosophical cause, and it was also a strength-building, restorative tonic. Too weak to carry a musket, he shouldered the burdens of statesmanship.

On January 2, 1775, Madison was present at the meeting of the Orange County Com-

COURTESY OF ALBERT E. LEEDS

The above miniature of Madison was painted sometime between 1780 and 1783 by Charles W. Peale.

Montpelier, Madison's home in Virginia, was depicted by the Baroness Hyde de Neuville, wife of the French minister to the United States, in 1818.

mittee of Safety at which his father was elected chairman. Seventeen months later Madison attended the Virginia Convention of 1776, which within a month's time made two crucial decisions: on May 15 it instructed the Virginia delegates to the Continental Congress to declare for independence from Great Britain, and on June 12 it passed the Virginia Declaration of Rights, which established fundamental guarantees of personal liberty and later became the model for the Bill of Rights. The chief draftsman of the Declaration of Rights was George Mason, but Madison prompted a subtle but important change in the wording of one key passage. While Mason had wanted to ensure governmental "toleration" of religious dissent, Madison prevailed on the Convention to have the passage state that "all men are equally entitled to the free exercise of religion, according to the dictates of conscience."

Madison was the youngest delegate to the Continental Congress, which in 1781 established a government of the United States. He was well aware, however, that the Articles of Confederation were imperfect. Because the powers to tax, regulate commerce, and raise armies had been left to the states, the federal government was impotent to enforce legislation until the states decided to supply the means for enforcement.

On May 25, 1787, the Constitutional Convention convened in Philadelphia. Among the fifty-five delegates were some who wanted broad, almost authoritarian power conferred on a central government and others who favored retention of state sovereignty and wanted only to close the loopholes of the Articles of Confederation; most delegates occupied positions somewhere between. The most effective debater, dialectician, and advocate of a strong new constitution was James Madison, who had been instrumental in calling the Convention and who had written extensively about the defects of the Articles of Confederation.

Convention sessions were held behind closed doors, and discussions were not recorded; but Madison kept notes on the principal proceedings. His own speeches were among the most significant, containing as they did such passages as this on the system of checks and balances: "A people deliberating in a temperate moment, and with the experience of other nations before them, on the plan of government most likely to secure their happiness, would first be aware that those charged with the public happiness might betray their trust. An obvious precaution against this danger would be to divide the trust between different bodies of men, who might watch and check each other."

That the President, Congress, and Supreme Court would form the three branches of the government was agreed upon with comparatively little dispute, but the composition of the legislature did not so easily emerge from the debates. The Virginia Plan, which Madison had written, suggested representation proportionate to population; the New Jersey Plan retained the Confederation system of one-state one-vote. Connecticut delegates proposed an acceptable compromise, which incorporated both plans in a two-chambered legislature. But another problem remained: since Congress had decided to apportion the House of Representatives on the basis of total population (as opposed to number of voters), the Southerners claimed that slaves should be counted, while the Northerners (paradoxically) had to take the position that a slave did not belong to the population at all. The compromise, which Madison had suggested as early as 1783, declared five slaves equal to three freemen in congressional apportionment.

Although he was largely responsible for it, the idea that the Constitution of his country contained wording that made a Negro three-fifths of a man must have been repugnant to James Madison, who pleaded for the "eventual extinguishment of slavery in the United States." But he conceived the "federal ratio" because he cared most about forging a strong national government.

The signing of the document on September 17, 1787, was only the first step in effecting it. Each state had to ratify it; and however awesome it seems today, the Constitution was by no means without opponents at its inception. At the Virginia Ratification Convention Madison promised to press for a series of amendments protecting individual freedom. His speeches helped secure the necessary votes. True to his word, he later led the fight for the Bill of Rights.

With Hamilton and John Jay, Madison contributed to a series of articles that during 1787 and 1788 appeared in the New York press over the signature "Publius." Probably the most persuasive of all defenses of the Constitution, the series was published in a single volume called *The Federalist*. Madison's tenth *Federalist* essay attracted the most attention. His theme was the danger that one group might gain domination over the nation. Developing his ideas in a tight, reasonable sequence, he found the antidote to be the tri-branched, two-housed political arrangement made possible by the Constitution. When New York ratified on July 26, 1788, much of the credit belonged to *The Federalist*.

In 1788 Madison was elected to the House of Representatives. During his four terms

there, the Federalist party formed behind Hamilton. It was Madison who organized the followers of Jefferson's opposing philosophy into the Democratic-Republican party. During the stormy administration of John Adams, Madison fought against the Alien and Sedition Acts. To counter their effectiveness, he wrote the Virginia Resolutions, which assumed for states the right to refuse to comply with a law they deemed unconstitutional.

When Jefferson entered the White House in 1801, Madison became his Secretary of State. Although the affairs of state during his eight years in the Cabinet were of lasting significance, they cannot be honestly credited to Madison, for Jefferson chose to be his own Secretary of State. But if Madison's achievements in the Jefferson administration were negligible, they were at least not political hindrances; and in the election of 1808, with the support of Jefferson, Madison ran for President, defeating Charles Cotesworth Pinckney, the Federalist candidate, by an electoral vote of 122 to 47.

James Madison was, of course, new to the duties of the Presidency, but his wife, Dolley, was used to being the First Lady, since she had acted as Jefferson's hostess. Madison had married Mrs. Dolley Payne Todd, a widow, on September 15, 1794, just three months after he had written a letter to a mutual acquaintance, Aaron Burr, asking him to arrange a meeting. As First Lady, Mrs. Madison began to entertain on a lavish scale, dazzling Washington with the splendid formality of her state dinners and the gay spontaneity of her private parties.

The gaiety of the White House social functions did not, however, reflect the atmosphere of Madison's administration. Like the three Chief Executives before him, the President found himself deeply involved in issues connected with European wars. England's Orders in Council assumed for British ships the right to stop and search neutral, specifically American, vessels suspected of bearing contraband, and Napoleon declared that an American ship that permitted itself to be boarded by the British would be con-

" TO THE GRAVE GO SHAM PROTECTORS OF " FREE TRADE AND SAILORS RIGHTS"—AND ALL THE PEOPLE SAY AMEN :"

The cartoon above shows Madison being dragged down by the unpopular Anglo-American trade restrictions.

sidered fair game for French guns. The one issue that cut deepest into the young nation's pride was the impressment of American sailors: British naval officers dismissed the validity of naturalization papers and, on boarding American ships, pressed into service any sailor who acted suspiciously or spoke or looked like an Englishman. Jefferson's embargo had been no solution, for it evaded confrontation only at the expense of the economy and national pride. Repealed in 1809, three days before Madison's inauguration, it was replaced by the Nonintercourse Act, which reopened trade with all nations except France and England and gave the President authority to restore trade whenever either or both belligerents withdrew its edicts against American shipping. When neither did so, Congress naïvely sought to force their hands by passing, in 1810, Macon's Bill No. 2, which restored trade with the warring powers and gave them until March 3, 1811, to revoke their edicts. Should one of the powers acquiesce, the President of the United States would declare a ninety-day suspension of trade with the other, and if its decrees were not withdrawn in that time, America would revive the Nonintercourse Act against the offending nation. Calculated to play France and England against each other, the bill in reality gave them a year to trade with the United States

and to harass American ships with impunity.

The country was sharply divided in its sympathies. New England Federalists were, as usual, anti-French; the Republicans—especially those of the frontier states—remained anti-English. Ironically, despite the fact that the growing rallying cry for war was "free trade and sailors' rights," shippers in the Northeast were quite unready for war. They blamed Republican incompetence for their troubles more than they did British intervention, and they were making enough profit from the ships that penetrated the blockade to make up for their losses. The Westerners, on the other hand, many of whom had never seen a ship, were most militant. Led by Henry Clay of Kentucky, these "war hawks" talked about national pride, but they thought about national expansion and looked longingly to Canada and West Florida.

The United States wanted Florida, and the Napoleonic Wars provided an excuse to begin taking it. On October 27, 1810, after receiving word that the people of Spanish West Florida (most of whom were American and French) had declared independence, President Madison signed a proclamation declaring West Florida American territory. The area, Madison claimed, had officially been American since the Louisiana Purchase.

Meanwhile, in the Northwest, Governor William Henry Harrison of the Indiana Territory was having trouble with the Indians. Upset that the Indians had the audacity to regard a 1795 boundary agreement as binding, Harrison wrote to Madison that Tecumseh—the Shawnee chief who was inciting many tribes by advocating unity, firmness in regard to land sales, abstinence from alcohol, and other radical measures—was "insolent and his pretensions arrogant." There could be, to Harrison and much of the nation, only one force behind Tecumseh's hostility: Great Britain. At first Madison turned down Harrison's request for permission to assault the Indian Territory because he did not want to divert troops from West Florida, but in 1811 he gave the go-ahead, and on November 7 Harrison engaged the

Shawnee and their allies in the bloody Battle of Tippecanoe.

While America waited for French and English replies to Macon's bill, the nation prospered from the increased customs receipts resulting from the resumption of trade. Prosperity hung by a thread, however, because the charter of the Bank of the United States was due to expire on March 4, 1811. As Madison's biographer, Irving Brant, points out, the President was a victim of a "lifelong unwillingness to make a public display of political inconsistency." With war a possibility, and with the country's money interests so obviously opposed to war with the probable enemy, Madison needed the Bank and wanted it rechartered; but he would not appear before Congress to make his wants known, for he had once denied the constitutionality of the Bank. When the Senate voted 17 to 17 on recharter, Vice President George Clinton broke the tie with a negative vote. As the Bank went out of existence, a depression began, hitting hard in the frontier states.

In December, 1810, after agreeing to honor American shipping rights (thereby compelling America to declare nonintercourse with England), Napoleon sequestered all American ships in French ports and declared all ports in the French alliance closed to American trade. With impenetrable logic, the Emperor claimed that his actions were designed to compel Britain to revoke its Orders in Council. The effects of Macon's bill had backfired: now France was in the strong position and throughout the year made only minor concessions to the United States. Britain, meanwhile, claimed that France had not in fact revoked its decrees (which it had not); and American Federalists said that France was the enemy, not England, and that Madison had been tricked by Napoleon (which he had) into an anti-English posture. Nevertheless, the President held firm and demanded that Parliament repeal the Orders in Council. Faced with serious economic problems at home, British Prime Minister Spencer Perceval finally decided to endorse repeal, but was assassinated before he could act. It was not until June 16, 1812, that England withdrew the orders.

A day later the United States declared war. On June 1, President Madison had appeared in Congress to list "the spectacle of injuries and indignities which have been heaped on our country. . . ." Deploring the fact that "our moderation and conciliation have had no other effect than to encourage perseverance and to enlarge pretentions," he placed the decision of "opposing force . . . in defense of national rights" into the hands of Congress. So war was declared after the principal acknowledged reason for war had been removed. In those days of slow communications, word of the repeal of the Orders in Council did not arrive until later.

National division, reflected in the congressional war vote—79 to 49 in the House, 19 to 13 in the Senate—prevailed throughout the War of 1812. Although it had wanted war, Congress was sluggish about voting funds to increase the size of the Army and Navy; and just as the frontier states united to wage war, the New England states united in refusing to have anything to do with it. In the Northeast, governors would not allow their state militias to join the national Army, and as Madison had feared, financiers refused to grant loans for the war effort. The war was the central issue in the presidential election of 1812; five out of six New England states voted for New York's DeWitt Clinton, but Madison won a second term.

Whether the War of 1812 was "the second war of American independence," as the war hawks claimed, or "Mr. Madison's War," as the Federalists chose to call it, was and is a matter of broad disagreement. While historian Bradford Perkins thinks that the President "seemed to drift rather than to direct policy" during the prelude to war, Irving Brant says that Madison encouraged the war movement in order to make his bid for peace from a position of strength, but that he was sabotaged by the Federalists, whose "active support of Great Britain and vituperation of their own government as . . . imbecile . . . created a dual delusion which poured on London in two lines of communi-

*The Octagon House, above, was spared when the British burned Washington;
the Madisons lived there while the gutted White House was being restored.*

cation." But however debatable his responsibility for the events of his first term, Madison was certainly not an effective Commander in Chief. No one commander was appointed to function as Washington had in the Revolution, and the various military operations were uncoordinated. In the summer of 1812, for instance, General William Hull marched boldly into Upper Canada, but realized too late that he might at any time be cut off at the Great Lakes by the British. Hurriedly retreating to Detroit, he waited for the British to besiege; they did, and on August 16 Hull surrendered his troops and the city to the enemy. When Buffalo fell the next year, American hopes of waging war principally on British soil were again dashed.

It was at sea, surprisingly, that America was most successful. Against the most formidable navy in the world, warships of the United States not only held their own in combat but frequently outmaneuvered their adversaries in matters of pure seamanship. If British complacency was shaken, American morale was boosted by several well-timed and widely quoted comments. "Now boys," said Captain Isaac Hull, "pour it into them," as his frigate *Constitution* battered the H.M.S. *Guerrière* into submission. "Old Ironsides" became the symbol of America's underdog sea strength, but even sinking ships sometimes left legacies of slogans: "Don't give up the ship!" said Captain James Lawrence as his *Chesapeake* went down with him aboard. And on September 10, 1813, Commodore Oliver Hazard Perry won the Battle of Lake Erie. "We have met the enemy and they are ours," he reported. When the British left Detroit, William Henry Harrison followed them into Canada and won the Battle of the Thames.

As American troops halted British advances in the Northwest, the war was stalemated. But in the summer of 1814, with Napoleon exiled to Elba, London was able to turn its full attention to America. In August, a company of British troops landed at Chesapeake Bay. After scattering the Americans at Bladensburg, Maryland, they proceeded to Washington.

On the morning of August 24, as the sound of cannon neared, Dolley Madison remained in the White House waiting for the President, who was at a meeting at the Navy yard. She spent the day looking through her spyglass, supervising the removal of Gilbert Stuart's portrait of George Washington, and writing a letter to her sister. In the afternoon she wrote: "Mr. Madison comes not; may God protect him! Two messengers covered

133

with dust come to bid me fly; but I wait for him. . . ." Later, a note from Madison arrived, explaining that he had left the city and that she must do the same. Gathering up what silver she could, she fled to Virginia. Soon Washington was in flames.

The British then moved on to Baltimore, which is situated behind a hilly peninsula that creates a bottleneck in Chesapeake Bay. As the British ships sailed near the peninsula, they were held off by the guns of Fort McHenry and by a civilian army in the hills. Through the night of September 13 the British bombarded the fort. By dawn's early light, Francis Scott Key, aboard an American dispatch boat, noted that the flag was still there.

The battles at Baltimore and the American victory at Plattsburg, New York, strengthened the position of the American commission at Ghent, Belgium, where the belligerents were trying to negotiate settlement of an unnecessary war. On Christmas Eve, 1814, the Treaty of Ghent was signed, and the two nations returned to the prewar situation. American sea rights were not guaranteed, and Canada remained British. The last battle was waged after the peace had been made: on January 8, 1815, Jackson defeated the British at New Orleans.

James Madison emerged from the war with enhanced prestige and without political opposition. Regarded in the popular imagination as the little President who had tolerated no nonsense from the world's strongest empire, he was also thought of by Americans as the architect of victory even though neither side had won.

Warning Congress not to abruptly revoke all war measures, Madison abandoned his faithfulness to consistency. The author of the Virginia Resolutions, which asserted the rights of states, now denounced states' rights as subversive to the Constitution; and the onetime foe of the Bank of the United States decided, in 1816, to support its re-establishment. That same year, Madison signed a tariff bill of the kind he had once steadfastly opposed. There were, however, some limits to Madison's flexibility.

Although he went before Congress and urged the establishment of "a comprehensive system of roads and canals, such as will have the effect of drawing more closely together every part of our country," he vetoed an internal improvements bill. An amendment, he believed—not a bill—was needed.

At the end of his second term, in 1817, the Madisons returned to Montpelier, their Virginia home. There James Madison assumed the role of gentleman farmer, and Dolley continued playing hostess to the gentry. After several years in retirement, however, Madison again began taking active part in the affairs of his state and nation. In 1826, he succeeded Jefferson as rector of the University of Virginia. As a delegate to the Virginia Constitutional Convention of 1829 he protested the disproportionate power of the eastern slaveholders in the state legislature. Throughout Monroe's two terms, Madison wrote newspaper articles defending administration decisions and was a foreign policy adviser. He continued to work for the abolishment of slavery; he wrote his autobiography; and he rewrote his journal of the Constitutional Convention.

Madison's small body weakened, but his mind remained alert to the end. On June 27, 1836, he spent several hours dictating a letter. The next morning breakfast was brought to him in bed, but he could not swallow. When his niece asked him what was wrong, he replied, "Nothing more than a change of *mind*, my dear." And then, according to his servant, James Madison "ceased breathing as quietly as the snuff of a candle goes out."

In the House of Representatives, Congressman John Quincy Adams summarized James Madison's importance in American history: "Is it not in a pre-eminent degree by emanations from his mind, that we are assembled here as the representatives of the people and the states of this Union? Is it not transcendently by his exertions that we address each other here by the endearing appellation of countrymen and fellow-citizens?"

—VINCENT BURANELLI

James Madison

A PICTURE PORTFOLIO

Presidential medals, such as this one depicting Madison, were presented to Indian chieftains as symbols of American friendship and good will.

FATHER OF
THE CONSTITUTION

When James Madison arrived in Philadelphia for the Constitutional Convention of 1787, he had with him two original essays, "Vices of the Political System of the United States" and "Study of Ancient and Modern Confederacies." Although all the delegates acknowledged the inadequacies of the Articles of Confederation, they were sharply divided in their views on a strong federal government. Madison, armed with his two scholarly documents, presented example after example of nations gaining strength and longevity under a central authority, or faltering and dy-

The portrait above, by Gilbert Stuart, shows James Madison in his mid-fifties as Secretary of State under Thomas Jefferson, some sixteen years after the Constitution had been ratified. The sculpture by Lee Lawrie, at right, is entitled "Drafting the Constitution," and is part of a frieze at the State Capitol of Nebraska. Seated left to right are Benjamin Franklin, George Washington, and Alexander Hamilton; Madison is the fourth standing figure from the left, his coat partially obscured by Franklin's chair. Among the others are James Wilson, Elbridge Gerry, Edmund Randolph, Rufus King, Gouverneur Morris, and Roger Sherman. After some two months of initial deliberations, the Constitutional Convention adjourned on July 26, 1787, to allow a committee of detail to compose a first draft. From August 6 until September 10 the assembly examined the nascent Constitution. A committee of style polished the document, and on September 15, at six in the evening, the Convention was ready to vote. "On the question to agree to the Constitution, as amended," Madison recorded, "All the States ay." The document was signed two days later and ratified in 1788.

ing when confederation was subordinate to individual elements. But although Madison was probably the most effective advocate of a powerful federal government, it was his willingness to compromise that made him the "Father of the Constitution." Most of the great compromises that made ratification of the Constitution possible—the two legislative branches, the "federal ratio" (slaves were counted as three-fifths of a man) that helped maintain a balance in representation of Northern and Southern states, suffrage restrictions—were suggested by Madison, as were many of the checks and balances. He was equally effective in the effort to win ratification of the document, and in pressing for the adoption of the Bill of Rights. Madison served in the new nation's Congress for four terms, during which he organized the Antifederalists behind Jefferson as the Democratic-Republican party. In 1801, when the party won the Presidency, James Madison became Jefferson's Secretary of State. The obvious choice to succeed Jefferson in the White House, Madison beat Charles Cotesworth Pinckney easily, and on March 4, 1809, he took the oath of office as the nation's fourth President.

DOLLEY

When Dolley Madison made her entrance into Long's Hotel for the inaugural ball of 1809, characteristically dressed in pale velvet, plumed turban, and pearls, she confirmed a friend's earlier appraisal of her as "all dignity, grace and affability." More somber was her husband James, whose face already reflected the cares of his new office. Certainly not among those cares was the running of the White House: that was Dolley's bailiwick, as it had been when she was official hostess for widower Thomas Jefferson. Her cheerful informality had complemented Jefferson's domestic simplicity, but now that she was actually living in the manor to which she had become accustomed, Dolley intensified the social schedule. The First Lady's weekly receptions and "drawing rooms," her teas, lawn parties, and dinners, belied her Quaker upbringing, and a few detractors noted that Dolley took snuff and was "said to rouge"; but her career as a hostess and *grande dame*, spanning nearly half a century, was a spectacularly popular one. Her aplomb at White House functions often was a political asset to her reticent husband, and in crises she could display a cool common sense: among the few things she saved before the British burned the White House in 1814 were some vital state documents and Gilbert Stuart's portrait of George Washington. Dolley faithfully nursed James Madison through his retirement at Montpelier, and when he died in 1836, she became a widow for the second time (her first husband, John Todd, had died of yellow fever in 1793). Although financial troubles plagued her for the rest of her life, Dolley maintained her poise: as a contemporary described Dolley's extraordinary quality, "'Tis not her form, 'tis not her face, it is the woman altogether. . . ."

LIBRARY OF CONGRESS

The daguerreotype above, attributed to Mathew Brady, was made on July 4, 1848. Dolley had returned to Washington in 1837 and had resumed her role as a leader of society in the Capital. Her last appearance was at a ball for James K. Polk in 1848; she died the following July, at the age of eighty-one.

The picture by Ezra Ames (left) captures the cheerful, almost puckish charm of Dolley in her prime.

RUNNING MATES AND RIVALS

GEORGE CLINTON

When Vice President George Clinton voted against rechartering the Bank of the United States in 1811, he broke a Senate tie, thereby killing the measure and affirming an abiding animosity for President James Madison, who had supported the bill. Madison was angry but not surprised; the Vice President he had inherited from Jefferson had always been a thorn in his side. A staunch supporter of state sovereignty since the Revolution, Clinton had opposed ratification of the Constitution. Extremely popular with New York voters, he was elected governor of that state seven times. He was nominated as Jefferson's running mate in 1804 because he was a Republican in a normally Federalist state, but he disapproved of Jefferson's policies, and as the election of 1808 approached, he charged that Madison would "make our situation still worse if possible." The Republicans, not wishing to lose support in New York and expecting Clinton to refuse renomination because of his age (he was sixty-five in 1804), offered him the chance to run again—and he accepted. He then proceeded to campaign openly for the Presidency against Madison, but was re-elected Vice President. In April, 1812, after a long period of poor health, Clinton became the first Vice President of the United States to die in office.

ELBRIDGE GERRY

Both of James Madison's Vice Presidents died in office. Like George Clinton of the first administration, Elbridge Gerry was in his sixties when nominated and was considered valuable to the ticket because he was a popular Republican from a Federalist state. Born in Massachusetts in 1744 to a wealthy shipping family, Gerry was a follower of patriot Samuel Adams. After national independence had been won, his inconsistencies on political issues began to negate the value of his breeding, integrity, and willingness to work. He opposed the Constitution because of its departures from pure republicanism, yet supported Alexander Hamilton's Federalist financial policies. Sent to Paris in 1797, his lack of trust in his diplomatic colleagues and his excessive trust in Talleyrand helped sabotage the peace commission, and when he returned home he was snubbed by the Federalist war hawks and embraced by the pro-French Republicans. In 1810, while Massachusetts was still a Federalist stronghold, Gerry, running as a Republican, won the governorship. To help his party, he sponsored a bill that redistricted the state in such a way that each Republican state senator represented considerably fewer voters than each Federalist senator; this technique is now known as "gerrymandering."

CHARLES C. PINCKNEY

When Federalist Charles Cotesworth Pinckney was defeated by James Madison in the presidential election of 1808, it was the third time he had failed in a bid for national office. Nominated for the Vice Presidency in 1800 (although Alexander Hamilton had worked furtively for his election to the Presidency), Pinckney received 64 votes but finished behind Thomas Jefferson, Aaron Burr, and John Adams. In 1804, his party chose him to oppose Jefferson's all-but-certain re-election; Pinckney lost by a landslide, 162 votes to 14. Born in South Carolina and educated in England, Pinckney was a brigadier general during the Revolution, a member of the South Carolina legislature, and a prominent delegate to the Constitutional Convention. He declined President Washington's offer to appoint him commander of the Army, a Supreme Court justice, or Secretary of State or War; but he accepted the post of minister to France in 1796, during the early stages of the Franco-American crisis. The French Directory refused to receive him, but a year later he returned to Paris on a mission that culminated in the notorious XYZ Affair. Despite his three electoral defeats, Pinckney remained active in various public affairs until his death in Charleston in 1825.

DeWITT CLINTON

As a presidential candidate in the election of 1812, DeWitt Clinton, usually a master of the game of politics, overplayed his hand. Nominated by the prowar New York Republicans, he won the Federalist endorsement by representing himself as one who would end the war. His double-dealing caught up with him during the campaign, and he lost to Madison by an electoral vote of 128 to 89. A New Yorker, Clinton was elected to the state senate in 1798, when he was twenty-nine. Gaining control of the council of appointments, he advanced his career by use of the spoils system. He held the New York City mayoralty for ten of the twelve years between 1803 and 1815, during which time he supported public education and health facilities and took special interest in developing the shipping trade. In 1816 the state legislature approved the canal system he had long advocated; the following year he was elected governor. After two terms in Albany he retired, but he held the post of canals commissioner until political infighting led to his dismissal. In 1824, however, he was elected to the state house once again. Clinton therefore had the well-earned honor of presiding at the openings of both the Erie and Champlain canals. He died in Albany in 1828, at the age of fifty-eight.

AN UNWANTED WAR

It appears," wrote James Madison in April, 1812, that the British "prefer war with us to a repeal of their Orders in Council. We have nothing left therefore, but to make ready for it." During his three years as President, Madison had tried diplomatic persuasion, commercial restrictions, and even threats of war, to make England and France cease their harassment of American vessels and seamen. None of his efforts had succeeded, however, and now he concluded that war with Britain, with whom lay "the original sin against the neutrals," was the only solution. Madison was acutely aware of the national disunity which would hamper an effective war effort; he knew that the Treasury was inadequate and that the armed forces were deficient in both men and matériel. Observed South Carolina's John C. Calhoun: "He reluctantly gives up the system of peace." But in his war message of June 1, President Madison cited "evidence of hostile inflexibility in tramping on rights which no independent nation can relinquish." A bitterly divided Congress, urged on by expansion-minded Southerners and Westerners ("The militia of Kentucky are alone competent to place Montreal and Upper Canada at your feet," trumpeted Speaker of the House Henry Clay), agreed to war, which was formally declared by the President on June 19.

The U.S.S. Constitution *engaged and destroyed the English ship* Guerrière *on August 19, 1812 (above). In October, Americans took Queenston Heights during the Niagara campaign in Canada. But when New York's militiamen refused to reinforce the position, a British force (below) recaptured the prominence easily.*

WASHINGTON AFLAME

In the summer of 1814 a large British force struck at selected points along the Eastern seaboard to divert attention from the Northern campaign. Ordered to destroy whatever they could, General Robert Ross and Rear Admiral Sir George Cockburn sailed up the Patuxent River in mid-August, bent on sacking Washington in reprisal for the destruction of the Upper Canadian capital, York. Although outnumbered, the British rolled through Bladensburg, Maryland, on August 24, scattering the heterogeneous, ineptly led American force. President Madison, who had watched the debacle, retired to Virginia. At dusk, Ross and Cockburn led a raiding party of two hundred men into an undefended Washington. They set the House and Senate ablaze and, wrote Congressman Charles Jared Ingersoll of Pennsylvania, left "the Capitol wrapped in its winding sheet of fire." At the White House, the marauders feasted on food that Dolley Madison had left for American troops before she fled earlier that day; with Dolley's wine, the British drank the President's health, "for being such a good fellow as to leave us such a capital supper." Cockburn and his men took whatever souvenirs pleased them and then, according to an American witness, put the Executive Mansion to the torch "with the ruthless firebrand of the Red Savages of the wood." Only a violent thunderstorm prevented the total destruction of the White House. The desecration of the federal Capital united the country in wrath. In September, American victories at Fort McHenry and Plattsburg ended the British threat in the East and North; Andrew Jackson ended it in the South and West early in 1815.

In the British cartoon above, Americans and British both scorn President Madison's flight from Washington.

The walls of the White House (above) survived the fire the British set in 1814, but the inside was gutted.

The roof of the House of Representatives (below in an 1815 sketch) collapsed during the conflagration.

HEROES OF THE WAR OF 1812

ZEBULON PIKE

The American goal in the North during 1813 was to gain control of the Great Lakes, thus forcing the British to find more hazardous ways of getting supplies to the marauding Indians. A key figure in the reduction of England's power on Lake Ontario was Zebulon Pike, who during the first decade of the century had established himself as a military explorer. He had led expeditions to the headwaters of the Mississippi, Red, and Arkansas rivers, and had reconnoitered vast areas of the Southwest. (The Colorado peak that bears his name commemorates this period of Pike's life.) Cleared of charges associating him with Aaron Burr's scheme in 1807 to carve a Western empire, the New Jersey-born Pike rose to the rank of brigadier general. In April, 1813, Commodore Isaac Chauncey and Pike sailed from Sackets Harbor, New York, with 1,800 men, intending to destroy British ships at York (Toronto) prior to joining the main army for an attack on Fort George on the Niagara River. While leading the successful assault on York, Pike and thirty-eight others were killed when a British powder magazine exploded. But during the battle a thirty-gun English ship was burned, a sixteen-gun vessel was captured, and seven hundred British soldiers were taken prisoner. The capital of Upper Canada was in the hands of the Americans.

STEPHEN DECATUR

Stephen Decatur was born of seafarers, and his skill and bravado in three wars proved him worthy of his ancestry. Made an acting lieutenant in 1799, he served in the Caribbean during the undeclared naval hostilities with France. With two Mediterranean cruises behind him, he was given command of a ship in November, 1803, during the Tripolitan War. Decatur's cunning destruction of the captured American frigate, the *Philadelphia*, earned him a captaincy in 1804; he participated in the two bombardments of Tripoli in August of that year. His brilliance as a naval strategist was evincing itself, and his courage in combat won him widespread respect. Decatur's service in the War of 1812 was highlighted by his seizure of the *Macedonian*, pride of the English fleet, near Madeira. A few weeks after the Treaty of Ghent was signed, Decatur's *President* was pursued by four blockading English ships: he disabled one but surrendered to the others; later a court of inquiry found the surrender justified. In 1815, Decatur was instrumental in stopping demands for tribute by Algiers, Tunis, and Tripoli, and exacted payment from them for the damages they inflicted on American ships during the War of 1812. He served for almost five years on the Board of Navy Commissioners, and was mortally wounded in a duel in 1820.

OLIVER PERRY

In a little over three hours on September 10, 1813, Master Commandant Oliver Perry accomplished two major objectives: he substantially reduced the criticism of President Madison by those who felt that American war efforts in the North were ineffectual, and he wrote his name indelibly into American naval history. The ambitious Perry, who at twenty-eight already had a long record of creditable service, had been granted earlier that year his request for command of the forces on Lake Erie. When the British commander, Robert Barclay, briefly lifted his blockade of Perry's small fleet, Perry sailed into open water and pursued the enemy to its station at Amherstburg. Short of supplies, Barclay sailed out on September 9, and the next morning the two fleets engaged in battle. The United States flagship *Lawrence* was disabled, but Barclay suffered heavier losses, and the British were forced to capitulate. It was the first capture of an English fleet by the American Navy, and when Perry reported, "We have met the enemy and they are ours," he was an immediate hero. Control of the lake facilitated successful American campaigns in Canada, giving weight to United States territorial claims at Ghent. Perry went on to fight the British along the Potomac in 1814, and later held a command in the Mediterranean.

THOMAS MACDONOUGH

A year and a day after Oliver Perry's victory on Lake Erie, Master Commandant Thomas Macdonough engineered a parallel triumph on Lake Champlain. As in the earlier engagement, victory was due to the courage and tactical brilliance of the American commander. Macdonough was only sixteen when he became a midshipman in 1800. During the next ten years he rose through the ranks, serving tours of duty along the Atlantic coast, in the West Indies, and in the Mediterranean. When he was given command of the Lake Champlain forces in 1812, he was faced, as Perry had been, with building a fleet and gaining supremacy over the enemy on a crucial body of water. For two years, Macdonough was frustrated by shortages of men and matériel; the balance of power seesawed between his fleet and that of British Commodore George Downie. In late summer, 1814, Downie was supremely confident. But when the battle was joined on September 11 in Plattsburg Bay, Macdonough outmaneuvered the stronger British flagship and forced Downie's surrender. Deservedly lauded for his successful engagement, Macdonough continued his naval career with two more tours of duty in the Mediterranean. His health failed, however, and, in 1825, Thomas Macdonough died aboard a merchantman at forty-one.

"HUZZA HUZZA"

The Treaty of Ghent settled few of the issues over which the War of 1812 was fought: neither belligerent gained or lost territory, and American shipping rights were no more secure than they had been before the hostilities. Nevertheless, the citizens of the United States were jubilant, as the exultant kerchief at left indicates. The young nation's ships had held their own against—and had often beaten— the British navy, and Andrew Jackson's ragtag troops had routed "the conquerors of the conquerors of Europe" at New Orleans. The only real loser in the war was the Federalist party. Opposed to the conflict from the beginning, the New England Federalists had met in Hartford in 1814, where they had drafted a series of resolutions referring to the federal government in the second person and threatening secession. But news of the Treaty of Ghent arrived just as the Federalist delegation appeared in Washington to voice their dissent. "Their position," said French minister Louis Sérurier, "was awkward, embarrassing, and lent itself cruelly to ridicule." Federalism was not immediately replaced by another party; instead factionalism gave way to a surge of nationalism and, as Sérurier said, to the evolution of "a national character founded on a common glory for all." When James Madison retired to Virginia in 1817, he turned over to President James Monroe the leadership of a strong and proud United States, beginning an "era of good feelings."

FACTS IN SUMMARY: JAMES MADISON

CHRONOLOGY

UNITED STATES		MADISON			
			Whisky Rebellion	1794	*Marries Dolley Todd*
	1751	*Born March 16*	Adams elected President	1796	
Stamp Act	1765		Alien and Sedition Acts	1798	*Frames Virginia Reso-*
Virginia Resolves	1769	*Attends College of New Jersey (Princeton)*	Undeclared naval war with France		*lutions*
First Continental Congress	1774	*Becomes member of Committee of Safety*	Jefferson inaugurated as President	1801	*Appointed Secretary of State by Jefferson*
Lexington and Concord	1775		Tripolitan War		
Declaration of Independence	1776	*Attends Virginia Convention*	*Marbury v. Madison*	1803	
			Louisiana Purchase		
		Elected to Virginia legislature	Embargo Act passed	1807	
				1808	*Elected President*
Articles of Confederation	1777		Macon's Bill No. 2	1810	
	1778	*Elected to Virginia executive council*	West Florida annexed		
	1780	*Attends Continental Congress*	War of 1812 begins	1812	*Asks Congress for 60-day Embargo*
			Surrender of Detroit		
Yorktown	1781		U.S. defeated in Canada		*Proclaims war with Great Britain*
	1784	*Elected to Virginia legislature*	U.S. naval victories		*Re-elected President*
	1786	*Attends Annapolis Convention*	British blockade	1813	
			U.S. victories on Great Lakes and in Canada		
Constitutional Convention	1787	*Attends Continental Congress*	Creek War	1814	*Asks Congress to end Embargo*
		Attends Constitutional Convention	Washington burned		
			Hartford Convention		
Constitution ratified	1788	*Writes letters for* The Federalist	Treaty of Ghent		
			Battle of New Orleans	1815	*Vetoes bill for Second U.S. Bank*
		Attends Virginia Ratification Convention	Second U.S. Bank created	1816	
Washington elected President	1789	*Elected to U.S. House of Representatives*	Monroe elected President		
Bill of Rights					

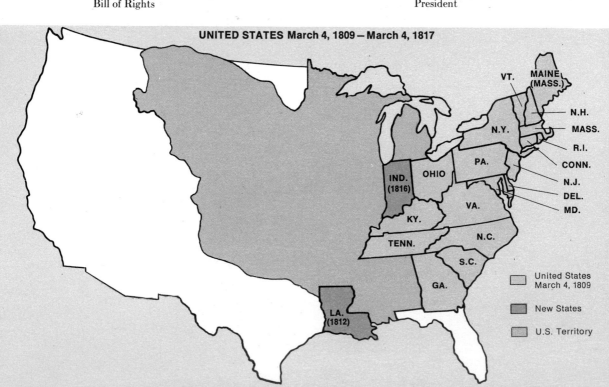

UNITED STATES March 4, 1809 — March 4, 1817

VT.   MAINE (MASS.)

N.H.

N.Y.

MASS.

R.I.

PA.

CONN.

IND. (1816)   OHIO

N.J.

DEL.

MD.

VA.

KY.

TENN.

N.C.

S.C.

GA.

LA. (1812)

United States March 4, 1809

New States

U.S. Territory

	1817	*Vetoes bill for internal improvements*
		Retires to Montpelier
Missouri Compromise	1820	
	1826	*Becomes rector of University of Virginia*
Jackson elected President	1828	
	1829	*Delegate to Virginia Constitutional Convention*
Nullification Controversy	1832	
Siege of the Alamo	1836	*Dies June 28*

BIOGRAPHICAL FACTS

BIRTH: Port Conway, Va., March 16, 1751
ANCESTRY: English
FATHER: James Madison; b. March 27, 1723; d. Feb. 27, 1801
FATHER'S OCCUPATIONS: Justice of the peace; vestryman; farmer
MOTHER: Eleanor Conway Madison; b. 1732; d. Feb. 11, 1829
BROTHERS: Francis (1753–?); Ambrose (1755–1793); William (1762–1843); Reuben (1771–1775)
SISTERS: Nelly (1760–1802); Sarah (1761–?); Elizabeth (1768–1775); Frances (1771–?)
WIFE: Dorothea (Dolley) Payne Todd; b. Guilford County, N.C., May 20, 1768; d. Washington, D.C., July 12, 1849
MARRIAGE: Harewood, Va., Sept. 15, 1794
CHILDREN: None
HOME: Montpelier, Va.
EDUCATION: Received early education at Donald Robertson's school in Virginia and from private tutor; awarded A.B. from the College of New Jersey (Princeton) in 1771; one year postgraduate study at Princeton
RELIGIOUS AFFILIATION: Episcopalian
OCCUPATION BEFORE PRESIDENCY: Politician
PRE-PRESIDENTIAL OFFICES: Member of Orange County Committee of Safety; Delegate to the Virginia Convention; Member of Virginia Legislature; Member of Virginia Executive Council; Delegate to Continental Congress; Delegate to Annapolis Convention; Delegate to Constitutional Convention; Member of the Virginia Ratification Convention; U.S. Congressman; Secretary of State
AGE AT INAUGURATION: 57
DEATH: Montpelier, Va., June 28, 1836
PLACE OF BURIAL: Montpelier, Va.

ELECTION OF 1808

CANDIDATES	ELECTORAL VOTE
James Madison Democratic-Republican	122
Charles C. Pinckney Federalist	47
George Clinton Independent-Republican	6

FIRST ADMINISTRATION

INAUGURATION: March 4, 1809; House of Representatives, Washington, D.C.
VICE PRESIDENT: George Clinton
SECRETARY OF STATE: Robert Smith; James Monroe (from April 6, 1811)
SECRETARY OF THE TREASURY: Albert Gallatin
SECRETARY OF WAR: William Eustis; James Monroe (from Jan. 1, 1813); John Armstrong (from Feb. 5, 1813)
ATTORNEY GENERAL: Caesar Augustus Rodney; William Pinkney (from Jan. 6, 1812)
POSTMASTER GENERAL: Gideon Granger
SECRETARY OF THE NAVY: Robert Smith; Paul Hamilton (from May 15, 1809); William Jones (from Jan. 19, 1813)
SUPREME COURT APPOINTMENTS: Joseph Story (1811); Gabriel Duvall (1811)
ELEVENTH CONGRESS (March 4, 1809–March 4, 1811):
Senate: 28 Democratic-Republicans; 6 Federalists
House: 94 Democratic-Republicans; 48 Federalists
TWELFTH CONGRESS (March 4, 1811–March 4, 1813):
Senate: 30 Democratic-Republicans; 6 Federalists
House: 108 Democratic-Republicans; 36 Federalists
STATE ADMITTED: Louisiana (1812)

ELECTION OF 1812

CANDIDATES	ELECTORAL VOTE
James Madison Democratic-Republican	128
DeWitt Clinton Fusion	89

SECOND ADMINISTRATION

INAUGURATION: March 4, 1813; House of Representatives, Washington, D.C.
VICE PRESIDENT: Elbridge Gerry
SECRETARY OF STATE: James Monroe
SECRETARY OF THE TREASURY: Albert Gallatin; George W. Campbell (from Feb. 9, 1814); Alexander J. Dallas (from Oct. 14, 1814); William H. Crawford (from Oct. 22, 1816)
SECRETARY OF WAR: John Armstrong; James Monroe (from Oct. 1, 1814); William H. Crawford (from Aug. 8, 1815); George Graham (from Oct. 22, 1816)
ATTORNEY GENERAL: William Pinkney; Richard Rush (from Feb. 11, 1814)
POSTMASTER GENERAL: Gideon Granger; Return J. Meigs, Jr. (from April 11, 1814)
SECRETARY OF THE NAVY: William Jones; Benjamin W. Crowninshield (from Jan. 16, 1815)
THIRTEENTH CONGRESS (March 4, 1813–March 4, 1815):
Senate: 27 Democratic-Republicans; 9 Federalists
House: 112 Democratic-Republicans; 68 Federalists
FOURTEENTH CONGRESS (March 4, 1815–March 4, 1817):
Senate: 25 Democratic-Republicans; 11 Federalists
House: 117 Democratic-Republicans; 65 Federalists

JAMES MONROE

In May, 1817, two and a half months after he had become President, James Monroe left Washington for a tour of the Northern United States. Intending to inspect all the shipyards, forts, and frontier outposts for which Congress had voted large appropriations, he was also hopeful that his appearance would solidify national unity. Almost at once he discovered that the trip was succeeding beyond his hopes: roadsides and riverbanks were spotted with people anxious to have a glimpse of him, and cheering crowds greeted his arrival at state capitals. "In principal towns," he wrote to Thomas Jefferson, "the whole population has been in motion, and in a manner to produce the greatest degree of excitement possible."

After enjoying the receptions of the Middle Atlantic states, Monroe, perhaps bracing himself, entered New England, the last stronghold of federalism; the third consecutive Democratic-Republican President, he had lost Connecticut and Massachusetts in the election of 1816. But Monroe's doubts about the enthusiasm of the Yankees were soon dissipated. On July 12, 1817, the Boston *Columbian Centinel* noted Monroe's visit in this paragraph: "ERA OF GOOD FEELINGS . . . During the late Presidential Jubilee many persons have met at festive boards, in pleasant converse, whom party politics had long severed. We recur with pleasure to all the circumstances which attended the demonstration of good feelings."

Whether or not feelings were really good during the "Era of Good Feelings" is a matter of conjecture, but the label became fastened to the Monroe administration, and the President profited. His popularity extended from the masses to many old political adversaries—the *Columbian Centinel*, for example, which was a dogmatic, consistently Federalist newspaper and a traditional foe of the Democratic-Republicans. Once a devoted party man,

This portrait of Monroe was made around 1820 by Rembrandt Peale.

According to James Monroe's descendants, this liquor chest accompanied the President on his travels.

Monroe found himself the personification of nonpartisan paternalism, credited with all the good but rarely blamed for the ills of his two terms. Even John Quincy Adams—who rather than say anything nice about anybody could usually be counted on to say nothing at all—wrote that the Monroe years would "be looked back to as the golden age of this republic."

The times were just right for James Monroe to assume the Presidency. In his Inaugural Address he said, "the United States have flourished beyond example. Their citizens individually have been happy and the nation prosperous. . . . The sentiment in the mind of every citizen is national strength. It ought therefore to be cherished." Americans agreed: the success of their Revolution, of their experiment with republicanism, of their military engagements—most recently the War of 1812—had buoyed their spirits and bolstered their national pride, unity, and ambition. Now the young country was growing, and a nationalistic generation, born under the American flag, was confident it could handle the problems expansion would raise. Still, Americans looked for leadership and example to the fathers of their independence. Washington was dead, Adams and Jefferson were old, and Madison was stepping down;

but there was Monroe: if he had not forged the Revolution he had at least helped to wage it, and, besides, he looked the part. Not yet sixty, he stood tall, angular, erect, his features large and chiseled, his blue-gray eyes at once penetrating and kind, and from a short distance he bore an unmistakable resemblance to George Washington. Wearing no-longer-stylish pantaloons, powdering his iron-colored hair, dressing from time to time in his old military uniform, he filled the role well, knowing, as the people knew, that he was the last of the great eighteenth-century figures who would lead the nation.

The Monroes were landowning farmers, neither rich nor poor, not quite aristocratic but quite respectable in Virginia's complex hierarchy. James Monroe, oldest of five children, was born in Westmoreland County on April 28, 1758. He probably became a patriot at an early age, for his father was an admirer of Patrick Henry and an occasional petitioner for colonial causes, and his mother's brother, Judge Joseph Jones, was a friend to Washington, Jefferson, and Madison. With his neighbor and classmate John Marshall, future United States Chief Justice, Monroe walked several miles a day to and from the school of Parson Archibald Campbell, reputedly "a disciplinarian of the sternest type. . . ."

In 1774, at the age of sixteen, Monroe was sent to Williamsburg to acquire an education and a Virginia gentleman's polish at William and Mary College. Before the year was out, his father died, but Judge Jones paid the bills to keep Monroe in school. Neither time nor place, however, was conducive to scholarship. Then the capital of Virginia, Williamsburg was a center of colonial discontent, and local ears were tuned to Philadelphia, where the First Continental Congress had convened. Monroe began drilling with student-formed military companies, and in 1775 received a lieutenant's commission in the Third Virginia Regiment.

In August, 1776, Congress ordered a number of state infantries, the Virginia Third among them, to New York. By the time the Virginians arrived, the city had been lost to the British; General Washington was holed up at Harlem Heights. Most of Monroe's earliest experiences with the Continental Army were devoted to retreating, the successful defense of White Plains being an exception. As November brought winter down the Hudson, Washington took his fast-shrinking army across it, through New Jersey, and across the Delaware River into Pennsylvania. Despite the diminished condition of his troops and supplies, the General decided to recross the Delaware, hoping that the holiday merriment of his opponents would serve as an equalizer. On Christmas night, while the Hessian mercenaries who occupied Trenton slept the sleep of the intoxicated feaster, the Americans penetrated the city. It was daylight when the Hessians realized what was happening. As they mobilized, Monroe led a column of troops in a victorious race to the arsenal. During the action a ball struck his shoulder, hitting an artery, and he needed two months in bed to regain his strength. During his convalescence, spent in the Pennsylvania home of a judge named Wyncoop, he learned that Washington had promoted him to the rank of captain, and he fell in love with his host's daughter, who was already spoken for.

Monroe was not yet nineteen, and a captain, but enlistments were so few that there were not enough men for the formation of a company for him to command. In August, 1777, he became an aide to Lord Stirling, Major General William Alexander, the self-proclaimed "American Earl." On September 11, after the rout at Brandywine Creek, Monroe tended the wounds of the French officer Lafayette, and the two soldiers became lifetime friends. Then Monroe participated in the abortive American attack of Germantown and was promoted to major.

In 1779, when the war shifted south, Monroe returned home, anxious to defend his state. In one of his rare letters of recommendation, General Washington wrote to the Virginia legislature suggesting that the major be given a command in the militia. "In every instance," the General wrote, Monroe "maintained the reputation of a brave, active, and sensible officer." Once again, however, he was a victim of the manpower shortage, and he received the commission but no company.

Advising Monroe to take advantage of the lull, Judge Jones suggested that he study with Thomas Jefferson, who, though he was then governor, still accepted a number of law students. Jones provided the introduction, the Washington letter provided the best of recommendations, and Monroe spent three years with the governor. They established a friendship that lasted until Jefferson's death in 1826.

It was easy to be friendly to James Monroe. "He is a man," said Jefferson, "whose soul might be turned wrong side outwards without discovering a blemish to the world." Straightforward, generous, not in the least pretentious, seldom discouraged for long, Monroe was trustworthy and trusting, and he had the ability to retain his friends even through profound political disagreements. Even his political limitations were often misplaced expressions of his personal qualities: he could be overgenerous, honest to the point of naïveté, and indiscreet.

He entered politics in 1782 as a member of the Virginia assembly and a year later was elected to the Continental Congress. In both state and national affairs he distinguished himself as a Jeffersonian agrarian-liberal, strongly sectionalist, a foe of centralized government, and a champion of frontier development. He made two trips "through the wilderness," and once seriously, though unofficially, suggested that the United States think about convincing Britain to relinquish Canada. As a member of the Virginia Convention of 1788, he originally opposed the Constitution on the grounds that it assigned too much power to the federal government. As for slavery, when a vote on some aspect of the issue came up, he absented himself.

Monroe ran for Congress in 1788 but was badly beaten by James Madison. In 1790, however, the Virginia legislature elected him to the United States Senate. During his four years in the Senate he was—with Jefferson's advice, Madison's cooperation, and Aaron

Monroe purchased these dueling pistols in Spain.

Burr's political expertise—instrumental in organizing opposition to the policies and philosophy of Alexander Hamilton. The result was a consolidation of Antifederalist factions that became the Democratic-Republican party.

In 1794 relations between the United States and France were beginning to worsen. Gouverneur Morris, the American minister to France, was a Federalist of aristocratic inclinations, hardly sympathetic to revolutionary France, whose government demanded his recall. Moreover, John Jay was in England negotiating a treaty, and the French were upset lest the United States become allied to Great Britain. To soothe the French, President Washington appointed a Republican minister, Monroe.

When he arrived in Paris, Monroe addressed the National Convention. Calling France "our ally and friend," he praised "the fortitude, magnanimity and heroic valor of her troops . . . the wisdom and firmness of her councils," and assured his audience that Jay would not weaken the relationship between the United States and France.

Across the Channel, the English read of Monroe's laudatory speech and found it disagreeable. Washington thought it not "well devised," and Secretary of State Edmund Randolph wrote the minister, reminding him to cultivate French friendship "with zeal, proportioned to the value we set upon it." Then, late in 1794, Monroe managed to secure the release of Thomas Paine, long a thorn in Washington's side, from prison, where he had been confined by extremists for his opposition to the execution of the King during the French Revolution. Paine

soon launched an attack on the American President, who could not have been pleased by Monroe's generosity to the patriot.

But Monroe's usefulness was gone anyway. The French were angered by the terms of Jay's Treaty, and the American minister obviously sided with the French. President Washington felt that a minister's responsibility was to defend his government's policy, and in December of 1796 Monroe was recalled. When he returned home, Monroe demanded without success that Washington make public the reasons for his recall and wrote a vindictive, damning attack on the General. It was not published until December, 1797, when John Adams was President. Adams employed the treatise in his propaganda campaign against the French, reminding Americans that the fine send-off the French had given "a disgraced minister, recalled in displeasure for misconduct, was a studied insult to the government of my country." Actually Monroe had been recalled for the good reason that his performance had been inconsistent with the position of the government he represented. But he kept the issue alive, published the unfortunate paper, and gave ammunition to the Federalists.

Monroe recovered. National sentiment was increasingly Republican, and he found that the French experience had gained him more in recognition than it had cost him in popularity. Washington, however, remained bitter—not without cause—about Monroe's attack. One December night in 1799, he returned home from a walk in the snow and was informed that James Monroe had just been elected governor of Virginia. Without changing his wet clothes, he sat before the fire and angrily discussed the news and his ex-soldier's ungrateful treachery. The snow on his apparel melted; he developed chills and the infection that led to his death.

In 1803 Monroe agreed to give diplomacy another try when President Jefferson asked him to return to France to engineer a treaty for free navigation of the Mississippi River. Before Monroe arrived in Paris, however, Robert Livingston negotiated the Louisiana Purchase, and Monroe was directed to Madrid to acquire Spanish Florida. When Spain refused to sell, Jefferson instructed him to go to London to see what could be done about ending Anglo-American tensions over shipping. On December 31, 1806, a treaty was signed, but since it made no reference to American rights on the high seas, the government disavowed it. Noting Monroe's record in the foreign service, Jefferson thought this an opportune moment to offer Monroe the governorship of the Louisiana Territory, "the second office in the United States in importance." Monroe refused and returned home in 1807. The next year, when James Madison was elected President, Monroe hoped for a Cabinet post, but was once again offered the governorship of Louisiana, which he did not want, and he returned to Virginia.

James Monroe's career resumed in 1810, when he was elected to the Virginia legislature, and from then on it virtually galloped to the Presidency. In 1811 he again became governor, but less than three months after taking office, he was asked to become Secretary of State, replacing Robert Smith. Smith had left the Department of State in chaos, and Monroe revealed his splendid administrative skills by creating an orderly, smooth-functioning agency. In 1814, during the war with England, Monroe also took charge of the disorganized Department of War, thus assuming a dual role in the Madison Cabinet. As Secretary of War, he built another well-oiled machine. The tide of war turned, and he became the most prestigious and logical Republican to receive the presiden-

DANIEL TOMPKINS

Daniel D. Tompkins seemed the ideal choice as James Monroe's running mate in 1816: the popular young governor of New York was a faithful Republican who had worked for improvements in educational facilities, a reformed penal code, and the abolition of slavery. The Monroe ticket won, but Tompkins had a difficult time during his tenure as Vice President. While governor of New York, during the War of 1812, he had accepted the command of the Third Military District and had secured badly needed loans (largely on personal credit) for both the New York and federal governments. But he had failed to keep accurate records of his transactions, and both governments claimed that he was heavily in debt to them. In 1821, New York settled the matter by declaring that Tompkins owed the state nothing and vice versa. The federal government took no action except to withhold his annual vice presidential salary of $5,000. Tompkins ran unsuccessfully for a fifth term as governor of New York in 1820, the same year in which he was re-elected Vice President. Depressed by his long campaign of self-vindication, he began to drink heavily and left Washington more than two years before the end of his second term. In 1824, Congress paid him $95,000, although he claimed he was owed $660,000. This "most injured of all men," as Martin Van Buren referred to Daniel Tompkins, died at the age of fifty in 1825.

tial nomination in 1816. The faltering Federalists were hardly a threat. Monroe won 183 electoral votes to 34 for Rufus King.

After his thirteen-state good-will tour, Monroe and his wife settled into the White House, which had been restored after the British had burned it in 1814. Monroe had married Elizabeth Kortright of New York in 1786. As First Lady she was quite a contrast to her spirited predecessor: whereas Dolley Madison had skipped about Washington paying social calls, Mrs. Monroe stayed at home, and the Capital's ladies came to her. Not that Elizabeth Monroe was antisocial— she was just formal. The spontaneity of Dolley's parties was replaced by the grandeur of Elizabeth's lavish dinners and balls.

Expansion was the prevailing issue of the Monroe administration, and expansion, of course, inspired or brought to the surface of government a number of greater issues. A nation could not simply annex territory. A nation first had to discover which land was its own and which was not; borders had to be defined; the development of new areas had to be planned; policies regarding foreign rights to neighboring territory had to be established. And the American nation had its own unique problem—slavery—to deal with: which, if any, annexed territory should be slave, and which, if any, free?

On the question of slavery, Monroe himself mirrored the paradox of the nation. Like most humanitarians, he opposed the institution, yet he owned slaves. He supported the American Colonization Society, which favored the establishment of a colony in the African state of Liberia to which American slaves would be deported. (Liberia liked the idea and named its capital, Monrovia, after the President.) American intellectuals of the time seldom considered the possibility of racial integration in the United States and chose to keep slaves and treat them well rather than release them into a society into which they could not become assimilated.

In 1819, when Missouri applied for admission to the Union, there were eleven slave states and eleven free states in the country. One way or another, the admission of Missouri would destroy this balance. Naturally, the North wanted Missouri admitted free, and the South, slave; the debates were ferocious. "I have never known a question so menacing to the tranquillity and even the continuance of our Union as the present one," Monroe wrote.

Another not-quite-forgotten issue that expansion fostered was that of internal improvements. A growing United States needed post offices, an interstate highway system, canals, and conservation programs. Like Jefferson and Madison, Monroe was emphatically in favor of federal legislation for the advancement of internal improvements, but he was also certain that the Constitution gave the government no such legislative powers. During his Northern trip in 1817, he thought he came up with a constitutional course to pursue: acting as Commander in Chief, he ordered the Department of War to repair a number of damaged roads in New York, claiming that maintenance of the roads was essential to national defense. Henry Clay of Kentucky, also an advocate of internal improvements, opposed congressional appropriation of the funds on the reasonable grounds that this was a roundabout method of handling a problem that required direct federal action. The President, however, having failed to convince Congress that a constitutional amendment should be passed, decided that he would have to veto bills for internal improvements.

And there was the problem of foreign policy. The United States was growing by leaps and bounds; how large it would ultimately get was becoming clearer: Americans were beginning to look to the wilderness between the Mississippi and the Pacific, but the definition of North-South borders was fuzzy. In 1817 Monroe dispatched a team of negotiators to London to settle the United States-Canada border, and the Convention of 1818 was arranged. The boundary was established along the forty-ninth parallel to the Rockies, beyond which was the Oregon Territory, where Americans and Canadians would enjoy equal rights. In the South, America wanted Spanish Florida to round off its Atlantic

coastline. In 1818 General Andrew Jackson and his men roamed at will through the Spanish possession. Madrid got the message. With the Spanish minister to Washington, Luis de Onís, Secretary of State John Quincy Adams worked out the details, and the Adams-Onís Treaty of 1819 added all of Florida to the United States.

Finally, in that same year, the Bank of the United States, established in 1816, failed, triggering the Panic of 1819 and a depression that lasted several years. Coming as it did the year before an election, the Panic could have been a great threat to Monroe's desire for a second term, but it was not. He was, after all, the symbol of the Era of Good Feelings. The ruined, the dispossessed and unemployed, blamed instead the symbol of finance. The Bank, which did not have to stand for public office, became the object of public fury. Monroe was not even opposed. The Federalists were still around, but on their last legs, and could not muster strength enough to put up a candidate. Except for one dissenting ballot cast to ensure George Washington's place in American history as the only President to win unanimously, Monroe would have received all the votes.

The issues of his first administration continued—in most cases were magnified—during the second. Two of the results were the Missouri Compromise, which Jefferson called "the death knell of the Union," and the Monroe Doctrine.

On March 3, 1820, Congress had passed a compromise bill whereby Missouri would be admitted as a slave state, Maine would be admitted as a free state (thereby maintaining

Fort Ross, built in northern California by the Russians in 1812, was one of the reasons for the formulation of the Monroe Doctrine eleven years later.

the balance), and slavery would be barred from the territories of the Louisiana Purchase north of latitude 36°30'. After the bill had been signed by the President, but before the official admission date of Missouri, the Missouri legislature itself revived the seemingly settled issue by passing a law excluding free Negroes from the would-be state. Outraged, antislavery factions wanted to abrogate Missouri's admission. In his first triumph as "the Great Compromiser," Speaker of the House Henry Clay came up with a solution: until the Missouri legislature gave assurance that it would not deny rights to any American citizen, statehood would remain suspended. The Compromise merely prohibited Missouri from passing any law contrary to the Constitution, and naturally Missouri agreed.

President Monroe did not miss the ambiguity of the wording of the Missouri Compromise; nor did the fact that it had accomplished less than it had postponed escape him. But he was genuinely puzzled by the constitutional questions that had been raised. First, the Constitution acknowledged slavery; it may not have favored it, but by declaring (for purposes of apportionment) each slave equal to three-fifths of a man, it recognized the existence of the institution. Second, in Monroe's opinion, Congress did not have the right to restrict slavery in any state, as slavery was a local issue. But Congress did have the right to admit or deny admis-

159

sion to any territory. In short, the Constitution provided no clear answer. With the advice of his Cabinet he signed the Compromise, perhaps agreeing with John Quincy Adams, who, though he had advised the President to sign, said, "I take it for granted that the present question is a mere preamble —a titlepage to a great, tragic volume."

Monroe never really settled the question of internal improvements. He sincerely believed that the government ought to provide for them, but when the House passed an internal improvements bill in 1822, he vetoed it because he thought Congress had no power to so legislate under the Constitution. His successor, John Quincy Adams, would face the problem in reverse: he wanted the improvements made, claiming that the Constitution implied the necessary power to Congress, but by then Congress would not pass the improvements bill.

The question of European activity in the Americas first came up in the Monroe administration in 1821, when the Czar announced that he was extending Russia's Alaska territory down the Pacific coast of North America to the fifty-first parallel, which was located well within the Oregon Territory. Monroe immediately took the issue to his Cabinet and found Secretary of State Adams' words most agreeable. Adams said that "we should contest the right of Russia to *any* territorial establishment on this continent, and that we should assume distinctly the principle that the American continents are no longer subjects for *any* new European colonial establishments." After the President ordered a protest lodged in St. Petersburg, the Czar proved conciliatory and agreed to withdraw north of the territory, to the parallel of 54°40'.

Adams was also the architect of United States policy toward Latin America. Spain had bungled its attempts at colonization there and had lost, through revolutions, most of its American territories. In 1822 rumors were circulating that the Spanish, with French aid, were seriously considering the possibility of re-entering their lost colonies and recapturing the governments. Great

Britain, anxious as ever to slap French hands, suggested that England and America publish a joint statement in support of the Latin countries, but Adams objected. "It would be more candid," he argued, "as well as more dignified, to avow our principles explicitly . . . than to come in as a cockboat in the wake of the British man-of-war."

Thus the Monroe Doctrine, written by Adams but made United States policy by James Monroe: "The American continents, by the free and independent condition which they have assumed and maintain, are henceforth not to be considered as subjects for future colonization by any European powers." Monroe drew the words from one of Adams' state papers and included them in his seventh annual message to Congress, on December 2, 1823. Although the Doctrine is only one sentence long, its implications have been gigantic. It has been employed as justification for a broad range of American actions—from the Spanish-American War to the Cuban Missile Crisis.

At the end of the Monroe administration the Marquis de Lafayette, after forty years' absence, returned for a visit to the United States. The reunion between the President and the foreign soldier who had become an American hero was moving, and the two men spent as much time as possible together during the next year. They said farewell on August 9, 1825, at a banquet given by the now ex-President.

Monroe retired to Oak Hill, his home in Loudoun County designed by architect Thomas Jefferson. In 1829 he returned to public service, becoming presiding officer of the Virginia Constitutional Convention. He led a battle for fair apportionment of legislative representation, opposed enlargement of the suffrage, and, once again, by and large avoided involvement with the slavery issue.

After Elizabeth died in 1830, Monroe, ailing and in financial difficulty stemming from his Presidency, sold Oak Hill and moved to New York to live with his daughter. He died there in 1831, the third of the nation's Presidents to die on the Fourth of July.

—DAVID JACOBS

James Monroe

A PICTURE PORTFOLIO

*This commemorative spoon honors the Monroe
Doctrine and the President who proclaimed it.*

When James Monroe was about twenty-four, he sat for the portrait at left by a now-forgotten artist. At that time, Monroe was a practicing attorney in Virginia.

In the painting at right, Monroe and Robert R. Livingston are shown purchasing Louisiana from Talleyrand.

In October, 1777, Monroe participated in the Battle of Germantown, depicted below in an 1850 painting by George Washington Parke Custis. General Washington, Monroe later recalled, took the British by surprise, and they were "driven before him." Although the Americans came close to victory, a morning fog confused the troops, and Washington was compelled to order them to retreat.

A CHECKERED CAREER

In spite of his diplomatic blunders abroad, James Monroe's political career flourished at home. Two reasons for his domestic successes were his extraordinary administrative skills and his fortunate friendships. During the Presidency of Washington (under whom he had served during the Revolution), Monroe was recalled from France in disgrace for having contradicted the policies of the administration he represented. But Jefferson, Monroe's mentor, and Madison, his friend, had organized the Democratic-Republican party, and Monroe's return to a well-established opposition party lessened the blow, making his recall seem a purely political matter. In 1799 Monroe was elected governor of Virginia, but in 1803 he failed again on a diplomatic mission abroad. Re-elected governor in 1811, he was called to Washington by Madison, whose Department of State was in chaos. Monroe straightened out the State Department, and with his organizational and supervisory abilities he also brought order to the War Department during the hostilities with England. His reward was the Presidency in 1817.

Entertainment at the White House during Monroe's Presidency was lavish and varied, befitting the Era of Good Feelings. On Inauguration Day, March 4, 1817, the band played a specially composed march that achieved some popularity, as evidenced by the sheet music pictured at left.

In 1821, sixteen Western Indians—"part of them all but naked," according to John Quincy Adams—were invited to the White House to stage a war dance for President Monroe and his guests. As Baroness Hyde de Neuville, wife of the French minister, watched, she drew the sketch below.

RUFUS KING

ERA OF GOOD FEELINGS

The election of 1816 was hardly a contest. By its opposition to the War of 1812, the Federalist party had wrecked its future and the chances of its candidate, Rufus King. Both William H. Crawford and James Monroe had supporters among the Democratic-Republicans, but Monroe's record during the war, as Secretary of the Departments of War and State simultaneously, was enough to secure the party's nomination. Winning the election itself was much simpler. King received only the electoral votes of the die-hard Federalist states, Massachusetts, Delaware, and Connecticut, losing even his own New York and all others to Monroe. The final tally was 183 electoral votes to 34. Then even the die-hard states moved into the Monroe camp. With prosperity high, and expansion and nationalism prevailing, it was difficult to fault the Chief Executive; the years of the Monroe administration were known as the Era of Good Feelings, a name coined in Federalist Massachusetts. There were, however, some bad feelings too: the voteless common man was beginning to resent the governing class; the free states and the slave states were finding less to like about each other; the prosperity was unstable and threatened to end at any moment. But none of this, in the people's eyes, had anything to do with the President. He would have been unanimously reelected in 1820 had not one elector wanted to preserve that honor for Washington.

The two presidential candidates in 1816 were in many ways the antithesis of each other. While Monroe was an efficient executive nominated by a prospering political party with the momentum of four successful electoral victories behind it, Rufus King, senator from New York, was a brilliant orator—"he is unequalled," Daniel Webster said—endorsed by a dying party. In contrast to Monroe's poor record in the field of diplomacy, King served as United States minister to Great Britain from 1796 to 1803, and has been called one of the most effective ambassadors the nation has ever had. A Harvard graduate, Rufus King was a congressman from Massachusetts before moving to New York; at the Constitutional Convention and then in the United States Senate, he was an eloquent spokesman for federalism. After being defeated as the Federalist vice presidential candidate in 1804, he retired to his Long Island home. Four years later he tried again for the same office and lost. King was vigorously opposed to the War of 1812, and in 1813 returned to the Senate to lead the opposition—an opposition, as it turned out, that destroyed the Federalist party; he was its last presidential candidate. Remaining in Congress, King turned his eloquence against the institution of slavery, proposing a plan for the resettlement of freed Negroes. In 1825, President Adams appointed him minister to England. But he soon became ill and had to return home, where he died in 1827.

A FORMAL FAMILY

An unfamiliar tenant named protocol moved into the White House in 1817, and informality was evicted. The First Family was not "at home" to the casual visitor, and the First Lady did not return calls as her predecessors had. Seldom responsive to invitations, the Monroes often sent their oldest daughter, Eliza Hay, and her husband to represent them at banquets and embassy balls. Educated in Paris, the classmate of princesses, Eliza was herself largely responsible for all the Old World formality; but to Secretary of State Adams she was just an obstructive and "obstinate little firebrand" carrying on a "senseless war of etiquette." Before long angry Washington wives turned Mrs. Monroe's receptions into predominantly stag affairs. Eliza even involved her sixteen-year-old sister's wedding in her feud. Maria Hester Monroe's 1820 marriage to Samuel Gouverneur was the first White House wedding. Eliza, in charge of the arrangements, announced a "New York style" wedding; only the family and intimate friends of the Monroes were invited. Lacking precedent, the Russian minister politely inquired how he might acknowledge the marriage of the President's daughter. The diplomatic corps, Eliza replied brusquely, were to ignore it. Thus did the social-minded Eliza Hay rudely reject the opportunity to establish a "Washington style" wedding.

Badly burned by the British during the War of 1812, the Executive Mansion had been restored adequately enough for the Monroes to move in in 1817. Congress appropriated $50,000 to buy new furnishings for the Mansion, above, which was still unfinished and without porticoes when the Monroes left it in 1825.

The Monroes brought to the Executive Mansion many of the furnishings they had purchased during diplomatic missions to Europe. A figurine of Hannibal adorns the gilt-bronze clock above. The chair below once belonged to Marie Antoinette.

It is possible that Elizabeth Kortright Monroe (above) was almost as snobbish as people said she was. Stately and reserved, she was a regal First Lady, a grande dame who tried to make the White House a grandiose court. But Mrs. Monroe also had great courage and a fighting spirit. An aristocrat, she nevertheless married a hard-drinking Republican and made a good marriage. She repeatedly overcame chronic poor health to travel with him during his ambassadorial years. In 1794, while in France, she gained permission to see the imprisoned wife of the Marquis de La-fayette on the day of her scheduled execution; Mrs. Monroe's interest may have helped secure the Marchioness' release the next day. Elizabeth also enjoyed being an innovator: in 1807 she dressed her daughter in French pantalettes and thus introduced the garment to an amazed Capital.

This enamel miniature of Clay was worn as a pin.

THE GREAT COMPROMISER

Speaker of the House Henry Clay did not design the Missouri Compromise of 1820, but because his efforts on its behalf were the primary reason for its passage, he became known, thereafter, as America's "Great Compromiser." It was a role for which the Kentuckian was well suited: he had an instinctive dislike for extremist positions, which he referred to as "entirely too ultra." Shrewd, realistic, and cynical, Clay was also optimistic and ever conscious of the odds. Once, when a woman offered Lucretia Clay sympathy because of her husband's penchant for gambling, Mrs. Clay replied, "he usually wins."

Clay did not win every hand, but he won enough to remain an active player in national politics for four decades. Born in Virginia in 1777, the tall, ungainly lawyer moved to Lexington, Kentucky, at the age of twenty. Specializing in criminal law, he attracted state-wide attention because, according to local lore, he never lost a client to the hangman. He received his first taste of national politics in the first decade of the nineteenth century when, as a state legislator, he was twice appointed to fill unexpired terms in the United States Senate. After running successfully for Congress in 1810, he became a "war hawk" and Speaker of the House in the Madison administration. He also served on the peace commission that concluded the War of 1812. In 1817, he was eager to be Secretary of State under Monroe. When John Quincy Adams received the appointment, Clay vengefully refused to allow the inauguration to take place in the House.

Although he was a slaveowner, Clay believed in a strong Union. His "American System," which he advocated throughout most of his career, was based on a broad interpretation of the federal government's constitutional powers. Ironically, the most bitterly opposed aspects of the system—a protective tariff and a national bank—met with considerable success, while the more widely admired internal improvements provision was never passed as a whole because many doubted that the national government had the right to appropriate money for roads, canals, and land development. President Monroe signed a watered-down version of the bill, and John Quincy Adams sponsored, without success, a constitutional amendment permitting internal improvements.

Clay was a perennial candidate for the Presidency. After finishing last in a four-man field in 1824, he threw his support to Adams, who won and subsequently appointed him Secretary of State. Elected to the Senate in 1831, Clay ran for President as an anti-Jackson National Republican a year later and was badly beaten. He sought the Whig party nomination in 1840, 1844, and 1848, receiving it in 1844 and losing narrowly to James K. Polk. In 1849, after a year's retirement in Kentucky, he saw the clouds of disunion forming again, and he returned to the Senate where he sponsored the Compromise of 1850. Clay died in 1852 at the age of sixty-five, believing that the Union had been preserved; he was spared the knowledge that nothing at all had been resolved by his compromises.

A FAMOUS DOCTRINE

The Monroe Doctrine has become the most famous of American foreign policy statements, but for many years after it was proclaimed in 1823, it was regarded as almost meaningless by other nations. There would be, President Monroe stated in Secretary of State John Quincy Adams' words, no "future colonization by any European powers" in the Western Hemisphere. America would stay out of Europe's wars, and Europe would be expected to keep out of American affairs. But these declarations of policy were made by the leader of a young, relatively weak nation, and it was the British navy, not the Monroe Doctrine, that made other European powers wary of molesting South America. In the 1830's and 1840's, England and France made incursions in Latin America, but there was no mention of the Doctrine by the United States government. Not until the end of the nineteenth century, when American strength had grown to formidable proportions, did the Monroe Doctrine become a meaningful policy. That adherence to the nonintervention clause was discarded in 1917 is evidence that the Doctrine is no more inflexible than any good foreign policy. As for the nations of Latin America, the promise of United States protection was not long applauded. At first, many doubted that the United States could or would come to their aid in the event of an attack. Later, they wondered who would protect them from the United States.

Theodore Roosevelt blended a generous portion of Monroe Doctrine into his "big stick" soup. The nutritional quality of the mixture is explained in this 1901 cartoon, in which Uncle Sam Rooster shelters the Latin chicks.

Franklin Delano Roosevelt's Good Neighbor Policy greatly improved United States relations with Latin America: trade was increased, and many American military bases were withdrawn. But as Hitler and Mussolini gobbled up one nation after another in Europe, the possibility that they might turn next to the Americas was anything but remote. As the cartoon at left, published in July, 1940, shows, the United States waved the Monroe Doctrine to remind them that aggression in the Western Hemisphere would never be tolerated.

The press was lavish in its references to the Monroe Doctrine during the Cuban Missile Crisis of 1962, when President John F. Kennedy reaffirmed it in spirit if not in name.

FACTS IN SUMMARY: JAMES MONROE

CHRONOLOGY

UNITED STATES		MONROE
	1758	*Born April 28*
Lexington and Concord	1775	*Leaves William and Mary to join army*
Bunker Hill		
Declaration of Independence	1776	*Promoted to first lieutenant*
Battle of Trenton		*Wounded at Trenton*
		Promoted to captain
Articles of Confederation adopted	1777	*Fights at Brandywine and Germantown*
	1778	*Fights at Monmouth*
	1780	*Appointed military commissioner of Southern army*
		Studies law under Jefferson
	1782	*Elected to Virginia House of Delegates*
	1783	*Elected to Continental Congress*
Shays' Rebellion	1786	*Admitted to the bar*
		Marries Elizabeth Kortright
		Elected to Virginia assembly
Constitutional Convention	1787	
	1788	*Elected to Virginia State Convention*
		Defeated in election for congressman
Washington elected President	1789	

	1790	*Elected to U.S. Senate*
Jay's Treaty	1794	*Appointed minister to France*
John Adams elected President	1796	*Recalled from France*
	1799	*Elected governor of Virginia*
Jefferson elected President	1801	
Louisiana Purchase	1803	*Participates in purchase of Louisiana Territory*
		Appointed minister to England
	1804	*Heads diplomatic mission to Spain*
Monroe-Pinkney Treaty	1806	*Appointed commissioner to negotiate treaty with England*
Jefferson refuses to send Monroe-Pinkney Treaty to Senate	1807	*Returns to America*
Madison elected President	1808	
	1810	*Elected to Virginia assembly*
	1811	*Elected governor of Virginia*
		Appointed Secretary of State
War with Britain	1812	
Treaty of Ghent	1814	*Appointed Secretary of War*
	1816	*Elected President*

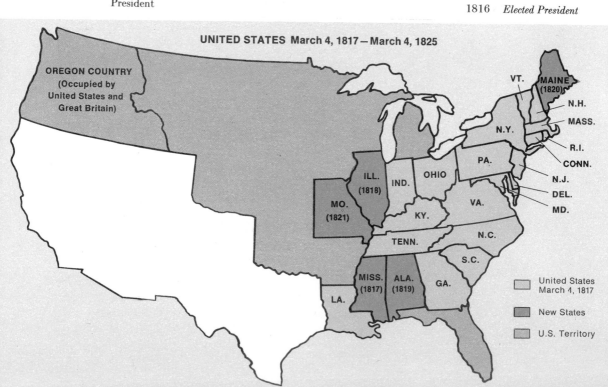

UNITED STATES March 4, 1817 — March 4, 1825

OREGON COUNTRY (Occupied by United States and Great Britain)

- United States March 4, 1817
- New States
- U.S. Territory

Rush-Bagot Agreement	1817	*Tours Northern states*
First Seminole War	1818	
Convention of 1818 signed in London		
Bank panic	1819	
Florida ceded by Spain		
Missouri Compromise	1820	*Re-elected President*
	1822	*Vetoes Cumberland Road Bill*
Monroe Doctrine	1823	*Announces Monroe Doctrine*
John Quincy Adams elected President	1825	
	1826	*Becomes regent of University of Virginia*
	1829	*Elected chairman of Virginia Constitutional Convention*
	1831	*Dies July 4*

BIOGRAPHICAL FACTS

BIRTH: Westmoreland County, Va., April 28, 1758
ANCESTRY: Scotch
FATHER: Spence Monroe; d. 1774
FATHER'S OCCUPATIONS: Carpenter; farmer
MOTHER: Elizabeth Jones Monroe
BROTHERS: Andrew (d. 1826); Joseph Jones (d. 1824)
WIFE: Elizabeth Kortright; b. New York, N.Y., June 30, 1768; d. Oak Hill, Va., Sept. 23, 1830
MARRIAGE: New York, N.Y., Feb., 1786
CHILDREN: Eliza (1787–?); Maria Hester (1804–1850)
HOMES: Ash Lawn, Charlottesville, Va.; Oak Hill, Loudoun County, Va.
EDUCATION: Parson Campbell's school; College of William and Mary
RELIGIOUS AFFILIATION: Episcopalian
OCCUPATION BEFORE PRESIDENCY: Lawyer
MILITARY SERVICE: Officer in Third Virginia Regiment and Continental Army (1776–1779)
PRE-PRESIDENTIAL OFFICES: Military Commissioner for Southern Army; Rep. to Va. Legislature; Member of Governor Jefferson's Council; Rep. to Va. House of Delegates; Rep. to Continental Congress; Rep. to Va. Assembly; Rep. to U.S. Senate; Minister to France; Minister to England; Governor of Va.; Secretary of State; Secretary of War
AGE AT INAUGURATION: 58
OCCUPATION AFTER PRESIDENCY: Writer
DEATH: New York, N.Y., July 4, 1831
PLACE OF BURIAL: Hollywood Cemetery, Richmond

ELECTION OF 1816

CANDIDATES	ELECTORAL VOTE
James Monroe Democratic-Republican	183
Rufus King Federalist	34

FIRST ADMINISTRATION

INAUGURATION: March 4, 1817; the Capitol, Washington, D.C.
VICE PRESIDENT: Daniel D. Tompkins
SECRETARY OF STATE: John Quincy Adams
SECRETARY OF THE TREASURY: William Harris Crawford
SECRETARY OF WAR: John C. Calhoun
ATTORNEY GENERAL: Richard Rush; William Wirt (from Nov. 15, 1817)
POSTMASTER GENERAL: Return Jonathan Meigs, Jr.
SECRETARY OF THE NAVY: Benjamin Crowninshield; Smith Thompson (from Jan. 1, 1819)
FIFTEENTH CONGRESS (March 4, 1817–March 4, 1819):
Senate: 34 Democratic-Republicans; 10 Federalists
House: 141 Democratic-Republicans; 42 Federalists
SIXTEENTH CONGRESS (March 4, 1819–March 4, 1821):
Senate: 35 Democratic-Republicans; 7 Federalists
House: 156 Democratic-Republicans; 27 Federalists
STATES ADMITTED: Mississippi (1817); Illinois (1818); Alabama (1819); Maine (1820)
END OF PRESIDENTIAL TERM: March 4, 1821

ELECTION OF 1820

CANDIDATES	ELECTORAL VOTE
James Monroe Democratic-Republican	231
John Quincy Adams Independent-Republican	1

SECOND ADMINISTRATION

INAUGURATION: March 5, 1821; House of Representatives, Washington, D.C.
VICE PRESIDENT: Daniel D. Tompkins
SECRETARY OF STATE: John Quincy Adams
SECRETARY OF THE TREASURY: William H. Crawford
SECRETARY OF WAR: John C. Calhoun
ATTORNEY GENERAL: William Wirt
POSTMASTER GENERAL: Return Jonathan Meigs, Jr.; John McLean (from July 1, 1823)
SECRETARY OF THE NAVY: Smith Thompson; Samuel L. Southard (from Sept. 16, 1823)
SUPREME COURT APPOINTMENT: Smith Thompson (1823)
SEVENTEENTH CONGRESS (March 4, 1821–March 4, 1823):
Senate: 44 Democratic-Republicans; 4 Federalists
House: 158 Democratic-Republicans; 25 Federalists
EIGHTEENTH CONGRESS (March 4, 1823–March 4, 1825):
Senate: 44 Democratic-Republicans; 4 Federalists
House: 187 Democratic-Republicans; 26 Federalists
STATE ADMITTED: Missouri (1821)
END OF PRESIDENTIAL TERM: March 4, 1825

JOHN QUINCY ADAMS

O f the second Adams-Jackson con-
test for the Presidency, historian Edward Channing wrote, ". . . it was more
honorable to have been defeated in 1828 than to have been elected." The re-
cipient of the honor was John Quincy Adams, by his own admission a man of
impeccable character, who during the mucky campaign was charged with
having entered into a "corrupt bargain." Self-defense or countercharge was
out of the question: refusing to sink to the level of his opponents, Adams remained tight-lipped, retained his dignity, and was soundly beaten. "The sun
of my political life," he confided to his diary, "sets in the deepest gloom."

His political sun was in fact not ready to set. Before he achieved the Presidency, Adams had compiled a substantial record of service to his state and
country—a record that for one other than an Adams might have represented
the work of two lifetimes. But he was an Adams, and as such, work and service
were almost instinctive. Though sixty-one when he left the White House, he
soon began his career anew: for the last eighteen years of his life he sat, stood,
debated, and fought in the House of Representatives, where he came to be
known as Old Man Eloquent, one of the ablest and most effective congressmen of his or later days.

The second child and first son of John and Abigail Adams, he was born in
Braintree, Massachusetts, on July 11, 1767. When John Quincy was three, his
father temporarily retired from politics, and as his re-entrance was gradual,
John Adams was home often enough to establish an extremely close if not
demonstrative relationship with his son. With the Revolution in the making,
the precocious John Quincy Adams was quite receptive to his father's anti-
British sentiments and explanations of the issues. Before he was seven he had
become a faithful reader of the patriot press, and when with his mother he

Gilbert Stuart began the portrait of Adams
at left; it was completed by Thomas Sully.

witnessed the Battle of Bunker Hill in 1775; he saw testament to all he had read and heard; he remained biased against the English for life.

In 1778 and again the next year, John Quincy accompanied his father to Europe on diplomatic missions. Educated in Paris, Amsterdam, and Leyden, and by his father, the youth developed sophisticated interests, ranging from history to agriculture, from economics to gastronomy. In many respects these years marked the end of childhood; one hesitates to call the teen-aged John Quincy Adams anything less than a mature adult. Even his strongly opinionated father allowed him to make his own decisions. In 1781, at the age of fourteen, John Quincy was invited to leave school to go to St. Petersburg to serve as private secretary to Francis Dana, American minister to Russia. Despite his age, young Adams was a valuable aid to the consul; he enjoyed Russia and the exposure to diplomatic circles. After a year, however, displaying an extraordinary objectivity about himself, he decided it would be best for him to return to his studies in the Netherlands.

Slowed by the Scandinavian and North German winter, the journey to The Hague took six months, during which John Adams was largely uninformed about his son's whereabouts. No sooner had John Quincy settled down with his books when his father appeared and removed him to Paris, where he could keep a closer eye on him. There John Quincy watched the signing of the Treaty of Paris, ending the American Revolution, and held his own in discussions with Franklin, Jay, Jefferson, his father of course, and whomever else he encountered, American or foreign, in several languages.

John Adams was sent to London in 1785, and John Quincy—again on his own—decided he had better get on with his education, this time without distractions. He returned to the United States and enrolled at Harvard. Understandably, after his experiences abroad, he found college life dull, but he graduated in two years and entered the law offices of Theophilus Parsons in New-

John Quincy Adams, sketched when he was sixteen

buryport, Massachusetts. Passing the bar in 1790, he set up practice in Boston, though he had no intention of spending his life as a lawyer. But since his father was by then Vice President of the United States, John Quincy worried about charges of nepotism and was overcautious about entering governmental service.

For four years John Quincy Adams was one of the most prolific political writers in America. Most of his articles were defenses of the Washington administration, and the President was impressed. In 1794, George Washington dismissed the Adamses' reservations and appointed John Quincy minister to the Netherlands. During his three years at The Hague, Adams was twice called to London to help negotiate John Jay's treaty; there he met and courted Louisa Catherine Johnson, daughter of the Maryland-born American consul. Louisa had been born and raised in Europe and had in fact never seen the United States. They were married in July, 1797, a few months after John Adams had been inaugurated in Philadelphia as the second President of the United States.

The sensitive Adams wanted to appoint John Quincy minister to Prussia, but again he hesitated. Finally, however, he named his son to the post, but not before securing a strong endorsement from George Washington, who wrote from Mount Vernon that the President had no right to deny the country the services of John Quincy Adams just because he was an Adams, and added that he "will prove himself to be the ablest of all our diplomatic corps." The difficulty of the assignment was illustrated to the couple even before they entered Berlin. As recorded in Adams' diary, he and Louisa arrived at the gates to the city and were there detained "by a dapper lieutenant who did not know, until one of his private soldiers explained to him, who the United States of America were." Although many of his duties were routine, Adams did manage to conclude a treaty of commerce and friendship, and his stay, if uneventful, was regarded at home as successful. In 1801, however, shortly before his departure from office, the President recalled his son. It is possible that Adams wanted to dramatize the cleavage between himself and his successor, or that he wanted to spare Jefferson the embarrassment of having an Adams in his service; but although his motives have never been clearly defined, it is perhaps most likely that Adams, knowing that the new President would in fact retain the valuable John Quincy, could not bear the thought of being indebted to Jefferson for anything. In any case, the young Adams arrived home in the autumn of 1801 and soon re-opened his Boston law office.

But being an Adams meant that John Quincy belonged in public service. It meant that he was a statesman, not a politician, and as such it meant that he followed a carefully delineated set of rules—all his own— for statesmanly conduct. It meant that membership in a political party was a convenience—nothing more—and that his being a Federalist would make him no more predictable than his election by a constituency would make him faithful to its interests. In

April, 1802, forty-eight hours after he took his seat in the upper chamber of the Massachusetts legislature, the Federalists who had elected him began to question the wisdom of their choice: Adams voted in favor of giving the opposition Democratic-Republican minority a proportionate voice in that chamber. He pursued his independent ways as a United States senator between 1803 and 1808, voting for the Louisiana Purchase, which his party opposed, and for Jefferson's Embargo Act of 1807, although passage was regarded as disastrous to New England commerce. However often he voted with the Republicans he was not one of them: he bore no affection for the man in the White House and accused Jefferson of taking credit for being an economizer when in fact his economic measures were wasteful of "national safety, of national honour, of national glory. . . ."

Under persistent attack from all sides, Adams noted in his diary that when independence is besieged, "The qualities of mind most peculiarly called for are firmness, perseverance, patience, coolness, and forbearance." He did not have to acquire these traits; he had inherited them. Reserved, moral, able to labor twice beyond ordinary human exhaustion, vain one day and self-abusive the next, devotion to country un-

John Adams wrote the letter at right, introducing his first son to the American minister in London.

concealed by a transparent air of detachment, self-righteous, irritable, compelled to write, possessed with a firmness of purpose fluctuating between virtuous determination and stubborn inflexibility—this was the Adams character, fused in the father, solidified in the son. Moreover, to even a greater extent than his father, John Quincy Adams was practically paranoid about the family name. It was inconceivable to him that anyone might oppose him on reasonable grounds; his adversaries were out to get the Adamses, of that he was sure. Fortunately, he restricted most of his personal rantings to his diary, which in parts reads like a drama cast with the damned and set in hell. (In 1835, for example, he listed thirteen men, including a former ally or two, whose entire faculties, he said, were devoted to "base and dirty tricks to thwart my progress in life.")

After three years the Federalist-dominated Massachusetts legislature had had enough of Senator Adams' independence and symbolically censured him by electing a successor to his seat nine months in advance of the March, 1809, expiration date. Adams immediately resigned in a huff, thereby essentially ending his affiliation with the Federalist party. He retired to Cambridge, where three years earlier, in 1805, he had been appointed Boylston Professor of Rhetoric and Oratory at Harvard. Although he still yearned for a political career, his star was dim indeed. His record offended most New Englanders, and his anti-British bias was not then widely shared (it would take the War of 1812 to restore him to good graces on this point). Like

Adams always kept these small bronze busts of classical writers and philosophers on his mantelpiece.

his father, he found himself a man without a party and without a political base; but his father, at least, had waited until he was President before driving away support. Adams found himself futureless at forty-one.

It was James Madison, two days after his inauguration in March, 1809, who rescued the political career of John Quincy Adams by appointing him minister to Russia. He arrived in St. Petersburg in October and became a friend and confidant to Czar Alexander I. Two years later he received word that the President had appointed him to the Supreme Court. Much to his surprise the Senate had unanimously confirmed the appointment; but with characteristic objectivity Adams regarded himself as unfit for the judiciary and declined. Though there is no evidence to suggest that Adams regretted turning down the offer, he was before long eager to return to America. The War of 1812 was being fought at home, and the Russians were busy with Napoleon; Adams felt out of touch with the big events. In 1814, however, Madison asked him to leave Russia not for home but for Ghent, Belgium, where he and four other American commissioners were to try to conclude a peace with England. A treaty was signed on December 21, 1814, but not before seven miserable months had passed, not before Adams' dislike of the British had been countless times confirmed, and not before he riled and was, in turn, countless times riled by his fellow bargainer Henry Clay.

Then Adams was asked to go to London as minister to the Court of St. James's. The wisdom of appointing an anti-English consul to represent America immediately after a British-American conflict may be questioned, but Adams went. He had about as much success with the Crown as his father had had in the same position following the Revolution: very little. Besides, England, too, was busy with Napoleon, and Adams' duties were again rather routine. On April 16, 1817, he received notice to set sail as soon as possible; President James Monroe had appointed him Secretary of State.

To comprehend the breadth of Adams' accomplishments as Secretary of State, one need not look any further than to the overall record of the Monroe administration. It was the Adams-Onís Treaty of 1819 that added Spanish Florida to the United States. It was Adams who settled the Canada-United States border controversy in negotiations with England, and it was Adams' firmness that convinced the Russians not to go ahead with their plans to penetrate the Pacific Coast of North America. Most notably, when the President included in a State of the Union address the key phrase that became the Monroe Doctrine, it was Adams' policy, word for word, that he read. While there have been a number of Presidents who have taken exclusive control of policy-making, employing their Cabinet members merely as agents or pawns, Monroe was one who believed strongly in delegating responsibility. His greatest skill was that of an administrator, and as such he was a master at the art of choosing, rejecting, and distilling various contributions in order to assemble his own, no less personal, policy. The prevailing issue of his two terms was national expansion, which shaped all the smaller issues, domestic and foreign, and which made the State Department what it had not been before: a hub

Secretary of State Adams gave a ball for Andrew Jackson on January 8, 1824, the anniversary of the Battle of New Orleans. The men shown (from left to right) are John Calhoun, Daniel Webster, General Jackson, Henry Clay, and John Quincy Adams.

around which all the now-related issues revolved. Monroe was fortunate in having Adams as Secretary of State, and he knew it: that he chose to make Adams' policies his policies is indicative not of his lack of imagination but of his sound executive judgment.

Adams had been a fine diplomat, but his abruptness, which often came across as orneriness, had prevented him from becoming a great one. Now, as a statesman, Adams channeled his articulateness, inexhaustible energy, and creative intellect to his new responsibilities, and thanks to the paternal Monroe, who discreetly edited the cantankerousness from Adams' papers, he became a superb, perhaps matchless, Secretary of State. His day began at four thirty in the morning and seldom ended before eleven or

179

twelve at night, and the operations of his department went so smoothly that his labors were taken for granted. When Congress asked him to prepare a report on weights and measures, he agreed and produced a lengthy treatise, largely ignored in America, but applauded abroad, which is to this day widely regarded as one of the definitive expositions of the subject. Despite his feelings toward the British, his objectivity took priority over his prejudice, and he forged a series of alliances with England that planted once and for all the seeds of lasting friendship.

He wanted to be President, but although Adams was the most distinguished member of the Monroe Cabinet, his successes were somewhat neutralized by his lack of friends and organizational backing. There was only one party at the time—the Democratic-Republican—and a congressional caucus gave the presidential nomination to Secretary of the Treasury William H. Crawford of Georgia. This was not a popular choice in most states, and by election day, November 2, 1824, there were three other candidates: Senator Henry Clay, General Andrew Jackson, and Adams. Adams received his nomination from a New England that had long forgiven him and had come to view him as the man who would save the nation from the rabble-rousing "Old Hickory." Secretary of War John Calhoun, originally a presidential candidate, accepted the vice presidential nomination and became a supporter of Jackson. Calhoun won his race easily.

But none of the presidential candidates received a majority of electoral votes, so the election was placed in the hands of the House of Representatives. Because Jackson had led the balloting with 99 votes to Adams' 84, and had received over forty thousand more popular votes, his supporters claimed the House had no choice but to declare for the General. Clay, however, had been eliminated, finishing last with 37 votes despite the fact that Crawford, with four more, had suffered a paralytic stroke during the campaign. The election hinged on Clay's instructions to his small but devoted band of enthusiasts. After what must have been considerable soul-searching on his part, Clay endorsed his old adversary, Adams, and Adams won. The decision was not made official until three weeks before the inauguration.

When Adams announced that he had appointed Henry Clay Secretary of State, the Jackson-Calhoun forces cried foul. According to a Jacksonian newspaper, there had obviously been "a corrupt bargain." In Tennessee, Jackson's home, the legislature passed a resolution of condemnation: "Mr. Adams desired the office of President; he went into the combination without it, and came out with it. Mr. Clay desired that of Secretary of State; he went into the combination without it, and came out with it." Making the charges seem credible was the past relationship between the two men, which had been marked by petty personality clashes and general animosity. No evidence, then or since, has ever clarified the matter one way or the other; but even if there had been a deal, Clay had acted from conviction because he could have made the same arrangement with any candidate, and Adams, not one to rationalize, made it clear in his diary and personal correspondence that he thought Clay the best man for the job. Nevertheless, the charge of corruption echoed throughout

Mrs. Adams used this china in the White House.

the Adams administration, branding it. It was hardly an administration at all.

What made the circumstances of Adams' Presidency doubly unfortunate for American history was the potential for greatness that the man exhibited. His character, capacity for work, statesmanship, and intellect were well-known; but in his first message to Congress, Adams revealed that he also had vision. Now that the vast expansion of the Monroe years had slowed and questionable border definitions were settled for the time being, Adams directed himself to the internal improvement of the country. His progressive program called for huge federal expenditures to establish an interstate network of roads and canals, a department of the interior to regulate use of natural resources, expeditions to map the country, a naval academy, a series of astronomical observatories, and government aid to education. Each provision, of course, did eventually become reality, but not in the Adams administration; it took Congress four years to debate and defeat each and every proposal.

The most vehement opposition came from the Jacksonians, who claimed that the President's plans placed too much power in the grip of the federal government. Yet, if passed, the program would actually have favored the common people for whom the Jacksonians expressed devotion. Development of the land and education of the people would have been expedited, thus providing "grass roots" Americans with the economic and intellectual strength to fight the Eastern, urban, big-money powers the Jacksonians so despised. Unfortunately, as Samuel Eliot Morison has pointed out, the Jacksonians, however significant their political accomplishments, did not always favor universal education. They sought support from whatever sources available, and if it was easier to appeal to the people's passions than to their minds, then forget education and condemn those who used it. The rise of the Jacksonians coincided with the rise of bigotry in the United States.

On the other hand, the anti-Jacksonians, who were beginning to call themselves Na-

A Creek chief, Selocta, wears a medal of President Adams in the portrait above. Beginning in 1827, the Creek were moved from Georgia to lands in the West.

tional Republicans, made no bones about their desire to limit suffrage to the moneyed and the educated. But, unlike the more aristocratic and now all but extinct Federalists, the National Republicans wanted that moneyed and educated class to eventually embrace all Americans. They opposed slavery and rallied behind President Adams' conscience-stricken plea for justice for the American Indian. Denouncing the "crying sins for which we are answerable before a higher jurisdiction," Adams wanted to provide the Indians with territory in the West and guarantee their rights there. But the more popular attitude was reflected in Jackson's treatment of the Indians in Florida—a blend of eviction and extermination—and Congress defeated the Adams plea. On issue after issue, the National Republican and Jacksonian wings drifted further apart, and two-party politics returned to the nation.

Adams wanted no part of it. He did not like partisan politics; he would not stoop to patronage; he would not make appointments on the basis of party affiliation. And when the partisan, highly regional issue of tariffs came up, Adams refused to take a stand, announcing that he would abide by the decision of Congress. So committed, when a bill creating an absurdly high tariff was passed and placed on his desk, he had no alternative but to sign, thereby losing what support he had in the South. Still, every previous President but one had won re-election, and in 1828 Adams was a candidate once again.

In his favor were the Chesapeake and Ohio Canal (one internal improvement for which Adams had been able to secure federal funds), a couple of commercial agreements with European countries, and the establishment of Pan-American rapport, as well as his character (if it could withstand the "corrupt bargain" charge) and a gracious First Lady presiding over social functions with such elegant restraint that almost nobody heard of them outside Washington. Against Adams were the corruption charges, his reputation for being antislavery and pro-Indian, a domestic program that was generally regarded as idiotic, a tariff that *was* idiotic, and an opponent who was the most popular military hero in America since George Washington, and who was backed by a well-organized machine that had been campaigning for four years. Naturally, Adams did not electioneer. Adamses serve but they do not campaign for office. Adamses also do not win second terms.

Nor do Adamses lose gracefully. Like his father, John Quincy Adams refused to attend the inauguration of his successor. Perhaps the younger Adams had better reason: he was beaten, his reputation muddied by a man he had once championed.

In 1830 the ex-President was elected Massachusetts delegate to the House of Representatives. He almost immediately displayed the old objectivity and even supported the position of President Jackson every now and then. He had not softened, though: he refused to attend when Jackson received an honorary degree from Harvard.

Always antislavery, Adams the congressman conducted a long, successful campaign to restore debate on abolition petitions, which had been halted by a "gag rule." On the grounds that it would extend slavery he opposed annexation of Texas. He was one of the few public figures who dared call the conflict with Mexico "a most unrighteous war." Instrumental in the establishment of the Smithsonian Institution, he also pressed for government provisions to make education available to all Americans. In 1843 the first observatory in America was finally established, and he was invited to lay the cornerstone on the hill site near Cincinnati that had been named Mount Adams.

In 1846 Adams suffered a paralytic stroke. Four months later he returned to the House, weak and with his speech impaired, and as he walked—with help—to his desk, the whole chamber rose and stood in homage. At that desk on February 21, 1848, he had another stroke. He was carried to the Speakers Room, where he remained until he died two days later. He regained consciousness only once. "Thank the officers of the House," he said. "This is the last of earth. I am content."

John Quincy Adams was not among America's more lovable figures, but he cared very deeply about the character of his people and country. He thought he knew what was best —often he did—for the nation that so frequently resisted him. But if he had had his way, he would have taken America by the hand and showed it the way, just as he had done with his six-year-old grandson, Henry Adams. In his third-person autobiography, Henry recalled: ". . . one summer morning [Henry had] a passionate outburst of rebellion against going to school . . . [when] the door of the President's library . . . opened, and the old man slowly came down. Putting on his hat, he took the boy's hand without a word, and walked with him, paralyzed by awe, up the road to the town . . . the boy reflected that an old gentleman close on eighty would never trouble himself to walk near a mile on a hot summer morning over a shadeless road to take a boy to school . . . but the old man did not stop, and the boy saw all his strategical points turned, one after another, until he found himself seated inside the school. . . . Not till then did the President release his hand and depart."

—DAVID JACOBS

John Quincy Adams

A PICTURE PORTFOLIO

A portrait of John Quincy Adams adorns this colorful sewing box, a campaign item in the hotly contested election of 1824.

Sliding down "ice hills," above, without sleds, was a popular activity in St. Petersburg during Adams' stay.

John Quincy Adams, as a neutral minister in St. Petersburg, was in an ideal position to watch the mobilization for the war between Russia and France. Above, Russian soldiers parade before the royal palace of Alexander I.

MINISTER TO RUSSIA

John Quincy Adams' success as minister to Russia saved him from the political scrap heap to which he had been relegated by those who deplored his disregard for party lines. He had already represented the United States at The Hague and in Prussia, where he had seen the rise of the tensions which beset Europe in the early 1800's. His mission in Russia was to urge freedom of the seas, to seek favorable treatment for American shipping in Russian waters, and to reaffirm the desire of the United States to avoid entanglement in continental policies. The Adamses arrived in St. Petersburg late in 1809 and soon were part of the capital's social whirl. (Adams grumbled, as had his father in Paris in the 1770's and 1780's, that such socializing wasted valuable time.) When fifty-two American ships were seized by Danish privateers, Adams appealed to Alexander I, who was eager for American friendship, to intercede. Through the Czar's efforts, the ships were released. By late 1810, Adams had convinced the Czar to discontinue the detainment of American ships (charged with carrying contraband) in Russian ports. The Czar's decision was in defiance of Napoleon's system of trade restrictions, and marked the beginning of the rapid deterioration of the Franco-Russian alliance. Open warfare between France and Russia began in 1812, one week after the outbreak of the Anglo-American conflict, which the Czar offered to mediate. Adams, who was later commended for his alacrity, immediately accepted the chance to end the war. But England refused the Czar's offer; she was winning the war and was deaf to offers of mediation on maritime issues. Peace would have to be negotiated directly, at Ghent.

Adams married European-born Louisa Johnson (above) in 1797. Her portrait is by Charles Bird King; John Singleton Copley painted Adams (below) in 1795, when the diplomat was twenty-eight.

The seal above was used at the signing of the Treaty of Ghent, and now is on display at the Adams National Historic Site in Quincy, Massachusetts. The city of Portsmouth, New Hampshire, was "in a perfect uproar of joy, shouts, illuminations, &c. &c." according to the broadside, below, that proclaims the end of the war.

PEACE!

Treaty of PEACE signed & arrived!

CENTINEL-OFFICE, *Feb.* 13, 8 *o'clock in the morning.*

WE have this instant received in Thirty-two hours from N. York, the following

Great and Happy News!

To BENJAMIN RUSSELL, *Esq. Centinel-Office,* Boston,
New-York, Feb. 11, 1815.—Saturday Evening, 10 o'clock.

SIR—

I HASTEN to acquaint you, for the information of the Public, of the arrival here this afternoon of H. Br. Majesty's Sloop of War FAVORITE, in which has come passenger Mr. CARROLL, American Messenger, having in his possession a

TREATY OF PEACE

Between this Country and Great-Britain, signed on the 26th December last.

Mr. BAKER also is on board, as Agent for the British Government, the same who was formerly Charge de Affairs here.

Mr. Carroll reached town at eight o'clock this evening. He shewed to a friend of mine who is acquainted with him, the pacquet containing the Treaty, and a London Newspaper of the last date of December, announcing the signing of the *Treaty*.

It depends, however, as my friend observed, upon the act of the President to suspend hostilities on this side.

The gentlemen left London the 2d Jan. The *Transit* had sailed previously from a port on the Continent.

This city is in a perfect uproar of joy, shouts, illuminations, &c. &c.

I have undertaken to send you this by Express—the rider engaging to deliver it by *Eight* o'clock on Monday morning. The expense will be 225 dollars—If you can collect so much to in lemnify me I will thank you so to do.

I am with respect, Sir, your obedient servant,

JONATHAN GOODHUE.

Printed at the Portsmouth Oracle-Office.

1815

MAKING A PEACE

The American delegation at Ghent faced many problems in addition to the demands of Britain's representatives. The war news during the summer of 1814 was depressing; and the growing threat of secession by New England Federalists weakened the American position at the conference table. And there were personality clashes within the United States delegation. John Quincy Adams found Henry Clay ir-

ritating, "dogmatical, over-bearing," and given to late hours and gambling. With typical candor, Adams acknowledged his own irascibility. He was annoyed when his drafts for the treaty were revised by his countrymen, but he admired James Bayard's "real self-command," and worked well with Albert Gallatin. At first, the British demanded that an Indian barrier territory be established between the United States and Canada, that the United States not fortify its Northern boundary, and that English navigation be permitted on the Mississippi. But by the end of 1814, England was increasingly concerned with European affairs and alarmed by American victories. She offered a peace which deferred many of the essential questions to further negotiation but which would at least end the fighting. On December 24, the Treaty of Ghent was signed.

Above, chief plenipotentiaries John Quincy Adams, center, and Lord Gambier conclude the Treaty of Ghent.

WILLIAM CRAWFORD

It is probable that only a series of paralyzing strokes in 1823 kept William Crawford from becoming the sixth President of the United States. The tall, handsome, engaging Southerner had served in the Senate since 1807, and had made many influential friends in Washington, yet he remained the maverick conservative he had been in the Georgia legislature. Basically a states' righter, he did advocate a moderate protective tariff and favored rechartering the National Bank. He was minister to France from 1813 to 1815; later, during Madison's second term as Chief Executive, he was Secretary of War and then of the Treasury. Declining to run for President in 1816, he was Monroe's Secretary of the Treasury for eight years, working effectively for internal improvements. His ambition and influence were strong, and he knew the power of patronage: "Crawford's Act" of 1820 limited the tenures of minor federal appointees to four years. In the free-for-all to succeed President Monroe, John Quincy Adams, Henry Clay, and Andrew Jackson all knew they had to beat Crawford, who had the support of Van Buren, Madison, and Jefferson. Then Crawford was stricken, and his nomination by a small congressional caucus was merely a gesture of respect and friendship. Winning only forty-one electoral votes, he ran a distant third in the race. Crawford then faded from national prominence. He died in 1834.

VICTORY AND DEFEAT

John Quincy Adams brought the office of Secretary of State to full flower under James Monroe. His firmness prevailed over the chicanery of Spanish minister Onís, and Spain gave up Florida and all claims to the Pacific Northwest. In dealing with Russia over Pacific Coast claims, Adams said in July of 1823, ". . . the American continents are no longer subjects for any new European colonial establishments." Five months later Monroe made that position a matter of doctrinaire policy.

Adams watched with distaste as men began to vie to succeed Monroe; he hated political manipulating and remained aloof: "I had neither talent nor inclination for intrigue." He was a man of old-fashioned ideals caught in a wave of new and seamy methods of competition. The virulence of the attacks on him during the close election of 1824 and following his appointment of Henry Clay as Secretary of State was only a prelude to what has been called Adams' "four years' martyrdom." Adams long had acknowledged that he was not a "popular man"; his personal and governmental ethics were in somber and stoical contrast to the Jacksonian democracy that was sweeping the nation. A solidly antiadministration Congress scrapped President Adams' vast domestic program, and he was ousted in the election of 1828. The acrimonious campaign left him embittered yet hopeful: "The cause of Union and of improvement will remain," Adams wrote in 1829. ". . . I have duties to it and to my country yet to discharge."

The cartoon above, drawn by David Claypoole Johnston in 1824, has Adams in the lead in the presidential race; William Crawford is just behind him, with Jackson third. An outdistanced Henry Clay scratches his head, at right. The drawing is rife with plays on words. "Hurra for our Jackson," shouts a supporter of Old Hickory, while John Adams cheers on "our son Jack."

"A FIG FOR THE
CONSTITUTION"

I bore some humble part in putting down the dynasty of John the First," shrilled John Randolph as John Quincy Adams was about to assume the Presidency. "I hope to aid in putting down the dynasty of John the Second." Adams, in turn, saw Randolph as the "superscription of a great man stamped upon base metal." Throughout his twenty-six years in Congress, Randolph never gave his opponents a respite; he was the unrelenting whip of the "Quids," the Old Republican element, and was an opponent of all legislation that threatened state sovereignty.

He was first elected to the House from his native Virginia in 1799, and soon became the Republican floor leader. But he split with Jefferson over the Louisiana Purchase and other questions. Rigid in his antifederalism, he was incensed that the administration was not, and he became leader of the conservative opposition. He hated Madison, says Irving Brant, because "peace with a man who outstripped him politically was no more possible to Randolph than marriage"—and Randolph was sexually impotent. He at first supported Monroe as Jefferson's successor, but later called Monroe a "Judas" for aligning himself with Madison. In discussing the moderate tariff of 1824, Randolph said ominously, "I do not stop to argue the constitutionality of this bill; I consider the Constitution a dead letter. . . . A fig for the Constitution . . . there is no magic in this word *union*." That year he promised to use "every . . . means short of actual insurrection" to block the passage of an internal improvements act.

Some saw Randolph as merely an obstructionist, while to others he was the most articulate champion of the fading states' rights cause. But all feared this enigma whose slashing wit often paid little heed to party lines. His rhetorical vitriol and flamboyant dress and manner (he often appeared in the House booted, spurred, and carrying a whip; he was a pistol brandisher, and his obscenity was notorious) bespoke a disturbed temperament and vanity. A fascinated contemporary described Randolph as "lean and sallow," with a small head and a face lined with "premature and unhealthy wrinkles." His limbs were "unnaturally . . . protracted. To his short and meager body are attached long legs which . . . grow larger as they approach the floor . . . giving his whole person the appearance of a sort of pyramid. His arms are the counterparts of his legs. . . ." Randolph was almost beardless; his voice was soprano. Manifestly brilliant and sensitive, he was deeply affected by his physiological misfortune. To a man who taunted him on his impotency, he retorted haughtily: "You pride yourself upon an animal faculty, in . . . which the negro is your equal and the jackass infinitely your superior!" And there is a proud pathos in his statement, "There *was* a volcano under my ice, but it is burnt out." In his stormy last terms he bitterly denounced the Adams-Clay coalition. His vituperative eccentricity waxed as his sanity waned. He died at fifty-nine in 1833, to the end believing his own epigram: "Asking one of the States to surrender part of her sovereignty is like asking a lady to surrender part of her chastity."

John Randolph, painted by Chester Harding

This daguerreotype of Adams was made shortly before his death. (None of his predecessors in the Presidency had ever posed for a camera.) Adams was stricken in Congress on February 21, 1848, and died two days later. Thomas Hart Benton, his old foe, said, "Where could death have found him but at the post of duty?"

"OLD MAN ELOQUENT"

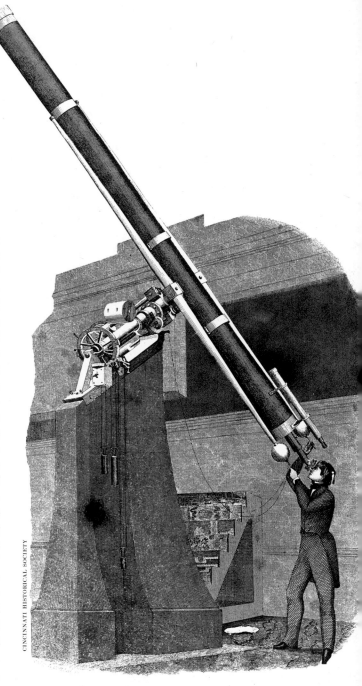

I adhere to the right of petition," said John Quincy Adams to his fellow congressmen in 1837. "Where," he challenged, "is the degree of vice or immorality which shall deprive the citizen of the right to supplicate for a boon, or to pray for mercy?" Adams, who had feared that he might fall into indolence after his defeat in 1828, was overjoyed at his election to the House two years later. He took on his new job with a rejuvenated independence of mind and spirit. After 1836, when the House passed a gag rule prohibiting the discussion of slavery petitions, Adams devoted much of his energy to fighting the rule. Though opposed to the extension of slavery and hopeful of eventual emancipation, he was not a rabid abolitionist (he decried their "senseless and overbearing clamor"), but he regarded the gag rule as "a direct violation of the Constitution." Annually he badgered the House not to renew it; when ignored, he read antislavery petitions anyway, rushing his words to beat the Speaker's angry gavel. He even read proslavery petitions, including one that asked for his own expulsion from Congress. Often he was hooted at, howled down, threatened with censure. But he persisted, and the gag rule was finally revoked in 1844. Adams' seventeen years in the House of Representatives were his greatest days. Even his adversaries admiringly referred to him as Old Man Eloquent.

Devoted to science, Adams felt astronomy was "one of the most important [subjects] that can engage the attention" of man. In 1843, he gave the address at the cornerstone ceremonies at the observatory on Mount Adams, Ohio (above). Adams also oversaw the creation of the Smithsonian Institution in 1846.

FACTS IN SUMMARY: JOHN QUINCY ADAMS

CHRONOLOGY

UNITED STATES		ADAMS			
	1767	*Born July 11*	Jefferson inaugurated as President	1801	*Returns to U.S.*
Declaration of Independence	1776			1802	*Elected to Mass. senate*
Articles of Confederation adopted	1777		Louisiana Purchase	1803	*Elected to U.S. Senate*
Franco-American alliance	1778	*Sails to France with father*		1805	*Appointed professor at Harvard*
	1779	*Attends school in Amsterdam*	Madison elected President	1808	*Resigns from Senate*
Articles of Confederation ratified	1781	*Enters Leyden University*		1809	*Named minister to Russia*
		Travels to St. Petersburg as secretary to American minister	War with England	1812	
			British burn Washington	1814	*Signs Treaty of Ghent*
Treaty of Paris	1783	*Resumes studies at The Hague*		1815	*Appointed minister to Great Britain*
		Accompanies father to Paris	Monroe elected President	1816	
	1785	*Returns to U.S.*		1817	*Named Secretary of State*
Constitutional Convention	1787	*Graduates from Harvard*		1819	*Negotiates Adams-Onís Treaty annexing Spanish Florida*
Washington elected President	1789		Missouri Compromise	1820	
	1790	*Admitted to the bar*	Monroe Doctrine	1823	*Helps draft Monroe's message to Congress*
Jay's Treaty	1794	*Appointed minister to the Netherlands*	Democratic-Republicans split into two factions	1825	*Elected President by House of Representatives*
John Adams elected President	1796		Death of Thomas Jefferson and John Adams	1826	*Nominates delegates to Panama Congress*
	1797	*Marries Louisa Johnson in London*	Jackson elected President	1828	*Signs "tariff of abominations" into law*
		Named minister to Prussia			*Ends presidential term*

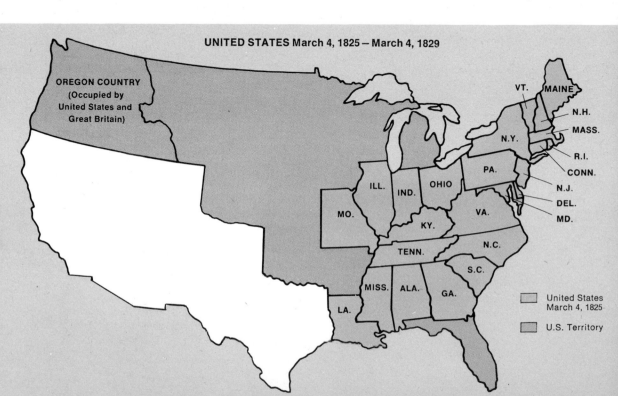

UNITED STATES March 4, 1825 – March 4, 1829

OREGON COUNTRY
(Occupied by
United States and
Great Britain)

VT.   MAINE
N.H.
MASS.
N.Y.
R.I.
PA.
CONN.
ILL.   IND.   OHIO
N.J.
DEL.
MO.   MD.
VA.
KY.
TENN.
N.C.
S.C.
MISS.   ALA.   GA.
LA.

United States
March 4, 1825

U.S. Territory

The "Old House" in Quincy, seen above as it appeared when John Quincy Adams died, was periodically enlarged.

	1830	*Elected to U.S. House of Representatives*
	1831	*Delivers eulogy on James Monroe*
Van Buren elected President	1836	*Opposes extension of slavery*
Tyler assumes Presidency	1841	*Argues Amistad case before Supreme Court*
	1843	*Lays cornerstone of first observatory on Mt. Adams*
Polk elected President	1844	
	1846	*Suffers paralytic stroke*
	1848	*Dies February 23*

BIOGRAPHICAL FACTS

BIRTH: Braintree (Quincy), Mass., July 11, 1767

ANCESTRY: English

FATHER: John Adams; b. Braintree (Quincy), Mass., Oct. 19, 1735; d. Quincy, Mass., July 4, 1826

FATHER'S OCCUPATIONS: Lawyer; statesman; President

MOTHER: Abigail Smith Adams; b. Weymouth, Mass., Nov. 11, 1744; d. Quincy, Mass., Oct. 28, 1818

BROTHERS: Charles (1770–1800); Thomas Boylston (1772–1832)

SISTERS: Abigail Amelia (1765–1813); Susanna (1768–1770)

WIFE: Louisa Catherine Johnson; b. London, England, Feb. 12, 1775; d. Washington, D.C., May 14, 1852

MARRIAGE: London, England, July 26, 1797

CHILDREN: George Washington (1801–1829); John (1803–1834); Charles Francis (1807–1886); Louisa Catherine (1811–1812)

EDUCATION: Studied in Paris, Amsterdam, Leyden, and The Hague; received B.A. (1787) from Harvard; studied law (1788–1790) with Theophilus Parsons

RELIGIOUS AFFILIATION: Unitarian

OCCUPATIONS BEFORE PRESIDENCY: Lawyer; professor

PRE-PRESIDENTIAL OFFICES: Minister to the Netherlands; Minister to Prussia; Member of Mass. Senate; Member of U.S. Senate; Minister to Russia; Minister to Great Britain; Secretary of State

POLITICAL PARTY: Federalist, to 1808; Democratic-Republican, to 1825; National Republican (Whig) thereafter

AGE AT INAUGURATION: 57

OCCUPATIONS AFTER PRESIDENCY: Congressman; writer

DEATH: Washington, D.C., Feb. 23, 1848

PLACE OF BURIAL: First Unitarian Church, Quincy, Mass.

ELECTION OF 1824

(Although Jackson received more votes than Adams, no candidate had a majority, so the election was submitted to the House of Representatives, which chose Adams.)

CANDIDATES	ELECTORAL VOTE	POPULAR VOTE
Andrew Jackson	99	153,544
John Quincy Adams	84	108,740
William H. Crawford	41	46,618
Henry Clay	37	47,136

THE ADAMS ADMINISTRATION

INAUGURATION: March 4, 1825; Hall of the House of Representatives, Washington, D.C.

VICE PRESIDENT: John Calhoun

SECRETARY OF STATE: Henry Clay

SECRETARY OF THE TREASURY: Richard Rush

SECRETARY OF WAR: James Barbour; Peter Buell Porter (from June 21, 1828)

ATTORNEY GENERAL: William Wirt

POSTMASTER GENERAL: John McLean

SECRETARY OF THE NAVY: Samuel Lewis Southard

SUPREME COURT APPOINTMENT: Robert Trimble (1826)

19th CONGRESS (March 4, 1825–March 4, 1827):
Senate: 26 Administration; 20 Jacksonians
House: 105 Administration; 97 Jacksonians

20th CONGRESS (March 4, 1827–March 4, 1829):
Senate: 28 Jacksonians; 20 Administration
House: 119 Jacksonians; 94 Administration

ANDREW JACKSON

I have never seen such a crowd before," said Daniel Webster. "Persons have come five hundred miles to see General Jackson, and they really seem to think that the country has been rescued from some dreadful danger."

The people had come to see "the People's President" inaugurated. They had been descending on Washington for days, by the thousands, filling every inn, sleeping several in a bed, or on billiard tables, or on the floors. Finally the great day arrived: March 4, 1829. It dawned cloudy, but as the vast crowd assembled, the sun broke through and warmed the people who had clogged the streets and were packed onto every terrace, portico, and balcony along Pennsylvania Avenue.

At midmorning the tall, sixty-one-year-old General departed from Gadsby's Tavern, where he had been staying. Some boys perched on nearby window sills caught sight of him and called out excitedly; cannons boomed, and a cheer rose up and resounded down the avenue. As he advanced toward the Capitol, the ailing hero was slowed by the press of the crowd, but he did not seem to mind and he shook every offered hand.

As journalist Anne Royall noted, Andrew Jackson was the most plainly dressed man at the inaugural ceremonies. In deep mourning for his wife, who had died less than three months earlier, the President-elect was attired all in black. He was "thin and pale, and his hair . . . was almost white, and his countenance was melancholy." When he delivered his address, he spoke stiffly and softly, and the pages of the manuscript were seen to tremble in his hand as he turned them. Just as solemn was the Federalist Chief Justice, John Marshall, who must have regarded with extreme distaste the assignment of administering the presidential oath of office to Andrew Jackson.

Andrew Jackson, portrayed in 1833 by Ralph E. W. Earl

As their new President rode horseback to the White House, the crowd followed, sweeping down the avenue, bursting past startled doormen into the Executive Mansion, fighting, scrambling, elbowing, scratching all the while. In the East Room, the mob hurled itself on the refreshments; to the sound of crystal breaking and china smashing, women fainted, fights erupted—noses, clothing, and furniture were bloodied. Presently the riotous assembly—"a regular Saturnalia," one witness called it—became too much for the President to bear. With the help of a wedge of armlocked men, he escaped through a back door and returned to Gadsby's. "The reign of King Mob," observed Supreme Court Justice Joseph Story, "seemed triumphant."

The riot came as no surprise to Jackson's opponents. Throughout the decade preceding the election of 1828, as one state after another eliminated property qualifications for voting, the snowballing power of the common man had placed fear in the hearts of the American upper class. James Kent, the New York jurist, called attention to the "tendency in the poor to covet a share in the plunder of the rich . . . the industrious and the virtuous; and *there is a tendency in ambitious and wicked men, to inflame these combustible materials*." Jackson and his supporters were, of course, Kent's ambitious and wicked men. Their campaign to rally the masses behind their cause began in 1824, and casting President John Quincy Adams and his administration in the role of tyrannical oppressors, they captured the Presidency with relative ease in 1828. The rejected political establishment went numb: Secretary of State Henry Clay spent most of the winter at home, lying on his couch under a black cape, as though in mourning; other Cabinet members complained of peculiar diseases; President Adams waited out his term in the White House without a word for his successor and stole away from Washington the night before the inauguration. If any of Jackson's opponents considered the possibility that the people might be something

Among the many gifts Jackson received while in office was a 1,400-pound cheese, four feet in diameter and two feet thick. The People's President offered it to the voters, above, at one of his public receptions.

more than a merciless mob, the disastrous inaugural reception dispelled their doubts. "The country," said John Randolph, "is ruined past redemption."

It was not, of course. But the country had changed. Under the leadership of four Virginia aristocrats and the two Adamses, American farmers, artisans, mechanics, and tradespeople had prospered and blended into a large and ever-growing middle class. By 1828 the nation was theirs, and they declared their ownership official by electing Andrew Jackson to the Presidency. In the spirit of the new America, Jackson changed the office, expanding its scope and power, and reinterpreting its responsibilities.

Andrew Jackson won the people's support for a variety of reasons, but perhaps most significantly because he embodied what was then, and what would remain long after, the American dream. Born poor in a near-wilderness, he had forged success largely on his own, by his strength, his iron will, his exertions and convictions. The people placed him alongside George Washington in their affections—but there was a difference. While Washington was a gentleman-hero, venerated for his devotion to the common cause, Jackson was one of them, a backwoodsman.

Jackson was born in the Waxhaws, a wooded frontier region on the North and South Carolina border, on March 15, 1767. He never knew his father; two weeks before the birth of his third son, the Irish immigrant lifted a heavy log, ruptured something, and died. Andrew's brothers, Hugh and Robert, and an uncle in South Carolina provided him with male companionship and a degree of guidance. He was no scholar, but by the age of five he had been responsive enough to his erratic education to have learned to read, and by eight, to write.

Jackson grew tall and agile, and as a blue-eyed, freckle-faced teen-ager with a thatch of hair as unruly as his hair-trigger temper, he would fight under the least provocation. "Jackson never would give up," recalled one schoolmate, who claimed the ability to "throw him three times out of four," but complained that "he would never *stay* throwed."

When the Revolution came to the Waxhaws in 1780, the Jackson boys joined up. Only Hugh was old enough to be a soldier, and he was killed in battle. Andrew, at thirteen, was a mounted orderly, a carrier of messages, but he did participate in an occasional skirmish. Following one encounter, he and Robert, who was sixteen, were taken prisoner. When Andrew refused a British officer's order to clean his boots, the officer slashed Jackson with a saber, cutting his left arm to the bone and leaving a gash on his head; for good measure, he slashed Robert, too. During a subsequent forty-mile march to a military prison, the Jacksons' wounds were untended, and the boys contracted smallpox. Presently Elizabeth Jackson appeared and persuaded the British commander to release her ailing sons in her custody. Drenched by rain through the long walk home, both boys became delirious. Robert died, but Andrew was saved by his incredible (later legendary) stamina.

Her one surviving son on the mend, Mrs. Jackson set out for Charleston Harbor, where two Jackson cousins lay feverish and in need of nursing aboard a British prison ship. Before long, Andrew received a bundle containing his mother's clothes and a note informing him that she had been buried with other plague victims in an unmarked grave. "I felt utterly alone," Jackson later recalled.

To the people who remembered him, Andrew Jackson emerged from his loneliness "the most roaring, rollicking, game-cocking, horse-racing, card-playing, mischievous fellow . . . the head of rowdies hereabouts. . . ." But Jackson's wildness was not shiftlessness, for he was also extraordinarily ambitious. Not long after his mother's death, he traveled to Salisbury, North Carolina, where he became a law student. In 1788, after completing his studies, he accompanied his friend John McNairy to the Western District of North Carolina (now Tennessee). McNairy had been elected superior court judge for the district, and Jackson went along as public prosecutor.

The Western District was accessible only by an arduous trip through Indian country.

On the Cumberland Road, one hundred and eighty miles beyond civilization, was the settlement of Nashville, where the settlers lived in blockhouses to protect themselves from hostile Indians. It was a developing region, an ideal arena for a young, inexperienced, but eager attorney.

Andrew Jackson moved into the blockhouse of the Widow Donelson, whose daughter, Rachel Robards, had separated from her husband. Rachel's voluptuous beauty attracted the attentions of many men, and Lewis Robards was too jealous to bear having his wife admired. Several months after she left him, however, he arrived at the Donelson house to attempt a reconciliation and was before long suspicious of Andrew Jackson. When Jackson heard about this, he challenged Robards to a duel; the husband refused, and Jackson moved out of the blockhouse. Robards and Rachel eventually returned to Kentucky together, but in 1790, Mrs. Donelson informed Jackson that her daughter again wished to leave her husband. Jackson rode to Kentucky to pick up Rachel and escort her back to the Cumberland Valley. Alleging misconduct between his wife and Jackson, Robards petitioned the Virginia legislature for a bill of divorce. Although the legislature simply gave him permission to take his case to court, Robards allowed the circulation of a rumor that the divorce had taken effect, and in August, 1791, Jackson and Rachel were married.

The divorce would not in fact be effected until two years later, but Jackson was unaware of this and returned to Nashville to resume his career. As a public prosecutor Jackson had been vigorous—in thirty days he had enforced seventy writs of execution— and conservative, generally siding with creditors against debtors. He speculated in land, slaves, and horses, and in that backwoods community he became a man of substance. He satisfied an interest in the military by becoming judge advocate of the county militia, a humble enough beginning for the hero of New Orleans. Skillful with a gun, anti-English and anti-Indian, condescending toward the Tidewater aristocracy, Jackson was, in sum, representative of most border gentlemen.

In December, 1793, Jackson learned that his wife had been legally divorced for only three months. At first he refused to consider remarriage: his pride would not allow him to accept the implication that the first marriage had not been valid; but he was persuaded to reconsider. The second ceremony took place in January, 1794.

In June of 1796, the territory became the state of Tennessee—a name Jackson reputedly gave it—and the rising young attorney was elected, unopposed, to the United States House of Representatives. Albert Gallatin saw him in the House chamber, "a tall, lanky, uncouth-looking personage . . . queue down his back tied with an eel skin . . . manners . . . of a rough backwoodsman." In his one term, Jackson managed to acquire for his state almost twenty-three thousand dollars as compensation for militiamen who had participated in an Indian raid that had taken place against the orders of the federal government. He also distinguished himself by stubbornly refusing to vote for the farewell tribute Congress wanted to tender George Washington. (Jackson disapproved of Jay's Treaty and especially of Washington's gentleness to Indians.) Following his term in the House and a year in the Senate, he resigned his seat to return to Tennessee, for he had been appointed to the superior court of the state. Future reports of his radicalism notwithstanding, the judge was again inclined to be conservative, favoring land barons.

Although Jackson had position and influence, he had not lost his "roaring, rollicking" tendencies, and back in Tennessee, where he was vulnerable to comments regarding his wife and marriage, he had ample opportunity to yield to them. One Saturday morning in October, 1803, on the steps of Jackson's courthouse, Governor John Sevier was elaborating on his own great worth to the state when Jackson stepped forward to recite his contributions. At one point, Sevier sneered, "I know of no great service you have rendered the country, except taking a trip . . . with another man's wife." Jackson instantly

Jackson was commissioned a major general in the United States Army in May of 1814 as a result of successes against the Creek Indians in encounters such as the one at right.

jumped upon Sevier with a howl of rage, clubbing the old soldier with his walking stick. He then challenged Sevier to a duel, but when the two met on the field of honor, they began screaming at each other. Jackson ran at his adversary, threatening to cane him, and Sevier drew his sword, all of which frightened Sevier's horse, which ran away with his pistols. Not a shot was fired.

More serious was Jackson's duel three years later with Charles Dickinson, a dandy who had twice alluded to Rachel's matrimonial record. Jackson took his enemy's shot in the chest, then straightened and aimed. Dickinson, confident of his own aim, staggered back in horror, thinking he had missed; and under the rules (Jackson had not yet fired) he had to return to the mark. Standing with his arms crossed, Dickinson took Jackson's .70-caliber ball in the groin and died a slow, agonizing death. So close was Dickinson's bullet to Jackson's heart that it could not be removed, and Jackson carried it with frequent pain for the rest of his life.

Perhaps Jackson's most famous brawl was one with the Benton brothers, Jesse and Thomas Hart (later a political ally). Tom Benton had criticized Jackson's role as second for a friend in a duel. One day in 1813,

Jackson arrived in Nashville, spotted his critic, and armed with a horsewhip, pursued Benton into a hotel to teach him a lesson. During the melee that followed, Jackson was shot twice. His shoulder was shattered by a bullet, but he refused to have his arm amputated and it was saved.

Jackson's set-to with the Bentons took place during the War of 1812, in which the judge, despite his martial spirit and his credentials (he was then a major general in the United States Volunteers), had participated only briefly. In 1812, Jackson had organized a division and brought it down to Natchez to fight the British, but as soon as he arrived, an order came from Washington to disband —eight hundred miles from home, without supplies or rations. Jackson flatly refused, grumbling about "the wicked machinations" of politicians, and resolved to take the two thousand men home at his own expense. During the difficult journey, one soldier remarked that Jackson was "tough as hickory." Soon the troops were referring to him as Old Hickory.

In 1813, Old Hickory rose from a bed— still bloodstained from the wounds inflicted on him by the Benton brothers—to fight the Creek Indians. The campaign lasted into

1814 and proved to the leaders in Washington that Jackson had tactical skills that could not be ignored. (After his victory, however, Jackson imposed on the Creek a treaty so harsh that the federal government subsequently repudiated much of it. His implacable hostility to Indians was probably his least attractive characteristic.) When the major theater of war shifted south in 1814, the defense of New Orleans fell to him.

First—and without official authorization—Jackson led his men into Spanish Florida and drove the British from Pensacola, which he "liberated" because he felt it should be American (which it soon became). Then he headed for New Orleans, where he tried to block off the six major water routes to the city. Hearing, however, that the British had already taken one, Lake Borgne, and were pressing inland within eight miles of the town, Jackson reportedly sprang up, slapped his hand down on a table, and cried, "By the Eternal, they shall not sleep on our soil!" His counterattack that night is credited by many military historians with having saved the city. Twenty-four hundred British troops had halted their march at the Villeré plantation to await the arrival of reinforcements, another twenty-four hundred men. While they waited, Jackson sent the schooner *Carolina* downstream to shell the British; then he attacked. The following morning, with the enemy thrown off balance by the surprise assault, Jackson retired to defensive positions at the Rodriguez Canal. Then he assembled his men and increased his numbers in preparation for the assault he knew would soon come. To his unit of Kentucky and Tennessee frontiersmen he added regulars and irregulars—Creole dandies, free Negroes, a handful of Choctaw braves, and Jean Lafitte and his pirate crew.

On January 8, 1815, the British regulars —"the conquerors of the conquerors of Europe"—marched into a torrential cross fire. Unable to seize the artillery batteries, which they had planned to turn against the Americans, they found huge chunks blasted from their evenly spaced ranks. The battleground, a flat field with cane stubble, offered no place to hide; the only escape was to the rear. As the front ranks melted away, the following ranks hesitated, then broke. "Never before had British veterans quailed," noted one subaltern sadly, but "that leaden torrent no man on earth could face." After the battle, more than five hundred troopers rose from the heaped mounds of dead comrades to come forward as prisoners. "I never had so grand and awful an idea of the resurrection," said General Jackson. The American casualties: 8 dead, 13 wounded, about 19 missing; the British combined casualties numbered 2,036.

The victory electrified the nation. Ironically, the war was already over (word of peace had not reached Jackson), but the battle gave the young country a needed psychological lift. Andrew Jackson became America's deliverer, its greatest hero since George Washington. At the Place d'Armes in New Orleans, under a triumphal arch, a little girl sang to the General while dozens of others strewed flower petals in his path.

After the war, Andrew Jackson solidified his new national eminence by keeping active in the Florida area, where expansionist eyes had logically turned. The Spanish had had much difficulty controlling East Florida, locale of considerable privateering with many rebels claiming to represent an assortment of governments. Aided by unauthorized British soldiers, Seminole and Creek raided the Georgia border; American troops arrived and chased the Indians deeper into Florida, and American settlers promptly moved in. As the Indians retaliated, President Monroe sent Jackson to lead troops against them but instructed him not to attack those who retreated into Spanish forts. Jackson, however, anxious to take "the whole of East Florida," seized the town of St. Marks in 1818, which he claimed was under Indian attack. He then marched to a Seminole village and burned it down; then he accused two British subjects of aiding the Indians and executed them. In May, he advanced on Pensacola and deposed the Spanish governor, installing in his place one of his own officers. President Monroe

Jean François Vallée, obviously influenced by portraits of Napoleon, made a miniature of General Jackson, right, at New Orleans in 1815. Edward Livingston, to whom Jackson presented the painting with the inscription above, had the confidence of many of the region's key figures; he roused support for Jackson and helped plan the city's defense.

denied ever giving Jackson permission to enter the Spanish colony, but there is a letter from Secretary of War Calhoun to the governor of Alabama which says that Jackson had been "vested with full power to conduct the war as he may think best." In any case, despite the misgivings of some in the Capital, Jackson's activities were widely championed in rural America. In 1821, Monroe appointed him governor of Florida, which had been officially ceded by Spain in 1819. Jackson served only four months and then returned to Nashville, where he was called on by a steady stream of politicians and men of public affairs. They wanted him to be President of the United States.

Jackson was not immediately amenable to the idea. "Do they think," he asked, "that I am such a damned fool as to think myself fit for President of the United States? No, sir; I know what I am fit for. I can command a body of men in a rough way; but I am not fit to be President." Within a year, however, the idea began to take hold of him. It was not unusual in 1822 to see newspaper items similar to the one in the Nashville *Whig* of July 17: "GREAT RACING!! . . . The prize to be run for is the *Presidential Chair*. . . . There have already four states sent their nags in. Why not Tennessee put in her stud? and if so, let it be called *Old Hickory*. . . ."

There were at least two good reasons why he should not make the attempt. First,

Rachel would have preferred that he did not. Each of her husband's public services left her bereaved, anxiously awaiting his return. And second, Jackson's health was in a perilous state. "He is not a well man and never will be unless they allow him to rest," wrote Rachel to her niece. "In the thirty years of our wedded life . . . he has not spent one-fourth of his days under his own roof. . . ." But Jackson's ability to ignore the frailty of his body and to overcome his various infirmities was nothing short of incredible: during the Creek campaign he came down with severe dysentery, from which he never fully recovered. In 1821, he wrote to a friend that in addition to a chronic cough and lung inflammation, "I have been recently vissitted by my old bowwel complaint, which has weakened me very much . . . in short Sir I must take rest or my stay here on Earth cannot be long. . . ." By 1822, however, the General was clearly reconciled to the role of undeclared candidate. Taking advice from Senator John Henry Eaton of Tennessee, he refused Monroe's offer of a ministerial appointment, but, against his wishes, he was elected senator and went to Washington.

The year 1824 was one of transition in the United States. Property qualifications for voting were eliminated in some states but retained in others; electors were chosen here by state legislators, there by districts, elsewhere by blocks. All the candidates were

203

Jeffersonian Republicans. John Quincy Adams was expected to take the urban Northeast and share the old Federalist vote with William H. Crawford, who would be strong in the South. The new popular vote and Western vote were sought by Henry Clay and Andrew Jackson. The final count on election day was Jackson 99, Adams 84, Crawford 41, and Clay 37. In the absence of a majority, the election was thrown to the House, where after weeks of intrigue, Clay threw his support to Adams, and Adams won. Jackson resigned his Senate seat and immediately began the campaign to win in 1828. Sabotaging Adams' programs whenever they could, his supporters kept the President under an unfriendly spotlight for four years.

As the election date neared, the campaign became low beyond all tradition. Colonel Charles Hammond, editor of the Cincinnati *Gazette* and a crony of Henry Clay's, asked in a pamphlet, "Ought a convicted adultress and her paramour husband to be placed in the highest offices of this free and christian land?" As a presidential candidate, Jackson could not demand a duel but he fervently vowed that "a day of retribution . . . [for] Mr. Clay and his tool Colonel Hammond must arrive. . . ." *The Coffin Handbill* was a widely circulated pamphlet detailing through words and pictures the deaths of John Woods (a mutineer Jackson had executed during the Creek War) and six Tennessee militiamen executed in Alabama. The handbill also showed Jackson sticking a sword into the neck of someone who had stopped to pick up something from the street. Nevertheless, the Adams-Clay forces were on the defensive; the common man was in charge now, and he wanted Jackson, who won by an electoral vote of 178 to 83.

Perhaps the most pathetic victim of the campaign was Rachel Jackson. A visitor found her "once a form of rotund and rubiscund beauty . . . now very plethoric and obese. . . . [She] talked low but quick, with a short and wheezing breath." On December 17, 1828, she suffered an apparent heart attack and a few days later developed symp-

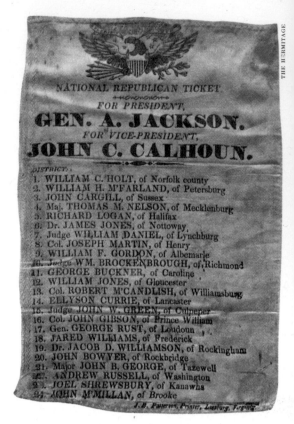

Ambitious John Calhoun of South Carolina settled for second spot on the Jackson ticket, above.

toms of pleurisy. On the night of the twenty-second she told her maid that she would "rather be a door-keeper in the house of God than to live in that palace [the White House]." Twenty minutes later, General Jackson, in the adjoining room, heard her say, "I am fainting." He rushed to her, lifted her to the bed, and felt the convulsion of her muscles as her life ended. At the funeral Jackson wept bitterly. He spoke of "those vile wretches" who had destroyed his "dear saint." Out loud he cried, "May God Almighty forgive her murderers, as I know she forgave them. I never can."

The next month the President-elect set out for Washington. Along the route the people came out to see him, but they were quiet, respecting his grief. On the boat from Cincinnati to Washington, according to a contemporary account, "a greasy fellow" said to him, "'General Jackson, I guess?'

The General bowed assent. 'Why they told me you was dead.' 'No! Providence has hitherto preserved my life.' 'And is your wife alive, too?' The General, apparently much hurt, signified the contrary, upon which the man concluded by saying, 'Ay, I thought it was the one or the t'other of ye.'"

So Andrew Jackson arrived in Washington, and the American republic became the Jacksonian democracy, where an ambitious, young, and vigorous people placed all their trust in an aging, ill, and mournful man who was, they thought, a symbol of themselves. To the factions he had defeated, Old Hickory was a radical; yet in political service he had tended to be conservative. In truth, no one knew what sort of President Andrew Jackson would be. "My opinion is," wrote Daniel Webster, "that when he comes he will bring a breeze with him. Which way it will blow, I cannot tell. . . ." Senator William Marcy of New York once commented that the politicians of his state "see nothing wrong in the rule that to the VICTOR belong the spoils of the ENEMY." Rotation in office was nothing new—Thomas Jefferson had removed 10 per cent of the officials in John Adams' administration when he took office—but the phrase "spoils system" had a dirty ring to it. When during his first eighteen months in office Jackson replaced about the same percentage of appointees, his opponents contended that he had "introduced corruption into the central government. . . ." The President never denied employing the system; he did deny that it was corrupt. Rotation in office, he explained, broke up an entrenched bureaucracy and prevented government from becoming a continuous "engine for the support of the few at the expense of the many."

Jackson's first major crisis in the White House was not outwardly a political matter, although it did have great political repercussions. Margaret O'Neale, daughter of a tavern keeper who was a friend of Jackson's and Senator John Eaton's, was a dark-haired, round-faced vamp, pampered, self-centered, and vivacious. Before she was sixteen, she had to her credit one suicide, one duel, one

nearly ruined and greatly damaged military career, and one aborted elopement. Then, at sixteen, she married a landlocked Navy purser, John B. Timberlake. Presently, Eaton, infatuated with Peggy, had Timberlake sent to sea and kept there, and sought out the young bride in order to console her. The plan apparently worked, and Washington society watched with great concern the scandalous developments of the affair. The First Lady, Mrs. James Monroe, ostracized the couple, and the other ladies of the Capital followed suit. In 1828, Timberlake died at sea from disease or drink, although Washington preferred to believe that Timberlake had cut his throat because of his wife's unfaithfulness. President-elect Jackson, who was either terribly naïve, terribly realistic, or just plain sympathetic—he was certainly sensitive to the problems of a woman's reputation—told Eaton, whom he intended to name Secretary of War, that he must marry Peggy Timberlake to "shut their mouths." The couple married on January 1, 1829.

Jackson's Cabinet was divided down the middle by the affair. Vice President John C. Calhoun, a brilliant, arrogant gentleman who wanted to be tapped for the presidential succession, could not (and apparently did not try to) bring his wife and the wives of other Cabinet members into line. They continued to ostracize Mrs. Eaton. On the other hand, Secretary of State Martin Van Buren, a widower with presidential aspirations of his own, remained perfectly courteous to the Eatons. Calhoun hoped that by embarrassing Eaton he would force the Secretary to resign, thus weakening the influence of Van Buren. But Eaton would not resign, nor would the President ask him to. Until April, 1831, the Eaton affair continued to divide the administration and interfere with the business of government; then, suddenly and simply, Van Buren, the "Little Magician," produced a magic cure: he resigned. When Eaton took the hint and resigned, too, Jackson was able to ask the rest of the Cabinet—the Calhoun wing—for resignations. It was as though a great weight had fallen from the General's shoulders.

205

The statuette above of King Louis Philippe and Jackson is carved from hickory and commemorates the payment of a French indemnity to the United States.

Jackson's Cabinet was rebuilt, and Van Buren sailed for London as minister to the Court of St. James's to wait for his reward in 1832. Calhoun and the President fell further apart, a process accelerated by Jackson's discovery that the Vice President had, contrary to his claims, spoken against the General's Florida adventure in 1818, and by Calhoun's success at getting the Senate to deny confirmation of Van Buren's London appointment. Amos Kendall, a frontier editor who had once been pro-Clay, became fourth auditor of the Treasury and chief adviser in Jackson's "Kitchen Cabinet." Now that he had his own men around him and the intra-administration problems were behind him, Jackson was ready to enforce his program.

He felt that the Chief Executive was responsible for the protection of "the liberties and rights of the people and the integrity of the Constitution against the Senate, or the

House of Representatives, or both together." And to make certain that the few never gained at the expense of the many—the measurement he generally used before taking a stand on an issue—he was prepared to use all the muscle at the disposal of the Presidency. He had already indicated that he would not hesitate to employ a veto. In 1830, Jackson had vetoed the Maysville Road bill, which committed government funds to the construction of roads entirely within the state of Kentucky, on the grounds that it benefited too small a percentage of those who would have to pay for it. Jackson thus came out against the internal improvements plank of Henry Clay's "American System." He would use the veto more frequently than any prior President, and Clay would deplore the "concentration of all power in the hands of one man."

Jackson also took aim at another keystone of the American System—the Bank of the United States. In his first annual message to Congress, the President voiced doubts about both the constitutionality and expediency of the Bank. No action was then necessary, however, because the Bank charter was not due to expire until 1836. But, as early as 1831, Jackson told Charles Carroll, last surviving signer of the Declaration of Independence, that he intended to stand for re-election "upon the principle of putting the bank down. . . . No bank and Jackson— or bank and no Jackson." His hostility reflected his suspicion of paper money and his conviction that the Bank created an alliance between business and government and resulted in benefits to the few at cost to many. The president of the Bank, Nicholas Biddle, tried in 1830 and 1831 to woo Jackson, but when his efforts proved fruitless, he agreed to have Clay and Webster make the Bank the major issue of the election of 1832.

In June the recharter passed the Senate. In July it passed the House. That evening, while a nightlong victory celebration rocked Biddle's lodgings, Jackson looked over the recharter bill with Van Buren, who had just returned from England to be Jackson's vice presidential candidate. "The bank, Mr. Van

Buren," said the President, "is trying to kill me." Then he matter-of-factly added, *"but I will kill it!"*

A week later, on July 10, Jackson sent his veto message to Congress: "It is to be regretted that the rich and powerful too often bend the acts of government to their selfish purposes. . . . Distinctions in society will always exist under every just government . . . but when the laws undertake to add to these natural and just advantages artificial distinctions . . . to make the rich richer and the potent more powerful, the humble members of society—the farmers, mechanics, and laborers—who have neither the time nor the means of securing like favors to themselves, have a right to complain of the injustice of their Government." The veto held, despite Biddle's cries of outrage.

Although the Bank was not rechartered, it was not yet dead, but before issuing his final thrust Jackson had other matters to deal with. South Carolina had been giving Jackson trouble since the start of his administration. The tariff of 1828, known as the "tariff of abominations," was the object of much animosity in the South because the protection of Northern manufacturing necessarily produced a loss in the South of overseas trade. John Calhoun wrote the *South Carolina Exposition*, which included the "Protest Against the Tariff of 1828 and the principles of Nullification." When another, equally oppressive, tariff was passed in 1832, the state legislature adopted the Ordinance of Nullification, which declared the tariff void, not "binding upon this State, its officers or citizens."

Jackson had clashed with Calhoun over the issue before, at a dinner honoring Thomas Jefferson on April 13, 1830. Following twenty-four carefully prepared toasts, mostly in support of South Carolina, the President rose and waited out the cheers. Van Buren was so excited he climbed onto his chair to watch. Jackson fixed his attention on Calhoun and paused to savor the drama of the moment. Finally he raised his glass: "Our Union: It must be preserved." In the charged atmosphere, all rose to drink, including Calhoun, clearly shaken to the core. The Vice President's hand trembled; wine trickled down the side of his glass. When order was restored and he was called on for a toast, Calhoun stuck to his guns: "The Union, next to our liberty, most dear."

South Carolina's Ordinance of Nullification and threats of secession were a clear challenge to federal authority. Jackson acted swiftly. "No state or states has a right to secede . . ." he said. "Nullification therefore means insurrection and war; and other states have a right to put it down." But in his annual message, on December 4, 1832, he was more conciliatory, proposing a lowered tariff as a compromise. John Quincy Adams, who had returned to Washington as a congressman, believed this to be "a complete surrender to the nullifiers." But before the week was out, he issued a proclamation to the people of South Carolina, a statement strong enough even for Adams, Webster, and

PLAIN SEWING DONE HERE

TENNESSEE HISTORICAL SOCIETY

SYMPTOMS OF A LOCKED JAW

Henry Clay was successful—as the cartoon on the left clearly indicates—in quashing Jackson's protest against Senate censure of his anti-Bank policies.

207

Emily Donelson, the President's young niece and hostess, sat for the portrait above in 1830. She snubbed Peggy Eaton, much to Jackson's displeasure.

the other staunch Unionists: "Disunion by armed force is *treason*. Are you ready to incur its guilt?" Then he had a bill introduced in the Senate that would authorize the President to use force to sustain federal authority. Jackson was prepared to send an army to South Carolina, but his will proved stronger than the pride of the nullifiers. A token compromise tariff was passed, which enabled the state to rescind its ordinance.

The Union had been preserved, and Jackson's popularity was soaring. He and Van Buren had overwhelmingly won the 1832 election, and the next spring, Jackson set out on a triumphal tour. In Baltimore, Philadelphia, New York, even in New England, where he had gained prestige through his vigorous defense of the Union and his new cordial relations with Daniel Webster, the old General was received with tumultuous welcomes.

Because of his failing health and developments in his war against the Bank of the United States, Jackson cut his tour short and returned to the Capital. The Bank char-

ter was about to expire, and the President's veto of the recharter had not been overridden. His more conservative advisers, Van Buren among them, suggested that Jackson had done enough; but the more radical, led by Kendall, thought that the government should remove its funds from the Bank, for otherwise the unchartered Bank would remain solvent. That being the case, a Congress fearful for the future of its deposits might well reconsider and vote for recharter after all. After first removing Secretary of the Treasury William J. Duane and replacing him with Roger B. Taney, who supported removal of public funds, Jackson dictated that after October 1, 1833, no federal deposits were to be made, and issued the first call for removal of funds.

Nicholas Biddle fought back ferociously. "All the other Banks and all the merchants may break," he wrote to a friend, "but the Bank of the United States shall not break." Biddle had given the nation its strongest currency, and he was not about to see his accomplishments undone. Tightening credit, calling in loans, reducing discounts, he meant to demonstrate the power of the Bank by creating a panic—and he succeeded. Some of those ruined were the Bank's most vigorous supporters. Finally, in 1834, Biddle succumbed to the pressure and eased up on his restrictive policies, unwittingly proving that his ruinous measures had not been necessary in the first place. Ironically, the Bank was enjoying a period of expansion when the charter expired in 1836. Rechartered as a state bank in Pennsylvania it eventually failed, and countless depositors were ruined.

The President's victory was a mixed blessing. The public deposits that had been transferred to state banks—Jackson's "pet banks," the opposition called them—and the loosening of credit led to an increased production of paper money. As a result of the inflation that followed, Jackson issued his "Specie Circular" of July 11, 1836, which stated that thenceforth the government would accept only specie, gold or silver, in land payments. As a result, inflation was curbed, but a depression struck in 1837 nonetheless.

During his last days in the White House, Jackson was concerned with an international matter: since 1821, American slaveowners had been settling in Texas. When Mexico won its independence, its government declared Texas a state but left it open for colonization. On April 8, 1830, however, the Mexicans passed a law forbidding slavery and the further colonization of Texas by Americans. Throughout the following five years, the American settlers took steps to separate from Mexico, and in 1835, Santa Anna abolished all local rights in the state and took an army of six thousand across the Rio Grande to deal with the insurrectionists. While the dictator-soldier was defeating the rebels at the Alamo, a convention declared Texan independence on March 2, 1836. Seven weeks later, Sam Houston reversed the trend and whipped the Mexicans at San Jacinto.

Congress passed resolutions calling for recognition of Texas early in July, but the President hesitated. The United States had recognized the Mexican republic, and Jackson felt that he was obliged to honor that government's sovereignty in what was technically an internal struggle. Moreover, the Whigs opposed recognition on the grounds that it was a Southern trick to broaden slavery. Personally, Jackson owned slaves and saw nothing wrong with the institution, but 1836 was an election year; his hand-picked successor, Martin Van Buren, was a candidate, and he did not wish to hurt his chances in the North by allowing the slavery issue to creep into the campaign. On March 3, 1837, however, with Van Buren safely elected, the President appointed an American representative to Houston's government, thereby effecting recognition of the new republic.

Texas insurgents took Fort San Antonio de Bexar (above) in 1835, but early the following March some three thousand Mexicans regained the town after besieging a 187-man force at the Alamo for thirteen days.

The next day the Presidency of Andrew Jackson ended. In eight years he had thoroughly altered the course of American government. His mistakes had been many, his prejudices legion, his actions guided less by law than by ego and instincts; yet his impact on the office has been matched by few.

Jackson represented a complete break from his sophisticated, intellectual predecessors. While their paternalistic attitude toward the common man may have been outdated, their concern for the people was in many ways greater than Jackson's. Thomas Jefferson and John Quincy Adams wanted all Americans to have education in advance of suffrage; Jackson was content to take advantage of the broad suffrage and was in no rush to educate the people. The first six Presidents wanted slavery abolished; most made at least token attempts to treat the Indians fairly. Jackson was for equality for all white men.

Jackson often referred to the law to justify his actions, but his positions were really assumed on the basis of how Jackson felt about them. His stated opposition to the Bank of the United States was spotted with references to constitutionality, yet an 1819 Supreme Court decision had declared the Bank perfectly constitutional. The almost sanctified concept of "Union" was enough to justify his firmness with regard to South Carolina's Ordinance of Nullification; but because he had no liking for Indians, Jackson did nothing when Georgia nullified a federal treaty. On Georgia lands guaranteed by the United States, the Cherokee Indians were laboring to develop a civilized society based on their own folkways but updated to be compatible with American society. They had renounced war, had cooperated with whites, and were well on their way to establishing a system of self-government when Georgia, claiming the right to overrule federal law, ordered the Cherokee off the land. The Indians remained committed to the rule of law. Instead of raising arms they took their case to the Supreme Court—and won. Again insisting it had the right to nullify the rule of any federal branch, Georgia proceeded to ex-pel the Cherokee. This was in 1832, at the same time that Jackson was telling South Carolina that nullification was "treason."

Yet Jackson is considered a great President. The first popularly elected Chief Executive, he pitted himself against the congressmen and senators who served some, while he acted for all. What Jackson grasped was not necessarily the essential fiber of an issue but the way people felt about it. Thus, his wisdom was the wisdom of the masses, his accomplishments the people's. As Clinton Rossiter wrote, "more than one such President a century would be hard to take. Yet he was a giant in his influence on our system . . . and second only to Washington in terms of influence on the Presidency."

Jackson was seventy when he retired to "The Hermitage," his home in Tennessee. Unfortunately, the monumental inability of his adopted son, Andrew, Jr., to hold on to a dollar made his retirement less leisurely than the General might have liked, and he had to spend much of his time going over books and trying to raise funds. He retained an interest and considerable power in his party—enough to dictate the nomination of the dark horse Polk, his protégé, for the Presidency in 1844.

He wrote to Polk on June 6, 1845, revealing that his mind was still vigorous; but according to historian J. W. Ward, "his flesh from the waist down had literally to be wrapped to his body to keep it from falling away." On June 8, he fainted, and a spoonful of brandy was administered to revive him. Late in the afternoon Andrew, Jr., asked the General if he knew him. Jackson said he did and asked for his spectacles. Shortly thereafter he died.

The Jacksonian Era continued, however. In the years between the election of Old Hickory and the election of Lincoln the only way the opposition could loosen the Jacksonian hold on the Presidency was by nominating two old soldiers who reminded the people of Jackson. Lincoln ended the Jacksonian Era. But even he would use the Jacksonian concept of the Presidency to fashion his own power and preserve the Union.

—SAUL BRAUN

Andrew Jackson

A PICTURE PORTFOLIO

I CROAK FOR THE JACKSON WAGON

The life-sized cast-iron bullfrog depicted above is one of the unique items from Jackson's campaigns.

GAVEL AND SWORD

In 1787, twenty-year-old Andrew Jackson was well equipped to make a name for himself in North Carolina's Western District. An arduous childhood had left him tall, straight, and spare with a thin, fair face and arresting blue eyes. A fine horseman and superior marksman, he was athletic, intelligent, ambitious—and already a licensed lawyer. In the next dozen years he served as district attorney, helped draw up the constitution when the District became Tennessee, sat in Congress in Washington, and was elected to the state superior court. Jackson bought The Hermitage and seemed

When a British officer, above, slashed his insubordinate prisoner, Andy Jackson, with his saber in 1781, he left the youth with a permanent scar on his hand and an equally permanent antipathy toward the English.

to aspire only to the life of a country gentleman. But he was elected major general of
the state militia in 1802; when he resigned
his judgeship in 1804 to retire to private life,
he retained his military commission. It would
be the sword, not the gavel, that would ultimately lead him to the Presidency.

*The miniature above of Jackson in Army uniform
was painted on ivory by Anna Claypoole Peale.*

*The certificate below, issued in 1796, permitted
Jackson to practice law in the new state of Ten-
nessee. The document was signed by Governor
John Sevier, who became Jackson's bitter enemy.*

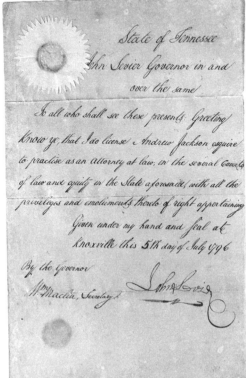

VICTORY
AT NEW ORLEANS

I will smash them, so help me God!" thundered Andrew Jackson upon hearing that an advance British force was nearing New Orleans. The engagement that evening, December 23, 1814, was indecisive, but it forestalled the British build-up for two weeks. Jackson's men had time to create and fortify an earthen embankment along a canal traversing the only route the enemy could take to New Orleans. On the morning of January 8, 1815, a heavy fog lifted and Jackson saw some 5,300 well-drilled redcoats marching directly toward the embankment. Three waves of Britons were raked by artillery and devastating rifle fire from rows of Jackson's sharpshooters. Only one Englishman gained the rampart unhurt; he looked behind him and discovered that his men "had vanished as if the earth had swallowed them up." More than two thousand British were killed or wounded that day, while American casualties totaled about forty. It was an overwhelming victory for General Jackson, who learned two months after the battle that a peace treaty between England and the United States had been signed in Europe in December.

The medal above was authorized by a joint congressional resolution on February 27, 1815. The resolution lauded Jackson and his motley troops for "uniform gallantry and good conduct" on January 8, when they won "a most signal victory . . . with a disparity of loss . . . unexampled in military annals."

West. Del.

BATTL AND DEAT

At the center of the painting below, Major General Sir Edward Pakenham, commander of the British forces at New Orleans, lies dying from a charge of grapeshot. Historian Marquis James likened the redcoats, falling from their ranks under the murderous gunfire, to "teeth snapping from a comb."

NEW ORLEANS
GENERAL PACKENHAM
January 1815.
Published and Sold by J. Yeager Nº 103 Race Sᵗ Philadᵃ

Jackson always kept with him the miniature of Rachel, above, by Anna C. Peale.

"I HAVE NEVER WISHED IT"

Slander and separation beset Rachel Donelson Jackson throughout her adult life; in 1828, they killed her. The slander arose from her mismarriage to Lewis Robards, and her subsequent, invalid first wedding to Andrew Jackson. The resultant calumny was an enduring source of sorrow to her and a forge of bitterness, anger, and frustration for Jackson. Rachel loved her husband with absolute devotion, but the trauma of her first marriage understandably abetted her wish to share with him a quiet life of simple, private pleasures at The Hermitage. As Jackson rose in the uncertain realms of politics and the military, Rachel's dreams of that life were only intermittently realized. ". . . you have served your Country Long Enough . . ." she wrote the General in 1814, "you have been gon six monthes. . . . oh Lord of heaven how Can I beare it." Since the early 1790's Rachel had been alone often, as her husband had pursued his legal career as a means to money and reputation. When he sat in Congress in 1796, he left her behind. Friends crowded The Hermitage when Jackson was elected to the state superior court in 1798, but Rachel was shy of them. She often spoke of Andrew as "Mr. Jackson," never "Judge," seldom "General."

Florida claimed much of Jackson's time after the War of 1812, and Rachel regretted his acceptance of its governorship. But when he resigned in October of 1821 she was happy at the prospect of returning to The Hermitage for, as Jackson put it, the "ballance of our lives." But her apprehensions soon were rekindled: in 1822 she wrote, "They talk of his being President. . . . But I hope he may not be called again to the strife and empty honors of public place." And when he was called, in 1828, she said, "For Mr. Jackson's sake I am glad. For my own part I have never wished it." Small wonder—for in that election campaign her name had been dragged through the mud again and again, and candidate Jackson could not settle matters with a pistol as citizen Jackson had done in earlier years. In late December of 1828, the years of casual gossip and outright slander, and of anxiety for her adored husband, took their toll on Rachel. Over the grave of his "dear saint," the grief-stricken President-elect warned that "those vile wretches who have slandered her must look to God for mercy."

A FOUL CAMPAIGN

TENNESSEE HISTORICAL SOCIETY, EMIL HURYA COLLECTION

Jackson Men,
Look out for the
SPURIOUS TICKET.
The Democratic Electoral Ticket, with Forty Three names on it, is circulated by the Opposition.
If you vote that Ticket, your Vote is lost to the Good Cause.

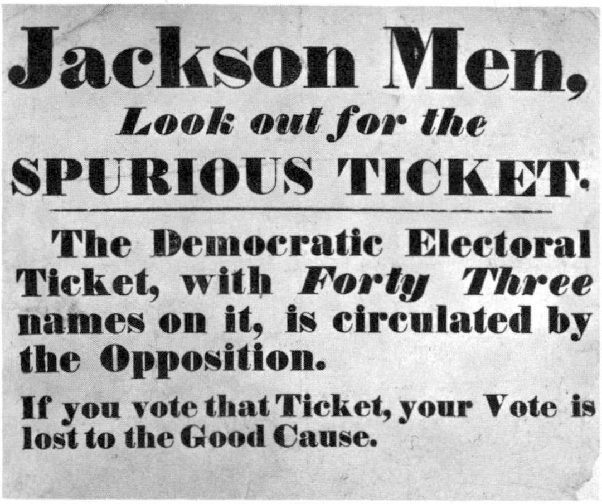

The poster above is indicative of the deviousness to which the 1828 campaigning descended. In the pell-mell rush to assassinate Jackson's character, administration forces sometimes acted rashly. Jackson's early dealings with Aaron Burr were deplored—until it was recalled that Secretary of State Henry Clay had been a defense attorney for one of Burr's associates.

"All that is necessary for you is to be still and quiet," advised Senator John Eaton in 1826. "Say nothing and plant cotton." Presidential aspirant Andrew Jackson did pretty much just that: he was enjoying a prolonged residence at The Hermitage for the first time in years. The excitement over the "corrupt bargain" between Henry Clay and President John Quincy Adams was clearly working against the administration. In Washington, a corps of counselors labored effectively on Jackson's behalf. The only real issues of the day, the tariff and internal improvements, found Jackson and Adams in substantial accord; it seemed certain that the election of 1828 would be decided on the basis of the candidates' personalities, and the 1824 campaign had proven that Jackson was more popular than Adams. But late in 1826, the slander against Rachel Jackson began in earnest, and the campaign became one of the most putrid in American history; Jackson himself was called the son of a prostitute and a mulatto. The Jackson press, to the disgust of its candidate, countered with allegations of premarital impropriety between President and Mrs. Adams. From the mire of the election rose an extremely popular—but newly widowed and embittered—President.

THE HERMITAGE

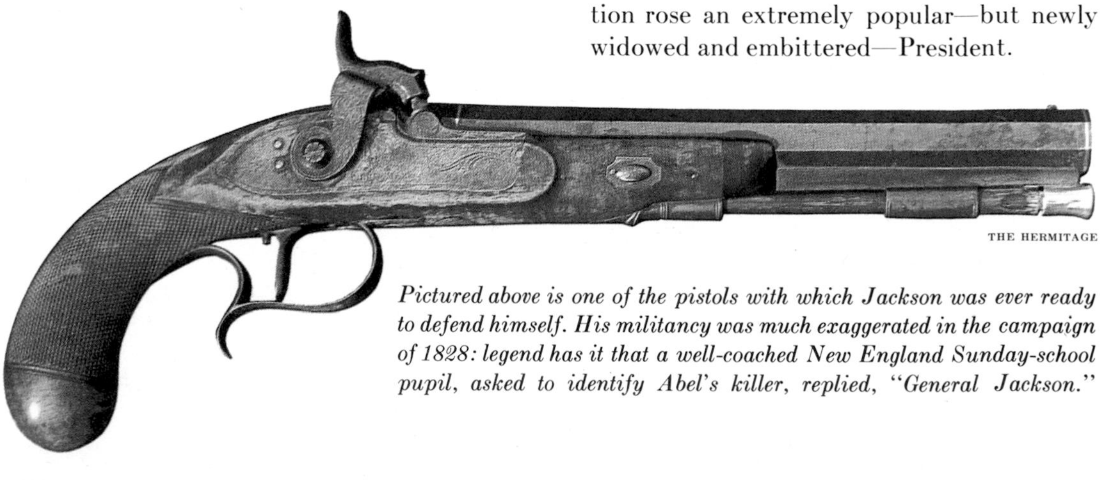

Pictured above is one of the pistols with which Jackson was ever ready to defend himself. His militancy was much exaggerated in the campaign of 1828: legend has it that a well-coached New England Sunday-school pupil, asked to identify Abel's killer, replied, "General Jackson."

Some Account of some of the Bloody Deeds of
GEN. JACKSON.

Jacob Webb.   David Morrow.   John Harris.   Henry Lew'.   David Hunt.   Edward Lindsey.

The Coffin Handbill, *above, condemned Jackson as a bloodthirsty disciplinarian for ordering the execution of six mutinous militiamen in 1815. The broadside was circulated during the campaign of 1828.*

"Jackson is to be President, and you will be HANGED."

The hanged man is unidentified, but it is clear that presidential nominee Jackson is the executioner.

Peggy Eaton (shown at right, in a daguerreotype made long after the political storm she caused was over) was said to have lived with Secretary of War John Eaton before their marriage, and to have given birth to two of Eaton's children while she was still Mrs. John Timberlake. Jackson, who recalled only too well the slander directed against his own wife, was infuriated by the malicious gossip. He called a special Cabinet meeting (depicted below; Peggy did not attend the actual conference, however) to discuss the matter. Finding no "complete establishment" of a case against her, Andrew Jackson thought Peggy vindicated. But the defamation campaign, led by John Calhoun's wife, Floride, continued unabated until the Jackson Cabinet was reorganized in 1831.

THE EATON AFFAIR

I f you love Margaret Timberlake," said President-elect Jackson to his old friend Senator John Eaton in 1828, "go and marry her . . . forthwith." Eaton did as he was told, but Washington gossips remained convinced that the pretty widow had a long history of promiscuity. Peggy Timberlake Eaton was summarily snubbed by the town's elite, but as the time for naming a Cabinet drew near (Eaton was to be Jackson's Secretary of War), the slander campaign eased, only to be redoubled after the inauguration. The sniping soon resulted in a full-scale political war of nerves: the President stoutly defended Eaton and his wife ("She is as chaste as a virgin!"), and Secretary of State Van Buren supported him. Vice President Calhoun, vying with Van Buren to succeed Jackson, was in opposition—were Eaton to fall, and drag Van Buren with him, Calhoun would have clear sailing. "Calhoun leads the moral party," was John Quincy Adams' wry comment, "Van Buren that of the frail sisterhood." Cannily, Van Buren resigned in 1831, permitting a reorganization of the Cabinet. Van Buren was clearly in line for the Vice Presidency, and Calhoun had yet another wound to lick.

"King Andrew the First," as Jackson's detractors called him, is depicted in a cartoon of 1832, above, as a veto-wielding tyrant who has trampled on the Constitution, the Supreme Court, and the National Bank.

221

"THE SOUTH,
THE POOR SOUTH"

If one drop of blood be shed [in South Carolina] in defiance of the laws of the United States," growled Andrew Jackson in 1832, "I will hang the first man of [the Nullifiers] I can get my hands on. . . ." Such drastic measures were never necessary, but Jackson always regretted not being able to hang John Caldwell Calhoun, the very voice of nullification.

In 1810, at the beginning of his congressional career, Calhoun was an ardent nationalist. Declaring that "our true system is to look to the country . . . to advance the general interest," he supported the War of 1812, internal improvements, a national bank, and protective tariffs. After seven years as Monroe's Secretary of State, he joined the 1824 presidential free-for-all and won the Vice Presidency under John Quincy Adams. But Calhoun sensed the imminent swing to Jackson, and as Senate president, permitted antiadministration oratory from Adams' detractors. ("Calhoun veers round in his politics . . ." Adams charged, "and makes his intellect pander to his will.") He was rewarded by being re-elected to the Vice Presidency under Jackson, whom he hoped to succeed. But Calhoun's animosity toward Peggy Eaton and his attempts to discredit Van Buren rankled Jackson, who was also furious when he discovered that Calhoun had criticized his conduct during the Florida campaign of 1818. But it was Calhoun's espousal of nullification that made the break with Jackson final.

In earlier years, Calhoun had been reprimanded by the Southern press for failing to abandon his protectionist stance. By 1827, however, he had come to believe that high tariffs and growing antislavery sentiment posed dire threats to the Southern economy.

His *South Carolina Exposition*, published anonymously in 1828, presented the theory that any state could annul a federal law it disapproved. Hopes that Jackson would support this states' rights principle were dashed at a Jefferson Day dinner in 1830, when Jackson, staring directly at Calhoun, made his famous toast: "Our Union: It must be preserved."

The Nullification Crisis reached its boiling point in 1832, when South Carolina proclaimed federal tariffs not "binding upon this State." When Jackson issued a proclamation stating that nullification could not be abided, Calhoun resigned the Vice Presidency, was appointed senator from South Carolina, and, amid saber rattling on both sides, led the fight in the Senate. A compromise tariff averted violence, but Calhoun's course was irrevocably plotted. In the Senate, as Secretary of State under Tyler, and in his writings, he feverishly deplored abolition and outlined his theory of "concurrent majorities." Rule by a numerical majority, he held, was "but Government of the strongest interests," which, "when not efficiently checked, is the most tyrannical and oppressive that can be devised. . . ." He stated flatly that "the will of a majority is the will of a rabble. Progressive democracy is incompatible with liberty." Out-of-power interests, namely the South, should be given the "right of self-protection": each state should have, he said, the power to concur in or veto any federal legislation.

"If trampled upon," he warned the nation in 1847, "it will be idle to expect that we will not resist." Frustration, failing health, and his own humorless intensity ground Calhoun down. He died in 1850, lamenting to the end the fate of "the South, the poor South."

The polar changes in the political philosophy of John Calhoun were mirrored in his physiognomy, as the illustrations on the left so strikingly indicate. The portrait, top, a copy of a painting by Charles B. King, shows him in his nationalist period when he was, said John Quincy Adams, "above all sectional and factious prejudices . . ." and was something of an idol for the youth of the country. The daguerreotype by Mathew Brady, bottom, captures the strain and frustration of Calhoun's last years. John Randolph remarked, when Martin Van Buren won the struggle for Jacksonian favor, that "Calhoun . . . must be in Hell. . . . He is self mutilated like the Fanatic that emasculated himself." In his cold, intellectual aloofness and his absolute devotion to the cause of Southern states' rights, Calhoun, who died early in 1850, was, to Harriet Martineau, "the cast iron man who looks as if he had never been born, and never could be extinguished."

TRAIL OF TEARS

Although the Indian Removal Act of 1830 simply authorized the President to negotiate for land, Andrew Jackson's "requests" were in fact orders. Resigned to their fate, the Choctaw and Chickasaw began the long journey from the Southeast to Arkansas and Oklahoma. But the Creek, who had disastrously encountered Jackson in 1813 and 1817, knew better than to believe his promise of guaranteed territory west of the Mississippi. Standing their ground in 1832, they extracted a treaty that said "they shall be free to go or stay, as they please." Four years later, their chiefs in chains and guns at their backs, the

As the Sauk, trying to return to their home east of the Mississippi, started to cross the river at Bad Axe,

Creek joined the exodus. In 1832, the Sauk were driven from their Illinois villages and across the Mississippi, leaving possessions and food stores behind. When Chief Black Hawk sent his braves to negotiate with the military, their white flags were ignored. After several skirmishes, the desperate leader tried to lead his starving people back home, but they were stopped at the river.

That pathetic series of events, known as the Black Hawk War, cost hundreds of Indian lives. In Georgia, the peaceful Cherokee sought and won from the Supreme Court a favorable decision, to which neither the state officials nor President Jackson paid any attention. Like the other Indian tribes, the Cherokee embarked on a long journey to the West, along a "trail of tears."

the Warrior *arrived, ignored Chief Black Hawk's white flags, and opened fire, killing hundreds of Indians.*

Thomas H. Benton.

"OLD BULLION"

When Andrew Jackson remarked in 1832 that he would start hanging South Carolina nullifiers at the first sign of trouble, Senator Thomas Hart Benton added, "When Jackson begins to talk about hanging, they can begin to look for the ropes." Benton knew his man. A daily visitor to the White House, the senator from Missouri was Jackson's confidant and leader of the administration forces in the Upper House. And he knew from personal experience the intensity of Jackson's wrath: in 1813 in Nashville, after Benton had made some critical remarks about Jackson, the latter attacked him with a horsewhip and started a celebrated donnybrook during which Jackson was shot in the arm. Ten years later, Benton found himself seated beside a new Senate colleague from Tennessee—Andrew Jackson. Benton, a man of imposing physique and every bit as stubborn and egotistical as Jackson, was not cowed; neither man acknowledged the other for days. Finally Jackson, chairman of a committee of which Benton was a member, turned and said, "We are on the same committee; I will give you notice when it is necessary to attend." Benton replied guardedly, "General, make the time to suit yourself." Shortly thereafter the two shook hands, beginning a firm friendship.

An early supporter of Henry Clay, Benton backed Jackson for the Presidency in 1824, and worked for the General's election four years later. Like Jackson, Benton was a hard-money man; he led the struggle against the National Bank. "Gold and silver is the best currency for a republic," boomed Benton. A "workingman's party" and a "hard-money party" were synonymous to him. In 1831 he introduced a resolution to allow the Bank charter to expire; and it was Benton who drew up the Specie Circular of 1836. "Old Bullion," as Benton was called, fought to expunge from the Senate record a resolution censuring Jackson's conduct in the removal of deposits from Mr. Biddle's Bank. He succeeded in 1837 and gave Jackson the pen that struck the resolution from the ledger. It was Benton's bill that raised the gold-to-silver ratio to 16 to 1, generating a healthy increase in gold coinage. Ever the Democrat—or, as he himself put it with magnificent vanity, "Benton and the people, Benton and Democracy are one and the same, sir . . ."—Benton strove to reduce Western land prices to facilitate settlement. In the latter days of his thirty-year Senate tenure he opposed the annexation of Texas on constitutional grounds and favored compromise over war in the determination of the Oregon boundary. Benton's Unionist opposition to the admission of California as anything but a free state prompted Mississippi's Senator Henry Foote to brandish a pistol at him on the Senate floor.

Benton served briefly in the House of Representatives and was a gubernatorial candidate in Missouri in 1856. He died of a wrackingly painful intestinal cancer in 1858, after completing his *Thirty Years View*, a masterful personal account of his political era. In that book's description of Van Buren's inauguration, Benton paid his final tribute to Andrew Jackson: "For once the rising was eclipsed by the setting sun."

"THE GOLDEN CALF"

Ido not dislike your Bank," said Andrew Jackson in 1829 to Nicholas Biddle, president of the Bank of the United States, "any more than all banks." It had taken Jackson some time to arrive at this position: early in the 1820's, in apparent support of Biddle's institution, he had warned against the inflationary practices of the West's "printing-press banks." But now he viewed the National Bank as a monopoly, a "hydra of corruption, dangerous to our liberties," benefiting a wealthy coterie at the expense of the common man. Whatever *rapprochement* Nicholas Biddle and Jackson might have reached was precluded by presidential aspirant Henry Clay, who persuaded Biddle to lobby for an early rechartering of the Bank as campaign ammunition against Jackson in 1832. Jackson picked up the gauntlet by vetoing the recharter, and ran successfully for re-election on an anti-Bank platform. "We shall crush the Kitchen Cabinet," seethed Biddle when Jackson began to withdraw federal deposits from the doomed Bank. Biddle tightened credit and financed a congressional and editorial campaign to censure Jackson's policies. But the President stood firm: "Is Andrew Jackson to bow the knee to the golden calf?" he thundered when businessmen complained of hardship resulting from Biddle's maneuvers. "If you want relief, go to Nicholas Biddle!" Biddle eventually capitulated, and the House in 1834 passed four definitive anti-Bank resolutions. "The fate of the Bank," said Jackson, was "sealed forever."

The Greek temple, above, on Chestnut Street in Philadelphia was the seat of the Bank of the United States. From his office Nicholas Biddle controlled twenty-seven branches—and the commercial activities of the nation.

The graphic cartoon above shows pro-Bank men Henry Clay, Daniel Webster, and John Calhoun consulting on the grave illness that is causing Mother Bank to cough up her deposits. Jackson, left, looks on with pleasure.

Jackson attacks the Bank with his veto stick in the cartoon above. Van Buren, standing at center, helps kill the monster, whose many heads represent Biddle (in top hat) and directors of the state branches.

FRIENDS AND ENEMIES

NEW YORK CITY HALL ART COMMISSION

EDWARD LIVINGSTON

The friendship between Edward Livingston and Andrew Jackson began in Congress in the 1790's; from that time on, Livingston was at Jackson's side at every critical phase of the latter's career. Livingston was forced to abandon his ascent in New York City politics in 1803: deeply in debt because of dishonest subordinates, he left to practice law in New Orleans. He organized support for Jackson before the Battle of New Orleans, and became the General's aide-de-camp, confidant, and secretary. (He wrote most of the formal war dispatches.) In 1825, back in the House, Livingston completed a universally admired criminal code commissioned by the state of Louisiana. In 1828, he campaigned for Jackson, to whom he had suggested the Presidency as early as 1815; Livingston himself was elected to the Senate. His loyalty was rewarded with the post of Secretary of State in 1831. While Livingston was a moderate on the Bank issue, he agreed fully with Jackson's opposition to nullification: he wrote the Proclamation of 1832 from presidential notes. Minister to France in 1833, Livingston initiated attempts to make France pay American claims dating from the Napoleonic Wars. Britain finally mediated the controversy, but not before Jackson's saber rattling had brought the two nations to the edge of war. Livingston died in 1836.

CULVER PICTURES

AMOS KENDALL

"Amos Kendall . . . is supposed to be the moving spring of the Administration," wrote the English economist and writer Harriet Martineau in 1838, "the thinker, the planner, the doer. . . ." Kendall was indeed one of the most influential men in the Jackson fold. Jackson always rewarded friendship and service, and Kendall, editor of a powerful Kentucky newspaper, had campaigned hard for the General in 1828. When he was appointed fourth auditor of the Treasury, he approached the job "in the spirit of reform" and did in fact substantially reduce corruption in his department. But more importantly, Kendall was a member of the "Kitchen Cabinet" of confidants to whom Jackson continually turned for advice. Kendall was responsible for much of the President's paperwork and many of his speeches (annual messages, administration correspondence, the 1832 Bank veto message to Congress) and helped to found the *Globe*, the administration's official newspaper in Washington. Appointed Postmaster General in 1835, Kendall again brought about reforms but winked at Southern postmasters' suppression of antislavery mail. After some financial duress in the early 1840's, he associated himself with Samuel F. B. Morse and made enough money to spend his last decade as a political writer and philanthropist.

NICHOLAS BIDDLE

Andrew Jackson's opponent in the "Bank War" was as antithetical to him personally as he was philosophically. Nicholas Biddle, born to an old Pennsylvania family, had long displayed a precocious diversity of talent in the classics, language, literature, and diplomacy; he was a sophisticated, polished gentleman. He had been secretary of the American legation at the Court of St. James's; later, President Monroe prevailed upon him to become a director of the Bank. Only thirty-seven when he became president of the institution in 1823, Biddle believed that a strong National Bank was the foundation of a strong economy. He used the Bank's broad charter to curtail extravagant lending by state banks. Many saw him as "Czar Nicholas," while only a handful believed that his conservative policies were the best means to stabilize the nation's currency. The conflict revealed the worst in Biddle: he was arrogant ("I have been for years in the daily exercize of more personal authority than any President") and misguided, allying himself with a loser, Henry Clay. Nevertheless, Biddle's policies would have averted the depression that followed the Bank's demise in 1836. Rechartered as a state bank, the institution failed in 1841; Biddle's creditors charged fraud, but they were paid and Biddle was ultimately exonerated. He died in 1844.

JOSEPH STORY

A distinguished member of the Supreme Court since 1811, Joseph Story was the logical successor to Chief Justice John Marshall in 1835. But Story, a former member of the Massachusetts and federal legislatures, was a nationalist and a supporter of John Quincy Adams, and he was not surprised when Jackson bypassed him in favor of Roger B. Taney. Nevertheless, Story remains a dominant figure in the Court's early history. His opinions in admiralty cases during the War of 1812 became models of international law, and in 1818 he established the Court's right to judicial review of state court decisions. Upholding the broad view of the Constitution, he argued in 1837 that Congress had exclusive right to regulate state and foreign commerce. His antipathy to slavery was reflected in the *Amistad* case of 1841, in which he freed a cargo of mutinous slaves, who were then returned to Africa. Story's writings were notable for their sagacity and range of subject matter. In 1832 he began his *Commentaries on the Constitution of the United States*, which appeared in three volumes. He accepted a chair at Harvard Law School in 1829, and in his teaching, as in his writings, he played a major role in the establishment of American equity jurisprudence. Story died in Cambridge, Massachusetts, in 1845, at the age of sixty-six.

A PRESIDENT'S POSSESSIONS

Stickpin and watch

A footscraper from *The Hermitage*

A silver wine caddy

The President's barber chair

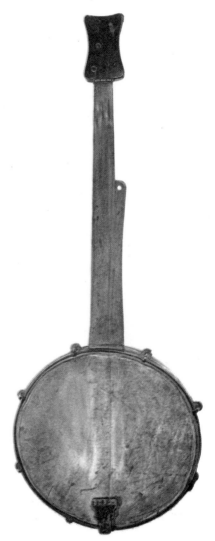

Jackson's banjo

A brass spittoon

DEATH OF A HERO

Hard of hearing, nearly blind in one eye, and suffering from the agonizing after-effects of a tubercular hemorrhage, Andrew Jackson lived by his own words: "I have long found that complaining never eased pain." An active interest in politics was the old chieftain's best tonic. Jackson advised Van Buren on fiscal policies; when the latter was defeated for re-election, Jackson was roused to write, *"Beaten but I trust not conquered. . . ."* Stung by Van Buren's apostasy on Texas—whose annexation he considered vital to national security—Jackson found "Joyfull news" in "Young Hickory" Polk's nomination in 1844. A year later, Jackson's letters persuaded Sam Houston to reconsider withholding Texas from the United States. Houston arrived at The Hermitage on June 8, 1845, the day his old military colleague died. In tears, Houston led his small son to the room in which General Jackson's wasted body lay. "My son," he said, "try to remember that you have looked on the face of Andrew Jackson."

The daguerreotype at left was made shortly before Jackson died. His face and body swelling with painful dropsy, he had to spend his last days in a cushioned chair, his nights sitting up in bed. But his spirit and spark remained; his mind to the end was occupied with national affairs— Texas, Oregon, President Polk's appointments. Before he died, he said to his family and servants: "Oh, do not cry. Be good children, and we shall all meet in Heaven."

The Hermitage, near Nashville, was inspired by Mount Vernon, as the lithograph of 1848, below, indicates. Rachel selected the site of the mansion, which was completed in 1819, and tended its extensive gardens. The house, rebuilt after a fire in 1834, is now a national shrine.

FACTS IN SUMMARY: ANDREW JACKSON

CHRONOLOGY

UNITED STATES		JACKSON
Townshend Acts	1767	Born March 15
Declaration of Independence	1776	
Yorktown	1781	Captured by the British
	1784	Begins law study
Constitution ratified	1788	Establishes law practice in Nashville
Washington elected President	1789	
	1790	Appointed attorney general of Western District of N.C.
	1791	Marries Rachel Robards
		Appointed judge advocate of Davidson County militia
Washington's Farewell Address	1796	Elected to House of Representatives
John Adams inaugurated	1797	Elected to U.S. Senate
Alien and Sedition Acts	1798	Elected judge of Tennessee superior court
Jefferson inaugurated	1801	
	1802	Elected major general of Tennessee militia
Jefferson re-elected	1804	Retires to private life
War with Great Britain	1812	Commands volunteer army in Creek War
Washington burned	1814	Defeats Creek forces at Horseshoe Bend
		Commissioned major general of U.S. Army

		JACKSON
	1815	Wins Battle of New Orleans
Rush-Bagot agreement	1817	Commands forces in First Seminole War
	1818	Captures St. Marks and Pensacola in Spanish East Florida
	1821	Appointed governor of Florida Territory
Monroe Doctrine	1823	Elected to U.S. Senate
	1824	Fails to win majority in presidential election
John Quincy Adams elected President by Congress	1825	
Tariff of Abominations	1828	Elected President
Webster-Hayne debates	1830	Makes pro-Union toast at Jefferson Day dinner
		Vetoes Maysville Road bill
Eaton affair	1831	Breaks with Calhoun
		Reorganizes Cabinet
Black Hawk War	1832	Vetoes bill for U.S. Bank recharter
South Carolina declares Tariff Act null and void		Issues Proclamation to the People of South Carolina
Calhoun resigns as Vice President		Re-elected President
Compromise tariff passed	1833	Approves force bill
		Removes deposits from the Bank of the U.S.
Second Seminole War	1835	Narrowly escapes assassination

UNITED STATES March 4, 1829 — March 4, 1837

OREGON COUNTRY
(Occupied by
United States and
Great Britain)

VT. MAINE
N.H.
MASS.
N.Y.
MICH. (1837)
R.I.
PA.
CONN.
ILL. IND. OHIO
N.J.
DEL.
MO.
VA.
MD.
KY.
TENN.
N.C.
ARK. (1836)
S.C.
MISS. ALA. GA.
LA.

United States March 4, 1829

New States

U.S. Territory

Texas declares independence	1836	*Issues Specie Circular*
		Supports Van Buren as presidential candidate
Siege of the Alamo		
Van Buren elected President		
Bank panic and depression	1837	*Publishes Farewell Address*
Polk elected President	1844	*Supports Polk for Presidency*
Texas annexed	1845	*Dies June 8*

BIOGRAPHICAL FACTS

BIRTH: The Waxhaws, S.C., March 15, 1767

ANCESTRY: Scotch-Irish

FATHER: Andrew Jackson; b. Ireland; d. 1767

FATHER'S OCCUPATIONS: Linen weaver; farmer

MOTHER: Elizabeth Hutchinson Jackson; b. Ireland; d. Charleston, S.C., 1781

BROTHERS: Hugh (1762–1780); Robert (1765–1780)

WIFE: Rachel Donelson Robards; b. Halifax County, Va., June 15, 1767; d. Nashville, Tenn., Dec. 22, 1828

MARRIAGE: Natchez, Miss., August 1, 1791; second ceremony: Nashville, Tenn., Jan. 17, 1794

CHILD: Andrew Jackson, Jr. (adopted) (1810–?)

HOME: The Hermitage, Nashville, Tenn.

EDUCATION: Attended public schools; studied law in Salisbury, S.C.

RELIGIOUS AFFILIATION: Presbyterian

OCCUPATIONS BEFORE PRESIDENCY: Lawyer; soldier; politician

MILITARY SERVICE: Judge advocate of Davidson County militia (c. 1791); major general of Tennessee militia (1802–1812); major general of U.S. Army (1814–1821)

PRE-PRESIDENTIAL OFFICES: Attorney General of Western District of N.C.; Delegate to Tennessee State Constitutional Convention; Member of U.S. House of Representatives; Member of U.S. Senate; Tennessee Supreme Court Judge; Governor of Florida Territory

AGE AT INAUGURATION: 61

DEATH: Nashville, Tenn., June 8, 1845

PLACE OF BURIAL: The Hermitage, Nashville, Tenn.

ELECTION OF 1828

CANDIDATES	ELECTORAL VOTE	POPULAR VOTE
Andrew Jackson Democratic	178	647,286
John Quincy Adams National Republican	83	508,064

FIRST ADMINISTRATION

INAUGURATION: March 4, 1829; the Capitol, Washington, D.C.

VICE PRESIDENT: John Calhoun (resigned Dec., 1832)

SECRETARY OF STATE: Martin Van Buren; Edward Livingston (from May 24, 1831)

SECRETARY OF THE TREASURY: Samuel D. Ingham; Louis McLane (from Aug. 8, 1831)

SECRETARY OF WAR: John H. Eaton; Lewis Cass (from Aug. 8, 1831)

ATTORNEY GENERAL: John M. Berrien; Roger B. Taney (from July 20, 1831)

POSTMASTER GENERAL: John McLean; William T. Barry (from April 6, 1829)

SECRETARY OF THE NAVY: John Branch; Levi Woodbury (from May 23, 1831)

SUPREME COURT APPOINTMENTS: John McLean (1829); Henry Baldwin (1830)

21st CONGRESS (March 4, 1829–March 4, 1831):
Senate: 26 Democrats; 22 National Republicans
House: 139 Democrats; 74 National Republicans

22nd CONGRESS (March 4, 1831–March 4, 1833):
Senate: 25 Democrats; 21 National Republicans; 2 Others
House: 141 Democrats; 58 National Republicans; 14 Others

ELECTION OF 1832

CANDIDATES	ELECTORAL VOTE	POPULAR VOTE
Andrew Jackson Democratic	219	687,502
Henry Clay National Republican	49	530,189
John Floyd Nullifier	11	
William Wirt Antimasonic	7	

SECOND ADMINISTRATION

INAUGURATION: March 4, 1833; House of Representatives, Washington, D.C.

VICE PRESIDENT: Martin Van Buren

SECRETARY OF STATE: Edward Livingston; Louis McLane (from May 29, 1833); John Forsyth (from July 1, 1834)

SECRETARY OF THE TREASURY: Louis McLane; William J. Duane (from June 1, 1833); Roger B. Taney (from Sept. 23, 1833); Levi Woodbury (from July 1, 1834)

SECRETARY OF WAR: Lewis Cass

ATTORNEY GENERAL: Roger B. Taney; Benjamin F. Butler (from Nov. 18, 1833)

POSTMASTER GENERAL: William T. Barry; Amos Kendall (from May 1, 1835)

SECRETARY OF THE NAVY: Levi Woodbury; Mahlon Dickerson (from June 30, 1834)

SUPREME COURT APPOINTMENTS: James M. Wayne (1835); Roger B. Taney, Chief Justice (1836); Philip P. Barbour (1836)

23rd CONGRESS (March 4, 1833–March 4, 1835):
Senate: 20 Democrats; 20 National Republicans; 8 Others
House: 147 Democrats; 53 Antimasons; 60 Others

24th CONGRESS (March 4, 1835–March 4, 1837):
Senate: 27 Democrats; 25 Whigs
House: 145 Democrats; 98 Whigs

STATES ADMITTED: Arkansas (1836); Michigan (1837)

MARTIN VAN BUREN

In succeeding Andrew Jackson as President, Martin Van Buren—in a commanding sense—succeeded himself in the White House. Van Buren was, after all, the prime architect of the Democratic party structure that helped to elect Jackson. He managed Old Hickory's campaign and delivered the support of New York's powerful machine. After the election, he served Jackson as Secretary of State, Vice President, phrasemaker, and confidant. Their relationship was so close that a tired Jackson once considered resigning from the Presidency during his second term, permitting Van Buren to replace him. In short, there would have been no President Jackson, as we know him, without Martin Van Buren.

As Arthur M. Schlesinger, Jr., has written, "Van Buren's understanding of the new functions of public opinion, as well as of Congress, furnished the practical mechanisms which transformed Jackson's extraordinary popularity into the instruments of power. . . . Without them, the gains of Jacksonian democracy would have been impossible." Van Buren lacked Washington's grandeur, Jackson's dash, and Jefferson's patrician intellect. But for all his rough edges and weaknesses, he grasped intuitively three central political facts of the time: that Congress had declined in power and influence; that a stronger judiciary had emerged; and, pre-eminently, that executive power was to be gained by popular persuasion rather than by presidential pleading with Congress. The common man controlled the nation now, and the masses needed to be told the whys and hows of political processes. It was to the development of this presidential method, especially in Jackson's two terms, that Martin Van Buren applied his great political talent. He became in the process the United States' first systematic national politician.

Born on December 5, 1782, in the village of Kinderhook in New York's Co-

G. P. A. Healy's portrait of Van Buren hangs in the White House.

lumbia County, he was the son of Abraham and Maria (Hoes) Van Buren, both Dutch. Although a more sophisticated Van Buren would suggest in post-presidential retirement that his ancestors might have been nobles, his father was, in fact, a truck farmer and tavern keeper who fought in the Revolution, served as Kinderhook town clerk, raised his son in the Dutch Reformed Church, and owned slaves.

Traditionally, American Presidents lisp republican principles from their trundle beds and seem destined at twelve to command ships of state. Not so Van Buren. His education was limited to a few years at a provincial academy, and he openly confessed to a secondary intellect. He preferred light reading to heavy, and action to abstraction. At some point, however, he acquired a penchant for law and polemics, and at fourteen entered the law firm of Francis Silvester, a Federalist. He swept floors, served as scrivener, studied law, and, as a burgeoning Republican, talked himself out of a job. Van Buren then moved to New York City, where he campaigned for Jefferson in 1800—his political baptism—and pursued his law career under attorney William P. Van Ness, a disciple of Aaron Burr.

Little Van, so named because he was only five feet six inches tall, returned to Kinderhook, was admitted to the bar in 1803, and began a systematic ascent to the summits of local, state, and national power. He kept a strict and circumspect counsel, avoiding controversial commitments and uniting antagonistic factions whenever possible. He married a distant kinswoman, Hannah Hoes, on February 21, 1807 (she died twelve years later), and fathered four sons, one of whom, John, would share some of his father's distinction and promise as a leader in the Free-Soil movement. Another son, Abraham, was to serve during his father's Presidency as a White House secretary.

By 1808, the truck farmer's son was surrogate of Columbia County. In 1812, he was elected—on an anti-U.S. Bank platform—to the state senate. There he supported the War of 1812, the construction of the lucra-

tive Erie Canal, and the revision of New York State's constitution. Van Buren also sponsored a bill to abolish imprisonment for debt—one of the first legislators to do so in the United States.

During his second term as state senator, Van Buren was appointed New York State attorney general, and successfully prosecuted General William Hull for cowardice and neglect of duty in surrendering Detroit to the British in the War of 1812; Hull's sentence, however, was remanded by President Madison.

Van Buren slowly assumed command of New York's Republican "Bucktail" wing, which was formally committed to a strict adherence to Jeffersonian principles and opposed to DeWitt Clinton's tolerance for Federalists. In securing control of the Bucktails, Van Buren learned a lesson that would serve him well in the White House: the great advantage of a friendly press. His organ in Albany was the *Argus*, edited by hand-picked Van Buren disciples. Without a paper managed by "a sound, practicable, and above all discreet republican," he stated with candor, "we may hang our harps on the willows." In Washington, Francis Blair's friendly *Globe* would serve Van Buren's purposes with comparable efficiency.

Van Buren was elected to the United States Senate in 1821. Before leaving for Washington, however, he made certain that the New York sheep would not play while the "Red Fox of Kinderhook" (another of his many nicknames) was away: he sealed an already tightly capped party machine—since known as the Albany Regency. Its structural informality notwithstanding, the Regency governed political patronage, defined party policy, ran campaigns, and—after freewheeling, secret party caucuses—assured its members' public loyalty with the threat of prompt removal from office for any departure from the party line. Working in tandem with Tammany Hall in New York City, the Regency assured Martin Van Buren's hegemony in the state, which from 1830 to 1860 contained one-seventh of the population of the United States.

In 1824 Van Buren led William H. Crawford's unsuccessful presidential campaign against John Quincy Adams, Henry Clay, and—of all people—Andrew Jackson. But Van Buren swiftly learned the lessons of Adams' victory and carefully moved to unify the supporters of Jackson, Calhoun, and Crawford into a viable political force. The objective for 1828: an appealing synthesis of Jackson's popularity and Jefferson's principles, packaged and sold by a new Democratic party. To sew up New York's pivotal vote for the General, Van Buren himself gave up his Senate seat to run for governor of New York, thus adding his own popular name to the ticket.

Van Buren's tactical coalition won. It was a mean campaign, and his lieutenants sank low to win. It was a contest, they said, between "John Quincy Adams, who can write" and "Andrew Jackson, who can fight." This unfair campaign technique would one day help to unseat Van Buren himself as President. But it worked for Old Hickory, even though the Adams forces lowered their campaign to the same level. The General was in the White House.

Van Buren was back in Albany—but only for a short time. In two and a half months, he resigned as governor and was promptly named Jackson's Secretary of State. He was easily the most powerful man in either the official or "Kitchen Cabinet." As Secretary of State, Van Buren's achievements were impressive. The world's chancelleries had been initially appalled by the mercurial and crotchety frontier President, and Van Buren—cordial, discreet, and immaculate—buffered the fray. A French minister would praise Van Buren's "certain ease, which makes him superior, as a man of the world, to those of his compatriots I have seen until now." When Washington Irving was in the diplomatic corps, he noted that Van Buren was "one of the gentlest and most amiable men I have ever met with." Highly respected in London, Van Buren reached a settlement with the Crown on West Indian trade; he also negotiated American access to the Black Sea with Turkey and persuaded

RICHARD M. JOHNSON

After receiving only a plurality in the election of 1836, Richard Mentor Johnson became the sole Vice President ever elected by the Senate. Like Van Buren, he had been Jackson's personal choice, but in contrast to the suave Van Buren, Johnson was a frontiersman, born in Kentucky in 1780. He was a brilliant soldier and an eccentric and careless dresser. Thus he brought to the ticket an appeal to the backwoods vote that the fastidious Van Buren did not have. Although Johnson had been prominent in both the Kentucky and national legislatures, urging government-sponsored education, he was an inconspicuous Vice President. But he became a problem for his party in 1840. When the Democrats nominated the unmarried congressman in 1836, they knew that he was the father of two daughters by a mulatto girl. Not until 1840 did Southern opposition to him solidify, and then even Jackson thought Johnson would be "dead wait [sic]" on the ticket. Johnson was not renominated, but he ran anyway. The Whig campaign of 1840 centered on Harrison's victories over the Indians, and inadvertently reminded the voters that Johnson had allegedly killed Tecumseh during the Battle of the Thames. Barnstorming throughout the nation to the chant, "Rumpsey dumpsey, Colonel Johnson shot Tecumseh," he displayed his battle scars wherever he went. But the Democratic ticket was defeated and Johnson retired.

the French to pay American damage claims from the Napoleonic Wars.

But Van Buren's importance to Jackson, even as Secretary of State, remained primarily political. He and Jackson agreed that only with the support of a strong political party could the President exercise effective leadership. To build this base of power, the lessons learned in Albany were systematically applied. There was no such thing as nonpartisanship: to the faithful belonged the jobs, and the key was patronage. Largely administered by Van Buren, the spoils system was dangled over the heads of the politically uncertain. "We give no reasons for our removals," said Van Buren, and the opposition seized on the patronage concept to paint a corrupt portrait of the administration. Actually, the number of dismissals of government employees was relatively modest—estimates range from one-eleventh to one-eighth, about the same proportion that Jefferson had removed.

With equal intensity, Van Buren pressed hard for Jackson's legislation in Congress. He drafted the General's veto of Congress' bill authorizing federal investment in the sixty-mile Maysville Road in Kentucky. Such support, Van Buren argued, was an unconstitutional federal intrusion in state affairs—even if the state wanted the intrusion. Most of the time, however, Martin Van Buren preferred to operate outside of congressional chambers. In the corridors, in drawing rooms, in his offices, he wheeled and dealt, playing faction against faction, molding consensus toward his own ends, earning his titles "Red Fox" and "Little Magician."

Among his impressive political tricks was his disposal of Vice President Calhoun as a rival for succession to the Presidency. Like all good tricks, it was simply executed. In 1830 Jackson and Calhoun had clashed over the principle of nullification, which the Vice President had espoused. Van Buren dutifully reminded Old Hickory that Calhoun had also opposed Jackson's military intervention in Florida in 1818—and not without point, for Calhoun had assured General Jackson that he had supported the action.

In the famed Eaton affair, the political war escalated. Calhoun's wife and those of most Cabinet members had ostracized Secretary of War and Mrs. Eaton, persuaded that the couple had been living together long before the death of Mrs. Eaton's first husband. No doubt because his own wife, Rachel, had suffered gravely at the hands of rumormongers, Jackson decreed Peggy Eaton's virtue and championed her cause. But Cabinet husbands and wives remained undissuaded despite the suspension of Cabinet meetings by Jackson, who demanded that Peggy be invited to the social events of the Capital. In the ensuing stalemate the President found himself hog-tied. He could not provide the Whigs with a critical issue by firing all Calhoun men in his Cabinet, but neither could he capitulate and accept Eaton's resignation. Van Buren, who had valued the Eatons' friendship, reached into his magic hat and pulled out his own resignation! Jackson was nonplused until Old Kinderhook explained that his resignation as an apparent neutral in the imbroglio would make it possible for the entire Cabinet to resign. Van Buren's strategy worked; Eaton withdrew and Jackson ordered the rest of the Cabinet to follow suit. The Eaton embarrassment was thus cleverly resolved, and in the process Martin Van Buren earned himself the Vice Presidency in 1832.

In the interim Little Van served as minister to Great Britain while Congress was in recess. But when the reconvened Senate was asked to confirm his appointment, Calhoun openly opposed it. The Senate's tie vote gave him his opportunity for revenge: as Vice President he had the power to break the tie, and he gleefully voted Nay. Triumphant, he sneered: "It will kill him dead, sir, kill him dead. He will never kick, sir, never kick." But Senator Thomas Hart Benton could not agree. To a Calhoun lieutenant sitting beside him Benton observed: "You have broken a minister, and elected a Vice President." Benton was right. An angry Jackson chose Van Buren as his running mate in 1832, and in 1835 named him his successor in the White House.

In November, 1836, "Old Kinderhook" (Van Buren's campaign initials gave birth to the expression "O.K."), running on a Jacksonian platform of democracy versus aristocracy, was elected the eighth President of the United States. His chief rival was a general named William Henry Harrison.

It was a wild—and cruel—political era. As Vice President, Van Buren had felt the need to hide two pistols beneath his jacket. In the campaign of 1836, the redoubtable William Seward called Van Buren "a crawling reptile, whose only claim was that he had inveigled the confidence of a credulous, blind, dotard, old man." Even the staid John Quincy Adams recorded in his diary as perhaps credible a rumor that Van Buren was the illegitimate son of Aaron Burr. To his detractors, Van Buren was the American Talleyrand, devious, hypocritical, professionally noncommittal. "The searching look of his keen eyes," observed one hostile contemporary, "showed that he believed, with Talleyrand, that language was given to conceal thought." John Randolph said of Van Buren: "He rowed to his object with muffled oars." The mud was not restricted to one camp, however. Van Buren's own party organ, the *Globe*, had itself pilloried General Harrison as a "superannuated old woman . . . a red petticoat general" and referred to him as "the hero of forty defeats."

Seminole Indians attack a federal fort in Florida in the 1837 lithograph above. They refused to be moved west and fought fiercely for seven years.

Yet despite all the invective, Martin Van Buren entered the White House with roseate good cheer. In his Inaugural Address in March, 1837, he recalled that he was the first President born after the Revolution began; "whilst I contemplate with grateful reverence that memorable event," he said, "I feel that I belong to a later age. . . ." Then, he addressed himself to the issues of the time, revealing that the inclinations of the New York politician would not be discarded by the new Chief Executive. To help unify the Democratic party, he dismissed Southern nullification of federal law as an embarrassment," a "partial and temporary evil," and blandly appealed for the old caucus consensus, for "free and fearless discussion, blended with unimpaired fraternal feeling." On the eve of one of America's worst depressions, he assured the nation that prosperity was now "perfectly secured." Faced already with angry rumblings of secession, he hailed the Founding Fathers' respect for "distinct sovereignties" within the nation and for "institutions peculiar to the various portions" of the country. But he urged that the unrest of Southerners not be "exaggerated through sinister designs. . . ."

"I must go into the Presidential chair," Jackson's heir proclaimed, "the inflexible and uncompromising opponent of every attempt on the part of Congress to abolish slavery in the District of Columbia against the wishes of the slaveholding States, and also with a determination equally decided to resist the slightest interference with it in the States where it exists." Promising to veto any bill "conflicting with these views," Van Buren urged "forbearance" with "the delicacy of this subject [slavery]." He assured the nation that his beliefs were "in accordance with the spirit that actuated the venerated fathers of the Republic. . . ." "I throw myself without fear on [the country's] justice and its kindness," he said. "May her ways be ways of pleasantness and all her paths be peace."

But the nation's ways were not pleasant, nor was America kind—or particularly just —to the chief Albany regent. Within days of his accession, Van Buren faced a major na-

tional depression—the Panic of 1837—which was to plague his administration for the length of its days. Ironically, the Panic was largely due to the execution of and opposition to Jackson's Specie Circular. "In destroying the bank," Schlesinger writes, "Jackson had removed a valuable brake on credit expansion; and in sponsoring the system of [federal] deposit in state banks, he had accelerated the tendencies toward inflation."

The basic cause of the crash was business' defiance of Jackson's hard-money policy in overextending paper credit to finance the boom in land speculation, manufacturing, transportation, and banking that had begun under Adams. Hard money was withdrawn en masse from the banks to pay for Western lands. The wheat crop of 1836 failed badly. The price of cotton fell by almost one-half. Food and fuel prices and rents soared, sometimes doubled. New Yorkers rioted over the cost of flour. Banks and businesses collapsed

Also struck by a depression, England and France asked Van Buren for payment of debts in hard money (above). But their reduction of American imports and tightened credit had already worsened the specie shortage here.

under pressure from England and Europe for repayment of short-term loans precisely when hard-money deposits were being depleted. Suffering was rife, poorhouses were crowded. The government alone lost nine million dollars in the failure of state banks. Nearly every bank in the country suspended specie payments.

By May, 1837, President Van Buren could temporize no longer. He summoned Congress into special session to deal with the Panic. His own solutions: stand fast for hard money; remove the federal deposits from all banks, state and national; establish an independent treasury that would wrest control of the government from the moneyed class. But a predictable coalition of state banking interests, Whigs, and conservative Democrats prevented passage of his Independent Treasury bill. Not until 1840, the last year of his administration, did the bill pass. Van Buren would hail its passage as a "Second Declaration of Independence," and would delight in having won Jackson's battle with Nicholas Biddle, but the Independent Treasury, in fact, would not be established on a permanent basis until 1846.

Van Buren's struggle for an Independent Treasury was by no means his only achievement as President. Despite his repeated belief that the federal government had no constitutional right to intervene in the economy, he issued in March, 1840, an Executive Order limiting to a ten-hour day the work of all laborers on federal projects. In 1837, Canada seized in American waters the U.S. steamer *Caroline*, which was illegally carrying supplies to the insurgents in a Canadian uprising. Van Buren defied both British bluster and American jingoist cries for vengeance by disarming intervening American zealots and smoothing the Crown's ruffled feathers. Similarly, in 1840, when Maine citizens clashed with Canadians over the boundary of the Northeast United States, Van Buren quietly ended the conflict and initiated a diplomatic dialogue concluded in the Webster-Ashburton Treaty of 1842.

Despite these displays of executive authority, the image of Van Buren as an eva-sive manipulator, unwilling to take an unpopular stand, remained. Even Jackson lost patience with his old alter ego when Van Buren, fearing war with Mexico, opposed both Jackson and Sam Houston on the annexation of Texas. Old Hickory looked increasingly to James K. Polk as a more tractable heir to his tradition.

Van Buren's ambivalence was due not only to political machination but equally to a highly limited view of the presidential and federal roles in the life of the nation and to a fundamentalist approach to the principles of Jefferson. This interpretation of Jeffersonianism was restricted to an embrace of states' rights as a screen for federal inaction and of limited government to perpetuate the status quo. Van Buren's view of the Constitution was ambiguous. On the one hand, he anointed it as "a sacred instrument," while on the other, he defied one of its fundamental principles by favoring an elective judiciary. He approved of Congress' explicit right to collect taxes, but he felt that the Constitution gave Congress no authority to spend these taxes—even after all basic expenses of government had been met —on internal improvements: public roads, schools, or canals. He also believed that the federal government had no constitutional right to correct inequities, resolve crises, or influence events. His fight for the Independent Treasury excepted, Van Buren's administration was the apotheosis of laissez-faire government. In international affairs, he declared his opposition to "all forms of . . . alliances." Precedents set in our foreign relations, he explained, left "little to [his] discretion, unless, indeed, I were willing to run counter to the lights of experience and the known opinions of my constituents." Historians also agree that his appointments, even on the highest levels, were capricious and inept. A "little magician" in securing and sustaining power for others, Van Buren himself was weak in the exercise of power.

Van Buren's perennial fence-sitting earned him enemies everywhere. He was blamed, as Hoover would be blamed, not only for the depression during his administration but for failure to combat it head on. He was regarded as proslavery in the North and antislavery in the South. And despite his victory over Biddle and the announcement of an Independent Treasury, he faced, in the campaign of 1840, a most hostile nation.

The tone of the campaign—one of the most visceral in American history—was sounded by Pennsylvania Congressman Charles Ogle in the House of Representatives on April 14, 1840. Commenting on a routine appropriation of $3,665 for White House maintenance and repairs, Ogle began an impassioned appeal for the election of William Henry Harrison, with an incredible assault on the person of the President. Van Buren, declared Ogle, wore the same perfume fancied by Queen Victoria, actually preferred Madeira to hard cider, and used "Fanny Kemble green glass finger cups." Moreover, Ogle raged on, the President had purchased—in Europe of all places—Brussels carpets, "dazzling foreign ornaments," French taborets for royal audiences, and other "womanish" contrivances. Van Buren, he said, actually slept in a Louis XV bed and used "gold-framed mirrors 'as big as a barn door' to behold his plain Republican self."

Reigning from his "royal establishment" at the cost of the nation, Ogle said, Van Buren looked down upon the people as "suckers" and "fawning spaniels" as he luxuriated in "sloth and effeminacy." The cost of three White House curtains alone, Ogle maintained, would build at least three goodly log cabins with money to spare to "treat the folks who came to the '*raisin*' with as much HARD CIDER as they can stow away under the belts of their linsey-woolsey hunting shirts."

The campaign was on. Like the Democrats in 1828, the Whigs nominated a military hero, William Henry Harrison. And also like the Democrats in 1828, the Whigs equated refinement with sexual aberration and intellect with weakness.

In contrast to Van Buren's sybaritic and royal splendor, Harrison was hailed as a frontier messiah, champion of the little people of whom God in His wisdom had made so many. When the votes were counted, it was found that many conservative Democrats had defected to the Whigs, and Old Tippecanoe had won by a plurality of 150,000 in a smashing electoral victory of 234 votes to 60. Van Buren even lost his own state, New York.

Of the Presidency, Van Buren said, agreeing with Jefferson, that "the two happiest days of his life were those of his entrance upon the office and of his surrender of it." He returned to Kinderhook, moving into "Lindenwald," a remodeled Italo-Gothic mansion. In 1844, after turning down President Tyler's politically motivated offer of a seat on the Supreme Court, Van Buren tried for the Democratic presidential nomination, but failed because of his continued opposition to the annexation of Texas, a slave state. In 1848, he was renominated by antislavery Democrats (the "Barnburners") in coalition with Free-Soilers and liberal Whigs. The Democrats nominated Lewis Cass; the Whigs, Zachary Taylor. With the New York Democrats thus split, Taylor carried the state and won the election. In the course of the 1848 campaign, Van Buren finally concluded that slavery and freedom could not coexist and wrote a moving appeal for free soil with his son John and future presidential candidate Samuel Tilden.

In retirement, besides playing patroon at Lindenwald, Van Buren traveled for several years in Europe. Without fear of political retribution, he was able to poke around ancestral Dutch towns and indulge himself in the purchase of the European finery he enjoyed so much. At the Villa Falangola in Sorrento, Italy, in 1854, the seventy-one-year-old former Chief Executive wrote his story for his countrymen.

Back in Kinderhook, Van Buren seethed over the policies of Presidents Pierce and Buchanan. In 1861, mourning the commencement of the Civil War, he expressed his confidence in Abraham Lincoln. Plagued by asthma for many months, Martin Van Buren died in the second year of the conflict, on July 29, 1862.

—WILSON SULLIVAN

A PICTURE PORTFOLIO

On this 1836 campaign item, candidate Martin Van Buren is encircled in a star surrounded by a star-studded horseshoe.

FROM THE WARDS
TO THE WHITE HOUSE

His soldierly posture and immaculate grooming made Martin Van Buren appear taller than his 5 feet 6 inches. This portrait was painted when he was governor of New York, in 1829, by Henry Inman. The building in the background is the Albany capitol.

Martin Van Buren was as shrewd, manipulating, and intensely partisan a politician as his reputation suggested. But if he was indeed the prototype of the latter-day ward heeler, he differed from the Tweeds and Pendergasts of American history because he sought and won power for himself through high elected office, not by managing the careers of others. Fighting tooth and nail in political arenas, he was, at the same time, as honest as he was intriguing, as generous in his public relations as he was wily in his politics. He could not understand why he should not be able to maintain personal friendships with political enemies; it was usually his opponents, not he, who confused the two.

As a staunch young Republican, he learned law in the office of an equally staunch Federalist. After battling his way to the leadership of New York State's Republican organization, he managed, in 1820, to have a Republican legislature elected in the same year that Federalist DeWitt Clinton was reelected governor. A year later, he went to Washington as a senator, and in 1827 he joined the political camp of General Andrew Jackson. Van Buren's own power had been solidified by the Albany *Argus*, a partisan newspaper owned in part by his brother-in-law; and the senator, who was perhaps the first American politician to understand the importance of a friendly press, began employing the *Argus* to strengthen Jackson's position in the Northeast. To help the General carry New York in the presidential election of 1828, Van Buren ran for governor. Both men won, and Van Buren, after just two and a half months in Albany, returned to Washington as Jackson's Secretary of State and, next, as his Vice President. Eight years later, Van Buren became the eighth President of the United States.

The rejected Minister,
*We never can make him President,
without first making him Vice-president.*
Vide webb.

In the struggle for power between John C. Calhoun and Martin Van Buren during Jackson's first administration, the Little Magician from New York always managed to turn the Vice President's triumphs into defeats. When Calhoun cast the deciding vote in the Senate against the appointment of Van Buren as minister to England, the Southerner thought that he had disposed of Van Buren once and for all. But as the cartoon at left indicates, the rejected minister came home to take the Vice Presidency away from Calhoun in 1832 and to become Jackson's obvious heir apparent. In 1837, after Van Buren had beaten Whig candidates William Henry Harrison, Hugh L. White, and Daniel Webster, Calhoun had to watch the scene depicted below: Van Buren's inauguration.

249

The snuffbox above, decorated with an idealized portrait of presidential candidate Martin Van Buren, was a souvenir of the campaign of 1836.

Nothing in the Little Magician's bag of tricks was equal to the crisis that burst in his face a few weeks after he took office. Andrew Jackson's execution of the Bank of the United States and the resulting Specie Circular of 1836—which demanded payment in hard money for all government lands—led to the Panic of 1837. The cartoon at right makes it clear that Old Hickory (Lady Macbeth) and his allies (a Southern planter who dealt in specie anyway and a city workingman who had no money and could also afford to be anti-Bank) were the real assassins of commerce, but its ghost haunts not them but Van Buren. While it may have been true that the new President was almost as frightened as he appears here, he was not helpless; and when some of his advisers suggested that he rescind the Specie Circular, Van Buren resisted the temptation. He labored, instead, to establish a permanent arrangement under which the nation's finances could be conducted: an Independent Treasury.

TROUBLED TIMES

Triggered by Jackson's victory over the National Bank, a depression engulfed the country during Van Buren's administration. "The less government interferes with private pursuits the better for the general prosperity," the President said; and instead of suggesting ways to end the depression, he turned his energies to winning passage of his Independent Treasury bill, under which all federal funds would be kept in government vaults, not in state or

250

private banks. The bill passed in 1840, but in the meantime even foreign affairs were affected by the financial problems. American inability to pay debts to creditors worsened Anglo-American relations, which were already tense due to the efforts of United States citizens to aid Canadian insurrectionists. In 1837, on the Niagara River, Canadian troops seized an American ship, the *Caroline*, which was bringing arms to the rebels. One American was killed, and in response to patriotic indignation, Van Buren sent troops to the border. Despite the President's pleas for neutrality in Canadian troubles, further incidents kept tensions high. Then, in 1839, Canadians began cutting timber in the Aroostook area, claimed by Maine. War seemed likely until Van Buren dispatched Winfield Scott to arrange a truce. Anglo-American differences were not settled until 1842, but by then Tyler, not Van Buren, was the occupant of the White House.

MACBETH.   BANK-OH'S! GHOST.

NO HOG AND HOMINY

Soon after the widower-President and his four sons moved into the White House, Dolley Madison came to call. Appalled by the conspicuous absence of a woman, the former First Lady turned matchmaker and sent for her pretty young South Carolina cousin, Angelica Singleton, who was just the right age for Abraham, Van Buren's eldest son. Less than a year later, Washington had its hostess. In the portrait by Henry Inman above, Angelica stands alongside a bust of the President.

When Martin Van Buren became President, he practiced what he had always preached: that political enemies could be personal friends. A long-time gourmet, the Chief Executive employed an English chef and, with characteristic generosity, invited Whig and Jacksonian alike

to frequent dinner parties, kept small to ensure the quality of the cuisine. Even John Calhoun and Henry Clay came often. Complimenting their host, his comradely enemies prepared to stab his political back—fair play according to Van Buren's own standards. What, his opponents asked publicly, was the meaning of all these exclusive little dinners? Was this elegant host who allegedly redecorated the Executive Mansion with European finery really a Democrat? A good American, they charged, was not even allowed in the White House if his shoes were muddy. The Whigs, said a Whig, were happy with "fried meat and gravy, or hog and hominy," and, of course, hard cider. Van Buren had no complaint: these were the tactics he had himself developed to elect Andrew Jackson to the Presidency in 1828. Turned against him in 1840, they beat him.

The romanticized etching above of Tiber Creek and the southern grounds of the White House was made in 1839 or 1840. About forty years later, the creek was filled in and was transformed into Constitution Avenue.

DISAPPOINTMENTS

In 1848, Martin Van Buren bolted the Democratic party and ran for the Presidency on the Free-Soil ticket. Eight years earlier, as Whigs throughout the nation gleefully chanted "Van is a used-up man," he had lost the office to William Henry Harrison. But he had subsequently toured the West and Southwest, demonstrating that he was not at all used up and tightening his seemingly secure grip on the 1844 nomination. At the last minute, however, his refusal to come out unequivocally for the annexation of Texas had cost him the nomination, and James Polk had won the candidacy and the Presidency. But in the next four years, the old habits of hesitation and fence-sitting were replaced by candor and forcefulness, as Van Buren clearly expressed his opinion that slavery should not be extended. When, in 1848, the Democrats nominated Lewis Cass, the old Barnburner wing of the party joined with other antislavery groups to form the Free-Soil party, and Van Buren was named to head its ticket. He won enough votes in New York to deprive Cass of victory in a close race with Zachary Taylor. In the last years of his life, Van Buren broke his own precedent of not allowing political differences to affect his personal relationships; he staunchly refused to have anything to do with President James Buchanan because of the latter's failure to avert the Civil War.

The cartoon above reminded voters in 1848 of the Free-Soil candidate's legendary political straddling—a posture that Martin Van Buren had largely abandoned. The daguerreotype opposite may have been made that year.

FACTS IN SUMMARY: MARTIN VAN BUREN

CHRONOLOGY

UNITED STATES		VAN BUREN
Peace negotiations begin in Paris	1782	Born December 5
Washington's Farewell Address	1796	Becomes clerk in law firm of Francis Silvester
John Adams elected President		
	1800	Made delegate to the congressional caucus in Troy
Jefferson inaugurated as President	1801	Works in New York law office as clerk
Louisiana Purchase	1803	Admitted to the bar
Lewis and Clark expedition		Becomes law partner of James Van Allen
	1807	Marries Hannah Hoes
Madison elected President	1808	Appointed surrogate of Columbia County, N.Y.
War with Great Britain	1812	Elected to New York State senate
Washington burned	1814	
Treaty of Ghent		
Battle of New Orleans	1815	Chosen regent of the University of New York
Monroe elected President	1816	Re-elected senator
		Chosen attorney general of New York

UNITED STATES		VAN BUREN
Bank panic and depression	1819	Wife dies
		Removed from attorney generalship
Missouri Compromise	1820	
	1821	Attends third New York State constitutional convention
		Elected to U.S. Senate
Monroe Doctrine	1823	
	1824	Supports Crawford for Presidency
John Quincy Adams elected President	1825	
	1827	Re-elected senator
Tariff of Abominations	1828	Supports Jackson for Presidency
Jackson elected President		Elected governor of New York
	1829	Appointed Secretary of State
Antimasonic party established	1831	Resigns as Secretary of State
Nullification controversy	1832	Appointment as minister to Great Britain rejected by Senate
Jackson vetoes Bank recharter		Elected Vice President
Jackson re-elected		

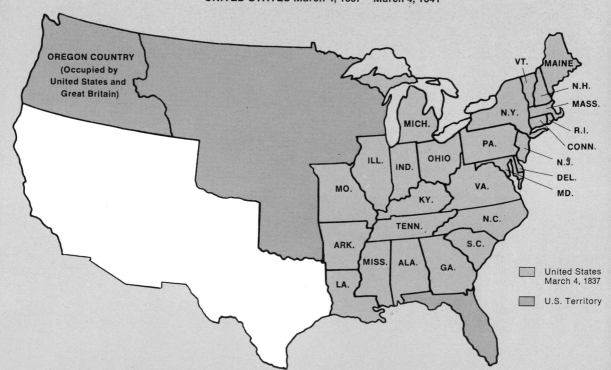

UNITED STATES March 4, 1837 — March 4, 1841

OREGON COUNTRY (Occupied by United States and Great Britain)

VT. MAINE N.H. MASS. N.Y. R.I. CONN. N.J. DEL. MD. MICH. PA. ILL. IND. OHIO MO. KY. VA. TENN. N.C. ARK. S.C. MISS. ALA. GA. LA.

United States March 4, 1837

U.S. Territory

Whig party formed	1834	
Texas declares independence	1836	*Elected President*
Siege of the Alamo		
Specie Circular issued		
Bank panic and depression	1837	*Fights for Independent Treasury*
Caroline affair	1838	*Issues neutrality proclamation*
Aroostook War	1839	*Sends General Winfield Scott to Maine to negotiate truce*
Harrison elected President	1840	*Independent Treasury established*
		Loses bid for re-election
Tyler becomes President	1841	*Retires to Kinderhook*
Independent Treasury Act repealed		
Webster-Ashburton Treaty	1842	
Polk elected President	1844	*Tries unsuccessfully for Democratic presidential nomination*
Texas annexed	1845	
War with Mexico	1846	
Oregon settlement		
Independent Treasury revived		
Wilmot Proviso		
Treaty of Guadalupe Hidalgo	1848	*Runs unsuccessfully for President on Free-Soil ticket*
Taylor elected President		*Retires*
Compromise of 1850	1850	
Buchanan elected President	1856	
Harpers Ferry	1859	
Lincoln elected President	1860	
Civil War begins	1861	
Battle of Shiloh	1862	*Dies July 24*

BIOGRAPHICAL FACTS

BIRTH: Kinderhook, N.Y., Dec. 5, 1782
ANCESTRY: Dutch
FATHER: Abraham Van Buren; b. Albany, N.Y., Feb. 17, 1737; d. April 8, 1817
FATHER'S OCCUPATION: Farmer
MOTHER: Maria Hoes Van Alen Van Buren; b. 1747; d. Feb. 16, 1817
BROTHERS: Lawrence (1786–1868); Abraham (1788–1836)
SISTERS: Derike (1777–1865); Hannah (1780–?)
HALF BROTHER: James Isaac Van Alen (1776–1870); two others
WIFE: Hannah Hoes; b. Kinderhook, N.Y., March 8, 1783; d. Albany, N.Y., Feb. 5, 1819
MARRIAGE: Kinderhook, N.Y., Feb. 21, 1807

CHILDREN: Abraham (1807–1873); John (1810–1866); Martin (1812–1855); Smith Thompson (1817–1876)
HOME: Lindenwald, Kinderhook, N.Y.
EDUCATION: Village schools; studied in law office
RELIGIOUS AFFILIATION: Dutch Reformed
OCCUPATIONS BEFORE PRESIDENCY: Lawyer; politician
PRE-PRESIDENTIAL OFFICES: Surrogate of Columbia County, N.Y.; New York State Senator; Attorney General of New York; Delegate to Third New York State Constitutional Convention; U.S. Senator; Governor of New York; Secretary of State; Vice President
POLITICAL PARTY: Democratic, during Presidency; Free-Soil, from 1848
AGE AT INAUGURATION: 54
OCCUPATION AFTER PRESIDENCY: Politician
DEATH: Kinderhook, N.Y., July 24, 1862
PLACE OF BURIAL: Kinderhook Cemetery, Kinderhook, N.Y.

ELECTION OF 1836

CANDIDATES	ELECTORAL VOTE	POPULAR VOTE
Martin Van Buren Democratic	170	765,483
William H. Harrison Whig	73	
Hugh L. White Whig	26	739,795
Daniel Webster Whig	14	
Willie P. Mangum Anti-Jacksonian	11	

THE VAN BUREN ADMINISTRATION

INAUGURATION: March 4, 1837; the Capitol, Washington, D.C.
VICE PRESIDENT: Richard M. Johnson
SECRETARY OF STATE: John Forsyth
SECRETARY OF THE TREASURY: Levi Woodbury
SECRETARY OF WAR: Joel R. Poinsett
ATTORNEY GENERAL: Benjamin F. Butler; Felix Grundy (from Sept. 1, 1838); Henry D. Gilpin (from Jan. 11, 1840)
POSTMASTER GENERAL: John M. Niles
SECRETARY OF THE NAVY: Mahlon Dickerson; James K. Paulding (from July 1, 1838)
SUPREME COURT APPOINTMENTS: John Catron (1837); John McKinley (1837); Peter V. Daniel (1841)
25th CONGRESS (March 4, 1837–March 4, 1839):
Senate: 30 Democrats; 18 Whigs; 4 Others
House: 108 Democrats; 107 Whigs; 24 Others
26th CONGRESS (March 4, 1839–March 4, 1841):
Senate: 28 Democrats; 22 Whigs
House: 124 Democrats; 118 Whigs

WILLIAM
HENRY
HARRISON

We could meet the Whigs on the field of argument and beat them without effort," claimed the Jacksonian New York *Evening Post*. "But when they lay down the weapons of argument and attack us with musical notes, what can we do?" When the election of 1840 ended, William Henry Harrison had, as politician Philip Hone put it, been "sung into the Presidency."

The Whigs had deliberately conducted a campaign fat with songs, slogans, and chants, and thin on real issues. Attempting to beat the Jacksonian incumbent at the Jacksonian game, they selected as their candidate the hero of Tippecanoe, casting him in Andrew Jackson's image, assuming for themselves the role of the people's party, and depicting President Martin Van Buren as a fop with indulgent tastes and highfalutin ways: "Old Tip he wears a homespun coat, He has no ruffled shirt-wirt-wirt. But Mat he has the golden plate, And he's a little squirt-wirt-wirt."

When a Jacksonian newspaper in Baltimore, alluding to Harrison's lack of intellectual depth, suggested that the candidate would be content with a log cabin and a barrel of hard cider, the Whigs immediately seized upon the idea and turned it to their advantage. In an era when Davy Crockett was a hero epitomizing masculine virtues, a log cabin and hard cider presidential candidate was made to order.

The "log cabin" in which the candidate was born on February 9, 1773, was a three-story brick mansion at "Berkeley," the Harrison family plantation in Charles City County, Virginia. His father, Benjamin, was a wealthy planter and a signer of the Declaration of Independence. Tutored privately at home until 1787, William Henry Harrison then entered Hampden-Sidney College, and after graduating, became a medical student. In 1791, Harrison changed

The picture of Harrison at left is probably the first daguerreotype ever made of a President in office.

his mind about being a physician and enlisted in the United States Infantry.

"All this story about the log cabin . . . is a mean fraud," the Democrats protested. But the Whigs persisted on a technicality. Avoiding reference to Old Tip's birthplace, they pictured him on their posters as the rough-hewn, hard-drinking, plow-pushing farmer of North Bend, Ohio, where, sure enough, Harrison did own a log cabin. In 1795, Lieutenant Harrison, stationed in Ohio, had become engaged to Anna Symmes, daughter of a prosperous North Bend farmer and judge. Before the wedding, he had bought a piece of land and built for his bride a five-room log cabin. Three years later he resigned from the Army and began to improve his property and take an active part in the affairs of the Northwest Territory. By 1840 the log cabin was only a corner of a much-annexed house—but it became the center of the Whig campaign.

Making the most of the symbol, the Whigs built a network of log cabin campaign headquarters, gave out log cabin songbooks, and dispensed log cabin cider. When the Jacksonians pointed out that Whiggery was a conglomeration of rich bankers, merchants, and planters, they failed to impress the voters. No matter who was behind the party, its campaigners, such as honest Abe Lincoln, the Rail Splitter, championed Old Tip in the vocabulary of the frontier. Even Chang and Eng, the famous Siamese twins, announced their collective support of Harrison. Against such forces, the Democrats found all their logic wasted, and by the time they came down to the Whig level, they found themselves in the path of a ball rolling too fast to be stopped:

What has caused the great commotion; motion, motion, Our country through?
It is the ball a rolling on.
For Tippecanoe and Tyler too—Tippecanoe and Tyler too.

Throughout the campaign, the Democrats called Harrison "Granny" (he was sixty-seven when he was nominated) and "General Mum" because of his reluctance to speak out on major issues. Pointing out that "all his ambitious efforts in legislative assemblies, as in the field, [were] unfortunate failures," they noted his "total want of qualifications."

While it was true that Harrison had suffered a number of political embarrassments and was at the time of his nomination nothing more than a county recorder in Ohio, he had had long experience in politics. In 1799, as the first representative to Congress from the Northwest Territory, he was instrumental in securing passage of a bill that divided the vast land into two smaller territories: Ohio and Indiana. In 1800 Harrison was appointed governor of the Indiana Territory. His principal problems as governor were slavery and Indians. In 1791, he had been a member of an abolition society, yet after 1802 he took the position that citizens of the territory should have the right to own slaves. It is possible that Harrison simply changed his mind. It is also possible that he opposed both slavery and the right of the federal government to regulate or curb property rights. An early Harrison biographer, Dorothy Goebel, suggests that he sided with the proslavery factions because most Indianians favored the institution.

On matters of criminal law, Harrison earned a reputation for being fair and compassionate, deploring the prevailing practice of punishing Indians for crimes committed against whites but ignoring crimes of whites against Indians. On issues of property, however, he was less magnanimous. President Jefferson had instructed him to secure as much Indian land for the United States as possible, and in 1802 Harrison was awarded full power to negotiate and conclude treaties. Since the Indians were badly organized, it was not difficult to purchase huge tracts of land from a needy tribe.

About 1805, two Shawnee brothers, Tecumseh and Tenskwatawa, known as the Prophet, began to work against United States expansion. While the Prophet warned against whisky and intertribal warfare, Tecumseh went from tribe to tribe, organizing a united front. So successful was the work of the Shawnee brothers that the United States was unable to arrange any significant land deals with the Indians of the Northwest Ter-

This portrait of Anna Symmes Harrison hangs in the house of her grandchild, Benjamin Harrison.

ritory from 1806 until 1809. Then, on September 30, 1809, Harrison managed—through a careful combination of fair bargaining, whisky distribution, and threats—to conclude the Treaty of Fort Wayne with the Miami tribe, which transferred two and a half million acres of Indian land to the United States. Tecumseh refused to recognize the deal, claiming that the land was not the Miami's to sell. After a meeting between the governor and Tecumseh in 1810, Harrison reported to President Madison that he had explained to the Indian chief that the treaty was legal and that the United States now wished to survey the land. According to Harrison, Tecumseh replied: "When you speak to me of annuities I look at the land and pity the women and children. . . . Should you cross [into Indian Territory] I assure you it will be productive of bad consequences." This Harrison called Tecumseh's "harangue"; he told the President that the Indians were the pawns of the British. Madison, however, was concerned with the possibilities of battle in West Florida and, wanting no military diversion in the Northwest, instructed Harrison not to cross the boundary just yet.

On August 22, 1811, Harrison finally received permission to assemble forces. A month later, while Tecumseh was away, Harrison led a thousand troops across the old boundary and slowly advanced toward the Prophet's encampment in an Indian town located where the Tippecanoe River empties into the Wabash. On October 1, the soldiers stopped to erect Fort Harrison, and they did not reach the vicinity of the town until November 6. As they approached, Harrison's officers advised him to attack; the governor was inclined to agree, but the President's orders had been specific: no effort should be made to take the town by force until the Prophet had been given the option to abandon it voluntarily. Thus an armistice was negotiated with the Prophet's messengers, and discussions were scheduled for the next day, November 7. The soldiers camped for the night by the Tippecanoe River.

At 4 A.M., the Indians attacked. In a short and bloody battle, 188 Americans and a few dozen Indians were killed or wounded. After the initial rout, American numerical superiority began to tell and on November 8 the town, abandoned by the Indians, was taken by the Americans and burned.

The Battle of Tippecanoe accomplished nothing except to drive the Indians into the outstretched arms of the British. Harrison himself was both praised and criticized. He had indeed performed bravely and had erected a fort that would be valuable to the United States during the coming war; but there were many critics who thought that he should have attacked the Indians first, others who accused him of being careless about his selection of a campsite, and still others who claimed that he had no right being where he was in the first place.

Nevertheless, Harrison, who had been commissioned a brigadier general of the Army, was appointed supreme commander in the Northwest in September, 1812. His chief responsibility was to raise, feed, and clothe an army for defense against further British advances. When Perry defeated the British fleet on Lake Erie on September 10, 1813, Harrison immediately led his troops toward Detroit, capturing it on September 29. The British retreated into Canada, and Harrison pursued, overtaking them at a little town on the Thames River. There, a battle was fought, the British fled, Tecumseh was killed, and Indian participation in the War of 1812 was ended. As the British never tried to re-take the area, Harrison's duties became routine; he resigned his commission and returned to his farm at North Bend.

In 1816 he was elected to the House of Representatives, where he became a follower of Henry Clay. Harrison became a state senator in 1819, but failed to win re-election—probably because of his ambiguous stand on slavery. Six years later, he won a United States Senate seat and resumed his association with Clay, through whose influence he was appointed, in 1828, minister to Colombia. He did not distinguish himself there, for he was outspokenly sympathetic with the republican opponents of Simón Bolívar.

Harrison was a Whig for the same reason that Daniel Webster, Henry Clay, and John Quincy Adams were Whigs: he was opposed to Andrew Jackson. After the sweeping Democratic victory of 1828, abolitionists and slaveowners, anti-Bank men and pro-Bank men, Masons and Antimasons, Neofederalists and states' rights advocates, champions of the tariff and crusaders against it, found it convenient to blame the Jacksonians for whatever they did not like. Thus the Whig party was formed.

In 1836 Harrison was one of three Whig candidates for President; he proved an effective vote getter. Four years later, bypassing Clay and Webster, whose views were too well-known to assure victory, the Whigs again nominated the popular, noncommittal, and tractable William Henry Harrison and refused the singing voice of no man, woman, or child in this first musical campaign.

The beautiful girls, God bless their souls,
souls, souls, The country through.
Will all, to a man, do all they can
For Tippecanoe and Tyler too.

All the charges and doubts about the battles of Tippecanoe and the Thames were revived by the Jacksonians during the campaign. Accusing Harrison of having "cannon fever," the Democrats called him a "*sham hero.*" They pointed out that Harrison had resigned his commission from the Army before the end of the War of 1812, thus letting his country down "in the time of her utmost need." Moreover, the Jacksonians insisted that Vice President Richard M. Johnson, who had served as a colonel under Harrison in the War of 1812, had shot Tecumseh.

But, the Whigs countered, what had Van Buren accomplished in the Indian wars?

When Martin was housed like a chattel,
Opposed to the war as you know,
Our hero was foremost in battle,
And conquered at Tippecanoe.

How did Harrison react to the utterly tasteless campaign? We can only conclude that if he had any objections to it, he kept them to himself. Yet he was a considerate, genial, and generous man, and his success, Miss Goebel, his biographer, suggests, was probably due to his "fine personality"; he attracted attention with his character, rather than with his political record, which was mediocre at best. He would promise anything to a friend, and if sincerity alone could keep promises, he would never have reneged on one. Unfortunately, he promised Cabinet posts two and three times over, and after his election, he was besieged at North Bend and in Washington by spoils seekers. As a British traveler wrote: "Whoever called to pay him a visit was sure to be asked to dinner; whoever called for a place [in the government] was sure to get a promise; whoever hinted at a want of money was sure to receive a draft; until it became the common talk that the President was overdrawing his account, overpromising his partisans, and overfeeding his friends."

He was an old man, and all the activity was taxing. On March 27, 1841, he came down with pneumonia; he suffered a relapse on April 3, and around midnight said: "Sir—I wish you to understand the true principles of Government. I wish them carried out. I ask nothing more." The words were assumed to be addressed to the absent Vice President, John Tyler. On April 4, one month after becoming President, he became the first to die in office. As John Quincy Adams said, Harrison was "taken away thus providentially from the evil to come."

—DAVID JACOBS

W H Harrison

A PICTURE PORTFOLIO

This flag was part of the torrent of paraphernalia that helped sweep Harrison to victory in the election of 1840.

KURZ & ALLISON LITHOGRAPH

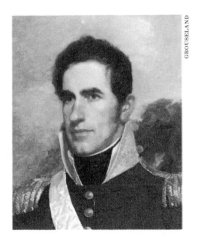

GROUSELAND

Harrison, above, was named governor of Indiana Territory in 1800.

INDIAN-FIGHTER

Sell a country! Why not sell the air, the clouds, and the great sea. . . ." Tecumseh, a Shawnee chief, was furious because some tribes were selling their lands to the expanding United States. His efforts to put an end to the practice were successful, and Governor William Henry Harrison of the Indiana Territory found it all but impossible to buy new areas. In 1809, however, he was able to conclude a deal with the Miami, a deal that Tecumseh refused to recognize. Two years later, Harrison led his troops into the disputed territory while Tecumseh was away; the result was the bloody, but almost meaningless, Battle of Tippecanoe on November 7, 1811. Appointed supreme commander of the Army of the Northwest in 1812, Harrison engaged Tecumseh again at the Battle of the Thames in 1813. The chief was killed, and Harrison's reputation as an Indian-fighter and a hero was solidified. He did not consider himself an Indian-hater, however, and when a Hoosier publicly suggested that he was, Harrison sued him for slander and won the case.

The Battle of Tippecanoe (left) was, Harrison wrote, the worst defeat the Indians had received "since their acquaintance with the white people." Actually, American casualties exceeded those of the Indians, although the latter were driven off.

The log cabin and a barrel of hard cider were the trade-marks of Harrison's campaign, but in the poster below, a heralding angel implies that Old Tippecanoe's candidacy was blessed by heaven, too.

OUR CAUSE OUR COUNTRY. OUR CHAMPION GENERAL

W^M. H. HARRISON, OUR BRAVE DEFENDER.

J. PIERSON.

BENJAMIN HARRISON HOME

LOG CABIN
CAMPAIGN

When William Henry Harrison was a Whig candidate for President in 1836, Nicholas Biddle, former president of the Bank of the United States, suggested that he "say not one single word about his principles or his creed—let him say nothing—promise nothing . . . [not] a single word about what he thinks now and will do hereafter." Harrison lost that election, but he remembered Biddle's advice four years later when he ran for the Presidency once again. In this campaign, the wealthy Ohio planter was represented as a simple backwoodsman; his dubious achievement at the Tippecanoe was hailed as a major act of military heroism. When an unsympathetic Democratic newspaper suggested that given "a barrel of Hard Cider, and . . . a pension of $2,000 a year," Harrison would be content to "sit the remainder of his days in his Log Cabin . . . and study moral philosophy," the Whigs cleverly turned the derogatory words into their campaign theme. In the months before the election, issues and programs were ignored; the Presidency would be won by the candidate who proved himself to be nearest to the people. When the log cabin campaign was over, Harrison had defeated Martin Van Buren by an electoral vote of 234 to 60.

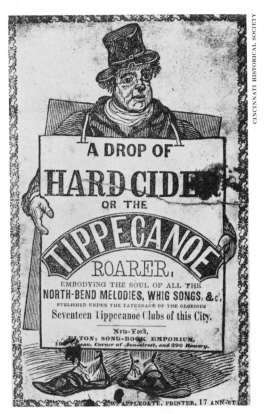

The Whigs promoted General Harrison's candidacy with hard-cider song sheets like the one above, which indicated that there were seventeen Tippecanoe clubs in New York City alone. Log cabins were built as campaign headquarters.

"The ball a rolling on" for the Whig team was more than just a campaign slogan in 1840. Pushing a huge paper ball (above) from city to city, Whig partisans gave to posterity the phrase "Keep the ball rolling."

"I CANNOT BEAR THIS"

Exhausted by his victorious campaign, President-elect Harrison was besieged by office seekers and self-appointed advisers. With characteristic courtesy, the defeated President, Martin Van Buren, volunteered to vacate the White House early so that the sixty-seven-year-old Harrison might find privacy there and get some rest. But Old Tip decided instead to visit his daughter in Virginia. While he was away, a notice appeared in the papers announcing that Harrison would shake no hands at the inauguration: his arm was sore and his hand swollen. The Presidency itself provided no respite. As Harrison passed from one part of the Executive Mansion to another, he was stopped by patronage seekers and by party men anxious for him to turn out non-Whig officeholders. Late in March, he caught cold. His responsibilities continued to trouble him as he grew weaker and became delirious: "I cannot bear this," the President muttered, "don't trouble me." Harrison died on April 4, 1841.

268

The people who had supported and worked for General Harrison during the campaign of 1840 were well represented at his inauguration (left); he spoke for one hour and forty minutes despite bitter cold weather.

One month later, to the day, Harrison died. Seen mourning in the Currier & Ives lithograph below are (left to right) Secretary of the Treasury Thomas Ewing, Secretary of State Daniel Webster, a physician, a minister, the Chief Executive's niece and nephew, and Postmaster General Francis Granger. Mrs. Harrison had been ill and never arrived in Washington to serve as First Lady. The new President, John Tyler, came just in time for the magnificent funeral, which according to the newspapers was "better arranged" than the procession following the inauguration.

The nation grieved over the loss of its first President to die in office. Many citizens wore black arm bands or special ribbons like the one above.

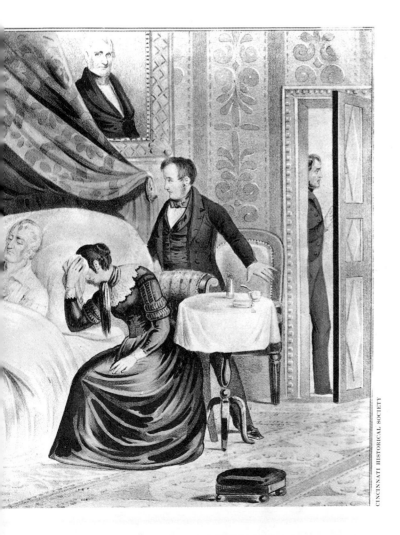

269

FACTS IN SUMMARY: WILLIAM HENRY HARRISON

CHRONOLOGY

UNITED STATES		HARRISON				
Boston Tea Party	1773	*Born February 9*			1799	*Elected U.S. representative from Northwest Territory*
First Continental Congress	1774				1800	*Named governor of Indiana Territory*
Lexington and Concord	1775		Jefferson becomes President	1801		
Second Continental Congress					1802	*Granted power to make treaties with Indians*
Bunker Hill						
Declaration of Independence	1776		Louisiana Purchase	1803		
Siege of Yorktown	1782		Madison elected President	1808		
Treaty of Paris	1783				1809	*Concludes Treaty of Fort Wayne*
Constitutional Convention	1787	*Enters Hampden-Sidney College*			1811	*Defeats Indians in Battle of Tippecanoe*
Washington elected President	1789		War with England	1812		*Appointed supreme commander in the Northwest*
	1790	*Graduates from Hampden-Sidney College*	Perry defeats British on Lake Erie	1813		*Reoccupies Detroit*
First National Bank chartered	1791	*Enlists in United States Infantry*				*Wins Battle of the Thames*
Whisky Rebellion	1794		British burn Washington	1814		
Jay's Treaty			Treaty of Ghent			
	1795	*Marries Anna Symmes*	Battle of New Orleans	1815		
John Adams elected President	1796		Monroe elected President	1816		*Elected to House of Representatives*
	1798	*Resigns from Army*			1819	*Elected to Ohio senate*
		Appointed secretary of Northwest Territory	Missouri Compromise	1820		

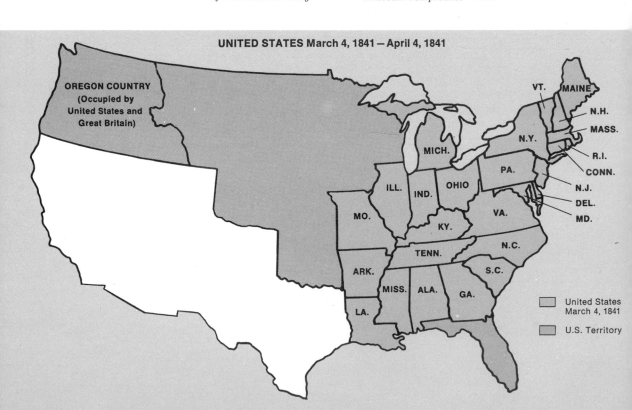

UNITED STATES March 4, 1841 — April 4, 1841

OREGON COUNTRY (Occupied by United States and Great Britain)

VT. MAINE N.H. MASS. R.I. CONN. N.J. DEL. MD. N.Y. MICH. PA. ILL. IND. OHIO MO. VA. KY. N.C. TENN. S.C. ARK. MISS. ALA. GA. LA.

United States March 4, 1841

U.S. Territory

Monroe Doctrine	1823	
John Quincy Adams elected President	1825	*Elected to U.S. Senate*
Jackson elected President	1828	*Named minister to Colombia*
Nullification Crisis	1832	
Jackson vetoes Bank recharter		
Jackson re-elected		
Rise of Whig Party	1834	
Siege of the Alamo	1836	*Runs unsuccessfully for President*
Van Buren elected President		
Bank panic	1837	
Independent Treasury Act	1840	*Elected President*
Tyler becomes President	1841	*Dies April 4*

BIOGRAPHICAL FACTS

BIRTH: Charles City County, Va., Feb. 9, 1773

ANCESTRY: English

FATHER: Benjamin Harrison; b. Charles City County, Va., April 5, 1726; d. Charles City County, Va., April 24, 1791

FATHER'S OCCUPATIONS: Planter; politician

MOTHER: Elizabeth Bassett Harrison; b. Charles City County, Va., Dec. 13, 1730; d. Charles City County, Va., 1792

BROTHERS: Benjamin (1755–1799); Carter Bassett (?–1808)

SISTERS: Elizabeth (1751–?); Ann (1753–1821); Lucy (?–1809); Sarah (1770–1812)

WIFE: Anna Tuthill Symmes; b. Morristown, N.J., July 25, 1775; d. North Bend, Ohio, Feb. 25, 1864

MARRIAGE: North Bend, Ohio, Nov. 25, 1795

CHILDREN: Elizabeth Bassett (1796–1846); John Cleves Symmes (1798–1830); Lucy Singleton (1800–1826); William Henry (1802–1838); John Scott (1804–1878); Benjamin (1806–1840); Mary Symmes (1809–1842); Carter Bassett (1811–1839); Anna Tuthill (1813–1845); James Findlay (1814–1817)

HOME: Grouseland, Vincennes, Indiana

EDUCATION: Private tutoring; attended Hampden-Sidney College

RELIGIOUS AFFILIATION: Episcopalian

OCCUPATIONS BEFORE PRESIDENCY: Soldier; politician

MILITARY SERVICE: U.S. Army (1791–1798), rose from ensign to captain; as governor of Indiana Territory, fought Indians at Tippecanoe (1811); commissioned major general of Kentucky militia (1812); U.S. Army (1812–1814), rose from brigadier general to major general in command of the Northwest

PRE-PRESIDENTIAL OFFICES: Secretary of Northwest Territory; U.S. Representative; Governor of Indiana Territory and Superintendent of Indian Affairs; Ohio State Senator; U.S. Senator; Minister to Colombia

AGE AT INAUGURATION: 68

DEATH: Washington, D.C., April 4, 1841

PLACE OF BURIAL: William Henry Harrison State Park, North Bend, Ohio

THE
HARRISON ALMANAC
1841.

NEW-YORK:
PUBLISHED BY J. P. GIFFING.
SUCCESSOR TO SAMUEL COLMAN,

This almanac shows Harrison as a gentleman farmer.

ELECTION OF 1840

CANDIDATES	ELECTORAL VOTE	POPULAR VOTE
William Henry Harrison Whig	234	1,274,624
Martin Van Buren Democratic	60	1,127,781

THE HARRISON ADMINISTRATION

INAUGURATION: March 4, 1841; the Capitol, Washington, D.C.

VICE PRESIDENT: John Tyler

SECRETARY OF STATE: Daniel Webster

SECRETARY OF THE TREASURY: Thomas Ewing

SECRETARY OF WAR: John Bell

ATTORNEY GENERAL: John J. Crittenden

POSTMASTER GENERAL: Francis Granger

SECRETARY OF THE NAVY: George E. Badger

27th CONGRESS (March 4, 1841–March 4, 1843):
Senate: 28 Whigs; 22 Democrats; 2 Others
House: 133 Whigs; 102 Democrats; 6 Others

JOHN TYLER

At dawn on April 5, 1841, Daniel Webster's son, Fletcher, rode up to a large garden-edged home in Williamsburg, Virginia, dismounted wearily, and hammered on the front door. He had been on the road all night, bearing, in a letter from the Cabinet addressed to "John Tyler, Vice President of the United States," the news of President William Henry Harrison's death.

The door was opened by Tyler himself—a tall, skinny, sharp-featured man with a thin and prominent Roman nose. He had not even known that Harrison was ill. Unfortunately, there is no record of his reaction to the news, but he must have been stunned. Like most Vice Presidents, he had deliberately buried any ideas of emergency succession. Unlike future Vice Presidents, he had no precedent to guide him in the immediate constitutional problem of his status in the government.

Tyler hurriedly packed and ate breakfast. Two hours after Fletcher Webster's arrival they began the long trip to Washington, which waited and buzzed with speculation. Was Tyler actually President, or only Acting President? Would he follow Harrison's policies, such as they were? How would he treat the hobbles on the Executive fashioned for Harrison by the Whig leadership? John Quincy Adams, former President and now a Whig representative from Massachusetts, was alarmed. He thought it highly unfortunate that John Tyler should be the agent of the first test of the Constitution's succession clause. "No one," Adams wrote in his diary, "ever thought of his being placed in the executive chair."

Adams' consternation was understandable. The chickens of the 1840 nominating convention were on their way home to roost. Tyler was not a vague and bewildered old general like Harrison. He was not even a Whig—certainly not

John Tyler, portrayed by G. P. A. Healy

in the terms in which Adams, Clay, Webster, and other Neofederalist party leaders defined themselves. Like many Southerners, Tyler had walked backward into the Whig alliance in protest against Andrew Jackson's "dictatorship." A strict constructionist, he had consistently opposed protective tariffs, the National Bank, and federally sponsored internal improvements—measures that were at the heart of the "American System," and which the Whig leaders had hoped to promote under Harrison. The Whigs had nominated Tyler as Vice President simply to balance the ticket. They had played with fire, and they—and perhaps the whole country—had been burned.

John Tyler was born March 29, 1790, on his family's plantation in Charles City County, Virginia. His father was Judge John Tyler, a friend of Thomas Jefferson's and a leading member of Virginia's Revolutionary generation. His mother, Mary Armistead Tyler, bore the Judge eight children before she died of a stroke the year young John was seven. Little else is known about Tyler's boyhood, but there are indications that his mother's death made him unusually dependent on his strong and active father, and that throughout his life he held himself up against standards he had not created and could not change.

He graduated from the College of William and Mary in 1807. Four years later, at the age of twenty-one, he began practicing law and was elected to the Virginia House of Delegates for the first of several terms he was to serve there. He was elected to Congress in 1816, to the governorship of Virginia in 1825, and to the Senate in 1827.

His career before 1840 was typified by a consistency of opinion that bordered on stubbornness and by the unbending honesty and courage that such consistency demanded. The root of his political philosophy was the idea that the federal government derived its power from the initiative of the states, and that it should not be allowed to extend such power on its own. In the Missouri Compromise debate, for example, Tyler fought against permitting Congress to concern itself

with slavery on a national basis—although as a slaveowner he wished the problem did not exist and was willing to outlaw the importing and auctioning of slaves in the District of Columbia. In the South Carolina Nullification Crisis he never satisfied himself that nullification was proper, but he was more concerned with the federal reaction to the problem. He supported Jackson's lowering of the tariffs to levels acceptable to South Carolina, but violently opposed the President's threat to move troops into that state. After helping to relieve the crisis by promoting the lower tariffs, Tyler voted against authorizing the President to use arms, if necessary, to enforce federal law in South Carolina. With most Southern members conveniently absent, the Senate approved the measure, 32 to 1. Tyler's negative vote was not based on the likelihood that the troops would actually be used, but on the principle that the federal government had no right to use troops against a state.

Tyler won the Vice Presidency despite an apparent disdain for the office. Late in 1835 a Democratic majority in the Virginia legislature cynically began to prepare a resolution instructing the two Virginia Whig senators, Benjamin Leigh and John Tyler, to vote to expunge from the Senate *Journal* the 1833 censure of Andrew Jackson. Tyler was being asked to repudiate his earlier vote for the censure, and he felt that removing anything from the record was unconstitutional. But he believed in the right of a state legislature to control the votes of the senators it appointed. Should he follow the instruction, or resign? Senator Leigh intended to ignore the order, and Whig leaders argued that the expunction would make a good campaign issue if both Virginia senators took the same course. They spoke pointedly of a vice presidential nomination for Tyler. But he refused to be swayed, and at the end of February, 1836, he resigned. Still, he was nominated for Vice President on two of the three regional Whig tickets that year—those headed by William Henry Harrison and Hugh L. White of Tennessee—and then ran third in a four-man race for the second office.

The tenth President, as he looked at about twenty

Less than two years later he was back in the Virginia House of Delegates, again being mentioned for the Vice Presidency. He decided to run for the Senate in 1839, and in the contest that followed he deadlocked with the incumbent, who had the support of Clay Whigs. Tyler admired Clay, but he would not step aside, even when Clay promised the Vice Presidency as a reward. Tyler's stubbornness forced the state legislature to postpone the senatorial election; this upset the Whigs in Virginia, who refused to back him for the vice presidential nomination. Tyler went on to support Clay for President, despite Clay's role in the senatorial contest and despite the fact that Clay's nomination would weaken his own chances for the Vice Presidency. When Clay lost the nomination to Harrison, the Whigs cast about among several possibilities for a running mate; they finally settled, without much enthusiasm, on John Tyler as a geographical, factional, and political counterweight to Harrison.

Personally Tyler was a kind, charming, generous man. Just as good breeding had given him this gracefulness, along with a rigid code of political behavior, it forbade his revealing details of his personal life to outsiders, or even appearing as if he had problems. He was almost always in financial difficulty; and Letitia Christian Tyler, to whom he had been happily married for twenty-seven years and who had borne him seven children, was now virtually an invalid, the result of a stroke. (She died in 1842.) But Tyler's worries remained out of sight, behind the smile, the attentive gaze, the handsome compliment, the beautifully turned phrase of a Virginia gentleman.

John Tyler reached Washington before sunrise on April 6, 1841, prepared to cope with the problem of his constitutional status. Probably the Founding Fathers had intended that when a President resigned, became too ill to serve, or died, the Vice President would take over as Acting President; at least that is the position usually taken by modern historians. However, the succession clause was not explicit:

"In case of the Removal of the President from Office, or of his Death, Resignation, or Inability to discharge the Powers and Duties of the said Office, the same shall devolve on the Vice President, and the Congress may by law provide for the case of Removal, Death, Resignation or Inability, both of the President and Vice President, declaring what Officer shall then act as President, and such Officer shall act accordingly, until the Disability be removed, or a President shall be elected."

What did "the same" refer to? Did the "Powers and Duties of the said Office" devolve on the Vice President, or "the said Office" itself? Secretary of State Webster and other members of the Cabinet chose the latter interpretation. How much of this attitude was communicated to Tyler by Webster's son during the twenty-one-hour journey to the Capital is not known. But Tyler's course was clear in his mind by the time he arrived: he would become President.

With the Cabinet and Tyler in agreement on this, the only remaining questions concerned the formalities. Webster held that Tyler should take the presidential oath. Tyler believed that his vice presidential

275

Among the many colorful devices used in the wild 1840 presidential campaign was the Harrison-Tyler kerchief above, emblazoned with Whig party slogans.

oath to support the Constitution was sufficient, but bowed to Webster's opinion. At Brown's Indian Queen Hotel, some fifty-three hours after Harrison's death, John Tyler was sworn in as the tenth (and, at fifty-one, the youngest up to that time) President of the United States.

If, as some claimed, Tyler was knowingly usurping an office to which he had no right, he had the support not only of most or all the members of the Cabinet but also of a majority in Congress. Attempts were made in the legislature to reverse Tyler's precedent, but these efforts received only cursory attention and scant support.

The best argument against Tyler's decision was offered in the Senate by William Allen of Ohio, who pointed out its implications for the future: whatever Tyler became now, a subsequent Vice President would also become if he substituted for a President who was ill; if the Vice President became President and the man he replaced recovered, who would be President then? Allen foresaw a struggle. But Senator John C. Calhoun said "that as none of those circumstances

existed which had been supposed [by Senator Allen], there could be no special occasion for discussion of this subject." The Senate then voted, as the House had already done, to style Tyler "President."

Within hours of his arrival in the Capital, Tyler was confronted by his first challenge from the party managers. Under Harrison, Webster said, executive decisions had been made in the Cabinet, with the President having one vote; would Tyler follow the same procedure? Certainly not, said Tyler. He wanted to keep the Harrison Cabinet, but he alone would lead. If the Cabinet members did not approve, they could resign. He would not only become President in name, but he would be President in fact.

The stage was set for conflict. The Whigs had a number of programs they wanted to effect, and they were led by men who interpreted the Constitution from a Northern and Western bias. In the executive chair sat a man of opposite political prejudices, who had declared his right to independent judgment and action. And there was another, more crucial factor: Henry Clay wanted to be President. Harrison had promised to serve only one term. Clay had planned to use that time to promote his nationalist program in Congress and solidify his control over the Whig party so that he would win the 1844 nomination. Now the situation had changed. Tyler might be able to develop enough personal strength to block Clay's path to the White House. Clay concluded that he had better grasp control while he could.

For the next two years the Clay-dominated Congress passed determinedly nationalistic bills; Tyler declared in advance that he would not sign them and then, with politely stern explanations, vetoed them on constitutional grounds, to the accompaniment of loud and somewhat theatrical howls from the nationalists. By September 14, 1841, five months after Tyler became President and five days after his second veto of a national bank bill, he had been burned in effigy in many cities, his entire Cabinet, except Webster, had resigned in a body, and he had been solemnly expelled from the Whig party—for trespassing against principles that the Whigs had not dared to write into a platform for 1840. "Tyler, Too" became "Old Veto." There were charges of "executive dictation," assassination threats, an effort to force Tyler's resignation, and an abortive attempt to impeach him; he was isolated from partisan support, and the legislature refused to act on some of his routine requests, demonstrating petty vindictiveness by failing to appropriate funds for repairs to the White House.

In foreign affairs, however, Tyler's record was impressive. The Webster-Ashburton Treaty, in which he played a dominant role, not only settled boundary disputes along the Canadian border, thus easing dangerous tension between Great Britain and the United States, but also made the United States a participant in policing the African coast to prevent illegal slave trading. Tyler enlarged the territory covered by the Monroe Doctrine to include the Hawaiian Islands, and a commercial treaty with China was signed in 1844.

Motivated by a long-standing continental image of the United States, Tyler also attempted to solve the boundary question in Oregon and to annex California. He was unsuccessful, but he provided the capstone for his administration, during its last days, by clearing the way for the annexation of Texas.

He was concerned, practically from the beginning of his Presidency, that he be remembered favorably. In October, 1841, he wrote Webster about bringing Texas into the Union. "Could anything throw so bright a lustre around us?" he asked. As his term drew on, he thought of Texas annexation more and more as the means of assuring himself a respected place in history. It became bound up in his search for a national political base and in the presidential campaign of 1844.

When, in the mid-term elections, the Whig majority was swept from the House of Representatives and replaced by a sizable Democratic majority, Tyler interpreted it as a public reproof to the Whigs for their opposition to the administration, and he decided that he could build out of the conservative Democrats and uncommitted Whigs an effective third force—a Tyler party. He probably would have accepted a term as President in his own right, but it is not likely that he thought he had a chance of winning the election in 1844 without the backing of one of the two major parties; in mid-term such backing seemed a faint hope. What he had in mind was the creation of "cells" in several important states in order to give himself political leverage and help him achieve something memorable as President. At the same time, he began to remove political enemies from federal offices.

The idea of Texas annexation had been under national consideration for about five years. The theory was that Texas would eventually be subdivided, into perhaps four states, and consequently the central problem of annexation was slavery. Tyler argued that the slavery issue should be left alone; slavery would seek its economic and geographic limits and eventually its own destruction. He urged, instead, concentration on the commercial advantages of having Texas in the Union—among other things, a

This gilt fruit basket on a base of porcelain was used at the White House during Tyler's Presidency.

virtual cotton monopoly for the United States—and its importance in terms of a continental vision.

The argument did not, however, convince Webster. In May, 1843, he resigned, still friendly to Tyler but disapproving of his use of the spoils system. With his Northeastern constituency to consider, Webster was unable to bring himself to work hard for Texas annexation. Tyler appointed Virginian Abel P. Upshur to replace him. By October, Tyler and Upshur had begun secret negotiations with Texas, and before the end of the year it was apparent that annexation would have the necessary two-thirds support in the Senate. Tyler's playing down of the slavery question had succeeded, and his third-party drive had gained momentum. By mid-February, 1844, the last important details of the treaty were worked out with Texas President Sam Houston. Then, as Tyler stood within reach of his goal, tragedy struck: Upshur was killed in an accident, and Tylerite Henry A. Wise let it be known that Calhoun would be chosen to replace Upshur. Tyler had no such intention, but felt that he could not deny the report because of the discord it would create in the South. So Calhoun, slavocracy's leading intellectual, took over as chief negotiator of the Texas treaty, and the nationalist feeling that Tyler had worked so hard to create on the issue rapidly vanished. Slavery became the central point, and as the senators were forced to take sides, support for annexation dwindled away.

In the words of Robert Seager II, Tyler's most recent major biographer, "Tyler reluctantly reached for a political blackjack." The Democrats met in Baltimore on May 27 to nominate a candidate; the Tyler party also convened in the same city that day— as a reminder of the inroads Tyler had made in the conservative wing of the Democratic party—and nominated Tyler on the slogan "Tyler and Texas." The strategy worked. Van Buren, who opposed annexation, failed to get the Democratic nomination; the pro-annexation James K. Polk was chosen as the candidate instead, and an annexation plank was included in the party's platform.

Exultant, Tyler now offered to withdraw from the race if the Texas treaty was ratified. But the damage done by the slavery issue could not be easily repaired. Annexation was defeated badly in the Senate on June 8. So in New York, New Jersey, and Pennsylvania the Tyler organizations began to make plans to field candidates for every possible office in the fall elections, in competition with Democratic slates. This frightened Democratic party leaders, and in late July they capitulated, as Andrew Jackson communicated assurances about Texas and federal jobs for Tyler men. New York's Tammany Hall came to terms in August, and Tyler threw his support to Polk.

When Polk won in November, Tyler moved quickly to collect part of his debts. He declared that Polk's election represented a mandate concerning Texas. Congress sidestepped the constitutional demand for a two-thirds Senate ratification of the treaty and approved a joint resolution calling for the admission of Texas as a state. On March 1, with less than three days left in his term, Tyler signed the bill.

With his new bride, Julia Gardiner Tyler, whom he had married in June of 1844, President Tyler retired to a plantation in Virginia and raised wheat, corn, and a new family of seven. As a leading moderate he remained a possible presidential nominee every four years until 1860. In 1861, he presided over the Washington peace conference that attempted to avoid civil war. In mid-conference he became a secessionist, hoping he could help create a pacifying balance of military power between the two sections. When Richmond became the Confederate capital, Tyler accepted a seat in the Confederacy's Provisional Congress and won election to the Confederate House of Representatives in November, 1861. But by now he was ill and tired. On January 12, 1862, he suffered a stroke; six days later he was dead. His body lay in state in the Confederate Congress and then was buried beside the grave of James Monroe.

—MICHAEL HARWOOD

John Tyler

A PICTURE PORTFOLIO

This painted leather fire bucket recalls Tyler's status as an emergency President.

The drawing of John Tyler, left, is by the inventor Samuel F. B. Morse, for whom Congress—deadlocked with the President—produced one of its very few pieces of constructive legislation, an appropriation of $30,000 for an experimental telegraph line.

The lithograph at right depicts the climax of Dorr's Rebellion in Rhode Island in May, 1842, when the insurgents attempted to capture the state arsenal. The uprising stemmed from the fact that Rhode Island's antiquated laws allowed less than half the state's adult males to vote. Reformers, led by Thomas W. Dorr, wrote a new constitution, set up a rival government, and asked Tyler for support. Tyler backed the old government and threatened to send federal troops. The rebellion soon collapsed, however.

VETOES AND VENGEFULNESS

He was an unexpected and, on the whole, unwanted President. Self-exiled from the Democratic party, and never more than nominally a Whig, John Tyler soon found himself cast out by the Whigs for vetoing two bills with which they had hoped to re-establish a national bank. Without partisan support in Congress, Tyler's administration produced little legislation of note. Neither did the hostile Congress. President Tyler vetoed a total of ten bills (the greatest number of bills rejected by a one-term Chief Executive before Andrew Johnson) and earned the sobriquet "Old Veto." He was the first President to have a veto overridden by Congress, an event that occurred on the last day of his term. The struggle between the Executive and the legislature manifested itself even at the President's Mansion. Congress would allocate no funds for upkeep. A reporter described the result. Alas, he said, the White House was changed "since the days of yore: its virgin white sadly sullied—its beautiful pillars . . . besplattered with saliva of tobacco . . . the gorgeous East Room reflecting, from its monstrous mirrors, patched carpets . . . the splendid drapery falling in tatters all around time's rude hand. . . ."

Only a few months after Tyler succeeded Harrison, it was apparent that he had little chance of winning an election in his own right. The cartoon at left, "Foot Race, Pennsylvania Avenue," depicts the campaign of 1844. Tyler, who received a splinter-party nomination, is shown quitting the race, "used up," to follow Julia Gardiner (whom he married that year) down the road to Texas. But, in fact, although hopelessly out of contention, he exploited the campaign with great skill to win passage of Texas annexation while he was still in office. Henry Clay and Theodore Frelinghuysen were the Whig nominees. Their confidence proved to be ill-founded, for after the President withdrew, James Knox Polk rode the annexation issue to victory.

SHIPBOARD DISASTER

THE WHITE HOUSE COLLECTION

Julia Gardiner, above, married John Tyler four months after the Princeton *tragedy. Wealthy, vivacious, queenly, she was twenty-four, thirty years younger than her husband. Tyler credited her parties, which enlivened the last year of his Presidency, with playing a major role in securing annexation of Texas. He gave her the gold pen with which he signed the Texas bill, and, true to character, the First Lady wore the pen proudly around her neck.*

The lithograph at right, by Currier & Ives, shows the "Peacemaker" exploding; eight men were killed, and nine others aboard the frigate were injured.

On February 28, 1844, John Tyler and some three hundred and fifty other dignitaries went for a cruise on the Potomac aboard the steam frigate *Princeton*, which carried the "Peacemaker," a bow gun of new design. In midafternoon most of the company was belowdecks, drinking champagne, when word came that the Peacemaker, which had been demonstrated earlier that day, was to be fired again. Tyler, in the

company of his Secretary of State, Abel P. Upshur, started toward the ladder himself, but then he stopped to listen to his son-in-law sing a song, and before the singing was over, the roar of the Peacemaker was heard. Suddenly a ship's officer rushed in, shouting for a surgeon. The gun had blown up, killing eight men, including Upshur, Secretary of the Navy Thomas W. Gilmer, and David Gardiner, father of Julia, Tyler's fiancée.

Julia fainted, and Tyler carried her across the gangplank to a rescue boat; halfway across she awoke and began to struggle, nearly pitching them both into the Potomac. Then, on the day of the mass state funeral, Tyler's horses ran away with his carriage and could not be checked for some distance. The United States had thrice narrowly missed losing two Chief Executives within a single four-year term.

"THE GODLIKE DANIEL"

His friends often referred to him as "the godlike Daniel." And Ralph Waldo Emerson said that "Webster . . . alone does not disappoint the eye and ear, but is a fit figure in the landscape." The expansive forehead underlined by heavy eyebrows; the wide, dark eyes; the deep, impressive actor's voice; and the brilliant grasp of oratorical effect made him one of the leading figures of the national capital for nearly forty years.

To John Tyler, Webster was, if not godlike, certainly a godsend. The Secretary of State defined the Vice President's role in the first succession crisis and supported Tyler's decision to become President; and it was Webster, alone among the members of the Harrison Cabinet, who stuck by Tyler when Henry Clay, trying to isolate Tyler from the Whig party to aid his own drive toward the Presidency, engineered a mass Cabinet resignation on September 11, 1841. "Where am I to go, Mr. President?" asked Webster late on that unsettling day, knowing that if he did not quit, too, his party would make him suffer for it. "You must decide that for yourself . . ." said Tyler. "If you leave it to me, Mr. President," Webster replied, "I will stay where I am." Tyler shot to his feet and declared, "Give me your hand on that, and now I will say to you that Henry Clay is a doomed man." Diplomatically and politically Webster was of inestimable value to the President. Among their diplomatic successes was the Webster-Ashburton Treaty with Great Britain, setting the northern boundary of Maine and arranging United States participation in putting a stop to the African slave trade. When Webster at last felt forced to resign in 1843 because of the slavery implications of Texas annexation, there was no bitterness on either side, merely respect for each other's courage.

Webster was born January 18, 1782, the son of a New Hampshire farmer and political leader. A frail and bookish child, unfit for farming, Daniel was sent away to school at fourteen. He left after a few unhappy months but continued his studies under a tutor. Within a year he was at Dartmouth College, where he made his mark as a facile student and a budding orator. For a while after graduation he vacillated between the law and teaching, finally choosing the law, and by 1808 he was making his presence felt both in the courts and in politics. New Hampshire sent him to Congress in 1813, and from then until his death in 1852 he spent most of his life as a legislator and statesman. He was twice Secretary of State. Throughout, he kept one eye on the Presidency and sometimes trimmed his sails hoping to catch the breeze that might waft him closer to the White House. But he distinguished himself, nonetheless, by his nationalist vision and his grasp of issues. He rose to real greatness on occasion: the brave and patriotic support he gave Tyler; the thundering voice replying to Hayne against nullification; the declaration of allegiance, not to Massachusetts (his home after 1816), nor to the North, but to Union and the Compromise of 1850. "You have manifested powers of intellect of the highest order," John Tyler told him in 1843, "and in all things a true American heart."

Webster, painted around 1848 by G. P. A. Healy

The patrician image of former President Tyler at sixty, right, was caught by a daguerreotyper around 1850.

The view of San Antonio's Main Plaza, below, was painted in 1849, four years after President John Tyler had engineered the admission of Texas into the Union. War with Mexico came in 1846, and by the time W. G. M. Samuels, sheriff of San Antonio's Bexar County, made this lively canvas, the United States had won the war and had acquired territory that is now the states of California, Nevada, and Utah, and portions of Arizona, New Mexico, Colorado, and Wyoming.

IN SELF-DEFENSE

In March, 1845, four days after Congress at last acceded to his desire that Texas be annexed, Tyler retired to his Virginia plantation. From that vantage point he observed with uneasiness the growing sectionalism, waited in vain for another call to serve in the White House, and—ever conscious of his reputation—rebutted criticisms of his Presidency. Especially wounding were misrepresentations of his Texas policy. Calhoun implied it had been a pro-South effort. A newspaper charged that Tyler had been influenced by land and stock speculators. Angrily Tyler declared that his concern had been not for "this or that section," but for "the glory of the whole country. . . ." He told his son hopefully, "If the tide of defamation and abuse shall turn . . . future Vice Presidents who may succeed to the Presidency may feel some slight encouragement to pursue an independent course."

FACTS IN SUMMARY: JOHN TYLER

CHRONOLOGY

UNITED STATES		TYLER		UNITED STATES		TYLER
	1790	*Born March 29*		Monroe elected President	1816	*Elected U.S. representative from Virginia*
Washington re-elected President	1792			Missouri Compromise	1820	
Whisky Rebellion	1794			Monroe Doctrine	1823	*Re-elected to Virginia House of Delegates*
Jay's Treaty				John Quincy Adams elected President	1825	*Elected governor of Virginia*
John Adams elected President	1796				1827	*Elected to U.S. Senate*
XYZ Affair	1798			Tariff of Abominations	1828	
Undeclared naval war with France				Jackson elected President		
Alien and Sedition Acts					1829	*Attends Virginia constitutional convention*
Jefferson elected President	1801			Nullification controversy	1832	
Louisiana Purchase	1803			Bank recharter vetoed		
	1807	*Graduates from College of William and Mary*			1833	*Opposes force bill*
				Van Buren elected President	1836	*Resigns Senate seat*
Madison elected President	1808					*Renounces Democratic party*
	1809	*Admitted to the bar*				*Chosen Whig candidate for Vice Presidency*
	1811	*Elected to Virginia House of Delegates*		Aroostook War	1838	*Re-elected to Virginia House of Delegates*
War with England	1812			Harrison elected President	1840	*Elected Vice President*
	1813	*Marries Letitia Christian*		Harrison dies April 4	1841	*Becomes President*
		Serves as captain of volunteer company		Independent Treasury Act repealed		*Vetoes U.S. fiscal bank bills*
Battle of New Orleans	1815			Cabinet resigns		

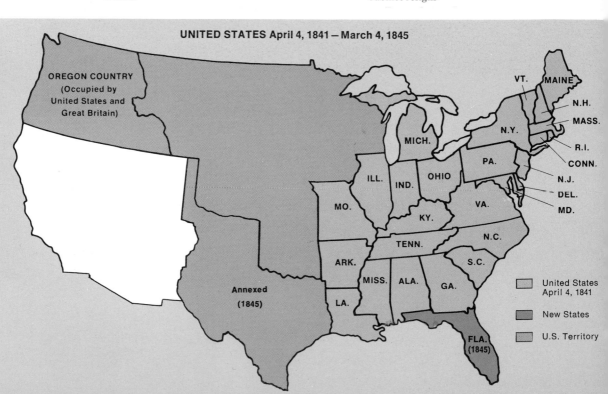

UNITED STATES April 4, 1841 — March 4, 1845

OREGON COUNTRY (Occupied by United States and Great Britain)

VT. MAINE N.H. MASS. N.Y. R.I. CONN. N.J. DEL. MD. MICH. PA. ILL. IND. OHIO MO. VA. KY. N.C. TENN. S.C. ARK. MISS. ALA. GA. LA.

Annexed (1845)

FLA. (1845)

United States April 4, 1841

New States

U.S. Territory

Dorr Rebellion	1842	*Signs Webster-Ashburton Treaty*
		Letitia Tyler dies
Polk elected President	1844	*Urges annexation of Texas*
		Marries Julia Gardiner
Annexation of Texas	1845	*Retires to Virginia*
Florida admitted to Union		
War with Mexico	1846	
Taylor elected President	1848	
Fillmore becomes President	1850	
Compromise of 1850		
Pierce elected President	1852	
Buchanan elected President	1856	
Lincoln elected President	1860	*Becomes chancellor of College of William and Mary*
Fort Sumter	1861	*Presides over Washington peace conference*
Civil War begins		*Elected to the Confederate House of Representatives*
	1862	*Dies January 18*

BIOGRAPHICAL FACTS

BIRTH: Charles City County, Va., March 29, 1790

ANCESTRY: English

FATHER: John Tyler; b. James City County, Va., Feb. 28, 1747; d. Charles City County, Va., Jan. 6, 1813

FATHER'S OCCUPATIONS: Judge; governor of Virginia

MOTHER: Mary Marot Armistead Tyler; b. 1761; d. April, 1797

BROTHERS: Wat Henry (1788–1862); William (?–1856)

SISTERS: Anne Contesse (1778–1803); Elizabeth Armistead (1780–1824); Martha Jefferson (1782–1855); Maria Henry (1784–1843); Christianna Booth (1795–1842)

FIRST WIFE: Letitia Christian; b. New Kent County, Va., Nov. 12, 1790; d. Washington, D.C., Sept. 10, 1842

FIRST MARRIAGE: New Kent County, Va., March 29, 1813

SECOND WIFE: Julia Gardiner; b. Gardiner's Island, N.Y., May 4, 1820; d. Richmond, Va., July 10, 1889

SECOND MARRIAGE: New York, N.Y., June 26, 1844

CHILDREN: (by first wife) Mary (1815–1848); Robert (1816–1877); John (1819–1896); Letitia (1821–1907); Elizabeth (1823–1850); Alice (1827–1854); Tazewell (1830–1874); (by second wife) David Gardiner (1846–1927); John Alexander (1848–1883); Julia (1849–1871); Lachlan (1851–1902); Lyon Gardiner (1853–1935); Robert Fitzwalter (1856–1927); Pearl (1860–1947)

HOME: Sherwood Forest, Charles City County, Va.

EDUCATION: Local Virginia schools; graduated from College of William and Mary (1807)

RELIGIOUS AFFILIATION: Episcopalian

OCCUPATION BEFORE PRESIDENCY: Lawyer

MILITARY SERVICE: Captain of volunteer company in Richmond, Va. (1813)

PRE-PRESIDENTIAL OFFICES: Member of Virginia House of Delegates; U.S. Representative; Governor of Virginia; U.S. Senator; Vice President

AGE AT INAUGURATION: 51

OCCUPATION AFTER PRESIDENCY: Lawyer

DEATH: Richmond, Va., Jan. 18, 1862

PLACE OF BURIAL: Hollywood Cemetery, Richmond

THE TYLER ADMINISTRATION

INAUGURATION: April 6, 1841; Indian Queen Hotel, Washington, D.C.

SECRETARY OF STATE: Daniel Webster; Abel P. Upshur (from July 24, 1843); John C. Calhoun (from April 1, 1844)

SECRETARY OF THE TREASURY: Thomas Ewing; Walter Forward (from Sept. 13, 1841); John C. Spencer (from March 8, 1843); George M. Bibb (from July 4, 1844)

SECRETARY OF WAR: John Bell; John C. Spencer (from Oct. 12, 1841); James M. Porter (from March 8, 1843); William Wilkins (from Feb. 20, 1844)

ATTORNEY GENERAL: John J. Crittenden; Hugh S. Legare (from Sept. 20, 1841); John Nelson (from July 1, 1843)

POSTMASTER GENERAL: Francis Granger; Charles A. Wickliffe (from Oct. 13, 1841)

SECRETARY OF THE NAVY: George E. Badger; Abel P. Upshur (from Oct. 11, 1841); David Henshaw (from July 24, 1843); Thomas W. Gilmer (from Feb. 19, 1844); John Y. Mason (from March 26, 1844)

SUPREME COURT APPOINTMENT: Samuel Nelson (1845)

27th CONGRESS (March 4, 1841–March 4, 1843):
Senate: 28 Whigs; 22 Democrats; 2 Others
House: 133 Whigs; 102 Democrats; 6 Others

28th CONGRESS (March 4, 1843–March 4, 1845):
Senate: 28 Whigs; 25 Democrats; 1 Other
House: 142 Democrats; 79 Whigs; 1 Other

STATE ADMITTED: Florida (1845)

END OF PRESIDENTIAL TERM: March 4, 1845

After his Presidency, Tyler lived at Sherwood Forest, above, where he and Julia raised seven children.

The lifelike miniature of President James Knox Polk, above, is by an unknown painter.

JAMES KNOX POLK

Americans, said Andrew Jackson in 1837, were chosen by Providence to be "the guardians of freedom to preserve it for the benefit of the human race." The American people wholeheartedly agreed. Confident of their ability to read the mind of God, convinced of the superiority of their customs and institutions, they believed all their causes just and all their endeavors moral: what was good for them was good for everyone. Thus, in the 1840's, as the country reached across the wilderness toward the Pacific Ocean, Americans thought about and talked about expansion as though it were a great crusade. "It is for the interest of mankind," said Walt Whitman, the young editor of the Brooklyn *Eagle*, that America's "power and territory should be extended—the farther the better." And as New York newspaperman John L. O'Sullivan put it, our claims to the land lay in the right of "our manifest destiny to occupy and to possess the whole of the Continent which Providence has given us."

It was this ambitious, cocksure, destiny-enraptured America that President James K. Polk was elected to lead. In the two decades preceding his election in 1844, missionaries, explorers, whalers, and traders in furs and hides had blazed new trails to the West. Then the pathfinders—the John C. Frémonts and Kit Carsons—cleared the way for settlers. By 1844, Americans had reached and crossed the Western boundaries of their country. But California was Mexico's, and the Oregon Territory, in accordance with an 1818 treaty, was to be shared by the United States and Great Britain. The American people wanted these Pacific lands for their own, and they elected Polk because he accepted the "manifest destiny" justification for national expansion.

Shortly after his inauguration in 1845, Polk confided to Secretary of the Navy George Bancroft that he had four goals for his administration. Slapping his thigh for emphasis, he enumerated them: "one, a reduction of the tariff; another, the independent treasury; a third, the settlement of the Oregon boundary question; and, lastly, the acquisition of California." These were not just Polk's goals; they were the nation's. Regarding his election as the people's mandate, he concentrated his energies on realizing their will. While accomplishing all four goals, he added more than a million square miles of territory to the United States and became one of the country's most effective Presidents.

Polk was not originally intended to become President at all. His nomination resulted from a deadlocked convention, and as the Democrats' compromise choice, he became the first dark horse in presidential history. "Who is James K. Polk?" the Whigs asked throughout the campaign.

He was born in Mecklenburg County, North Carolina, on November 2, 1795, the first of ten children. His father, Samuel Polk, a prosperous farmer, was, if not irreligious, apparently indifferent to the pious Presbyterianism of his wife Jane, whose great joy, a friend of Polk's reported, lay in "the Bible, the Confession of Faith, the Psalms and Watt's Hymns." On the occasion of James's baptism, Samuel engaged the minister in a bitter quarrel; the sacrament was not consummated, and Polk was not baptized until fifty-four years later as he lay on his deathbed.

Nevertheless, Polk's upbringing was religious, and he seems to have gained strength from his faith. Always frail and sickly, he was strong-willed enough to survive a gallstone operation performed in his seventeenth year, without anesthesia or antiseptics, on a bare wooden table in Danville, Kentucky.

In contrast to Polk's physical disposition, "his moral conduct," according to his teacher, Parson Henderson, was "unexceptionable and exemplary," and he "never missed a recitation nor omitted the punctilious performance of any duty."

All the Polks were keenly interested in politics, and James prepared himself for a political career. After graduating with honors from the University of North Carolina in 1818, he traveled to Tennessee, where he studied law for two years and was admitted to the bar. He became a prominent lawyer in that rugged young state and renewed his acquaintance with his father's friend, General Andrew Jackson, who had become America's foremost national hero. Polk's lifelong friendship and political association with Jackson would be mutually beneficial.

In 1824, following two years in the Tennessee legislature, Polk was a candidate for the House of Representatives, running as a Democratic-Republican on a ticket headed by Old Hickory. Jackson lost, but Polk did not, and he journeyed on horseback and by stagecoach to Washington, where he attracted attention as an industrious Jacksonian and a thorn in the side of President John Quincy Adams. The Chief Executive found Polk to have "no wit, no literature . . . no elegance of language . . . no pathos, no felicitous impromptus; nothing that can constitute an orator but confidence, fluency, and labor." A political opponent, George McDuffie of South Carolina, was also both impressed and annoyed by Polk's performance in the House and credited the congressman "with a tact and skill and zeal worthy of a better cause."

Somber, stern, thin-lipped, James Knox Polk was physically undistinguished. He was slender and of medium height; he had cold, penetrating eyes, a large, broad forehead, and he wore his hair combed straight back. Carrying himself stiffly erect, he was formal, dignified, and fastidious. Although Arthur Schlesinger, Jr., credits him with "an exceptionally winning smile," Polk apparently was stingy with it, and he was reluctant to express his personal feelings. Archibald Yell, one of Polk's closest friends and later governor of Arkansas, once wrote to Polk: "I am not able to even conjecture how your feelings are after all your long letters." It was indeed one of Polk's great pleasures to be secretive, to be sly, to hoard knowledge and say little. In May, 1838, a phrenologist, O. S. Fowler, felt Polk's skull and made some shrewd observations. Polk's cranium

Flanking Ralph E. W. Earl's 1830 portrait of Congressman James K. Polk are paintings of his mother (left, attributed to Washington Cooper) and his wife (right, by G. P. A. Healy).

suggested to Fowler a man who "thinks well of himself; often asks advice, and does just as he pleases; is one of the firmest of men; slow in committing himself, but once committed, does all in his power to carry through his measures . . . has many acquaintances, few bosom friends. . . ." Fowler also suggested that Polk would have succeeded on the stage—he apparently had a well-developed mimetic sense.

During the administrations of Andrew Jackson and his hand-picked successor, Martin Van Buren, Polk's career flourished. In 1832 he achieved membership on the House Ways and Means Committee, where he supported Jackson's opposition to the United States Bank. Three years later he became Speaker of the House, a position that exposed him to bitter attack. Called Young Hickory and accused of being the lackey of the President, Polk was also the convenient whipping boy for anti-Jacksonians who did not wish to incur public wrath by assaulting the heroic President himself. Henry A. Wise, the Southern radical, tried more than once to provoke Polk into a duel. "You are a damned little petty tyrant," Wise shouted heatedly during a House debate. "I mean this personally—pocket it!" Polk, however, would not be provoked. As the Speaker completed his term, he said: "It has been made my duty to decide more questions of parliamentary law and order

. . . than had been decided . . . by all my predecessors, from the formation of this Government." He was not exaggerating.

In 1839, the Democratic party of Tennessee drafted Polk as its candidate for governor. Although he would have preferred to remain in Washington, he accepted the draft and was elected. In his bid for re-election two years later, and in another try in 1843, he was defeated by a preference for the Whigs that had affected much of the nation. Van Buren, too, had lost his re-election bid to William Henry Harrison. John Tyler, Harrison's successor, soon alienated himself from his party. As the election of 1844 approached, Henry Clay, the oft-beaten, oft-thwarted Whig aspirant, looked forward to a victorious race against Van Buren, who appeared to be the logical Democratic choice. And Polk, due to his long and faithful service to the Jacksonians, seemed to have earned the right to his party's vice presidential nomination.

The story is told that Henry Clay was relaxing at his home when his son rushed in and asked him to guess who had won the Democratic nomination. "Why Matty of course," said Clay. His son shook his head. "Then Cass." Again the younger Clay gestured negatively. "Then Buchanan." No. "Then who in the hell is he?" Told that James Polk would oppose him, Clay reportedly groaned, "Beaten again, by God."

Clay's prophecy came true chiefly because he temporized on the Texas issue—the same issue that cost Martin Van Buren his party's nomination. Immediately after the United States recognized the independence of Texas, the former Mexican region applied for admission to the Union; but since statehood would have destroyed the delicate balance between slave and free states that had existed since 1820, American politicians generally avoided the issue. In April, 1844, President Tyler, hearing that Texas was negotiating a treaty with England, asked Congress to hedge no longer and approve annexation, but the legislators were unsure about the people's reactions and refused to vote for annexation in an election year. Both Clay and Van Buren announced that they intended to keep Texas out of the approaching campaign. At The Hermitage, meanwhile, Andrew Jackson was much surer about public sentiment. Summoning several Democratic leaders, including Polk, to his Tennessee home, he told them that Van Buren's anti-Texas position was political suicide. Making "All of Oregon, all of Texas" a campaign pledge, he said, would satisfy North and South and the people's desire to expand. Polk was from the Southwest, Polk was for annexation, Polk could win. Following Old Hickory's advice, the Jacksonian leaders deadlocked the party convention in Baltimore for seven ballots (two-thirds of the delegate votes were required for nomination), then brought forth the dark horse Polk, who won on the ninth.

Despite the fact that Andrew Jackson had indeed measured the people's sentiments correctly, the odds were against a Polk victory. The people wanted all of Oregon and all of Texas, and they liked the Democratic slogan, "54° 40' or Fight!" but Henry Clay was infinitely better known than Polk and had always been popular in the frontier states. Polk's service had been principally in party and legislative circles, but Clay was a national figure who had seldom strayed from the center of activity. The election was much closer than was expected in a nation so sure of its manifest destiny. Because of

his hedging on the Texas question, Senator Clay lost votes in New York to a third candidate, abolitionist James Birney. As a result, Polk captured a small plurality of the New York vote, and its 36 electoral votes gave him the election, 170 to 105.

Who, indeed, was this James K. Polk, the dark horse Jacksonian whose significance was dismissed by many contemporaries and whose reputation has grown steadily and continues to grow in our own time? According to Bernard De Voto, "Polk's mind was rigid, narrow, obstinate, far from first-rate. . . . But if his mind was narrow it was also powerful and he had guts. If he was orthodox, his integrity was absolute and he could not be scared, manipulated, or brought to heel. No one bluffed him, no one moved him with direct or oblique pressure. Furthermore, he knew how to get things done, which is the first necessity of government, and he knew what he wanted done, which is the second. . . . He was to be the only 'strong' President between Jackson and Lincoln. He was to fix the mold of the future in America down to 1860, and therefore for a long time afterward. That is who James K. Polk was."

Polk was also indefatigable, and his tenacity served him well in the White House. Once, vexed with his secretary for taking an unscheduled pleasure trip, he accused the young man of not giving "that close and systematic attention to business which is necessary to give himself reputation. . . ." This was Polk's own prescription. He worked so hard that he had "but little opportunity to read newspapers," and called himself "the hardest-working man in this country." Finding that too much time was lost daily to office seekers, favor seekers, businessmen, and visiting Indians, he resolved to see no one after noon. He also inveighed against the spoils system, which so exhausted the nation's chief patronage dispenser. Polk was, in sum, a man who rose to fit the job, who worked as hard as was necessary to do whatever had to be done.

He brought to Washington a First Lady much like his mother. He had married Sarah

Childress in 1824, when she was a plain but vivacious twenty-year-old. A woman of unflinching Presbyterianism, she banned dancing in the White House, but she was considerably more popular in the Capital than her husband. Henry Clay once gallantly informed her that there was "a general approbation expressed of her administration . . . [whereas] there was some difference of opinion about her husband's administration."

Polk first tackled the Oregon boundary question. Since 1818 the Oregon Territory had been held jointly by the United States and Great Britain, with both nations having the option to terminate the agreement on a year's notice. Although "54° 40' or Fight!" had been the Democratic slogan during the election, Polk had instructed his Secretary of State, James Buchanan, to suggest the forty-ninth parallel as a final border between the United States and Canada. When England refused, holding firm in its demands for all land north of the Columbia River, Polk decided to exercise the termination clause of the agreement. In his first annual message to Congress he said that "the extraordinary and wholly inadmissable demands of the British Government" could not be countenanced. A few days later he told a visiting congressman: "The only way to treat John Bull was to look him straight in the eye . . . if Congress faltered or hesitated in their course, John Bull would immediately become arrogant and more grasping in his demands." Congress was willing to gamble on war and authorized termination on April 23, 1846. Meanwhile, partly due to the pacific policies of British Foreign Minister Lord Aberdeen, public opinion in England inclined toward a settlement at the forty-ninth parallel, and in June, Buchanan received almost the same offer that Britain had turned down the year before. A rejection of the new proposal would mean war; in view of the growing crisis with Mexico, Polk and most of his Cabinet decided to avoid the risk by accepting the offer.

Buchanan, however, aspired to the Presidency. He hesitated to endorse or reject the British settlement until he could determine

GEORGE M. DALLAS

George M. Dallas won the Democratic nomination for Vice President almost by default when Silas Wright, a loyal Van Buren supporter in the contest for the presidential nomination, refused to be Polk's running mate. The convention's second choice was, nonetheless, an eminently qualified candidate. Born in Philadelphia and a graduate of the College of New Jersey (Princeton), Dallas was appointed secretary to Albert Gallatin on a peace mission to Russia in 1813. Returning to the United States, he established a law practice in Philadelphia and became prominent in state and local politics. He served as a United States senator from 1831 to 1833 and later as minister to Russia. In the campaign of 1844, it was "Polk, Dallas, and Texas." His championship of Texas annexation was an important factor in his nomination and was remembered by the state, which named a county after him. As Vice President he supported Polk's policies. In 1846 his loyalty to the President overrode his own protectionist views when he broke a tie in favor of the low-tariff bill sponsored by the administration. At the end of his term, Dallas retired from public life until Pierce appointed him minister to Great Britain in 1856. He proved an able diplomat, negotiating a settlement of conflicting Central American interests in the Dallas-Clarendon Convention. Dallas was seventy-two years old when he died in 1864.

where political capital could be made; after pursuing a soft line, he gradually turned truculent. The rest of the Cabinet advised the President to lay the proposal before the Senate, but Buchanan, mumbling something about "caking out from 54° 40'," sulkily refused to help Polk prepare the message. But Polk was always stronger than his Cabinet or any one member: the message he prepared was accepted, and the treaty was signed on June 15, 1846.

Repercussions came immediately from the Western war hawks. Senator William Allen of Ohio resigned the chairmanship of the Committee on Foreign Relations. Senators Edward Hannegan of Indiana, James Semple of Illinois, and David Atchison of Missouri "lashed themselves into a passion" over the loss of the whole of Oregon and immediately crossed the aisle to vote with the Whigs. Worse, as Polk noted, "they oppose, too, and embarrass the military bills for the prosecution of the war against Mexico."

That war was already a month old. Throughout 1845 President Polk had not hesitated to admit that he had "California and the fine bay of San Francisco as much in view as Oregon." He instructed Commodore John D. Sloat to occupy San Francisco in the event of a Mexican war, and he employed Thomas Larkin, a Boston businessman with affairs in Monterey, California, as a special consul. In November, John Slidell was sent to Mexico to offer up to forty million dollars for Upper California, New Mexico, and the Rio Grande as a boundary for Texas, but the Mexican government refused to receive the American representative. Finally, in April, 1846, in a disputed area in Texas between the Nueces River and the Rio Grande, a battle began; the presence of Americans there suggested to the Mexicans that Mexico had been invaded; the presence of Mexicans meant to Americans that the United States had been invaded. Polk had planned to declare war anyway, but the battle provided the excuse, and on May 13, 1846, Congress declared war.

There were those in the North who felt that Polk had started the war in connivance with the Southern states for the acquisition of more slave territory. In *The Biglow Papers* James Russell Lowell wrote: "They just want this Californy/ So's to lug new slave-states in/ To abuse ye, an' to scorn ye/ An' to plunder ye like sin." Though Polk was a slaveowner with a Tennessee plantation, he determined to avoid the issue insofar as his policy decisions were concerned, but Congress would not let him. Convinced that Mexico would not agree to peace terms unless it acquired enough money to at least pay its army, the President requested two million dollars be made available. Pennsylvania Congressman David Wilmot attached to the appropriations bill a proviso that slavery be excluded from any lands acquired from Mexico. The Wilmot Proviso did not pass, but neither did the appropriations bill. "What connection slavery had with making peace with Mexico it is difficult to conceive," wrote Polk. Deprived of working funds, he now had to acquire territory solely by military means; unfortunately, the military aspect of the war had become just as political as the congressional battlefield.

When "Old Rough-and-Ready," General Zachary Taylor, engaged and defeated the Mexicans with his underdog forces in southern Texas, he became a national hero and, to Eastern Whig leaders, a potential presidential candidate. In Washington, Winfield Scott, another Whig presidential hopeful and commanding general of the Army, was anxious to follow up Taylor's victories with an immediate invasion of Mexico. President Polk, however, had other ideas. In the first place, he was by no means anxious to assist either general into the White House, and in the second, he still had hopes of acquiring New Mexico and California by diplomacy. To increase his chances of diplomatic success, Polk agreed to enlist the services of former Mexican dictator Santa Anna, who was in exile in Cuba. Santa Anna was, naturally, anxious to regain power in Mexico. He was to be afforded safe conduct through the American blockade and, having resecured his place in government, cooperate with the

In 1849, the President retired to "Polk Place," his mansion in Nashville. It was demolished in 1900.

United States in negotiating a settlement. In the meantime, he would supply the Americans with military advice. On August 16, Santa Anna arrived in Veracruz and immediately condemned any attempt to negotiate with the United States. Within a month he was back in uniform, and before the end of the year he was elected President of Mexico.

As soon as Santa Anna revealed that he had no intention of working for the United States, President Polk no longer had reason to prevent an invasion of Mexico. After Taylor took Monterrey in September, nine thousand of his men were transferred to Scott's army. Nevertheless, Taylor met Santa Anna at Buena Vista and won a bloody battle. In March, 1847, Scott took Veracruz and proceeded inland through the spring and summer, reaching Mexico City by the middle of September. Santa Anna retreated to Guadalupe Hidalgo and renounced the Presidency. Two months later the Mexican ad interim government named a commission to negotiate a treaty.

Negotiating for the United States was Nicholas P. Trist, chief clerk of the State Department. Dispatched in April, 1847, Trist had been empowered to offer fifteen million dollars (although he could go as high as twenty) for "the Rio Grande as a boundary and the cession of New Mexico and Upper California." (California had actually been in American hands throughout much of the hostilities, and uprisings of Mexicans were considered "insurrections.") The mission was supposed to be secret, but less than a week after Trist's departure from Washington, an item in the New York *Herald* gave all the details of the assignment. After that, Polk lost confidence in the mission. When word reached him in October that the Mexicans had refused the terms offered by Trist, the President decided to recall his negotiator and to pursue a program of total victory over Mexico. Even the possibility of annexing all of the country was considered. Trist refused to be recalled, however, and the President was furious—the whole affair had gotten out of his control; Trist, he said, was "arrogant, impudent, and very insulting to his government . . . destitute of honor and principle . . . a very base man." Yet, on February 19, 1848, when the Treaty of Guadalupe Hidalgo—signed seventeen days earlier by Trist and the Mexican commissioners— arrived in Washington, Polk had to submit it to the Congress. It contained provisions for everything he had wanted: the Rio Grande became the final border; New Mexico and California became American; and the Mexicans settled for fifteen million dollars. As the New York Whig Philip Hone put it, the treaty, ratified March 10, was "negotiated by an unauthorized agent, with an unacknowledged government, [and] submitted by an accidental President to a dissatisfied Senate."

Nevertheless, the treaty achieved the last of Polk's four goals. In the Jackson administration, when Polk had been chairman of the House Ways and Means Committee, he had labored long and hard against the Bank of the United States. Largely through Polk's efforts, Congress had agreed to withdraw public funds from the Bank and allow its charter to expire. As Speaker during the Van Buren administration, Polk had been able to help establish an Independent Treasury, but the Whig victory in 1840 led to its repeal a year later, and the management of public money was left to the Secretary of the Treasury, who had no legal guidelines to follow. Polk restored the Independent Treasury Act in 1846.

After an arduous struggle, Polk also managed to enact the Walker Tariff of 1846, which greatly reduced the duties set on imports by the Whig Tariff of 1842. Northern industrialists denounced it bitterly, but it was one of the few issues on which the President had the full support of John Calhoun. The significance of the tariff lay in the impetus it provided to free trade, a trend that lasted until the Civil War.

On December 5, 1848, in his last annual message to Congress, President Polk announced that gold had been discovered in California. The announcement gave impetus to the westward movement, and within months the gold rush was on. Yet, despite the obvious potential of the West, Congress had failed to provide territorial governments for New Mexico and California in preparation for eventual statehood. The reason for the hesitation was the slavery question. Polk did not want that issue to interfere with the future of the nation that now spanned the continent. He said:

"In the eyes of the world and of posterity how trivial and insignificant will be all our internal divisions and struggles compared with the preservation of this Union of the States in all its vigor and with all its count-less blessings! No patriot would foment and excite geographical and sectional divisions. No lover of his country would deliberately calculate the value of the Union."

By 1848, the Whigs and everybody else knew who James Knox Polk was. He knew what he wanted done; he said he needed only one term to do it; and he was true to his word. He had achieved much and won little applause for it, although he had worn himself out in the process: his hair had turned gray, his step was feeble, his health was ruined. And for this he was known as Polk the Mendacious.

Polk did not run for the Presidency again. Zachary Taylor won the election of 1848, and at his inauguration in March, 1849, Polk found his successor "exceedingly ignorant of public affairs, and . . . of very ordinary capacity." Then the ex-President retired to Polk Place, his home in Tennessee. The chronic diarrhea that had plagued him during his administration recurred, but he had left his resiliency in the White House. He died on June 15, 1849, and was buried in Nashville.

Like Andrew Jackson, Polk regarded himself as the tool and representative of the people. He opposed Clay's American System because he thought it was unconstitutional in that it benefited few at the expense of many. He accepted the manifest destiny concept of American expansion because the people accepted it. He lowered the tariff because he felt the people—not the manufacturers—should choose their own goods from the greatest possible market. He re-established the Independent Treasury because he thought the people's money should be protected by law and not handled by the judgment of one man. He was able to carry out his program because he was a superb administrator, keeping his fingers in every crevice of government, leading every department, and by his own tenacity setting an example he expected all to follow. A moderate in the midst of radicals and reactionaries, he won the enmity of both sides and the admiration only of history.

—SAUL BRAUN

A PICTURE PORTFOLIO

POLK HOME, COLUMBIA, TENN.

JAMES K. POLK.
THE PEOPLES CHOICE.

Artist Nathaniel Currier lithographed this poster for the 1844 presidential campaign.

As indicated by the poster at right, Whig support of American industry was stressed by candidate Henry Clay in the campaign of 1844. The people, however, were more interested in land than in factories, and Polk, the Democratic expansionist candidate, won.

In the 1846 cartoon above, titled "This is the House that Polk Built," the President sits brooding over—and dangerously under—his tenuously balanced young administration. He seems to be planning ways to prevent the Oregon boundary dispute, the conflict with Mexico, and tariff problems from collapsing on his head. By the end of his term, Polk had turned the house of cards into a fortress.

WHO IS POLK?

Compared with Whig candidate Henry Clay, James Knox Polk was a political novice, a man little known outside Tennessee and Washington. He had been a congressman for fourteen years and Speaker of the House under Van Buren; but unlike the colorful, ubiquitous Clay, Polk had always worked inconspicuously, behind the scenes. Thus, when in 1844 he became the first dark horse to receive the presidential nomination, the Whigs asked, laughingly and often, "Who is James K. Polk?" A devoted Jacksonian, Polk, who was sometimes called Young Hickory, was the Democratic candidate because Old Hickory had chosen him. Reading the national temperament more accurately than the Whigs, Jackson felt that Clay's popularity could be neutralized by his evasiveness with regard to the Oregon boundary dispute and the annexation of Texas. Demanding "All of Oregon, all of Texas!" Polk won New York's 36 electoral votes, which gave him his 170 to 105 victory. After the rain-soaked inauguration, President Polk plunged into the issues that made his administration one of the most eventful single terms in presidential history. A believer in America's manifest destiny, he settled the Oregon boundary dispute with England, fought and won a profitable war with Mexico, and gained the breadth of the continent for the United States.

A gift from her husband, the fan Mrs. Polk carried at the inauguration was decorated with pictures of all the Presidents through Polk. On the other side, the signing of the Declaration of Independence is shown.

TO THE PACIFIC

Although President Polk had ridden to victory on slogans such as "All of Oregon" and "54° 40′ or Fight!" he knew full well that England had large investments in northern Oregon and would never cede the whole territory. Having no desire to go to war with England, he settled for a border along the forty-ninth parallel, thus achieving his aim of extending the United States to the Pacific. Polk then turned his attention to California, which Mexico had refused to sell and over which he was quite willing to fight. He had pledged to acquire "All of Texas," and a small, disputed area north of the Rio Grande provided the excuse for a war of conquest against Mexico. The conflict was a smashing success: the American Army learned to invade, pursue, hold, and occupy; the Navy learned to use its muscle off the Pacific coast. And in the Treaty of Guadalupe Hidalgo, signed on February 2, 1848, Mexico relinquished all claims to Texas, California, and New Mexico, adding more than a million square miles to the United States. And yet, perhaps because it was so obviously aggressive, the Mexican War was not universally popular. Even with the enemy defeated, on his knees in his own capital, President Polk insisted on paying fifteen million dollars for the lands he had taken—conscience money, the payment has been called. Critics of the war were legion, but no one ever seriously suggested that the United States give back to Mexico the vast expanse of territory it had gained from the war.

In 1846, a war over Oregon was not imminent, but it was a possibility. Sent to observe the American settlement at Oregon City, Army officer Henry Warre painted the picture above. A year later, the American Army and Navy joined forces in the fight for California. Commodore Robert F. Stockton secured Los Angeles when he defeated the Mexicans at La Mesa. One sailor, William Meyers, painted the scene below.

On September 14, 1847, the American offensive through Mexico ended in Mexico City.

Leading the column, on a brown horse, is the triumphant General Winfield Scott.

PROPONENTS OF THE WEST

NEW YORK PUBLIC LIBRARY

LIBRARY OF CONGRESS

GEORGE BANCROFT

George Bancroft's Democratic affiliations and expansionist views were strangely out of place in the New England society in which he was bred. Educated at Harvard and the University of Göttingen in Germany, he was co-founder of the Round Hill boys' school in Massachusetts, where he taught before embarking on his career as a historian and statesman. By 1840, he had published three volumes of his famous ten-volume *History of the United States*, which he completed in 1874. (The first volume, noted a contemporary critic, was "redolent of the ideas of the new Jacksonian democracy.") Bancroft worked to secure the Democratic presidential nomination for Polk in 1844, and as the latter's Secretary of the Navy supported the President's acquisitions of Oregon and California. Bancroft established the Naval Academy at Annapolis, and at the outbreak of the Mexican War, issued instructions to the Pacific fleet for the occupation of California's ports. Appointed minister to Great Britain by Polk, he later served as minister to Berlin under Johnson and Grant. Throughout his life he continued to write; when he died at the age of ninety, the *Harvard Graduates' Magazine* justly noted that George Bancroft's "position as Father of American History is as unshaken as that of Herodotus among the Greeks."

BRIGHAM YOUNG

"Brigham Young," observed a French visitor to Salt Lake City, "is . . . the Mormon pope; he is at the same time, by election of the people, a prophet, 'revelator,' and seer." An early convert to Mormonism, Young became a zealous missionary, rose quickly in the hierarchy of the church, and soon ranked second only to the prophet Joseph Smith. When Smith was murdered by a mob in 1844, Young, then forty-three, became the leader of the Mormon church. Threatened with expulsion from Illinois, the persecuted Mormons prepared to leave their home in Nauvoo. The exodus began in the winter of 1846 and was completed the following year. In one of the epic colonizing ventures of America's westward movement, the Mormon leader shepherded his people across the plains to the barren valley of the Great Salt Lake in Mexico Territory. Displaying a genius for social and economic organization, Young laid out a city, instituted a system of irrigated agriculture, and ruled his colony with a despotic hand. When the land was ceded to the United States and was named Utah Territory, he was made its first governor; near the end of his life he boasted of ". . . the founding of over 200 cities, towns and villages." The Mormon patriarch, who had fifty-six children and a score of wives, died at the age of seventy-six.

WASHINGTON IRVING

"It is a fact well known," declared the Boston *Post* in 1838, "that with few exceptions, our first literary men belong to the democratic party." Washington Irving—an intimate friend of President Van Buren's—was no exception. He served his party and his country as a diplomat abroad, and was minister to Spain from 1842 through the first year of Polk's administration. It was in the capacity of an author, however, that he made his greatest mark on the course of American democracy. His stories of the Western frontier captured the imagination of the American people and sparked the contemporary interest in the growing westward movement. Best known for his comic *History of New York* and for such charming tales as *Rip Van Winkle* and *The Legend of Sleepy Hollow*, it was not until 1832 that he turned his attention to Western themes. In that year he accompanied an expedition to the lands of the Osage and Pawnee Indians, collecting material for *A Tour on the Prairies*, published in 1835. *Astoria*, published in 1836, and *The Adventures of Captain Bonneville, U.S.A.*, in 1837, told the story of the fur trade and stimulated American interest in the region of the Pacific Northwest. Near the end of his life he began a five-volume biography of Washington, which he completed in 1859, the year of his death.

SAMUEL HOUSTON

"Gov. Houston," wrote Washington Irving of the hero of the Texas Revolution, was a "tall, large, well formed, fascinating man . . . given to grandiloquence." Friend and defender of the Cherokee nation, Sam Houston led the rugged life of a frontier soldier and statesman. He fought in the Creek War with Andrew Jackson, became district attorney for Nashville, served two terms in Congress, and in 1827 was elected governor of Tennessee. Two years later, when his bride of three months left him, Houston resigned the governorship, went to live among the Cherokee in Indian Territory, and became an Indian trader on the Verdigris River. Establishing himself at Nacogdoches in 1835, he was soon enmeshed in the struggle for Texan independence. As commander of the Texas troops, he defeated Santa Anna's army at the San Jacinto in 1836 and was rewarded with the presidency of the new republic. Elected for a second term in 1841, Houston yielded to the popular cry of the expansionists and guided Texas into the Union. For thirteen years he served as a United States senator from Texas, and in 1859 he was elected governor. Opposed to secession and refusing to acknowledge the authority of the Confederate government, Houston resigned in 1861. Two years later the Texas patriot died at the age of seventy.

A PIOUS FIRST LADY

Sarah Childress Polk was the first active, bona fide First Lady to move into the White House since Mrs. John Quincy Adams. While the lovely and spirited young women who had served as hostesses in the interim had directed a lively social calendar, only one—John Tyler's child bride, Julia—had been a real First Lady, and she was a lame-duck one at that. But if anyone anticipated a return to the more homey tenure of Dolley Madison or the regal years of Elizabeth Monroe, he was in for a surprise. A pious Calvinist, as strong-willed and earnest as her husband, Mrs. Polk established a new order: wine, dancing, and card-playing were forbidden in the White House, and at public receptions no refreshments were served. Ironically, it was the wine-drinking, card-playing, snuff-taking octogenarian Dolley Madison who prevented a pall from completely enveloping the Capital. Receptions in her Lafayette Square home were frequent and lively, and her presence at White House functions countered the austerity of Mrs. Polk. But in fairness to the First Lady, it must be added that her tenure was well suited to the needs of her husband and his administration. One of the hardest-working Presidents in history, Polk had a distaste for "time unprofitably spent." When after a year in office it became apparent that he was wearing himself down, Mrs. Polk lightened his work load by becoming his competent confidential secretary. Not until his last year in office did Polk agree to take a vacation; then it was too late. The eleventh President died three months after leaving the White House.

The recently discovered daguerreotype at left was made during Polk's administration. President and Mrs. Polk are in the center. At the extreme left of the picture is Secretary of State and future President James Buchanan with his niece, Harriet Lane. The lady (second from right) who moved while the shutter was open is none other than the perennially popular former First Lady, Mrs. James Madison.

FACTS IN SUMMARY: JAMES KNOX POLK

CHRONOLOGY

UNITED STATES		POLK
	1795	*Born November 2*
John Adams elected President	1796	
XYZ Affair	1798	
Undeclared naval war with France		
Alien and Sedition Acts		
Jefferson elected President	1801	
Louisiana Purchase	1803	
	1806	*Moves to Tennessee*
Madison elected President	1808	
Battle of Tippecanoe	1811	
War with England	1812	
Battle of Lake Erie	1813	
Battle of the Thames		
British burn Washington	1814	
Treaty of Ghent		
Jackson wins Battle of New Orleans	1815	*Enters University of North Carolina*
Monroe elected President	1816	
Missouri Compromise	1820	*Admitted to the bar*
Monroe Doctrine	1823	*Elected to Tennessee legislature*

	1824	*Marries Sarah Childress*
		Elected to U.S. House of Representatives
John Quincy Adams elected President	1825	
Jackson elected President	1828	
Nullification controversy	1832	*Named to House Ways and Means Committee*
Jackson vetoes Bank recharter		
Rise of Whig party	1834	
	1835	*Becomes Speaker of the House*
Siege of the Alamo	1836	
Van Buren elected President		
	1839	*Elected governor of Tennessee*
Independent Treasury Act	1840	
Harrison elected President		
Tyler becomes President	1841	*Defeated in bid for re-election as governor*
Independent Treasury Act repealed		
Webster-Ashburton Treaty	1842	

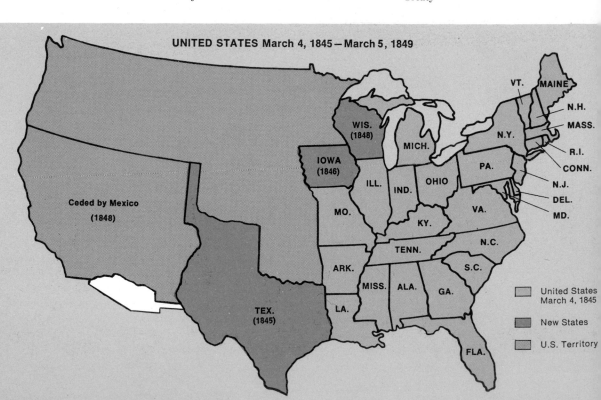

UNITED STATES March 4, 1845 — March 5, 1849

VT. MAINE
N.H.
MASS.
WIS. (1848)
MICH.
N.Y.
R.I.
CONN.
IOWA (1846)
ILL.
IND.
OHIO
PA.
N.J.
DEL.
MD.
MO.
KY.
VA.
Ceded by Mexico (1848)
TENN.
N.C.
ARK.
S.C.
MISS. ALA. GA.
LA.
TEX. (1845)
FLA.

United States March 4, 1845
New States
U.S. Territory

1844	Elected President
Texas annexed	1845	*Authorizes Slidell mission to Mexico*
U.S. Naval Academy opened		*Recommends tariff revision*
Texas admitted to Union		
War with Mexico declared	1846	*Restores Independent Treasury*
Battle of Palo Alto		
Oregon boundary settled		*Enacts Walker Tariff*
Wilmot Proviso		
Monterrey captured		
Treaty of Cahuenga ends hostilities in California	1847	*Sends Trist to negotiate peace with Mexico*
Battle of Buena Vista		
Capture of Veracruz		
Winfield Scott's troops take Mexico City		
Gold discovered in California	1848	*Signs bill establishing territorial government for Oregon*
Treaty of Guadalupe Hidalgo		
Taylor elected President		
	1849	*Retires to Nashville Dies June 15*

Sarah Polk wore this cameo of her husband as a pin.

POLK HOME, COLUMBIA, TENN.

BIOGRAPHICAL FACTS

BIRTH: Mecklenburg County, N.C., Nov. 2, 1795
ANCESTRY: Scotch-Irish
FATHER: Samuel Polk; b. Tryon, N.C., July 5, 1772; d. Maury County, Tenn., Nov. 5, 1827
FATHER'S OCCUPATION: Farmer
MOTHER: Jane Knox Polk; b. Iredell County, N.C., Nov. 15, 1776; d. Maury County, Tenn., Jan 11, 1852
BROTHERS: Franklin Ezekiel (1802–1831); Marshall Tate (1805–1831); John Lee (1807–1831); William Hawkins (1815–1862); Samuel Wilson (1817–1839)
SISTERS: Jane Maria (1798–1876); Lydia Eliza (1800–1864); Naomi Tate (1809–1836); Ophelia Clarissa (1812–1851)
WIFE: Sarah Childress; b. Murfreesboro, Tenn., Sept. 4, 1803; d. Nashville, Tenn., Aug. 14, 1891
MARRIAGE: Murfreesboro, Tenn., Jan. 1, 1824
CHILDREN: None
HOME: Polk House, Columbia, Tennessee
EDUCATION: Private school; received B.A. from the University of North Carolina
RELIGIOUS AFFILIATION: Presbyterian
OCCUPATION BEFORE PRESIDENCY: Lawyer
PRE-PRESIDENTIAL OFFICES: Member of Tenn. Legislature; U.S. Representative; Speaker of the House of Representatives; Governor of Tennessee
AGE AT INAUGURATION: 49
OCCUPATION AFTER PRESIDENCY: Retired
DEATH: Nashville, Tenn., June 15, 1849
PLACE OF BURIAL: State Capitol Grounds, Nashville, Tenn.

ELECTION OF 1844

CANDIDATES	ELECTORAL VOTE	POPULAR VOTE
James K. Polk Democratic	170	1,338,464
Henry Clay Whig	105	1,300,097
James G. Birney Liberty	—	62,300

THE POLK ADMINISTRATION

INAUGURATION: March 4, 1845; the Capitol, Washington, D.C.
VICE PRESIDENT: George M. Dallas
SECRETARY OF STATE: James Buchanan
SECRETARY OF THE TREASURY: Robert J. Walker
SECRETARY OF WAR: William L. Marcy
ATTORNEY GENERAL: John Y. Mason; Nathan Clifford (from Oct. 17, 1846); Isaac Toucey (from June 29, 1848)
POSTMASTER GENERAL: Cave Johnson
SECRETARY OF THE NAVY: George Bancroft; John Y. Mason (from Sept. 9, 1846)
SUPREME COURT APPOINTMENTS: Levi Woodbury (1845); Robert Cooper Grier (1846)
29th CONGRESS (March 4, 1845–March 4, 1847):
Senate: 31 Democrats; 25 Whigs
House: 143 Democrats; 77 Whigs; 6 Others
30th CONGRESS (March 4, 1847–March 4, 1849):
Senate: 36 Democrats; 21 Whigs; 1 Other
House: 115 Whigs; 108 Democrats; 4 Others
STATES ADMITTED: Texas (1845); Iowa (1846); Wisconsin (1848)

ZACHARY TAYLOR

O n the night that "Old Rough-and-Ready" Zachary Taylor entered Washington for his inauguration as President he was greeted by a crowd said to be the largest ever seen in the Capital up to that time; bonfires crackled, fireworks burst in the night sky, and cannon thudded salutes. When he died, sixteen months after taking office, more than one hundred carriages and a procession nearly two miles long accompanied his body to the grave, while thousands upon thousands of mourners lined the route. He was a national hero and a popular President.

Time, however, has reduced his stature. Taylor's modern-day obscurity is particularly curious because in the tug of war that created and characterized the crisis of 1850, the President held one end of the rope; and that ephemeral pacifier, the Compromise of 1850, became law only over Taylor's dead body.

Zachary Taylor was an offspring of Virginia's aristocratic Revolutionary generation. His father, Richard Taylor, was descended from a line of wealthy planters and served in the First Virginia Regiment during the War for Independence, rising to lieutenant colonel. Richard's wife, Sarah Dabney Strother, was similarly wellborn and had been educated by European tutors. In 1784, after five years of marriage, Richard, his pregnant wife, and their two sons left their comfortable home near the Rapidan River to strike out for Kentucky and a new life. On November 24, in a rough-hewn outbuilding on a relative's estate that lay along the way, Sarah bore Richard a third son, whom they named Zachary. After a few months he was taken to a wilderness settlement on Beargrass Creek, near Louisville, where the family began to farm. "Here," wrote a visitor of Taylor's early childhood, "we were saluted every night with the howling of wolves." Here, also, Indians harassed the settlers. On the frontier, Zachary received a rudimentary education; first from a wandering Con-

Zachary Taylor, as he appeared in about 1848

313

necticut schoolteacher, and then from an Irish scholar who set up a school in the neighborhood. Richard and Sarah passed on to their children the respect for culture and education inherent in Virginia society; politics was doubtless a frequent dinner table topic.

At twenty-three, Zachary Taylor accepted a commission as a first lieutenant in the Army. During the next forty years, except for one brief hiatus after the War of 1812, he remained an Army officer. In 1810 he married Margaret Mackall Smith; they had six children, only four of whom—three daughters and a son—survived infancy. Husband, father, career soldier, Taylor was also a professional farmer, owning land and slaves in Louisiana and Mississippi. Acquaintances remarked how he preferred discussing crops, the weather, and farming methods to any other kind of talk. But he had to do most of his farming by mail, through plantation managers, as his Army service took him from Illinois to the Gulf of Mexico, from the District of Columbia to Minnesota. He fought the British and the Indians; he gained a reputation for courage and improvisational skill in battle and for fairness in administering Indian affairs. He built roads, bridges, and forts, and commanded numerous Army posts. He played a substantial, sometimes a key, role in opening the West to settlement. Promotions came slowly, but in 1844 he was a brevet brigadier general and commanding officer of the First Department, United States Army, at Fort Jesup, Louisiana.

"He looked like a man born to command," a fellow officer had written in 1832. Yet in many ways General Zachary Taylor's appearance was rather odd. His large head and torso did not match his unusually short legs. A typical uniform for him consisted of baggy cotton pants, a plain coat bearing no insignia, and a farmer's wide-brimmed straw hat. He reviewed his troops or observed a battle's progress seated sideways on his war horse, "Old Whitey," with one leg thrown over the pommel of his saddle. From a distance he may have seemed merely an eccen-

tric. But in his seamed and craggy face could be read a remarkable depth of spirit. His gaze was direct—as he was. His concern for matters at hand was wholehearted.

General Taylor's assignment in Louisiana in 1844 was part of American preparations for Texas annexation; the Mexicans threatened war over the republic, which they still considered theirs despite a successful rebellion. When a Texas convention accepted annexation in July, Taylor moved in with his forces and set up a base camp at Corpus Christi. There the growing army was drilled until early in 1846. By then Mexico seemed less decisive about opposing annexation, but there was something else to fight about: Texas claimed the Rio Grande as her southern boundary, and Mexico protested that the border should be farther north. Taylor began to move toward the Rio Grande.

The first skirmish of the war was fought on April 25, when an American scouting party was ambushed. Taylor hastened to inform Washington, but by the time war was formally declared by Congress—on May 13 —two major battles had already been fought, at Palo Alto and the Resaca de la Palma. Taylor's army, although greatly outnumbered, had won both. Within a few days these engagements in the cause of manifest destiny had made General Taylor a national hero. Before a month was out he had also become a pawn in the game of national politics: Thurlow Weed, New York editor and boss of the "out" party, the Whigs, predicted to the general's brother, Joseph, that Taylor would be elected President. Nonsense, said Zachary. The idea "seems to me too visionary to require a serious answer. . . . [It] never entered my head, nor is it likely to enter the head of any sane person." But during the summer of 1846, while Taylor received a promotion to major general, organized his army for a southward sweep to Monterrey in Mexico, and tried to cope with a barely manageable flood of volunteers that increased his forces to 14,000 men, the presidential talk continued. Support for Taylor came from all over the political spectrum; meetings of Democrats, Whigs, and

Native Americans (precursor of the anti-Catholic, anti-immigration "Know-Nothing" party of the 1850's) nominated him for an election that was more than two years away. Although there was some popular confusion as to Taylor's political leanings, President Polk correctly thought of him as a Whig, and thus a serious threat to Democratic power. For Polk the crisis came when Old Rough-and-Ready's army stormed Monterrey and took it after a bloody house-to-house battle. When it was over, Taylor held most of the town, but the Mexicans had holed up in a strong defensive position, and he would have been hard pressed to dislodge them: the fighting had already lasted three days and American supplies were dwindling. Moreover, it was known that Polk was offering to negotiate peace, and under the circumstances Taylor felt that "it would be judicious to act with magnanimity towards a prostrate foe. . . ." He let the surviving Mexicans leave Monterrey with their arms.

Polk, observing how the victory further enhanced Taylor's chances for the White House, was constrained to feel that the general—by letting the Mexicans go—had missed a chance to end the war in Monterrey. Whether or not the President had a point, politics demanded that he remove Taylor from the spotlight and diminish his command. Polk turned over active prosecution of the war to the Army chief of staff, General Winfield Scott. Taylor was told to stay at Monterrey (most of his best troops were transferred to Scott) and was ordered to conduct only defensive operations. But Polk's plot backfired. General Scott's letter to Taylor about the transfer of troops fell into the hands of the Mexican commander, Santa Anna. Taylor and his drastically reduced force looked like an easy conquest, and the Mexicans needed a victory. Twenty thousand Mexican troops marched toward Monterrey. Meanwhile, Taylor had grown bitter at being—as he saw it—victimized by the intrigues of Scott and Polk. Disobeying orders, he moved five thousand of his troops a few miles to the southwest of Monterrey. As Santa Anna advanced, the

UNCLE SAM'S TAYLORIFICS

America cuts up Mexico (with Taylor's troops) while England fishes for Oregon in this cartoon of 1846.

main body of the Americans took up positions in a mountain valley, near a ranch called Buena Vista. There, on February 22 and 23, 1847, Taylor's outnumbered band hung desperately on the edge of annihilation; but at the end they had fought the Mexicans to a standstill. Though they had lost more than seven hundred men, they had suffered less than half the number of Mexican casualties. That night, Santa Anna retreated.

Coming at the end of a string of successes against superior numbers, Buena Vista virtually made the old farmer-general President of the United States. Of course with the possible exception of George Washington, no man, no matter how great a hero, has become President by spontaneous combustion. Hard work was needed by men with political power, and Taylor got it—from such leaders as John J. Crittenden of Kentucky, Abraham Lincoln of Illinois, and Alexander H. Stephens of Georgia. And as Taylor's friends and a multitude of letter writers began to wean Taylor from his aloofness from politics, the general himself displayed evidence of a native political sharpness that stood him in good stead. He avoided making deals and remained relatively noncommittal on the issues. He politely accepted nominations from local political groups of all stripes, and continued to assert, well into 1848, that he did not want to be a party candidate bound by party principles. Not until six weeks before the Whig National Convention were close friends able to convince him to come out openly as a Whig in order to assure himself a meaningful nomination. Even then he maintained that he was no party "ultra," and promised the public that "if elected I would not be the mere president of a party—I would endeavor to act independent of party domination, & should feel bound to administer the Government untrammelled by party schemes. . . ."

The Democrats put forward the pro-expansionist Lewis Cass of Michigan. This caused Barnburners—free-soil Democrats—to bolt the party in New York; they nominated Martin Van Buren for President. Early in August, a Free-Soil convention attended by abolitionists and Whigs of the Northeast, as well as Barnburners, seconded this nomination. Cass's chances in crucial New York were ruined. In November he ran third in the state, behind Van Buren, who was second; Taylor won the state's thirty-six electoral votes with less than a popular majority. Pennsylvania's twenty-six votes also went to Taylor, helped by a Whig alliance with Know-Nothings in Philadelphia.

Zachary Taylor is believed not to have voted in 1848, thus perpetuating a perfect record of never having voted in a presidential election. To some he seemed an utterly apolitical figure who would have to depend heavily on experienced politicians around him. But he had always been interested in government, and he had opinions of his own, which he made known after his inauguration.

The central issues of his administration were national expansion and slavery extension. The founding of the Free-Soil party indicated the increasing political potency in the North of antislavery feelings. The country was being bombarded by abolitionist writings; the South (and Taylor too) was concerned about what the movement and its inflammatory propaganda would bring. When slaves escaped northward, their capture and return was difficult, and growing more so. Slave insurrections were feared, as was, of course, abolition itself. Southerners felt that if the North won political control in the Congress, abolition was a certainty, and there were signs that the North would soon win that control: its industries were attracting thousands of immigrants, swelling its voting population; the Missouri Compromise had shut out slavery from the Northern states; and the Oregon Territory had been created, in August, 1848, with slavery excluded. For all these reasons many Southerners favored expansion of the United States to the south and west, enlarging the slave territory and maintaining the sectional equilibrium intended by the Missouri Compromise. Free-Soil activists naturally tried to block them.

Civil government for the land wrested from Mexico was a responsibility assumed

*In this engraving made from a daguerreotype,
Taylor is shown wearing his general's uniform,
which he seldom donned except to pose for portraits.*

by the United States as soon as the Treaty
of Guadalupe Hidalgo was signed in February, 1848. Then, as the news began to fan
out from the Sacramento Valley that gold
had been discovered there, territorial organization or statehood for California became
crucial. The military government and the
remnants of Mexican civil authority simply
could not handle the wild conditions that
rapidly developed in California in 1848 and
1849. New Mexico's predicament was different: Texas wanted land the New Mexicans
believed was theirs, and full-blown armed
hostility in the region between the Pecos
River and the Rio Grande was a possibility.

Because of the slavery issue, Polk was unable to push through Congress territorial
bills for either area, and responsibility for
solving the problem fell to Taylor. The
twelfth President sent word to both California and New Mexico that applications for
statehood would be welcome; since congressional debate on territorial status would
raise great bitterness between the sections,
Taylor hoped by this method to present
Congress with a *fait accompli*, with the slav-

ery status of the two regions already settled
by the inhabitants. Both would probably
apply for admission as free states, which he
approved and may have encouraged. He
wanted to stop congressional debate on slavery permanently; he and a good many moderate Southerners felt that this could be
accomplished by halting the extension of
slavery and guaranteeing the status quo in
the extant slave states.

In August, Taylor let the country know
what he had in mind. In a speech at Mercer,
Pennsylvania, he said, "The people of the
North need have no apprehension of the
further extension of slavery." That summer
he hemmed in the slavocracy in another
way, by issuing a proclamation against a
filibustering expedition then being prepared
for the conquest of Cuba. In his annual message in December he noted the probability
of applications for statehood from California
and New Mexico, suggesting that until they
arrived, sectional arguments were not in
order. The South was growing alarmed;
Taylor's moderate Southern Whig backing
began to dissolve and secessionist talk grew
loud. Now his inexperience in government
would start to tell; he had few political
friends, no backlog of political debts to call
in, and the only power that remained to promote his wishes was the prestige and force of
the Presidency—sufficient to create an
angry stalemate, but no more.

Henry Clay, the Great Compromiser, now
tried to move into the leadership vacuum.
He suggested the admission of California on
its own terms, but included also the creation
of territorial governments for New Mexico
and the Mormon empire of Deseret (Utah),
a western boundary for Texas somewhat
farther east than the Texans wanted, the
abolition of slave trading in the District of
Columbia, creation of a fugitive-slave law
more effective than the one then in force,
and denial to Congress of the power to legislate over interstate slave trade. Although
Clay won to his support such leaders as
Daniel Webster, Stephen Douglas, and
Lewis Cass, along with most of the congressional Democrats, and although talk of com-

317

promise put brakes on the secessionist movement in the South, he really only succeeded in intensifying the stalemate. Taylor refused to budge: California—which applied for free statehood in March, 1850—had to come in by itself, and if the Southern states tried to secede, he would, he swore, personally lead the Army to put down the rebellion.

Taylor kept the pressure on. At his behest, New Mexico requested admission (as a free state) in June. He believed that once New Mexico was a state, the boundary dispute with Texas could be settled by the Supreme Court. Texas wanted none of it and prepared to raise troops to seize the disputed territory, then being protected by United States forces. It appeared that the South might fasten on this issue to test federal reaction to a state rebellion.

Through the month of June, the forces of Clay and Taylor, and of Texas and Taylor, remained locked, with debate raging on about the Compromise—now wrapped up in an omnibus bill—and with Taylor giving every evidence of readiness to veto the bill.

The President was having other troubles. His Cabinet appointments had not been popular, and now, in the spring of 1850, the Secretaries of War and the Treasury and the Attorney General were revealed to have participated in a legal action that had netted the Secretary of War, George Crawford, a lot of money. Just how wrong their actions were is debatable, but they certainly looked bad, and the scandal got tangled in the California-New Mexico debate.

One problem that resulted from the California gold rush concerned a project to cut a canal across Central America. Because of British interests in that region, it seemed necessary to work out with Great Britain an agreement to neutralize the area before digging got under way. Secretary of State John Clayton began discussions with English diplomat Sir Henry Lytton Bulwer in January, 1850. Laced with maneuverings and misunderstandings that required President Taylor's personal attention, the negotiations dragged on until July 4, when the Clayton-Bulwer Treaty was finally signed.

That hot and sunny Independence Day of 1850, President Taylor attended ceremonies at the unfinished Washington Monument. When he arrived back at the White House he took some refreshment—evidently uncooked vegetables or fruit, and large amounts of cold milk or water. Within the next day or so, he came down with acute gastroenteritis, and suddenly, on the evening of July 9, he died.

How is Taylor to be ranked among the Presidents? It is common to think of him either as a naïve, goodhearted, tough old man, his nationalism conditioned by a lifetime of faithful Army service—a habit, not a creed; or as a man whose political doctrine was formed by New York's antislavery senator William H. Seward. Seward did have some influence at the White House, but one must remember that Taylor had political friends to whom he felt a deeper personal commitment than he did to Seward, including the outspoken slavocrat, Jefferson Davis, his son-in-law, whom he greatly admired. It would seem that Taylor depended on Seward because Seward agreed with him, not the other way around; that Taylor was more his own man than even many of his contemporaries realized.

His great weakness as Chief Executive was his lack of practical preparation for many aspects of his job. But even so, he held his own in the central conflict of his Presidency. As Holman Hamilton, Taylor's major biographer, points out, the President held the key to passage or defeat of the Compromise, which surely would not have become law over his veto; Clay, Douglas, and Cass did not have the votes. At the time, the alternative seemed to be war in the Southwest, late in August, 1850. This war might have been smaller and shorter than the one that would begin eleven years later, but would such a war have been a final solution? Or was the United States destined for Armageddon—a conflict in which one side would become so crippled for so long as to permit the reshaping of the nation's policy toward Negroes?

—MICHAEL HARWOOD

Z. Taylor.

A PICTURE PORTFOLIO

Taylor is depicted at the center of this kerchief; at the corners are scenes from the battles of Buena Vista, Monterrey, Resaca de la Palma, and Palo Alto.

The above sketch of General Taylor was made during the Mexican War.

"A BRAVE OLD FELLER"

After nearly forty years of relative obscurity as a United States Army officer, Zachary Taylor suddenly found himself propelled to prominence by the war with Mexico. He had long been respected by his colleagues for his obvious ability to lead soldiers and for his bravery and effectiveness as a frontier commander. Although Andrew Jackson told James Polk that Taylor would be "the man to lead our armies" in any war with England, junior officers crit-

icized General Taylor's lack of organization. But General Taylor was at his best once a fight was under way, improvising, and inspiring his men. It is said his sudden appearance on the battlefield at Buena Vista, and his coolness while his clothes were ripped by bullets, were enough to rally the American Army from the verge of defeat. He became an instant legend and a potential presidential candidate. "Zachary Taylor was a brave old feller," went one popular song:

Brigadier General A No. 1.
He fought twenty thousand Mexicanos;
Four thousand he killed, the rest they
  'cut and run.'
In the thickest of the fight Old Zachary
  appear-ed,
The shot flew about him as thick as any
  hail,
And the only injury he there receiv-ed
Was a compound fracture of his brown
  coattail.

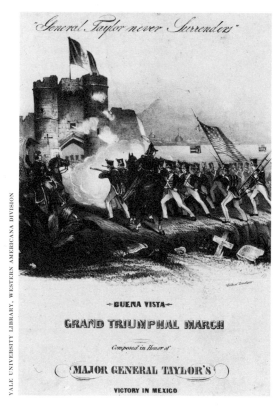

The sheet-music cover above honored General Taylor's role in the great victory at Buena Vista.

The Battle of Palo Alto (left) on May 8, 1846, was the first major engagement of the war. Even though Taylor's troops were outnumbered, their superior artillery helped them to rout the enemy.

LEWIS CASS

Rotund Lewis Cass might have been the twelfth President had it not been for Martin Van Buren and the slavery issue. In New York antislavery Democrats were so unhappy with Cass's expansionist views that they nominated Van Buren to compete for Democratic and "Conscience Whig" votes in 1848; Old Kinderhook drew off enough support from Cass in New York to give Taylor the state and the victory. Born October 9, 1782, in Exeter, New Hampshire, Cass went west in 1799, practiced law in Ohio, and served as an officer in the War of 1812. He became governor of the Territory of Michigan in 1813, and remained at that post for eighteen years. Andrew Jackson made him Secretary of War and then, after five years, sent him to France as minister. Quitting that job in a bitter public debate with John Tyler's Secretary of State, Daniel Webster, Cass came home and ran unsuccessfully for the Democratic presidential nomination in 1844. He went to Washington as Michigan's senator the next year, and became the Democratic presidential candidate in 1848. Cass advocated expansion into Oregon, Mexico, and Yucatan, and fought the Wilmot Proviso, which would have barred slavery from land won from Mexico. Returning to the Senate after his defeat, he was made Buchanan's Secretary of State in 1857, although by then he was too old and infirm to be much more than a figurehead. He resigned in the midst of the secession crisis and died at eighty-four in 1866.

A RELUCTANT CANDIDATE

Taylor refused at first to believe that he might be seriously considered as a presidential candidate. It is said, perhaps apocryphally, that when someone raised the topic while in Taylor's tent in Mexico, the general gruffly suggested that the speaker shut up and drink his whisky. But the dozens of reporters, artists, and politicians who flocked to see him, and the many testimonials and notifications of nomination that were sent to him, made a believer of him. Daniel Webster, another potential candidate, wrote after Buena Vista, "Gen. Taylor's popularity seems to spread like wild fire. They say it is likely to break down party divisions, entirely, in the South & West." Even when this became clear to Taylor, he still was not convinced that he should run; he knew he was inexperienced in statecraft, he disliked practical politics, and Mrs. Taylor was opposed because the wearying Mexican adventure had affected her husband's health. Nevertheless, flattered by the attention he was receiving, he decided that he would serve if elected. But he wanted to be tied to no one party, and for months it appeared that if he were to be elected on his own terms, it would have to be the result of a nonpartisan grass-roots movement, without the official support of either of the major parties. In the end General Taylor reluctantly agreed to accept the Whig presidential nomination, vowing that, even so, he would be a national, not a partisan, Chief Executive.

In the campaign poster above, each letter of Taylor's name is decorated with scenes from the Mexican War. As the Taylor-for-President boom developed, the general received nominations, at the local level, from political groups of all colors, and he accepted them all. The cartoon below reflects the resulting national puzzlement; a phrenologist studies Taylor's skull in an attempt to divine his true political attitudes.

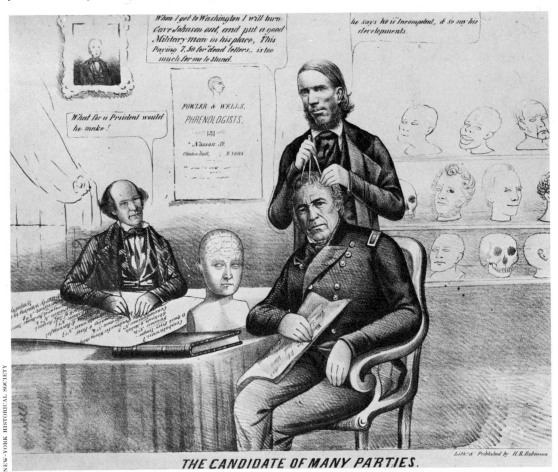

THE CANDIDATE OF MANY PARTIES.

COMPROMISE?

To the surprise of many, Taylor proved to be a strong-willed President. He suffered for never having held a political post before he entered the White House; his lack of experience made it difficult for him to pick his Cabinet members and gave him few personal friends in government on whom he could rely. But in the one major issue of his short tenure—statehood for California and New Mexico—he took a reasonable, defensible position and stuck to it in the face of opposition from the leaders of his party. He believed he could end disruptive congressional debate on slavery by guaranteeing the rights of the South, by taking the state-creating initiative away from Congress, and by stopping the spread of slavery. He asked California and

Henry Clay, standing at center above, opened the debate on the Compromise of 1850 on February 5. Webster, who was to support Clay, is shown sitting at left, his head on his hand. Calhoun stands second from right.

New Mexico to begin the statehood process themselves, knowing they would apply as free states. The South was not pleased; the leading Northern Whigs wished to compromise, but President Taylor was adamant and met threats of a Southern rebellion with a firm promise to suppress it by force. Only after Taylor's sudden death could the temporizing Compromise of 1850 be effected.

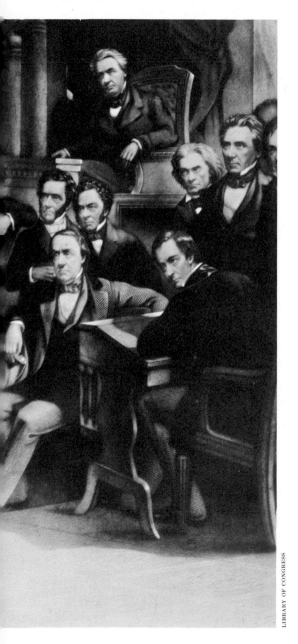

President Taylor died on July 9, 1850, worn out by war, politics, and illness. Grief-stricken, the nation put on mourning ribbons like the one above. In the House, Robert Winthrop, a Massachusetts Whig, remarked sadly, "He has fallen . . . at a moment when some of us were looking to him to render services to the country, which we . . . thought no other man could perform. Certainly . . . he has died too soon for everybody but himself."

FACTS IN SUMMARY: ZACHARY TAYLOR

CHRONOLOGY

UNITED STATES		TAYLOR				
	1784	*Born November 24*	John Quincy Adams inaugurated	1825		
Constitutional Convention	1787		Jackson elected President	1828		
Washington elected President	1789			1829	*Takes command of Fort Snelling*	
Adams elected President	1796			1832	*Takes command of Fort Crawford*	
Jefferson elected President	1801				*Appointed colonel*	
Louisiana Purchase	1803	*Serves as volunteer in Kentucky militia*			*Fights in Black Hawk War*	
Madison elected President	1808	*Appointed first lieutenant, 7th Infantry*	Texas War for Independence	1836		
	1810	*Appointed captain*	Van Buren elected President			
	1811	*Marries Margaret Smith*		1837	*Named a brigadier general for heroism against the Seminoles in the battle of Lake Okeechobee*	
		Takes charge of Fort Knox				
War with Britain	1812	*Defends Fort Harrison against Indians*		1838	*Commands Department of Florida*	
War embargo	1814	*Commissioned major*				
Creek War			Harrison elected President	1840		
Battle of New Orleans	1815	*Receives honorable discharge*	Tyler becomes President	1841		
Monroe elected President	1816	*Reinstated as major, 3rd Infantry*	Webster-Ashburton Treaty	1842		
Bank panic	1819	*Appointed lieutenant colonel, 4th Infantry*	Polk elected President	1844	*Assumes command of Fort Jesup*	
Missouri Compromise	1820		Annexation of Texas	1845	*Commands Army of Occupation on Mexican border*	
	1822	*Establishes Fort Jesup in Louisiana*				

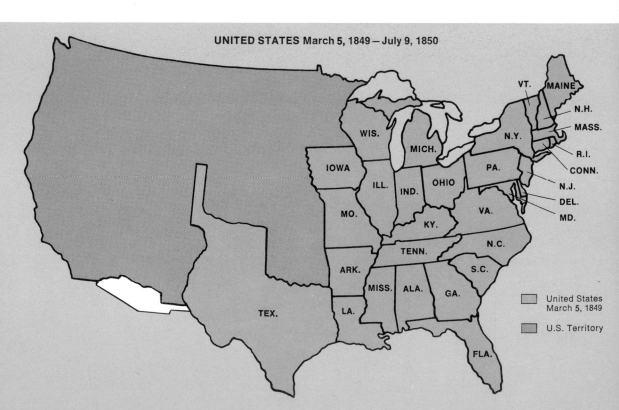

UNITED STATES March 5, 1849 — July 9, 1850

United States March 5, 1849

U.S. Territory

The lithograph above depicts Cypress Grove Plantation in Mississippi, which General Taylor purchased in 1842.

Mexican War begins	1846	*Fights at Matamoros*
		Defeats Mexicans at Palo Alto
		Routs Mexicans at Resaca de la Palma
		Becomes major general
		Takes Monterrey
	1847	*Fights Santa Anna at Buena Vista*
Treaty of Guadalupe Hidalgo	1848	*Nominated for Presidency by Whig party*
		Elected President
	1849	*Resigns from Army*
		Inaugurated as President
Compromise of 1850 Clayton-Bulwer Treaty	1850	*Fights Compromise of 1850*
		Dies July 9

BIOGRAPHICAL FACTS

BIRTH: Orange County, Va., Nov. 24, 1784
ANCESTRY: English
FATHER: Lt. Col. Richard Taylor; b. Orange County, Va., April 3, 1744; d. near Louisville, Ky., Jan. 19, 1829
FATHER'S OCCUPATIONS: Soldier; landowner; civil servant
MOTHER: Sarah Dabney Strother Taylor; b. Dec. 14, 1760; d. Dec. 13, 1822
BROTHERS: Hancock (1781–1841); William Dabney Strother (1782–1808); George (1790–1829); Joseph Pannill (1796–1864)
SISTERS: Elizabeth Lee (1792–1845); Sarah Bailey (1799–1851); Emily Richard (1801–1841)
WIFE: Margaret Mackall Smith; b. Maryland, Sept. 21, 1788; d. Aug. 18, 1852
MARRIAGE: Jefferson County, Ky., June 21, 1810
CHILDREN: Anne Mackall (1811–1875); Sarah Knox (1814–1835); Octavia Pannill (1816–1820); Margaret Smith (1819–1820); Mary Elizabeth (1824–1909); Richard (1826–1879)
EDUCATION: Limited tutorial education

RELIGIOUS AFFILIATION: Episcopalian
OCCUPATIONS BEFORE PRESIDENCY: Soldier; farmer
MILITARY SERVICE: Volunteer in Kentucky militia (1803); rose from first lieutenant to major general in U.S. Army (1808–1849)
AGE AT INAUGURATION: 64
DEATH: Washington, D.C., July 9, 1850
PLACE OF BURIAL: Jefferson County, Ky.

ELECTION OF 1848

CANDIDATES	ELECTORAL VOTE	POPULAR VOTE
Zachary Taylor Whig	163	1,360,967
Lewis Cass Democratic	127	1,222,342
Martin Van Buren Free-Soil	—	291,263

THE TAYLOR ADMINISTRATION

INAUGURATION: March 5, 1849; the Capitol, Washington, D.C.
VICE PRESIDENT: Millard Fillmore
SECRETARY OF STATE: John M. Clayton
SECRETARY OF THE TREASURY: William M. Meredith
SECRETARY OF WAR: George W. Crawford
ATTORNEY GENERAL: Reverdy Johnson
POSTMASTER GENERAL: Jacob Collamer
SECRETARY OF THE NAVY: William B. Preston
SECRETARY OF THE INTERIOR: Thomas Ewing
31st CONGRESS (March 4, 1849–March 4, 1851):
Senate: 35 Democrats; 25 Whigs; 2 Others
House: 112 Democrats; 109 Whigs; 9 Others

MILLARD FILLMORE

As the greatest debate in congressional history entered its sixth month, Vice President Millard Fillmore began to consider the possibility that the Senate might divide evenly in a vote, leaving the final decision to him. The debate was over Henry Clay's Compromise of 1850; the issue was slavery, and the Union was at stake.

Since January of 1850, the Vice President, presiding over the Senate, had watched the debate unfold and passions rise. He had watched a great triumvirate dominate the chamber for the last time: a mellowed Daniel Webster, the Yankee; a dying John C. Calhoun, the Southerner; a fast-aging Henry Clay, the Great Compromiser of the West. Now, a few days before he would have to recess the Senate for the Fourth of July holiday, Fillmore decided to call on President Zachary Taylor, who opposed the Compromise and any other legislation that placed the slavery question in the hands of the federal government. If, Fillmore later recalled telling the President, the vote were to deadlock, "and if I should feel it my duty to vote for it, as I might, I wished him to understand that it was not out of any hostility to him or his Administration, but the vote would be given, because I deemed it for the interests of the country."

After the Independence Day recess, Fillmore reconvened the Senate with a clear conscience. He was prepared to act against the wishes of the administration, but at least he had been open and aboveboard about it. His independence, however, was never asserted: on July 9, 1850, Zachary Taylor died. Fillmore was inaugurated the next morning, and later that day he accepted the resignation of the Cabinet. The greatest stumbling blocks to passage of the Compromise—administration pressure and the threat of presidential veto—were eliminated, and within eleven weeks the five bills of the Compromise were

Millard Fillmore, by G. P. A. Healy

signed into law. "The Country Saved," trumpeted one newspaper.

It was not, of course. The provisions of the Compromise were offensive to both North and South. The fifteen slave states resented abolishment of the slave trade in the District of Columbia and the admission of California as a free state and of New Mexico and Utah as territories open to "popular sovereignty." The fifteen free states abhorred the provision that declared a runaway slave the private property of his owner, even in a free state. The conflict had not been resolved; it had been left to simmer and intensify. Like the three other Presidents directly preceding Lincoln, Fillmore was unable to understand what the abolitionists and secessionists knew: the country was compromising on an issue that defied compromise.

Millard Fillmore was not cast from the same mold as Abraham Lincoln, the man who would ultimately deal with the conflict, but he traveled the same route to political prominence. He was born in a log cabin on January 7, 1800, in central New York State, and his parents were poor but hard-working farmers. A bright child, quick to learn when he could find the tools, he had little formal education and was seventeen before he saw a dictionary. At eighteen he began to call on a local lawyer, a Quaker, who hired him as a clerk and impressed him with the idea that the law could lead him to honor and distinction. By 1822 Fillmore was clerking in a Buffalo law office, and within a year his assurance and good judgment convinced his associates that he was ready to be admitted to the bar.

As a young lawyer living in East Aurora, near Buffalo, Fillmore found it easy to make friends, to gain a reputation as an able and honest man, and to make money. At twenty-six he married his sweetheart of seven years, Abigail Powers, a minister's daughter. Before he was thirty he realized that he had all the raw materials with which to build a career in politics: humble origin (almost a must in these early years of the Jacksonian era), friends, reputation, money, a wife and a son. Tall and husky, good-natured and

straightforward, Fillmore retained the rugged appearance of the backwoodsman; he looked as if he were accustomed to hard physical labor, his hair fell across his forehead, his face was ruddy and lined. To this he added dignity. His voice was deep and masculine, but he spoke softly and carefully, in short, unembellished sentences. He was logical, at times witty, and he projected himself not as a showman, but as a good, sober citizen.

As the vehicle for his entrance into politics Fillmore chose the Antimasonic party. The rise of the common man in the 1820's was marked by an instinctive dislike of clubs and fraternities with their policies of exclusiveness. Secret societies of all kinds were distrusted, including Freemasonry, which had counted among its members many of the Founding Fathers of the nation. It was also an era in which political parties were formed to rally for or against single issues; when the issue died, so did the party. In 1826, after a New York bricklayer was allegedly kidnapped and murdered for betraying Masonic secrets, the Antimasonic party was born.

Fillmore never explained his reasons for joining the Antimasons, but he helped organize the party in New York and in 1828 was elected to the state assembly. During his three years in Albany, he distinguished himself by drafting a law abolishing prison terms for inability to pay debts but making fraudulent bankruptcy a punishable crime. He also established a close association with editor Thurlow Weed, a political boss who supported Fillmore's successful candidacy in 1831 for the United States House of Representatives. When Weed led the Antimasons into the new Whig party in 1834, Congressman Fillmore followed.

Throughout the 1830's the fortunes of Millard Fillmore and Thurlow Weed advanced together. When the Whigs finally captured the Presidency in 1840, Fillmore became chairman of the House Ways and Means Committee, and Weed, along with other party leaders, watched him closely. Here was a politician to be reckoned with.

When Fillmore became President, the California gold rush was in full swing. These prospectors (and friend) were photographed at work in 1852.

He was handsome, he had an attractive family, and all through his career he had demonstrated a remarkable ability to win votes. When Democrats had won landslide victories, Fillmore had won elections; in Whig years he had led the ticket. In any future national election, his ability to win in New York, with its large electoral vote, had to be considered.

As Ways and Means chairman, Fillmore played a significant role in the passage of a Whig relief plan to deal with the depression that had been lingering since 1837, a protective tariff advantageous to American manufacturing, and a congressional appropriation to help Samuel Morse develop the telegraph. Yet, with his reputation never higher, Fillmore astonished the politicians by declining to stand for re-election in 1842. John Quincy Adams, lamenting Fillmore's apparent retirement to his law practice in Buffalo, said, "I hope and trust he will soon return for whether to the nation or to the state, no service can be or ever will be rendered by a more able or a more faithful public servant." Congressman Adams need not

have worried, for Fillmore had no intention of retiring. He hoped to be elected to the Senate, and he had been mentioned as a possible vice presidential candidate in 1844; Weed urged him to try for the New York governorship instead. Reluctantly Fillmore agreed. The elections of 1844 were disastrous for the Whigs, and Fillmore was defeated for the first time in his life. He lost to Silas Wright, one of the most popular men in the state.

The Whigs found it difficult to regroup in advance of the 1848 elections, for the slavery issue divided two main party elements— the Southern planters and the Northern industrialists. At the nominating convention they settled on a military hero, General Zachary Taylor, a slaveowner regarded as essentially pro-Union. To satisfy Northern Whigs, the Taylor camp suggested the nomination of Massachusetts textile manufacturer Abbott Lawrence for Vice President, though Weed and Fillmore felt this would not satisfy the Northerners because a Taylor-Lawrence ticket would be a slate of two cotton men. Weed's personal choice was William H. Seward, a former governor of New York, but the powerful faction that had supported Kentucky's Henry Clay for the Presidency nominated Fillmore, who won the nomination on the second ballot.

331

Fillmore and Weed had always had cordial relations, but Fillmore had never been a tool of the boss. Yet, for some reason that has never been clarified, Fillmore regarded Weed as essential to Whig fortunes, and he agreed to help Weed elect Seward to the Senate. After the narrow Whig victory, Weed and Seward immediately worked their way into President Taylor's confidence and excluded Fillmore. So far as patronage was concerned, Weed gloated, "We could put up a cow against a Fillmore nominee and defeat him." He was right: the Vice President could not even have the man of his choice appointed port collector in his own city of Buffalo. Fillmore could only preside over the Senate and watch as North and South battled over the question of slavery in the territories won from Mexico.

In December, 1849, President Taylor proposed that California be granted statehood and that a border dispute between Texas and New Mexico be settled by the Supreme Court. Slavery was not mentioned, the implication being that the states would themselves decide that question. The slave state of Texas, however, would fight rather than have its western border shaved by New Mexico, which, like California, was sure to enter the Union as a free state. Clay's compromise was designed to avert conflict, but Taylor did not approve of it and restated his intention to admit New Mexico as a territory and to defend its boundaries with troops. In June, a convention was called in Nashville, where representatives from the slave states met to solidify resistance to Clay's compromise and to federal interference. Texas was prepared to assemble an army of 2,500 men to meet the federal troops; and in the House of Representatives Alexander Stephens of Georgia said, "The first federal gun [fired] against Texas . . . will signal . . . freemen from the Delaware to the Rio Grande to rally to the rescue."

The guns were cocked for civil war when Taylor suddenly fell ill and almost as suddenly died. For Fillmore, who had learned of the gravity of Taylor's condition only a few hours before his death, this abrupt turn of events was overwhelming. He sent a brief message to the seven members of the Cabinet—men who had always ignored him or accorded him the barest civility—then locked his door and spent a long, sleepless night in sober reflection.

Fillmore had, as he later put it, a "prejudice" against slavery that he had "drunk in with his mother's milk," but he was determined to be President of the whole country, even if that meant losing friends and encountering "their reproaches." Weighed against a national disaster, he concluded, personal unpopularity was unimportant.

The next day, after being sworn in before a joint session of Congress, he accepted the resignation of the Cabinet but asked its members to remain for a month. They agreed to a week. Presently, Fillmore selected their replacements. Three, including Secretary of State Daniel Webster, were Northerners, two were Southerners, and two were from border states. All were pro-Union men, and all favored compromise.

Fillmore hesitated before signing the Fugitive Slave Law of the Compromise for political as well as moral reasons. His Attorney General, John Crittenden, assured him that it was constitutional, but his wife pointed out that signing it would be political suicide. But sign he did, convinced that he had no constitutional alternative. The President then had to send troops to put down a threatened insurrection in the South, where secessionists were certain that the Compromise was just a prelude to further federal action, and he was forced to pledge the same action in the North to deal with resistance to the Fugitive Slave Law. While abolitionists vowed to "trample the law under our feet," and while Harriet Beecher Stowe's *Uncle Tom's Cabin* stirred resentment to the law, Fillmore threatened to use troops to enforce it. "With what face," he asked, "could we require the South to comply with their constitutional obligations, while we in the North openly refuse to live up to ours?"

When the clamor subsided and a measure of tranquillity came to the country, Fill-

THE CHAMPION OF THE LIGHT WEIGHTS ON HIS GUARD.

This Fillmore cartoon appeared in Young America *magazine during the presidential campaign of 1856.*

more seized the opportunity to develop and encourage an expanding economy. With the West bursting with gold seekers, there was a need for railroads, and Fillmore cooperated with Illinois Senator Stephen A. Douglas' efforts to secure federal grants for railroad construction. Always friendly to American commerce, the President sought to open new markets abroad. The principles of the Monroe Doctrine, strengthened by Polk, had not endeared the United States to the other nations of the hemisphere. Fillmore tried to better relations by formulating a good neighbor policy, which also helped American businessmen. He began to restore diplomatic harmony with Mexico, and an American-built railroad was constructed across the Isthmus of Tehuantepec. He negotiated to cut a canal through Nicaragua, and he resisted the efforts of American capitalists to seize Peruvian guano—seafowl excrement which made a good fertilizer—and by so doing established with Peru an honorable

agreement that ultimately proved pacific and profitable to both nations. When Spain executed a band of Americans who had attempted to overthrow the colonial government of Cuba, President Fillmore adamantly refused to retaliate.

Farther afield, American ships roamed the Pacific. The Chinese trade had begun in 1843, but the Japanese were aloof and suspicious. Fillmore twice sent letters to the Japanese Mikado urging trade. Although the letters revealed a complete lack of American understanding of Japanese ways or protocol, the Emperor eventually sent a favorable response. This occurred a year after the end of Fillmore's Presidency, but it gave him satisfaction to know that it was his administration that had finally broken the Japanese barrier.

As the Oriental trade ripened during the 1840's, Hawaii became an important Pacific supply depot. When Napoleon III seized Honolulu in 1849, the Americans protested, and although the French withdrew, there were rumors that they were going to return. In the United States a movement grew in favor of annexation, but Fillmore resisted it. Then, in 1851, the French gave the Hawaiian King a list of demands that would essentially make the islands a French protectorate. Through Secretary of State Webster, Fillmore told Napoleon that if Hawaii was going to lose its independence, it would be to America. But the basic issue was the independence of a backward nation, which Fillmore pledged to protect. The French acquiesced, retiring from the islands. But significant though they were, Fillmore's accomplishments in foreign affairs were made at the expense of a smoldering domestic issue, the controversy over slavery.

Millard Fillmore's biographers have made a point of describing their subject's lack of personal ambition, and the facts seem to bear them out. On the day he took the oath of office as President, he said that he would not seek re-election; he allowed his name to be placed before the convention of 1852 only because his friends had convinced him that he was the only Whig with a chance to win.

Thurlow Weed, powerless yet eager to regain political prominence, took a well-timed trip to Europe in order to avoid conflict. Seward, however, with his implacable hostility toward the President, launched a divisive campaign that was destined to split the party and doom it to extinction. After fifty-three ballots, the party nominated General Winfield Scott. He carried only four states, losing the election to Franklin Pierce, who captured 254 electoral votes.

Inauguration Day, 1853, was raw and snowy. Never in the best of health, Abigail Fillmore shivered in the cold. The next day she fell sick, and three weeks later she died. Grief-stricken, and uncertain about his future, the ex-President turned instinctively to politics, which had been his life.

But a politician must have a party, and the Whigs had been reduced to a nonentity. Fillmore's dilemma was not unique. He was pro-Union, but he did not believe the federal government had the right to restrict slavery, which he personally hated. The Republican party was just one of several rising new political organizations. In 1854, after touring the South and West, Fillmore demonstrated that he had lost touch with the realities of American politics by deciding that the American, or Know-Nothing, party —not the Republicans—represented the wave of the future.

He had come full circle from his Antimasonic days, for the American party which he joined was the child of an anti-Catholic secret society, the Order of The Star-Spangled Banner. The elaborate ritual and stern discipline of the order far outdid that of the Masons; when members were queried by outsiders they were instructed to reply, "I know nothing." What they did know, however, was that the Vatican wanted to control the United States; that foreigners, especially Irish and Germans, brought dangerous, un-American ideas with them to these shores; that Marxists and other radicals were ready to seize the republic at any moment. The party nominated its candidates secretly, and in some cities hired plug-uglies to man the polls and plug with a carpenter's awl potential voters who did not give the Know-Nothing password. The party did well in the elections of 1854 and 1855 and nominated Millard Fillmore for President in 1856, thus running an antislavery candidate on a proslavery platform. By the time the presidential election was held, however, most Americans realized that the time for compromise had passed. What little strength Fillmore had was in the border states; he ran a poor third, winning only 8 electoral votes to Democrat James Buchanan's 174 and Republican John C. Frémont's 114.

Fillmore retired from politics for good. In 1858 he married a wealthy widow, Caroline McIntosh, and in their impressive mansion they entertained Abraham Lincoln, who was on his way to the White House. When the Civil War came, Fillmore helped recruit volunteers for the Union army. "Our Constitution is in danger," he said, "and we must defend it!" But in 1864, Fillmore decided that the Republican administration meant "national bankruptcy and military despotism." "I have no faith," he wrote, "in that policy which proposes to exterminate the South, or hold it by military subjugation," and he announced his support of General McClellan for President. For these opinions he was accused of lack of patriotism and even treason. Deeply hurt, he withdrew completely from public life. Only in April, 1865, did he make an exception: when Lincoln's funeral train passed from Batavia to Buffalo, Fillmore headed the committee that served as escort.

Fillmore died on March 8, 1874, shortly after suffering a stroke. Had he led his country a decade earlier or twenty years later, he might have been judged a good President, for he was a selfless public servant and a fine administrator, and he accomplished much in a term of less than three years. But Millard Fillmore became President in 1850, and history in its judgment cannot divorce his achievements from the needs of the times. He is counted among the mediocre because of what he did not and could not do.

—DAVID JACOBS

Millard Fillmore

A PICTURE PORTFOLIO

In 1856, three years after vacating the office he had inherited in 1850, Millard Fillmore sought the Presidency. The ribbon above was worn in a losing cause.

TRIBULATIONS

When Vice President Millard Fillmore was informed of the death of President Zachary Taylor, he closed himself in his room and spent a sleepless, introspective night. The new Chief Executive was not accustomed to sleeplessness. Stocky and robust, an abstainer from drink and tobacco, Fillmore took good care of himself; he was widely regarded as one of the handsomest American Presidents. But as though the pressures of the office were not

Frail and sickly, Abigail Powers Fillmore (above) passed on many of her responsibilities as First Lady to her daughter. But Mrs. Fillmore was not totally inactive. Horrified by the absence of books in the Executive Mansion, she managed to secure a congressional appropriation to establish a new White House library.

President Fillmore (seated on a black horse in the painting at right) tips his hat as he passes the Governor General of Canada (who is sitting in the carriage beneath the American flag). The occasion was a jubilee on Boston Common in 1851, celebrating the joining of the Canadian and United States railroad systems.

LIBRARY OF CONGRESS

taxing enough, the White House itself threatened to damage his health. The walls were damp, the food was prepared primitively in an open fireplace, and the Potomac River's mosquitoes made malaria a feared possibility. Fillmore countered as best he could, making certain he got plenty of rest and keeping his Sundays free. To the distress and bewilderment of the cook, the President purchased a closed, "small hotel size" cooking stove, then had to go to the Patent Office to learn how the thing worked. One of his most effective health-preserving techniques was departure from the Mansion. Completion of the Erie Railroad and the opening of other lines in 1851 provided opportunities for tours which Fillmore used for political ends. Taking Cabinet members from the Deep South with him to the Northern states, he hoped to promote national unity, an impossible cause which dominated Millard Fillmore's administration.

THE MARE'S NEST, or Cuba Preserved.

AN EXTRAVAGANZA, IN ONE ACT.

President of the United States—MR. FILLMORE.   *Chief of the Filibusters*—GEORGE LAW, *his first appearance in that part*
The other characters by MESSRS CONRADE, HUGH MAXWELL, BRADY, *and the whole strength of the Company.*

Obstructing the concept of manifest destiny, Fillmore resisted attempts to annex Cuba to the United States.

COMPROMISE
AND AGITATION

By eliminating administration opposition, Zachary Taylor's death and Millard Fillmore's ascension to the Presidency facilitated passage of the Compromise of 1850. The Compromise was unpopular in both the North and the South. To slave states it was evidence that the federal government could and would pass legislation concerning slavery, which they considered the province of the state; and to the North the Fugitive Slave Law, which obligated free states to return escaped slaves to their masters, was intolerable. When he learned that a group of Southern agitators was planning to seize the federal fort at Charleston, South Carolina, the President dispatched troops to strengthen fortifications there. At the same time, when Northerners continued to aid fugitive slaves, Fillmore insisted that they be prosecuted. Moreover, when he discovered that some Southerners anxious to annex Cuba to the United States were encouraging Americans to join a Cuban insurrection, the President warned against their participation. In defiance of his warning the agitators did join the uprising, which was unsuccessful. Most were captured, and a few were executed, but Fillmore refused to retaliate against Spain. The President continued to resist American attempts to secure Cuba. When expansionist George Law, an American shipper who did business in the Caribbean, tried to incite a war with Spanish authorities in Cuba, Fillmore stopped Law's ships from sailing and settled permanently the matter of Cuban annexation.

Although Fillmore (above) wanted to enforce the Fugitive Slave Law, Northern juries, their indignation aroused by Harriet Beecher Stowe's novel (advertised on the poster below), seldom convicted the offenders.

A MISGUIDED CANDIDATE

Guarding the Baltimore polls in 1856 was a band of rowdies called plug-uglies, who wore this ribbon and bullied prospective anti-Fillmore voters.

Millard Fillmore began his career in the Antimasonic party, a political alliance based on opposition to secret societies in the United States. Twenty-seven years later, in 1855, the ex-President received the secret rites of the Order of the Star-Spangled Banner, an anti-Catholic, antiforeigner fraternal order. After the initiation, the presiding officer told the new member: "Mr. Fillmore, you have taken this step which will certainly land you in the presidential chair at Washington." "I trust so," said Fillmore.

The election of Franklin Pierce in 1852 stimulated the breakdown of the two-party system in the nation. His own Democratic party was faction ridden and fast declining, and the Whigs were so bewildered and demoralized by his election that they disintegrated. New parties sprang up everywhere, among them the Republican party and the American, or Know-Nothing, party. To Fillmore's discredit, he decided that the Know-Nothings, a political extension of the Order of the Star-Spangled Banner, represented the wave of the future. Opposition to foreigners united the party, for immigration was at a peak and some of the newcomers were fugitives from the radical European revolutions of 1848. President Pierce refused to acquiesce to the manufactured hysteria and even appointed several naturalized American citizens to ambassadorial posts. "Where," asked Fillmore, "is the true-hearted American whose cheek does not tingle with shame . . . to see our highest and most courted foreign missions filled by men of foreign birth to the exclusion of the native-born?" The answer to his question: everywhere but in Maryland, the only state that Millard Fillmore carried in 1856.

The partisan cartoon above appeared during the presidential campaign of 1856. Labeled "The Right Man for the Right Place," it depicts peacemaker Fillmore between Republican John C. Frémont (with rifle) and Democrat James Buchanan (with knife). Below: the first page of Fillmore's autobiography.

Sketch of the early life of Millard Fillmore by himself, commenced Feby. 8. 1871.

I have been requested to state some of the early incidents of my life for the benefit of the Buffalo Historical Society, and in compliance with that request I proceed at once to the task. Believing that an humble origin affords no just cause of concealment or shame,—and certainly not, even when fortune has smiled, for vain boasting and self glorification,—I shall content myself by stating, that I am the second child and eldest son of Nathaniel Fillmore and Phebe Millard. I was born

FACTS IN SUMMARY: MILLARD FILLMORE

CHRONOLOGY

UNITED STATES		FILLMORE			
	1800	*Born January 7*	Independent Treasury Act	1840	*Becomes chairman of House Ways and Means Committee*
Jefferson elected President	1801		Harrison elected President		
Madison elected President	1808		Tyler becomes President	1841	
War with England	1812		Webster-Ashburton Treaty	1842	
Washington burned	1814	*Works in a clothier's mill*		1844	*Defeated in bid for governorship of New York*
Monroe elected President	1816		Annexation of Texas	1845	
	1818	*Becomes law clerk*	War with Mexico	1846	*Becomes chancellor of the University of Buffalo*
Missouri Compromise	1820				
Monroe Doctrine	1823	*Admitted to the bar*	Gold discovered in California	1848	*Elected Vice President*
John Quincy Adams elected President	1825		Treaty of Guadalupe Hidalgo		
	1826	*Marries Abigail Powers*	Taylor elected President		
Tariff of Abominations	1828	*Elected to New York State assembly on Antimason ticket*	Taylor opposes Compromise of 1850	1850	*Supports Clay's compromise*
Jackson elected President			Clayton-Bulwer Treaty		*Becomes President*
	1830	*Moves to Buffalo*			*Enforces Fugitive Slave Law*
	1831	*Elected to U.S. House of Representatives*	Taylor dies		
Rise of the Whig party	1834	*Supports Whig party*		1851	*Opposes French annexation of Hawaii*
Siege of the Alamo	1836		*Uncle Tom's Cabin* published	1852	*Loses Whig presidential nomination*
Van Buren elected President			Pierce elected President		
Bank panic	1837				

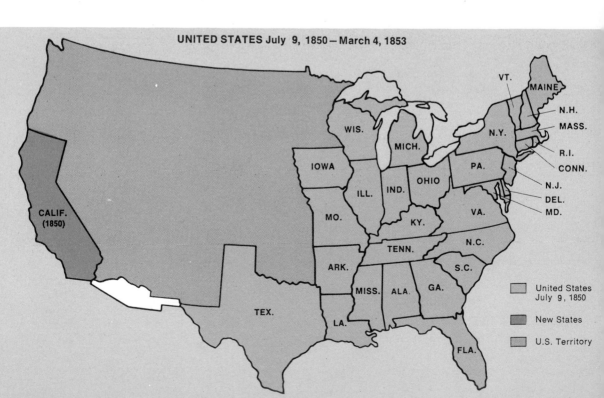

UNITED STATES July 9, 1850 — March 4, 1853

VT. MAINE N.H. MASS. R.I. CONN. N.J. DEL. MD. N.Y. PA. VA. N.C. S.C. GA. FLA. WIS. MICH. IOWA ILL. IND. OHIO KY. MO. TENN. ARK. MISS. ALA. LA. TEX.

CALIF. (1850)

United States July 9, 1850

New States

U.S. Territory

Gadsden Purchase	1853	*Abigail Fillmore dies*
Kansas-Nebraska Act	1854	*Joins American party*
Republican party formed		
Civil war in Kansas	1856	*Runs unsuccessfully for President*
Buchanan elected President		*Retires from politics*
Dred Scott decision	1857	
	1858	*Marries Caroline Mc- Intosh*
John Brown's raid at Harpers Ferry	1859	
Lincoln elected President	1860	
South Carolina secedes		
Civil War begins	1861	
Battle of Shiloh	1862	
Emancipation Proc- lamation	1863	
Gettysburg Campaign		
Lee surrenders at Appomattox	1865	
Lincoln assassinated		
Andrew Johnson be- comes President		
Johnson impeached	1868	
Grant elected President		
	1874	*Dies March 8*

The young Millard Fillmore was active in New York politics when Thomas Sully sketched this portrait.

BIOGRAPHICAL FACTS

BIRTH: Locke, Cayuga County, N.Y., Jan. 7, 1800

ANCESTRY: English

FATHER: Nathaniel Fillmore; b. Bennington, Vt., April 19, 1771; d. March 28, 1863

FATHER'S OCCUPATION: Farmer

MOTHER: Phoebe Millard Fillmore; b. Pittsfield, Mass., 1780; d. May 2, 1831

BROTHERS: Cyrus (1801–?); Almon Hopkins (1806–1830); Calvin Turner (1810–?); Darius Ingraham (1814–1837); Charles DeWitt (1817–1854)

SISTERS: Olive Armstrong (1797–?); Julia (1812–?); Phoebe Maria (1819–1843)

FIRST WIFE: Abigail Powers; b. Stillwater, N.Y., March 13, 1798; d. Washington, D.C., March 30, 1853

FIRST MARRIAGE: Moravia, N.Y., Feb. 5, 1826

SECOND WIFE: Caroline Carmichael McIntosh; b. Morristown, N.J., Oct. 21, 1813; d. Buffalo, N.Y., Aug. 11, 1881

SECOND MARRIAGE: Albany, N.Y., Feb. 10, 1858

CHILDREN (by first wife): Millard Powers (1828–1889); Mary Abigail (1832–1854)

EDUCATION: Attended public schools; studied law in Cayuga County and Buffalo, N.Y.

RELIGIOUS AFFILIATION: Unitarian

OCCUPATION BEFORE PRESIDENCY: Lawyer

PRE-PRESIDENTIAL OFFICES: Member of N.Y. Legislature; Member of U.S. House of Representatives; Vice President

POLITICAL PARTY: Whig, during Presidency; American, from 1854

AGE AT INAUGURATION: 50

OCCUPATIONS AFTER PRESIDENCY: Politician; chancellor of the University of Buffalo

DEATH: Buffalo, N.Y., March 8, 1874

PLACE OF BURIAL: Forest Lawn Cemetery, Buffalo, N.Y.

THE FILLMORE ADMINISTRATION

INAUGURATION: July 10, 1850; Hall of the House of Representatives, Washington, D.C.

SECRETARY OF STATE: Daniel Webster; Edward Everett (from Nov. 6, 1852)

SECRETARY OF THE TREASURY: Thomas Corwin

SECRETARY OF WAR: Charles M. Conrad •

ATTORNEY GENERAL: John J. Crittenden

POSTMASTER GENERAL: Nathan K. Hall; Samuel D. Hubbard (from Sept. 14, 1852)

SECRETARY OF THE NAVY: William A. Graham; John P. Kennedy (from July 26, 1852)

SECRETARY OF THE INTERIOR: Thomas M. T. McKennan; Alexander H. H. Stuart (from Sept. 16, 1850)

SUPREME COURT APPOINTMENT: Benjamin R. Curtis (1851)

31st CONGRESS (March 4, 1849–March 4, 1851):
Senate: 35 Democrats; 25 Whigs; 2 Others
House: 112 Democrats; 109 Whigs; 9 Others

32nd CONGRESS (March 4, 1851–March 4, 1853):
Senate: 35 Democrats; 24 Whigs; 3 Others
House: 140 Democrats; 88 Whigs; 5 Others

STATE ADMITTED: California (1850)

FRANKLIN PIERCE

The wife of Senator Clement Claiborne Clay of Alabama recalled that before Franklin Pierce became President of the United States she had "seen him bound up the stairs with the elasticity of a schoolboy. He went out after four years," she added, "a staid and grave man, on whom the stamp of care and illness was ineradicably impressed." So, she might have said, was the stamp of failure.

If the storm that climaxed in the Civil War can be likened to a hurricane, then Franklin Pierce came to the White House in the hurricane's eye. To many, the Compromise of 1850 seemed to have settled the major differences between North and South. Indeed, when Charles Sumner of Massachusetts arrived in the Senate in 1851, Thomas Hart Benton of Missouri told him, "You have come upon the scene too late, sir. There is nothing left to settle except petty, sectional disturbances over slavery."

But the quiet was deceptive. The eye of the hurricane was moving past, and Pierce—charming, kind, introspective, an old-fashioned Democratic party regular raised in the political backwater of New Hampshire—would be battered by the storm and swept away. He never comprehended the central moral issue of the day: slavery. He could not understand the abolitionists and for years fought them for stirring up trouble. Like many other men dedicated to the preservation of the Union, he could not see that the Compromise of 1850—particularly that part of it known as the Fugitive Slave Law—contained the seeds of continued bitterness between the sections; it created moral indignation in the North and fed the abolition movement, which in turn aroused the South. How little of this Pierce understood was indicated by his inaugural pledge to the country to preserve the Union by adhering to the Compromise. In many ways, Pierce was an anachronistic figure. His ideals,

Franklin Pierce, by G. P. A. Healy

345

Bennie Pierce, seen above with his mother when he was nine, was killed before his twelfth birthday.

learned from his father (who had been a general during the Revolutionary War), were those of a far less complicated age. His heroes were the men who had signed the Constitution of the United States, and he longed for a return to the conciliatory spirit that had marked the Constitutional Convention of 1787, seventeen years before his own birth on November 23, 1804, in Hillsboro, New Hampshire.

Politically speaking, Pierce came into the world with a silver spoon in his mouth: his father was a leading figure in the state and was subsequently its governor. A lawyer at twenty-two, the future President became a state legislator two years later. He was speaker of the legislature at twenty-six, a member of Congress at twenty-nine, and a senator at thirty-three. But though his mastery of New Hampshire politics led to the 1852 presidential nomination, it did not train him to run a national party that was splitting along sectional lines. Nor was he emotionally equipped. Pierce was a follower, not a leader. He followed the advice of his father and of the leaders of his party, right

up to his entry into the White House. Always, he was too anxious to please others.

His home life was unsatisfactory: his wife, the former Jane Means Appleton, daughter of the president of Bowdoin College, Pierce's alma mater, did not like either Washington or politics. She was a withdrawn, deeply religious neurotic and frequently an invalid. In deference to her, Pierce retired from the national scene in 1842 and returned to New Hampshire to practice law. But he continued to participate in state politics, with a brief hiatus during the Mexican War, when he served as a brigadier general in Winfield Scott's drive on Mexico City.

Pierce capped his New Hampshire achievements in 1850 and 1851 when his party's gubernatorial candidate began to show free-soil sympathies. Pierce led the move to replace him with a man who supported compromise. The latter's victory in the subsequent election was regarded throughout the nation, and especially in the South, as a triumph for Pierce. As the 1852 nominating convention approached, he began to loom as a dark-horse alternative to the Democratic front-runners—Lewis Cass, Stephen Douglas, James Buchanan, William O. Butler, and William Marcy—who seemed destined to deadlock the convention. Because he knew his wife would not approve, Pierce could not show much enthusiasm; he did not, however, repudiate the use of his name at the convention, and his supporters managed to win the nomination for him, as a compromise candidate, on the forty-ninth ballot. According to his friend Nathaniel Hawthorne, Pierce received the news "with no thrill of joy, but a sadness." When a rider brought them the report, Mrs. Pierce fainted. The strength and the openness of her antipathy to her husband's political ambitions were revealed in a letter that her eleven-year-old son, Bennie, wrote to her: "Edward brought the news . . . that Father is a candidate for the Presidency. I hope he won't be elected for I should not like to be at Washington and I know you would not either."

In the campaign that followed, Pierce

said and wrote little, as was the custom of the period, allowing the party chiefs to garner votes for him. They nicknamed him Young Hickory, casting back to the glorious days of the Democratic party. In the fall of 1852, he defeated the Whig candidate, General Winfield Scott, 254 electoral votes to 42. His popular-vote margin was only about 216,000, but the defeat effectively put an end to the Whig party.

"I have come seriously to the conclusion," wrote Hawthorne about the President-elect, "that he has in him many of the chief elements of a great ruler. His talents are administrative, he has a subtle faculty of making affairs roll onward according to his will, and of influencing their course without showing any trace of his action. . . . He is deep, deep, deep."

Pierce immediately began to lay plans for his administration: it would have a strong foreign policy; it would seek peaceful expansion; it would be frugal and honest; it would stand by strict construction, the Compromise, and the rights of the Southern states. His Cabinet, he hoped, would unify the unstable party organization. Eventually it included both the breakaway Barnburner elements and some Southern states' rights advocates; notable among the latter was Jefferson Davis, the Secretary of War.

The vigor with which he pursued his pre-inaugural plans came to an abrupt end in January, 1853. As the Pierces traveled from Boston to Concord, New Hampshire, the railroad car in which they were riding rolled off the track and their young son, Bennie, was killed. The parents were virtually unhurt, but at that instant their lives were shattered. Bennie was the third child they had lost. Their first son had died at the age of three days, and another had succumbed to typhus when he was four. Bennie had been their pride and the center of their marriage. The melancholy Mrs. Pierce interpreted the tragedy as a sign from God that her husband was not to be preoccupied with thoughts of a family so that he could better carry out the responsibilities of the Presidency. From then on, Jane Pierce rarely made public appearances, and when she did, it was with an air of martyred sadness.

Pierce was smothered by guilt and despair. Those who dealt with him found him timid and distracted. His journey to Washington for the inauguration was characteristic. Mrs. Pierce did not accompany him. Stopping off in New York, he avoided the crowds that had turned out to greet him. He did the same in Washington; instead of allowing himself to be welcomed by the mayor, he got off at the rear of the train and went to the Willard Hotel, where he stayed until the inauguration on March 4.

Yet his Inaugural Address showed flashes of positiveness. Always a skillful speaker, he had committed the speech to memory— the first President to do so. In it he outlined his goals and drew admiration from his audience for his choice of words as much as for his sentiments. In deference to Pierce's mourning, there was no inaugural ball, but a swarm of people descended on the White House for a reception that lasted all afternoon. That evening the new President and his private secretary, Sidney Webster, lit a candle and searched through the Mansion for a place to sleep; nothing was ready for them. At last Pierce gave up. He pointed to one room and said to Webster, "You had better turn in here and I will find a bed across the hall."

Mrs. Pierce arrived soon after, accompanied by her aunt, Mrs. Abby Kent Means —who became the official White House hostess in lieu of the First Lady—and took to her bedroom, where she wrote pathetic notes to her dead Bennie. The Executive Mansion took on an air of somber New England piety, with Mrs. Pierce asking the servants to attend church "for her sake" each Sunday. One visitor commented that "everything in that mansion seems cold and cheerless. I have seen hundreds of log cabins which seemed to contain more happiness."

Meanwhile, the President met the first problems of his administration. Patronage was one. Distributing the spoils of government to deserving party members was made particularly difficult by the existence of bickering factions within the party. Pierce could not please one group without angering another. His job was made no easier by his deep desire to please everyone. He backed and filled, listened to advice from all quarters, and agreed on appointments one day and changed his mind the next. His difficulties with appointments helped weaken his position with Democrats of all stripes.

There were troubling policy questions as well, almost all of which were complicated by sectional debate. Pierce bent all his efforts toward compromise, trying to avoid clashes. But unfortunately this meant compromising in favor of the South, which seriously threatened to break up the Union. To begin with, there was the question of a transcontinental railroad. The month Pierce was inaugurated, Congress authorized the War Department, under Jefferson Davis, to survey four transcontinental railroad routes. Southerners thought that the best route might be one running from New Orleans, across Texas and the New Mexico Territory, to San Diego. In May, Pierce's advisers prevailed upon him to negotiate with Mexico for a small portion of territory across which the railroad might run, and in December James Gadsden signed a treaty with Mexico in which the United States agreed to purchase a 29,640-square-mile rectangle of land for $15,000,000—a price later reduced by a third. However, the land speculations of many powerful men, not a few of whom were members of the national legislature, were also involved. This group included Senator Stephen Douglas, the "little giant" from Illinois, who began plumping for a central route out of Chicago that followed emigration trails west and went through the Great Plains, which were not yet territorialized. To clear the way for this line, his Senate committee issued a bill establishing the Territory of Nebraska. Since an earlier attempt to organize Nebraska had not won support from the South, and since there were indications that this new bill would fail for the same reason, Douglas tried to draw Southern votes to his side by including in the bill the proviso that the slave or free

status of the territory would be settled by its inhabitants. But the Great Plains had been closed to slavery by the Missouri Compromise, and the effect of Douglas' Nebraska Act would be to repeal *ipso facto* that Compromise. Southern senators soon called for an amendment to repeal the Missouri Compromise outright. Pierce did not favor the amendment, preferring to force the question into the Supreme Court where, he was positive, the Compromise would be declared unconstitutional. But the Southern bloc in the Senate would not back down, and Pierce found himself trapped; his administration's success depended on the support of Southern Democrats. With deep misgivings, Pierce went along with their amendment. The new bill also included division of the territory into Kansas and Nebraska. It was therefore possible that the southernmost, Kansas, would become a slave state through emigration from Missouri. Having made an unpleasant choice, Pierce threw his support completely behind the Kansas-Nebraska Act, and he whipped enough Democratic dissenters into line to win its passage. At the time, he felt he had achieved a major victory.

Kansas then became the scene of a bitter civil war, as settlers and land speculators from the slave state of Missouri and from abolitionist New England flocked into the territory and fought for control of the government. In the first two elections, "border ruffians" from Missouri flooded over the state line and elected proslavery representatives. This government set up its capital at Lecompton and was recognized as official by the territorial governor (who feared that he would be killed if he acted otherwise); it was therefore recognized by President Pierce. The antislavery men countered by creating another government in Topeka.

The Kansas-Nebraska Act was the great tragedy of Pierce's administration. It cost him, first, control of his party: Northern Democrats, their passions aroused by the repeal of the Missouri Compromise, defected; and Southern Democrats quickly grew impatient at the President's consequent inability to pass other pro-South measures. Then it cost the Democrats control of the House, as Know-Nothings and the new, antislavery Republican party made notable gains in the mid-term elections.

Increasingly hobbled by the sectional breakup inside and outside his party, Pierce struggled to cope with numerous other problems. The annexation of Cuba had long been urged by Southerners, and James K. Polk had tried with no success to buy it from Spain. The situation was complicated for Pierce by the belligerent attitude of certain segments of the American public; they were for taking whatever they wanted by force, and they organized filibustering expeditions that Pierce did not know how to handle. Furthermore, there were indications that Britain and France were encouraging Spain to free the slaves in Cuba, with an eye toward preventing American expansion southward; the island would thus appear less attractive to those Southerners who were planning to turn it into a slave state. Spain herself tended to excoriate relations with the United States, and on the 28th of February, 1854, Cuban authorities committed the blunder of seizing the cargo of an American ship for a minor violation of the rules of the port of Havana. This stirred anti-Spanish feelings in the United States and brought forth loud demands for war. Secretary of State William L. Marcy prevailed with cooler counsel, however. In a comic postlude, the American ministers to Spain, France, and Great Britain, under instructions to plan diplomatic maneuvers to wrench Cuba from Spain, met in Ostend and issued a manifesto, which was not a united diplomatic policy, but rather a suggestion that the United States either buy the island or, if Spain would not sell, wrest it from her. Pierce was right back where he had started, with Northerners angry at his attempts to annex a possible slave state.

The President also considered the annexation of Hawaii. A treaty was drafted in November, 1854, which would bring the island kingdom into the Union as a state in return for cash to the royal family, but Pierce knew the treaty would have difficulty in the Sen-

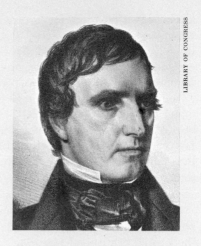

WILLIAM R. KING

In March, 1853, William R. King was sworn into the Vice Presidency under "the clear sky of the tropics." By a special act of Congress, the Vice President-elect, suffering from tuberculosis, was permitted to take the oath of office in Havana, where he was struggling to regain his health. In April he died, never having served in the office for which his long years in Congress had so ably prepared him. A graduate of the University of North Carolina, King was admitted to the bar in 1806 and was elected to the House of Representatives four years later. In 1818 he moved to Alabama. Representing his state in the Senate from 1820 to 1844, he chaired a committee on public lands, became an ardent follower of Jackson, and served as president pro tempore of the Senate for five years. In 1844 President Tyler appointed him minister to France, where he worked to prevent French interference in the annexation of Texas. Returning to the Senate in 1848, he supported the Compromise of 1850, worked toward the ratification of the Clayton-Bulwer Treaty, and, when Fillmore acceded to the Presidency, became president of the Senate. When the Democratic convention met in 1852, the delegates settled on the winning team of "gallant Pierce and King." King's death one month after his inauguration left the United States without a Vice President until Kentucky's John C. Breckinridge assumed the office in 1857.

ate if presented there for approval. Britain was against it; France seemed to be also. At the least, the treaty would have to be rewritten. But before it could be, the Hawaiian king was dead and so was annexation.

But there were successes in foreign policy under Pierce. Commodore Matthew C. Perry opened Japan to American trade in 1854. Disagreements between Great Britain and the United States over commercial fishing rights along the North American shores were settled by the Canadian Reciprocity Treaty in mid-1854. The treaty also eliminated import duties on certain goods traded between the United States and Canada.

A dispute between Great Britain and the United States over Central America—only a few years after the signing of the Clayton-Bulwer Treaty—threatened to result in war. The treaty had provided that neither country would ever "occupy, or fortify, or colonize, or assume or exercise any dominion over Nicaragua, Costa Rica, the Mosquito Coast [east coast of Nicaragua and Honduras] or any part of Central America." But there was disagreement over whether that meant the British were to vacate their pretreaty holdings in the area—the Bay Islands, Greytown (Nicaragua), and the Mosquito Coast. There was also a dangerous moment when an American naval officer sent by Fillmore to protect American interests in Greytown captured that community in 1853. Two years later, Pierce did nothing to prevent a free-lance filibuster named William Walker from taking over civil-war-torn Nicaragua, in order to protect the interests there of an American firm, the Accessory Transit Company. The President issued a proclamation against the filibustering, but after refusing to receive one emissary from the Walker government, he decided to see the next in 1856, thus in effect recognizing the government. When Cornelius Vanderbilt, who took over control of the Accessory Transit Company, brought about Walker's downfall, the situation was relieved: Britain ceded, as free territories, the Bay Islands to Honduras, and Greytown and the Mosquito Coast to Nicaragua.

Pierce began to gather strength of purpose as the 1856 nominating convention approached; he wanted to stay in the White House. But "Bleeding Kansas" ruined him. He continued to stand by the principle of local sovereignty and the constitutional rights of the slave states in the slavery question, and he castigated the abolitionists as fanatics. As far as the North was concerned, he was anathema, and the Southern Democrats felt that his loss of strength in the North made him an unacceptable candidate for 1856. The convention nominated, instead, James Buchanan of Pennsylvania.

After he left office, he and Mrs. Pierce went to Europe for about two years. When they returned, they found that there was a movement to run him again for the Presidency. But by this time he wanted no part of it, and Pierce forbade his supporters to nominate him.

When the Democratic party fell apart in 1860 and Abraham Lincoln won the election for an obviously sectional party, Pierce was dismayed. Dismay became bitter opposition to Lincoln during the Civil War. Pierce was sharply criticized for his position by his neighbors; the most crushing blow to his reputation came on July 4, 1863, when he spoke at a Democratic rally in Concord. He condemned this "fearful, fruitless, fatal Civil War." That afternoon, while the meeting went on, news circulated through the crowd of a great Northern victory at Gettysburg.

Two further blows followed. His wife died at the end of that year. The next spring, he and Hawthorne went off together on a trip to the White Mountains—an attempt to restore the writer's health. But Hawthorne died one night in a bedroom adjoining Pierce's. At Hawthorne's funeral the former President was pointedly snubbed by the New England literati and was not included among the pallbearers. A broken man, Pierce himself died on October 8, 1869.

"I can not . . . bow to the storm," he had written his wife shortly before her death. And he did not. But like a stiff and brittle tree he had been shattered by the hurricane.

—MARTIN LURAY

Franklin Pierce

A PICTURE PORTFOLIO

The Democrats were the party of compromise in 1852, and to adorn their campaign banners they chose two moderates—one a Yankee, the other a Southerner.

Franklin Pierce, shown (at right) on a commemorative medal, was, at forty-eight, the youngest President yet inaugurated. He was also one of the best looking (he was nicknamed Handsome Frank) and most charming: "Courtly and polished," one senator's wife described him. Mrs. Jefferson Davis noted that Pierce scolded so gently "the sting was all taken out." And his good manners were not saved just for influential Washingtonians. The President "gives me the compliments of the morning," testified the White House doorkeeper, "as grandly as he does General Scott."

GAS AND GLORY.

Nathaniel Hawthorne spoke in awed tones of Pierce's good luck, but in the Mexican War, Brigadier General Pierce was anything but fortunate. At the start of his first major action, outside Mexico City, his horse—startled by exploding shells—bucked and tossed him forward so that the pommel of his saddle was driven into his groin. He fainted; the horse fell, broke its leg, and tore Pierce's knee. In the confusion an officer shouted that the unconscious Pierce was a coward—a report that spread. Despite his injuries and intestinal infections, Pierce kept forcing himself into action during the rest of the campaign, but he never managed to find the opportunity for heroic redemption of his reputation—as the uncomplimentary cartoon above indicates.

WINFIELD SCOTT

Andrew Jackson had called him a "hectoring bully," and Polk termed him "visionary," but in the eyes of the nation General Winfield Scott was nothing less than a hero when the Whigs offered him the presidential nomination in 1852. Publicly acclaimed for his courage at Chippewa and Lundy's Lane in the War of 1812, he was brevetted a major general. He fought in the Black Hawk War, and when, in 1837, Jackson ordered an inquiry into General Scott's handling of the Creek and Seminole campaigns, the court praised the soldier's "energy, steadiness, and ability." His accomplishments as peacemaker in 1838 and 1839 were no less impressive. In little more than a year, he restored peace along the Canadian border; pacified some sixteen thousand dispossessed Cherokee; and averted a war with Great Britain in the Maine boundary dispute. As general in chief of the Army during the Mexican War, he led the victorious assault on the enemy capital and again won public applause. National sentiment was not strong enough, however, to make him President, and in the election of 1852 he was roundly defeated by Pierce. Resuming his military duties, he averted a serious conflict with Great Britain in 1859 over possession of San Juan Island off the Pacific coast. During the Civil War, he remained loyal to the Union, serving briefly as general in chief. He retired in 1861 and died five years later, at eighty.

AN UNEXPECTED VICTOR

When the 1852 Democratic convention, after laboring long, gave birth to a dark horse from New Hampshire, Senator Stephen A. Douglas commented dryly, "Hereafter, no private citizen is safe." For the dark horse, Franklin Pierce, it was a breath-taking turnabout. He had risen rapidly and had become a United States senator in 1837, at the age of thirty-three; but his wife hated Washington, and after only one term he had exchanged a career in national politics for a Granite State law practice. His subsequent service as a general in the Mexican War was undistinguished. In 1850, though Pierce was still leader of the New Hampshire Democratic party, he seemed about as far from the White House as from the moon. Yet by the time of the national convention, three factors had intervened: the Compromise of 1850 gave the nation hope for settlement of the slavery issue; Pierce successfully fought disruptive free-soil infiltration of the state party during the 1851 gubernatorial campaign, thus earning favorable notice nationally; and the leading contenders for the Democratic presidential nomination proved strong enough only to block each other. A deadlock breaker—someone acceptable to the South—was needed, and Pierce was chosen on the forty-ninth ballot. His electoral vote margin in the election that fall, 254 to 42, was the largest since that of James Monroe in 1820.

EXPANSION

Commodore Matthew C. Perry, shown above in a portrait by a Japanese artist, was sent by President Fillmore to open isolationist Japan to American trade; during Pierce's term, Perry succeeded in negotiating an advantageous treaty. Below is a Japanese depiction of one of the black warships under Commodore Perry's command.

America at mid-century was expansion minded, seeking more trade abroad, more land on the American continent. Pierce planned to encourage the nation's growth as a world power, and he succeeded, to some extent, with the help of his able Secretary of State, William L.

Marcy. They completed a record number of treaties for a four-year administration, including the Gadsden Purchase, the Canadian Reciprocity Treaty (which involved North Atlantic fishing rights and commerce between the United States and Canada), and trade treaties with the Netherlands and Denmark. They sent a consul general to Japan to follow up Commodore Perry's success there. But their attempt to attach Cuba to the United States came to naught. The blustering tone of the Ostend Manifesto and the filibustering of William Walker in Central America epitomized a problem that Pierce did little to solve: America's enthusiasm for expansion was giving the country a black eye overseas. Muttered a British diplomat, "These Yankees are . . . totally unscrupulous and dishonest and determined somehow or other to carry their Point."

The painting above by Albert J. Fountain, Jr., depicts the July 4, 1854, celebration of the Gadsden Purchase in Mesilla, New Mexico Territory. The land (now southern Arizona and New Mexico) was bought at the urging of Pierce's Secretary of War, Jefferson Davis, to clear the way for a transcontinental railroad across the South.

"BLEEDING KANSAS"

Kansas was the shoal on which the Pierce administration came to grief. Senator Stephen A. Douglas, ardent nationalist, would-be President, and investor in lands around Chicago, had been trying to get the Great Plains territorialized so that a transcontinental railroad might be built, using Chicago as one terminus. The South had its own proposed route and was not interested. So when a bill to organize the plains region was introduced in 1854, Douglas' Senate Committee on Territories tried to sweeten it a bit for the slavery interests, and the result was explosive—a bill creating the territories of Kansas and Nebraska and repealing the Missouri Compromise, thus opening all the Northern territories to slavery. Pierce was reportedly furious but because he needed Southern support for anything he might want to do in the future, he backed the bill. Kansas was soon the setting for a wild war over land and slavery and quickly became an explosive national issue. As his party began to crumble under the stresses this created, Pierce found himself to be the object of abuse from many sides.

The uproar caused by Kansas was unprecedented in its ferocity. The atmosphere in Congress was highly charged with epithets, threats, and violence. Senator Charles Sumner, reformer and abolitionist from Massachusetts, was, for one, a wellspring of vitriol. As he viciously attacked Stephen Douglas and the absent Andrew P. Butler of South Carolina in an 1856 debate over Kansas, Douglas remarked, "That damn fool will get himself killed by some other damn fool." He was not far wrong. Two days later, Senator Butler's nephew, Representative Preston Brooks, caught Sumner at his Senate desk and caned him into insensibility (above). With the family honor thus peculiarly satisfied, and with Sumner incapacitated for, as it turned out, three years, Brooks was censured by the House and resigned; he was re-elected—a triumph for sectional rancor.

The bitter cartoon at left blames the administration Democrats for the excesses of the proslavery forces in "Bleeding Kansas," while conveniently ignoring the excesses of antislavery Kansans. Secretary of State William L. Marcy and the Democrats' 1856 presidential nominee, James Buchanan, are shown stealing a corpse's belongings. Pierce, whose weakness for alcohol was often used against him, and Lewis Cass terrorize Miss Liberty, as Douglas gaily scalps a victim.

FACTS IN SUMMARY: FRANKLIN PIERCE

CHRONOLOGY

UNITED STATES		PIERCE				PIERCE
Jefferson re-elected President	1804	*Born November 23*	Webster-Ashburton Treaty	1842	*Resigns from Senate*
Madison elected President	1808		War declared on Mexico	1846	*Declines to serve as U.S. Attorney General*
War with England	1812			1847	*Commissioned brigadier general of volunteers*
Missouri Compromise	1820				*Marches to Mexico City with Winfield Scott's expedition*
Monroe Doctrine	1823				
	1824	*Graduates from Bowdoin College*	Treaty of Guadalupe Hidalgo	1848	*Resigns from Army*
	1827	*Admitted to the bar*	Compromise of 1850	1850	*Elected president of N.H. constitutional convention*
Jackson elected President	1828			1852	*Elected President*
	1829	*Named to the New Hampshire legislature*	Gadsden Purchase	1853	
	1831	*Chosen speaker of the state legislature*	Perry opens Japan to American trade	1854	*Signs Kansas-Nebraska Act*
Jackson vetoes bill to recharter Bank of the U.S.	1832		Kansas-Nebraska Act		
			Canadian Reciprocity Treaty		
	1833	*Begins term in U.S. House of Representatives*	Birth of Republican party		
Rise of Whig party	1834	*Marries Jane Means Appleton*	Ostend Manifesto		
		Nominated for second term in Congress		1855	*Issues proclamation against William Walker's invasion of Nicaragua*
Siege of the Alamo	1836	*Elected to U.S. Senate*	Civil war in Kansas	1856	
Van Buren elected President			Buchanan elected President		
Harrison elected President	1840		Dred Scott decision	1857	*Travels to Europe*

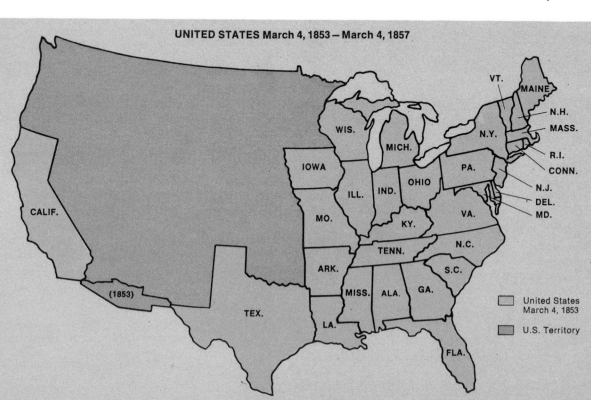

UNITED STATES March 4, 1853 — March 4, 1857

United States March 4, 1853

U.S. Territory

This view of Bowdoin College in Maine was painted in 1821, three years before Pierce graduated.

Lincoln-Douglas debates	1858	
John Brown's raid	1859	*Returns to United States*
Lincoln elected President	1860	
Civil War begins	1861	
	1863	*Jane Pierce dies*
Lincoln assassinated	1865	
Johnson becomes President		
Grant elected President	1868	
	1869	*Dies October 8*

BIOGRAPHICAL FACTS

BIRTH: Hillsboro, N.H., Nov. 23, 1804

ANCESTRY: English

FATHER: Benjamin Pierce; b. Chelmsford, Mass., Dec. 25, 1757; d. April 1, 1839

FATHER'S OCCUPATIONS: Soldier; farmer; governor of New Hampshire

MOTHER: Anna Kendrick Pierce; b. 1768; d. Dec., 1838

BROTHERS: Benjamin Kendrick (1790–1850); John Sullivan (1796–1824); Charles Grandison (1803–1828); Henry Dearborn (1812–1880)

SISTERS: Nancy M. (1792–1837); Harriet B. (1800–1837)

HALF SISTER: Elizabeth Andrews (1788–1855)

WIFE: Jane Means Appleton; b. Hampton, N.H., March 12, 1806; d. Andover, Mass., Dec. 2, 1863

MARRIAGE: Amherst, N.H., Nov. 19, 1834

CHILDREN: Frank Robert (1839–1843); Benjamin (1841–1853)

HOME: Pierce Homestead, Hillsboro Upper Village, N.H.

EDUCATION: Attended public school and Hancock Academy; graduated from Bowdoin College (1824)

RELIGIOUS AFFILIATION: Episcopalian

OCCUPATIONS BEFORE PRESIDENCY: Lawyer; politician; soldier

MILITARY SERVICE: Brigadier general in U.S. Army (1847–1848)

PRE-PRESIDENTIAL OFFICES: Member and Speaker of N.H. Legislature; Member of U.S. House of Representatives; Member of U.S. Senate; President of N.H. Constitutional Convention

POLITICAL PARTY: Democratic

AGE AT INAUGURATION: 48

OCCUPATION AFTER PRESIDENCY: Retired

DEATH: Concord, N.H., Oct. 8, 1869

PLACE OF BURIAL: Old North Cemetery, Concord, N.H.

ELECTION OF 1852

CANDIDATES	ELECTORAL VOTE	POPULAR VOTE
Franklin Pierce Democratic	254	1,601,117
Winfield Scott Whig	42	1,385,453
John P. Hale Free-Soil	—	155,825

THE PIERCE ADMINISTRATION

INAUGURATION: March 4, 1853; the Capitol, Washington, D.C.

VICE PRESIDENT: William R. King (died April 18, 1853)

SECRETARY OF STATE: William L. Marcy

SECRETARY OF THE TREASURY: James Guthrie

SECRETARY OF WAR: Jefferson Davis

ATTORNEY GENERAL: Caleb Cushing

POSTMASTER GENERAL: James Campbell

SECRETARY OF THE NAVY: James C. Dobbin

SECRETARY OF THE INTERIOR: Robert McClelland

SUPREME COURT APPOINTMENT: John A. Campbell (1853)

33rd CONGRESS (March 4, 1853–March 4, 1855):
Senate: 38 Democrats; 22 Whigs; 2 Others
House: 159 Democrats; 71 Whigs; 4 Others

34th CONGRESS (March 4, 1855–March 4, 1857):
Senate: 40 Democrats; 15 Republicans; 5 Others
House: 108 Republicans; 83 Democrats; 43 Others

END OF PRESIDENTIAL TERM: March 4, 1857

JAMES BUCHANAN

James Buchanan was the last in a string of Presidents, Northern men with Southern principles or vice versa, who stood for compromise between two bitterly opposed groups of radicals; the last in a line chosen because, it was thought, they would not press for a nation-splitting decision on the slavery issue. During their service, the situation had grown more dangerous despite continued legal and political compromises. Pierce had been broken by it. Now it was Buchanan's turn.

When he assumed the Presidency, this son of a Pennsylvania storekeeper had been in public life for more than forty years. Born April 23, 1791, near Mercersburg, Pennsylvania, he was graduated from Dickinson College in 1809 and began the practice of law three years later. He became a Federalist state legislator in Pennsylvania in 1814 and a member of Congress in 1821.

Buchanan was a gentle, diplomatic person, religiously fatalistic in his approach to life. He stood six feet tall and was a heavy man, but because his sight was uneven (one eye being nearsighted, the other farsighted), he cocked his head down and to one side when addressing or listening to someone, giving the impression of shyness and humility. Considered charming and good-looking, he nevertheless remained a bachelor all his life. He came closest to the altar when he was in his late twenties, but his devotion to work got in the way of his courting, and misunderstandings followed; his fiancée, Ann Coleman, broke off the engagement. Because Ann was a wealthy girl, and because her parents had felt all along that Buchanan was marrying her for her money, he was afraid that protestations of love would be suspect. So he did not offer them. Ann died soon afterward, apparently as a result of a hysterical fit. Buchanan's role in the tragedy was characteristic; he considered all the angles and was not ruled by his emotions. Success came to him in politics because he

The portrait of James Buchanan is by G. P. A. Healy.

played it like a game of chess—cautiously, step by step. He habitually kept his financial records accurate to the penny and knew how every cent was spent; before long he had amassed a considerable fortune. With similar care he observed and took advantage of the constantly shifting schisms in politics and eased his way upward through the maze. After ten years' service in Congress, during which he left the moribund Federalists for the Jacksonian Democrats, he went to Russia as United States minister in 1832. He was elected to the Senate in 1834 and was re-elected twice. Not a moving speaker as either a lawyer or a legislator, he was a conscientious committee member and was meticulously detailed when presenting a case. Contemporaries found his plodding caution irritating—but worthy of respect nonetheless.

By 1844 he had become a possibility for the Presidency. He lost the Democratic nomination to Polk that year, then worked hard to bring Pennsylvania into the Democratic column; as a result he was awarded the post of Secretary of State. Buchanan and Polk respected each other, but they battled constantly during the next four years. Polk had made all his Cabinet members promise that they would not actively seek the presidential nomination of 1848, but Buchanan had taken the post for the prestige it would bring him, and he competed with Polk for leadership and laurels in foreign policy. "If I would yield up the government into his hands," wrote Polk, "and suffer him to be in effect President . . . I have no doubt he would be cheerful and satisfied." Toward the end of his term in the State Department, Buchanan began to campaign quietly for votes at the convention. But he lost to Lewis Cass of Michigan and retired to a new estate, "Wheatland," outside Lancaster. Then the maneuvering for the presidential nomination began again, and failed again in 1852, as Franklin Pierce won on the forty-ninth ballot.

In the spring of 1853, President Pierce convinced Buchanan to represent him in Great Britain. Although his ministry was not a great success—he became involved in the controversial Ostend Manifesto—his absence from the country during Pierce's administration proved fortunate: he was not a participant in the Kansas-Nebraska debate and, therefore, had no responsibility for "Bleeding Kansas."

Kansas, and the larger question of slavery in the United States, were to be the major issues of the 1856 campaign. Buchanan was known as a conservative, a compromise man. "I am not friendly to slavery in the abstract . . ." he had said, "[but] the rights of the south, under our constitutional compact, are as much entitled to protection as those of any other portion of the Union." Consistently he had held to the view that the abolitionists should be quiet and that everyone should show forbearance toward one another. This position was popular with the South and with Unionists in the North; Buchanan, a Northerner, thus fitted into the category from which the Democrats had been selecting their nominees.

After he returned from England, Buchanan began to emerge as the leading candidate because, unlike President Pierce and Senator Stephen A. Douglas, he had made no enemies over Kansas, which divided the Democrats as it did the country as a whole. After twelve ballots at the convention, Pierce was out of the running. Douglas withdrew after four more, and Buchanan was nominated by acclamation.

In November he polled less than half the popular vote, but won in the electoral college, 174 votes to 114 for the Republican, John C. Frémont, and 8 for the Know-Nothing, Millard Fillmore. Ominously, though Buchanan won New Jersey, Pennsylvania, Indiana, Illinois, and California, the bulk of his strength lay in the South. The Republican party, in its first major test, had swept the Northeast.

Thus, Buchanan came into the office of President as a contradiction: the Unionist elected without the votes of one of the contending sections. He saw the danger: "The great object of my administration," he wrote, "will be to arrest, if possible, the agitation of the slavery question at the North, and to destroy sectional parties."

The Kansas issue was the first crucial problem he had to meet, and for a while he did so with determination. Before he was inaugurated he suggested to friends on the Supreme Court that the Dred Scott case, then under consideration, be used as a platform for defining Congress' role in the slavery question. Scott was a slave who had been taken from Missouri into Wisconsin Territory and Illinois during the 1830's by his master, an Army doctor. Scott eventually sued in Missouri for his freedom on the grounds that his temporary removal to a free area had automatically given him the right to be free. Shortly after Buchanan entered office, the Court announced its decision: Scott was a slave, not a citizen, and thus could not sue for anything; and because the Missouri Compromise had forbidden slavery north of the Mason-Dixon Line, it had deprived Southern slaveowners of the right to take their property wherever they wished and had therefore been unconstitutional. Congress, the Court said, could not legislate concerning slavery in a territory, and this implied that neither could any territory created by Congress. All territories were open to slavery and could exclude slavery only when they became states.

Buchanan had had a considerable effect on the Court's pronouncement. Not only had he suggested elaboration of the decision, but he had put pressure on an associate justice from Pennsylvania, Robert C. Grier, to support it. He hoped that this would settle the Kansas controversy, but it did the opposite, increasing the anger in the North against the South.

To cope with the immediate situation in Kansas, Buchanan selected Robert J. Walker of Mississippi to be territorial governor and to oversee the territory's progress toward statehood. The best choice yet for that position, Walker was a levelheaded, no-nonsense Unionist. But even he was not able to bring order out of the chaos.

Sooner or later Kansas was going to become a free state. Douglas had thought so;

LIBRARY OF CONGRESS

JOHN C. BRECKINRIDGE

Because the Democrats needed a Southern candidate to balance their ticket in 1856, thirty-five-year-old John C. Breckinridge of Kentucky was nominated for the Vice Presidency. Breckinridge had entered politics through the Kentucky legislature in 1849, was elected to Congress in 1851, and was soon one of the party's most prominent members. As Buchanan's Vice President from 1857 to 1861, he strove to maintain order in a divided Senate, advocating adoption of the Crittenden Compromise as a solution to the bitter slavery conflict between North and South. In 1860 he was nominated for President by the Southern wing of the badly split Democratic party. Opposing Douglas of the Northern Democrats and Lincoln of the Republicans, he defended himself against charges of promoting disunion, maintaining that he "never did an act nor cherished a thought that was not full of devotion to the Constitution and the Union." After Lincoln's election, Breckinridge represented his state in the Senate, defending her neutral position in the Civil War. When Kentucky later befriended the Union, however, Breckinridge joined the Confederate army and was expelled from the Senate as a traitor. In 1865 he was made Confederate secretary of war, escaping to Europe after Lee's surrender. In 1869 the federal government permitted him to return to Lexington, where he died in 1875.

so had Pierce; so did Buchanan. The odds were strongly against the proslavery men; they were already outnumbered in the territory by about four to one. Any fair process of producing a state constitution would result in a prohibition of slavery. However, early in 1857 the proslavery faction ran the government recognized as official in Washington and could control the election of delegates to a constitutional convention. When voter registration for that election began, the Free-Soilers assisted their opponents by refusing to register; they wanted nothing to do with the Lecompton (proslavery) government and hoped to discredit it by making the election appear unfair. As a result, proslavery delegates were elected. Then elections to the territorial legislature were held; for the first time the two factions contested for seats in the same legislature. When Walker discovered and threw out fraudulent returns from two areas, the antislavery party won a majority. Walker's action caused an uproar in the South. In that atmosphere the constitutional convention met at Lecompton. It is generally agreed that the delegates were a motley crowd of roughnecks, unequipped to write a constitution that would calm the situation. Furthermore, they were under pressure from the South not to submit their product to the people of the territory for approval. When they finished, they had decided to present only one question to popular vote: Should more slaves be allowed into Kansas?

In the constitution, they had provided that Kansas slaveowners could keep the approximately two hundred slaves then in Kansas if slavery were voted down. This "abolition" clause was similar to property-protection measures taken earlier by various Northern states when they outlawed slavery. But under the circumstances it was like waving a red flag. The Republicans blew it up out of all proportion. Considering, in addition, that the whole constitution was not to be submitted to a vote, and that it specified that no amendments were to be made until 1864, the proponents of slavery did appear to be engaging in trickery.

For months Buchanan had vacillated between calling for a referendum only on slavery or for one on the entire constitution. Finally he had promised Governor Walker he would support the latter course. But when the results of the territorial election and the Lecompton convention were received in Washington, Buchanan's Southern advisers, armed with threats of secession from several slave states, convinced him to change his mind again. He concluded that although the Lecompton measures would cause some trouble, they were, after all, legal, and that establishing Kansas as a state—any kind of a state—would end the national quarrel over the territory.

Senator Douglas, who had assured everyone during the Kansas-Nebraska debate that Kansas would enter the Union as a free state as the result of a popular vote, saw the actions of the Lecompton body as a violation of the popular sovereignty principle. Moreover, he was up for re-election in Illinois, where the Lecompton government was thoroughly disliked. If he backed Buchanan's decision, he would lose, and his chances for the Presidency in 1860 would be diminished. He hurried to the White House to talk to the President. At the end of an angry conference, he told Buchanan he would have to oppose the administration if it allowed the Lecompton constitution to come to Congress without a vote on the en-

At left, Buchanan receives the first Japanese ambassadors to the United States, in May, 1860. Above is one of the Japanese gifts, "The Emperor's Bowl," the largest known porcelain in the world.

tire paper by the inhabitants of the territory. Buchanan, in turn, warned Douglas against fighting the administration and reminded him of how Andrew Jackson had ruined Democrats who opposed him. "Mr. President," said Douglas. "I wish you to remember that General Jackson is dead!"

In his annual message, delivered less than a week after Douglas broke with him, Buchanan told Congress he would send it the Lecompton constitution following the "with-slavery, without-slavery" vote. Within two weeks, in a referendum held under the aegis of the Lecompton convention, Kansas voted 6,226 to 569 for the constitution with slavery. Then the new Free-Soil legislature in the territory called for another vote and offered the whole constitution, as well as the slavery question, for the approval of the voters. The constitution was disapproved 10,226 to 162. Even so, Buchanan sent the constitution to Congress in February, 1858, and advised that Kansas be admitted. The debate that followed was long and bitter. But on April 1, 1858, Douglas Democrats, Republicans, and Know-Nothings combined to prevent passage of the Lecompton instrument in the House. Kansas would not become a state, as it turned out, until 1861.

A disastrous step had been taken toward war. Buchanan had given way to pressure from the South. Certainly, anything he did at the time was bound to stir up bitterness.

But the Southern extremists, who were encouraged by their success with him and enraged by the defeat of the Lecompton constitution in Congress, grew more clamorous.

Other forces were at work to aid them. In August, 1857, a business panic broke out in the North. To the South, aroused by religious revivalism and the denominational schisms reflecting the slavery controversy, the financial ruin in the North seemed a just retribution for the abolition movement and for the cluttered, seamy life of the cities. In the 1840's, Ralph Waldo Emerson had written, "Cotton thread holds the Union together. . . ." But the South was barely troubled by the Panic of 1857, and it began to feel that the North needed *it* far more than vice versa; Southern society was stable, Northern society was corrupt and at the mercy of financiers. If the North did not conform to Southern wishes, the South would break the thread of the Union and flourish.

More dramatic, and just as important, was an incident at a small town in Virginia in the fall of 1859. With a handful of whites and Negroes, a madman named John Brown, who had led a massacre in Kansas in 1856, seized the federal arsenal and a rifle factory at Harpers Ferry. He intended to start a Negro insurrection. Although he failed—federal troops soon captured Brown, who was tried and hanged—he became in both North and South a symbol of noncompro-

365

mise. Even Southern moderates began to feel forced to choose between the idea of Union and protection of a familiar way of life against a dangerous enemy.

Slavery was not the only issue of Buchanan's administration. Nor was Kansas the only territory that proved a problem for him. "Deseret," the Mormon promised land, established by the Compromise of 1850 as the Territory of Utah, had been treated as an ill-favored stepchild for several years. Its applications for statehood had been ignored, and in 1855 Pierce had made three federal judiciary appointments for the territory that were remarkable for their inappropriateness: all three men were enemies of the Mormon community. The judges were unable to exercise much authority in the territory, mainly because the inhabitants ignored them; so in 1857 they came east to complain. Buchanan named a new governor, Alfred Cumming, to replace Brigham Young and ordered west a 2,500-man army to help sustain the law. Lack of communications from Washington left the Mormons with the impression they were being invaded. The Mormon War began, highlighted by severe harassment of the approaching troops and a massacre of Californian emigrants by Mormons and Indians. At last, Thomas L. Kane of Philadelphia, a

friend of Buchanan's and a Mormon sympathizer, suggested that he be sent to Salt Lake City to talk to Young. Buchanan agreed, and gradually the matter was ironed out, with Cumming accepted as governor.

Foreign policy was always Buchanan's strong suit. Despite the restrictions imposed on him by the growing domestic crisis, it was in this area that he achieved his greatest successes as President. Using his diplomatic contacts in Great Britain, he developed with the British an interpretation of the troublesome Clayton-Bulwer Treaty—an attempt to guarantee nonintervention in Central America by the United States and Great Britain—that was satisfactory to both sides.

At the same time, the President labored to enlarge United States influence in Central and South America, partly as a step toward national expansion and partly because the constant political turmoil south of the border invited intervention by European powers. While discouraging filibustering, he brought American power to bear on—among others —Nicaragua (winning the right to protect routes across the isthmus with American arms) and Mexico (which agreed to let the United States send troops into the country whenever uprisings threatened the Mexican government). The Senate refused to ratify

"Picturesque and elegant," one visitor called Wheatland, Buchanan's home in Pennsylvania. Comfortably spacious and surrounded by wheat farms, its grounds were patrolled by a pair of large pinioned eagles.

these treaties, but had Buchanan been President in a quieter time, he might today be remembered as an empire builder.

From the beginning of his term Buchanan had to deal with a chaotic situation in Congress. Though the reigning Democrats were a national party in form—and the only one then remaining in American politics—they were not national in substance. They were divided along sectional lines—North versus South versus West. Washington was full of lobbyists for various enterprises, who had liquor to pour and money to spend. As sectionalism weakened party discipline, and rising Republican strength foreshadowed an 1860 defeat, Democratic congressmen tended to look after their private and local power rather than national needs, and failed to provide the President with the national "consensus" he so ardently desired. What small chance there was for party unity vanished in the Lecompton fight; this left the Douglas Democrats and the Southern extremists antagonistic to the administration and cost the party control of the Lower House after the mid-term elections.

Buchanan's legislative program, an ambitious one which included the purchase of Cuba and enlargement of the armed forces, was wrecked by sectionalist bickering and the vengefulness of congressmen who could not have their own way. Even ordinary appropriation bills, needed to keep the government in operation, had trouble passing.

Buchanan stood curiously disconnected from the realities. After seeing the dismaying returns in the mid-term elections, he could still make the amazing statement that "the prospects are daily brightening. From present appearances the party will ere long be thoroughly united." Yet every day the South drew further away from the ideal of the old Union. At odds with the North and West, trapped, as it felt, by the weight of increasing Northern population, frightened by the possibility of slave emancipation or insurrection, insulted and angered by William Lloyd Garrison, Harriet Beecher Stowe, and their kind, the South looked upon the North as a foreign government keeping it in

In twenty-three words—at the close of a volume defending his Presidency—James Buchanan capsuled the tragedy of a good man out of his depth.

thrall and in danger. They saw Northern Democrats pulling out of line, as Douglas had done, and knew what this meant for 1860. The election of a President representing a purely Northern party—either William Seward or Abraham Lincoln—would be sufficient cause, all by itself, for setting up a Southern confederacy. Even before Lincoln's election, preparations were being made for that eventuality.

Buchanan had decided before his inauguration not to stand for re-election; he thought two terms were too long for any man to be President. The Democrats were unable to unify behind anyone else, and Lincoln won with much less than a popular majority. On the morning after the election, the federal district judge in South Carolina resigned his post and other representatives of the national government there did the same.

The calls for secession were growing louder in Georgia, Alabama, Mississippi, Louisiana, and Florida, but South Carolina, the old home of nullification, presented the most immediate danger to the Union. Because there was talk of the possible capture of the forts in Charleston Harbor by the secessionists, Colonel John L. Gardner, commanding the garrison there, decided to remove federal arms from the arsenal in the middle of Charleston as a precaution. But his plans were stymied by an outraged mob.

Buchanan scolded the North for the abolition movement and begged the Southern states to wait and see what Lincoln did before they took any precipitous action. If the abolitionists continued to plague the South, or if Lincoln were to "invade" the constitutional rights of the slave states, he said, then a rebellion might be justified. On the other hand, secession was illegal. But the federal government had no means to prevent it or to suppress it once it occurred. The present administration had the right to protect federal functions and property within a state, Buchanan said, but only defensively. It could not act unless attacked. It could not declare war against a state. The government would stay in Charleston to guard the forts and collect tariffs. But otherwise the maintenance of federal responsibility in South Carolina was peculiarly hampered, Buchanan said, by the fact that a number of federal officers there had resigned. Thus, certain official functions, particularly those pertaining to the enforcement of federal law (including putting down a rebellion), could not be sustained by force because there were no law officers.

The appeal to reason had reached, at last, the nadir of its futility. Buchanan was every inch the high-minded gentleman. As a lame-duck President his position was already weak, and he made it weaker by his self-restricting legalism. He denied himself powers that other Presidents before him had felt able to use in like emergencies—notably Washington in the Whisky Rebellion and Jackson in the Nullification Crisis.

South Carolina seceded before Christmas, followed quickly by Mississippi, Florida, Alabama, Georgia, Louisiana, and Texas. A provisional Confederate government had been organized by February 9, 1861. All over the South federal forts and arsenals were captured. Buchanan believed that by law he was still powerless to act. Practically speaking, he had only a few hundred troops at his disposal should he decide to use arms. And if he used them, would not war be inevitable? He begged Congress to give the government new powers on the one hand and to create a legal solution to the crisis on the other. He felt that the best solution lay in a clarifying amendment to the Constitution that would guarantee slavery in the states that wanted it. With Congress refusing to act, he tried to remain in the middle, giving in to no one, but pacifying both sides until a solution could be worked out. Those Northerners who support the South "are almost literally between two fires," he had once told John Calhoun. "I desire to come between the factions as a daysman with one hand on the head of each, counselling peace," he said now. And after leaving office he told his niece, "I acted for some time as a breakwater between the North and the South, both surging with all their force against me."

When he retired to Wheatland that March, he left the crisis intact for Lincoln to deal with. In many ways this was appropriate, for neither Lincoln nor his party had been willing to help Buchanan. But in short order he was made the scapegoat for the havoc that followed. He was unfairly accused of having been proslavery and of having helped the South to arm for war. His failure to act at once in November to cut off secession was also criticized—justly, if one also gives him credit for seeking to maintain not just the Union, but his idea of constitutional government as well.

He supported Lincoln and the war, saying that he would have done as Lincoln did, once Fort Sumter was fired on. Lincoln was not grateful; he needed someone to blame for the war and led off the attack on Buchanan—an attack that continues to this day. "It is one of those great national prosecutions," wrote Buchanan himself before he died in 1868, ". . . necessary to vindicate the character of the Government. . . ." The world, he said, had "forgotten the circumstances" and blamed his "supineness."

It was a mild—and characteristically aloof—observation. But his appeal to "the circumstances" cannot be ignored. The intersectional struggle had evaded real control by the executive branch ever since John Tyler had come to office in 1841. The conciliating James Buchanan reaped a whirlwind that had been decades in the making. His administration was a failure, yet in many aspects it was less his administration than that of the "irrepressible conflict."

—MICHAEL HARWOOD

James Buchanan

A PICTURE PORTFOLIO

Above Buchanan's head on an 1856 campaign ribbon is a rooster, then the symbol of the Democratic party.

Buchanan was not alone in the North in his belief that law and good will could hold the crumbling Union together. His election campaign was, like his predecessor's, founded on that idea, as is shown in the advertisement at right, published by Buchanan's supporters in Connecticut. Nonetheless, Republican John C. Frémont swept New England and New York, while Buchanan won by taking the whole South.

In many respects the new Republican party was the party of dissent and change. Louis Maurer's lithograph, done for Currier & Ives during the 1856 campaign, acidly makes this point, demonstrating that the Democrats, while preaching Union, were less than conciliatory toward a large segment of the electorate.

A MISCAST PRESIDENT

JOHN C. FRÉMONT

Buchanan inherited an exceedingly unsettled situation when the election of 1856 made him President. His nation was growing at a breath-taking pace; railroads, steamboats, and the telegraph were changing the age-old rhythm of human communication; the industrial revolution had come to America. Scientific thought and philosophy were being infiltrated by exciting, radical ideas; religion was in revivalist ferment; social institutions were being questioned, broken, remade. It was a time when much of the world had outlawed human slavery, but the United States remained half free, half slave. An increasingly large segment of its population, caught up in the spirit of change, angrily opposed the institution. Buchanan thought that the sectionalist clash thus precipitated was capable of reasonable, legal solution. Thus he believed that by winning a Supreme Court ruling—in the Dred Scott case—that delineated congressional powers over slavery in the territories, he had solved the problems of Kansas. Buchanan was emotionally isolated from the fervor that enveloped America. He had traveled little in the United States; he had seldom explored outside diplomacy, practical politics, and the law. He lacked both the experience and the temperament to fight the national fires with fire: not when they repeatedly flared up over Kansas, not when they wrecked his legislative program, not even when the South began its secession.

Explorer, soldier, and "Pathfinder" of the West, John C. Frémont was the first presidential candidate of the Republican party. Running against Buchanan on a free-soil platform, Frémont was chosen largely for his national prestige. His fame was linked to a series of important explorations—through South Pass in 1842 and to Oregon, the Sierra Nevada, and California in 1843 and 1844. An expedition on the eve of the Mexican War involved him in the conquest of California. His excessive zeal resulted in a court-martial, but made him a national hero. After a year as a United States senator and two more expeditions, he was adopted by the new party. "Free soil, free speech, and Frémont" was the Republican slogan, and among those distinguished citizens who supported him were Emerson, Bryant, and Longfellow. Support by the intellectuals and Northern abolitionists was insufficient, however, to counteract Unionist fears of Southern secession; and Frémont lost to the compromising Democratic candidate, Buchanan. When Civil War broke out, Frémont commanded the Department of the West, but his radical antislavery actions in Missouri led to his removal. Given a command in western Virginia, he soon resigned. In 1864 he was nominated for the Presidency by a group of Radical Republicans, but was persuaded to withdraw. Before his death in 1890, Frémont served for six years as the governor of Arizona Territory.

In the fall of 1859, John Brown (shown above in a modern painting by John Steuart Curry) led eighteen whites and Negroes in a raid on the arsenal and rifle factory at Harpers Ferry, Virginia, hoping to spark a slave rebellion. It did not work. Buchanan ordered in federal troops; Brown was captured and brought to trial. But the incident seemed to crystallize sectional antipathies, making President Buchanan's chosen role as compromiser more and more agonizing, increasingly untenable.

A SHAKY UNION

There is a body of opinion in America, wrote New Hampshire abolitionist Nathaniel Rogers, which "abhors slavery in the abstract . . . but denies the right of any body or any thing to devise its overthrow, but slavery itself and slaveholders. It prays for the poor slave, that he might be elevated, while it stands both feet on his breast to keep him down." The description fitted Buchanan's views exactly. Admitting to a personal dislike of slavery, he nevertheless railed at abolitionists such as William Lloyd Garrison and John Brown for fomenting disunion. But, to his horror, the abolitionists did not want a union with slavery. As Garrison put it, *they*, at least, would not equivocate, and they would be heard.

A Pictorial History of the Negro in America

As the above cartoon portrayed him, Buchanan was only a candle end, stubbornly flickering on despite fierce winds, while providing little light.

Frank Leslie's Illustrated Newspaper

"If it is deemed necessary that I should forfeit my life . . . and mingle my blood . . . with the blood of millions [of slaves]," Brown told his accusers, ". . . I say, let it be done." It was. On December 2, 1859, he was hanged at Charlestown, and as the abolition hymn was soon to promise, John Brown's truth went marching on—to war.

DISCORDANT VOICES

FREDERICK DOUGLASS

Without the verification of history, the story of Frederick Douglass would seem to be an improbable piece of fiction. The son of a slave and an unknown white man, Douglass was reared in bondage in Maryland. Despite laws forbidding the education of slaves, he learned to read and write, increasing his fierce desire to be free. In 1838, at the age of twenty-one, he succeeded: he fled to New York, and then to New Bedford, Massachusetts, where he worked as a laborer and lived with the realization that his "runaway" status might be discovered at any time. His impressive physique and commanding voice soon made Douglass a spokesman for the state's antislavery society; in 1845 he daringly sharpened the sword hanging over his head by publishing his life story, *Narrative.* Two years later he arranged to buy his freedom and established a newspaper, the *North Star*, firmly setting his own policies despite conflicting advice from abolitionist friends. He lectured widely, advocated woman suffrage, and, during the war, recruited two Negro regiments, exhorting them, "Better even die than to live slaves. . . . The iron gate of our prison stands half open. One gallant rush . . . will fling it wide. . . ." During Reconstruction, he agitated for Negro civil rights, and by the time of his death in 1895, Douglass had held a number of federal offices, including that of minister to Haiti.

ROGER B. TANEY

Roger B. Taney's proslavery opinion in the Dred Scott case of 1857 should have surprised no one, for it was wholly in accord with the strict-constructionist, states' rights philosophy he had held since Jackson had appointed him Chief Justice of the Supreme Court in 1836. Groomed for politics in upper-class tidewater Maryland, Taney had been a Federalist state legislator early in the century but swung to Jackson in 1824; by 1831 he was Old Hickory's Attorney General. In 1834 the Senate refused to confirm him as Secretary of the Treasury, but not before Taney, who like Jackson saw the National Bank as a predator, had placed federal funds in "pet banks" while interim Secretary. Once installed on the high bench, Taney began to reverse the nationalist trends of his predecessor, John Marshall, by increasing the power of the states over corporations in the Charles River Bridge case and by construing the Constitution's commerce clause narrowly. Taney held that states should be free to act unless the Constitution specifically authorized federal intervention; a strong, Northern-dominated federal government, he felt, would stifle the South. Ironically, his Dred Scott decision speeded the South's downfall. During the war, Taney opposed President Lincoln's suspension of the writ of habeas corpus. Weak from recurrent illness, he died in 1864.

nothing to excite ambition for education."
In the one-room schools of the day, formal
education embraced nothing more than reading (*Dilworth's Speller*), a little writing, and,
as Lincoln later said, "cipherin' to the rule
of three."

Despite this stifling environment, Lincoln
rose to knowledge. Wherever he could find
or make light, he read: *Aesop's Fables, Rob-
inson Crusoe*, the Bible. Even at work in the
field, when his horse rested, Lincoln's book
would be out of his pocket. Books like Parson Weems's lyrical life of Washington affected him deeply. When he borrowed the
Weems book and got it wet, he worked three
days on a farm to pay for it and own it.

For all his introspection, Lincoln was a
powerful young man—tough, muscular, a
rough foe in any bout. By nineteen, he was
six feet four inches tall. Despite a relatively
small chest and a slim waist, he had powerful shoulders and large limbs.

In February, 1830, Thomas Lincoln pulled
up stakes again, this time moving to Macon
County in Illinois. The next year, Abe struck
out on his own: hired by Denton Offut, he
worked on a flatboat carrying goods to New
Orleans. It was a decisive trip, for Offut
took a liking to him and offered him a job as
a clerk in a general store and mill in New
Salem, Illinois. And on this passage Lincoln
first saw the horror of slavery: Negroes in
chains, whipped and sold like cattle.

He arrived in New Salem in July, 1831,
and soon thereafter squared off in a wrest-
ling match with the town tough, Jack Armstrong. Some say he beat Armstrong; others
call it a draw. But unmistakably, Lincoln
won Jack's and the townspeople's respect.
Affable behind the counter, good to children,
obliging to widows (for whom he chopped
wood), Lincoln earned a reputation for kindness, reliability, and honesty. Also, clerking
afforded him leisure for reading. Weems gave
way to Voltaire and Thomas Paine, to Burns
and Blackstone, to Indiana statutes and the
Constitution, to Shakespeare (*Macbeth* was
his favorite). Friends lent him books, the
cooper opened his shop to him at night so
that he could read by a fire of shavings, and

schoolmaster Mentor Graham polished Lincoln's command of the English language.

In 1832 Lincoln served one brief term as
a soldier in the field. When the Sauk, under
Black Hawk, took to the warpath, the governor issued a call for volunteers, and Lincoln promptly signed up. He saw no battle,
but served competently in two independent
companies as a scout.

Returning to New Salem, the popular Lincoln campaigned for a seat in the Illinois
general assembly as an anti-Jackson Whig.
His approach was disarmingly to the point:
"Fellow Citizens, I presume you all know
who I am. I am humble Abraham Lincoln. . . .
My politics are short and sweet like the old
woman's dance. I am in favour of a national
bank. I am in favour of the internal improvement system and a high protective tariff. . . .
If elected, I shall be thankful; if not, it will
be all the same." Predictably, Lincoln lost
this first election in hard-nosed Jacksonian
territory. But he won almost all the votes of
his neighbors, Democrats or not.

He was soon back in the grocery business,
in partnership with William F. Berry, who
had served with him during the Black Hawk
War. On credit and on Lincoln's high reputation in the town, the two veterans took over
three stores. But the enterprises foundered:
Berry liked liquor too much, and Lincoln,
the law, which he was studying in spare moments. It took him fifteen years of self-denial
to pay off all his—and Berry's—creditors.

When the job of postmaster fell vacant in
May, 1833, Lincoln was named to the office.
In charge of the mails, he could be less than
efficient, keeping his postal receipts in an old
blue sock and the mail in his hat. But on
his rounds, he was more than dutiful. He
would walk miles to deliver a letter he knew
was eagerly awaited. The postmaster's salary
was based on receipts and ranged from $25
to $80 a year. So, probably through the in-
fluence of a Democratic friend, Lincoln was
offered the more lucrative post of deputy
county surveyor. He learned about surveying by poring over books late into the night.

Meanwhile, love had found Lincoln, in the
person of Ann Rutledge, daughter of a tav-

ern keeper. Ann was auburn-haired, blue-eyed, slender, and fair. Lincoln loved her, courted her, and became engaged to her. But Ann died of typhoid, and Lincoln was thrust into a profound melancholy.

A seat in the Illinois assembly remained Lincoln's goal: when he sought election again in 1834, he won. Through the first session of the legislature, he remained observant and silent in his new sixty-dollar suit. But in succeeding sessions, he rose to the leadership of his party, becoming the Whigs' perennial candidate for speaker of the house in the strongly Democratic assembly. He supported the removal of the state capital to Springfield, to which he himself moved in 1837. In the capital, he boarded free with a tradesman named Joshua Speed, who took pity on his poverty and melancholy face. These legislative years saw a maturing of Lincoln's moderate Whig philosophy and his development as an adroit partisan advocate and orator. Admitted to the bar in 1836, he fared well, not only as a capital attorney, but also as a circuit lawyer.

Of primary interest in his Springfield years is his position on slavery. The Illinois constitution of 1818 had granted the vote to all adult white male residents, without qualification. Consequently, Lincoln's campaign appeal of 1836 that "all whites . . . who pay taxes or bear arms" be given the vote was radical only in his suggestion that taxpaying females be allowed to vote.

Indeed, Lincoln remained highly ambivalent on the subject of slavery. In response to the rise in Illinois of overt antislavery sentiment, the Illinois legislature in 1837 passed resolutions condemning abolitionism and denying the right of the federal government either to abridge slavery in the states or to abolish it without a vote in the District of Columbia. In a dissenting resolution, Lincoln and a friend, Dan Stone, addressed themselves not only to abolitionism, but to the institution of slavery itself. Slavery, they said, was "founded on both injustice and bad policy. . . ." On the other hand, they argued, the abolition of slavery was also wrong because "the promulgation of aboli-

tion doctrines tends rather to increase than to abate" the evils of slavery. As for the role of the federal government, Lincoln and Stone agreed that the federal government could not constitutionally interfere with slavery in any state but that it could abolish it in the District of Columbia, though "that power ought not to be exercised unless" the people of the District so requested.

But all was not politics in Springfield. Lincoln had fallen in love again. As a popular and respected legislator, he had access to the hub of Springfield's social life, the Ninian Edwards' mansion, which was overseen by Mrs. Elizabeth Todd Edwards, sister of Mary Todd of Lexington, Kentucky. Twenty-one-year-old Mary was well educated and charming, if high tempered. In its initial stage, her courtship with Lincoln lasted for about twelve months, and their wedding was set for January 1, 1841.

What happened at that first scheduled wedding of Mary and Abraham has been the subject of passionate controversy. Some biographers insist that Lincoln simply did not show up. Others say that he went to Mary and said he could not go through with the marriage. There is no disagreement, however, over the fact that after he left Mary Todd, Lincoln experienced a profound emotional breakdown lasting almost a year and a half. Joshua Speed and Speed's mother nursed him back to mental health.

By mid-1842, Lincoln was moving toward stability, and Mary Todd was still willing. They reconciled and repledged their troth. On November 4, 1842, they were married in an Episcopal ceremony. A week later, Lincoln concluded a business letter with an enigmatic remark: "Nothing new here except my marrying, which to me, is matter of profound wonder."

Lincoln's marriage to Mary was indisputably rocky. They fought hard and bitterly, often and audibly. Lincoln seems to have met Mary's assaults with a saddened forbearance, avoiding conflict when possible. A common love for their children bound them together: Robert, the eldest, who would go on to Exeter and Harvard and service as

Secretary of War under Presidents Garfield and Arthur; Edward, who would die at three; William, who would die at eleven in the White House; and frail Thomas ("Tad"), who was afflicted with a stammer.

In 1846 Lincoln was elected to the Thirtieth Congress by the largest majority in the history of his district. When he arrived in Washington, the United States was only several weeks short of victory in the Mexican War. In Congress Lincoln joined the shrill Whig attack on the Democratic President, James K. Polk. On January 12, 1848, Congressman Lincoln explained his position. He rejected as the "sheerest deception" Polk's claim that the first American blood spilled by Mexicans was spilled on American soil. Mexico was not the aggressor; the United States was. Back home in his Illinois district, the reaction to Lincoln's stand against the war was one of fury and shock. But the congressman stood his ground. "Allow the President to invade a neighboring nation whenever he shall deem it necessary to repel an invasion ..." Lincoln wrote, "and you allow him to make war at pleasure. . . ."

In Congress Lincoln consistently favored the exclusion of slavery in the territories ceded by Mexico, but he still remained opposed to federal interference with slavery in the states where it already existed. A lame-duck congressman (by prearrangement with other party leaders in Illinois), he introduced, in January, 1849, an amendment to a resolution instructing the Committee on the District of Columbia to report out a bill abolishing slavery in the District. Lincoln urged that children born of slaves in Washington after January 1, 1850, should be free, but should be apprenticed to their masters until they came of age. Masters wishing to free a slave would be compensated by the federal government. All fugitive slaves escaping into the District, under Lincoln's plan, were to be returned to their masters. The resolution did not become law.

In 1848 Lincoln took to the stump for the Whig presidential candidate, Zachary Taylor. He organized demonstrations and rallies and toured New England in a bid to unite Whigs and Free-Soilers behind the war hero. Taylor won, and after the inauguration the congressman looked for a patronage plum: the office of commissioner of the general land office. When he failed to get this position, a disillusioned Lincoln, now aged forty,

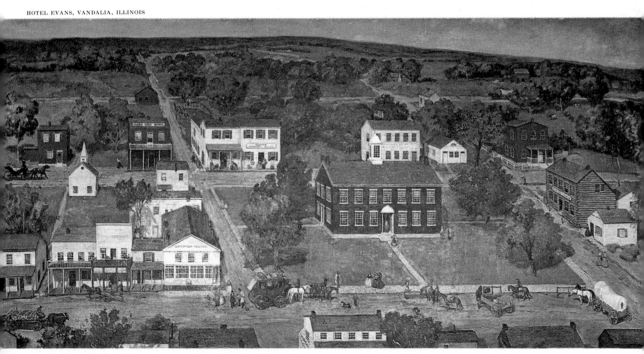

Vandalia was the Illinois capital until 1839. When Lincoln joined the legislature in 1834, the brick State-house, although only ten years old, was in such disrepair that laws had to be framed amidst falling plaster.

retired for a five-year lull in public political activity. Again he was a circuit lawyer, a natural politician who liked a good joke.

But the "irrepressible conflict" was approaching, presaged even more formidably by the passage in 1854 of the Kansas-Nebraska Act. Sired by Illinois's Democratic senator, Stephen A. Douglas, the act, in effect, opened up the entire area of the Louisiana Purchase to slavery. In the Northwest the reaction to the act was bitter and violent. On March 20, 1854, anger gave way to organized political rebellion when a coalition of Whigs, Free-Soilers, and antislavery Democrats met at Ripon, Wisconsin, and formed the Republican party.

Lincoln joined the new party in 1856 and campaigned hard for its first presidential candidate, John C. Frémont. By plumping for the party slate, he built his own reputation, county by county. According to Horace White, secretary of the Illinois Republican state committee, Lincoln was "one of the shrewdest politicians of the state. . . ." Nobody, White said, "knew better than he what was passing in the minds of the people. Nobody knew better how to turn things to advantage politically, and nobody was readier to take such advantage, provided it did not involve dishonorable means."

Two days after the inauguration of President Buchanan in 1857, Chief Justice Roger B. Taney's heavily Southern Supreme Court handed down its decision in the Dred Scott case: it ruled that slaves were property, and declared the Missouri Compromise unconstitutional. In Springfield, Senator Douglas defended the Court's decision. "The Courts," Douglas said, "are tribunals prescribed by the Constitution. . . . Hence, whoever resists the final decision of the highest judicial tribunal aims a deadly blow at our whole Republican system of government. . . ."

Lincoln, now emerging as the major spokesman for free-soil Republicanism, spoke in Springfield on June 26, 1857. He derided Douglas' pious homily on the Court's pre-eminence, pointing out that Douglas himself had defied the Court's ruling on the United States Bank by applauding President Jackson's refusal to abide by its decision. Lincoln condemned the alliance of American business interests, educators, and theologians, who were, he said, joining forces to imprison the Negro forever. Any man who justifies the enslavement of others, he added, justifies his own. If color is the excuse, and the lighter man has a right to enslave the darker, the lighter may himself be enslaved by a still lighter man. If intellectual superiority justifies slavery, all men are at the mercy of those more brilliant than they. If business interest justifies slavery, anyone with an interest in a man, white or black, may enslave him.

Lincoln's logic, now fired by political passion, was unassailable. To Douglas' statement that Lincoln's views were held only by people who wanted "to vote, and eat, and sleep, and marry with Negroes," Lincoln replied that the fact that he did not want to have a Negro woman for a slave did not imply that he must have her for a wife. Could he not just leave her alone? "In some respects," he said, "she certainly is not my equal; but in her natural right to eat the bread she earns with her own hands without asking leave of any one else, she is my equal, and the equal of all others."

Lincoln's reply to Douglas initiated a verbal exchange that thrust him into national fame. On June 16, 1858, he was named by the Republicans to run for Douglas' Senate seat. That same day, he delivered his acceptance speech at the Illinois Republican state convention. Noting the rise of impassioned agitation against slavery, Lincoln told his party: "In *my* opinion, it *will* not cease, until a *crisis* shall have been reached, and passed." Then he turned to the language of the Bible: "'A house divided against itself cannot stand.' I believe this government cannot endure, permanently half *slave* and half *free*. I do not expect the Union to be *dissolved*—I do not expect the house to *fall*—but I *do* expect it will cease to be divided. It will become *all* one thing, or *all* the other. Either the *opponents* of slavery, will arrest the further spread of it, and place it where the public mind shall rest in the belief that it is in course of ultimate extinction; or its *advocates* will push it forward, till it shall become alike in *all* the States, *old* as well as *new—North* as well as *South.*"

To a critic who complained that the speech was too strong, Lincoln replied: "If I had to draw a pen across my record, and erase my whole life from sight, and I had one poor gift or choice as to what I should save from the wreck, I should choose that speech and leave it to the world unerased."

Then he challenged Douglas to a series of debates which began at Ottawa, Illinois, on August 21, 1858, and ended at Alton on October 15, amidst banners, brass bands, raucous crowds, and sweating reporters. At Freeport, on August 27, Douglas made a major ideological concession—his famed "Freeport Doctrine"—that would cost him Southern Democratic support and would nourish Democratic disunion. To Lincoln's question, "Can the people of a United States territory, in any lawful way, against the wish of any citizen of the United States, exclude slavery from its limits prior to the formation of a state constitution?" Douglas answered Yes. Further, he said, "it matters not what way the Supreme Court may hereafter decide as to . . . whether slavery may or may not go into a territory under the Constitution, the people have the lawful means to introduce it or exclude it as they please. . . ."

At the last debate, at Alton, Douglas assailed Lincoln's "house divided" speech as a "slander upon the immortal framers of our Constitution," who founded the country, he said, both free and slave, under state sovereignties. He ridiculed Lincoln's egalitarian view of the Declaration of Independence, which was meant, Douglas said, for colonial and British whites only. And he condemned Lincoln's "crusade against the Supreme Court" following the Dred Scott decision.

Lincoln replied that if the Founding Fathers were as wise as Douglas agreed, why did he defy their permissive attitude on slavery by introducing his divisive Kansas-Nebraska bill? Lincoln envisioned new United States territories open to "*free white people everywhere*—the world over. . . ." He dismissed

THE UNDECIDED POLITICAL PRIZE FIGHT.

Attended by a Negro, Lincoln and Douglas engage in "The Undecided Political Prize Fight" of 1860.

Douglas' charges that he sought a sectional war over slavery or favored "introducing a perfect social and political equality between the white and black races. . . ." The whole question, Lincoln said, was reduced to a choice between "the common right of humanity" or "the divine right of kings."

Actually, the debaters were less at odds than they appeared to be. Lincoln fully shared Douglas' horror of miscegenation. "Agreed for once—a thousand times agreed," he said in 1857. "There are white men enough to marry all the white women, and black men enough to marry all the black women; and so let them be married." Though affirming in July, 1858, that he had "always hated slavery . . . as much as any Abolitionist," he insisted that he had never intended to do anything about it where it already existed. And finally he declared in Chicago on July 10, 1858, that he wished that all talk of "inferior" people be discarded. Yet only two months later, in Charleston, Illinois, he contradicted himself:

"I will say then that I am not, nor ever have been in favor of bringing about in any way the social and political equality of the white and black races—that I am not nor ever have been in favor of making voters or jurors of negroes, nor of qualifying them to hold office, nor to intermarry with white people. . . . And inasmuch as they cannot so live, while they do remain together there must be the position of superior and inferior, and I as much as any other man am in favor of having the superior position assigned to the white race."

In the Senate election, held on November 2, 1858, Lincoln polled a popular majority of some four thousand votes over his opponent. But Douglas, through gerrymandered apportionment, won electoral control of the assembly, which re-elected him to the Senate 54 to 46. Lincoln described his reaction to the defeat in words that would one day be echoed by another Illinoisan, Adlai E. Stevenson II. Likening himself to the little boy who stubbed his toe, he said, "It hurt too bad to laugh, and he was too big to cry." But friends assured a disappointed Lincoln that more and more influential people were eying him for the Presidency. Replied Lincoln, "I . . . admit that I am ambitious, and would like to be President . . . but there is no such good luck in store for me. . . ."

Still, friends pressed the issue, urging Lincoln to make himself even better known. Calls for speeches poured in from Iowa, Pennsylvania, Missouri, New York. On February 27, 1860, at Cooper Institute in Manhattan, he argued wholly from tradition, citing the personal attitudes and constitutional provisions of the Founding Fathers to support a policy of nonintervention with slavery in states where it existed and the barring of it in the territories. Lincoln denied that the Republican appeal for the restriction of slavery was sectional, urging the South to give it a chance at the polls. George Washington himself, he said, had heartily signed Congress' Northwest Ordinance barring the extension of slavery. Was Washington sectional, too?

Rejecting the extremism of both abolitionists and secessionists, Lincoln disproved Taney's claim that the Constitution "distinctly and expressly" affirmed the right of property in a slave. The Constitution, he said, certainly guaranteed property. But as for

The country saw a determined Abraham Lincoln in this medal from the 1860 presidential campaign.

the slave, Lincoln explained, the Constitution cited him specifically as a "person," alluding to his master's claim over him solely in terms of "service or labor which may be due." To the South's claim that the election of a Republican President would destroy the Union, Lincoln replied: "That is cool. A highwayman holds a pistol to my ear, and mutters through his teeth, 'Stand and deliver, or I shall kill you, and then you will be a murderer!' " Slaveowners, he said, would apparently be appeased only if opponents of slavery would agree that slavery was morally proper and should be given "a full national recognition . . . as a legal right, and a social blessing." The South, he said, was demanding that the righteous, not the unrighteous, be called to repentance. "*Right*," Lincoln concluded, "*makes might*. . . ." New York applauded.

Lincoln moved on to Providence, then to New Hampshire, where he was hailed by Governor Frederick Smith as "the next President of the United States." In May his political ship made for home port at the Illinois Republican state convention in Decatur. When John Hanks, Lincoln's old Mississippi flatboat companion, entered the convention hall bearing two rails allegedly split by Abe, the delegates erupted with joy.

The Republican National Convention of 1860, held in Chicago, ratified the decision made at Decatur. Senator William H. Seward of New York, who had called American civil war "irrepressible," entered the convention city a brassy and confident candidate. Others in the field were Salmon P. Chase, Edward Bates, and Simon Cameron.

A great roar went up for Seward when he was nominated, but there was an even greater cry for Lincoln. "The uproar" for Abe, a journalist reported, "was beyond description. Imagine all the hogs ever slaughtered in Cincinnati giving their death squeals together. . . ." Then the Republican party voted. Needed to win: 233 votes. First ballot: Seward, 173½; Lincoln, 102 votes. Favorite-son votes for Bates, Cameron, Chase, and others. Second ballot: Seward, 184½; Lincoln, 181. "I've got him," cried Lincoln in Springfield when the news flashed to the capital. Third ballot: Lincoln, 231½. Ohio rose: four votes for Lincoln, Republican candidate for President of the United States.

In Springfield a nervous Lincoln, who had played ball during the day to relieve his tension, heard the news and went off to tell Mary. He seemed calm, Lamon said, "but a close observer could detect in his countenance the indications of deep emotion."

The Republican platform of 1860 called for noninterference in slave states and for exclusion of slavery from the territories. It pledged a homestead act to grant free land to settlers. In addition, the party called for a rigid tariff to protect burgeoning American industries, railroad subsidies to unite the country economically, improved mail and telegraph lines, and whatever would aid the development of a brash, progressive American capitalism.

At the Democratic convention, meeting at Charleston, South Carolina, eight cotton states, indignant over the party's refusal to endorse slavery, withdrew from the hall. Rump conventions nominated Douglas as the official Democratic candidate; John C. Breckinridge of Kentucky as the Southern candidate; and Tennessee's John Bell as candidate of the new and moderate National Constitution Union party. Lincoln directed a campaign strategy aimed at further deepening the critical schisms within the Democratic party. His running mate, Senator Hannibal Hamlin of Maine, was an ex-Democrat who had turned Republican.

It was not an inspiring campaign. Northern propagandists portrayed the politically sophisticated Lincoln as an ingenuous but patriotic plowman sacrificing farm and security to save his country; or, despite Lincoln's oft-stated compromises on slavery, as a veritable abolitionist. Nor was the South lacking its own barrel of distortions. A Republican victory, it declared, would mean the end of states' rights, of respect for private property, and of freedom itself.

Though his three opponents polled 60 per cent of the popular vote in the election of November 6, 1860, Lincoln won 180 electoral votes out of 303, carrying all eighteen free states. But Republican joy was overshadowed by dark clouds of rebellion in the South, now thoroughly persuaded that Lincoln meant to destroy its economy and political foundations.

In Congress compromise measures were advanced, among them the Crittenden proposal to sustain existing slavery and to divide the territories between slavery and freedom at the old Missouri Compromise line. But while the President-elect maintained public silence, he moved powerfully behind the scenes, instructing Republicans to vote against any compromise measure that allowed the extension of slavery.

The Southern storm broke on December 20, 1860, in a slow roll of secessionist thunder. On that day, South Carolina declared at Charleston that "the union now subsisting between South Carolina and other States under the name of the United States of America is hereby dissolved." On February 4, 1861, seven Southern states met at Montgomery to proclaim the Confederate States of America. The threat of decades had become a reality: the house was divided.

On February 11, Lincoln bade farewell to Springfield: "To this place, and the kindness

of these people," he said, "I owe everything. . . . I now leave, not knowing when,
or whether ever, I may return, with a task
before me greater than that which rested
upon Washington."

Lincoln's journey to the national capital
was protracted to twelve days to permit
speeches and receptions along the way. In
Philadelphia, word reached the party of a
plot to murder Lincoln in Baltimore, and
plans were made to curtail the President-
elect's journey immediately and to send him
by private coach to Washington. While
agreeing to bypass Baltimore, Lincoln insisted on going ahead with Washington's
Birthday ceremonies at Independence Hall,
which were highlighted by his raising of a
34-star flag, hailing Kansas' admission to
the Union as a free state.

Within hours, Lincoln was hidden as an
invalid in a Pullman berth, and he began his
secret midnight journey to Washington. At
six o'clock in the morning, Saturday, February 23, 1861, a muffler around his neck, he
slipped into the Capital and quietly checked
in at the Willard Hotel. There he received
well-wishers, heard patronage requests, and
organized his Cabinet. Delegates to the celebrated "Peace Conference"—an attempt
by representatives from twenty-one states to
restore the Union—met with him, but Lincoln was firm before all insistence that in
the interest of national unity he permit the
extension of slavery: "My course," he said,
"is as plain as a turnpike road. It is marked
out by the Constitution."

On March 4, 1861, seated in an open carriage with Buchanan, protected at all points
of the route to the Capitol by cavalry and
infantry and by riflemen perched in windows, Lincoln rode to his destiny. Speaking
from the east portico of the Capitol, he offered massive reassurances and concessions
to the South: "I have no purpose, directly

THE EAGLE'S NEST.

Chillingly ferocious, the Union eagle crushes its deformed and rebellious offspring in this 1861 cartoon.

or indirectly, to interfere with the institution of slavery in the States where it exists." He cited the Republicans' platform promise to maintain states' rights. He abjured an armed invasion of states by any domestic power as "the gravest of crimes" and upheld the Fugitive Slave Law's provision that runaway slaves must be returned to their masters. Then Lincoln turned to the crisis of secession. Even if the Constitution were merely a voluntary contract, he reasoned, one party to that contract could not declare it null and void. The Union was inviolable.

"I therefore consider that . . . the Union is unbroken," Lincoln declared, "and . . . I shall take care, as the Constitution itself expressly enjoins upon me, that the laws of the Union be faithfully executed in all the States." In pursuit of this policy, he added, "there needs to be no bloodshed or violence; and there shall be none, unless it be forced upon the national authority." Then the President called the South back home: "In *your* hands, my dissatisfied fellow countrymen, and not in *mine*, is the momentous issue of civil war. The government will not assail *you*. You can have no conflict, without being yourselves the aggressors. . . ."

Then Chief Justice Taney arose. The author of the Dred Scott decision, his hands shaking, his face ashen, stepped forward to administer the oath of office: "I, Abraham Lincoln, do solemnly swear that I will faithfully execute the Office of President of the United States, and will to the best of my Ability, preserve, protect and defend the Constitution of the United States." He was President.

But the South had made its decision; there was no going back. By the time Lincoln took his oath, Confederates had seized all federal forts and Navy yards in the states under their control, except Fort Pickens in Pensacola, Florida, and Fort Sumter at Charleston, South Carolina.

Lincoln's Cabinet was a formidable collection of Whigs, converted Democrats, and moderate and radical Republicans. His primary appointments were all men of extraordinary ability and integrity: William H.

The indulgent Lincoln ignored his son Tad's mischief. "Let him run," he remarked. "There's time enough for him to learn his letters and get pokey."

Seward, the antislavery senator from New York, as Secretary of State; the abolitionist Republican Salmon P. Chase of Ohio as Secretary of the Treasury; Simon Cameron of Pennsylvania as Secretary of War (he was replaced in January, 1862, by the articulate, unreconstructed but efficient Democrat Edwin M. Stanton); and Gideon Welles of Connecticut in the critical post of Secretary of the Navy. It was a Cabinet with massive potential for inner dispute, but it functioned well, largely through Lincoln's own personal ability to separate chaff from wheat.

Early in the administration, however, Lincoln's authority was challenged by Secretary Seward. The New Yorker clearly considered Lincoln his inferior in education, political experience, and good judgment, and he moved swiftly to establish his position as *de facto* President. In an incredible memorandum to Lincoln on April 1, 1861, Seward lamented what he called the President's lack of firm policies, domestic or foreign, after one month in office. He urged Lincoln, among other things, to shift his emphasis from slavery to Unionism and to divert attention from American disunion by precipitating a war with Spain and France. Further, he said, if the President was unwilling to pursue these policies, he would do it himself. To this contemptuous and irresponsible letter, President Lincoln responded with quiet grandeur. Whatever had to be done by executive authority, he told Seward, he would do as President. "Still . . . I wish, and suppose I am entitled to have, the advice of all the cabinet."

War now seemed imminent as the South demanded the evacuation of Fort Sumter. On the day after his inauguration, Lincoln had received word from the fort's commander that he and his men had scant provisions in the face of still silent Confederate shore batteries. A month later, the President had still not decided whether to provision the fort or to arm it further to repel a threatened Confederate assault. Ultimately, he decided to send food to the fort, making clear his decision against sending arms.

At 4:30 A.M. on April 12, 1861, the Confederate States of America fired upon Sumter. They were the first shots in a war that would kill 600,000 American men. Lincoln moved quickly to meet the assault. He called for 75,000 volunteers and ordered a blockade of the South. The Capital city itself made new preparations for siege. Virginia, angered by what it considered Lincoln's despotic call for volunteers, left the Union, followed by Arkansas, North Carolina, and Tennessee.

On July 4, President Lincoln addressed a saddened special session of Congress. The Confederates, he said, knew full well that he had sent bread and not bullets to Sumter and that the fort, hemmed in by Confederate guns, could scarcely have attacked them. Why, then, the assault? To destroy, Lincoln said, "the visible authority of the Federal Union, and thus force it to immediate dissolution. . . . This issue," said the President, "embraces more than the fate of these United States. It presents to the whole family of man, the question, whether a constitutional republic, or a democracy . . . can, or cannot maintain its territorial integrity against its own domestic foes . . ."; whether, in fact, republics had an "inherent and fatal" flaw.

The United States, Lincoln declared, had no alternative: it must "resist force, employed for its destruction, by force, for its preservation."

On July 21, the North was decisively defeated at Bull Run (Manassas) in the first major encounter of the war. Lincoln replaced his field commander, General Irvin McDowell, with General George B. McClellan; he was confident that McClellan would press the war forward with dispatch. When, on November 1, General Winfield Scott, ill and cantankerous, resigned his post as general in chief of the Union forces over policy differences, McClellan was named his successor. But although he was an efficient organizer, McClellan proved to be dilatory in executing his plans and was smitten, besides, with an overweening egotism. He and Lincoln disagreed as to strategy; the President preferred a massive frontal assault at Manassas, while McClellan proposed a direct march from the rear on the Confederate capital at Richmond. In January, 1862, McClellan had still not begun his offensive, and an impatient Lincoln ordered him to move by February 22.

In early February, however, Lincoln deferred to McClellan's plan to march on Richmond. On March 8, the President reorganized the Army in four corps, relieving McClellan of all duties except those of commander of the Army of the Potomac. McClellan moved by water to the mouth of the James River, then up the Virginia peninsula between the James and the York rivers. In a series of bloody encounters he faced General Robert E. Lee, whose forces drove McClellan's men from the peninsula in the Seven Days' Battles, ending at Malvern Hill on July 1. When McClellan blamed Lincoln for not sending reinforcements, the President replied that he had sent as many as he could. Losses in the campaign were heavy, and Lincoln appealed for 300,000 more men.

The year 1862 was a bitter one for the President. In February his son, eleven-year-old Willie, died after a bout of cold and fever. Lincoln was shattered. Mary, who wore mourning black for almost two years, collapsed in "paroxysms of grief." Even the sorrowing President, immured in his own anguish, warned her on one occasion that she would have to be committed to a mental hospital if she could not control herself.

Stricken with family grief, and with the hard news of mounting Union casualties in a war he had hoped would be brief, Lincoln was also harassed by a divided and personally ambitious Cabinet; by abolitionists calling for total war on slavery and for the unconditional surrender of an occupied South; by the defeatism of those who demanded peace before Union; by uncooperative states; by the insubordinate and vacillating McClellan; by desertion in the Army; and by virulent abuse in the press.

"As a general rule," the President would say in his last public address, "I abstain from reading the reports of attacks upon myself, wishing not to be provoked by that to which I cannot properly offer an answer." But some attacks could not go unanswered. Among these was an assault by Horace Greeley, editor of the New York *Tribune*, in August, 1862. In an open letter to the President, Greeley berated Lincoln for capitulating to the South by failing to issue immediately a decree emancipating the slaves.

It is true that Lincoln vacillated on the slavery question. A political realist, he knew that basic institutions were not changed by the stroke of a pen or a sword or by the dictates of personal idealism; he realized that even when the North won the war it would still have to face the issues of slavery and lingering disloyalty. He could not go forward, he believed, unless the people were with him, step by step.

He had, however, appealed to the border states to free slaves gradually and to compensate their owners with the assistance of the federal government. Congress had already passed legislation freeing the slaves of "disloyal" masters and those in the District of Columbia and in the territories. Then, in July, 1862, the President summoned his Cabinet and laid before it for discussion an emancipation proclamation. Seward agreed on principle, but advised postponement. Current Union military reverses, he argued, might encourage some to consider the measure "the last *shriek* on our retreat." Lincoln concurred.

A month later, in his reply to Greeley, Lincoln placed the Union above all other considerations. "My paramount object in this struggle *is* to save the Union, and is *not*

The Monitor *(foreground) and the* Merrimac *exchange fire off Hampton Roads on March 9, 1862. The* Merrimac *finally retired, but neither vessel was seriously damaged in this first battle between ironclad warships.*

either to save or to destroy slavery. . . . What I do about slavery, and the colored race, I do because I believe it helps to save the Union; and what I forbear, I forbear because I do *not* believe it would help to save the Union. . . . I have here stated my purpose according to my view of *official* duty; and I intend no modification of my oft-expressed *personal* wish that all men everywhere could be free."

To restore the Union, Lincoln considered no measure ultimately too severe. "These rebels," he reasoned, "are violating the Constitution to destroy the Union; I will violate the Constitution, if necessary, to save the Union. . . ." Accordingly, President Lincoln unilaterally increased the size of the Army and Navy, imposed a blockade of the South, suspended the writ of habeas corpus where necessary, placed treason suspects in military custody, and forbade the use of the mails for "treasonable correspondence." In the actual military conduct of the war, Lincoln functioned literally as Commander in Chief, personally mapping strategy.

Despite such victories as the capture of Fort Donelson on the Cumberland River in Tennessee by General Ulysses S. Grant and the occupation of New Orleans by Flag Officer David Farragut, the North was being bled in battle after battle. Thirteen thousand Union troops became casualties at Shiloh in April. In August the Union suffered another crushing defeat at Bull Run. In September Stonewall Jackson captured twelve thousand Union troops at Harpers Ferry. Then Lee and Jackson met McClellan at Antietam on September 17, 1862, in a bloody but indecisive battle.

Now, on September 22, Lincoln issued the Preliminary Emancipation Proclamation, publishing the final version on January 1, 1863. "Things had gone from bad to worse," he confessed later, "until I felt we had reached the end of our rope on the plan of operations we had been pursuing; that we had about played our last card, and must change our tactics or lose the game."

The proclamation was issued, Lincoln said, as "an act of justice" as well as "a fit

and necessary war measure." It freed slaves only in those areas of the Confederacy still in rebellion, not in Southern areas already occupied by the Union army, or in loyal slave states.

Secretary Seward was astonished: "We show our sympathy with slavery," he said, "by emancipating the slaves where we cannot reach them and holding them in bondage where we can set them free." And in fact the proclamation did not go nearly so far as the second Confiscation Act, which had provided freedom to slaves of disloyal owners, regardless of state of residence.

Documents notwithstanding, the war went on. An angry Lincoln fired McClellan on November 7, appointing General Ambrose Burnside to succeed him as commander of the Army of the Potomac. In January, 1863, after Lee's victory at Fredericksburg, Burnside was replaced by General Joseph Hooker, who would himself be succeeded by General George Meade in June.

In May, 1863, Chancellorsville saw a crushing defeat of the Union forces. Then, as Grant was laying siege to Vicksburg in Mississippi, Lee led the entire Army of Northern Virginia through the Shenandoah Valley to southern Pennsylvania, where he met the Union army in the greatest and most decisive battle of the war, at Gettysburg. After three days of battle (July 1–3) with massive losses on both sides, Lee was forced to withdraw on July 4 to a position west of Sharpsburg, where the flooded Potomac blocked his passage to Virginia. Lincoln issued orders to pursue the foe and to destroy his army. But Meade hesitated; the Potomac subsided, and Lee escaped. Lincoln despaired, blaming Meade: "He was within your grasp, and to have closed upon him would . . . have ended the war. As it is the war will be prolonged indefinitely."

Over five thousand men, in both gray and blue, had been killed in the savage encounter at Gettysburg; their bodies had littered the field. On November 19, 1863, President Lincoln joined in the consecration of a new national cemetery at the site where the men had fallen. Edward Everett, a renowned orator, held forth for two hours in a verbal crescendo filled with classical allusions. Then Lincoln rose to offer ten sentences of splendid simplicity that told—and still tell—what the war was all about:

"Four score and seven years ago our fathers brought forth on this continent, a new nation, conceived in Liberty, and dedicated to the proposition that all men are created equal.

"Now we are engaged in a great civil war, testing whether that nation, or any nation so conceived and so dedicated, can long endure. We are met on a great battle-field of that war. We have come to dedicate a portion of that field, as a final resting place for those who gave their lives that that nation might live. It is altogether fitting and proper that we should do this.

"But, in a larger sense, we can not dedicate—we can not consecrate—we can not hallow—this ground. The brave men, living and dead, who struggled here, have consecrated it, far above our poor power to add or detract. The world will little note, nor long remember what we say here, but it can never forget what they did here. It is for us the living, rather, to be dedicated here to the unfinished work which they who fought here have thus far so nobly advanced. It is rather for us to be here dedicated to the great task remaining before us—that from these honored dead we take increased devotion to that cause for which they gave the last full measure of devotion—that we here highly resolve that these dead shall not have died in vain—that this nation, under God, shall have a new birth of freedom—and that government of the people, by the people, for the people, shall not perish from the earth."

Response to this timeless address was largely disdainful. The Chicago *Times* asserted that the "cheek of every American must tingle with shame as he reads the silly, flat, and dish-watery utterances of the man who has to be pointed out to intelligent foreigners as the President of the United States." History, however, would agree with the Chicago *Tribune* that Abraham Lincoln's words would "live among the annals of men."

STANLEY KING COLLECTION

GEORGE B. McCLELLAN

Presidential candidate George McClellan had no more success *against* Lincoln in 1864 than General in Chief George McClellan had had *for* Lincoln in the Civil War's early days. A graduate of West Point (he ranked second in his class) and a veteran of the Mexican War, he had seemed the logical choice to lead the Union forces in 1861, but his egotism and overcautiousness plagued Lincoln. Calling his critics "traitors," McClellan continually asked for reinforcements and maintained that he could "do it all" if only he had more men. Lee and Jackson exploited his hesitancy during the bloody Peninsular Campaign. A Confederate general, speaking of the battle of Antietam, said that "Lee's army and everything it had" could have been captured by McClellan if he had not failed to pursue the retreating enemy. Shortly thereafter, an exasperated Lincoln sacked the man for whom the huge Army of the Potomac had been merely a "bodyguard." Two years later, the Democrats nominated McClellan for the Presidency, depicting him as a victim of administration callousness and an example of its ineptness. His chances were good until a series of Union victories re-established the voters' faith in Lincoln, who was returned to office. General McClellan soon faded from view but emerged to serve as governor of New Jersey from 1878 to 1881. The Connecticut-born general died at fifty-seven in 1885.

In late November, the Union cause was buttressed by Grant's victory at Chattanooga, where Confederate soldiers were driven from Tennessee. Grant's services to the Union were rewarded on March 12, 1864, when the ruddy field soldier was named, at last, general in chief of the Union armies.

In May, at the Wilderness (the area south of the Rapidan River near Richmond, Virginia), at Spotsylvania, and at Cold Harbor, Grant's forces suffered over sixty thousand casualties. Then Grant shifted his troops, moving south toward Petersburg, hoping to cut Richmond off from the Rebel states. Lee met him, and the siege of Petersburg began. For ten months Grant's forces were holed up in their trenches by a rugged Confederate defense.

On June 8 the Republican party nominated Lincoln at Baltimore for a second term. Andrew Johnson, a pro-Union Democrat who had been appointed military governor of Tennessee, was named for the Vice Presidency. A week earlier, Republican Radicals had met in Cleveland to nominate John C. Frémont for President. In August the Democrats chose General George B. McClellan to oppose Lincoln. Both the regular and rump Republican conventions affirmed support for a constitutional amendment to abolish all slavery forever, and Lincoln gave the proposed amendment his approval: "In the joint names of liberty and union," he said, "let us labor to give it legal form, and practical effect." (The President was to give the Thirteenth Amendment vital support in its consideration and adoption by Congress. Passed by the Senate in April, 1864, it was finally approved by the House of Representatives in January, 1865.)

It was a divisive political campaign. Lincoln was assailed in newspapers and campaign tracts. Horace Greeley pronounced the President "already beaten." Lincoln himself was doubtful about his chances of winning. "It seems exceedingly probable,"

Frank Bellew's drawing for Harper's Weekly *late in November of 1864 summed up the electorate's feeling: it was titled "Long Abraham a Little Longer."*

Harper's Weekly

he wrote confidentially, "that this Administration will not be re-elected."

But good news from the front—especially of the capture of Atlanta on September 1 by General William Sherman—aided Lincoln's cause. On September 22, Frémont withdrew. Even so, while Lincoln won the election on November 8 by an electoral victory of 212 to 21, his popular margin was not large: 2.2 million to 1.8 million.

On March 4, 1865, the President, appearing markedly older, again took the oath of office. He could look with satisfaction on the success of the Union armies. At Nashville, Union forces had decimated John B. Hood's troops. Sherman had completed his march to the sea, had forced the evacuation of Savannah, and had then swung north to seize Columbia, South Carolina. In February Union forces had occupied Charleston.

"Fondly do we hope—fervently do we pray—that this mighty scourge of war may speedily pass away," Lincoln said in his second Inaugural Address. "With malice toward none, with charity for all; with firmness in the right, as God gives us to see the right, let us strive on to finish the work we are in; to bind up the nation's wounds; to care for him who shall have borne the battle, and for his widow, and his orphan—to do all which may achieve and cherish a just, and a lasting, peace, among ourselves, and with all nations."

On April 3, the time for making peace was upon the President: Richmond had fallen. At 4 P.M., April 9, 1865, General Lee, given generous terms by Lincoln through Grant, surrendered at Appomattox Court House.

Lincoln's plans for Reconstruction were already well defined. In July, 1864, he had pocket vetoed Congress' vindictive Wade-Davis bill, which would have allowed the readmission of a state only after the majority of its electorate pledged past as well as present loyalty. At a preliminary conference with Confederate officials on board a ship off Hampton Roads, Virginia, on February 3, 1865, he had been conciliatory, excluding any punitive unconditional surrender by the South, promising pardons, urging only that

Southern Americans once again embrace the Constitution. He even suggested that the South might adopt the Thirteenth Amendment slowly, perhaps over a five-year period, and hinted at millions of dollars in federal compensation for freed slaves. And in a face-saving gesture to the South, he prevailed in his view that new state governments might be formed once 10 per cent of a state's qualified voters took an oath of loyalty to the United States and agreed to the emancipation of the slaves.

On April 11, 1865, Lincoln spoke from a White House window to a delirious victory throng. He called for an end to debate over the "pernicious abstraction" as to whether the Southern states had ever truly left the Union. "Finding themselves safely at home," Lincoln said, "it would be utterly immaterial whether they had ever been abroad."

The President cited Louisiana as a model of Reconstruction. He conceded that a larger electorate would be desirable and that "very

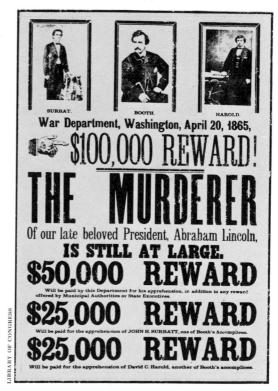

Twenty-eight men were directly involved in Booth's death; their bounties were finally awarded in 1866.

397

intelligent" Negroes might properly be given the vote. But which was the wiser course, he asked: to take Louisiana as it was and improve it, or to discard its antislavery government and start again? Louisiana, he said, was well on its way to harmony with the Union, now that it had empowered its legislators to give the Negro the vote, adopted a free constitution, and voted to ratify the Thirteenth Amendment. "We shall sooner have the fowl by hatching the egg than by smashing it," he said. Reconstruction, he warned, was a complex process to be pursued with realism and patience.

At 11 A.M., Good Friday, April 14, 1865, Lincoln met with his Cabinet, mapping Reconstruction until 2 P.M. Then the President went for a carriage drive with his wife. They rejoiced that the bitter war years were over and looked forward to that evening at the theater. General and Mrs. Grant were unable to join them in the presidential box at Ford's Theater, but Miss Clara Harris and Major Henry Rathbone—the daughter and stepson of Senator Ira Harris of New York —had accepted the Lincolns' invitation to see the comedy *Our American Cousin.*

The presidential party arrived late at Ford's. The actors stopped when they saw the President, and the band burst into "Hail to the Chief." Lincoln sat back, his hand in Mary's.

In a barroom near Ford's, a few minutes before 10 P.M., a twenty-six-year-old pro-slavery extremist, actor John Wilkes Booth, finished his drink; he departed and entered the theater. His movements planned step by step, Booth made his way to the door of the hallway leading to the President's box. Once inside, he bolted the door.

With a pistol in one hand and a dagger in the other, Booth opened the unguarded door of the box, aimed his pistol at Lincoln's head, and fired. Rathbone lunged at Booth, who stabbed him violently in the arm. Then the actor leaped from the box to the stage. Flashing his knife, Booth cried, "*Sic semper tyrannis!*" and escaped.

Lincoln sat mute and immobile, his head fallen forward. He was, said a doctor, fatally wounded. Booth's bullet had torn through the President's brain and had lodged behind an eye. Carried across the street to a boardinghouse owned by a Mr. Peterson, Lincoln was laid diagonally across a bed too small for his massive frame.

As the President lay dying, word spread that most of the Cabinet had been murdered, too. In fact, Seward, confined to bed by a bad fall, had been savagely bloodied by a Booth accomplice. But the rest of the Cabinet was safe.

At the Peterson house, Mrs. Lincoln, convulsed by a new, insupportable grief, moved closer to mental derangement. Robert, his head on the shoulder of Senator Sumner, sobbed aloud as his father slowly slipped away. At about six o'clock in the morning, April 15, 1865, rain began falling. At 7:22 A.M., Abraham Lincoln died.

His body lay in state in the East Room of the White House on a black-draped catafalque. Thousands of the nation's stunned citizens came to see the dead President. Some had seen him before, others had merely heard of him: "Old Abe," "Honest Abe," the "Rail Splitter" of Illinois and Indiana, the savior of the Union, dressed now in his First Inaugural suit for a final ascent to greatness.

On April 19, Lincoln's body was borne from the White House to begin a long journey to Illinois. The cortege stopped for homage in many cities along the way. Finally, on May 4, the coffin of the "Great Emancipator" was closed, and Lincoln was buried at Oak Ridge Cemetery in Springfield.

"What is to be will be," Lincoln had said, "or rather, I have found all my life as Hamlet says: 'There is a divinity that shapes our ends, Rough-hew them how we will.' " Healing when others wounded, hoping when others despaired, assuring when others feared, he grew in the Presidency taller than himself. He remains a symbol of liberty, his memory nourished by his own great words and deeds.

"Now," said a sorrowing Stanton for the nation, "he belongs to the ages."

—WILSON SULLIVAN

Abraham Lincoln

A PICTURE PORTFOLIO

*The Lincoln lantern above was attached to the end of a pole
and was carried in 1864 campaign parades in New York.*

The daguerreotype at right, made in 1846, is the earliest known photograph of Abraham Lincoln—freshman congressman from Illinois. Below is an 1868 view of part of Springfield's business section; Lincoln practiced law with the volatile William Herndon in the second building from the right. The men worked well as a professional team, but Herndon did not get on with Mrs. Lincoln and was much aggravated by Lincoln's reading newspapers aloud and permitting his children to use the office as a rumpus room. When Lincoln moved there, raw and sprawling Springfield was trying to comport itself properly as the new state capital, but hogs roamed at will in the streets, which often were seas of mud and impossible to navigate.

ON THE RISE

In 1834 Abraham Lincoln, still politically wet behind the ears, was elected to the legislature of the equally raw young state of Illinois. At the primitive capital, Vandalia, legislators wrangled and bargained, and Lincoln soon learned the techniques of political infighting. Sagacious vote swapping enabled him to lead the movement to transfer the capital to Springfield, his own base from 1837. Highly respected there, Lincoln still retained some rough edges. Once he leaped out of a window, trying to prevent a quorum because a vote would have hurt the state bank, one of his pet projects. But prudence began to temper him: when his biting satire provoked a challenge from an opponent, Lincoln shrewdly chose long cavalry broadswords as weapons, and his shorter-armed foe let matters drop. Lincoln also ran a thriving, if cluttered, law office (he kept an envelope marked, "When you can't find *it* any where else, look into this"). He and Mary lived modestly, but in a far more comfortable fashion than he had known as a youth in Kentucky and Indiana. A four-term legislator, the Lincoln of the early 1840's could no longer call himself "a piece of floating driftwood." Indeed, he was eagerly seeking a seat in the United States Congress and was thinking of even greater things.

ABRAHAM LINCOLN'S RESIDENCE.

At the end of 1843 the Lincolns moved into the frame house above, just beyond the Springfield business section. The house, lot, carriage shed, and barn—where Lincoln kept a horse and a milking cow—cost fifteen hundred dollars. Robert Todd Lincoln was five months old; three other sons would be born there, but only he would live to maturity. The family lived there until shortly after the November evening in 1860 when Lincoln returned from the telegraph office and announced, "Mary, we're elected." He was never again to return to Springfield.

THE "LITTLE GIANT"

If each State will only agree to mind its own business," boomed Stephen A. Douglas at Quincy, Illinois, in October, 1858, ". . . this republic can exist forever divided into free and slave States. . . ." Twelve thousand people attended this segment of the seven-part touring debate between the "Little Giant" and the challenger for his Senate seat, Abraham Lincoln; the tour's aggregate audience would be about seventy-eight thousand, and the newspapers would carry the debaters' statements to the entire nation.

At Quincy, Lincoln rose and thanked Douglas for revealing that his "policy in regard to . . . slavery contemplates that it shall last forever." His somber irony pointed up Douglas' chief liability, an essentially cynical, amoral attitude toward slavery, which he thought of only as an issue that interfered with the nation's expansion. Apparently blind to the backlash that stung neutrals in the 1850's, Douglas had long held that territorial slavery should be left up to the settlers. This "popular sovereignty" proposal was the basis of his Kansas-Nebraska bill of 1854; since Douglas wanted the Nebraska territory organized (thus clearing the way for a transcontinental railroad that would benefit Northern speculators, of which he was one), he wooed Southern support for the bill by including in it repeal of the Missouri Compromise. The bill became law, but anti-Douglas demonstrations in the North and the subsequent violence in Kansas indicated that the father of popular sovereignty had sired an unmanageable son. When, in 1857, Buchanan supported Kansas' fraudulent Lecompton constitution, Douglas (who knew that most of his constituents opposed the proslavery document) led the fight for con-

gressional rejection of the constitution. "I have taken a through ticket," he said, snapping defiance at Buchanan and the Southern Democrats, "and checked my baggage."

Although Douglas was keenly ambitious, it would be unfair to say that his popular-sovereignty concept had been devised solely for political or economic gain. After his election to Congress from Illinois in 1843, he blossomed into a popular, persuasive nationalist of the Henry Clay mold. Short, muscular, modishly dressed, and flamboyant, he was to his contemporaries a "steam engine in britches," as he urged that all of Oregon be taken, supported the Mexican War, and guided the Compromise of 1850 through Congress. But Douglas miscalculated the mood of the nation, and his stand on slavery made him an agent of party schism. When, during a debate with Lincoln at Freeport, he suggested that the Dred Scott decision could be circumvented by the states and territories, he calcified the rift between Northern and Southern Democrats. In the senatorial election of 1858, Douglas lost the popular vote, but was re-elected because the Democrats retained narrow control of the legislature; his seat was saved but his party was shattered.

Two years later Douglas was the presidential candidate of the Northern and Western Democrats. He knew that he could not win, but he toured the South, pleading for loyalty to the next President, ignoring the jeers and eggs that were directed at him. In 1861 Douglas bid every American to "rally around the flag"; that June, typhoid fever claimed the life of the forty-eight-year-old gamecock who had helped dress the national stage for secession and who, in his debates with Lincoln, had helped make a President.

Senator Stephen A. Douglas, the "Great Debater"

The 1860 campaign flag above deploys its thirty-three stars—one for each
state then in the Union—to form one large star with stars at each angle.

The poster above, issued in September of 1860 and obviously pro-Lincoln,
shows him easily outsprinting (from left) Bell, Breckinridge, and Douglas.

LINCOLN: PRESIDENT-ELECT

Only events can make a President," said a cryptic Abraham Lincoln in 1858—and by May of 1860 he was the Republican candidate, an almost sure winner against the fragmented Democrats. In the interim he had toured widely, his speeches had been published, and he had kept in touch with party leaders; and while Southern saber rattling was met by radical denunciations from many Republican hopefuls, Lincoln had remained moderate, opposing only slavery's territorial extension and deploring John Brown's raid. Even so, his nomination was not assured. His managers had to pack the convention hall with leather-lunged boosters and wheel and deal with delegations from the key states. The subsequent campaign was not lacking the usual hoop-la and smear, but it was dominated by the slavery issue; Lincoln became the most sectionally chosen President ever. The Atlanta *Confederacy* trumpeted, "Whether . . . Pennsylvania Avenue is paved ten fathoms deep with mangled bodies . . . the South will never submit to . . . the inauguration of Abraham Lincoln." But even as the Cotton South seceded, Lincoln remained as firm as "a chain of steel" on slavery's extension. With Southern delegates having walked out of the Peace Conference in February, the new President took office on a day which was, portentously, now sunny, now cloudy, and cold and windy throughout.

HANNIBAL HAMLIN

Hannibal Hamlin, a prominent Maine Republican and a leading opponent of slavery, was the logical choice for Lincoln's running mate in the election of 1860. Formerly associated with the Jacksonian Democrats, Hamlin renounced his allegiance in 1856 over the issue of slavery and joined the new Republican party. His political career began when as a young lawyer in Hampden, Maine, he was named to the state legislature, where he served for five years. In 1842 he was elected to Congress, and in 1848 he became a United States senator. After quitting the Democratic party, he was elected governor of Maine on the Republican ticket in 1856. He served in his new post for only a few weeks before resigning to renew his anti-slavery crusade in the Senate. Elected to the Vice Presidency in 1861, he soon became impatient with Lincoln's cautious approach to the problems of emancipation. In 1863 he complained: "The slow and unsatisfactory movements of the government do not meet my approbation. . . ." As convention time approached, Hamlin's association with the radical elements of Congress worked against him, and he lost the bid for renomination. In 1868 he was again elected to the Senate, where he served until his appointment as minister to Spain in 1881. Returning to his native state, he was influential in the Republican party organization until his death at the age of eighty-two in 1891.

THE·NEW·YORK

WHOLE NO. 8982. SECOND EDITION—SATURDAY, APRIL 13, 1

THE WAR BEGUN.

Very Exciting News from Charleston.

Important Correspondence Between General Beauregard, Major Anderson and the Southern Secretary of War.

The Summons to Major Anderson to Surrender.

MAJOR ANDERSON'S REFUSAL.

Bombardment of Fort Sumter Commenced.

Terrible Fire from the Secessionists' Batteries.

Brilliant Defence of Maj. Anderson and His Gallant Garrison.

Reckless Bravery of the Confederate States Troops.

SIXTEEN HOURS FIGHTING.

Breaches in the Walls of Fort Sumter.

Several of Major Anderson's Guns Silenced.

Partial Cessation of the Firing for the Night.

THE SCENE OF

Charleston and Its Defences---Plan of the Harbo and Moultrie, Cummings Point Iron Floating Battery and Ot

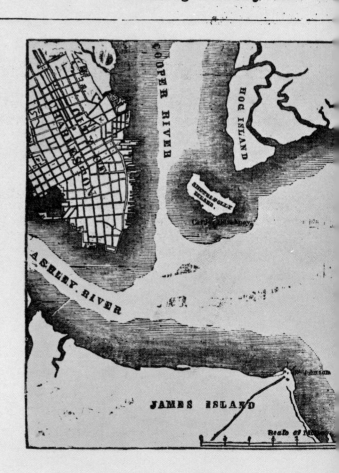

lives and at every shot jump upon the rampart observe the effect, and then jump down, cheerg.

A party on the Stevens battery are said to have played game of the hottest fire.

The excitement in the community is indescribable. With the very first boom of the gun thousands rushed from their beds to the harbor front, and all day every available place has been thronged by ladies and gentlemen, viewing the solemn spectacle through their

Major Anderson is busy repairing damages. He received twenty-nine full shots from Stevens' battery alone, making the bricks fly from the walls in all directions.

It is estimated that from twelve to eighteen hundred balls and shells were fired during the day. Over one hundred shells took effect inside the fort.

Orders have been issued to send Major Anderson a bomb from all the batteries every twenty minutes during the night, to keep him wide awake

It is re the bar.

The fir renewed tempt is arrange

The Pa are repo Troops

RATIONS.

ing the Position of Forts Sumter
y, Fort Johnson, the
tifications.

e war vessels are outside

ON, April 12—Evening.
or the night, but will be
e morning, unless an at-
ce the fort, which ample
made to repel.
ane, and a third steamer,

every train.

CHARLESTON AND ITS DEFENCES.

The news of the bombardment of Fort Sumter by the
Confederate forces, which we publish this morning, in-
duces us to give a full description of the scene of operations, embracing the city of Charleston, its harbor and
fortifications. The plans of the forts and batteries, showing the stronghold of Major Anderson and the position of
the attacking forces under General Beauregard, cannot
fail to interest our readers.

FORT SUMTER—THE STRONGHOLD OF MAJOR AN-
DERSON.

THE WAR BEGINS

President Lincoln had vowed to "hold, occupy, and possess" federal property, and Fort Sumter in Charleston Harbor became a symbol of the North's determination. If Major Robert Anderson and his small force were to surrender Sumter, the North would in effect be recognizing the Confederacy and the disunion it had been denying. But Anderson was short of food, and Lincoln had to decide whether to precipitate a crisis by provisioning the fort. He refused to be stampeded into a hasty decision—not by a Cabinet that advised against sending supplies nor by a Secretary of State who proposed a foreign war to reunite the nation. Lincoln hoped to arrange an eventual withdrawal from Sumter that would keep Virginia in the Union ("A State for a fort is no bad business"), but he received no promises from Richmond. And because Secretary Seward, acting on his own, had advised the Confederacy of Sumter's imminent evacuation, the South regarded Lincoln's ultimate decision to provision the fort as a broken promise. On April 11, Anderson refused a demand that he surrender, saying that he would do so only when—and if—food ran out. He was then told that shore batteries would open fire. Early the next morning they did, and the Civil War began. The fort surrendered on the 13th, as festive Charlestonians watched the bombardment. None seemed to recall Andrew Jackson's dire warning issued during the Nullification Crisis of 1832: "Disunion by armed force is treason. Are you really ready to incur its guilt?"

The map of Charleston Harbor, left, showed the North what Anderson was up against. Sumter was encircled by Rebel batteries from Fort Moultrie and Castle Pinckney—in Confederate hands since late December—and from Fort Johnson and Cummings Point (off the map to the right). Only one defender died in the thirty-four-hour bombardment of Sumter; he was killed when a federal cannon exploded.

407

408 On July 21, 1861, at Bull Run in northern Virginia, North and South clashed in the first major battle of the war. The 1889 lithograph above mistakenly shows the Union's "Fire Zouaves" in their gaudy dress uniforms, and more erroneously, gives the impres-

sion that there was some semblance of order on the battlefield. Actually, Bull Run was a confused and bloody encounter between two green armies, and a victory for the Confederacy, to the horror of those Washingtonians who had come out to watch a federal triumph.

409

HEROES OF THE UNION

GEORGE THOMAS

Asked once if some dead soldiers should be buried according to their state of origin, General George Thomas said, "No, no. Mix them up. I am tired of State rights." But doubts of the Virginia-born officer's loyalty persisted, enhanced by Thomas' chronic sluggishness. (He often catnapped through councils of war.) Not until late in the Civil War would all question of his allegiance, ability, and courage be swept away. Thomas, who had served continuously in the Army since his graduation from West Point in 1840, earned the sobriquet "the Rock of Chickamauga" for his determined stand there in September, 1863, amidst a defeat which sent the rest of the Army of the Cumberland scrambling toward Chattanooga. Promoted to brigadier general, he took over the command of the unstable William Rosecrans. Thomas worked smoothly with Grant and Sherman in breaking the Confederate siege of Chattanooga; his own troops secured the victory with a daring assault on Missionary Ridge on November 25, 1863. Having led Sherman's vanguard into Atlanta, Thomas was assigned to prevent John Hood's Confederate troops from slipping north to aid Lee. Battle was decisively joined in Nashville on December 15 and 16, 1864, after what Lincoln had considered too long a delay. But General Hood was defeated by Thomas in one of the war's major routs.

WILLIAM T. SHERMAN

General William Tecumseh Sherman believed in total war. In 1863 he wrote that "talk of compromise is bosh" and urged the North to hound the South to its "innermost recesses" to make its people "so sick of war that generations would pass away before they would again appeal to it." A brooding and temperamental man, Sherman had firm friendships with Southerners and espoused a liberal peace. But he felt that waging war in the Confederate hinterland would enervate local morale and hasten the end of bloodshed. After graduating from West Point in 1840, Sherman had tried several civilian pursuits in the 1850's, none successfully. He re-entered the Army in 1861 and was widely criticized for his role in the early campaigns, but he was vindicated at Vicksburg and Chattanooga and was commander of the Western armies by 1864. That year's plan was simple: Grant was to contain Lee in the North while Sherman crushed the Southern opposition. By September 1, he had beaten a bloody path to Atlanta; soon sixty thousand men would begin their march to the sea under the man Carl Sandburg called a "lean, restless, hawk-eyed rider of war and apostle of destruction." Georgia despoiled, Sherman swung north; the vise tightened, and the Confederacy was doomed. Sherman retired as general of the Army in 1883 and died in 1891, at the age of seventy-one.

PHILIP SHERIDAN

"Little Phil" Sheridan, commander of the cavalry of the Army of the Potomac, was up for promotion early in 1864. Although he had distinguished himself the year before, notably at Chickamauga and Chattanooga, most of official Washington knew only that the short, slight Ohioan looked more like a jockey than a general. But U. S. Grant had noted Sheridan's leadership in combat and his abilities as an intuitive strategist: in August he was given command of the newly formed Army of the Shenandoah. That autumn Sheridan thrice defeated the forces of Jubal Early—once, at Cedar Run, by audaciously rallying his men to turn a near rout into a signal victory. So ordered by Grant, he despoiled the Shenandoah Valley, with staggering losses to the Confederacy of food and munitions. He had given Lincoln's bid for re-election a much-needed boost; the President later told him he had always felt "a cavalryman should be at least six feet four high, but I have changed my mind— five feet four will do in a pinch." Sheridan, by then a major general in the regular army, helped apply the *coup de grâce* to Lee's forces the following spring. After the war he commanded the military forces in Louisiana and Texas, later serving as military governor and leading operations against hostile Indians. Sheridan was elevated to the rank of full general before he died in 1888.

DAVID FARRAGUT

Captain David Farragut, sixty years old in the winter of 1862, was not hopeful of realizing his ambition to become a distinguished naval leader. He had been a midshipman in the War of 1812 and had served routine tours since; not even the Mexican War had brought the active duty he so keenly sought. A firm Unionist, Farragut had moved north from Virginia in 1861; a year later he had his chance: he was given command of the West Gulf Blockading Squadron, assigned to capture New Orleans and open the Mississippi. After ineffectually bombarding two forts defending the city, Farragut decided on April 24, 1862, to sail past the forts, contrary to his orders. Successful, he defeated the flotilla lying between him and New Orleans; he took the city, and the forts surrendered. Farragut was then elevated to the newly created rank of rear admiral. In August of 1864 he engineered the capture of Mobile Bay, the last gap in the blockade. Again he faced fortresses, a flotilla, and mines, but again his sagacious daring produced victory. Sailing under the guns of Fort Morgan, he thundered, "Damn the torpedoes [mines]!" The fleet followed him through, and the victory at Mobile paralleled that of New Orleans. Farragut, a national hero, was commissioned admiral in 1866; the next year he led a naval squadron on a good-will tour of European ports.

In the drawing on the right, the President and General Winfield Scott review a regiment of three-year volunteers marching down Pennsylvania Avenue early in the war. The Commander in Chief was always eager to see troops as they came through the Capital. According to Robert Lincoln, the presidential carriage once stopped to allow a line of soldiers to pass. Lincoln called out to a group of nearby workmen, "What is that, boys?"—in hopes they knew the soldiers' home state. The reply: "It's a regiment, you damned old fool," and the President had a hearty laugh at his own expense.

Below, the New York Excelsior Brigade makes its charge in the inconclusive Battle of Fair Oaks during the abortive Peninsular Campaign of early 1862.

"PEGGING AWAY"

I don't amount to pig tracks in the War Department," said President Lincoln, but he was there, day after weary day, poring over wires from the front, answering them with encouragement or gentle admonition, always feeling the anguish of fraternal war, firmly resolved "to keep pegging away." Some of his wartime measures were severely criticized, notably the suspension of habeas corpus and the national conscription act, but he saw them as essential to victory, to "proving that popular government is not an absurdity." He ached for peace, but had it for less than two of the nearly fifty months he served; he wielded the sword longer than any other American Commander in Chief. Finally he found an able leader and left the war to him. When visitors complained that General Grant would not tell them about the Army's movements, President Lincoln said, "Neither will he tell me."

Skirmish between h Brooklyn 14ᵗʰ and 300 Rebel Cavalry.

The skirmish at Antietam, above, is by Alfred R. Waud, as are the other sketches on these pages. The English illustrator, a "war artist" for Harper's, was a familiar figure in Union camps throughout the conflict.

413

THE OTHER PRESIDENT

No man is fit to take hold," wrote Henry Adams about both the North and the South, "who is not as cool as death." But whereas Lincoln rose to greatness as leader of the Union, circumstances and his own character conspired against Jefferson Davis, the President of the Confederacy. He was not the South's first choice for leadership: Alexander Stephens, a Georgia congressman, was offered the Presidency initially, but refused because he would not "strike the first blow." Davis himself accepted the office reluctantly ("as a man might speak of a sentence of death," said his wife); he would have preferred a military commission. Although he had been successful in politics, serving in Congress in the 1840's and 1850's and as Secretary of War under Franklin Pierce, he was proudest of his Army record. Born in Kentucky and raised in Mississippi, Davis had won appointment to West Point in 1824. Although he had served without distinction in the Black Hawk War in the early 1830's, he had been acclaimed a hero during the Mexican War when he made a stand at Buena Vista that saved Zachary Taylor from defeat. Davis' first wife was Taylor's daughter, who had died a few months after their marriage, in 1835. Ten years later, Davis married into the Mississippi aristocracy, embracing all its social and philosophical tenets. As a plantation owner and as a politician, he came to regard the South as a country within a country and served as the region's spokesman in Washington. He was a tall, slim, elegant man noted for "the grace of his diction, and the rare charm of his voice"; as Carl Schurz said, he had "that kind of dignity which does not invite familiar approach. . . ."

Jefferson Davis, by Swiss artist Carl Gutherz

Accompanying that dignity, unfortunately, was an imperious and humorless egotism.

At first, Davis opposed total secession, espousing a "dominion status" for the South. But when Mississippi seceded, he resigned his Senate seat and on February 18, 1861, was inaugurated as provisional President of the Confederacy; later that year he was elected to a full six-year term. He headed a would-be nation whose economy was ill-suited to war; the Northern blockade prevented European aid; and the Confederacy's fiscal structure was chaotic. But Davis himself was no help. Because of his thwarted military ambitions, he repeatedly thrust his own stratagems upon his generals, often hampering field operations. And his uncompromising federalist viewpoint gave rise to political antipathies. As he strove for centralization, favoring general conscription and the suspension of the writ of habeas corpus, many in the government came to regard him as a despot, unsympathetic to states' rights. The Richmond *Whig* spoke for the opposition: "This Confederacy is not a nation, but a league of nations." But to the end Davis maintained "we are fighting for independence, and that, or extermination, we *will* have." He refused to negotiate for peace on any basis other than between "the two countries," bearing out Lincoln's remark that "he affords us no excuse to deceive ourselves." After the war, Davis supported himself as a private businessman and author until his death at eighty-two in 1889. Although he had been indicted for treason and had served two years in prison, he was never brought to trial. To those who insisted that Davis be hanged, Lincoln had replied softly, "Judge not, that ye not be judged."

The advertisement on the right was not unlike the ones young Abe Lincoln saw on flatboat trips to New Orleans in 1828 and 1831. Legend has it that his reaction to a slave auction there was, "If I ever get a chance to hit that thing, I'll hit it hard." His Emancipation Proclamation did not hit it all that hard, but it paved the way for the Thirteenth Amendment, ratified eight months after his murder. The allegorical painting below, by A. A. Lamb, was made in 1865. Lincoln, escorted by some Union soldiers and heralded by Liberty, tenders his proclamation to a crowd of unfettered Negroes while the sun breaks through storm clouds over the Capitol.

$1200 TO 1250 DOLLARS! FOR NEGROES!!

THE undersigned wishes to purchase a large lot of NEGROES for the New Orleans market. I will pay $1200 to $1250 for No. 1 young men, and $850 to $1000 for No. 1 young women. In fact I will pay more for likely

NEGROES,

Than any other trader in Kentucky. My office is adjoining the Broadway Hotel, on Broadway, Lexington, Ky., where I or my Agent can always be found.

WM. F. TALBOTT.

LEXINGTON, JULY 2, 1853.

EMANCIPATION

Issued in September, 1862, the Preliminary Emancipation Proclamation was clearly a warning—and an offer. Confederate states renouncing rebellion by electing federal congressmen could retain slavery; elsewhere in the South it would be outlawed. Only two Louisiana districts complied. Fearing further secession, Lincoln chose to leave border-state slavery alone, thereby infuriating the abolitionists. Republican losses in the elections that fall indicated dissent to the new policy. Even Lincoln knew that the decree was as enforceable in the South as "the Pope's bull against the comet!" But he stood firm. The proclamation, enacted in January, prevented European recognition of the South. And although many Northerners were at first unenthusiastic ("I don't think enough of the Niggar to go and fight for them," said one Ohio soldier), Negroes were soon in uniform, fighting for themselves. And gradually more Northerners began to regard the tragic war as a crusade for freedom as well as for preservation of the Union.

Characteristic of the South's propaganda during the Civil War is the vicious drawing above, entitled "Under the Veil," which portrays Lincoln as a Negro. The Richmond Enquirer *asked rhetorically, "What shall we call him? Coward, assassin, savage, murderer of women . . . ?" It settled for "Fiend."*

417

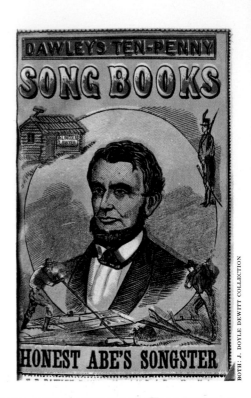

The 1864 campaign item above was a child's "ball-shot" game featuring Lincoln and prominent Union generals. The cover of the contemporary songbook on the right is embellished by scenes from the President's early life.

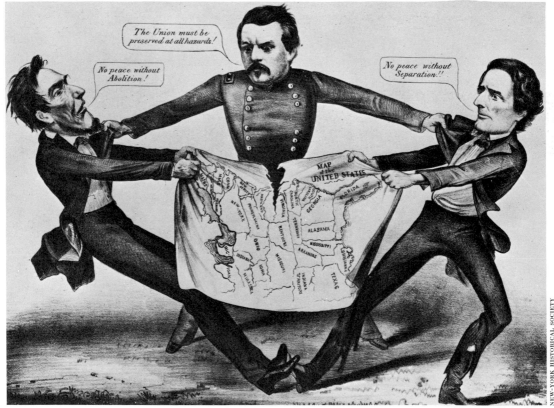

George McClellan (center, above) is depicted as the answer to the schism created by Lincoln and Davis. In the event of McClellan's election, Lincoln planned to work with him to try to end the war quickly. Secretary Seward later remarked that McClellan would have said, "'Yes, yes' . . . and would have done nothing at all."

TEARS AND LAUGHTER

Under Lincoln the White House was full of activity. Initial swarms of office seekers gave way to queues of congressmen, soldiers, and petitioners to whom the accessible President listened patiently in his daily "public opinion baths." There were regular receptions and levees, which Lincoln endured (calling ceremonial gloves "cruelty to animals"), but which his wife craved. Troubled Mary Lincoln was a mixed blessing as First Lady. Rumors that she was a spy (she had kin in both armies) distressed her already unstable mind. She had severe headaches, periods of deep depression, outbursts of temper; her prolonged agonizing over young Willie's death from typhoid fever prompted Lincoln to threaten to place her in an asylum. The grieving mother consulted spiritual mediums, and more than once an incredulous Abraham Lincoln witnessed séances in the Red Room. Passionately bent on being Washington's social leader, Mary spent money lavishly— in four months she bought three hundred pairs of gloves. She exceeded a White House refurbishing budget by seven thousand dollars, and her clothing debts ran to twenty-seven thousand. She had good cause to rejoice when her husband defeated George McClellan in the election of 1864. Often the theater or opera took Lincoln's mind off his troubles, and he usually carried a copy of a Shakespearean play to bed with him. A constant tonic was Tad, his youngest son— active, excitable, ubiquitous. He sometimes sat on his father's knee during policy discussions; he often slept in his father's bed. When Tad sentenced a doll to death for insubordination, his father solemnly wrote: "The doll Jack is pardoned. By order of the President. A. Lincoln." Tad once startled some visitors by driving a pair of pet goats through the East Room. Like any other wartime home, the White House was a place of bitter tears and grateful laughter.

MESERVE COLLECTION

The picture above shows Mary Lincoln around 1863. In later years, with a husband murdered and three sons dead, her mind gave way. She thought herself impoverished, yet continued to spend wildly. She would murmur, "I am afraid; I am afraid," with no apparent reason. When Robert Lincoln felt it necessary to have her committed, she accused him of robbery and "wicked conduct." Adjudged insane in 1875, she was, however, later found to be competent.

THE END IN SIGHT

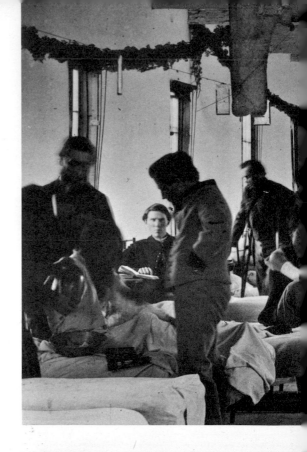

The President's face, reported Horace Greeley in March of 1865, "was haggard with care and seamed with thought and trouble." Well it might have been, for the past few months had been as strenuous as any he had endured. He had told Congress in December that he would stop prosecuting the war "whenever it shall have ceased on the part of those who began it." But he realized the South "would accept nothing short of severance of the Union," so—"casual as a locomotive," in Carl Sandburg's phrase—he called for three hundred thousand more men to fight the staggered Confederacy. He was equally intent on implementing emancipation. The House vote on the Thirteenth Amendment would be extremely close, and he issued an imperative to two congressmen: "I am President of the United States . . . and I expect you to procure those votes." They did as they were told. In the spirit of his recent Inaugural Address, Lincoln planned for the liberal treatment of an enemy whose surrender was imminent. To his commander at evacuated Richmond he said, "I'd let 'em up easy, let 'em up easy." Four years of war had exhausted Lincoln, but he could not find the balm for "the *tired* spot." He had told Harriet Beecher Stowe: "I shall never live to see peace. This war is killing me." Early in April, Lincoln was "strangely annoyed" by a dream in which he saw a catafalque in the East Room. "Who is dead . . . ?" asked the President. A military guard replied that it was Lincoln himself, "killed by an assassin!"

To the right, above, is a photograph of wounded soldiers in Washington's Carver Hospital; at least 375,000 men were wounded, but not killed, in the war. At right is a view of Charleston after Sherman's men had burned it early in 1865. "The men 'had it in' for [South Carolina]," wrote one Northern officer, "and they took it out in their own way."

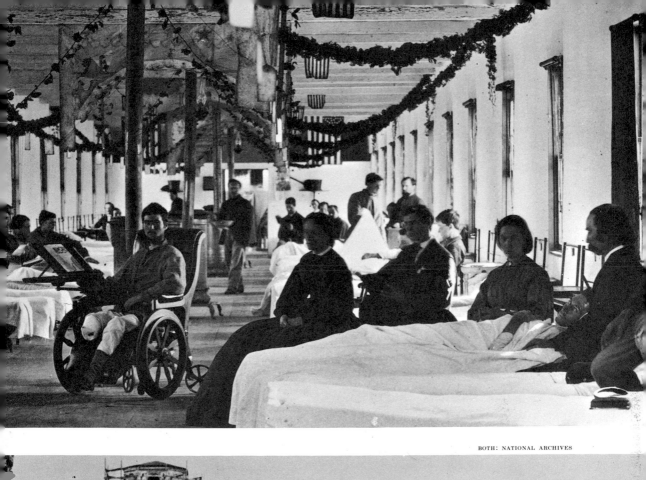

ASSASSINATION

Our country owe[s] all her troubles to him," wrote John Wilkes Booth shortly before he murdered Abraham Lincoln, "and God simply made me the instrument of His punishment." But Booth was less an avenging angel than a guilt-ridden Southerner who had done nothing for the cause. Now, with an egotistical thirst for immortality whittling away at his sanity, he burned to redeem himself. (Co-conspirators were Lewis Paine, George Atzerodt, and David Herold—a motley, drifting crew who intended to kill William Seward and Andrew Johnson while Booth performed in the scheme's mad limelight—and Mary Surratt, who had sheltered them. These four would be hanged in July.) On Good Friday of 1865 Booth learned Lincoln would be at Ford's Theater that evening. Quickly he arranged for a horse, bored a peephole in the door of the President's box—and took time to tell a hotel clerk that there would be "some fine acting" at Ford's that night. When the time came, Booth coolly flashed his card at presidential guard John Parker, who accepted him as a halfhearted watchdog would accept a burglar with a scrap of meat. Seconds later, a handmade lead ball just under a half inch in diameter augered through Lincoln's brain. Booth broke his left shin in his leap from the box to the stage, but he was still able to escape. A doctor, Charles Leale, rushed up from the audience and removed a blood clot from the President's wound, slightly easing the pressure on the brain. Leale's prognosis: "It is impossible for him to recover." For nearly nine hours in a nearby rooming house, Lincoln lay unconscious, his life seeping away. The doctors were as helpless as the stunned dignitaries who crowded into the nine by fifteen room. Secretary of State Seward, stabbed at his home, would live; but in the morning, as a steady, cold rain fell, Abraham Lincoln died.

Harper's Weekly

The drawing above mistakenly shows Booth assailing Lincoln from the side. He actually came up from the rear, took careful aim at the back of the head (three inches from and in line with Lincoln's left ear), and fired his brass derringer. Opposite is one of the last pictures of Lincoln.

THE ROAD HOME

The search for Booth was on, spurred by a War Department offer of $50,000 for his capture; the Radical press was accused of having incited the assassination; the die-hard Copperheads gloated. But the citizenry at large was stunned. The nation's front doorways wore crepe, and men wept quietly with their wives and uncomprehending children. It was a silent, pervasive grief, ultimate and inconsolable. Easter sermons that April 16, 1865, were calls for retribution, panegyrics for a leader lost, apologies from preachers who could not find words. Thousands viewed the body in the White House—dignitaries, wounded soldiers, citizens black and white—as did tens of thousands more later in the week under the Capitol's new dome. On Friday, April 21, the casket was aboard a nine-car train that retraced to Springfield the route President-elect Lincoln had traveled fifty months before. The mourners varied—subdued by rain at Baltimore, nearly panicking in a mad crush in Philadelphia—but their numbers were impressive (at Newark, New Jersey, they stood a mile square). The train was in Albany on the twenty-sixth, the day that John Wilkes Booth, cornered by soldiers in a burning barn in Virginia, was mortally shot. His enigmatic last words: "Useless. Useless." On the train went, through Ohio, Indiana, to Chicago and, at last, home. On the fourth of May, Abraham Lincoln was buried, Henry Ward Beecher's peroration of Easter Sunday yet echoing, "Give him place, oh, ye prairies. . . . Ye winds . . . of the West, chant his requiem!"

The lantern slide on the left shows the funeral procession inching its way down Broadway toward New York's City Hall on April 24, 1865. The next day, with scalpers selling window space to spectators, nearly one hundred thousand marched to the depot to see the body of the President on its way.

FACTS IN SUMMARY: ABRAHAM LINCOLN

CHRONOLOGY

UNITED STATES		LINCOLN				
Madison inaugurated as President	1809	*Born February 12*	Clay's compromise	1850	*Son Edward dies*	
War with Great Britain	1812		*Uncle Tom's Cabin* published	1852		
Monroe elected President	1816	*Moves with family to Indiana*	Pierce elected President			
Jackson elected President	1828		Kansas-Nebraska Act	1854	*Denounces slavery in "Peoria Speech"*	
Webster-Hayne debates	1830	*Moves to Illinois*	Republican party formed			
	1831	*Works in Offut's store*		1855	*Runs unsuccessfully for U.S. Senate*	
Jackson re-elected	1832	*Serves as volunteer in Black Hawk War*	Civil war in Kansas	1856		
		Runs unsuccessfully for Illinois assembly	Buchanan elected President			
Jackson removes deposits from Bank of the U.S.	1833	*Appointed postmaster for New Salem*	Dred Scott decision	1857		
		Appointed deputy county surveyor		1858	*Debates with Douglas during campaign for Senate seat*	
	1834	*Elected to Illinois general assembly*	Brown's raid at Harpers Ferry	1859		
Van Buren elected President	1836	*Re-elected to Illinois general assembly*	South Carolina secedes from Union	1860	*Elected President*	
		Admitted to the bar	Fort Sumter fired upon	1861	*Orders Fort Sumter reprovisioned*	
Financial panic	1837	*Moves to Springfield*	First Bull Run		*Issues call for 75,000 volunteers*	
Webster-Ashburton Treaty	1842	*Marries Mary Todd*	*Trent* affair		*Orders blockade of South*	
Polk elected President	1844		Battle of Shiloh	1862	*Issues Preliminary Emancipation Proclamation*	
War with Mexico	1846	*Elected to House of Representatives*	Second Confiscation Act passed		*Son William dies*	
Oregon boundary settled		*Opposes Mexican War*	Battle of Antietam			
Taylor elected President	1848	*Campaigns for Taylor*	Battle of Fredericksburg			

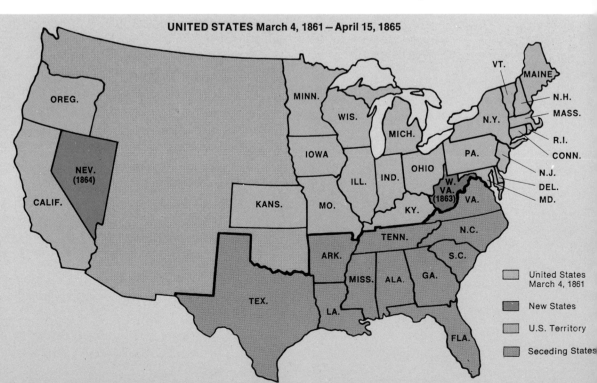

UNITED STATES March 4, 1861 — April 15, 1865

OREG.

NEV. (1864)

CALIF.

MINN.

WIS.

MICH.

IOWA

KANS.

MO.

ILL.

IND.

OHIO

KY.

TENN.

ARK.

MISS.

ALA.

GA.

TEX.

LA.

FLA.

S.C.

N.C.

VA.

W. VA. (1863)

PA.

N.Y.

VT.

MAINE

N.H.

MASS.

R.I.

CONN.

N.J.

DEL.

MD.

United States March 4, 1861

New States

U.S. Territory

Seceding States

Conscription Act	1863	*Issues Emancipation Proclamation*
Chancellorsville		
Vicksburg Campaign		*Delivers Gettysburg Address*
Battle of Gettysburg		
Battle of Chattanooga		*Proposes moderate Reconstruction policy*
Battle of the Wilderness	1864	*Names Grant general in chief of Union armies*
Spotsylvania		*Re-elected President*
Fall of Petersburg	1865	*Visits Richmond*
Lee surrenders at Appomattox		*Shot by John Wilkes Booth*
		Dies April 15

BIOGRAPHICAL FACTS

BIRTH: Hardin County, Ky., Feb. 12, 1809
ANCESTRY: English
FATHER: Thomas Lincoln; b. Rockingham County, Va., 1778; d. Coles County, Ill., Jan. 15, 1851
FATHER'S OCCUPATIONS: Farmer; carpenter
MOTHER: Nancy Hanks Lincoln; b. Va., Feb. 5, 1784; d. Spencer County, Ind., Oct. 5, 1818
STEPMOTHER: Sarah Bush Johnston; b. Hardin County, Ky., Dec. 12, 1788; d. Charleston, Ill., April 10, 1869
BROTHER: Thomas (b. and d. 1812)
SISTER: Sarah (1807–1828)
WIFE: Mary Todd; b. Lexington, Ky., Dec. 13, 1818; d. Springfield, Ill., July 16, 1882
MARRIAGE: Springfield, Ill., Nov. 4, 1842
CHILDREN: Robert Todd (1843–1926); Edward Baker (1846–1850); William Wallace (1850–1862); Thomas ("Tad") (1853–1871)
HOME: Eighth and Jackson streets, Springfield, Ill.
EDUCATION: Local tutors; self-educated
OCCUPATIONS BEFORE PRESIDENCY: Store clerk; store owner; ferry pilot; surveyor; postmaster; lawyer
MILITARY SERVICE: Served in volunteer company for three months during Black Hawk War (1832)
PRE-PRESIDENTIAL OFFICES: Member Illinois General Assembly; Member U.S. House of Representatives
AGE AT INAUGURATION: 52
DEATH: Washington, D.C., April 15, 1865
PLACE OF BURIAL: Oak Ridge Cemetery, Springfield

ELECTION OF 1860

CANDIDATES	ELECTORAL VOTE	POPULAR VOTE
Abraham Lincoln Republican	180	1,865,593
Stephen Douglas Democratic	12	1,382,713
John C. Breckinridge Southern Democratic	72	848,356
John Bell Constitutional Union	39	592,906

FIRST ADMINISTRATION

INAUGURATION: March 4, 1861; the Capitol, Washington, D.C.
VICE PRESIDENT: Hannibal Hamlin
SECRETARY OF STATE: William H. Seward
SECRETARY OF THE TREASURY: Salmon P. Chase; William P. Fessenden (from July 5, 1864)
SECRETARY OF WAR: Simon Cameron; Edwin M. Stanton (from Jan. 20, 1862)
ATTORNEY GENERAL: Edward Bates; James Speed (from Dec. 5, 1864)
POSTMASTER GENERAL: Montgomery Blair; William Dennison (from Oct. 1, 1864)
SECRETARY OF THE NAVY: Gideon Welles
SECRETARY OF THE INTERIOR: Caleb B. Smith; John P. Usher (from Jan. 1, 1863)
SUPREME COURT APPOINTMENTS: Noah H. Swayne (1862); Samuel F. Miller (1862); David Davis (1862); Stephen J. Field (1863); Salmon P. Chase, Chief Justice (1864)
37th CONGRESS (March 4, 1861–March 4, 1863):
Senate: 31 Republicans; 10 Democrats; 8 Others
House: 105 Republicans; 43 Democrats; 30 Others
38th CONGRESS (March 4, 1863–March 4, 1865):
Senate: 36 Republicans; 9 Democrats; 5 Others
House: 102 Republicans; 75 Democrats; 9 Others
STATES ADMITTED: West Virginia (1863); Nevada (1864)
END OF PRESIDENTIAL TERM: March 4, 1865

ELECTION OF 1864

(Because eleven Southern states had seceded from the Union and did not participate in the presidential election, eighty-one electoral votes were not cast.)

CANDIDATES	ELECTORAL VOTE	POPULAR VOTE
Abraham Lincoln National Union	212	2,206,938
George McClellan Democratic	21	1,803,787

SECOND ADMINISTRATION

INAUGURATION: March 4, 1865; the Capitol, Washington, D.C.
VICE PRESIDENT: Andrew Johnson
SECRETARY OF STATE: William H. Seward
SECRETARY OF THE TREASURY: Hugh McCulloch
SECRETARY OF WAR: Edwin M. Stanton
ATTORNEY GENERAL: James Speed
POSTMASTER GENERAL: William Dennison
SECRETARY OF THE NAVY: Gideon Welles
SECRETARY OF THE INTERIOR: John P. Usher
39th CONGRESS (March 4, 1865–March 4, 1867):
Senate: 42 Unionists; 10 Democrats
House: 149 Unionists; 42 Democrats
END OF PRESIDENTIAL TERM: April 15, 1865

ANDREW JOHNSON

T he Constitution-breakers are trying
the Constitution-defender," wrote Secretary of the Navy Gideon Welles on
March 24, 1868; "the conspirators are sitting in judgment on the man who
would not enter into their conspiracy, who was, and is, faithful to his oath,
his country, the Union, and the Constitution. What a spectacle!" Welles's
"Constitution-defender" was President Andrew Johnson, who had been impeached for "High Crimes and Misdemeanors" by the United States House
of Representatives. Now he was being tried by the Senate; conviction would
result in his removal from the Presidency.

There could be no mistake about the nature of the "spectacle": it was the
Constitution that was on trial; and the real reason for Johnson's impeachment
was his defiance of the Republican party. Even Senator Charles Sumner of
Massachusetts, one of the most powerful leaders favoring conviction of the
President, admitted as much: the trial, he said, "is political in character—
before a political body—and with a political object." The main issue was the
post bellum South, how it should be reconstructed and by whom. Johnson
wished, as had Lincoln, to bind the nation's wounds: "If a State is to be
nursed until it again gets strength," he said, "it must be nursed by its friends,
not smothered by its enemies." The Radical Republicans, on the other hand,
intended to treat the South as a defeated belligerent. Beneath their moralistic
rhetoric, however, the Radicals had a not-so-moral aim: if the South were regarded as a conquered foreign nation, its states could not be represented in
the Congress. Without the South, the Democratic party was small and impotent; without a Democratic opposition, the Republicans could rule with
complete impunity. Between their aims and reality stood President Andrew
Johnson and the constitutional system of checks and balances in government.

Johnson posed for Mathew Brady in 1865.

The Radicals' solution was to eliminate the President and to ignore the Constitution.

Andrew Johnson was in many respects an ideal victim for the Radicals. He was a Southerner, a Democrat, a pale and clumsy successor to the martyred Abraham Lincoln. But in other respects, he might have been the ideal leader to guide the nation to a just reunion. He was, after all, a Southerner *and* a staunch Unionist, capable of understanding the motives of both the men who fought to preserve the Union and those who fought for their state's right to leave it.

Johnson was born in a shack in Raleigh, North Carolina, on December 29, 1808. In his desolate childhood—he was fatherless from the age of three—there was little time for anything but work, certainly none for school. He made his first real contact with books when at the age of fourteen he was apprenticed to a local tailor. The apprentices were read to as they worked, and Johnson, once exposed, hungered for more education and taught himself to read.

At eighteen he moved to Greeneville, a poor mountain village in eastern Tennessee. There, for the first time in his life, he found himself among equals—independent mountain folk who worked with their hands and performed with dignity their tasks as cobblers, farmers, and bricklayers. They did not fear competition from slaves, for few slaveowners lived in the area.

A year after his arrival in Greeneville, Johnson married Eliza McCardle. Determined that her husband should amount to something, she encouraged him to continue educating himself: she hired a man to read to him as he worked and to teach him to write. He joined two debating societies and soon began attracting attention as a public speaker. Presently his tailor's shop became a gathering place for the townspeople who, during the course of discussions, decided that they should have a voice in the local government. The man they chose to represent them was Andrew Johnson; he was elected alderman at the age of twenty, then mayor for two years, and state legislator after that. All the while he was developing his skills as a stump speaker; and in 1843 he was elected as a Democrat to the United States House of Representatives.

Andrew Johnson was a good congressman, industrious and sincerely dedicated to the needs of the working people. He pressed for economy in government, opposed high tariffs that would raise the cost of living, and advocated a homestead act which would issue land to settlers. Ever conscious of his lack of formal education, he drove himself to study, to assemble facts, to read omnivorously. He armed himself with statistics on every conceivable issue, trying to anticipate any topic that might come up in Congress. He practiced his elocution and, with his rich and mellow voice, held his own in an age of brilliant orators. A *New York Times* reporter wrote that in his speeches Johnson "cut and slashed right and left, tore big wounds and left something behind to fester and remember. His phraseology may be uncouth, but his views are easily understood and he talks strong thoughts and carefully culled facts in quick succession."

Johnson lived simply, in a boardinghouse, and he dressed simply, always in black. Sturdily built, of medium height, he had black hair and piercing eyes set in a face that visitor Charles Dickens called "remarkable . . . indicating courage, watchfulness, and certainly strength of purpose."

An admirer of Jefferson and Jackson, Johnson was a Democrat but by no means a faithful party man. The needs of the people came first: he spoke for religious liberty, freedom of speech, and adherence to popular will. Once, foreshadowing a position he would take later on, he defended the presidential veto, calling it "a breakwater . . . to arrest or suspend for the time being hasty and improvident legislation until the people . . . have time and opportunity to consider of its propriety." His independent posture frequently irritated Democrats as well as Whigs, and he was often the victim of bipartisan attack. Vexed by the congressman's opposition to increased appropriations for West Point, Jefferson Davis sneered on the floor of the House: "Can a blacksmith or tailor

According to Greeneville lore, the moment Eliza McCardle (above) first saw Johnson she stated, "There goes my beau." They married a year later.

construct . . . bastioned field-works . . . ?" But Johnson was proud of having made his way "by the sweat of his brow," and he resented any slur on any workingman. "Sir," he once responded to one such insult, "I do not forget that I am a mechanic. I am proud to own it. Neither do I forget that Adam was a tailor and sewed fig leaves, or that our Saviour was the son of a carpenter."

While he antagonized his Southern colleagues, he continued to please his constituency, which re-elected him four times. In 1852, unable to defeat him at the polls, the Tennessee Whigs gerrymandered his district out of existence. Their shrewdness promptly backfired: the ex-congressman returned home and was elected governor of the state. Once installed, Johnson drove his victory home, establishing Tennessee's first public-school system and placing the needs of the working people over those of the slaveowning aristocracy, for whom he never hesitated to express contempt. The Whigs attacked him savagely, calling him "an apostate son of the

South," a "leveler," "low, despicable and dirty." In responding, Johnson only solidified his position with the common man. "Whose hands built your Capitol?" he once asked. "Whose toil, whose labor built your railroads and your ships? . . . I say let the mechanic and the laborer make our laws, rather than the idle and vicious aristocrat." In 1855, during a bitter campaign against Whigs and Know-Nothings, he was advised to tone down his attacks on the opposition and his defense of Catholics and foreigners. "I will make that same speech tomorrow," he responded, "if it blows the Democratic party to hell." He won the election, and in 1857 the state legislature named him to the United States Senate. "I have," he said, "reached the summit of my ambition."

Back in Washington Johnson resumed his fight for passage of his homestead act, which would give 160 acres of land to the head of any family that would settle on it for five years. Congress, however, was preoccupied with slavery, and while the North embraced the bill—seeing it as a remedy for the evil of slavery—the Southerners opposed it, seeing in it eventual loss of their congressional power. Johnson's reaction: "Why lug slavery into the matter?" He did not like slavery because it lowered the value of the white laborer, but he accepted it as a fact of life, a local institution peculiar to the states and beyond the province of Congress.

In 1860 the Tennessee delegation to the Democratic National Convention gave Johnson its favorite-son votes for the Vice Presidency, but what little chance he might have had was nullified when the Southern states withdrew over the slavery issue and nominated John C. Breckinridge to oppose the regular Democrats' choice, Stephen Douglas. Johnson campaigned for Breckinridge only because he was pro-Union. But asked what he would do if the South used the election of Lincoln as a pretext to secede, Johnson answered: "When the crisis comes I will be found standing by the Union."

Between Lincoln's election and inauguration, Andrew Johnson, alone among Southern congressmen and senators, called on

431

Congress to act to prevent secession; and he pledged himself—"my blood, my existence" —to save the Union. In the North his words were acclaimed; in the South he was hanged in effigy. After the inauguration, he hurried back to Tennessee, disregarding threats on his life, narrowly escaping a lynch mob, to try to keep his state from seceding. His mountain and valley people voted overwhelmingly to remain in the Union, but the richer and more populous western districts were too strong, and Tennessee joined the Confederacy. Branded a traitor, Johnson was obliged to flee to Kentucky.

In Washington, Johnson pressed for the military deliverance of East Tennessee, whose people were suffering for their Union sympathies. Like many Unionists, Johnson's wife and youngest son were turned out of their home. (His two older sons were in the Union army, and his son-in-law was engaged in guerrilla fighting in the Tennessee mountains.) Then, early in 1862, Grant took Nashville and part of western Tennessee, and President Lincoln appointed Johnson military governor of the state, ordering him "to provide . . . peace and security to the loyal inhabitants of that state until they shall be able to establish a civil government" to conform with the Constitution. Johnson accepted the mission, but not until late in 1863, when all of Tennessee had been cleared of Confederate troops, could he begin to establish a civilian government.

Two years later, the Republican convention (meeting under the name of National Union party) acknowledged Johnson's remarkable services to the nation by nominating him for the Vice Presidency. After the victorious election, Johnson returned to Tennessee to continue Reconstruction. By the end of February, 1865, the job had been done; all that remained was the election of a civil governor, and that was set for March 4, which was also Johnson's inauguration day.

Ill, anxious, and exhausted, Johnson asked to take his oath of office in Nashville. Lincoln, however, felt that the inauguration of a Southerner would symbolize the national unity he hoped to restore. So, at the President's request, Johnson returned to Washington, arriving a day or two before the inauguration, still ill and further exhausted by the trip. As he sat waiting for the ceremonies to begin, he said he did not feel well and asked for a stimulant. Some brandy was sent for; he had a sizable drink, then two more. The delays and the heat of the stuffy Senate chamber put the brandy to work. When he was called upon to speak, he slurred his words uncharacteristically and spoke extemporaneously and irrationally, as a condemning assembly and a compassionate Lincoln looked on. Evidence indicates that this was the first time Andrew Johnson had ever been intoxicated. Nevertheless, in gossip and press, he became "Andy the Sot." Lincoln, who had privately sent an investigator to Tennessee, learned that Johnson was a temperate drinker and defended him. But "Andy the Sot" he remained. His reputation as a drunkard, however, was the least of his troubles.

Forty-one days after the inauguration, less than a week after Appomattox, Andrew Johnson—tailor, reputed drunkard, Southerner, Democrat, and staunch Unionist—became President of the United States. He took the oath on the morning of April 15, 1865, in the parlor of his hotel. Secretary of the Treasury Hugh McCulloch wrote that Johnson was "grief stricken like the rest, and he seemed to be oppressed by the suddenness of the call upon him to become President . . . but he was nevertheless calm and self-possessed."

On the day of Lincoln's death the Radical Republicans met in caucus and, remembering Johnson's consistent opposition to Southern aristocratic leadership, agreed that his accession to the Presidency "would prove a godsend to the country." They proposed a harsh, vindictive peace in which land would be confiscated, Confederate sympathizers disenfranchised, white suffrage severely limited, and Negro suffrage restrictionless. But it took the Radicals only one month to discover that Johnson meant to continue Lincoln's magnanimous policy. Why fight a war to preserve the Union, his logic went, if after its conclusion the victors prevent Union from being re-established? Reconstruction of the South, he felt, should be based on a faith in its people; if reasonable terms were offered to Southerners, Johnson believed they would carry them out.

At first the people of the North agreed with President Johnson: with the exception of Maine, Massachusetts, and Pennsylvania, summer and autumn conventions of state Republicans enthusiastically endorsed the President's program. Moreover, the leading Union generals—among them Sherman, Meade, and Grant—supported Johnson, and by December every Confederate state but Texas had met the Reconstruction qualifications and had elected local officials, congressmen, and senators.

The Radicals, however, had not been idle. Their propaganda campaign against the President, the moderates, and the hated Rebels had mounted steadily, and they had managed to attract the support of Northern industrialists (who had everything to gain from a government-occupied agricultural South) as well as that of the abolitionists. As their alliance broadened, Johnson's obvious limitations became glaring. Greatest of these were the facts that he was a Democrat and a Southerner and not even a member of the party in power. His Cabinet had been selected by Lincoln, and at least one member —Secretary of War Edwin Stanton—was secretly allied with the Radicals. To make matters worse, although Johnson began to realize how much power the Radicals had mustered, he stubbornly refused to use patronage as a weapon. Not knowing whom he could trust, he resisted the advice of many well-meaning Northerners and became, in effect, his own enemy (though not his worst) as the tragedy unfolded.

The newly elected senators and congressmen from the South were not turned away from Washington, but the Radicals managed to "delay" their seating until a committee could investigate "conditions of the so-called Confederate States and . . . report . . . if any were entitled to be represented in Congress. . . ." This move retained the

THE REPENTANT (?) ENEMIES OF THE REPUBLIC APPLYING FOR PARDON TO UNCLE SAM.

As this cartoon indicates, diplomacy in Johnson's administration got off to an embarrassing start, since most of the foreign powers with which he dealt had obviously hoped that the South would win the Civil War.

When the President vetoed the Reconstruction Act of 1867, which gave suffrage to Southern Negroes only, the Radical press ignored Johnson's known antislavery sentiments and implied that he was a bigot.

overwhelming Republican majority. But the Radicals were not yet strong enough. Although they managed to pass a bill extending the powers of the Freedmen's Bureau, they could not override Johnson's veto.

Johnson had vetoed the bill on constitutional grounds, since the bureau would have been empowered to restrict the constitutional rights of white Southerners, whom he still considered American citizens. Enraged, the Radical press called the President an "insolent, drunken brute" and circulated rumors that he had been involved in Lincoln's assassination, that he maintained a harem of harlots, and that he was scheming with Southern Rebels to usurp Northern power. Thaddeus Stevens said that he was an "alien enemy, a citizen of a foreign state . . . and therefore not now legally President."

Early in 1866 the Radicals managed to unseat a New Jersey senator, a Democrat, on a trivial technicality. Thus Johnson's margin of safety was reduced. When he vetoed a Senate civil rights bill, again on constitutional grounds, the Congress overrode

his veto. The taste of victory only whetted the Radicals' appetite for more power, and as they sought it they made it perfectly clear that so meager a roadblock as the Constitution—and its system of checks and balances —would not stand in their way. Congress, Senator Sumner said, must have "plenary powers, the Executive none, on reestablishing the Union." Andrew Johnson must learn, remarked Stevens, that "as Congress shall order he must obey." For his part Johnson saw himself as the tribune of the people, the defender of the Constitution against congressional despotism. "I intend to assert the power which the people have placed in me," he said firmly. It was, however, becoming more and more obvious that the Radicals would employ any means to gain their end— absolute control of the federal government.

The importance of the election of 1866 was understood by both sides. Some members of both parties had long urged the President to call a convention of the National Union party, which had nominated him and Lincoln in 1864, in order to organ-

434

ize his supporters as a political force. However, Johnson hesitated. Not until August, 1866, did he call the assembly, and that, just three months before the elections, was too late. This was probably his greatest single mistake. Johnson had more supporters than he imagined: well-organized, running for office as National Union candidates (which would have instantly identified them as pro-Johnson), they might have demonstrated this support. Instead, there was little feeling of a national movement behind the President, little to counter the well-organized, expertly staffed, press-endorsed influence of the ubiquitous Radicals, whose position was strengthened by the understandable resentment in the North toward the South. The war, after all, had ended just a year before, and the wounds were still fresh. Identification with the National Union party would have associated the pro-Johnson candidates with the forces behind Union victory. Running as plain Democrats or Republicans, however, they were vulnerable to the traitor, or Copperhead, label, which the Radicals pinned on them as they consistently salted the nation's wounds. When Johnson made a national speaking tour in favor of moderate candidates, the Radicals sent hecklers and ruffians to disrupt every gathering. Sadly, the President could not ignore the taunts, and more than once his replies turned speeches into shouting matches, meetings into riots. It was a close election, but the Radicals won a clear majority.

Claiming a popular mandate to reconstruct the South on their terms, the Radicals stated their aims. "Reconstruction," as Wendell Phillips put it, "begins when the South yields up her idea of civilization, and allows the North to permeate her channels and to make her over. . . ." Thaddeus Stevens and the other leaders had already drafted the harsh measures to do this: military rule, disfranchisement of the Rebels, and unrestricted Negro suffrage to make the former slaves the rulers—rulers, incidentally, who would vote Republican.

When Johnson vetoed another Radical civil rights bill early in 1867, the House sent an impeachment resolution to the Judiciary Committee, which had to determine whether the President was guilty of trying "to overthrow, subvert or corrupt the Government of the United States." The Radicals probably hoped that the very presence of the resolution would convince the President to watch his step. But Johnson was contemptuous: "Let them impeach and be damned"; he had no intention of suspending his right to veto.

The Radicals were firmly in the saddle, and they passed one act after another over Johnson's head. Their arrogance reached its peak on March 2, 1867, when they passed three major bills—all of them unconstitutional. The first Reconstruction Act re-established martial law in the South, limited white suffrage, and conferred universal suffrage (but in the South only) on Negroes. To the Army Appropriations Act was attached an illegal rider that stripped the President of his role as Commander in Chief. To veto the bill, however, would have meant denying the Army funds, so Johnson signed it, after taking care to note its unconstitutionality. Finally, the Radicals passed the Tenure of Office Act over Johnson's veto. This law—which again was actually a constitutional amendment masquerading as a simple law—forbade the President to remove, without the consent of the Senate, any officeholder whose appointment had required Senate approval.

Meanwhile the House Judiciary Committee was having trouble finding evidence with which to impeach the President. It was Johnson himself who came to the Radicals' rescue. On August 5, convinced that Secretary of War Stanton was in league with the Radicals (which he was: Stanton had drafted the unconstitutional statute in the Army Appropriations Act), the President asked for his resignation. Stanton refused, and Johnson suspended him, appointing in his stead General Grant, whom no man dared defy. An impeachment bill of December, 1867, failed. But 1868 would be an election year, and Grant began to act like a presidential candidate. When in January the Senate insisted that Stanton be reinstated, the General quietly withdrew. Johnson was firm, however: Tenure of Office Act or no, he had a constitutional right to remove Stanton, and he appointed Major General Lorenzo Thomas Secretary of War. Stanton refused to leave and swore out a warrant for Thomas' arrest, charging him with seizing his office. "Very well, that is the place I want it," Johnson said, "in the courts."

"Didn't I tell you so?" demanded Thaddeus Stevens. "If you don't kill the beast it will kill you." The House closed in quickly. The Joint Committee on Reconstruction resolved to impeach the President. There were two days of one-sided debating. On February 24, 1868, by a vote of 126 to 47, Andrew Johnson became the first and only American President to be impeached.

The word "impeachment," which is sometimes erroneously used to mean removal from office, is actually the parliamentary equivalent of the legal term "indictment." Under the Constitution, "the sole Power of Impeachment" belongs to the House of Representatives, which functions as a grand jury. The Senate has the sole responsibility for conducting a trial; conviction requires a two-thirds majority vote of the senators and may result in the President's removal.

At one o'clock on March 5, Chief Justice Salmon Chase, impressive in his robes, took his seat on the Senate rostrum. The chamber and the galleries were filled to overflowing.

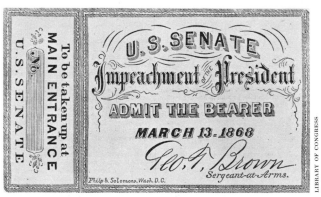

A ticket such as this was hard to come by during Johnson's trial. People had poured into Washington by the thousands, hoping to watch the spectacle.

In the front and to the right of the rostrum sat the President's counsel. (But not the President. He wanted to attend, but his advisers had insisted that he stay away.) To the left sat the seven managers of impeachment for the House. The senators occupied the first two rows of seats; behind them were the accusers, the members of the House of Representatives. With great pomp Chase swore in the senators, and the trial began. It would last for three months.

The first eight articles of impeachment charged the President with intent and conspiracy to violate the Constitution and the Tenure of Office Act. The ninth dealt with his violation of the Army Appropriations Act. The tenth charged him with having disgraced the Congress and the Presidency and with having made some of his speeches "in a loud voice." The eleventh was a catchall, reiterating the first ten and accusing the President of plotting to violate two other laws the Radicals had passed. In sum, the indictments were blather and buncombe: "a mountain of words," Welles wrote in his diary, "but not even a mouse of impeachment material. . . . Those who may vote to convict . . . would as readily vote to impeach the President had he been accused of stepping on a dog's tail."

Johnson's lawyers based their defense on two points: that the President had appointed General Thomas as Secretary of War in order to test the constitutionality of the Tenure of Office Act; and that, constitutional or not, the act could not apply in this case because Stanton was Lincoln's appointee. The prosecution consistently objected to testimony regarding Johnson's intent—seventeen times the Senate overruled the Chief Justice's decisions regarding the admission of evidence. Nor were members of the Cabinet allowed to testify for the President. Because of their prestige, however, Generals Sherman and Thomas were allowed to testify on his behalf.

Johnson went about his business, anxious to stride up to the Senate rostrum and do some "plain speaking." His temper, understandably, was quick, and each day he remained tense until some bearer of news would return from the Capitol and tell him what was going on. The irony of the affair caused him the greatest anguish. "Impeach *me* for violating the Constitution?" he growled. "Damn them!"

There were fifty-four senators at the time. Thirty-six votes were needed for conviction; the Radicals were sure of thirty, Johnson of twelve, leaving another twelve—Republicans all—in doubt. As the days passed, Johnson learned that five of the twelve were going to vote for conviction. That meant the Radicals had to swing the support of just one of the remaining seven. The pressure on those seven, and on Johnson, mounted as the trial drew near its conclusion. Thaddeus Stevens, too ill to deliver his fanatical closing plea for conviction, had it read for him: those who voted for acquittal could expect to be eternally "tortured on the gibbet of everlasting obloquy." On May 7 the trial ended, and the Senate adjourned until May 11. During the recess, as before, the pressure from the newspapers, from constituents, from colleagues, party leaders, preachers, Army officers, and lobbyists closed in on the seven doubtfuls: Convict!

When the Senate reconvened, four of the undeclared—Fessenden of Maine, Trumbull of Illinois, Grimes of Iowa, and Fowler of Tennessee—revealed that they would vote to acquit. This made the Radicals frantic: they managed to have the vote, originally scheduled for the twelfth, postponed until the sixteenth. That same afternoon Senator Grimes buckled under the pressure and had a stroke that left him partially paralyzed. The sad news was coupled, however, with a hopeful word for Johnson: Van Winkle of West Virginia could be depended on, and Henderson of Missouri would probably vote for acquittal. That left one senator: Ross of Kansas, a freshman Radical, devoted to his party but silent throughout the trial. As for Grimes—whether or not he could make it to the Senate chamber was a matter of doubt.

The chamber had never been more closely packed. Senator Fessenden rose to ask a half hour's delay to await the arrival of the

Johnson's defense was based on his executive powers as defined in the Constitution, but not even that document was spared his enemies' ridicule.

stricken Grimes. The Radicals had no time to object, for as Fessenden spoke, Senator Grimes was helped to his seat by friends. That left it all up to Ross. When his turn to vote came, fourteen senators had voted for acquittal and four more minority votes were guaranteed. The final decision, then, was Ross's; his answer would not simply convict or acquit Johnson, it could, perhaps, preserve or destroy the Constitution, and it would, certainly, make or break his own future in politics. He rose—all eyes were on him, the faces of those present "pale and sick under the burden of suspense." His face gave away nothing. "Not guilty," he said quietly, and the spectacle was over. So, incidentally, was his political career.

There were ten more articles to be voted on, and although the Radicals managed a ten-day postponement, they could not retrieve even one of those seven precious votes. True, in less than a year they would be in control of the executive branch through

437

their nominee, General Grant; but at least what power they would have would be secured through constitutional means.

Understandably, Johnson had no love for the White House, but he thought the 1868 Democratic nomination for the Presidency would mean "a vindication such as no man had ever received." But while the party was loud in its praise, it nominated Horatio Seymour, who lost to Grant.

In December, 1868, with Grant safely elected and the Radicals anxious to get their administration under way, Johnson appeared before Congress to give his last annual message. His warning was prophetic: "The attempt to place the white population under the domination of persons of color in the South . . . has prevented that cooperation between the two races so essential to the success of industrial enterprise. . . ." Already the Ku-Klux Klan was riding and the seeds of lasting hatred were sown.

On the night before the inauguration of Grant, which Johnson did not attend, Secretary Welles said good-by to the Johnson family and recorded his thoughts in his diary: "No better persons have occupied the Executive Mansion, and I part from them, socially and personally, with sincere regret. Of the President, politically and officially, I need not here speak further than to say he has been faithful to the Constitution, although his administrative capabilities and management may not equal some of his predecessors. Of measures he was a good judge, but not always of men."

The Johnson administration, for all its battles, and agonies, and turmoil, demonstrated an essential truth of American history—that the government goes on. That it did under Johnson is largely to the credit of most of the Cabinet members, especially Welles and William H. Seward.

Seward, once a leading presidential aspirant, supported the President consistently and wrote many of Johnson's veto messages; he was also one of the most active Secretaries of State since John Quincy Adams. During the Civil War, Napoleon III of France had sent troops to Mexico and had placed Austrian Archduke Maximilian on the Mexican throne. Early in 1866, with Johnson's approval, Seward decided to reassert the Monroe Doctrine and ordered the French to withdraw; for emphasis he sent General Sheridan and fifty thousand troops to the Mexican border. Napoleon acquiesced in the spring of 1867, but Maximilian was ambushed by a band of Mexican partisans and was executed. Later that year, the Midway Islands were claimed by the American fleet. In October, Seward negotiated the purchase of the Danish West Indies (the Virgin Islands), but the Senate killed the purchase bill.

Seward's most famous achievement was the purchase of Alaska from Russia for $7,200,-000. He submitted this bill to the Senate in March, 1867, after just three weeks' negotiation, and managed to have it passed by convincing Senator Sumner to support it. It was an unpopular purchase at first, and Alaska became known as "Seward's Folly" and "Johnson's polar bear garden."

So, thanks to Seward and others, Johnson's Presidency had not been devoid of accomplishments. But the ex-President still sought vindication. Back in Tennessee, he again grew active in state affairs, and in 1875 he ran for the United States Senate. (As he was waiting for the election results, he was so nervous that he had to steady himself with brandy. For the second time in his life—but this time privately—he got drunk.) He was elected, and in March he returned to Washington to attend a special session of Congress. Nervously he entered the chamber: from the galleries came a great burst of applause; he found his desk covered with flowers. When the senators—even those who had judged him guilty seven years before—pressed forward to shake his hand, he shook with them all. He had his vindication.

Andrew Johnson was only briefly a senator. He suffered a stroke at his daughter's Tennessee home and died on July 31, 1875. He was buried on a hilltop outside Greeneville, his winding sheet the flag, his pillow the Constitution.

—DAVID JACOBS

Andrew Johnson

A PICTURE PORTFOLIO

_This white china vase, a souvenir of the Lincoln-
Johnson inauguration in 1865, is decorated with
portraits of both of the victorious candidates._

Tennessee aristocrats were appalled when Andy Johnson, the town tailor, was twice elected alderman and thrice the mayor of Greeneville. To make matters worse, this common "mechanic" remained busy at his trade in his shop, above, while he served. At left is a pair of Johnson's shears.

As long as Andrew Johnson remained in Greeneville, his shop was a focal point for local political activities. Even when he was mayor, the town council met in the shop to do official business—as the page above from the Town Book reveals. Having a business of his own and living in a place where labor was not regarded as undignified meant a great deal to Johnson, whose self-confidence increased daily. And like the shop and the town, his wife Eliza, whom he had met in 1826, was a major force behind his perpetual self-improvement program. She did not, however, have to push her husband; the urge to better himself was there all the time.

TEN DOLLARS REWARD

Ran away from the Subscriber," read a notice in the Raleigh, North Carolina, *Gazette* in 1824, ". . . two apprentice boys, legally bound, named WILLIAM and ANDREW JOHNSON. . . . I will pay the above Reward [ten dollars] to any person who will deliver said apprentices to me in Raleigh, or I will give the above Reward for Andrew Johnson alone. All persons are cautioned against harboring or employing said apprentices. . . . JAMES J. SELBY, *Tailor*." The bounty was never collected, but a year later the Johnson boys returned to Raleigh on their own. Andrew, it seemed, had felt guilty and wanted to serve out his apprenticeship. Although Selby had closed his shop by this time, he remained unforgiving, and with the possibility of legal prosecution hanging over his head, the seventeen-year-old Johnson moved with his mother and various other relatives to the mountains of eastern Tennessee.

In 1827, after a year's transient labor, he heard that the tailor in Greeneville had retired. Johnson set up shop there and soon married his sweetheart. A year later, with the election of Andrew Jackson to the Presidency, the age of the common man began. In Andrew Johnson's shop ideas flowed back and forth. There, from his best friend, plasterer Blackstone McDaniel, Johnson received many of his democratic views. Active in regional debating societies, the tailor met Sam Milligan of Greeneville College, who became his political adviser and helped him to develop his skills as a stump speaker. After his friends elected him alderman in 1828, Johnson became mayor, a congressman, governor of Tennessee, and eventually a United States senator. He desired to rise no higher, but rise he did—tragically.

ANDREW JOHNSON NATIONAL MONUMENT

Senator Andrew Johnson of Tennessee (above) wore black at all times in Washington. Inconspicuous outside the Senate chamber, inclined to keep to himself, he lived simply and frugally. If he felt intimidated by his college-educated colleagues, he responded by working harder and longer—and by knowing the facts and the issues better—than most.

UNFORESEEN CONSEQUENCES

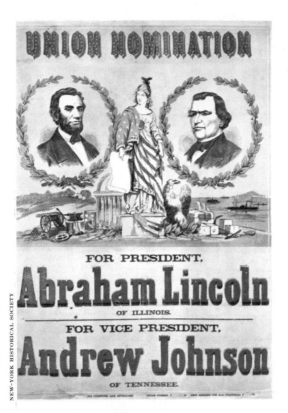

When Radical Republican Thaddeus Stevens heard that his party was considering the nomination of Tennessee Democrat Andrew Johnson as a running mate for Abraham Lincoln in 1864, he asked: "Can't you find a candidate for Vice-President in the United States without going down to one of those damned rebel provinces to pick one up?" Stevens had missed—or had caught and rejected—the point. Johnson's candidacy gave the ticket the strength it sorely needed at a time when Lincoln's popularity was low enough to make his chances of re-election seem slight. It made the anti-Lincoln Radicals appear unduly partisan in such troubled times (the campaign poster above makes no mention of the Republican party); it attracted Democrats; and it illustrated Lincoln's sincere belief that the nation must, at the end of the Civil War, return to being a united nation, a nation of North and South.

Senator Andrew Johnson was serving as military governor of Tennessee when he learned that the Republicans, under the name of the National Union party, had nominated him as their vice presidential candidate. To a group of Unionists in Nashville he said, "I accept the nomination on principle, be the consequences what they may. I will do what I believe to be my duty." The consequences, as things turned out, were greater than he could have imagined.

Johnson got off to a bad start, appearing drunk (probably for the first time in his life) at his inauguration. Then, seven weeks later, a deed and a nondeed made him President: Booth killed Lincoln; an accomplice, George Atzerodt, whose role in the conspiracy was to kill Johnson, had an eleventh-hour change of heart and did not attempt to carry out his assignment. Grief-stricken by Lincoln's death but self-possessed, Johnson took over the Presidency. The Radicals, led by Thaddeus Stevens in the House, Charles Sumner in the Senate, and Edwin Stanton in the Cabinet, at first adopted a cautiously optimistic attitude toward Johnson—was he not, after all, a vehement enemy of Southern aristocracy? But Johnson knew that the war had diminished that aristocracy, and he made it clear that he intended to be conciliatory. With Congress in recess, he began his magnanimous Reconstruction program. "If something is not done," said Stevens, "the President will be crowned King before the next Congress meets." The press joined the assault: Horace Greeley, in his New York *Tribune*, cried out against Johnson; and cartoons like the one on the opposite page (from *Harper's Weekly*) began to appear.

KING ANDY I.

HOW HE WILL LOOK AND WHAT HE WILL DO.

LONG LIVE KING ANDY I.

DO YOU WANT ANDREW JOHNSON PRESIDENT OR KING

YOU PAYS YOUR TAXES AND YOU TAKES YOUR CHOICE.

Th: Nast.

THE RUSSIAN SETTLEMENT

RECEIVED
WITH OPEN ARMS

THE FISH
BITE QUITE FREELY

THE OFFICIAL SEAL

ALL: *Harper's Weekly*

The anti-Johnson press had a fine time with the Alaskan purchase. Harper's Weekly *ran the cartoons above, and word spread that the only products of "Seward's Folly" were "polar bears and icebergs; the vegetation is mosses . . . the streams are glaciers."*

"READY FOR BUSINESS"

The battle raged almost without letup throughout 1867: it was one branch of the federal government against another, executive versus legislative, neither yielding, neither altering its strategy, Congress passing bills, Johnson vetoing them, Congress passing them over his veto. His service during the Civil War, however, had taught Secretary of State William Seward that a nation functioned even when it was at war with itself. One March night in that stormy year, Seward was having a game of whist at his Washington home when the Russian minister arrived with the news that the Czar was willing to sell "Russian America"—Alaska—for $7,200,000. Delighted, Seward wanted to close the deal (which had been pending for a month) immediately, and when the Russian reminded him that the hour was late, Seward replied, "Never mind that. Before midnight you will find me at the Department, which will be open and ready for business."

Seward wanted to work fast because Congress was approaching adjournment; a surprised Upper House received the treaty the next morning. Although the Senate ratified the treaty in less than a month, the inevitable newspaper assault ensued: nothing that Johnson approved, his opponents evidently believed, could possibly be beneficial to the nation. The House refused to vote the necessary appropriation. But fortunately Russia was willing to wait for its money, which was finally appropriated a year later. As 1867 turned to 1868 Seward, who had nearly been nominated for President in 1860 and who had been one of the most influential men in his party, continued to do his duty at the side of President Andrew Johnson. Together they shaped a respectable record in foreign affairs—especially remarkable in view of the fact that 1868 brought the impeachment of the President.

In 1861 England, Spain, and France formed a joint military expedition to protect their property and lives in turbulent Mexico. Equally troubled but fearful of a Mexico-Confederacy alliance, the United States could not join the compact. A year later, Louis Napoleon drove his allies away in disgust when they learned of his plans to remove the Mexican President, Benito Juárez, and to establish a French empire there. When the end of the Civil War finally gave Americans the time to look, they found Louis Napoleon's puppet, Archduke Maximilian, on the throne of Mexico. They demanded French withdrawal in editorial and song (left), and Secretary Seward promised aid to Juárez. In 1867, with more pressing problems at home, Napoleon pulled out his troops, leaving Maximilian behind. His execution was immortalized by Manet (below).

RADICALS AND STATESMEN

NATIONAL ARCHIVES

ANSCO COLLECTION

THADDEUS STEVENS

"Not only the slave states," declared Thaddeus Stevens in his first congressional speech, "but the general government, recognizing and aiding slavery as it does, is a despotism." Articulate, uncompromising, and grim, "Old Thad" was a dominant figure in the House of Representatives for nearly fifteen years, waging a relentless war on slavery. A Pennsylvania lawyer and businessman who had risen from dire poverty, Stevens was known to defend fugitive slaves without fee. After four years in the state legislature he entered Congress as a Whig in 1849 and served until 1853. Re-elected as a Republican in 1858, he served as chairman of the House Ways and Means Committee during the Civil War and urged harsher measures in dealing with the "Rebels" of the South. After Johnson's inauguration he was made House chairman of a joint committee on Reconstruction and launched an open battle against the moderate policies of the President. As virtual dictator of the Republican-dominated House of Representatives and leader of the Radicals, he succeeded in overriding presidential vetoes and imposing military Reconstruction on the South. He was one of the men chosen to conduct the impeachment case against Johnson, but failing health robbed him of his usual capacity for fiery leadership, and he died shortly after the President's trial.

EDWIN M. STANTON

Edwin McMasters Stanton, President Johnson's perfidious Secretary of War, was described by a contemporary as "'incorruptible' in the ordinary sense" but susceptible to corruption by his own "prejudice and passion." A brilliant and dynamic lawyer, Stanton began practice in Ohio, moved to Pennsylvania, and settled in Washington, D.C., in 1856. Acting as United States counsel in 1858, his masterful handling of fraudulent California land claims won him the Attorney Generalship in 1860. In spite of his Radical tendencies and initial distrust of Lincoln, he was appointed Secretary of War in 1862 and won the President's admiration for his vigorous administration of the War Department. It was possibly Lincoln's respect for Stanton that prompted Johnson to request his continuance in office after the assassination and to retain him long after his loyalty was suspect. Only after months of conspiracy with the congressional Radicals was the Secretary of War dismissed. Challenging the presidential order on the strength of the newly adopted Tenure of Office Act, he refused to vacate the post until impeachment proceedings exonerated the President and made Stanton's position untenable. Named an associate justice of the Supreme Court by President Ulysses S. Grant in 1869, the fifty-five-year-old Radical died before he could take his seat.

SALMON P. CHASE

Presiding over the impeachment trial of President Johnson, Chief Justice Salmon Portland Chase, the "high priest of radicalism," was determined to set aside Radical party pressures in an effort to conduct a fair hearing. "I do not believe . . ." he affirmed, "in the subversion of the executive and judicial departments . . . by Congress, no matter how patriotic the motive may be." Admitted to the bar in 1829, Chase settled in Cincinnati, where he often defended fugitive slaves. A founder of the Free-Soil party, he served in the United States Senate from 1849 to 1855, when he was elected governor of Ohio on the new Republican ticket. Appointed Secretary of the Treasury in 1861, he established the national banking system that became law in 1863. He was highly critical of Lincoln's policies, which he considered weak and ineffectual, and he sympathized with the subversive Radicals in the Senate. If his Cabinet loyalty was questionable, his judicial deliberations were above reproach. Appointed Chief Justice of the Supreme Court after he resigned from the Cabinet in 1864, he presided over the trial of Jefferson Davis and the impeachment trial of President Johnson with scrupulous objectivity. A presidential aspirant, Chase was continually defeated for the nomination and retained his seat on the Supreme Court until his death at sixty-five in 1873.

WILLIAM HENRY SEWARD

William Henry Seward's influence on the course of American politics spanned almost half a century, from the election of John Quincy Adams through the administration of Andrew Johnson. As a young lawyer in Auburn, New York, Seward boldly opposed the presidential candidate of the Albany Regency and spoke out for "John Quincy Adams—and better government." His independent spirit never wavered. As governor of New York for four years and United States senator from 1848 to 1860, he took a firm stand against slavery. Opposing the Compromise of 1850, he argued the inherent freedom of the territories on the basis of "a higher law than the Constitution" and saw in the whole slavery issue "an irrepressible conflict" between North and South. A masterful Secretary of State under Lincoln and Johnson, he skillfully averted European intervention in the Civil War and later secured France's promise of withdrawal from Mexico. An expansionist, he purchased Alaska in 1867. (It was promptly dubbed "Seward's Folly.") Favoring a moderate Reconstruction policy, he staunchly supported President Johnson during the impeachment proceedings; efforts to entice him into the Radical camp were met with the emphatic rejoinder: "I will see you damned first." Retiring from public service in 1869, Seward died three years later in Auburn.

447

"NOT GUILTY"

A White House aide named Andrew Johnson "The Grim Presence." Grim, indeed, was the President, justly so—and justly bitter, justly moody, justly frustrated. The Senate was trying him for the eleven high-sounding, low-in-substance charges on the House of Representatives' bill of impeachment. It was his trial, the trial of the century—The United States v. The President of the United States—but his counsel would not let him attend. So, from late March to mid-May, 1868, grumbling, cursing, waiting for daily reports, Andrew Johnson went about his duties. He began reading more, memorizing passages from English literature, studying philosophical books on the subject of immortality. Once he asked an aide to get him some material on the trial and execution of Charles I of England; he enjoyed reading that all but three members of the court which condemned the King met with untimely deaths. The aide thought that Johnson did not fear conviction and removal from office because he was sure fate would deal similarly with his persecutors. Nevertheless, Johnson wanted to take his case to the people, and despite the alarm of his advisers he invited reporters from friendly and neutral newspapers to the White House.

When the President violated the Tenure of Office Act, hoping for a court test of its constitutionality, he got a trial of a different sort. Above, left, the vindictive Thaddeus Stevens concludes his successful impeachment campaign in the House of Representatives. At right, Johnson is shown receiving a summons from the Senate.

From these unprecedented interviews emerged the traditional presidential press conference. Direct and vehement with the journalists, Johnson was inclined to conceal the awful helplessness he felt. But one morning, privately, he did reveal himself to a friend: "Here I am," he read from the Bible, "testify against me before the Lord. . . . Whose ox have I taken? Or whose ass have I taken? Or whom have I defrauded? Whom have I oppressed? Or from whose hand have I taken a bribe to blind my eyes with it?" As the President read from the Scriptures, the betting odds on the trial shifted back and forth. First there were twelve doubtful votes, then seven—Radical Republicans all; only one of them was needed to convict. It soon became apparent that six were going to choose conscience over party, political obscurity over power, by voting to acquit. The decisive vote belonged to freshman Radical Edmund Ross. His name was called. "I almost literally looked down into my open grave," he recalled. "Friendships, position, fortune, everything that makes life desirable to an ambitious man were about to be swept away by the breath of my mouth, perhaps forever." Senator Ross's decision to vote "Not guilty" saved President Johnson and probably the Constitution.

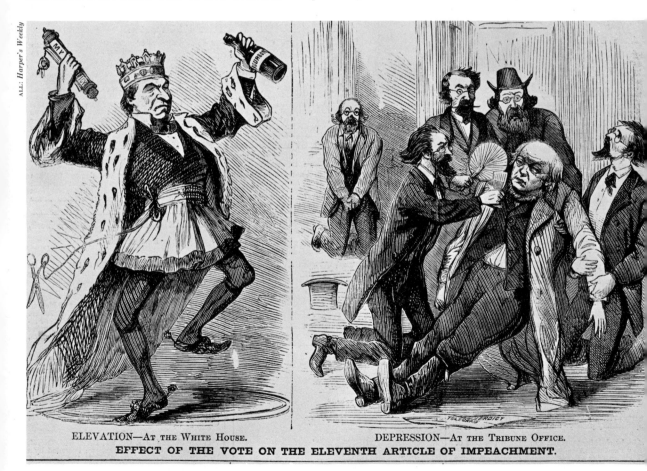

ELEVATION—At the White House.   DEPRESSION—At the Tribune Office.
EFFECT OF THE VOTE ON THE ELEVENTH ARTICLE OF IMPEACHMENT.

Impartial in its irreverence, Harper's Weekly *illustrated the different responses to Johnson's acquittal. At left, "King Andy" does a dance, his symbolic mace matched by a bottle of whisky, his tailor's scissors still fastened to his regal robes. At right, editor Horace Greeley faints in horrified shock after hearing the verdict.*

449

Because Mrs. Andrew Johnson was ill with tuberculosis, the President's daughter, Martha Johnson Patterson (left), served as White House hostess during his administration. The gold snuffbox above was a gift to Johnson from a visiting party of California gold miners. At an auction of Confederate booty held after the conclusion of the Civil War, Johnson purchased the elaborate coffee maker below. It had been owned by none other than his old Senate antagonist, Confederate President Jefferson Davis.

"I MISS MY OLD FRIENDS"

Andrew Johnson held no grudges. True, he sought complete vindication, but he did not try to degrade his impeachers. He regarded the underhandedness of War Secretary Stanton as contemptible, but he said little against Congressman Stevens and Senator Sumner, who had at least fought him openly. He buried the past; he was characterized by his secretary as having "a heart full of kindness." During his final months in office he allowed his daughter, Martha Patterson, to enliven the White House with a series of parties—formal parties and informal ones, parties for the important and unimportant, parties even for children. And he left Washington with a modest degree of popularity. Six years later he was back, the only former Chief Executive to take a seat in the United States Senate. His return was triumphant—it brought tears to his eyes—but created a problem for Senator Oliver P. Morton. Once Johnson's friend, he had done a turnabout and voted to convict; as his colleagues greeted and embraced the returned ex-President, Morton hovered in a shadow. Nevertheless Johnson spotted him, approached him, extended his hand, which, with great relief, Morton shook. "I miss my old friends," Senator Johnson said sadly as he took his seat, "Fessenden, Fowler, Trumbull, Grimes, Henderson, Ross, all are gone. . . ." Gone indeed: Andrew Johnson had named six of the seven Republican senators who had given up their legislative careers to vote for his acquittal in 1868.

Living with the Johnsons in the White House were their two sons, two daughters, and five grandchildren. Pictured above and below are Martha's two children, Mary Belle and Andrew.

451

FACTS IN SUMMARY: ANDREW JOHNSON

CHRONOLOGY

UNITED STATES		JOHNSON					
Madison elected President	1808	*Born December 29*	Annexation of Texas	1845			
War with England	1812		Oregon boundary settled	1846			
Monroe elected President	1816		War with Mexico				
Missouri Compromise	1820		Gold discovered in California	1848			
	1822	*Becomes tailor's apprentice*	Taylor inaugurated as President	1849			
Monroe Doctrine	1823		Fillmore becomes President	1850			
John Quincy Adams elected President by Congress	1825		Compromise of 1850				
			Uncle Tom's Cabin published	1852			
	1826	*Moves to Greeneville, Tennessee*	Pierce elected President				
	1827	*Marries Eliza McCardle*	Gadsden Purchase	1853	*Elected governor of Tennessee*		
Jackson elected President	1828	*Elected alderman*	Kansas-Nebraska Act	1854			
	1830	*Elected mayor of Greeneville*	Republican party formed				
	1835	*Elected to Tennessee legislature*		1855	*Re-elected governor*		
Van Buren elected President	1836		Civil war in Kansas	1856			
			Buchanan elected President				
Harrison elected President	1840		Dred Scott decision	1857	*Elected to U.S. Senate*		
Tyler becomes President	1841		John Brown's raid	1859			
	1843	*Elected to first of five terms in U.S. House of Representatives*	Lincoln elected President	1860	*Supports Breckinridge for President*		
			South Carolina secedes		*Opposes secession of Southern states*		

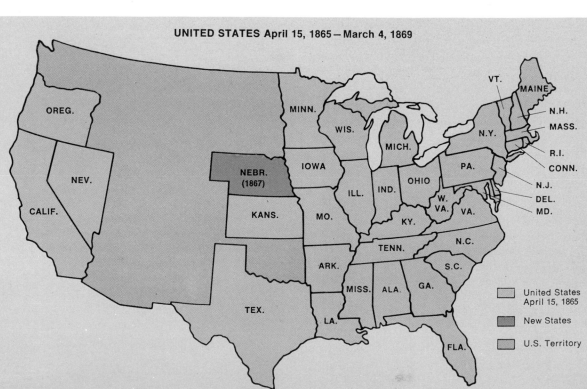

UNITED STATES April 15, 1865 — March 4, 1869

United States April 15, 1865

New States

U.S. Territory

Fort Sumter bombarded	1861	
First Bull Run		
Shiloh	1862	*Appointed military governor of Tennessee*
Antietam		
Emancipation Proclamation	1863	
Chancellorsville		
Vicksburg		
Gettysburg		
Lincoln re-elected President	1864	*Elected Vice President*
Lee surrenders at Appomattox	1865	*Becomes President*
		Issues proclamation of amnesty
Lincoln assassinated		
Congress opposes Johnson's Reconstruction program		*Clashes with Congress over Reconstruction*
Thirteenth Amendment ratified		
Civil Rights Act passed over veto	1866	*Vetoes New Freedmen's Bureau bill*
Congress refuses to seat delegates from South		*Orders U.S. troops to Mexican border*
New Freedmen's Bureau bill passed over veto		*Vetoes Civil Rights Act*
First Reconstruction Act passed over veto	1867	*Vetoes first Reconstruction Act*
		Authorizes purchase of Alaska
House of Representatives impeaches Johnson	1868	*Attempts to oust Secretary of War Stanton*
Grant elected President		*Impeached by the House of Representatives*
		Acquitted by the Senate
	1869	*Retires to Tennessee*
Grant re-elected President	1872	
	1874	*Elected to U.S. Senate*
	1875	*Dies July 31*

BIOGRAPHICAL FACTS

BIRTH: Raleigh, N.C., Dec. 29, 1808

ANCESTRY: Scotch-Irish and English

FATHER: Jacob Johnson; b. England; d. Raleigh, N.C., 1812

FATHER'S OCCUPATION: Laborer

MOTHER: Mary McDonough Johnson; d. 1856

BROTHER: William (1804–?)

WIFE: Eliza McCardle; b. Leesburg, Tenn., Oct. 4, 1810; d. Greene County, Tenn., Jan. 15, 1876

MARRIAGE: Greeneville, Tenn., Dec. 17, 1827

CHILDREN: Martha (1828–?); Charles (1830–1863); Mary (1832–1883); Robert (1834–1869); Andrew (1852–1879)

HOME: Greeneville, Tenn.

EDUCATION: Self-taught

RELIGIOUS AFFILIATION: No denomination

Harper's Weekly

This cartoon depicts Johnson (left) and Congressman Thaddeus Stevens as the drivers of colliding trains.

OCCUPATIONS BEFORE PRESIDENCY: Tailor; legislator

PRE-PRESIDENTIAL OFFICES: Alderman; Mayor; Member of Tenn. Legislature; Member of U.S. House of Representatives; Governor of Tennessee; Member of U.S. Senate; Vice President

POLITICAL PARTY: Democratic; elected Vice President on National Union ticket

AGE AT INAUGURATION: 56

OCCUPATION AFTER PRESIDENCY: Senator

DEATH: Carter County, Tenn., July 31, 1875

PLACE OF BURIAL: Andrew Johnson National Cemetery, Greeneville, Tenn.

THE JOHNSON ADMINISTRATION

INAUGURATION: April 15, 1865; Kirkwood House, Washington, D.C.

SECRETARY OF STATE: William H. Seward

SECRETARY OF THE TREASURY: Hugh McCulloch

SECRETARY OF WAR: Edwin M. Stanton; John M. Schofield (from June 1, 1868)

ATTORNEY GENERAL: Henry Stanberry; William M. Evarts (from July 20, 1868)

POSTMASTER GENERAL: Alexander W. Randall

SECRETARY OF THE NAVY: Gideon Welles

SECRETARY OF THE INTERIOR: James Harlan; Orville H. Browning (from Sept. 1, 1866)

39th CONGRESS (March 4, 1865–March 4, 1867):
Senate: 42 Unionists; 10 Democrats
House: 149 Unionists; 42 Democrats

40th CONGRESS (March 4, 1867–March 4, 1869):
Senate: 42 Republicans; 11 Democrats
House: 143 Republicans; 49 Democrats

STATE ADMITTED: Nebraska (1867)

ULYSSES SIMPSON GRANT

Nothing," said Ulysses S. Grant of presidential-hopeful General Winfield Scott in 1846, "so popularizes a candidate for high civil positions as military victories." Scott did not win the Presidency, but Grant, the supreme Union hero of the Civil War, proved his own point. When Lincoln issued a call for federal volunteers in April, 1861, thirty-eight-year-old "Sam" Grant was imprisoned by poverty and despondency: he was a West Point graduate with no prospects, performing menial odd jobs and haunted by the memory of forced resignation from the Army for excessive drinking. Three years later he would be general in chief of the Union armies. Seven years later he would be elected President.

Grant was born on April 27, 1822, in a two-room frame house overlooking the Ohio River at Point Pleasant, Ohio. After a solemn family assembly to vote the future hero a name, the child was christened Hiram Ulysses Grant; later the boy himself changed it to Ulysses Hiram Grant, to avoid initials that spelled "HUG." It was the beginning of Grant's continuing battle to secure his name against ridicule.

Grant's father, Jesse, was an enterprising tanner who had learned his trade under John Brown's father. Jesse was a Whig (he supported Jackson, however), a Methodist, and a Mason. He loved to talk politics, forging a second career out of letters to the local editor. Jesse had left Kentucky at twenty-one because, he said, "I would not own slaves and I would not live where there were slaves." Grant's mother, Hannah Simpson, was a farmer's daughter, quietly strong and direct, of whom her son said, "I never saw my mother cry."

In 1823 the Grants moved to Georgetown, Ohio, where Ulysses was to spend his boyhood. The family—Ulysses was one of six children—was free of both hardship and luxury. "Useless" Grant, as wags liked to call him,

U. S. Grant as he appeared in 1865

This oil painting depicts Grant's birthplace at Point Pleasant, Ohio. He lived there for only one year.

farmed, hauled wood, helped his father at the tannery, ran his own wagon-taxi to Cincinnati when he was ten, and earned a formidable reputation for breaking difficult horses. He attended school regularly until he was seventeen, recalling later that he had been assured that "a noun is the name of a thing" so often, he came to believe it.

Grant was a diffident, quiet boy, blue-eyed, russet-haired, pink-cheeked, and fair-skinned. A muscular five feet one inch at seventeen (he was to grow seven more inches at West Point), he had unusually small hands and feet. And though sometimes prankish, young Grant was essentially a pleasant, retiring boy who wanted to be called Hiram and be let alone.

In 1839 Jesse Grant received word that the West Point appointment he had sought for his son appeared certain. "But I won't go," Grant informed his father. Jesse said that he would most certainly go, and, said Grant, "I thought so, too, if he did."

Still, Grant was a reluctant soldier. He relished the initial trip to West Point chiefly as an opportunity to travel to New York and Philadelphia. "When these places were visited," he confessed, he "would have been glad to have had a steamboat or railroad collision, or any other accident happen" to make him unable to enroll at the Point.

"A military life," he was to say candidly, "had no charms for me, and I had not the faintest idea of staying in the army even if I should be graduated, which I did not expect." But for good or ill, he was now Cadet Ulysses Simpson Grant, his name in-

correctly registered by his congressman. From the first, he was to his classmates "Uncle Sam" or "Sam" Grant, as fellow students hailed "U. S. Grant" on the roster.

Cadet Grant detested Academy discipline and was an indifferent scholar. (He seized eagerly upon periodic reports in the newspaper that Congress wished to abolish the Academy as undemocratic.) He flavored the rigid curriculum with large doses of Sir Walter Scott and Frederick Marryat and was elected to preside over the cadet literary society, "The Dialectic." He also found diversion from regimen in perfecting his horsemanship; his equestrian high-jump record would remain unbeaten at the Point for twenty-five years.

As a cadet, Grant received numerous demerits for slovenly dress, unsoldierly bearing, and tardiness. Not a man for dancing or social etiquette, he preferred sauntering off to a local pub for off-limits drinking. Promoted to sergeant in his third year, he confessed that the higher rank was "too much" for him, and he willingly served his senior year as a private.

Despite these setbacks, Grant learned to admire the Academy as "the most beautiful place I have ever seen," as well as for the future security it promised. "I would not go away on any account," he wrote to a cousin. "If a man graduates here, he is safe for life, let him go where he will."

Grant graduated from West Point in 1843, academically 21st in a graduating class of 39, and 156th in conduct among the Academy's 223 cadets. The Academy's best horseman requested, but was denied, a coveted cavalry commission. He was named a brevet second lieutenant in the Fourth U.S. Infantry at $779 per year and was assigned to Jefferson Barracks near St. Louis.

While at Jefferson Barracks, Grant made the acquaintance of comely and pert Miss Julia Dent, sister of his fourth-year roommate at the Point. Julia was the amiable, sensible daughter of a well-to-do colonel, Frederick Dent, who owned a plantation near the barracks. A distinguished horsewoman, Julia caught Ulysses' romantic eye at first sight. They married on August 22, 1848, and enjoyed a stable and happy relationship throughout almost thirty-seven years of marriage. The Grants would have four children: Frederick, Ulysses Simpson, Jr., Jesse, and Nellie, who would marry an Englishman, Algernon Sartoris, in a sumptuous White House wedding.

Grant was stationed for two years in Missouri and Louisiana before joining Zachary Taylor's army at Corpus Christi, Texas, prior to the Mexican War. From July, 1846, he was a regimental quartermaster, fighting under both Taylor and Winfield Scott. Active in all major battles except Buena Vista, Sam Grant distinguished himself for bravery in hand-to-hand combat, once making a heroic dash through enemy-held territory to secure ammunition for his troops. He later marched with Scott from Veracruz to Mexico City, and he emerged from the war as a first lieutenant and brevet captain.

Like Lincoln, Lieutenant Grant was thoroughly opposed to the Mexican War, which was being waged, he said, as "a war of conquest." But despite his convictions, Grant obeyed the command to fight the Mexicans. "Experience proves that the man who obstructs a war in which his nation is engaged, no matter whether right or wrong, occupies no enviable place in life or history," he explained.

In Mexico Grant felt the injustice of the war even more deeply, his heart going out to the ragged and starving Mexicans. It was a side of Grant not often remembered during his later military victories or during the corruption of his Presidency. It was the Grant who, despite the vicious Civil War title of "Butcher," was horrified by the cruelty of hunting and found bullfights "sickening." It was the Grant, too, who preferred to sit out in the cold, drenching rain at Shiloh rather than in a warm tent where he might see the blood of his soldiers in surgery. "I never went into a battle willingly or with enthusiasm," he would confess in later years.

When the war ended, Grant was stationed at Sackets Harbor, New York. But whatever domestic pleasure he and Julia might have shared was roughly curtailed in 1852 when the captain was assigned to bleak frontier posts on the Pacific Coast. Julia, already a mother, did not accompany him. After a treacherous crossing of the Panama Isthmus, in which cholera killed one-third of his companions, he arrived in San Fran-

U.S. MILITARY ARCHIVES

That Grant loved horses is evident in this affectionate drawing, which he did while at West Point.

457

cisco, moving north to Fort Vancouver (near today's Portland, Oregon) in late September.

It was at Fort Vancouver that the great shadow that would sully Grant's name first began to descend: compulsive, excessive drinking. The thirty-year-old soldier missed his young wife, longed for a first look at his second son, Ulysses, Jr., and bitterly regretted the fact that he could not afford to bring them west. His excesses were noted by General George B. McClellan, among others. "It was not that Grant drank much," a friend recalled. "The trouble was that a very little would . . . thicken his never glib or lively tongue. On far less liquor than many a comrade carried without a sign, Grant would appear half stupefied."

Grant's tippling became a critical issue when he was summoned to Fort Humboldt at Humboldt Bay, California, in the summer of 1853. His mission: to take command of a company under Colonel Robert C. Buchanan, a fastidious officer with whom Grant had already exchanged angry words at Jefferson Barracks. Despondent, Grant found sedation in drinking—heavily, often, and straight.

In April, 1854, Sam Grant, then a commissioned captain, was discovered drunk in public by Buchanan, who promptly demanded that Grant either resign or stand trial. Fearing a scandal and the heartbreak a trial would bring to Julia, Grant chose to resign. He was relieved of his command on May 1, his resignation having been accepted as tendered by Secretary of War Jefferson Davis. "If you ever hear from me again," Sam told his comrades, "it will probably be as a well-to-do farmer."

Grant now faced eight ineffably bitter years of squalor and failure. He, Julia, and the family moved at first to a sixty-acre tract, twelve miles from St. Louis, that had been given to Julia by her father. Grant cleared the land, squared logs, and built a house. By the spring of 1855, he was plowing and planting, hauling cordwood for sale to St. Louis, and hoping to be free and clear within three years. But Grant lacked the capital to make the farm a paying enter-prise, and crop prices collapsed in the Panic of 1857. Grant leased the property and took over the old Dent farm, until "fever and ague" put him to bed. Subsequent efforts to earn money as a real-estate agent and collector of overdue accounts also failed.

In desperation, Grant appealed to his father, who offered him only an $800-per-year post as a clerk in his Galena, Illinois, leather shop under the patronizing direction of two younger brothers. There Grant lifted heavy stock, unloaded wagons, and kept books. Spiritually he was at rock bottom.

When President Lincoln issued his call for seventy-five thousand Union volunteers on April 15, 1861, Captain Sam Grant came to life, promptly offering to drill a company of Galena volunteers. He served next as a clerk in the state adjutant general's office. He appealed to the U.S. adjutant general in Washington to give him a regiment and let him fight, but his request went unanswered. McClellan, soon to command all the Union armies, refused to see him. Undeterred, Grant persevered and in June, 1861, was appointed a colonel to lead the 21st Illinois Volunteers. In August he was named a brigadier general in charge of troops in southern Illinois and southeastern Missouri.

Early in 1862 Grant's military star began its incredible national rise. He captured Confederate-held Fort Henry on the Tennessee River, then Fort Donelson on the Cumberland, pushing the enemy back to Tennessee. The North was jubilant; Grant was named a major general. The Battle of Shiloh, in which Grant drove the Confederates back despite initial misjudgments, took place in April, 1862; Memphis fell to the Union forces by June 6, establishing federal control of the Mississippi as far as Vicksburg. By July 4, 1863, Vicksburg itself had fallen; five days later Grant took Port Hudson, securing Union control of the entire Mississippi. In late November, in the Battle of Chattanooga, General Grant—then commander of the Union armies of the West—drove the Confederate forces out of Tennessee and opened the road to Georgia.

On March 9, 1864, a grateful Lincoln

This cartoon told Secretary of War Stanton literally to get off the back of the commanding general.

named Grant a lieutenant general and three days later placed him in charge of all the Union armies. There were still rumors of his drinking, still complaints of his shabbiness, still those who insisted that he was a disgrace to the Army. But in June, Grant began his historic siege of Petersburg. Almost a year later, the Confederate armies were caught between his forces in the north and Sherman's troops in the south. When Richmond surrendered on April 3, Grant pursued and surrounded Lee's men.

On Palm Sunday, April 9, 1865, General Lee surrendered to Grant in the Virginia village of Appomattox Court House. On this historic occasion, the Union's chief general appeared wearing a borrowed private's uniform (decorated only by his lieutenant general's shoulder straps) and muddy boots. As he looked at Lee in defeat, Grant could feel only compassion. He had considered the Confederate cause "one of the worst for which a people ever fought," but now he felt profoundly sad.

After chatting about old Army days in Mexico, Grant informed Lee of the magnanimous terms of surrender on which he and Lincoln had agreed. There would be no reprisals, no prisons, no hangings. The Confederate officers would be allowed to keep their side arms; to deprive them of these, Grant felt, would be an "unnecessary humiliation." The Confederate troops were only to sign paroles and were "not to be disturbed by the United States authority so long as they observe[d] their paroles and the laws in force where they reside[d]." Informed that Lee's men were hungry, Grant ordered Union rations shared with them immediately. As news of the surrender reached the troops, Union artillery burst in celebration, but Grant ordered it stopped. "We did not," Grant said later, "want to exult over their downfall."

But the victorious North did exult, and Grant's name shone second only to Lincoln's. Even the fallen South hailed Grant for his manly consideration and kind terms at Appomattox. Wherever the General went, he was mobbed by crowds. In Washington, Lincoln received him with deep emotion, inviting the Grants to join him and Mrs. Lincoln at Ford's Theater. Grant promptly accepted the invitation, but Julia decided that they should not go, offering the excuse that she wanted to get back to her children. It was a fateful decision, for Grant's name, too, was on the assassins' list. En route to New Jersey, Grant heard the shocking report of Lincoln's assassination and returned to the Capital. "It would be impossible for me," he wrote, "to describe the feeling that overcame me at the news. . . ."

Grant's position under President Johnson was extremely awkward. On the one hand, the new President was his constitutional Commander in Chief. On the other hand, both he and the President knew that Grant now stood first in the eyes of the nation, enjoying unprecedented esteem. Johnson also realized that Grant was the inevitable Republican presidential candidate for 1868.

Johnson tried to exploit Grant's popularity by sending him on a tour of the South in 1865. But he and the General were men of different mind and mettle; and any doubt of their basic disparity and popular standing was dispelled when the President, contrary to Grant's handwritten terms at Appomattox, sought to have General Lee arrested for treason. Grant was enraged that Johnson would even contemplate breaking the nation's—and his—solemn word at the surrender table. When Lee appealed to him, Grant intervened on his behalf, threatening to take his case to the people if the President did not desist. Johnson backed down.

For the most part, Grant maintained a studied public neutrality on divisive political issues, remaining outwardly impartial even during Johnson's impeachment proceedings. Even when Johnson tried to fire Edwin M. Stanton as Secretary of War, Grant—who had been named interim Secretary—maintained neutrality, resigning when Congress refused to permit Stanton's dismissal.

Gradually, however, Grant dropped the façade of neutrality. Though approached by both parties for the presidential nomination, he found himself drawn strategically to the Radical Republican position, which favored the immediate enfranchisement of the Negro, as a counterbalance to what he considered excessive Southern influence in the White House.

Grant was nominated for the Presidency by acclamation on the first ballot at the Republican convention of 1868 in Chicago. Speaker of the House Schuyler Colfax of Indiana was named his running mate. Only four words of Grant's reaction to the news of his nomination remain to posterity: "Let us have peace."

But if Grant wanted peace, his party did not. The campaign was grossly intemperate, clearly dominated by the incendiary Radicals. "Vote As You Shot," Republican posters proclaimed. Grant was apotheosized as the almost superhuman savior of the Union, the hero of Vicksburg, now trampling the Confederate flag in the dust. Grant's Democratic opponent, Horatio Seymour, wartime Unionist governor of New York, was pilloried as a Copperhead—a Northerner with Southern sympathies—and a tool of Tammany Hall. For all his popularity, however, Grant won the Presidency by a surprisingly small margin of only 300,000 votes.

"The office," said Grant in his Inaugural Address, "has come to me unsought; I commence its duties untrammeled." He hinted at what his relationship with Congress would be as Chief Executive: he would be a prime minister, a first among equals. "I shall on all subjects have a policy to recommend," he explained, "but none to enforce against the will of the people." As for the critical issues of Reconstruction, which his own campaign had further embittered, Grant now urged that they "be approached calmly, without prejudice, hate, or sectional pride. . . ."

The new President advocated prompt payments on the nation's staggering war debt of $400,000,000; a return, when possible, to specie currency; and a sounder national credit. Soon to profit from mining stocks,

MUSEUM OF FINE ARTS, BOSTON, M. AND M. KAROLIK COLLECTION

This bronze statuette, by Auguste Peyrau, commemorated the inauguration of Colfax, left, and Grant.

Grant saluted Providence's gift of "a strong box in the precious metals of the West, which we are now forging the key to unlock." Assuring industry and commerce encouragement, President Grant also urged fairer treatment of the Indians. He concluded by asking for passage of the Fifteenth Amendment, which would give Negroes the constitutional right to vote. (On March 30, 1870, the amendment was ratified.)

General Grant presided over the United States at the beginning of an era of fabulous growth and optimism, creativity and invention, glory and shame. It was the era of Mark Twain and New York's notorious Boss Tweed, of Susan B. Anthony, Horatio Alger, and J. P. Morgan. Two months after Grant's inauguration, the Union Pacific and Central Pacific railroads were linked in Utah. The thrust of Western settlement, spurred by the Homestead Act (passed under Lincoln), continued to carve farms out of prairies. From New York to the Mississippi, commerce hummed, quickened by industrial steam and the refrigerated railroad car.

It was a brash, heady era—the "Gilded Age"—in which no one wanted the federal government meddling in his affairs, unless that intervention took the form of railroad subsidies, grants of free public land, a protective tariff to stem foreign competition and keep prices up for consumers, or defense against the Indians as settlers moved west. In Ulysses S. Grant the movers of American society had precisely the man they wanted to preside over their expansion and pursuit of wealth. They desired a "chairman of the board" who would defer to their sound judgments in arcane matters of finance and legislation. And that is what Grant wanted, too. A President, he believed, should follow the will of the people and administer the laws passed by their elected representatives.

Grant's was a narrow interpretation of executive power, one calculated to please congressional bosses such as Roscoe Conkling, Simon Cameron, and James G. Blaine, who virtually governed the nation through control of patronage and federal disbursements. Grant's attitude was epitomized in his first annual message. "The appropriations estimated for river and harbor improvements and for fortifications are submitted . . ." he declared. "Whatever amount Congress may deem proper to appropriate for these purposes will be expended."

If hope lingered that the Grant administration would provide an inspired, reforming government, it died when the General announced his Cabinet appointments, most of which were made on the basis of personal friendship. An undistinguished congressman, Elihu Washburne, was elevated to Secretary of State. He was replaced two weeks later, however, by New York's highly competent Hamilton Fish, who would serve under Grant in lone distinction. As Secretary of War, Grant appointed General John Schofield, who, having enjoyed this honor for one week, stepped aside for Grant's Civil War confidant, General John A. Rawlins. A Philadelphia businessman, Adolph E. Borie (whose principal distinction seems to have been his wealth), was named Secretary of the Navy. The Senate confirmed the appointment of Alexander T. Stewart, a rich New York merchant, as Secretary of the Treasury, but then passed a law specifically forbidding anyone with a financial interest in business to head the Treasury Department. Unimpressed, Grant urged the Senate to make Stewart an exception. But the President was rebuffed, and the Treasury post went to George S. Boutwell of Massachusetts, a leader in the impeachment of Andrew Johnson.

It was a triumph of cronyism and idolization of the rich. "A great soldier," snapped Henry Adams, "might be a baby politician." When it became known that Stewart had sent costly gifts to Grant and that Borie had entertained him lavishly, the American people began to share Adams' indignation. Nor were minds relieved when the General nominated as minister to Belgium a friend who was a livery-stable supervisor.

President Grant functioned under major limitations: an unwillingness to consult with informed counselors who might have taken his chestnuts out of the fire or roasted them more palatably, and a consuming awe of the

Julia, with a cast in one eye, rarely faced a camera head on. Grant said he liked her eyes crossed.

world's rich and influential. His mistakes were titanic. He permitted himself, for example, to be entertained publicly by the infamous speculators James Fisk and Jay Gould, allowing them to wine and dine him aboard their yacht and to urge upon him their conviction that the government should stay out of the gold market, which Fisk and Gould were conspiring to corner. Their object: to buy relatively inexpensive gold in volume, drive its price up to maximum height, and sell it at exorbitant rates. They knew that the federal government could, at any time, decrease the price of gold by offering more of its vast gold reserves for sale. It was important for Gould and Fisk, therefore, that the government be persuaded either not to release its gold reserves or, that failing, that they be informed in advance about Treasury plans. Convinced they had persuaded the President to do nothing, Fisk and Gould made allies of Abel Corbin and Mrs. Corbin—the President's sister—who assured them information regarding Treasury intentions by securing the appointment of General Daniel Butterfield as United States subtreasurer in New York.

Informed by Horace Greeley and others,

the public became aware of the intended swindle. Grant's brother-in-law wrote to the President, begging him not to permit the government to sell gold. Julia Grant replied for the President, urging Corbin to get out while the getting was good. Grant, hoping against hope for a cordial way out, ultimately ordered the Treasury to release federal gold. The price of gold fell, and the conspiracy was foiled. But the administration, almost directly involved in the scandal, never escaped its taint.

In 1870 another scandal ripped through the administration, this time in connection with the Dominican Republic in the Caribbean. The dictator of that nation, Buenaventura Báez, surrounded and buttressed by financial speculators, informed the United States of his desire to sell the country at a profit to himself. Bypassing Secretary of State Fish, Grant sent his personal aide, Colonel Orville E. Babcock, to work out a deal with Báez. To Fish's dismay, Babcock returned with a treaty to which Grant promptly pledged full support. The President also dispatched warships to the island to protect Báez against threats to his life.

When he learned of these events, Secretary Fish threatened to resign. But Grant, in an almost unique display of executive will, remained adamant in support of the treaty. When Senate opposition to the deal flared, Grant personally visited the Capitol and lobbied in the Senate corridors. Still, the Senate refused to ratify the treaty. If only his plan had been adopted, Grant said, the recently freed Negroes might have been deported to a rich new country of their own.

Grant's first administration was also rocked by a scandal at the New York Custom House, whose collector, Thomas Murphy, had been a personal appointee and intimate race-track associate of the President's. Murphy inherited and sustained a system of graft under which a Colonel Leet, himself a former member of Grant's personal staff, used presidential influence to secure a monopoly on the storage of imports. Leet charged an entire month's rent for one day's storage in the Port of New York, reaping huge profits. Faced with a presidential election in 1872 and a congressional investigation of the scandal, the administration reluctantly sacked Murphy. Grant, however, paid tribute to his "honesty."

In the realm of Reconstruction, despite Grant's professed acceptance of Lincoln's policy of reconciliation, the administration pursued a frantic policy of vengeance. As President, Grant became both the victim and the instrument of his Radical support. Northern carpetbag governments in the South, established to advance Northern interests as much as to aid the Negro freedman, continued to anger Southern whites, who saw them for the ruse they were and who bristled under the Negro militia and stifling taxes imposed by the North. The South responded with the Ku-Klux Klan and other vengeful secret societies.

Spurred by the Radicals, the Union League, and other wavers of the "bloody shirt," Grant lent strong support in 1871 to the passage of the astonishing Ku-Klux Act, which authorized direct federal intervention in the legal structure of the South. The President was given the power to declare martial law and suspend the writ of habeas corpus at will anywhere in the South. Those accused of crimes were to be turned over directly to federal authorities, bypassing Southern courts and juries.

Incensed Southern whites were close to rebellion. In South Carolina, Grant used his new power to declare martial law in nine counties and suspend habeas corpus. Mass arrests and trials before packed juries followed. Under the act, some 7,400 were indicted, and while there were few convictions, this humiliation of the South wrote a new legacy of bitterness.

Grant's first term, however, was not totally without achievement. The government moved closer to responsibility in paying the national debt and in creating a stable currency and a more reliable national credit. Internationally, it was beginning to emerge from insularity. Under Secretary of State Fish—who graced the Grant Cabinet, as Richard Hofstadter has written, "like a

jewel in the head of a toad"—America negotiated with Great Britain an arbitrated settlement whereby Britain agreed to pay the United States $15,500,000 for damages inflicted on the Union by the vessel *Alabama*, which the British had sold to the Confederates. Washington and London also agreed on the southern Canadian border and on fishing rights in adjoining waters.

But not even Fish's unimpeachable integrity and distinction could compensate for the incredible presidential retinue of grafters, scheming speculators, and calculating merchants and industrialists or for the disproportionate influence of the military. And rumors of the President's inordinate drinking persisted, despite the insistence of friends that he had given up liquor immediately upon arrival at the White House.

Nor was the criticism of Grant limited to the Democrats. While Grant was easily renominated by the regular Republicans at the convention of 1872, dissident Republicans and other foes of his policies nominated Editor Horace Greeley for President in a newly organized Liberal Republican party. The Greeley men called for civil service reforms, less stringent Reconstruction policies, a general amnesty for the South, and impartial suffrage. In response the Grant forces pursued the same poster tactics used in 1868: Grant in his tanner's apron and military boots holding the Union shield. The President won re-election, 286 electoral votes to 66. Greeley, who had been endorsed by the Democrats, took only six states.

"I have been the subject of abuse and slander," Grant said at the end of his second Inaugural Address, "scarcely ever equalled in political history, which today I feel that I can afford to disregard in view of your verdict, which I gratefully accept as my vindication." He again expressed regret that the nation had failed to annex the Dominican Republic, urged the reform of the civil service, and asked for clemency toward the Indians. And in a statement that would please both Radicals and Southern white supremacists, he concluded: "Social equality is not a subject to be legislated upon, nor

HORACE GREELEY

Horace Greeley was more a social reformer than a politician when he ran for President in 1872. Founder and editor of the New York *Tribune*, Greeley had issued his first edition in 1841, pledging that his paper would stand "removed alike from servile partisanship" and "mincing neutrality." He succeeded in both objectives, shaping public opinion through the high moral tone of his editorials. Espousing Fourierism, homestead legislation, labor unions, and women's rights, he attacked all forms of social and economic tyranny. He supported the free-soil movement; and while he advocated preservation of the Union, he was willing to see it dissolved rather than allow the extension of slavery. A founder of the Republican party, he supported Lincoln in 1860 but attacked his cautious emancipation policy. Hailing Grant's election, he later denounced the administration as corrupt and illiberal toward the South. When the Liberal Republicans split from the regular party in 1872, Greeley became their candidate and was also endorsed by the Democrats in an effort to block Grant. Urging a conciliatory attitude toward the South, Greeley failed to carry a single Northern state. The vituperation of his opponents hurt him deeply. Crushed by the magnitude of his defeat, the death of his wife, and the loss of his editorship, Greeley died, tragically insane, soon after the 1872 election.

shall I ask that anything be done to advance the social status of the colored man, except to give him a fair chance to develop what there is good in him, give him access to the schools, and when he travels let him feel assured that his conduct will regulate the treatment and fare he will receive." The pattern of Reconstruction was now clear: it would simply be left to die. The South would be allowed to establish the *status quo ante bellum*, if not in words, most assuredly in fact. When the Democrats gained control of the House in 1874, in a clear repudiation of Radical Reconstructionism, the days of the fire-eaters were numbered.

If General Grant and his entourage hoped for a term less tempestuous than the first, they were to face major disappointments. A month before he was re-elected, another national scandal began breaking wide open and led to a congressional investigation ending in February, 1873. Even before Grant's first election to the Presidency, promoters of the Union Pacific Railroad had organized a camouflage company, Crédit Mobilier, to divert profits from railroad construction and to control charges levied by the railroad, itself heavily subsidized by the government.

The tone of the company's operations is typified by the fact that in 1868 its total dividends were more than 340 per cent of the total par value of the company's stock. One of the corporation's prime movers, Congressman Oakes Ames, realizing that Congress might one day investigate the fraud, had distributed blocks of the valuable stock among members of Congress, in whose hands, Ames reasoned, it would be most beneficial. Vice President Schuyler Colfax, dumped in the 1872 campaign because he dared presidential ambitions, was also given some of the stock, as were his successor, Henry Wilson, a number of Republican senators, and a congressman named James A. Garfield. While Grant himself owned railroad stock that would one day help to finance his world travel, it is not known whether he, too, was approached by Crédit Mobilier operators. It was a sorry spectacle of official corruption. And although the swindle had its genesis before Grant became President, the fact that it involved many of his associates and was exposed during his Presidency further tarnished his name.

Nor did the Panic of 1873, precipitated by uncontrolled credit, inflation, wild speculation, and overexpansion, enhance Grant's now-dwindling public stature. With the collapse of Wall Street's powerful Jay Cooke and Company and the subsequent stock market decline, pressure mounted for a new greenback bill to inflate the currency. Grant's veto of the popular greenback law passed by Congress further inflamed resentment toward his administration. In the wake of the panic, unemployment soared and businesses failed. Then, incredibly, new scandals broke.

The notorious "Whisky Ring" was uncovered in 1875. Headed by General John McDonald, supervisor of the United States Internal Revenue Bureau in St. Louis, the ring worked in cooperation with a network of revenue officers and distillers who had highly placed allies in the federal Treasury itself. Their system: abating taxes paid on whisky and diverting the unreported revenue to their own pockets or to Republican campaign coffers.

Previous complaints made directly to the President, urging that the ring be exposed and broken, elicited no response. Eventually an agent was sent to St. Louis to investigate, but he was silenced when he returned to Washington. Later Grant and his personal secretary, General Orville E. Babcock, were guests of McDonald in St. Louis, and Grant accepted as a gift from the Whisky Ring a costly team of horses.

With the advent of a new Secretary of the Treasury, Benjamin Bristow, the ring's days were numbered. Bristow uncovered the fact that Babcock had received a direct bribe from the ring to remain silent and to have the investigation called off. McDonald was indicted and jailed. Babcock, though indicted, retained Grant's undiminished support and was declared not guilty.

Corruption also engulfed the Post Office and Interior departments, and the payrolls

In a rare anti-Grant cartoon (called "In For It"), Thomas Nast depicted a full barrel of corruption.

of Navy yards were padded just before the elections by the Secretary of the Navy. But the crowning scandal of the Grant administration erupted when it was learned that the Secretary of War, General William W. Belknap, had received kickbacks from the sale of trading posts in the West. Again Grant rose to the defense of a man openly guilty of corruption, but his attempt to shield Belknap from impeachment was of no avail. Although Belknap resigned, an angry House voted impeachment proceedings. Administration efforts to bring the House investigating committee itself into court to discredit its case against Belknap were defied. But the trial in the Senate bordered on farce, the defense counsel ridiculing the accusers and anointing Belknap, who was acquitted, a loyal son of the Union.

The Belknap verdict was par for the course in an era in which Congress could increase its own pay, retroactive for two years, on the final day of its session in 1873. And although Congress also decreed equal pay for equal work for women in federal agencies and passed Grant's Resumption Act providing for specie payment by 1879, the prevailing tone on Capitol Hill was one of cynicism and chicanery.

Still, Grant's popularity was only slightly diminished, and there was some clamor for him to run again. But the House, in a 234–18 vote, declared that a third term would be "unwise, unpatriotic and fraught with peril to our free institutions." The General did not appear disappointed. "I never wanted to get out of a place as much as I did to get out of the Presidency," he would say. And he was quick to use his new leisure to realize an old boyhood dream: a trip around the world with all the fixings.

If Grant left the Presidency under a cloud, the world beyond the United States did not seem to know it. For the entire period of their travel abroad, the Grants were received everywhere as royalty. They dined with Queen Victoria at Windsor Castle and chatted with Disraeli and Bismarck. Mont Blanc and the Parthenon were illuminated in their honor. They sailed the Nile on the Khedive's own vessel, and they met Pope Leo XIII at the Vatican, Richard Wagner at Heidelberg, and the Czar in St. Petersburg. The Japanese Emperor gave his own sitting-room furniture to the Grants because Julia admired its lacquer finish.

Grant's popularity was again demonstrated by a series of receptions across the United States when he returned home in 1879. The scandals and cronies were forgotten, and the image of the plain soldier doing his job, sometimes let down by his friends but unblemished himself, emerged once more. The move by some Republican party leaders was predictable: Why not Grant for President again in 1880? Grant himself appeared open to a draft, and his name was placed in nomination. But the old soldier lost to Garfield.

Grant and Julia now turned their backs on politics. A fund of $100,000, raised by twenty friends, including A. J. Drexel and J. P. Morgan, enabled them to buy a mansion in New York City. In 1882 another friend, William H. Vanderbilt, lent Grant $150,000 to found a brokerage firm, Grant and Ward. Grant thus gave prestige and money to the fiscal operations of Ferdinand Ward and James D. Fish, who had earlier been in business with Grant's son, Ulysses, Jr. ("Buck"). In mid-1884 the firm suddenly failed, and Grant was left penniless and humiliated. Although Vanderbilt would gladly have written off the debt, the proud Grants turned all their property over to him.

Again Grant faced financial hardship. It would be somewhat relieved when Congress restored him to the rank and full pay of a general, but more money was needed to finance his household. To provide this, Grant accepted a generous offer by Mark Twain to publish his memoirs.

A few months earlier, Grant had felt the first stabbing pain of cancer in his throat. He had demanded, and received, the truth from his doctor: he was dying. It became difficult for the General to eat enough to live; the malignancy had spread to his tongue. But the old soldier had one final, personal battle to win, and despite the incessant pain and numbing sedation, he meant to win it. He would finish his memoirs.

Gradually, General Sam lost even the shy, quiet voice he had had. When he could no longer bear the pain of whispering dictation, he wrote himself. Eventually, he had to scribble his most elementary needs and wishes. As the memoirs neared conclusion, he laboriously wrote a confession to his doctor: "I am ready now to go at any time. I know there is nothing but suffering for me while I do live."

In June, 1885, Grant was moved to a cottage at Mount McGregor in the Adirondack foothills. There he was served tenderly and selflessly by Julia. On July 16, 1885, he completed his 295,000-word *Personal Memoirs*, which would earn $450,000 for Julia and his family within two years.

On July 22 the General, who had been forced to remain propped up in an armchair to avoid choking to death, asked to be put to bed. The next day he died.

Grant was buried on New York's Riverside Drive, in a funeral that rivaled Lincoln's in massive tribute. Four words are engraved on Grant's tomb: "Let us have peace." As Lincoln's favorite general, Grant had won peace for the nation. Now he had earned it for himself.

—WILSON SULLIVAN

A PICTURE PORTFOLIO

The brass matchbox above, one-tenth larger than its actual size, was a Grant presidential campaign item. Matches were struck on its underside.

OFFICER GRANT

Grant was about twenty-one years old and a brevet second lieutenant when the picture above was taken.

If the class had been turned the other end foremost I should have been near head," said Cadet U. S. Grant of his progress in French at West Point. Fearful of failing in his studies, Grant was also often out of step on parade and in drill; his informal nature was not suited to the Academy's spit-and-polish routine. But he came to excel in mathematics and envisioned a professorial career—first at the Point and then "in some respectable college." The Mexican War, however, derailed that train of thought. He emerged from it a brevet captain whose audacity at San Cosme, near Chapultepec, had helped break Santa Anna's inner lines at Mexico City. (Grant had set up a howitzer in a church belfry and peppered a crucial bastion.) Soon Grant was a happily married family man. Not particularly ambitious, Regimental Quartermaster Ulysses S. Grant appeared settled in a pleasant enough rut—that of an undistinguished officer in a small, peacetime army.

Lieutenant Grant took part in the fight for Chapultepec (the "hill of the grasshoppers") outside Mexico City

The aquatint of West Point, above, was made by W. J. Bennett in 1833, six years before Grant matriculated.

in September of 1847. The battle, depicted above by James Walker, hastened Santa Anna's surrender.

In 1860 Grant was in Galena, Illinois, clerking in his father's leather store, right, and trying to break a seemingly endless chain of bad luck. Years later, President Grant recalled the 1850's rather incredibly: "Those were happy days. I was doing the best I could to support my family." On the West Coast he had tried to supplement his Army income by selling farm produce and by running a billiard parlor; both enterprises failed. He drank, and his inability to hold his liquor ended his military career. Once, he compared experiences with another ex-officer—William Tecumseh Sherman, who called himself "a dead cock in a pit." Neither man knew then of the victories and cheers that would mark both of their futures.

The sketch above shows a Union charge at Shiloh where, on April 6 and 7, 1862, casualties totaled 23,741, nearly five hundred more Americans than fell in the Revolution, the War of 1812, and the Mexican War combined.

"HE FIGHTS"

I can't spare this man. He *fights*," said Lincoln to those urging him to sack Grant, whose unentrenched troops had sustained heavy casualties in a surprise Confederate attack at Shiloh. But Grant had stood his ground and the Rebels had been repulsed. Grant was a welcome change from the irresolute and bickering Union commanders who had plagued the President. (Later, commenting on rumors of Grant's drinking, Lincoln said that if he knew what kind of whisky Grant liked, he would send some to his other generals.) In the spring of 1861, a year before Shiloh, ex-Army officer Grant had led a mass meeting to raise volunteers at Galena; soon he was a state mustering officer; then he commanded a state regiment and by August was a brigadier general of volunteers. Six months later he displayed the firmness it would take to win the war: he demanded and got the "unconditional and immediate surrender" of Fort Donelson from General Simon Buckner, who had once lent Grant money. In the spring of 1863 Grant began his assault on Vicksburg, a campaign that would sunder the South and make him a major general in the regulars. He daringly isolated his army from other federal forces, chased the Confederates out of Jackson, wheeled, and pinned down Pemberton in Vicksburg. After his victories at Chattanooga, he was given supreme command. Grant knew total victory would come only through the relentless pressure of the North's superior numbers and matériel. Many cried "Butcher!" as casualty lists lengthened during the Virginia Campaign of 1864; but Grant had Lincoln's support, and the war of attrition at Petersburg brought the conflict close to an end. And as Grant dictated magnanimous terms at Appomattox, there were no Union hurrahs, but "an awed stillness rather," for Grant's vision of peace did not include subjugation of the vanquished.

LIBRARY OF CONGRESS; OVERLEAF: MUSEUM OF FINE ARTS, BOSTON, M. AND M. KAROLIK COLLECTION

Above, Lieutenant General Grant contemplates the action at City Point, Virginia, during the siege of Petersburg. The costly Virginia Campaign, with Petersburg its consummation, kept Lee bottled up, unable to aid Joe Johnston, who was retreating through the Carolinas pursued by Sherman's army.

The folk painting above fancifully depicts Grant's assault on General John Pemberton's defenses outside Vicksburg on May 19, 1863. Union morale was high: Johnston had been ousted from Jackson, and Pemberton's back was to the wall. Grant therefore ordered a number of direct assaults in an attempt to take the city by storm. But once inside their formidable works, the Rebels repulsed such maneuvers; the federals turned to the slow, sure expedient of siege, for Grant wanted Vicksburg badly (he reckoned it to be worth "the capture of forty Richmonds"). Under the blazing Mississippi sun Union soldiers widened and deepened their trenches; their outworks slowly veined toward the city; soon, mining of the Confederate trenches would be possible—and that would mean the eventual fall of the citadel. Said one despondent Rebel: "When the real investment began a cat could

not have crept out of Vicksburg without being discovered." There was much conversation between rival pickets. At one point, engineers calculated that two trenches being dug toward town would converge within Confederate lines. The result of an informal parley with Rebel pickets was that the defenders withdrew to allow work to proceed without bloodshed—"You Yanks will soon have the place anyway." And so they did. Federal reinforcements precluded Johnston's swinging back to take the pressure off Pemberton, and on Independence Day an exhausted, hungry Rebel garrison surrendered Vicksburg. The more than thirty thousand Confederate prisoners were paroled, but they would not fight again. For the second time in a year and a half General Ulysses S. Grant had captured an army, something officials in neither Washington nor Richmond could afford to ignore.

GENTLE WARRIOR

Union General George McClellan was relieved in the spring of 1862 to hear that Robert E. Lee had taken command of the army opposing him. He dismissed Lee as "wanting in moral firmness when pressed by heavy responsibility" and "likely to be timid and irresolute in action." The irony was monumental. While McClellan's words summarized his own military comportment, they did not apply at all to Lee, whose record contradicted such an appraisal. An exemplary member of the class of 1829 at West Point (where he was superintendent from 1852 to 1853), Lee had won praise for his bravery during the Mexican War. His stock was still high in 1861, and he was offered command of the Union armies. Although Lee could not "see the good of secession" and called slavery a "moral & political evil," his first allegiance was to his native state, which he vowed to follow "with my sword, and, if need be, with my life." For Lee was a thoroughbred Virginian, an aristocrat whose hero was George Washington; he was devoted to his birthright codes of loyalty and duty, socially and martially.

Lee was a robust fifty-five years old when he took command of the South's Army of Northern Virginia. Outnumbered, as he would be throughout the war, he immediately displayed the calculated daring and flair for psychological warfare that became his hallmark. After Stonewall Jackson's audacious raids in the Shenandoah Valley checked the Union offensive, Lee attacked in the Seven Days' Battles and in the rout at Second Bull Run. Weathering the bloody draw at Antietam, Lee engineered crushing victories at Fredericksburg and, in May of 1863, at Chancellorsville. While Lincoln continued to look for an effective commander, Lee marched boldly into Pennsylvania to divert federal strength from Vicksburg and to encourage Northern pacifism. But his army was newly reorganized, and at Gettysburg he was beaten as much by intramural confusion and reluctant cooperation from Generals Ewell and Longstreet as he was by Meade's forces. The attrition of war began to tell: it was a poorly fed, ill-equipped army that tried to thwart Grant's Virginia Campaign in 1864. On April 9, 1865, shortly after a ten-month siege at Petersburg, Lee surrendered to General Grant at Appomattox Court House. Lee's cool decorousness set the tone of the quiet, reserved meeting; he was as courteously dignified in his public role as he was warm and compassionate with intimates. Lee rode back to his men, some of whom cried, "We'll fight 'em yet." No, said Lee, dead set against a guerrilla continuation of hostilities. He bade his men go home peaceably and soon thereafter wrote of the "duty of every one to unite in the restoration of the country, and the establishment of peace and harmony. . . ."

Lee's personal credo was based on obedience to authority; silent on politics, he had had a working rapport with the difficult Jefferson Davis. That he did not demand a parallel respect from obdurate field subordinates was his one major flaw as a commander. Lee was indicted for treason, but the case was dropped after the general amnesty proclamation of 1868. In 1865 he had become president of Washington College (now Washington and Lee University) in Lexington, Virginia, where he lived simply and quietly with his family until his death from a stroke in 1870. Magnificently inspiring in victory, Lee had been a source of consolation in defeat; he was mourned throughout the South, where reverence for him as the apotheosis of the Christian gentleman-warrior was unabated.

Robert E. Lee, painted in 1865 by W. B. Cox

HORATIO SEYMOUR

"I could not accept the nomination if tendered," maintained Horatio Seymour at the Democratic convention of 1868. But when he was chosen on the twenty-second ballot, "the great decliner," as his enemies dubbed him, became a reluctant candidate for President. Seymour entered politics by serving as military secretary to New York's Governor William L. Marcy for six years. He was elected state assemblyman in 1841 and became mayor of Utica the next year. In 1844 he re-entered the assembly, and after pushing through important canal legislation, was elected speaker in 1845. Following the split in the New York Democratic party, Seymour played an important role as arbitrator between the opposing "Hunker" and "Barnburner" factions. Nominated six times for governor, he won the office twice, first in 1852 and again ten years later. Opposing Lincoln's election and the war, he nevertheless urged loyalty to the President; and during his second term as governor, he worked to maintain the state's quota in Union forces. Nominated in 1868 as a compromise candidate between Eastern and Western Democrats, Seymour campaigned vigorously, but was overshadowed by the more popular and magnetic Grant. After his defeat he continued to play a prominent role in the Democratic party, notably in his efforts to reform Tammany Hall and drive out bossism from New York City politics.

A DOWNWARD ROAD

At the crest," wrote Bruce Catton of U. S. Grant, "any road he took would lead downward." And when the adored hero succeeded Andrew Johnson, his first steps showed that the decline would be steady. He alienated the Republican leadership—and lost a potential power base—by handing out Cabinet positions on the basis of personal preference. Grant could not distinguish between talent and friendship (in eight years he appointed a total of twenty-three men to his Cabinet). Nor did he grasp the idea of compromise, of give-and-take. He did nothing for the legislators who backed him up in his attempt to annex the Dominican Republic and therefore could not expect their support when he established a Civil Service Commission that threatened their congressional pork barrel. Congress refused to finance the project, and Grant meekly said, "If Congress adjourns without positive legislation on . . . 'civil reform' I will regard such action as a disapproval of the system and will abandon it." If nothing else, he had meant it when he said he intended to function as "a purely administrative officer"; the commission atrophied. Scandals began to break, and one senator declared the Republicans to be "the [most] corrupt and debauched political party that has ever existed." Asked once if he liked Washington, Grant said that he would like it much better if it had a road on which he could race horses (he once was arrested for speeding, but the charge was not pressed). Grant was trying to learn his job as he went, but he was not an apt pupil. One of the President's visitors during his first term as Chief Executive noted "a puzzled pathos, as of a man with a problem before him of which he does not understand the terms."

The Puck cartoon above, entitled "*A Strong Man at the Head of Government,*" summed up U. S. Grant's two administrations as a time of wholesale corruption. Grant is shown clinging to Whisky and Navy rings while supporting various bosses and profiteers.

FAILURE AND CRISIS

Grant won re-election in 1872 less on his record than on the unpopularity of his Democratic-Liberal Republican opponent: vituperative, eccentric Horace Greeley. Reconstruction, Grant's primary concern, was failing miserably. Southern passion flared anew, fired by the increased military support given carpetbag rule. But Radicalism was losing its grip on the North, and as the South began to send more and more Democrats to Congress, Reconstruction became a dead letter. In 1872, as a sop to the South, the Freedmen's Bureau was

The engraving at left celebrates the Fifteenth Amendment, which provided for universal male suffrage. The amendment was ratified on March 30, 1870.

"The origin of the Ku-Klux Klan," wrote a contemporary Southern editor, "is in the galling despotism that broods like a nightmare over these Southern States." The Klan and other night-riding bands were determined to keep the freed Negro out of politics. Methods varied, depending on the nature of the resistance met. (One broadside threatened: "No rations have we, but the flesh of man—/And love niggers best—the Ku-Klux Klan.") The two Alabama Klansmen shown below were photographed in 1868.

abolished and the Negro was left to make his own way. Grant remained the weathercock, catching full in the face the storms of protest at unchecked corruption; and because of the disputed Hayes-Tilden election he lived with crisis right up to the end of his second term. But soon the White House would be out of mind and far, far out of sight.

VICE PRESIDENTS AND APPOINTEES

BOTH: LIBRARY OF CONGRESS

SCHUYLER COLFAX

Schuyler Colfax, with his dark beard and broad grin, seemed to the Republicans a perfect candidate for Vice President—"a good-tempered, chirping, warbling, real canary bird." Born in New York City in 1823, Colfax moved to Indiana in 1836 and began his career as an auditor, clerk, and newspaper correspondent. He became publisher of the leading Whig newspaper in northern Indiana and later helped to organize the Republican party in that state. Elected to Congress as a Republican in 1855, he served fourteen years in the House of Representatives. His position as Speaker during the last six years of his tenure gave him a considerable advantage over other vice presidential hopefuls at the Republican convention in 1868; and on the fifth ballot "Smiler" Colfax became Grant's running mate. Things did not go smoothly for the amiable Vice President. Six months before the end of his term he was implicated in the Crédit Mobilier affair— accused of accepting stock in the fraudulent company in return for political protection. During the investigations it was also disclosed that he had accepted a $4,000 gift from a government contractor while he was serving as Speaker of the House. Colfax was allowed to finish his term as Vice President, but the scandal ruined him politically, and he retired in January of 1873 in disrepute.

HENRY WILSON

Henry Wilson, born Jeremiah Jones Colbath, rose from poverty as an indentured farmer and cobbler to become the eighteenth Vice President of the United States. Changing his name to Wilson after his twenty-first birthday, he established himself at Natick, Massachusetts, and became a successful shoe manufacturer. In 1840 he was elected to the state legislature, where he served several terms. Leaving the Whig party in 1848 because of its evasiveness on the slavery issue, he helped to organize the Free-Soil party and became editor of its news organ, the Boston *Republican*. Briefly associated with the American party, or "Know Nothings," he exited when they refused to adopt a strong antislavery platform. In 1855 he entered the United States Senate as one of its most energetic abolitionists. Aligning himself with the Republicans, he campaigned for Lincoln and worked tirelessly as chairman of the Senate's military committee during the Civil War. After the war he joined extremists in opposing Johnson's moderate Reconstruction program and only later adopted a more sympathetic attitude toward the South. In 1872 Wilson was nominated by the Radicals for the Vice Presidency on the Republican ticket. His term was cut short by a stroke, however, and Wilson died in office on November 22, 1875.

HAMILTON FISH

An exception among Grant's appointees, Secretary of State Hamilton Fish neither sought high office nor descended to the cronyism and scandal that marred the administration. Fish, who was born in New York in 1808 and was admitted to the bar at the age of twenty-two, was elected to the House of Representatives in 1842; he was governor of New York from 1849 to 1850, and a year later began a six-year term as United States senator. Named to the State Department in 1869, he ensured Grant's support for his foreign policies by backing the President's scheme to annex the Dominican Republic. The settlement of claims against England, which had supplied warships to the Confederacy, was complicated by harsh reparation demands by the Radicals. Fish waited until they were out of Grant's favor, and in 1871 he concluded the moderate Treaty of Washington, which led to an equitable settlement and opened the way for an agreement on Canadian fishing rights and boundaries. In 1873 Spain captured the *Virginius*, a steamer that was being used by Cuban revolutionaries although it flew the American flag. Many of the crew—including some Americans—were executed. Fish averted a serious incident by proving that the ship was registered illegally and negotiated an $80,000 award for the men's heirs.

MORRISON R. WAITE

Morrison R. Waite was startled in January of 1874 to hear that he had been named Chief Justice of the United States. Although he came from a distinguished legal family and had been a capable counselor in the arbitration of Civil War claims against England, he was simply a former Ohio congressman who now had a solid private practice. But his fourteen years as Chief Justice proved him to be an energetic and far-seeing magistrate. The railroad interests of the Gilded Age had abused their privileged positions, and in 1877 (*Munn v. Illinois*) Waite held that when private property becomes "clothed with a public interest," it should be publicly regulated. In the companion Granger cases this view prevailed: state laws setting maximum passenger and freight rates for railroads were upheld and established a lasting precedent in matters concerning public utilities. Waite felt that "until Congress acts" (and it did not until the Interstate Commerce Act of 1887) such laws were essential to a given state's welfare, "even though . . . those without may be indirectly affected." In *Stone v. Farmers' Loan* (1886), however, he insisted on reasonable state laws by cautioning, "this power . . . of regulation is itself [not] without limit." No state, he warned, could take over "private property . . . without due process of law."

GRAND TOUR

The tour was a second honeymoon for the Grants—
a far cry from their wedding trip, which had taken
them by river boat up the Mississippi from Julia's
home in St. Louis to her husband's home in Bethel,
Ohio. The drawing above shows the Grants seated,
center, among the temple ruins at Karnak, Egypt.

If the General's repu-
tation had become somewhat tarnished in
the United States, abroad he was still every
bit the hero, as he discovered during a world
tour that began soon after he left the White
House. Banquets, parades, and ovations
greeted the Grants all along their winding
route through Europe and the Middle East;
Grant, once disdainful of applause, seemed
now to find it restorative. They saw the
sights, lived like—and with—royalty. At
Pompeii an ancient loaf of bread was dug
from the ruins for them. The Khedive of
Egypt gave them a palace to stay in and a
boat for exploring the Nile. Meanwhile, from
America came signs of a possible third term;
distance was making the American heart
grow fonder, it seemed, and Grant's advisers
told him to stay abroad as long as he could,
to come home only in time for the 1880 convention. Perhaps partly because of that, the
trip was extended to the Orient. At the Taj
Mahal the gardener gave roses to Julia. They
toured the palace of the Maharajah of Jai-
pur and turned down the chance to go on a
tiger hunt. ("Twice in my life I killed wild
animals," Grant had said to the Duke of
Sutherland in Scotland, "and I have regretted
both acts ever since.") In China they were
guests at a seventy-course dinner that included soles of pigeons' feet and suckling pig.
The reception in Japan was spectacular. But
the trip had to end; the General had to consider the future. Indeed, was there a future
at all for him? "I am both homesick and
dread going home," he wrote shortly before
they headed east across the Pacific for California. Some of his doubts began to fade
when, in San Francisco, a huge, enthusiastic
crowd cheered the return of the former
President. "Old World Splendor Eclipsed,"
boasted one of the city's newspapers in its
description of the tumultuous welcome.

Jushie Yoshida, Japan's diplomatic representative in Washington, was called home to take charge of the Grants' visit to the island nation. They were put up at the summer palace on the island of Enriokwan, and in a tradition-breaking ceremony, Grant accompanied the Emperor on a review of the army. Above is a painting of the festival of Ueno that was held in their honor. Below, an illustration from a biography published that year; depicting the famed General's visage only as a reflection in a mirror was typical Japanese deference.

A FINAL BATTLE

The cartoon above, "Grant As His Own Iconoclast," explains why he was not nominated for a third term in 1880. Evidence of corruption abounds, and not even his war record can sustain him as the American ideal. Democratic nominee W. S. Hancock watches.

I propose to fight it out on this line if it takes all summer," wrote Grant in 1884. He was fighting in the single combat of authorship, and, oddly, this would be the only civilian pursuit that ever gave his family a measure of financial security. He had been swindled into penury by Ferdinand Ward, but now, with his pen recalling the mightiness of his sword, he would recoup. As he struggled against time and cancer, loyal friends—Northern and Southern—visited him; even Jeff Davis wrote in sympathy. Grant's quiet sense of humor was intact. "I will have to be careful about my writing. I see every person I give a piece of paper to puts it in his pocket. Some day they will be coming up against my English." As a youth he had learned what a noun was; shortly before he died the former President scrawled, "A verb is anything that signifies to be; to do; or to suffer. I signify all three."

In 1879 the Grants explored a mine at Virginia City, Nevada. Julia (third from left, above) did not want to go down, but changed her mind when she heard that her husband, center, had bet a dollar she was afraid.

Rushing to finish his memoirs, Grant, with less than a month to live, is shown above at his retreat at Mt. McGregor, New York. With his writing now a scrawl, he had abandoned fine paper for a student's scratch pad.

FACTS IN SUMMARY: ULYSSES S. GRANT

CHRONOLOGY

UNITED STATES		GRANT
	1822	*Born April 27*
Jackson elected President	1828	
	1839	*Enters U.S. Military Academy*
	1843	*Serves as 2nd lieutenant in 4th Infantry*
Polk elected President	1844	
War with Mexico	1846	*Serves in Mexican War*
Battle of Buena Vista	1847	*Brevetted captain for gallantry at Chapultepec*
Scott captures Mexico City		
Treaty of Guadalupe Hidalgo	1848	*Marries Julia Dent*
Compromise of 1850	1850	
Pierce elected President	1852	*Moves with regiment to Pacific Coast*
	1854	*Resigns from Army*
		Works as farmer and real-estate agent
Buchanan elected President	1856	
Lincoln elected President	1860	*Works in father's store in Galena*
South Carolina secedes		
Civil War begins	1861	*Appointed colonel of 21st Illinois Volunteers*
Battle of Bull Run		*Named brigadier general*

Battle of Shiloh	1862	*Captures Fort Henry and Fort Donelson*
Second Bull Run		
Battle of Antietam		*Wins Battle of Shiloh*
Emancipation Proclamation	1863	*Captures Vicksburg*
Chancellorsville		*Wins Battle of Chattanooga*
Gettysburg		
Sherman marches through Georgia	1864	*Appointed general in chief of Union armies*
		Fights at the Wilderness, Spotsylvania, and Cold Harbor
Civil War ends	1865	*Captures Petersburg*
		Accepts Lee's surrender
Ku-Klux Klan founded	1866	*Commissioned general of the Army*
	1867	*Serves as Secretary of War, ad interim*
Johnson impeached	1868	*Elected President*
Transcontinental railroad completed	1869	*Orders sale of gold, ruining speculators*
		Attempts to annex Dominican Republic
Fifteenth Amendment ratified	1870	
Amnesty Act	1872	*Re-elected President*
Crédit Mobilier scandal		
"Salary Grab" Act	1873	
	1874	*Urges resumption of specie payments*

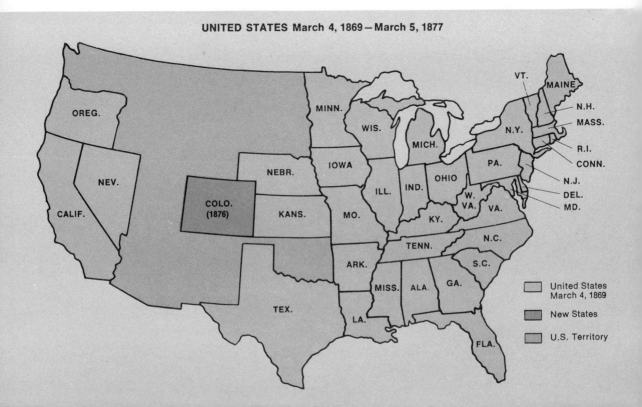

UNITED STATES March 4, 1869 — March 5, 1877

Legend:
- United States March 4, 1869
- New States
- U.S. Territory

Whisky Ring exposed	1875	
Secretary of War Belknap impeached	1876	
Hayes wins Presidency	1877	*Leaves for world tour*
Garfield elected President	1880	*Fails to win presidential nomination*
Cleveland elected President	1884	*Loses fortune through unwise investments*
	1885	*Writes memoirs*
		Dies July 23

BIOGRAPHICAL FACTS

BIRTH: Point Pleasant, Ohio, April 27, 1822

ANCESTRY: English-Scotch

FATHER: Jesse Root Grant; b. Westmoreland County, Pa., Jan. 23, 1794; d. Covington, Ky., June 29, 1873

FATHER'S OCCUPATION: Leather tanner

MOTHER: Hannah Simpson Grant; b. Montgomery County, Pa., Nov. 23, 1798; d. Jersey City, N.J., May 11, 1883

BROTHERS: Samuel Simpson (1825–1861); Orvil Lynch (1835–1881)

SISTERS: Clara Rachel (1828–1865); Virginia Paine (1832–1881); Mary Frances (1839–1898)

WIFE: Julia Boggs Dent; b. St. Louis, Mo., Jan. 26, 1826; d. Washington, D.C., Dec. 14, 1902

MARRIAGE: St. Louis, Mo., Aug. 22, 1848

CHILDREN: Frederick Dent (1850–1912); Ulysses Simpson (1852–1929); Ellen Wrenshall (1855–1922); Jesse Root (1858–1934)

EDUCATION: Local schools; U.S. Military Academy

RELIGIOUS AFFILIATION: Methodist

OCCUPATIONS BEFORE PRESIDENCY: Soldier; farmer; real-estate agent; custom house clerk; leather store clerk

MILITARY SERVICE: Commissioned 2nd lt. in 4th U.S. Infantry (1843), resigned as captain (1854); re-entered Army in Aug., 1861, as brig. general; became general in chief of Union armies on March 12, 1864

AGE AT INAUGURATION: 46

DEATH: Mount McGregor, N.Y., July 23, 1885

PLACE OF BURIAL: Grant's Tomb, New York, N.Y.

ELECTION OF 1868

CANDIDATES	ELECTORAL VOTE	POPULAR VOTE
Ulysses S. Grant Republican	214	3,013,421
Horatio Seymour Democratic	80	2,706,829

FIRST ADMINISTRATION

INAUGURATION: March 4, 1869; the Capitol, Washington, D.C.

VICE PRESIDENT: Schuyler Colfax

SECRETARY OF STATE: Elihu B. Washburne; Hamilton Fish (from March 17, 1869)

SECRETARY OF THE TREASURY: George S. Boutwell

SECRETARY OF WAR: John A. Rawlins; William T. Sherman (from Sept. 11, 1869); William W. Belknap (from Nov. 1, 1869)

ATTORNEY GENERAL: Ebenezer R. Hoar; Amos T. Akerman (from July 8, 1870); George H. Williams (from Jan. 10, 1872)

POSTMASTER GENERAL: John A. J. Creswell

SECRETARY OF THE NAVY: Adolph E. Borie; George M. Robeson (from June 25, 1869)

SECRETARY OF THE INTERIOR: Jacob D. Cox; Columbus Delano (from Nov. 1, 1870)

SUPREME COURT APPOINTMENTS: William Strong (1870); Joseph P. Bradley (1870); Ward Hunt (1872)

41st CONGRESS (March 4, 1869–March 4, 1871):
Senate: 56 Republicans; 11 Democrats
House: 149 Republicans; 63 Democrats

42nd CONGRESS (March 4, 1871–March 4, 1873):
Senate: 52 Republicans; 17 Democrats; 5 Others
House: 134 Republicans; 104 Democrats; 5 Others

ELECTION OF 1872

(Horace Greeley died shortly after the election, and the 66 electoral votes he had won were cast for several Democratic candidates.)

CANDIDATES	ELECTORAL VOTE	POPULAR VOTE
Ulysses S. Grant Republican	286	3,596,745
Horace Greeley Democratic	—	2,843,446

SECOND ADMINISTRATION

INAUGURATION: March 4, 1873; the Capitol, Washington, D.C.

VICE PRESIDENT: Henry Wilson

SECRETARY OF STATE: Hamilton Fish

SECRETARY OF THE TREASURY: William A. Richardson; Benjamin H. Bristow (from June 4, 1874); Lot M. Morrill (from July 7, 1876)

SECRETARY OF WAR: William W. Belknap; Alphonso Taft (from March 11, 1876); James D. Cameron (from June 1, 1876)

ATTORNEY GENERAL: George H. Williams; Edwards Pierrepont (from May 15, 1875); Alphonso Taft (from June 1, 1876)

POSTMASTER GENERAL: John A. J. Creswell; James W. Marshall (from July 7, 1874); Marshall Jewell (from Sept. 1, 1874); James N. Tyner (from July 12, 1876)

SECRETARY OF THE NAVY: George M. Robeson

SECRETARY OF THE INTERIOR: Columbus Delano; Zachariah Chandler (from Oct. 19, 1875)

SUPREME COURT APPOINTMENT: Morrison R. Waite, Chief Justice (1874)

43rd CONGRESS (March 4, 1873–March 4, 1875):
Senate: 49 Republicans; 19 Democrats; 5 Others
House: 194 Republicans; 92 Democrats; 14 Others

44th CONGRESS (March 4, 1875–March 4, 1877):
Senate: 45 Republicans; 29 Democrats; 2 Others
House: 169 Democrats; 109 Republicans; 14 Others

STATE ADMITTED: Colorado (1876)

RUTHERFORD BIRCHARD HAYES

The Civil War had been over for twenty-seven years, but again the sounds of marching feet echoed through the streets of Washington, D.C. The men of the Grand Army of the Republic were seeking, in the fall of 1892, to recapture the glory of the Union army's Grand Review of 1865. One of the marchers, Rutherford Birchard Hayes, had been President of the United States. But he came to the Capital that day not as the former Commander in Chief of the Armed Forces, but as the former commanding officer of the Twenty-third Regiment of Ohio Volunteers, a position that he had taken even more pride in than the Presidency itself.

Hayes's appearance in Washington, just four months before his death, symbolized his lifelong devotion to the cause of Union. As a student, he had impressed his elders with stirring renditions of Webster's "Reply to Hayne," with its peroration, "Liberty AND Union, now and forever, one and inseparable!" As a young man he had at first viewed with some tolerance the efforts by Southern states to secede from the Union, but on perceiving this course as folly, he had entered the Union army. As President, he had ended the ugly era of Reconstruction and had endeavored to bind the United States together in fact as well as in name. With characteristic equanimity he had persevered in the face of abuse from his contemporary critics (who called him "Rutherfraud"), and he is regarded today as an able President whose integrity and good sense brought a desperately needed respite to a country that was plagued by corruption and hate.

Hayes was born on October 4, 1822, in Delaware, Ohio. His father had left his store in Dummerston, Vermont, and had journeyed with his wife to Ohio in 1817. He was struck down by a fever in the summer of 1822 and died within a few days; two and a half months later Sophia Hayes gave birth to their last

Rutherford B. Hayes, during his Presidency

ALL: HAYES MEMORIAL LIBRARY

Hayes, at left in a portrait made when he was twenty-four, was deeply influenced by Fanny, his overly affectionate sister (center), and his hovering mother, Sophia Birchard Hayes (right).

child, the future President. The boy was sickly and emaciated, and his mother became overprotective. She had lost her husband, two sons, and a daughter; only Rutherford and another daughter, Fanny, two years older than he, still lived, and the mother was determined that this remnant of a family would survive. The pervasive feminine atmosphere made the boy yearn for a father, a role that was partly filled by an uncle, Sardis Birchard, who also helped finance Hayes's education.

The future President attended private schools in Ohio and Connecticut and then enrolled at Kenyon College in Gambier, Ohio. At nineteen, he wrote in his diary that he was "determined from henceforth to use what means I have to acquire a character distinguished for energy, firmness, and perseverance." After pondering several careers, he chose law, and upon his graduation from Kenyon in 1842, he entered Harvard Law School. His sister wanted Hayes to practice law in Columbus, where she lived with her husband. But although the town offered great opportunities for a young lawyer, Hayes knew that residing with Fanny was not advisable. Their affection for each other spilled over the customary bounds of sibling devotion. Even after her marriage—which Rutherford had refused to attend—she wrote to him constantly begging him to visit her and assuring him that he was "daily the object of my waking thoughts & almost

nightly of my dreams." After one visit from Rutherford in 1842, Fanny became violent, refused to believe that he had gone, and had to be briefly committed to an insane asylum. Hayes therefore chose to hang his shingle in Lower Sandusky (now Fremont), Ohio, the home of his Uncle Sardis. The decision was costly for his career; for five "doleful" years, his legal training was squandered on cases of little importance.

In 1849 Hayes took the firm step that would assure his success. He moved to Cincinnati, where he gained considerable renown in a number of sensational criminal trials. Marriage, too, came to the Cincinnati lawyer. He met Lucy Ware Webb, of Chillicothe, Ohio, then a student at Wesleyan Female College in Cincinnati, and was moved by her "soft" voice, "beautiful, dreamy" eyes, and "quiet" ways. After a long betrothal, they were married on December 30, 1852.

The marriage of Rutherford and Lucy Hayes was a success in every way. A potential source of difficulty was removed in 1856 when Fanny died after childbirth. To a friend, Hayes wrote: "Oh, what a blow it is! During all my life she has been the dear one. . . ." To his wife, whose reaction is not recorded, he wrote, "You are Sister Fanny to me now." In the years that followed, Hayes became the father of a daughter and seven sons; he once jokingly remarked that he and Lucy were in "the boy business."

Political activities had engaged Hayes's interest from childhood. At first he was a Whig, but when that party disintegrated, he helped form the Republican party in Ohio. Because of his stature in the community, he was often mentioned for public office, but he held none until 1858, when the city council chose him to fill the vacant post of city solicitor. In 1859 he was elected to a two-year term. Unlike some of his predecessors, he sought to serve the city's interests rather than his own. But Cincinnati voters, believing that the national Republican victory in 1860 had provoked disunion, turned against that party in 1861, and Hayes lost his office. After the attack on Fort Sumter, he knew where his duty—and his chance for military glory—lay. Entering the Army as a major in the Ohio Twenty-third Volunteers, he rose in rank to brigadier general. He craved action, was wounded five times, and won great respect from his men for his valour.

In the summer of 1864, while still in the Army, Hayes was nominated for Congress. He refused to campaign, assuring a supporter that "an officer fit for duty who at this crisis would abandon his post to electioneer for a seat in Congress ought to be scalped." He won the election, and the war ended in time for him to take his seat in the Thirty-ninth Congress. The freshman representative was assigned to the chairmanship of the "no-account" Library Committee. He had little stomach for the major controversy of the day, between the Radicals and President Andrew Johnson. Hayes always considered himself a party man, and he supported the Radical House leadership. But the mild-mannered, fair-minded Hayes could not fail to be dismayed by the temper of the times. Though re-elected, he welcomed an opportunity to leave Washington in 1867, when Ohio Republicans nominated him for governor. Hayes, in his campaign, called for the ratification of an amendment to the state constitution that would permit Negroes to vote. The amendment was defeated, and the state went Democratic for most offices. But Hayes's popularity pulled him through; he was elected by 3,000 votes.

During his two terms in office, Governor Hayes pressed for reform on several fronts. He supported voter registration to prevent election frauds, a state civil service system, state regulation of railroads, a safety code for mines, and improved conditions in prisons and mental hospitals. He helped establish the forerunner of Ohio State University. A conservative in matters of finance and taxes, he stood firm for sound money against greenback sentiment and for ratification of the Fifteenth Amendment guaranteeing the franchise to Negroes.

After his second term ended, he and Lucy resided briefly in Cincinnati. He agreed in 1872 to stand again for Congress, but opposition to "Grantism" was already running high in Cincinnati, and Hayes suffered defeat. Then he moved to Fremont and to the lovely estate, "Spiegel Grove," that Sardis Birchard had built. Hayes turned his attention to private business affairs and local civic activities, ignoring for the most part the requests of party leaders that he run for some office or other.

In 1875 he returned to the political arena. Though he supported another candidate, he accepted a Republican convention draft for a third term as governor, fully aware that if elected he would probably be a presidential possibility. (The Republican nomination seemed an empty honor, however, in view of widespread disenchantment with Grant.) Hayes won the election by about 5,500 votes, again defeating the Democrats on the issue of sound money versus inflation.

The presidential boom now began. Hayes was outwardly above the battle, but the office began to exert its inevitable attraction. His own self-assuredness was reflected in a diary entry for March, 1876: "It seems to me that good purposes and the judgment, experience, and firmness I possess, would enable me to execute the duties of the office well. . . . This all looks egotistical, but it is sincere."

Three months later Republican delegates convened in Cincinnati. Influential men were on the scene working for Hayes, but so were representatives of other, more promi-

The names of the Republican party's candidates in 1876 are emblazoned on the campaign banner above.

nent, candidates. The leading contender was the brilliant, able James G. Blaine of Maine. However, one of the periodic scandals that plagued his career had blossomed just before the convention, and many delegates were sensitive to the corruption issue. On the first ballot Blaine led with 285 votes, while Hayes trailed badly in fifth place with only 61, mostly from Ohio. Blaine thereafter gained slowly, and his opponents realized that they must unite on one candidate to defeat him. Hayes was the man. He had a loyal party record and no taint of corruption. He had proved he could win elections, and his war record was outstanding. Henry Adams, writing at the time, described Hayes's "availability" with considerably less sympathy: he was "a third rate nonentity, whose only recommendation is that he is obnoxious to no one." But on the seventh and final ballot Rutherford B. Hayes won the Republican presidential nomination, receiving 384 votes to Blaine's 351.

Republicans who wondered what manner of man they had nominated got some idea when Hayes released his Letter of Acceptance. He condemned the spoils system, said that he would serve only one term, supported the resumption of specie payments, and pledged his best efforts toward "a civil policy which will wipe out forever the distinction between North and South in our common country." Characteristically, he called for "simplicity and frugality in public and private affairs. . . ." His plea that a civil service merit system be established clinched the support of the reform Republicans.

The Democrats named as their presidential candidate Samuel J. Tilden, the reform-minded governor of New York. He matched Hayes's determination to return good government to Washington.

Hayes rarely appeared in public during the campaign of 1876, an exception being his trip to the Centennial Exhibition at Philadelphia in October. The crowds that flocked to see him must have been somewhat disappointed: Hayes was one of the most mediocre-looking men ever to run for President. He was short, rumpled in dress, and had a rat's-nest beard. *The New York Times* noted that he wore "a dreadfully shabby coat and a shockingly bad hat, all brushed up the wrong way."

To win, the Republicans had to get the voters' minds off the real issues. "Our strong ground," Hayes wrote to Blaine, "is the dread of a solid [Democratic] South, *rebel rule*, etc., etc. I hope you will make these topics prominent in your speeches. *It leads people away from 'hard times,' which is our deadliest foe.*"

On election night, Hayes went to bed believing that he had lost. Tilden had taken a substantial lead in the popular vote and seemed certain to win a majority of the electoral votes (the winner needed 185). He had apparently swept the South as well as the doubtful Northern states of New York, Indiana, Connecticut, and New Jersey.

But the presidential contest, far from being over, had in fact only barely begun. In his office at *The New York Times*, Managing Editor John Reid studied the returns until dawn. Finally he saw a way that Tilden might be robbed of his victory. With the acquiescence of Republican leaders, telegrams were sent across the nation, warning local Republicans of fraud and urging them to hold their states for Hayes.

Republican hopes centered on Florida, Louisiana, and South Carolina. Without those states, Tilden had only 184 electoral votes, one less than he needed; Hayes had 166. If Hayes could capture all the electoral votes of those states, he would win with 185. This was easier said than done, however, inasmuch as Tilden seemed to have popular majorities in all three. But carpetbaggers and Negroes, supported by the guns of federal soldiers, still ruled in South Carolina, Louisiana, and Florida, though their grip was weakening. The Republicans therefore controlled the state canvassing boards. These boards had no trouble turning up valid evidence of widespread intimidation of Negro voters by white Democrats.

An honest man would have had difficulty determining who won the election, but the politicians did not even try. National leaders of the Republican and Democratic parties hurried South to protect their respective interests, and rumors soon spread that they were engaged in vote buying. In each state a similar process was repeated. The canvassing boards refused to count the returns (largely Democratic) from districts where Negroes allegedly had been denied the right to vote. Tilden majorities were transformed into Hayes majorities. The Republican electors met, cast their votes for Hayes, and forwarded their votes to the Congress for tabulation. The Democratic electors, refusing to accept this outcome, also met, voted, and sent their votes to Congress.

In a further complication, Democrats in Oregon discovered that one Republican elector was a postmaster and therefore constitutionally ineligible, and they sought to replace him with a Democrat. That fight was also carried to Washington.

Hayes thought he had won fairly; "I have no doubt," he asserted in a letter, "that we are justly and legally entitled to the Presidency." But some Democratic hotheads threatened armed violence and a march on Washington to force Tilden's inauguration.

Congress, clearly, had to decide the issue. The Constitution provided that "The President of the Senate shall, in the Presence of the Senate and House of Representatives, open all the Certificates, and the [electoral] Votes shall then be counted." But who would count the votes? The president of the Senate was a Republican, but if the decision was put to the joint session of Congress, the Democrats would prevail because of their

WILLIAM A. WHEELER

"Who," asked Rutherford B. Hayes of his suggested running mate in 1876, "is *Wheeler?*" William A. Wheeler was virtually unknown outside his native New York when he was mentioned for the second spot on the Republican ticket. A successful lawyer and banker, Wheeler became active in local politics as a district attorney in 1846. In 1850 he entered the New York State legislature as assemblyman and was later elected to the senate. From 1861 to 1877 he spent a total of ten years in the United States House of Representatives, where he served capably but without particular distinction, his main contribution being the successful arbitration of a potentially disastrous 1874 election dispute in the state of Louisiana. His refusal to benefit from the "Salary Grab" Act of 1873 (Congress raised its own pay by 50 per cent) enhanced his reputation as a congressman of exceptional honesty. Nominated for the Vice Presidency to secure a sectional balance on the party ticket, he took an active part in the campaign, pledging his support to social, administrative, and civil service reforms. During his tenure as Vice President he became a close personal friend of President Hayes, who found him "a noble, honest, patriotic man." Little else is remarkable about his four years in office. Wheeler retired to his home in Malone, New York, in 1881 and, declining further public service, died a private citizen six years later.

majority in the House of Representatives.

A compromise was effected with the formation of an electoral commission, composed of five senators (three Republicans, two Democrats), five representatives (three Democrats, two Republicans), and five justices of the Supreme Court (two Democrats, two Republicans, and one independent). The findings of the commission could be overturned only by the action of both houses of Congress, voting separately. Because each party controlled one branch of Congress, it was certain that any findings by the commission would be final.

It was assumed that the key man on the commission would be Justice David Davis, a political independent. Had Davis actually served on the commission, it is likely that Tilden would have been declared elected. But just as Congress was completing action on the commission bill, Democratic members of the Illinois legislature confounded everybody by electing Davis to the U.S. Senate. Davis resigned from the Court. There was no alternative to replacing him on the commission with a Republican, because only two Democrats sat on the High Court. The Republicans thus held an 8 to 7 margin on the commission, and Tilden's cause was doomed.

Congress, meeting in joint session, began to count the electoral votes in alphabetical order. When the conflicting returns from Florida were announced, the Electoral Commission took over. It first had to decide whether to go behind the returns and conduct an investigation at the state level. The Republican majority rejected this approach, 8 to 7, arguing that with Inauguration Day less than a month away, time did not permit a full investigation. The commission merely voted—8 to 7, of course—to accept the returns from the Republican-controlled canvassing board. This procedure was repeated for Louisiana and South Carolina. The disputed Oregon vote also went to Hayes.

Many Democrats remained bitterly angry at what they regarded as a brazen steal. Some Democratic congressmen resorted to filibustering to slow down the vote count.

It appeared that the Congress might not complete its work in time for the inauguration. To break the stalling tactics, Republicans sought to drive a wedge between the Northern and Southern Democrats.

In January Republicans had signaled their willingness to establish good relations with the South. They gave strong support to the Texas and Pacific Railroad bill, which was much desired by the economically retarded South. Once the lines of communication had been opened between the Southerners and the Republicans, other aspects of a deal began to take shape. It was understood that Hayes, if elected, would include a Southerner in his Cabinet and that Southerners would share in patronage. Hayes had already said that he would withdraw all remaining troops from the South.

Hayes refused to be a party to a deal, but his representatives maneuvered in his behalf. To one of these, Senator John Sherman, he wrote: "I wish *you* to feel authorized to speak in pretty decided terms for me whenever it seems advisable—to do this, not by reason of specific authority to do it, but from your knowledge of my general methods of action."

When the South helped wear down the congressional filibuster, finally even Tilden gave up. At 4:10 A.M., Friday, March 2, the president of the Senate announced to both houses of Congress that Hayes had received 185 electoral votes, Tilden 184. Modern scholars believe that Hayes was probably entitled to the votes of South Carolina and Louisiana and that Tilden carried Florida. But Hayes, not Tilden, was the nineteenth President of the United States.

Because Inauguration Day fell on Sunday, Hayes took the oath of office privately at the White House on the evening of March 3. On Monday, March 5, in a public ceremony on the Capitol steps before thirty thousand persons, he again took the oath. In his Inaugural Address he pledged fair treatment for both whites and Negroes in the South. He surprised cynics by bringing up the civil service question again and made his oft-quoted statement that ". . . he serves his party best who serves his country best."

In a diary entry anticipating his election, Hayes had pledged "the firmest adherence to principle against all opposition and temptation" and asserted that "I shall show a *grit* that will astonish those who predict weakness." He had no band of organized followers, and his previous record was that of a loyal party man. Nonetheless, he determined to be independent of the old guard Republican leaders, who had humiliated Johnson and had controlled Grant.

He named a Cabinet with little consideration to the wishes of the spoilsmen. His Secretary of State, William Evarts, was a statesman and one of the most able lawyers in the country. John Sherman, the Secretary of the Treasury, was perhaps the most capable financial expert in public life. Carl Schurz, Secretary of the Interior, was an aggressive, uncompromising reformer.

Only two carpetbag governments—in Louisiana and South Carolina—remained; the one in Florida had collapsed. The President was convinced that no interpretation of the Constitution could justify a state government staying in power by force of arms. Upon investigation, Hayes determined that the Democrats had valid claims to the governorships of South Carolina and Louisiana. He extracted promises from the would-be Democratic governors that they would protect the constitutional rights of all citizens. Then the President ordered federal troops to withdraw. Republican rule collapsed, and the Southern whites were in control.

Former abolitionists and leaders of his own party deplored the President's action. But it was not Hayes's intention to abandon either the Negroes or the Republican cause in the South; he expected that the educated and prosperous white elements would eventually gravitate to the Republican party for economic reasons. His hopes were, of course, premature. Nonetheless, he had created a favorable atmosphere for reconciliation, and he furthered this spirit by touring the South in the fall of 1877.

President Grant had made a few ineffectual gestures toward upgrading the federal

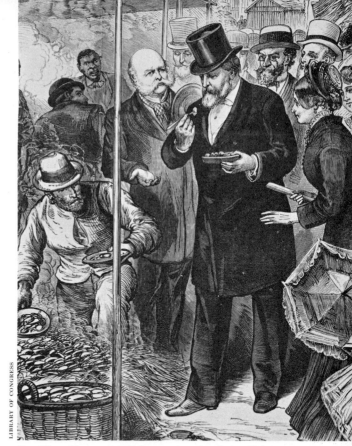

LIBRARY OF CONGRESS

President Hayes attended a reunion clambake of the Grand Army of the Republic in Rhode Island.

civil service, but it remained for Hayes to declare that the spoils system "ought to be abolished. The reform should be thorough, radical, and complete." On June 22, 1877, the President issued an Executive Order prohibiting all federal civil servants from taking part "in the management of political organizations, caucuses, conventions, or election campaigns. . . . No assessment for political purposes, on officers or subordinates, should be allowed."

Hayes's order had been precipitated by the report by a presidential commission of gross errors and inefficiency in the New York Custom House. The President soon demanded that the New York collector, Chester Alan Arthur, and his associate, Alonzo Cornell, either abandon their Republican political activities or resign their posts at the custom house. They refused. Senator Roscoe Conkling, boss of the New York Republicans, publicly broke with the President. Equally defiant, Hayes sent to

495

the Senate for its consent the names of two men to replace Arthur and Cornell. But the Senate would not approve the nominees because the senator from their state—Conkling—objected. Hayes bided his time, and after the Senate adjourned he removed Arthur and Cornell in favor of his own appointees. When the Senate reconvened, the fight was renewed. In the fervor of his attacks on Hayes, Conkling overplayed his hand. The number of Republicans supporting the President doubled, and with additional votes from Democrats, Hayes's nominees were confirmed. Hayes won the battle but not the war. In three annual messages he pleaded for a merit system, but the split in his own party precluded any reform legislation by Congress.

The monetary issue plagued Hayes as it would all Presidents of his era. The contest lay between the capitalist and the debtor—between the Easterner, who had money and lent it, and the Westerner, who needed money and owed it. The Westerners wanted legislation that would increase the money supply, raise farm prices, and help the debtor pay his obligations. The inflationists, who controlled the House in 1877, passed a bill providing for the free and unlimited coinage of silver at the ratio of 16 to 1 (silver to gold). This bill, supported by the Western silver bloc, overvalued the cheaper metal. To the relief of Eastern bankers, the Senate watered down the measure. Passed over Hayes's veto, the Bland-Allison Act provided for limited coinage of silver and required that the Treasury purchase between two and four million dollars of silver every month. Each month Treasury Secretary Sherman purchased the minimum amount, which was not enough to dilute the value of gold.

Meanwhile, Sherman had to prepare for the redemption of greenbacks in gold, as provided by a law passed in 1875. He was able to build up substantial gold reserves through the sale of bonds and as a result of a favorable balance of trade made possible by bumper harvests in the United States and by the crop failures of European na-tions. The time for the resumption of payments in specie—January 1, 1879—passed without crisis. Confidence in the green-backs was restored, and they were exchanged freely with gold and silver on a par value.

A widespread railroad strike in the summer of 1877 presaged years of labor strife. Many railroads east of the Mississippi River announced cuts in wages (already low) by another 10 per cent. After the reduction went into effect, rail workers seized the Baltimore and Ohio lines at many points, refusing to permit freight trains to move. The strike spread rapidly to the South and West. In response to pleas from governors, Hayes sent troops to West Virginia, Maryland, Pennsylvania, and Illinois. But rioting, sparked by radicals, criminals, and tramps, erupted in several cities. In Pittsburgh the militia killed a score of demonstrators, wounded many more, and barely escaped with their lives. Property damage in Pittsburgh alone totaled nearly three million dollars. Nevertheless, the strikers' demands were refused by management. But public attention was directed to the plight of wage earners, and the managers of the railroads realized that they must eventually improve their employees' lot.

Democratic attempts to deprive the federal government of its power to enforce the Fifteenth Amendment in the South prompted a demonstration of presidential backbone. Congressional Democrats attached to an appropriation bill a rider repealing the law that permitted use of the Army to maintain peace at election polls. A rider to another bill forbade United States marshals to act to enforce state election laws. In the course of protracted parliamentary maneuvering, Hayes used the veto six times. Though he conceded ground in minor particulars, he effectively rebuffed attempts by Congress to encroach on presidential authority; he also won back the support of his own party, which had virtually disowned him.

Foreign affairs during Hayes's administration failed to excite a population preoccupied with an industrial boom and the westward migration. Mexico was in revolutionary turmoil, and raiders from that country destroyed United States property in a number of border incidents. In June, 1877, the Secretary of War authorized American troops to chase the raiders across the border, and the Mexican government issued a counterorder to repel invaders by force. When Porfirio Díaz restored calm in Mexico, the order to the American troops was withdrawn.

When a French company headed by Ferdinand de Lesseps secured from Colombia a concession to build a canal in Panama, some Americans feared that circumstances might arise that would require French intervention to protect the interests of French nationals in Panama, and that such intervention would constitute a threat to the Monroe Doctrine. Many congressmen wanted the United States to dig its own canal, but President Hayes confined himself to the assertion that "the policy of this country is a canal under American control." The French began to dig a canal, but the enterprise failed and was abandoned.

In California, long-smoldering hatred for Chinese laborers flared up in the summer of 1877. White workers and shiftless elements ran amuck and stormed San Francisco's Chinatown, killing two Chinese. Orientals, who had been brought into the country to help build the Central Pacific Railroad, made up nearly one-tenth of California's population. Because they lived cheaply and in crowded conditions, they forced down the prevailing wage rates. The issue went to Congress as both parties vied for the support of the white California voters. Congress passed a bill requiring Hayes to tell China that sections of the Burlingame Treaty of 1868, which permitted free interchange of citizens, would be nullified. Hayes coura-

In the summer of 1877—for the third time in as many years—the railroads cut wages. President Hayes sent troops to Baltimore, Maryland (above), Pittsburgh, and other cities to quell the resulting strikes and riots.

geously vetoed the bill, asserting that Congress could not order him to abrogate part of a treaty. But Hayes knew that something had to be done. He and Evarts soothed the sensibilities of the Chinese and obtained a modification of the Burlingame Treaty, permitting the United States to "regulate, limit or suspend" the entry of Chinese laborers when national interests were jeopardized.

In 1878 a tattooed Samoan chief named Le Mamea arrived in Washington to sign a treaty which would grant to the United States the right to establish a coaling station in the harbor of Pago Pago in exchange for American protection against foreign powers. But Germany and England also had interests in Samoa, and in 1880 they joined with the United States in establishing a protectorate. The arrangement prevented a take-over by any one foreign power.

These, then, were the political and diplomatic issues of the Hayes administration. It was a relatively quiet time in Washington. The dark era of sectional conflict had passed, and the great issues that would shape modern America had not yet embroiled the Capital. Indeed only a perceptive eye could see the shape of the future—in the rising population figures, in the cities swelled by immigrants, in the soaring profits of John D. Rockefeller's oil enterprises, and in the laboratories of inventors such as Edison.

For all its vexations, life in the White House could not have been altogether unpleasant for Hayes, his wife, and children. The older ones were often away, but the younger ones (aged ten and six in 1877) brought life into the old Mansion. Hayes rose daily at 7 A.M. Breakfast was at 8:30, followed by prayers. Meetings with congressmen and Cabinet members usually occupied the late morning. Lunch came at 2 P.M., followed by ninety minutes of writing letters, then a long carriage ride. After a nap, it was time for dinner, with the evenings usually given over to more visitors and appointments. Hayes's attire—silk hat, frock coat, and black shoes—seldom varied.

If Hayes seems in some ways a caricature of old-fashionedness, it should be remem-bered that in some ways he was ahead of his times. He ended Reconstruction and turned away ·from the politics of the past. Civil service reform, not a continuation of the spoils system, was the wave of the future. He traveled more than any predecessor and was the first President to visit the West Coast.

But his effectiveness was limited by several factors. He had no charisma. He was an old-school statesman in an era that was beginning to demand aggressiveness and originality. His assertion that he would serve only one term, plus his feuds with Conkling and others, weakened his hold on the party. But most of all, he could not shake off the onus of his dubious election.

Lucy Hayes was the first college graduate to serve as First Lady. She was recognized for her cleverness, but associates remembered her most as a cheerful, kindly woman. She began the tradition of Easter-egg rolling on the White House lawn. Another of her customs did not survive: she would not allow alcoholic beverages in the Mansion.

After leaving the Presidency, Hayes lived in retirement for almost twelve years. He took a continuing interest in education and prison reform. He found happiness at reunions of his old regiment. And he grew increasingly concerned about the accumulation of wealth in the hands of the few.

Lucy died in 1889. Two years later Hayes wrote to a friend that he was "busy as ever —busier! Shoving on to the end!" On January 8, 1893, after a visit to Lucy's grave, he wrote in his diary: "My feeling was one of longing to be quietly resting in a grave by her side." Nine days later, he joined her.

Several years afterward, John Sherman appraised the nineteenth President in these words: "Hayes was a modest man, but a very able one. He had none of the brilliant qualities of his successor, but his judgment was always sound, and his opinion, when once formed, was stable and consistent. . . . Among the multitude of public men I have met I have known no one who held a higher sense of his duty . . . than President Hayes."

—DONALD YOUNG

R B Hayes

A PICTURE PORTFOLIO

This commemorative Rutherford B. Hayes medal was struck off, in bronze, at the mint in Philadelphia during Hayes's administration.

A LION FROM OHIO

The Republican party could avoid a disastrous split in 1876, warned its liberal wing, only by choosing a presidential nominee "whose very name is . . . conclusive evidence of the most uncompromising determination . . . to make this a pure government once more." Thus, though James Blaine was popularly thought to be the front-runner, his record was not entirely clean, and the Republican leaders began to focus their attention on Rutherford B. Hayes, governor of Ohio. Born in Delaware, Ohio, in 1822, "Rud" Hayes was a lawyer, well educated, happily married, with a good record as a Union officer; in the process of rising to the rank of brigadier general he

had won the admiration of his men. "Hayes is a lion of a leader . . ." wrote one. "*Who could not follow him in battle . . . ?*" While in the field in October, 1864, he had been elected to Congress. Re-elected in 1866, he resigned to begin the first of two consecutive two-year terms as Ohio's governor. Hayes built a reputation for clean and progressive leadership, while at the same time remaining a Republican party regular and a capable politician. He had not demonstrated any great ambition for high national office, but by 1875 he knew that if he won a third gubernatorial term, against the popular Democratic incumbent William Allen, he was "likely to be pushed for . . . President."

The marriage of Hayes and Lucy Ware Webb, whose daguerreotype portraits, above, were made about the time of their wedding in 1852, was fecund and happy. Hayes fondly called his wife "the Golden Rule incarnate."

BUCKLAND & HAYES,
ATTORNEYS AND COUNSELLORS AT LAW,
LAND & COLLECTING AGENTS,
RALPH P. BUCKLAND, }   *LOWER SANDUSKY,*
RUTHERFORD B. HAYES. }   Sandusky County, Ohio.

Hayes interrupted the practice of law (one of his advertisements is shown at left) to lead Union troops. He saw action at South Mountain and Cedar Creek and was wounded five times. The engraving, right, features his answer to a suggestion that he take a furlough in order to campaign for himself in 1864.

RUTHERFORD B. HAYES DURING THE WAR.

FOR PRESIDENT

R. B. HAYES, OF OHIO.

VICE PRESIDENT

Wᴹ A. WHEELER, OF N.Y.

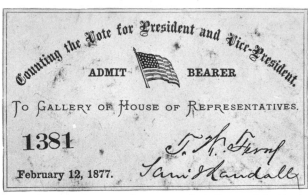

Counting the Vote for President and Vice-President.

ADMIT BEARER

To Gallery of House of Representatives.

1381

February 12, 1877.

It took Congress three months to count the ballots and decide the winner of the 1876 race; above is a pass to the House gallery.

HAYES
ELECTED.

TILDEN.

NUF CED.

The electoral debate was bitter, and partisans threatened violence, but just two days before the inauguration, Hayes and Wheeler (above, left) were declared winners. The Republicans crowed victoriously (right).

"A CONTESTED RESULT"

One of the dangers that he faced in the presidential election, wrote Hayes two weeks before the voters went to the polls, was "*a contested result.*" And sure enough, when the dust had cleared that November, Tilden had only 184 electoral votes, Hayes 165. The votes of Florida (4), Louisiana (8), and South Carolina (7) were in dispute; and one of Oregon's three Republican electors was possibly ineligible. Only 185 votes were needed to elect, and Tilden, who had won a popular majority, needed just one of the contested votes to become President; Hayes had to get them all. "No man worthy of the office . . ." said incumbent Ulysses S. Grant piously, "should be willing to hold it if counted in or placed there by fraud." But neither Hayes nor Tilden, both of whom sincerely favored government reform, was unaware that the weapons of their political duel had been and would be bribery, intimidation, the judicious deal. Tilden's nephew tried to buy Southern electors, but the price was too high. Hayes went so far as to declare against fraud by his supporters, but in the end he accepted his election from Congress despite the fact that it was based largely on the crookedness of three Southern Republican canvassing boards—which he then paid off with federal jobs. There was a kind of twisted logic to this: *he* knew he meant well, and he believed that had fair elections been held across the South he would have been awarded not just those nineteen contested ballots but "forty . . . at least. . . ."

SAMUEL J. TILDEN

Samuel J. Tilden rose to prominence in the Democratic party as one of the country's most successful champions of government reform. After an intermittent education at Yale and New York University, he was admitted to the bar in 1841 and soon became corporation counsel of the city of New York. He used his influence in New York State to help elect Polk in 1844; and in the Democratic party split that followed, he supported the free-soil "Barnburners" against W. L. Marcy's conservative "Hunkers." Gaining a reputation as a brilliant lawyer, he concentrated on railroad litigation and laid the foundations of a huge fortune. Remaining on the periphery of politics during the Civil War, he opposed Lincoln's election, encouraged opposition to the power of the central government, and supported Johnson's moderate Reconstruction policy. As chairman of the state Democratic committee from 1866 to 1874, he won national recognition in ousting New York City's infamous "Tweed Ring" of corrupt politicians and purifying the state's governmental and judicial bodies. Elected governor in 1874, he reformed the state's economic structure and smashed the fraudulent "Canal Ring" that was growing fat on funds allocated for canal improvements. Defeated by Hayes in the bitterly disputed presidential election of 1876, Samuel Tilden died ten years later, bequeathing a fortune to create the New York Public Library.

"THE OHIO IDEA"

Hayes was a reforming President, and his reforms were not universally popular. One that met special disapproval was the ban on alcoholic beverages at the White House—a move that public opinion blamed on Mrs. Hayes, who was consequently nicknamed Lemonade Lucy. Hayes declared that he made the rule himself. But whoever was responsible, it ruined many evenings in Washington. Total abstinence was called "the Ohio idea," but Representative James A. Garfield, for one, grumbled about "a State dinner at the President's wet down with coffee and cold water."

Secretary of State Evarts did not see how he could ask the diplomatic corps to attend such meals. A sympathetic steward, however, reportedly found a way to circumvent the rule: he served a confection known as Roman Punch—a kind of sherbet made of lemon juice, sugar, beaten whites of eggs, and a hearty dose of Saint Croix rum. At first he hid it inside oranges; then, more boldly, he served it in glasses. It looked innocent enough, and the practice was never discovered by the President or Lucy. The sherbet course—at mid-meal—came to be known as the Life-Saving Station.

HAYES MEMORIAL LIBRARY

"No matter what they build, they will never build any more rooms like these," Mrs. Hayes declared. Above is the Green Room, once Thomas Jefferson's dining room, but since then a parlor. A Hayes contemporary called it "Frenchy and pretentious," but it owed less to France than to the eclectic tastes of the Victorian era.

Lucy Hayes's sobriquet, Lemonade Lucy, implies that she was strait-laced. She did support temperance. But she was also sweet-tempered, generous, gregarious (she initiated the annual egg-rolling on the White House lawn), and the first First Lady to hold a college degree. She loved ornate, hand-painted chinaware (an oyster plate from a set that was used by the Hayeses is shown at left) and even decorated plates herself, as a hobby. She enjoyed evenings around the sitting-room piano, with the family and guests such as Vice President Wheeler joining in the singing. Pictured below with her are, from left, Carrie Paulding Davis, daughter of a friend, and Scott and Fanny, then the youngest of her offspring.

SERVANTS OF THE PEOPLE

CARL SCHURZ

In 1849 Carl Schurz was a cloak-and-dagger agent during a democratic uprising in his native Germany; thirteen years later he was fighting against a rebellion to destroy the union of his adopted country, the United States. Twenty-three years old when he emigrated in 1852, Schurz settled in Wisconsin, where he became a prominent opponent of slavery and a supporter of Lincoln. After serving briefly as minister to Spain, he returned in 1862 to urge immediate emancipation; in June he was appointed a Union general. His military career was marred by wrangles with field superiors and by unsupported charges that his German-American troops were cowardly under fire. Schurz made a postwar survey of the South and held a number of newspaper jobs before his election to the Senate in 1868. A civil service reformer, he was bitterly attacked by the pro-Grant press. Schurz helped to found the Liberal Republican party in the early seventies, but in 1876 he supported Hayes, who made him Secretary of the Interior. Schurz's dealings with the Indians were commendably fair; his establishment of an interdepartmental merit system for promotion was a landmark of reform. After 1881 he again turned to editorial writing and was a strong anti-imperialist. He wrote a biography of Henry Clay and his own *Reminiscences*.

WILLIAM EVARTS

William Evarts was one of the most active and versatile lawyers of the nineteenth century, combining a notable private practice with a varied political career. In 1860 he represented New York State in the Lemmon slave case; he successfully argued that freedom was due a slave who had set foot in a non-slave state during transit from one slave state to another. Evarts had served as assistant United States attorney for southern New York from 1849 to 1853; during the Civil War he was the government counsel in Supreme Court cases concerning the status of captured ships. He was the chief defense counsel in the impeachment of President Johnson, who made him Attorney General for the last eight months of his term. Evarts was one of the three American counselors at Geneva in 1871 and 1872 and was highly regarded by the British delegation. He successfully defended Henry Ward Beecher in a celebrated adultery case in 1874; two years later he was chief counsel for the Republican party in the Hayes-Tilden election litigation. As Secretary of State under Hayes, Evarts stressed the nation's "paramount interest" in a Central American canal. He had run unsuccessfully for the Senate in 1861; in a second try in 1885, he was elected. Evarts retired from public life in 1891 when he was seventy-three years old and died ten years later.

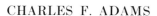

CHARLES F. ADAMS

Charles Francis Adams was considered for
the Liberal Republican presidential nomination in 1872 and still had support in 1876,
but he never received the "unequivocal call"
that would have allowed him to remain
above the bargaining he detested. A former
state and federal legislator, the antislavery
Bostonian had been the Free-Soil vice presidential nominee in 1848. During the Civil
War he was Lincoln's supremely capable
minister to England. When Britain verged
on recognizing the Confederacy by building
ironclads for the South, Adams wrote to
Foreign Secretary Lord John Russell: "It
would be superfluous in me to point out to
your lordship that this is war." England
backed down. As an arbitrator in Geneva in
1871 and 1872, Adams held that Britain
should have to honor only America's direct
war claims against her. Radicals pressed for
indirect damages, but Adams stood firm,
"representing all nations" in appealing
to the highest principles of international
law. His view prevailed. In the 1850's
Adams prepared an edition of the private
correspondence of his grandparents John
and Abigail Adams. (He did so with characteristic detachment—the volumes were
praised for being free of "all extrinsic mod-
elling.") He also published the memoirs of
his father, John Quincy Adams.

PETER COOPER

In all but solitary contrast to the robber
barons of the "Gilded Age" stood humorless,
virtuous Peter Cooper, who rose to the
heights of material success but then gave
much of his fortune away because he felt
"the object of life is to do good." He was
thirty years old in 1821 when he paid two
thousand dollars for a New York glue factory. In 1828 he established the Canton Iron
Works in Baltimore and designed and built
America's first steam locomotive, enabling
the faltering Baltimore and Ohio Railroad,
vital to his business, to remain operative. In
the next two decades he controlled foundries,
rolling mills, iron mines, and telegraph companies. Ever an innovator (as a boy he had
built a rudimentary washing machine),
Cooper produced the first structural steel for
fireproofing buildings. In 1859 New York's
Cooper Union for the Advancement of
Science and Art was opened, offering education to the poor. Cooper contributed heavily
to various New York City projects, including water sanitation and public schooling.
He was the Greenback party's presidential
candidate in 1876, but his views on government controls on unemployment, currency,
and monopolies were far too advanced for
his era, and he received only one per cent of
the popular vote. Resuming his philan-
thropies, he lived to be ninety-two years old.

In this 1880 cartoon by Joseph Keppler of Puck, "Cinderella" Hayes, who chose not to run for a second term and was not pressed by party leaders to change his mind, sits by his pot of Prosperity Soup in a spotless national kitchen, well stocked with the results of his labors; his evil older sisters—Ulysses S. Grant and Senator Roscoe Conkling—are ready to attend the Republican convention, where they will attempt to win a third term for Grant. Hayes's civil service reform had found a strong enemy in the senator, whose power in New York was based on the spoils system and graft. Hayes had, as an initial step, ordered federal officials not to involve themselves in political groups or elections, except as voters. The federal collector for the Port of New York, Chester A. Arthur, and one of his deputies, Alonzo B. Cornell, would not give up their important

roles in Conkling's machine, and Hayes fired them from the government. A confrontation on the issue in the Senate followed, and the senator lost. With his control at home in serious jeopardy, Conkling tried to regain strength by playing kingmaker: Grant had been useful to the old-line politicians before, and he was the obvious candidate. He had just returned from a triumphant world tour; hence the "stole" of tickets he is wearing in Keppler's drawing. Conkling was famed as an orator; his speeches were often billed (as his plumes, above, indicate) as his "greatest effort." The artist's view of him is a striking echo of James G. Blaine's sneer at the senator's "haughty disdain, his grandiloquent swell, his majestic, super-eminent, overpowering, turkey-gobbler strut." Despite Conkling's efforts, James Garfield, not Grant, was nominated by the Republicans.

FACTS IN SUMMARY: RUTHERFORD B. HAYES

CHRONOLOGY

UNITED STATES		HAYES
	1822	*Born October 4*
John Quincy Adams elected President	1825	
Jackson elected President	1828	
Siege of the Alamo	1836	*Attends academy at Norwalk, Ohio*
	1838	*Enters Kenyon College*
	1843	*Enters Harvard Law School*
Polk elected President	1844	
Texas annexed	1845	*Admitted to the Ohio bar*
War with Mexico	1846	
	1849	*Moves to Cincinnati*
Clay's compromise	1850	
Pierce elected President	1852	*Marries Lucy Webb*
	1855	*Serves as delegate to Ohio Republican convention*
Lincoln-Douglas debates	1858	*Named Cincinnati city solicitor*
Lincoln elected President	1860	
South Carolina secedes		
Civil War begins	1861	*Joins Union army as major*
Battle of Bull Run		*Promoted to lieutenant colonel*
Battle of Shiloh	1862	*Wounded in Battle of South Mountain*
Battle of Antietam		

UNITED STATES		HAYES
Battle of Chancellorsville	1863	
Battle of Gettysburg		
Lincoln re-elected	1864	*Promoted to brigadier general*
Lee surrenders to Grant	1865	*Promoted to major general*
Lincoln assassinated		*Begins term in House of Representatives*
	1866	*Re-elected to Congress*
	1867	*Elected governor of Ohio*
Johnson impeached	1868	
Grant elected President		
	1869	*Re-elected governor*
Grant re-elected	1872	*Loses congressional election*
	1875	*Re-elected governor*
Results of presidential election disputed	1876	*Named Republican candidate for President*
	1877	*Declared President by Electoral Commission*
		Withdraws troops from South Carolina and Louisiana
Bland-Allison Act passed over President's veto	1878	*Vetoes Bland-Allison bill*
		Suspends Chester Arthur as N.Y. customs collector

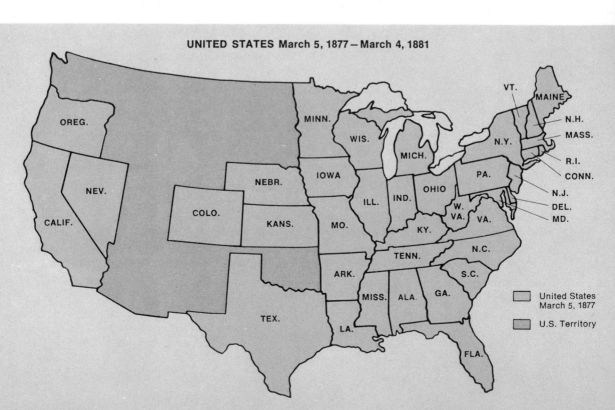

UNITED STATES March 5, 1877 – March 4, 1881

United States March 5, 1877

U.S. Territory

Specie payments resumed	1879	*Vetoes bill limiting number of Chinese allowed to enter U.S.*	
		Vetoes Army appropriation bill and other bills to prevent use of troops in congressional elections	
Garfield elected President	1880	*Visits Pacific Coast*	
Garfield shot	1881	*Retires to Fremont*	
Arthur becomes President			
Pendleton Act	1883	*Named president of National Prison Association*	
Cleveland elected President	1884		
Interstate Commerce Act	1887		
Harrison elected President	1888		
	1889	*Lucy Hayes dies*	
Sherman Antitrust Act	1890		
Cleveland re-elected President	1892		
	1893	*Dies January 17*	

BIOGRAPHICAL FACTS

BIRTH: Delaware, Ohio, Oct. 4, 1822

ANCESTRY: English

FATHER: Rutherford Hayes; b. Brattleboro, Vt., Jan. 4, 1787; d. Delaware, Ohio, July 20, 1822

FATHER'S OCCUPATION: Store owner

MOTHER: Sophia Birchard Hayes; b. Wilmington, Vt., April 15, 1792; d. Columbus, Ohio, Oct. 30, 1866

BROTHER: Lorenzo (1815–1825)

SISTERS: Sarah Sophia (1817–1821); Fanny Arabella (1820–1856)

WIFE: Lucy Ware Webb; b. Chillicothe, Ohio, Aug. 28, 1831; d. Fremont, Ohio, June 25, 1889

MARRIAGE: Cincinnati, Ohio, Dec. 30, 1852

CHILDREN: Birchard Austin (1853–1926); Webb Cook (1856–1934); Rutherford Platt (1858–1927); Joseph (1861–1863); George Crook (1864–1866); Fanny (1867–1950); Scott (1871–1923); Manning (1873–1874)

EDUCATION: Academy at Norwalk, Ohio; Isaac Webb's school at Middletown, Conn.; Kenyon College, Gambier, Ohio; Harvard Law School

HOME: Spiegel Grove, Fremont, Ohio

RELIGIOUS AFFILIATION: None

OCCUPATIONS BEFORE PRESIDENCY: Lawyer; soldier; politician

MILITARY SERVICE: Commissioned major in 23rd Ohio Volunteers (1861); resigned as major general in June, 1865

PRE-PRESIDENTIAL OFFICES: City Solicitor of Cincinnati; U.S. Congressman; Governor of Ohio

AGE AT INAUGURATION: 54

OCCUPATIONS AFTER PRESIDENCY: Philanthropist; president of the National Prison Association

DEATH: Fremont, Ohio, Jan. 17, 1893

PLACE OF BURIAL: Spiegel Grove State Park, Fremont, Ohio

A defiant Hayes shows a vetoed anti-Chinese bill to Denis Kearney, the labor leader who had said that California would secede if the bill was not passed.

ELECTION OF 1876

(The disputed electoral votes of Florida, South Carolina, Louisiana, and Oregon were awarded to Hayes by a commission appointed by Congress.)

CANDIDATES	ELECTORAL VOTE	POPULAR VOTE
Rutherford B. Hayes Republican	185	4,036,572
Samuel J. Tilden Democratic	184	4,284,020
Peter Cooper Greenback	—	81,737

THE HAYES ADMINISTRATION

INAUGURATION: March 3, 1877, the White House (private ceremony); March 5, 1877, the Capitol, Washington, D.C.

VICE PRESIDENT: William A. Wheeler

SECRETARY OF STATE: William M. Evarts

SECRETARY OF THE TREASURY: John Sherman

SECRETARY OF WAR: George W. McCrary; Alexander Ramsey (from Dec. 12, 1879)

ATTORNEY GENERAL: Charles Devens

POSTMASTER GENERAL: David M. Key; Horace Maynard (from Aug. 25, 1880)

SECRETARY OF THE NAVY: Richard W. Thompson; Nathan Goff, Jr. (from Jan. 6, 1881)

SECRETARY OF THE INTERIOR: Carl Schurz

SUPREME COURT APPOINTMENTS: John Marshall Harlan (1877); William Burnham Woods (1880)

45th CONGRESS (March 4, 1877–March 4, 1879): Senate: 39 Republicans; 36 Democrats; 1 Other House: 153 Democrats; 140 Republicans

46th CONGRESS (March 4, 1879–March 4, 1881): Senate: 42 Democrats; 33 Republicans; 1 Other House: 149 Democrats; 130 Republicans; 14 Others